# Text, Cases and Materials on Criminal Law

# Pearson

*Second Edition*

# Text, Cases and Materials on Criminal Law

Stuart Macdonald

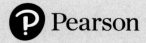

Harlow, England • London • New York • Boston • San Francisco • Toronto • Sydney
Dubai • Singapore • Hong Kong • Tokyo • Seoul • Taipei • New Delhi
Cape Town • São Paulo • Mexico City • Madrid • Amsterdam • Munich • Paris • Milan

**Pearson Education Limited**
KAO Two
KAO Park
Harlow CM17 9NA
United Kingdom
Tel: +44 (0)1279 623623
Web: www.pearson.com/uk

First published 2015 (print and electronic)
**Second edition published 2018** (print and electronic)

© Pearson Education Limited 2015, 2018 (print and electronic)

The right of Stuart Macdonald to be identified as author of this work has been asserted by him in accordance with the Copyright, Designs and Patents Act 1988.

Contains public sector information licensed under the Open Government Licence (OGL) v3.0.
http://www.nationalarchives.gov.uk/doc/open-government-licence/version/3/

Contains Parliamentary information licensed under the Open Parliament Licence (OPL) v3.0.
http://www.parliament.uk/site-information/copyright/open-parliament-licence/

Pearson Education is not responsible for the content of third-party internet sites.

ISBN:      978-1-292-21992-9 (print)
           978-1-292-21993-6 (PDF)
           978-1-292-21994-3 (ePub)

**British Library Cataloguing-in-Publication Data**
A catalogue record for the print edition is available from the British Library

**Library of Congress Cataloging-in-Publication Data**
Names: Macdonald, Stuart Keith, 1979- author.
Title: Text, cases, and materials on criminal law / Stuart Macdonald.
Description: Second edition. | Harlow [Engand] : Pearson Education Limited, 2018. | Includes
    index.
Identifiers: LCCN 2018008840 | ISBN 9781292219929 (print) | ISBN 9781292219936
    (pdf) | ISBN 9781292219943 (epub)
Subjects: LCSH: Criminal law—England. | LCGFT: Casebooks (Law)
Classification: LCC KD7869 .M33 2018 | DDC 345.42—dc23
LC record available at https://lccn.loc.gov/2018008840

10 9 8 7 6 5 4 3 2 1
22 21 20 19 18

Print edition typeset in 9.5/12 pt Charter ITC Std by iEnergizer Aptara®, Ltd.
Printed in Slovakia by Neografia

NOTE THAT ANY PAGE CROSS REFERENCES REFER TO THE PRINT EDITION

To

Sarah, Cara and Kai

# Brief contents

# Contents

# Preface

Criminal law is both a very important subject – the liberty of defendants is often at stake and victims may have suffered serious harm – and a very interesting one, involving a range of challenging theoretical issues, ethical questions and policy decisions. My aim in writing this text is therefore not only to help you get to grips with the subject and achieve your full potential during your course, but also to make your study thought-provoking, engaging and enjoyable.

*Text, Cases and Materials on Criminal Law* has been written specifically with the needs of undergraduates and conversion course students in mind. It uses a number of features to help make your reading as interesting and productive as possible:

- An engaging writing style, which is designed to communicate the material in a clear and comprehensible manner.
- Chapter objectives at the start of each chapter, and checklists at the end, so that you know exactly what you need to achieve and are able to assess your progress.
- Carefully selected extracts, to help you get used to reading judgments and academic writings, accompanied by facilitator questions, to help you identify key points and make your reading proactive.
- A variety of diagrams and illustrations, to provide an aid to understanding and help you learn how to structure exam answers.
- Self-test questions, which consolidate your understanding by providing an opportunity to apply the material you have studied.
- Further reading lists, to enable you to explore key issues in greater depth.

The text begins with two introductory chapters that provide your foundation for the study of the subject. In the 11 chapters that follow the objective will be to ensure that you have a good understanding of the relevant law and an ability to apply this to factual scenarios. Each chapter also identifies specific topics for further thought and evaluation. The aim here is to encourage you to think more deeply about the subject matter and help you to write an essay on the chosen topics. By nurturing these analytical skills the text will equip you for further study and help you develop into an independent learner.

If you have any comments on or suggestions for the text, please do get in touch with me at s.macdonald@swansea.ac.uk. I am also on Twitter (@CTProject_SM).

# Table of cases

Note: Cases are listed under the names of the accused whenever the usual method of citation would cause them to appear as 'R v' signifying prosecution by the Crown

# Table of European Court of Human Rights cases

# Table of statutes

# Table of statutory instruments

# Table of treaties and other international instruments

# Acknowledgements

Since the publication of the first edition of *Text, Cases and Materials on Criminal Law* I have benefited from the feedback offered by a great number of people, including the students on the Criminal Law module at Swansea University, who now endure my text as well as my lectures! I would particularly like to thank the anonymous reviewers for taking such time and care to provide detailed and constructive comments. I would also like to thank the team at Pearson for all their hard work on this new edition, especially Cheryl Stevart and Agnibesh Das.

I have taught criminal law for the past 18 years, and still enjoy it greatly. The students I have taught during this time have contributed to both my understanding of the subject and how I communicate it to others. I have also been fortunate to work with many gifted colleagues. Worthy of special mention is Mark Telford, with whom I taught criminal law at the University of Southampton. I am grateful to Mark for allowing me to use in this text some of the self-test questions that he designed during that time.

Most of all, I would like to thank my family for their love and support.

## Publisher's acknowledgements

*We are grateful to the following for permission to reproduce copyright material:*

### Text

Extract on chapter 1. from Woolmington v Director of Public Prosecutions [1935] AC 462, Incorporated Council of Law Reporting; Extracts on chapters 1., 2., 6. from R v Brown [1994] 1 AC 212, Incorporated Council of Law Reporting; Extract on chapter 1. from *The Enforcement of Morals*, Oxford University Press (Devlin, P. 1970) Republished with permission of Oxford University Press, permission conveyed through Copyright Clearance Center, Inc.; Extract on chapter 1. from 'The criminal law as last resort', *Oxford Journal of Legal Studies*, Vol 24(2), pp.207–235 (Husak, D. 2004), Republished with permission of Oxford University Press, permission conveyed through Copyright Clearance Center, Inc.; Extract on chapter 1. from 'Towards a modest legal moralism', *Criminal Law and Philosophy*, Vol 8(1), pp.217–235 (Duff, R.A. 2014), copyright © 2012, Springer Science + Business Media Dordrecht, with kind permission from Springer Science + Business Media; Extract on chapter 1. from Fair labelling in criminal law, *Modern Law Review*, Vol 71(2), pp.217–246 (Chalmers, J. and Leverick, F. 2008), Copyright © 2008 Chalmers, J. and Leverick, F. The Modern Law Review Limited; Extract on chapter 1. from 'Prevention and criminalization: Justifications and limits', *New Criminal Law Review*, Vol 15(4), pp.542–571 (Ashworth, A. and Zedner, L. 2012), Republished with permission of University of California Press, permission conveyed through Copyright Clearance Center, Inc.; Extracts on chapters 2., 6. from Fagan v Metropolitan Police

Commissioner [1969] 1 QB 439, Incorporated Council of Law Reporting; Extract on chapter 2. from Thabo Meli v R [1954] 1 WLR 228, Incorporated Council of Law Reporting; Extract on chapter 2. from R v Le Brun [1992] QB 61, Incorporated Council of Law Reporting; Extract on chapter 2. from 'Ignorance of the Criminal Law, and Duties to Avoid It', *Modern Law Review*, Vol 74(1), pp.1–26 (Ashworth, A. 2011), Copyright © 2011 Ashworth, A., The Modern Law Review Limited;; Extract on chapter 3. from Attorney-General's Reference (No 2 of 1992) [1994] QB 91, Incorporated Council of Law Reporting; Extract on chapter 3. from R v Stone & Dobinson [1977] QB 354, Incorporated Council of Law Reporting; Extract on chapter 3. from R v Miller [1983] 2 AC 161, Incorporated Council of Law Reporting; Extract on chapter 3. from Airedale NHS Trust v Bland [1993] AC 789, Incorporated Council of Law Reporting; Extract on chapter 3. from R v Cheshire [1991] 1 WLR 844, Incorporated Council of Law Reporting; Extract on chapter 3. from Environment Agency v Empress Car Co (Abertillery) Ltd [1999] 2 AC 22, Incorporated Council of Law Reporting; Extract on chapter 3. from R v Smith [1959] 2 QB 35, Incorporated Council of Law Reporting; Extract on chapter 3. from R v Williams & Davis [1992] 1 WLR 380, Incorporated Council of Law Reporting; Extract on chapter 3. from R v Blaue [1975] 1 WLR 1411, Incorporated Council of Law Reporting; Extract on chapter 3. from 'Causation in (Criminal) Law', *Law Quarterly Review*, Vol 133(3), pp.416–441 (Simester, A. P. 2017); Extract on chapter 4. from R v Cunningham [1957] 2 QB 396, Incorporated Council of Law Reporting; Extract on chapter 4. from R v Caldwell [1982] AC 341, Incorporated Council of Law Reporting; Extract on chapter 4. from Elliott v C [1983] 1 WLR 939, Incorporated Council of Law Reporting; Extract on chapter 4. from R v Parker [1977] 1 WLR 600, Incorporated Council of Law Reporting; Extract on chapter 4. from R v Woollin [1999] 1 AC 82, Incorporated Council of Law Reporting; Extracts on chapters 4., 11. from Re A (Children) (Conjoined Twins: Surgical Separation) [2001] Fam 147, Incorporated Council of Law Reporting; Extract on chapter 4. from Westminster CC v Croyalgrange Ltd [1986] 1 WLR 674, Incorporated Council of Law Reporting; Extract on chapter 4. from 'The man who caught a 4-year-old girl from the Grenfell Tower blaze pictured' *The Metro*, 16/06/2017 (White, C.); Extract on chapter 5. from R v Powell & English [1999] 1 AC 1, Incorporated Council of Law Reporting; Extract on chapter 5. from DPP v Newbury & Jones [1977] AC 500, Incorporated Council of Law Reporting; Extract on chapter 5. from R v Lamb [1967] 2 QB 981, Incorporated Council of Law Reporting; Extract on chapter 5. from R v Church [1966] 1 QB 59, Incorporated Council of Law Reporting; Extract on chapter 5. from R v Watson [1989] 1 WLR 684, Incorporated Council of Law Reporting; Extract on chapter 5. from Andrews v DPP [1937] AC 576, Incorporated Council of Law Reporting; Extract on chapter 5. from R v Adomako [1995] 1 AC 171, Incorporated Council of Law Reporting; Extract on chapter 5. from 'Anger and fear as justifiable preludes for loss of self-control', *The Journal of Criminal Law*, Vol 74(3), pp.223–241 (Edwards, S. 2010), copyright © 2010 by SAGE Publications, reprinted by permission of SAGE Publication; Extract on chapter 5. from 'Replacing Provocation in England and Wales: Examining the Partial Defence of Loss of Control', *Journal of Law and Society*, Vol 40(2), pp.280–305 (Fitz-Gibbon, K. 2013), Copyright © 2013 Fitz-Gibbon, K., Cardiff University Law School; Extract on chapter 6. from Collins v Wilcock [1984] 1 WLR 1172, Incorporated Council of Law Reporting; Extract on chapter 6. from R v Venna [1976] QB 421, Incorporated Council of Law Reporting; Extract on chapter 6. from R v Ireland & Burstow [1998] AC 147, Incorporated Council of Law Reporting; Extract on chapter 6. from R v Savage & Parmenter [1992] 1 AC 699, Incorporated Council of Law Reporting; Extract on chapter 6. from DPP v Smith [1961] AC 290, Incorporated Council of Law Reporting; Extract on chapter 6. from R v Cunningham [1957] 2 Q.B. 396, Incorporated Council of Law Reporting; Extract on chapter 6. from R v Richardson

[1999] QB 444, Incorporated Council of Law Reporting; Extract on chapter 6. from R v Wilson [1997] QB 47, Incorporated Council of Law Reporting; Extract on chapter 6. from 'Social disutility and the law of consent', *Oxford Journal of Legal Studies*, Vol 14(1), pp.121–135 (Kell, D. 1994), Republished with permission of Oxford University Press, permission conveyed through Copyright Clearance Center, Inc.; Extract on chapter 6. from 'Not Giving Up the Fight: A Review of the Law Commission's Scoping Report on Non-fatal Offences Against the Person', *The Journal of Criminal Law*, Vol 80(3), pp.188–200 (Demetriou, S. 2016), copyright © 2016 by SAGE Publications, reprinted by permission of SAGE Publications; Extract on chapter 6. from 'Getting their "act" together? Implementing statutory reform of offences against the person', *Criminal Law Review*, Vol 9, pp.597–617 (Gibson, M.J.R. 2016); Extract on chapter 7. from R v Olugboja [1982] QB 320, Incorporated Council of Law Reporting; Extract on chapter 7. from "Breaking boundaries? Sexual consent in the jury room", *Legal Studies*, Vol 26(3), pp.303–320 (Finch, E. and Munro, V.E. 2006), Copyright © 2006, John Wiley and Sons; Extract on chapter 7. from 'Alcohol-related rape cases: Barristers' perspectives on the Sexual Offences Act 2003 and its impact on practice', *The Journal of Criminal Law*, Vol 74(6), pp.579–600 (Gunby, C., Carline, A. and Beynon, C. 2010), copyright © 2010 by SAGE Publications, reprinted by permission of SAGE Publications; Extract on chapter 7. from 'Expanding Liability for Sexual Fraud Through the Concept of "Active Deception": A Flawed Approach', *The Journal of Criminal Law*, Vol 80(1), pp.28–44 (Sharpe, A. 2016), copyright © 2016 by SAGE Publications, reprinted by permission of SAGE Publications; Extract on chapter 7. from '"I Think it's Rape and I Think He Would be Found Not Guilty": Focus Group Perceptions of (un)Reasonable Belief in Consent in Rape Law', *Social & Legal Studies*, Vol 25(5), pp.611–629 (Larcombe, W., Fileborn, B., Powell, A., Hanley, N. and Henry, N. 2016), copyright © 2016 by SAGE Publications, reprinted by permission of SAGE Publications; Extract on chapter 8. from R v Kelly [1999] QB 621, Incorporated Council of Law Reporting; Extract on chapter 8. from R v Woodman [1974] QB 754, Incorporated Council of Law Reporting; Extract on chapter 8. from R v Morris [1984] AC 320, Incorporated Council of Law Reporting; Extract on chapter 8. from DPP v Gomez [1993] AC 442, Incorporated Council of Law Reporting; Extract on chapter 8. from Lawrence v MPC [1972] AC 626, Incorporated Council of Law Reporting; Extract on chapter 8. from R v Hinks [2001] 2 AC 241, Incorporated Council of Law Reporting; Extract on chapter 8. from R v Lloyd [1985] QB 829, Incorporated Council of Law Reporting; Extract on chapter 8. from R v Ghosh [1982] QB 1053, Incorporated Council of Law Reporting; Extract on chapter 8. from R v Collins [1973] QB 100, Incorporated Council of Law Reporting; Extract on chapter 8. from R v Walkington [1979] 1 WLR 1169, Incorporated Council of Law Reporting; Extract on chapter 8. from R v Steer [1987] 3 WLR 205, Incorporated Council of Law Reporting; Extract on chapter 8. from 'Thief or Swindler: Who Cares?', *Cambridge Law Journal* Vol 50, p.389 (Glazebrook, P. 1991); Extract on chapter 8. from 'Dishonesty: What the Jury Thinks the Defendant Thought the Jury Would Have Thought', *Cambridge Law Journal* Vol 41, p.222 (Spencer, J. 1982); Extract on chapter 8. from *'On the nature and rationale of property offences' by Simester, A. P. and Sullivan, G. R. In Defining Crimes: Essays on the Special Part of the Criminal Law*, Oxford University Press (Duff, R. A. and Green S.P. (eds) 2005) pp.168–195, Republished with permission of Oxford University Press, permission conveyed through Copyright Clearance Center, Inc.; Extract on chapter 8. from 'Can Dishonesty Be Salvaged? Theft and the Grounding of the MSC Napoli', *The Journal of Criminal Law*, Vol 74(1), pp.53–76 (Glover, R. 2010), copyright © 2010 by SAGE Publications, reprinted by permission of SAGE Publications; Extract on chapter 8. from 'Theft and fair labelling', *Modern Law Review*, Vol 56(4), pp.554–558 (Clarkson, C. 1993), Copyright © 1993

Modern Law Review; Extract on chapter 8. from 'Fraud by Abuse of Position and Unlicensed Gangmasters', *Modern Law Review*, Vol 79(2), pp.354–363 (Collins, J. 2016), Copyright © 2016 Modern Law Review; Extract on chapter 9. from R v Sheehan [1975] 1 WLR 739, Incorporated Council of Law Reporting; Extract on chapter 9. from Attorney-General of Northern Ireland v Gallagher [1963] AC 349, Incorporated Council of Law Reporting; Extract on chapter 9. from R v Bailey [1983] 1 WLR 760, Incorporated Council of Law Reporting; Extract on chapter 9. from R v Hardie [1985] 1 WLR 64, Incorporated Council of Law Reporting; Extract on chapter 9. from DPP v Majewski [1977] AC 443, Incorporated Council of Law Reporting; Extract on chapter 9. from R v Morgan [1976] AC 182, Incorporated Council of Law Reporting; Extract on chapter 9. from R v Kingston [1995] 2 AC 355, Incorporated Council of Law Reporting; Extract on chapter 9. from R v O'Grady [1987] QB 995, Incorporated Council of Law Reporting; Extract on chapter 10. from R v Sullivan [1984] AC 156, Incorporated Council of Law Reporting; Extract on chapter 10. from R v Hennessy [1989] 1 WLR 287, Incorporated Council of Law Reporting; Extract on chapter 10. from R v Burgess [1991] 2 QB 92, Incorporated Council of Law Reporting; Extract on chapter 10. from R v Quick [1973] QB 910, Incorporated Council of Law Reporting; Extract on chapter 10. from R v Kemp [1957] 1 QB 399, Incorporated Council of Law Reporting; Extract on chapter 10. from R v Windle [1952] 2 QB 826, Incorporated Council of Law Reporting; Extract on chapter 10. from R v Byrne [1960] 2 QB 396, Incorporated Council of Law Reporting; Extract on chapter 10. from *Simester and Sullivan's Criminal Law: Theory and Doctrine* 6th edition, Hart Publishing (Simester, A. P., Spencer, J. R., Stark, F., Sullivan, G. R. & Virgo, G. J. 2016) pp.751–754, 978-1849467223, Extract on chapter 10. from Simester and Sullivan's Criminal Law: Theory and Doctrine, 6th edition, Simester, A. P., Spencer, J. R., Stark, F., Sullivan, G. R. & Virgo, G. J., 2016, Hart Publishing, an imprint of Bloomsbury Publishing Plc.; Extract on chapter 10. from 'Pragmatism Preserved? The Challenges of Accommodating Mercy Killers in the Reformed Diminished Responsibility Plea', *The Journal of Criminal Law*, Vol 81(3), pp.177–200 (Gibson, M. 2017), copyright © 2017 by SAGE Publications, reprinted by permission of SAGE Publications; Extract on chapter 10. from 'Introducing a new diminished responsibility defence for England and Wales', *Modern Law Review*, Vol 74(5), pp.750–766 (Kennefick, L. 2011), Copyright © 2011 Kennefick, L., The Modern Law Review Limited; Extract on chapter 10. from 'The New Diminished Responsibility Plea in Operation: Some Initial Findings' *Criminal Law Review*, Vol 1, pp.18–35 (Mackay, R. and Mitchell, B.J. 2017); Extract on chapter 10. from 'Diminished Responsibility in Golds and Beyond: Insights and Implications', *Criminal Law Review*, Vol 7, pp.543–553 (Gibson, M.J.R. 2017); Extract on chapter 10. from 'Case Comment, Homicide: R v Golds (Mark Richard)', *Criminal Law Review*, p.316 (Laird, K. 2017); Extract on chapter 11. from Southwark LBC v Williams [1971] Ch 734, Incorporated Council of Law Reporting; Extract on chapter 11. from Johnson v Phillips [1976] 1 WLR 65, Incorporated Council of Law Reporting; Extract on chapter 11. from Re F (Mental Patient: Sterilisation) [1990] 2 AC 1, Incorporated Council of Law Reporting; Extract on chapter 11. from R v Howe [1987] AC 417, Incorporated Council of Law Reporting; Extract on chapter 11. from R v Hudson and Taylor [1971] 2 QB 202, Incorporated Council of Law Reporting; Extract on chapter 11. from R v Graham [1982] 1 WLR 294, Incorporated Council of Law Reporting; Extract on chapter 11. from R v Bowen [1997] 1 WLR 372, Incorporated Council of Law Reporting; Extract on chapter 11. from R v Clegg [1995] 1 AC 482, Incorporated Council of Law Reporting; Extract on chapter 11. from R v Martin (Tony) [2003] QB 1, Incorporated Council of Law Reporting; Extract on chapter 11. from Beckford v The Queen [1988] AC 130, Incorporated Council of Law Reporting; Extract on chapter 11. from Attorney-General's Reference (No 2 of 1983) [1984] QB 456, Incorporated Council of Law Reporting; Extract on chapter 11. from R v Bird [1985] 1 WLR 816, Incorporated Council of Law Reporting; Extract on chapter 11. from 'Duress and the criminal law: Another about turn by the House of Lords', *Cambridge Law Journal* Vol 47, p.61 (Milgate, H.P. 1988); Extract on chapter 12. from R v Griffiths & others [1966] 1 QB 589, Incorporated Council of Law Reporting; Extract on chapter 12. from R v Anderson [1986] AC 27, Incorporated Council of Law Reporting; Extract on chapter 12. from R v Gullefer [1990] 1 WLR 1063, Incorporated Council of Law Reporting; Extract on chapter 12. from R v Jones (Kenneth) [1990] 1 WLR 1057, Incorporated Council of Law Reporting; Extract on chapter 12. from R v Khan [1990] 1 WLR 813, Incorporated Council of Law Reporting; Extract on chapter 12. from 'Attempt: The conduct requirement', *Oxford Journal of Legal Studies*, Vol 29(1), pp.25–41 (Clarkson, C. 2009), Republished with permission of Oxford University Press, permission conveyed through Copyright Clearance Center, Inc.; Extract on chapter 13. from A-G's Reference (No 3 of 1992) [1994] 1 WLR 409, Incorporated Council of Law Reporting; Extract on chapter 13. from Attorney-General v Able [1984] QB 795, Incorporated Council of Law Reporting; Extract on chapter 13. from R v Calhaem [1985] QB 808, Incorporated Council of Law Reporting; Extract on chapter 13. from Attorney-General's Reference (No 1 of 1975) [1975] QB 773, Incorporated Council of Law Reporting; Extract on chapter 13. from Du Cros v Lambourne [1907] 1 KB 40, Incorporated Council of Law Reporting; Extract on chapter 13. from R v Bainbridge [1960] 1 QB 129, Incorporated Council of Law Reporting; Extract on chapter 13. from DPP for Northern Ireland v Maxwell [1978] 1 WLR 1350, Incorporated Council of Law Reporting; Extract on chapter 13. from Chan Wing-Siu v The Queen [1985] AC 168, Incorporated Council of Law Reporting; Extract on chapter 13. from 'Simply harsh to fairly simple: joint enterprise reform', *Criminal Law Review*, Vol 3, pp.5–21 (Wilson, W. & Ormerod, D. 2015); Extract on chapter 13. from 'Commentary on R v Johnson', *Criminal Law Review*, pp.216, 218 (Laird, K. 2017); Extract on chapter 13. from 'The taming of Jogee?', *Cambridge Law Journal* Vol 76, p.4 (Stark, F. 2017); Extract on chapter 13. from 'Jogee: not the end of a legal saga but the start of one?', *Criminal Law Review*, Vol 8, pp.539–552 (Ormerod, D. & Laird, K. 2016); Extract on chapter 13. from 'The demise of "parasitic accessorial liability": substantive judicial law reform, not common law housekeeping?', *Cambridge Law Journal* Vol 75, p.550 (Stark, F. 2016); Extract on chapter 13. from 'Accessory liability and common unlawful purposes' Law Quarterly Review, Vol 133(1), pp.73–90 (Simester, A. P. 2017)

# 1

# Your criminal law toolkit

## Chapter objectives

By the end of this chapter you should have:

- An understanding of the basic principles of criminal law
- An awareness of the definitional and other debates surrounding these principles
- An ability to apply these principles to particular situations.

 **Introduction**

As well as the standard academic texts, my collection of books on criminal law includes: *The World's Stupidest Laws*;[1] *The World's Funniest Laws*;[2] and *The Little Book of Loony Laws*.[3] According to these books:

- It is illegal to land a flying saucer in the vineyards of France.
- In Madagascar it is illegal for a pregnant woman to wear a hat.
- In Alaska it is illegal to push a live moose out of a moving aeroplane.
- In Scotland it is illegal to be drunk in possession of a cow.
- In Thailand you may not leave your house if you are not wearing underwear.

If these offences do indeed exist, they seem to be a strange use of the criminal sanction. That, after all, is why they appear in a book of loony laws! But why do they strike us as strange? Why is it inappropriate to use the criminal law in this way? How should the criminal sanction be used? That is the question that we will ask ourselves in this opening chapter. The chapter examines a range of important criminal law principles. The aim is to build a strong foundation for your study of this subject; these principles are the tools that we will use throughout the text to analyse and evaluate the criminal law. In the first half of the chapter we study the following principles:

- Individual autonomy
- The harm principle
- The offence principle
- Social welfare
- Legal moralism
- Legal paternalism
- Criminal law as the least restrictive appropriate intervention.

These are all concerned with the question: what conduct should the criminal law prohibit? In other words, they are relevant to criminalisation decisions, decisions as to what conduct should be criminal and what shouldn't.

In the second half of the chapter we study:

- The principle of legality
- The correspondence principle
- The presumption of innocence
- The ladder principle
- Fair labelling.

These are all concerned with the features of individual offences. They cover questions of definition, seriousness, proof and labels.

Before we turn to the individual principles, there are two preliminary points to bear in mind. The first is that the 12 principles do not always pull in the same direction. Often the

---

[1]Crombie, D. (2000) *The World's Stupidest Laws*. Michael O'Mara Books Ltd: London.
[2]Alexander, J. (2005) *The World's Funniest Laws*. Crombie Jardine Publishing Ltd: Cheam.
[3]Green, C. (2002) *The Little Book of Loony Laws*. Neil Wilson Publishing: Glasgow.

various principles will conflict. When this happens, a choice has to be made between the competing demands of different principles. One of the key skills that this chapter will help you to develop – and which you will need to use throughout the text – is the ability to recognise situations where the principles conflict, articulate the demands of the competing principles and explain which principles you believe should be given priority. Remember that not all of the principles that we study are of equal importance. As we work through them, you should consider which ones you believe to be the most important.

The second point is that a number of the extracts in this chapter are taken from works of legal theory and legal philosophy. Some of these extracts use technical terms which you may not have come across before. The following list therefore defines some of these terms for you. You may find it helpful to refer back to this list as you work through the chapter:

- **A priori:** To presume something without proof. So an a priori assumption is one that has not been proved.
- **Censure:** Expression of disapproval or blame.
- **Discourse:** The language and terminology used in a particular field, such as legal discourse or moral discourse.
- **Empirical:** Based on experience or observation (as opposed to abstract reasoning or theorising). So to test a claim empirically one must collect relevant information and evidence in order to determine whether or not the claim is justified.
- **Extra-legal:** Lying outside the boundaries of the legal system. So an extra-legal example is one which does not involve laws or legal principles.
- **Majoritarianism:** To defer to the decisions of a majority within a society.
- **Normative:** Based on evaluative standards. A normative claim is based on a person's values or norms. By contrast, a 'positive' claim is a statement of fact that can be tested and verified.
- **Polity:** A society that has an organised system of politics and government.
- **Prima facie:** At first sight, or on the face of it.
- **Proscription:** Banning or outlawing. Proscribed conduct is conduct that has been prohibited.

Some of the extracts also use the letters D and V to refer to the defendant and the victim. You will find this convention in much writing on criminal law, and it will be used throughout this text.

## Individual autonomy

We begin with the principle of individual autonomy. The premise of the principle of individual autonomy is that people have the freedom and the capacity to make their own decisions. The principle states that, since people have the ability to choose, we should respect their right to do so. Indeed, this is a person's most fundamental right: the right to decide how to live their own life. Of course, this cannot be an absolute right. Suppose that I decide that I really want to be a serial killer. By exercising my right to choose, I would be denying my victims the same right. The principle of individual autonomy therefore states that individuals should be given the right to choose how to live their lives as long as this does not involve denying the same right to others.

The principle of individual autonomy provides an answer to the question: why do we have the criminal law? The criminal law exists in order to protect the autonomy of individuals. By criminalising murder the criminal law prevents would-be killers from denying their victims the right to choose how to live their life. The same applies to other criminal offences. For example, the offence of rape protects individuals' right to choose whom to have sexual intercourse with. And the offence of theft protects individuals' right to choose what to do with their property.

## ACTIVITY

Protection of individual autonomy is not the only potential justification for criminal laws. Can you think of any others? (By the end of the chapter you should be able to list several more!)

The principle of individual autonomy also helps us to answer another question: when should people be held criminally responsible? Since we each have the ability to make choices, the principle states that we should be held responsible for the choices that we make. So if I choose to become a serial killer and murder people, I should be held responsible for my victims' deaths. As well as being held responsible for results that I choose to bring about, the principle also states that I should be held responsible for results that I choose to risk bringing about. So if I choose to play football next to my neighbour's greenhouse, aware that the ball might smash the glass, the principle of individual autonomy states that I should be held responsible when the ball smashes the glass since I chose to take the risk that this would happen.

Conversely, the principle of individual autonomy tells us that individuals should not be held criminally responsible for conduct they did not freely choose. So, for example, a defendant should not be criminally liable for another person's death if they did not freely choose to either cause the death or to risk causing the death. This provides an explanation for why children under the age of ten and defendants who establish a defence of insanity are not found guilty of any crime: they lack sufficient capacity to be held responsible for their conduct.

## ACTIVITY

You are at a party. Knowing that you have to drive home later, you only drink fruit juice. Unbeknown to you, someone spikes your drink. You do not taste the alcohol and, when you drive home later in the evening, you have no idea that you are over the legal limit. You are stopped by police conducting random spot checks and subsequently convicted of drink-driving (a crime that does not require any proof of fault). According to the principle of individual autonomy, should you be criminally liable? Can you think of any arguments to support imposing criminal liability in a situation like this one?

## ● ● ● The harm principle

Closely related to the principle of individual autonomy is the harm principle. The harm principle is the most common starting point for discussions of the scope of the criminal law. The nineteenth-century theorist John Stuart Mill famously described the harm principle as follows:[4]

> [T]he only purpose for which power can rightfully be exercised over any member of a civilised community against his will is to prevent harm to others. His own good, either physical or moral, is not a sufficient warrant.

As this extract illustrates, Mill's concern was to impose limits on the use of the criminal sanction. He emphasised that conduct should only be criminalised if it causes harm to others. Conduct which is not harmful should not be criminalised, even if the conduct is immoral or harmful to the person performing it. However, it does not follow from Mill's statement that all conduct that does cause harm to others should be criminalised. Take sports such as rugby or boxing as an example. Participants in these sports may well cause harm to their opponents (bruises, cuts, broken bones). Criminalising such sports may be compatible with Mill's version of the harm principle, but it does not follow that they should be criminalised. In other words, the harm principle expounded by Mill imposes a necessary, but not a sufficient, condition for criminalisation.

One of the most thorough examinations of the harm principle is Joel Feinberg's four-volume work *The Moral Limits of the Criminal Law*. In it, Feinberg discusses how the word 'harm' should be understood in this context. He argues that a person causes harm to another when: (1) he sets back that other person's interests; *and* (2) he wrongs the other person. Having defined harm, Feinberg states the harm principle as follows:[5]

> It is always a good reason in support of penal legislation that it would probably be effective in preventing (eliminating, reducing) harm to persons other than the actor (the one prohibited from acting) *and* there is probably no other means that is equally effective at no greater cost to other values.

So in contrast to Mill's negative formulation, Feinberg's statement of the harm principle specifies a set of conditions which *do* justify criminalisation. These are:

- The conduct causes harm to another person, in that it sets back that other person's interests.
- The conduct is wrongful.
- There is no other way of preventing the harm that is equally effective and has no greater cost to other values.

If these conditions are satisfied, there is 'good reason' to criminalise the conduct. The next step is to balance the arguments in favour of criminalisation against any competing considerations. Feinberg explains that, when performing this balancing exercise, a range of considerations should be taken into account including: the gravity of the possible harm; the probability of it occurring; and the value and usefulness of the dangerous conduct.

## ACTIVITY

Can you use Feinberg's account of the harm principle to explain why it is not a criminal offence for a boxer to harm his opponent?

---

[4]Mill, J.S. (1874) *On Liberty*. Longmans: London
[5]Feinberg, J. (1984) *The Moral Limits of the Criminal Law, Volume One: Harm to Others*. OUP: New York, 26.

## The offence principle

As well as the harm principle, Feinberg advocates another possible justification for criminalisation: the offence principle. He describes this as follows:[6]

> It is always a good reason in support of a proposed criminal prohibition that it is probably necessary to prevent serious offense to persons other than the actor and would probably be an effective means to that end if enacted.

So according to Feinberg's offence principle, conduct that is offensive to other people may potentially be criminalised even if it does not cause them any harm. Notice, however, that Feinberg insists that the offence must be 'serious'. He later expands on this:[7]

> Provided that very real and intense offense is taken predictably by virtually everyone, and the offending conduct has hardly any countervailing personal or social value of its own, prohibition seems reasonable even when the protected sensibilities are not.

This is intended to impose a high threshold. So whilst a person who dribbles, scratches, farts and belches on a crowded bus might cause disgust, the level of offence would not be sufficiently 'real and intense' to satisfy the offence principle. By contrast, if a passenger on a crowded bus performs a sexual act on a dog this may very well satisfy Feinberg's test of offensiveness.

Although Feinberg's offence principle requires a high level of offence, it has been argued that it still casts the net of criminal liability too wide. In the following extract Simester and von Hirsch argue that, whilst the offence principle does provide a valid justification for criminalisation, some further constraints on the principle are necessary.

### EXTRACT

In the following extract, Simester and von Hirsch argue that Feinberg's offence principle has too broad a scope. What reasons do they give for this?

According to Simester and von Hirsch, why does Feinberg's version of the offence principle dilute the requirement that only wrongful conduct should be criminalised?

### Simester, A.P. and von Hirsch, A. (2011) *Crimes, Harms, and Wrongs: On the Principles of Criminalisation.* Hart Publishing: Oxford, 95–97

The deficiency in Feinberg's analysis, in our view, lies in his equation of offence with affront to sensibility. If offence is defined in terms of displeasing activities (independent of any reasons why they are displeasing), its potential scope is vast. Anything you choose to do might irritate or exasperate me. A great deal depends, therefore, on how much weight is given to the various mediating principles Feinberg proposes.

As Feinberg acknowledges, this is not how offensiveness is understood in ordinary moral discourse. The mere fact that V dislikes what D is doing does not by itself make D's conduct offensive.

---

[6]Feinberg, J. (1984) *The Moral Limits of the Criminal Law, Volume One: Harm to Others.* OUP: New York, 26.

[7]Feinberg, J. (1985) *The Moral Limits of the Criminal Law, Volume Two: Offense to Others.* OUP: New York, 35.

Ordinarily, when someone objects to behaviour as offensive, she can be expected to give reasons for objecting that are ulterior to the fact that she dislikes it.

By way of illustration, consider the following extra-legal example. Suppose that D meets V one day when D is wearing a garish Day-Glo orange tie. V objects. Were harmful conduct at issue, V might say, 'That's *my* tie, and you've taken it without permission'. But if the issue is offence, the mere fact that V's sensibilities are affronted does not imply any similar transgression. It is insufficient for V to say, 'Day-Glo ties get on my nerves', for the tie-wearer has no general obligation to spare the viewer's aesthetic sensibilities. The objector would normally be expected to supply a further normative reason why the conduct should be considered objectionable.

It is true, as Feinberg points out, that the objector may not be able to say why he finds luminescent orange ties irritating, or other conduct disgusting. What irritates or disgusts has its roots in social conventions, and V may dislike D's tie because he has accepted certain traditional notions of proper dress. But breach of such a convention does not necessarily show that there is anything wrong with the behaviour – and charging someone with being offensive involves charging him with a kind of misconduct. Were V to say, 'It's simply not done to wear Day-Glo orange', that would suggest merely that D is being unconventional, not that he has acted in an improper manner.

What is needed, therefore, is the provision of reasons why D's conduct is offensive: reasons going beyond the fact that it affronts V's sensibilities. Those reasons may be various. The objector may cite a personal relationship with the actor that demands special regard for the former's sensibilities in the circumstances ('It's my birthday party, and you know how I hate Day-Glo orange'). Or the reason may concern the insulting character of the conduct ('But this is the Hibernian Society Ball on St Patrick's Day!'). Or there might be reasons of enforced togetherness warranting special attention to others' sensibilities ('We're stuck together in this confounded submarine for the next three months, and many of us detest Day-Glo orange'). But if the actor is a stranger to the objector, and no such special reasons can be cited, the mere fact that the conduct causes displeasure or exasperation is insufficient.

While one must be careful when drawing parallels between extra-legal examples and criminal policy, similar reasoning holds when one is considering the legal proscription of purportedly offensive conduct. It is not affronting the sensibilities of other persons (even many of them) that should justify possible state intervention, but affront *plus* valid normative reasons for objecting to the conduct. Where state intervention is involved, the range of eligible reasons could well differ from those in everyday life: for example, our birthday-party example of a special personal relationship would not provide reasons for state action. But reasons there still should be.

Feinberg explicitly disavows the need to supply such reasons. Admittedly, he does restrict the scope of the Offence Principle to states of affront 'caused by the wrongful (rights-violating) conduct of others'. But he then sidelines this requirement with the assertion that 'there will always be a wrong whenever an offended state [i.e. a disliked mental state] is produced in another without justification and excuse'. This reasoning supposes a general, prima facie duty not to generate offended mental states in others: consequently, the separate requirement for a wrong disappears. Since people are taken to have a right not to be affronted, Feinberg slides effortlessly from affront to wrong, subsuming the latter criterion within the former. Thus it is no surprise to find that the wrongfulness requirement is disregarded in the rest of the book. Absent further considerations, 'we don't like it' suffices. If enough people find Day-Glo ties upsetting, there would be a case for prohibition.

By withdrawing the normative element from V's objection, the justification of prohibition rests, ultimately, merely on conventional sensibilities. As Feinberg intends, this avoids rendering the Offence Principle into one version of legal moralism – but only at the risk of permitting a type of aesthetic majoritarianism. Perhaps it is true that whenever D's φing causes displeasure to V, or affront to V's sensibilities, there is in every case a prima facie *reason* (as opposed to duty) for D not to φ. But, even if this be conceded, assuming D is a private citizen, her reasons not to φ are not quite the point. What matters is *whether the state has a prima facie reason to prohibit D from φing*. On the latter question, our objection, in short, is that Feinberg's portals to the Offence Principle are too wide. Affront to sensibility, by itself, should never suffice to invoke the Offence Principle and therefore qualify for the sort of weighing exercise that both Harm and Offence Principles must then conduct.

Simester and von Hirsch accordingly argue that the offence principle should require both: (1) an affront to people's sensibilities; and (2) an element of wrongdoing. They go on to list three examples of behaviour that would satisfy these criteria:

- **Insulting conduct that is grossly derogatory:** Such conduct is not only offensive. It is also wrongful because it undermines the victim's human dignity.
- **Exhibitionism (e.g. a couple having sexual intercourse on a crowded bus):** This is wrongful because privacy does not only require the exclusion of others from one's personal domain. It also involves not having the private matters of others being involuntarily forced upon you.
- **Infringements of anonymity in public spaces:** This is wrongful because individuals have the right to be left alone. So if a stranger follows you and repeatedly asks you to give him some money, this infringes your right to anonymity in public spaces.

### ACTIVITY

Do you agree that these three examples satisfy the two criteria set out by Simester and von Hirsch? Can you think of any other examples?

## Social welfare

The three principles that we have examined so far each focused on individuals. The principle of individual autonomy emphasised protecting the right of each individual to choose how to live their own life. The harm principle emphasised protecting individuals from harm. And the offence principle emphasised protecting individuals from offence. The principle of social welfare, by contrast, does not focus on individuals. Instead, it focuses on society as a whole. It focuses on collective goals.

There are some criminal offences which are easier to explain in terms of social welfare than in terms of individual autonomy, harm or offence. Take crimes against the environment as an example. In cases involving such things as litter or air or water pollution, it may not be possible to identify specific individuals who can be described as victims. The same applies to other offences such as tax evasion or driving without a licence. These crimes may instead be understood as protecting society's collective interest in protecting the environment, requiring people to pay taxes and ensuring that only licensed drivers use public roads.

A key question for the social welfare principle is: what collective goals should society pursue? This is a question on which people may hold widely differing views, yet the demands of this principle depend on how this question is answered. For example, one person might strongly believe that it is in the best interests of society to uphold a traditional view of marriage, whereas there are many others who would disagree with this. It is important, therefore, that claims about the collective good are grounded in empirical evidence. An activity should not be criminalised on the basis of vague assertions that it harms society. Any attempt to invoke the social welfare principle should explain how the activity in question harms social welfare and produce supporting evidence.

## Legal moralism

If most members of a society regard a certain type of behaviour as immoral, is this a sufficient justification to criminalise it? Here we are not concerned with crimes like murder and rape. Whilst these are undoubtedly immoral, the existence of these crimes can be justified by reference to the harm principle. Our concern here is behaviour that does not cause harm to other people but is nonetheless regarded as immoral. Is it legitimate to criminalise such conduct? Take cruelty to animals as an example.[8] Most people would consider it wrong to cause an animal to suffer unnecessarily, notwithstanding the fact that other people are not harmed. Is this a sufficient reason to criminalise it?

The relationship between morality and the criminal law was debated in a famous exchange between Lord Devlin and Professor Hart. The context in which this exchange took place was the recommendation of the Wolfenden Report in 1957 that homosexual acts between consenting adult males in private should be decriminalised.[9] In the following extract Lord Devlin sets out the argument that criminal law may be used to prohibit immoral behaviour.

### EXTRACT

In the extract Lord Devlin says that he aims to answer the following three questions:

1. Has society the right to pass judgement on matters of morals? Or are morals always a matter for private judgement?
2. If society has the right to pass judgement on matters of morals, may it use the law to enforce these judgements?
3. If so, should it resort to using the law in all cases or only some? And if only some, how should it distinguish those cases where it should from those where it shouldn't?

How does he answer each of these questions?

Devlin also addresses another issue: how are we to identify society's opinion on moral issues? How does Devlin answer this?

Can you think of any difficulties with, or objections to, Devlin's argument?

---

[8]See, for example, the Animal Welfare Act 2006.
[9]Wolfenden Committee (1957) *Report of the Committee on Homosexual Offences and Prostitution* (Cmnd 247).

## Devlin, P. (1965) *The Enforcement of Morals*. OUP: London.

The institution of marriage is a good example for my purpose because it bridges the division, if there is one, between politics and morals. Marriage is part of the structure of our society and it is also the basis of a moral code which condemns fornication and adultery. The institution of marriage would be gravely threatened if individual judgements were permitted about the morality of adultery, on these points there must be a public morality. But public morality is not to be confined to those moral principles which support institutions such as marriage. People do not think of monogamy as something which has to be supported because our society has chosen to organize itself upon it; they think of it as something that is good in itself and offering a good way of life and that it is for that reason that our society has adopted it. I return to the statement that I have already made, that society means a community of ideas; without shared ideas on politics, morals, and ethics no society can exist. Each one of us has ideas about what is good and what is evil; they cannot be kept private from the society in which we live. If men and women try to create a society in which there is no fundamental agreement about good and evil they will fail; if, having based it on common agreement, the agreement goes, the society will disintegrate. For society is not something that is kept together physically; it is held by the invisible bonds of common thought. If the bonds were too far relaxed the members would drift apart. A common morality is part of the bondage. The bondage is part of the price of society; and mankind, which needs society, must pay its price.

The answer to the first question determines the way in which the second should be approached and may indeed very nearly dictate the answer to the second question. If society has no right to make judgements on morals, the law must find some special justification for entering the field of morality: if homosexuality and prostitution are not in themselves wrong, then the onus is very clearly on the lawgiver who wants to frame a law against certain aspects of them to justify the exceptional treatment. But if society has the right to make a judgement and has it on the basis that a recognized morality is as necessary to society as, say, a recognized government, then society may use the law to preserve morality in the same way as it uses it to safeguard anything else that is essential to its existence. If therefore the first proposition is securely established with all its implications, society has a prima facie right to legislate against immorality as such.

[...]

[I]t is not possible to set theoretical limits to the power of the State to legislate against immorality. It is not possible to settle in advance exceptions to the general rule or to define inflexibly areas of morality into which the law is in no circumstances to be allowed to enter. Society is entitled by means of its laws to protect itself from dangers, whether from within or without. Here again I think that the political parallel is legitimate. The law of treason is directed against aiding the king's enemies and against sedition from within. The justification for this is that established government is necessary for the existence of society and therefore its safety against violent overthrow must be secured. But an established morality is as necessary as good government to the welfare of society. Societies disintegrate from within more frequently than they are broken up by external pressures. There is disintegration when no common morality is observed and history shows that the loosening of moral bonds is often the first stage of disintegration, so that society is justified in taking the same steps to preserve its moral code as it does to preserve its government and other essential institutions. The suppression of vice is as much the law's business as the suppression of subversive activities; it is no more possible to define a sphere of private morality than it is to define one of private subversive activity. It is wrong to talk of private morality or of the law not being concerned with immorality as such or to try to set rigid bounds to the part which the law may play in the suppression of vice. There are no theoretical limits to the power of the State to legislate against treason and sedition, and likewise I think there can be no theoretical limits to legislation against immorality. You may argue that if a man's sins affect only himself it cannot be the concern of society. If he chooses to get drunk every night in the privacy of his own home, is any one except himself the worse for it? But suppose a quarter or a half of the population got drunk every night, what sort of society would it be? You cannot set a theoretical limit to the number of people who can get drunk before society is entitled to legislate against drunkenness. The same may be said of gambling.

In what circumstances the State should exercise its power is the third of the interrogatories I have framed. But before I get to it I must raise a point which might have been brought up in any one of the three. How are the moral judgements of society to be ascertained? By leaving it until now, I can ask it in the more limited form that is now sufficient for my purpose. How is the law-maker to ascertain the moral judgements of society? It is surely not enough that they should be reached by the opinion of the majority; it would be too much to require the individual assent of every citizen. English law has evolved and regularly uses a standard which does not depend on the counting of heads. It is that of the reasonable man. He is not to be confused with the rational man. He is not expected to reason about anything and his judgement may be largely a matter of feeling. It is the viewpoint of the man in the street – or to use an archaism familiar to all lawyers – the man in the Clapham omnibus. He might also be called the right-minded man. For my purpose I should like to call him the man in the jury box, for the moral judgement of society must be something about which any twelve men or women drawn at random might after discussion be expected to be unanimous.

[...]

There must be toleration of the maximum individual freedom that is consistent with the integrity of society. It is not confined to thought and speech; it extends to action, as is shown by the recognition of the right to conscientious objection in war-time; this example shows also that conscience will be respected even in times of national danger. The principle appears to me to be peculiarly appropriate to all questions of morals. Nothing should be punished by the law that does not lie beyond the limits of tolerance. It is not nearly enough to say that a majority dislike a practice; there must be a real feeling of reprobation [...] Not everything is to be tolerated. No society can do without intolerance, indignation, and disgust; they are the forces behind the moral law, and indeed it can be argued that if they or something like them are not present, the feelings of society cannot be weighty enough to deprive the individual of freedom of choice. I suppose that there is hardly anyone nowadays who would not be disgusted by the thought of deliberate cruelty to animals. No one proposes to relegate that or any other form of sadism to the realm of private morality or to allow it to be practised in public or in private. It would be possible no doubt to point out that until a comparatively short while ago nobody thought very much of cruelty to animals and also that pity and kindliness and the unwillingness to inflict pain are virtues more generally esteemed now than they have ever been in the past. But matters of this sort are not determined by rational argument. Every moral judgement, unless it claims a divine source, is simply a feeling that no right-minded man could behave in any other way without admitting that he was doing wrong. It is the power of a common sense and not the power of reason that is behind the judgements of society. But before a society can put a practice beyond the limits of tolerance there must be a deliberate judgement that the practice is injurious to society.

In the following extract Professor Hart responds to the arguments set out by Lord Devlin:

## EXTRACT

What are Hart's criticisms of Devlin's argument? How do Hart's criticisms compare to your own?

## Hart, H.L.A. (1963) *Law, Liberty and Morality*. OUP: London.

[T]hough [Lord Devlin] says that society has the right to enforce a morality as such on the ground that a shared morality is essential to society's existence, it is not at all clear that for him the statement that immorality jeopardizes or weakens society is a statement of empirical fact. It seems sometimes to be an *a priori* assumption, and sometimes a necessary truth and a very odd one. The most important indication that this is so is that, apart from one vague reference to "history" showing that "the loosening of moral bonds is often the first state of disintegration", no evidence is produced to show that deviation from accepted sexual morality, even by adults in private, is something which, like treason, threatens the existence of society. No reputable historian has maintained this thesis, and there is indeed much evidence against it. As a proposition of fact it is entitled to no more respect than the Emperor Justinian's statement that homosexuality was the cause of earthquakes. Lord Devlin's belief in it, and his apparent indifference to the question of evidence, are at points traceable to an undiscussed assumption. This is that all morality – sexual morality together with the morality that forbids acts injurious to others such as killing, stealing, and dishonesty – forms a single seamless web, so that those who deviate from any part are likely or perhaps bound to deviate from the whole. It is of course clear (and one of the oldest insights of political theory) that society could not exist without a morality which mirrored and supplemented the law's proscription of conduct injurious to others. But there is again no evidence to support, and much to refute, the theory that those who deviate from conventional sexual morality are in other ways hostile to society.

There seems, however, to be central to Lord Devlin's thought something more interesting, though no more convincing, than the conception of social morality as a seamless web. For he appears to move from the acceptable proposition that *some* shared morality is essential to the existence of any society to the unacceptable proposition that a society is identical with its morality as that is at any given moment of its history, so that a change in its morality is tantamount to the destruction of a society. The former proposition might be even accepted as a necessary rather than an empirical truth depending on a quite plausible definition of society as a body of men who hold certain moral views in common. But the latter proposition is absurd. Taken strictly, it would prevent us saying that the morality of a given society had changed, and would compel us instead to say that one society had disappeared and another one taken its place. But it is only on this absurd criterion of what it is for the same society to continue to exist that it could be asserted without evidence that any deviation from a society's shared morality threatens its existence.

It is clear that only this tacit identification of a society with its shared morality supports Lord Devlin's denial that there could be such a thing as private immorality and his comparison of sexual immorality, even when it takes place "in private", with treason. No doubt it is true that if deviations from conventional sexual morality are tolerated by the law and come to be known, the conventional morality might change in a permissive direction, though this does not seem to be the case with homosexuality in those European countries where it is not punishable by law. But even if the conventional morality did so change, the society in question would not have been destroyed or "subverted". We should compare such a development not to the violent overthrow of government but to a peaceful constitutional change in its form, consistent not only with the preservation of a society but with its advance.

Whilst Devlin's account has been subjected to much criticism, in recent years there have been a number of other attempts to construct legal moralist accounts of the criminal law. These accounts emphasise that the criminal law speaks with a moral voice. A criminal conviction expresses disapproval and condemnation. It is hard to see why a person deserves moral condemnation unless his conduct was wrongful. A prominent example is Antony Duff. In the following extract Duff outlines his argument for a version of legal moralism that is 'positive' and 'modest'.

## EXTRACT

Duff draws a distinction between positive and negative versions of legal moralism. What is the difference between these?

He also draws a distinction between ambitious and modest versions of legal moralism. What is the difference between these? Was Devlin's version of legal moralism modest or ambitious?

According to Duff, what kinds of wrongdoing may and may not be criminalised?

Applying Duff's approach, may: (1) animal cruelty; and (2) homosexuality be criminalised?

### Duff, R.A. (2014) 'Towards a Modest Legal Moralism'
### 8 *Criminal Law and Philosophy* 217

Negative Legal Moralism is, I believe, right, but it is also inadequately ambitious; it tells us when we may not criminalize a type of conduct (when that type of conduct is not wrong), but not when we should criminalize; it specifies a conclusive reason against criminalization, but does not tell us what could count as a good reason for criminalization. Although it is quite natural for theorists, faced by the apparently irresistible tendency of governments (at least in Britain and the United States) to reach for criminal law as a first rather than as a last resort, to look for negative principles that might constrain the tide of criminalization, we must also ask about the positive principles that should guide decisions about the scope of the criminal law; and positive Legal Moralism offers just such a principle.

However, a second distinction must now be drawn, between ambitious and modest versions of positive Legal Moralism. Moore's is an ambitious version, since he holds that every kind of moral wrongdoing is in principle worthy of criminalization, although other considerations, both principled and pragmatic, militate against criminalizing many kinds of wrongdoing, so that in the end the criminal law's scope might not be very different from that favoured by liberals who reject positive Legal Moralism. A modest Legal Moralism, by contrast, holds that only certain kinds of moral wrongdoing are even in principle worthy of criminalization; for many kinds of wrongdoing, the conduct's wrongness gives us no reason at all to criminalize it. A central task for a modest Legal Moralist is of course then to explain which kinds of wrongs are in principle criminalizable, and why.

The Legal Moralism that I favour is a modest one: the criminal law is, I believe, properly concerned not (even in principle) with every kind of moral wrongdoing, but only with wrongs that should count as 'public' rather than 'private'– which at once raises the question of how we are to distinguish public from private wrongs (see Marshall and Duff 1998, 2010). But it is a positive Legal Moralism, since I believe that the distinctive function of criminal law, the function that marks it off from other modes of legal regulation, is its focus on wrongdoing. It aims, in its substantive mode, to define the range of public wrongs that the polity is to mark and condemn as wrongs; and, in its procedural mode, to provide for those accused of committing such wrongs to be called to public account for them through the criminal trial. In a liberal republic of the kind in which we should aspire to live, the distinctive role of the criminal law is to define those wrongs for which we will be publicly called to answer by our fellow citizens, and to provide the formal, institutional mechanisms through which we can thus be called (see Duff 2007).

 **Legal paternalism**

According to legal paternalism, the state is justified in placing restrictions on individuals' freedom of choice if doing so is in their best interests. A simple example is the criminal law duty to wear a seat belt. The law restricts individuals' choice whether to wear a seat belt in order to protect them from the risk of harm. But whilst being required to wear a seat belt is not particularly objectionable, legal paternalism has the potential to be very intrusive indeed. In the following extract Paul Roberts sets out three reasons why legal paternalism is not as attractive as it might at first appear.

### EXTRACT

#### Roberts, P. (1995) 'Appendix C' in Law Commission *Consent in the Criminal Law* (Law Commission Consultation Paper No 139)

C.63 First, the paternalist argues from a philosophical slippery slope and is at constant risk of taking a tumble. The fact is that many of us make life-style choices which do not promote our immediate or long-term interests. Smoking certainly falls into this category of choices: for the paternalist it should be a clear target for criminalisation. But the point goes much further. If (as seems plausible) a balanced, healthy, diet and regular exercise would be in every person's interests the paternalist has a reason for criminalising fatty foods and sedentary life-styles. Risk-taking without good reason would also be ruled out. Sky-diving, mountaineering and most contact sports would have to be criminalised. In principle, the paternalist seems to be committed to using the criminal law to turn us all into super-fit, clean-living 'spartans', whether we like it or not. Paternalism seems less attractive when its implications are made apparent.

C.64 Secondly, some criminal prohibitions which have intuitive appeal and which are often justified by paternalist arguments are in fact best explained in terms of the harm principle and are therefore perfectly consistent with liberalism. Professor Glanville Williams gave an example of one such prohibition when he explained the rationale behind the criminalisation of duelling. At first sight this appears to be a paternalistic measure: (presumably) men who wanted to defend their honour in the traditional way were prevented from doing so *for their own good*. We are told, however, that many people were in fact hounded into duels against their will because prevailing social expectations effectively robbed them of any say in the matter. Once a man was slighted he was bound to offer a duel and his tormentor was bound to accept the challenge, even if neither wanted to fight. The duelling statute was therefore an exemplar of the harm principle. Far from interfering with people's choices in order to promote their welfare, by 'setting men free from the tyranny of custom' the statute gave effect to their authentic desires not to be injured at the hands of another. The liberal can and does support this type of statute without appealing to paternalistic arguments.

C.65 And thirdly, the liberal need not be as austere or uncompassionate as the paternalist paints her, because situations in which people might foolishly impair their own welfare do not present a straight choice between criminalisation and inaction. Modern-day liberals follow Mill in pointing out that the state can do a great deal to assist people to make the right choice without resorting to the coercion of criminal sanctions. The liberal state can educate, inform, remonstrate, persuade and exhort, and provided that it stops short of outright coercion it retains its liberal credentials. If, however, a man should freely and voluntarily consent to placing himself in permanent servitude, the consistent liberal will let him have his head. Although the paternalist's solution is apparently attractive in these extreme circumstances, it is purchased only with the sacrifice of autonomy, and that is too high a price for the liberal to pay.

To illustrate Roberts' final point – that liberals can assist people to make the 'right' choice' without resorting to the criminal sanction – consider Thaler and Sunstein's nudge principle, which they describe as a combination of liberalism and paternalism:[10]

> Libertarian paternalism is a relatively weak, soft, and nonintrusive type of paternalism because choices are not blocked, fenced off, or significantly burdened. If people want to smoke cigarettes, to eat a lot of candy, to choose an unsuitable health care plan, or to fail to save for retirement, libertarian paternalists will not force them to do otherwise – or even make things hard for them. Still, the approach we recommend does count as paternalistic, because private and public choice architects are not merely trying to track or to implement people's anticipated choices. Rather, they are self-consciously attempting to move people in directions that will make their lives better. They nudge.

So if the state wishes to discourage people from eating unhealthily, it does not have to resort to criminalising fatty foods. It can 'nudge' people in this direction (by, for example, ensuring that unhealthy snacks are not placed at checkouts) whilst still maintaining their freedom to choose. This leads us neatly on to the next principle.

## Criminal law as the least restrictive appropriate intervention

You will often hear people say that the criminal law should only be employed as a last resort. The suggestion is that, if there are other methods for tackling a particular form of misconduct (such as civil law interventions or administrative regulation), these other methods should be used instead. Only where there is no other alternative form of intervention should we resort to using the criminal law. It is easy to understand why such a principle is attractive. Concern has repeatedly been expressed about the rate at which new criminal offences are created. One study found that, in the twelve months from May 2010 to May 2011, a total of 1760 new crimes were created![11] Encouraging the use of the criminal sanction as a last resort could lead to greater restraint.

However, there are difficulties with the last resort principle. First of all, in terms of punishment and moral condemnation, the criminal law is unique. As Douglas Husak explains in the following extract, some further elaboration is needed in order to explain the significance of the uniqueness of the criminal sanction.

### EXTRACT

#### Husak, D. (2004) 'The Criminal Law as Last Resort' 24 *Oxford Journal of Legal Studies* 207

A superficial interpretation of the last resort principle is as follows: legislation has an objective. If non-criminal alternatives are preferable to the criminal law in attaining this objective, the former

---

[10]Thaler, R.H. and Sunstein, C.R. (2009) *Nudge: Improving Decisions about Health, Wealth and Happiness.* Penguin Books: London, 6.

[11]Chalmers, J. and Leverick, F. (2013) 'Tracking the Creation of Criminal Offences' *Criminal Law Review* 543. The Law Commission has also commented that: 'more than 2 and a half times as many pages were needed in Halsbury's Statutes to cover offences created in the 19 years between 1989 and 2008 than were needed to cover the offences created in the 637 years prior to that' (Law Commission (2010) *Consultation Paper on Criminal Law in Regulatory Contexts* (Consultation Paper No 195) para 1.17).

should be employed. I describe this interpretation as superficial because, as so construed, the principle says nothing distinctive about the criminal law, and seems equally applicable to *any* purposeful endeavour. In this respect, the principle is comparable to claims like 'the criminal law should not be used if it is not effective [in controlling conduct], or 'punishment ought not to be inflicted [where it] would produce more evil than the offence would'. Presumably, similar kinds of principles apply with equal force to *all* goal-directed activities; it is hard to see why *any* means should be employed that is known to be inferior to an alternative, ineffective, or counterproductive. These principles appear to be little more than requirements of practical reasoning. If a carpenter wants to turn a screw, why would he knowingly employ a means that will not succeed, would do more harm than good, or is worse than an alternative he rejects? I assume that the last resort principle is not simply a requirement of practical reasoning. A sensible interpretation of this principle must explain why it has a special (although not necessarily unique) application to the *criminal* law. This difficulty can be overcome by construing the last resort principle as a tie-breaker. The principle states that a criminal law should not be enacted unless other means are less effective in attaining the legislative objective.

So it is not merely that the criminal sanction should not be used if there are other forms of intervention that are more effective; the criminal sanction should also not be used if there are other forms of intervention that are equally effective.

However, as Husak goes on to discuss, this merely raises questions about what effectiveness means in this context. Suppose that lawmakers are considering making it a crime to do X. One possible measure of effectiveness is whether the number of incidents of X will decrease after it becomes a criminal offence. But the criminal law does not exist solely to prevent crimes. It also has an expressive function. It communicates our disapproval and condemnation of certain forms of conduct. So if X is regarded as a really serious wrong, we might still want to criminalise it even if the new offence will not result in any drop in the number of times X occurs. Husak explains this point in the following extract.

## EXTRACT

### Husak, D. (2004) 'The Criminal Law as Last Resort' 24 *Oxford Journal of Legal Studies* 207

Expressive theories are incompatible with the preventive interpretation of the last resort principle. The [preventive] version of the principle states that non-criminal alternatives should be employed when they are as good or better at preventing given kinds of conduct. Once we understand that the criminal law has both preventive and expressive functions, we need to provide a new interpretation of the last resort principle. Even though alternative modes of social control may do a better job reducing the incidence of criminality, they may fail to achieve an indispensable objective of the criminal sanction: expressing censure. To decide whether alternatives to the criminal law are equally effective, we would have to evaluate not only their ability to reduce crime, but also their efficacy as expressions.

The following example may be helpful in recognizing this point. Suppose that criminal sanctions for domestic violence were ineffective in reducing the incidence of batteries that take place behind closed doors. Imagine that empirical research demonstrated that a criminal law against domestic violence led significant numbers of battered wives to be less inclined to notify the police because they did not want their husbands to be arrested and prosecuted. Suppose the state could adopt non-criminal means to prevent domestic violence that were just as successful as an approach that invoked the criminal sanction. This empirical finding, although important for many purposes, would not provide a decisive objection to criminalizing acts of domestic violence. The point of this law is not only to reduce the incidence of the proscribed conduct, but also to censure those who engage in it. If we used these empirical studies to conclude that laws against domestic violence should not have been enacted, we would frustrate an objective of the legislature by failing to retain our conventional methods of condemning persons who are guilty of spousal abuse.

In the following extract Andrew Ashworth and Lucia Zedner seek to restate the last resort principle in a way that respects both the preventive and expressive functions of the criminal law.

## EXTRACT

Read the following extract from Ashworth and Zedner's article and then think back to the domestic violence example offered by Husak in the previous extract. Would Ashworth and Zedner's approach support criminalisation?

### Ashworth, A. and Zedner, L. (2012) 'Prevention and Criminalization: Justifications and Limits' 15 New Criminal Law Review 542

Like Bentham, Mill's view was that the criminal law should be used as a last resort, when it is clear that other methods of regulating behaviour will not succeed. However, this principle is concerned with the effectiveness of less censuring methods of regulation – an important element, but one that cannot be adopted without reference to the seriousness of the wrong itself. Some wrongs are so egregious that they ought to be subject to the censure of the criminal law and state punishment. Other, lesser wrongs may properly, and without undermining significant social values, be dealt with in some kind of lesser system of administrative offenses or civil wrongs. Assigning offenses to one category or the other will not be straightforward, but the exercise is no more difficult than many other contested issues in criminal justice. The important point is that the principle must take account not merely of the effectiveness of different modes of regulation but also of the seriousness of the wrong involved, and that it should avoid treating differently wrongs that have the same level of seriousness. As the principle of the least restrictive appropriate intervention, it has much to commend it. Thus:

[...] Criminalization should only be resorted to if it is the least restrictive appropriate response.

## The principle of legality

The principle of legality is often referred to as the rule of law. In *R v Rimmington* [2005] UKHL 63 Lord Bingham described the principle as follows:

> 33 [...] There are two guiding principles: no one should be punished under a law unless it is sufficiently clear and certain to enable him to know what conduct is forbidden before he does it; and no one should be punished for any act which was not clearly and ascertainably punishable when the act was done.

We will look at each of these requirements in turn:

**No one should be punished under a law unless it is sufficiently clear and certain to enable him to know what conduct is forbidden before he does it**

This has been described as the 'principle of maximum certainty': the wording of criminal laws should be as clear and as certain as possible.[12] The reason for this is rooted in

---

[12]Horder, J. (2016) *Ashworth's Principles of Criminal Law*. 8th edn. Oxford: OUP, 85–87.

the principle of individual autonomy. If individuals are to be held responsible for their choices, criminal offences must be defined clearly enough for individuals to know what conduct is and isn't criminal. It would be unjust to hold a person criminally liable for their conduct if they had not been given fair warning that their conduct constituted a criminal offence.

Consider, for example, the statutory definition of 'anti-social behaviour'. This states that conduct is anti-social if it causes, or is likely to cause, harassment, alarm or distress to another person.[13] This definition has been applied to a very wide range of conduct, including: drunken disorder; threatening behaviour; drug abuse; noise nuisance; graffiti; fly-tipping; fly-posting; littering; abandoned vehicles; mini-moto misuse; dog fouling; prostitution; begging; high hedges; and, young people hanging around.[14] Some of the items on this list may surprise you, but in fact the definition is capable of being applied even more broadly! The behaviour of the hypothetical bus passenger that we mentioned earlier – who dribbles, scratches, farts and belches in front of other passengers – is likely to cause other passengers harassment, alarm or distress. Even the person who has a barbeque in his back garden may satisfy the definition, if he happens to have a neighbour who does not like the smell of sausages.[15]

It is unsurprising, then, that critics of the definition of anti-social behaviour have argued that it is insufficiently clear and precise.[16] But in the eyes of supporters of the definition, this vagueness is beneficial since it ensures flexibility. This means that if new types of anti-social behaviour emerge which have not been foreseen, they will still fall within the scope of the legislation. One Government spokesman explained, '[W]idely drawn legislation with clarity of purpose, and with clear expectations placed on those who use it, can be a flexible method'.[17] But drafting deliberately far-reaching and imprecise laws in order to confer wide-ranging discretion on those using them is contrary to the principle of maximum certainty. It may not only fail to give individuals fair warning of what the law requires, it also creates the possibility that the discretion vested in officials will be applied in an inconsistent or discriminatory manner. Yet this legislative technique has also been applied in other contexts. For example, a number of the offences contained in the Terrorism Acts 2000 and 2006 have been criticised for being both overly broad and vague.[18]

So whilst the principle of maximum certainty is important, there are competing practical concerns that are sometimes given precedence by lawmakers. In fact, as we'll see in a moment, even though the principle of maximum certainty has been enshrined in Article 7 of the European Convention on Human Rights, the case law on Article 7 is weaker than one might expect. This leads us neatly to the second strand of the principle of legality.

---

[13]Anti-Social Behaviour, Crime and Policing Act 2014, s.2(1).

[14]See Macdonald, S. (2006) 'A Suicidal Woman, Roaming Pigs and a Noisy Trampolinist: Refining the ASBO's Definition of "Anti-Social Behaviour"' 69 *Modern Law Review* 183 and the sources cited therein.

[15]This example was discussed during the Parliamentary debates on the Crime and Disorder Act 1998.

[16]In addition to Macdonald (n 14 above) see: Ashworth, A., Gardner, J., Morgan, R., Smith, A.T.H, von Hirsch, A. and Wasik, M. (1995) 'Overtaking on the Right' 145 *New Law Journal* 1501; and, Ashworth, A., Gardner, J., Morgan, R., Smith, A.T.H., von Hirsch, A. and Wasik M. (1998) 'Clause 1 – The Hybrid Law from Hell?' 31 *Criminal Justice Matters* 25.

[17]Alun Michael (Home Office spokesman) HC Standing Committee B col 70 30 April 1998.

[18]A noteworthy example is the encouragement of terrorism offence (Terrorism Act 2006, s.1), on which see Marchand, S.A. (2010) 'An Ambiguous Response to a Real Threat: Criminalizing the Glorification of Terrorism in Britain' 42 *George Washington International Law Review* 123.

No one should be punished for any act which was not clearly and ascertainably punishable when the act was done

## ACTIVITY

Imagine that on 7 July 2019 John has sexual intercourse with Christine, even though at the time he is married to Valerie. Six months later Parliament creates a new law which states: 'It shall be a criminal offence to commit an act of adultery. This new offence shall apply retrospectively, from 1 January 2019'. John is subsequently arrested and charged with the new crime of adultery. What objections, if any, would you have to John being convicted of this crime?

In this example, the principal objection to John's conviction is that, at the time he committed adultery, he had no idea that his actions would subsequently be deemed to be a criminal offence. In other words, his conviction infringes the principle of individual autonomy because at no stage did he make a choice to break the criminal law. It is for this reason that the principle of legality insists that no one should be punished for an act which was not clearly punishable at the time it was done. This is known as the principle of non-retroactivity.[19] It is regarded as so important that it is enshrined in Article 7 of the European Convention on Human Rights as an absolute right (i.e. no exceptions are permitted, even in a time of war or other public emergency).

## EXTRACT

### Article 7 of the European Convention on Human Rights

#### No punishment without law

1.  No one shall be held guilty of any criminal offence on account of any act or omission which did not constitute a criminal offence under national or international law at the time when it was committed. Nor shall a heavier penalty be imposed than the one that was applicable at the time the criminal offence was committed.

As indicated above, however, there are competing considerations at play here. What makes our example involving John so powerful is that it was completely unforeseeable that Parliament would make adultery a criminal offence. The weight that you attach to the principle of non-retroactivity might change if the new law was more predictable, or even to be expected. Take the case of *R v R* [1992] 1 AC 599 as an example. The issue for the House of Lords in this case was whether the defendant could be guilty of raping his wife. The alleged offence took place in 1989. According to the law as stated in 1736, a husband could not be convicted of raping his wife. This was known as the marital rape exception, and was based on the view that a woman gave her consent upon marriage and could not later withdraw it. What made the case difficult was that at no stage between 1736 and 1989 had Parliament changed the law (in fact, the Law Commission urged

---

[19]Horder, J. (2016) *Ashworth's Principles of Criminal Law*. 8th edn. Oxford: OUP, 82–84.

Parliament to do so in 1990). The House of Lords handed down its judgment in 1991. It abolished the marital rape exception – stating that it was incompatible with the conditions of modern life – and upheld the defendant's conviction.

### ACTIVITY

Did the House of Lords' judgment infringe the principle of non-retroactivity? If so, was this justifiable?

Following the House of Lords' judgment the defendant in *R v R* pursued his case to the European Court of Human Rights. The European Court, in *SW v United Kingdom* (1995) 21 EHRR 363, held that the defendant's conviction did not violate Article 7. It explained the requirements of Article 7 as follows:

> 36. However clearly drafted a legal provision may be, in any system of law, including criminal law, there is an inevitable element of judicial interpretation. There will always be a need for elucidation of doubtful points and for adaptation to changing circumstances. Indeed, in the United Kingdom, as in the other Convention States, the progressive development of the criminal law through judicial law-making is a well entrenched and necessary part of legal tradition. Article 7 (art. 7) of the Convention cannot be read as outlawing the gradual clarification of the rules of criminal liability through judicial interpretation from case to case, provided that the resultant development is consistent with the essence of the offence and could reasonably be foreseen.

Applying this to the facts of the case, the Court stated that the abolition of the marital rape exception was 'consistent with the very essence of the offence' and that the evolution of the offence meant that the House of Lords' decision was 'a reasonably foreseeable development of the law'.[20] The Court added that:

> 44. [...] [T]he abandonment of the unacceptable idea of a husband being immune against prosecution for rape of his wife was in conformity not only with a civilised concept of marriage but also, and above all, with the fundamental objectives of the Convention, the very essence of which is respect for human dignity and human freedom.

So whilst the principle of non-retroactivity is important, it is clear from the decision in *SW v United Kingdom* that Article 7 leaves room for judges to develop the law, provided that these developments are reasonably foreseeable and consistent with the essence of the offence.

## The correspondence principle

The correspondence principle also focuses on how offences are defined. More specifically, it is concerned with the relationship between the different requirements that must

---

[20]Similar reasoning was employed by the Court of Appeal in *R v C* [2004] EWCA Crim 292. In this case the defendant was convicted in 2002 of having raped his wife in 1970.

be proved in order to establish liability for an offence. Ashworth and Campbell offer the following definition:[21]

> [I]f the offence is defined in terms of certain consequences and certain circumstances, the mental element ought to correspond with that by referring to those consequences or circumstances. If a mental element as to a lesser consequence were acceptable, this would amount to constructive criminal liability.

Figure 1.1 illustrates this. The diagram focuses on offences against people. On the left are different 'consequences', that is different levels of injury that a victim might suffer. On the right are different 'mental elements', that is different states of mind that the prosecution might have to prove for a conviction. According to the correspondence principle, the state of mind that is required for a conviction should align with the specified consequence. So, for example, death is the specified consequence in homicide offences. So, according to the correspondence principle, the required state of mind should also refer to death. A homicide offence would therefore satisfy the correspondence principle if it required either proof of an intention to kill or recklessness as to whether the victim would be killed.

*Consequence*              *Mental element*

Death

- Intention to kill V
- Recklessness whether V will be killed

Grievous bodily harm (GBH)

- Intention to cause V GBH
- Recklessness whether V will suffer GBH

Actual bodily harm (ABH)

- Intention to cause V ABH
- Recklessness whether V will suffer ABH

**Figure 1.1.** The correspondence principle (1)

In order to understand why the correspondence principle is important, consider an example. In Chapter 5, we will study the offence of murder. We will learn that: (1) only intention will suffice for the offence of murder, recklessness is insufficient; and (2) the defendant need not have intended to kill, it is enough that he had an intention to cause grievous bodily harm. Figure 1.2 incorporates these two points.

**An example: murder**

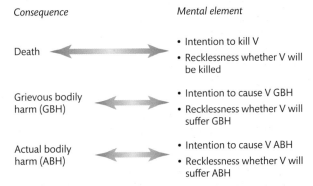

*Consequence*              *Mental element*

Death                      Intention to kill V

*Constructive liability*

Grievous bodily harm (GBH)           Intention to cause V GBH

Actual bodily harm (ABH)           Intention to cause V ABH

**Figure 1.2.** The correspondence principle (2): an example – murder

---

[21]Ashworth, A. and Campbell, K. 'Recklessness in Assault – and in General?' (1991) 107 *Law Quarterly Review* 187.

So the definition of murder requires that the victim died, but to secure a conviction it is sufficient to show that the defendant had an intention to cause the victim grievous bodily harm. In other words, as long as the defendant intended to cause the victim serious harm he can be convicted of murder – even if the possibility of the victim dying never crossed his mind. This violates the correspondence principle and is an example of what criminal lawyers call 'constructive liability'. Constructive liability is controversial because it is difficult to reconcile with the principle of individual autonomy.[22] If the possibility of the victim dying never crossed the defendant's mind, then it cannot be said that the defendant at least chose to take a risk that the victim would be killed.

## The presumption of innocence

The legality and correspondence principles each focus on how offences are defined. Once an offence has been defined, the next question which arises is: who should bear the burden of proving each element of the offence? The starting point here is a famous passage from the judgment of Viscount Sankey LC in *Woolmington v Director of Public Prosecutions* [1935] AC 462.

### EXTRACT

*Woolmington v Director of Public Prosecutions* [1935] AC 462

#### Viscount Sankey LC

Throughout the web of the English Criminal Law one golden thread is always to be seen, that it is the duty of the prosecution to prove the prisoner's guilt subject to what I have already said as to the defence of insanity and subject also to any statutory exception. If, at the end of and on the whole of the case, there is a reasonable doubt, created by the evidence given by either the prosecution or the prisoner [...] the prosecution has not made out the case and the prisoner is entitled to an acquittal. No matter what the charge or where the trial, the principle that the prosecution must prove the guilt of the prisoner is part of the common law of England and no attempt to whittle it down can be entertained.

Being convicted of a crime has serious repercussions for an individual. Add to this the fact that the state has far greater resources with which to conduct prosecutions than individuals have to defend themselves, and it seems right that no one should be convicted unless the state has proven their guilt beyond reasonable doubt. This is known as the presumption of innocence. Or, to put it differently, it is the principle that the prosecution should bear the burden of proof.

The presumption of innocence is enshrined in Article 6(2) of the European Convention on Human Rights.[23] In *Barberà, Messegué and Jabardo v Spain* (1988) 11 EHRR 360 the European Court of Human Rights explained the requirements of Article 6(2).

---

[22]See: Horder, J. (1995) 'A Critique of the Correspondence Principle in Criminal Law' *Criminal Law Review* 759; and Mitchell, B. (1999) 'In Defence of a Principle of Correspondence' *Criminal Law Review* 195.

[23]Article 6(2) states: 'Everyone charged with a criminal offence shall be presumed innocent until proved guilty according to law.'

## EXTRACT

*Barberà, Messegué and Jabardo v Spain* (1988) 11 EHRR 360

### European Court of Human Rights

77. Paragraph 2 (art. 6–2) embodies the principle of the presumption of innocence. It requires, inter alia, that when carrying out their duties, the members of a court should not start with the preconceived idea that the accused has committed the offence charged; the burden of proof is on the prosecution, and any doubt should benefit the accused. It also follows that it is for the prosecution to inform the accused of the case that will be made against him, so that he may prepare and present his defence accordingly, and to adduce evidence sufficient to convict him.

At the same time, however, the European Court has accepted that states may reverse the burden of proof – as long as these reverse burden provisions are kept 'within reasonable limits' and 'take into account the importance of what is at stake and maintain the rights of the defence'.[24] You may also have noticed that, in spite of his grand-sounding rhetoric, Viscount Sankey LC also envisaged exceptions to the presumption of innocence. One of these was the defence of insanity, which we will study in Chapter 10. The other exception mentioned by Viscount Sankey LC was more open-ended. He accepted that Parliament could create statutory exceptions to the presumption of innocence. A study by Andrew Ashworth and Meredith Blake in 1996 found that this exception was being employed routinely.[25] Ashworth and Blake examined 540 offences triable in the Crown Court (i.e. 540 of the most serious offences) and found that 219 (40 per cent) placed the burden of proof for at least part of the offence on the defendant. Their study concluded by warning that the 'apparent casualness' with which Parliament was creating reverse burden provisions was undermining the presumption of innocence.

Since the introduction of the Human Rights Act 1998, there have been signs that the courts in this country are now taking a stricter approach to the presumption of innocence. To understand this case law, it is important to appreciate the distinction between an evidential and a persuasive burden:

- **An evidential burden:** this requires the party to produce sufficient relevant evidence of a matter to justify the jury being asked to consider it. For example, a defendant who wishes to claim that he acted in self-defence must discharge the evidential burden. He must produce sufficient evidence that he did indeed act in self-defence to justify leaving the defence to the jury.

- **A persuasive burden:** once the evidential burden has been discharged, the next question is who should bear the burden of persuading the jury. In other words, should the prosecution or the defence bear the burden of proof? In our self-defence example, once the defence has discharged the evidential burden the prosecution would bear the burden of proof. The prosecution would be required to convince the jury beyond reasonable doubt that the defendant did not in fact act in self-defence.

---

[24]*Salabiaku v France* (1988) 13 EHRR 379, [28].
[25]Ashworth, A. and Blake, B. (1996) 'The Presumption of Innocence in English Criminal Law' *Criminal Law Review* 306.

In *R v Lambert* [2001] UKHL 37 the defendant, Steven Lambert, had been convicted of possessing cocaine with intent to supply. The relevant statute provided that it was for the defendant to prove that he neither knew, nor suspected, nor had any reason to suspect that he was in possession of the cocaine.[26] By a majority of 4–1, the House of Lords held that the statute placed an evidential, not a persuasive, burden on the defendant. Notwithstanding the public interest in combating the illegal drug trade, the majority held that it would be disproportionate and a breach of Article 6(2) to impose a persuasive burden on defendants charged with this offence. Their Lordships then explained that the Human Rights Act imposes an obligation to interpret legislation compatibly with the European Convention whenever possible. Even though the natural interpretation of the statutory wording was that it imposed a persuasive burden, the wording was deemed sufficiently flexible to be interpreted as only requiring an evidential burden.

Since then this approach has been adopted in other cases.[27] When deciding whether a persuasive burden is disproportionate, issues for the court to consider include the seriousness of the misconduct the offence targets and the difficulties both prosecutors and the defence will face proving the matter in question. For example, in a licensing case it may be justifiable to impose a persuasive burden on the defendant, since it may be easier for them to prove that they have a licence than it is for the state to prove that they do not have one.

## The ladder principle

The ladder principle is concerned with the relationship between different offences. In *R v Coutts* [2006] UKHL 39 Lord Bingham stated:

> 12 In any criminal prosecution for a serious offence there is an important public interest in the outcome (*R v Fairbanks* [1986] 1 WLR 1202, 1206). The public interest is that, following a fairly conducted trial, defendants should be convicted of offences which they are proved to have committed and should not be convicted of offences which they are not proved to have committed. The interests of justice are not served if a defendant who has committed a lesser offence is either convicted of a greater offence, exposing him to greater punishment than his crime deserves, or acquitted altogether, enabling him to escape the measure of punishment which his crime deserves. The objective must be that defendants are neither over-convicted nor under-convicted, nor acquitted when they have committed a lesser offence of the type charged.

As Lord Bingham explains, justice not only requires that the guilty are convicted and the innocent are acquitted. It also requires that the guilty are convicted of a crime that reflects the seriousness of their offence. They should not be 'over-convicted' or 'under-convicted'.

Building on this sentiment, the Law Commission has advanced the 'ladder principle'.[28] The ladder principle states that there should be a hierarchy – or ladder – of criminal offences. This ladder should reflect the seriousness of the different offences, with the most serious ones at the top and the least serious at the bottom. In addition, the Law Commission explained that there should be minimal overlap between the different

---

[26]Misuse of Drugs Act 1971, s.28(2).

[27]See in particular: *Sheldrake v DPP; Attorney-General's Reference (No 4 of 2002)* [2004] UKHL 43.

[28]See: Law Commission (2005) *A New Homicide Act for England and Wales? A Consultation Paper* (Law Commission Consultation Paper No 177); and Law Commission (2006) *Murder, Manslaughter and Infanticide* (Law Commission Report No 304) HC 30.

offences, and individual offences should not be so broad that they cover a large variety of conduct of widely differing levels of gravity. In short:[29]

> A ladder of offence seriousness is defensible so long as, by and large, the cases that fall within a particular tier are, other things being equal, more serious than the cases that, by and large, fall within the tier below.

---

### ACTIVITY

1. When we study the law of homicide in Chapter 5, we will encounter the following three scenarios. In your opinion, should each defendant be: convicted of murder; convicted of manslaughter or not convicted of any homicide offence?

   - A woman suffering from an incurable, incapacitating disease repeatedly begs her husband to end her life. One night, after she keeps him awake for most of the night pleading to have her life ended, he gives into her requests. He puts a pillow over her face and asphyxiates her.[30]

   - A terrorist plants a bomb and then contacts the authorities and warns them. He plants a live bomb instead of a fake one – so that the authorities will fear him and listen to him – but he doesn't want the bomb to explode because he fears that he will lose public support if innocent people are killed. He gives the warning some time before the bomb is set to explode, so that the public can be evacuated and a bomb disposal expert can defuse the bomb. However, the bomb explodes and kills the bomb disposal expert.[31]

   - During an operation, an inexperienced and exhausted anaesthetist fails to notice that the tube supplying oxygen to the victim has become disconnected. Four-and-a-half minutes later, an alarm sounds on the blood pressure monitor. Still not noticing the disconnected tube, the anaesthetist administers some drugs to raise the patient's pulse. A few minutes later the patient suffers cardiac arrest and dies.[32]

2. In Chapter 5 we will see that, under the current law of homicide, the outcomes of the three scenarios would be as follows:

   - The husband would be convicted of a more serious offence (murder) than the other two defendants.
   - The terrorist and the anaesthetist would be convicted of the same offence (manslaughter).

   Are these outcomes what you expected? In your opinion, are these outcomes consistent with the ladder principle?

---

## Fair labelling

Our final principle is fair labelling. This principle focuses on the names we give to criminal offences. It insists that the names that we attach to criminal offences should be fair. This immediately raises two questions: what does it mean for an offence label to be fair

---

[29]Law Commission (2006) *Murder, Manslaughter and Infanticide* (Law Commission Report No 304) HC 30), para 2.47.

[30]These are the facts of *R v Cocker* [1989] Crim LR 740, in which the defendant unsuccessfully appealed against his conviction for murder.

[31]As we will see in Chapter 5, although the terrorist in this hypothetical scenario acts recklessly he lacks the necessary intention to be convicted of murder.

[32]These are the facts of *R v Adomako* [1995] 1 AC 171, a leading case on gross negligence manslaughter.

and why is it important? In their article on this topic, James Chalmers and Fiona Leverick discuss a number of potential justifications for fair labelling:[33]

- Fairness to offenders requires that offence labels represent their wrongdoing accurately (e.g. most would agree that it would be unfair to apply the label 'murder' to every case of unlawful killing).
- Offence labels have an educative function – they make clear to offenders exactly what it is they have done wrong.
- Offence labels have a deterrent effect – they dissuade potential offenders who do not wish to be stigmatised from committing the crime in question.
- Fairness to victims requires that offence labels reflect the nature of the defendant's wrongdoing accurately.
- Excessively broad offence labels confer too much discretion on sentencers.
- Offence labels need to be accurate since they communicate information to criminal justice agencies, for example, sentencing judges have regard to previous convictions.
- Offence labels should also be accurate because they communicate information to agencies operating outside the criminal justice process, for example, potential employers.
- Offence labels should be accurate since they have a symbolic function, communicating the nature of an offender's wrongdoing to society at large.

## ACTIVITY

Which of these reasons do you believe are the most important? Are there any that you find unconvincing?

## EXTRACT

In the following extract Chalmers and Leverick explain which of the reasons they consider to be the most important. How closely does their assessment match your own?

Chalmers and Leverick draw a distinction between labelling in the sense of description and labelling in the sense of differentiation. What is the difference between these? Which form of labelling is most relevant to which groups of people?

### Chalmers, J. and Leverick, F. (2008) 'Fair Labelling in Criminal Law' 71 *Modern Law Review* 217

Why, then, does labelling matter? The first thing that can be said is that, of the justifications examined above, some of them – the sentencing discretion argument, the educative argument and the deterrence argument – are unconvincing or tangential. Others, while not entirely unconvincing, are insufficiently developed. Clearly labelling raises issues of fairness to the offender but the precise nature of the unfairness concerned needs to be articulated. The

---

[33]Chalmers, J. and Leverick, F. (2008) 'Fair Labelling in Criminal Law' 71 *Modern Law Review* 217.

interest in question is the offender's legitimate interest in protecting her reputation and on this basis the argument that insufficiently precise labels are unfair to the offender is one that has some force. At the very least, this is a convincing justification for labels that are not inaccurate or potentially misleading.

Another strong justification for fair labelling is that decision-makers rely on the offence name and the information it conveys in making decisions about the offender. These might be decisions within the criminal justice system – such as sentencing – or decisions made outside the criminal justice system, such as offers of employment. In both instances, the decision-maker uses the offence name to draw conclusions about the nature of the offender's previous criminal behaviour. Information on the length of sentence may or may not be available as an additional source of information (it would be for sentencing decisions, for employment decisions it may not), but while this can tell the decision-maker something about offence seriousness, it is not informative about the nature of the conduct. This does matter, for reasons of fairness both to the offender and for public protection, although the degree of information that is necessary to ensure fairness in this respect is another question.

Finally, it has been suggested that the victim (or her family) has a legitimate interest in fair labelling in that she deserves to have her suffering reflected by an offence of appropriate seriousness. But despite this legitimate interest, given that it would be unfair to the offender if the label over-represented her culpability and unfair to the public if it under-represented it, the victim's perspective appears to add little to those already considered.

Thus it can be said that the most convincing argument for fair labelling is that offence names communicate information about the offender to a number of different bodies – the public, agencies operating both within and outside the criminal justice system – and that members of these groups may form opinions or make decisions about the offender that turn on the information received. It is also clear, however, that what constitutes 'fair' labelling in each of these contexts may differ. Where information is being communicated to agencies and individuals operating outside the criminal justice system, no assumption of legal knowledge can be made. In addition, in the particular context of providing a signal to the public, information is likely to be filtered through media reports, which may distort the accuracy of the message. Fair labelling in this context is labelling that is fair in the *descriptive* sense – the use of simple, informative offence names that convey the essential nature of the wrongdoing and minimise the potential for misrepresentation or misunderstanding. To quote Ashworth's original formulation, 'the label applied to an offence ought fairly to represent the offender's wrongdoing'. What is important here is not so much the extent to which offences are differentiated but *the name itself*.

By contrast, in the context of decisions made by legal professionals, some reliance can be placed upon their legal knowledge, making the specific terms used to identify offences of less importance. What matters here is not so much the name itself but the differentiation of offences. Thus fair labelling in this context takes on a second meaning – labelling that fairly *differentiates* wrongdoing. For example, it was suggested earlier that the 'label' offered by section 20 of the Offences Against the Person Act 1861 may be unfair, in that it is liable to mislead the public as to the culpability of the defendant. But that is of little concern to a prosecutor who subsequently examines an individual's criminal record, as that prosecutor will be well aware of what is meant by section 20 of the 1861 Act. For her purposes, it is the fact that the individual has been deemed to have recklessly – rather than deliberately – caused grievous bodily harm to another that will be crucial. The wording of the 'label' which is used to communicate that fact is of little, if any, importance. For these purposes, the distinctions involved could just as validly be communicated by way of hieroglyphics, leaving aside the inefficiencies involved in such a system. It is differentiation rather than description which is crucial here.

 ## A case study: *R v Brown*

Having studied these different principles, it is helpful to consider how they might be applied in a particular case. The case study that we will use is the House of Lords' decision in *R v Brown* [1994] 1 AC 212. This case involved a group of homosexual middle-aged men who committed acts of violence against each other for sexual pleasure. The acts included: whipping; caning; applying stinging nettles to the genitals; inserting fish hooks into the penis; nailing the scrotum or foreskin to pieces of board and burning the penis with a candle. The activities were carried out in private and had been going on for a number of years. There was no evidence that any of the men had suffered permanent injury or ever sought medical treatment. The police discovered the group's activities by chance, when investigating other matters.

Five of the defendants were convicted of the offence of assault occasioning actual bodily harm. Three were convicted of the more serious offence of malicious wounding.[34] The prosecution accepted that the victims had consented to their injuries. The House of Lords had to decide whether consensually inflicting injury for the purpose of sexual gratification is a lawful or unlawful activity. By a majority of 3–2, the House of Lords held that it is an unlawful activity and upheld the men's convictions.

### ACTIVITY

Each of the following sets of questions concerns one of the principles that we have studied in this chapter. Think through the questions and write down your answers. (You may find it helpful to look back at the relevant pages as you do this.)

- Did the House of Lords' decision infringe the principle of individual autonomy? If so, whose autonomy was infringed?
- Can the decision be justified using the harm principle? Did the defendants' conduct cause harm to the victims? If so, was their conduct wrongful?
- Can the decision be justified using the offence principle? Who (if anyone) was caused offence?
- Does the decision advance social welfare? If so, what collective goals does the decision advance? Is there supporting evidence that shows that the defendants' conduct harms social welfare?
- Were the defendants' activities immoral? If so, should the criminal law enforce this particular moral standard?
- Were the victims placing themselves at risk? If so, should the criminal law intervene in order to protect their best interests?
- Were other forms of intervention available to regulate the men's activities? If so, would these have been equally effective and appropriate?
- Was the conduct in question a crime prior to the House of Lords' decision? If not, did the decision infringe the principle of legality?
- Do the offence labels offer a fair indication of the nature of the defendants' offences? If not, does this matter, and to whom?

Having answered each of these questions, look back over your answers. Weighing up both sides of the argument, do you believe the conduct in *R v Brown* should constitute a criminal offence?

---

[34]Offences Against the Person Act 1861, sections 47 and 20 respectively. We will study these offences in Chapter 6.

## EXTRACT

Read the following extracts from the judgments of Lord Templeman (majority) and Lord Mustill (minority). These extracts address some of the above questions. What answers do they offer to these questions? How do their answers compare to your own? Who do you find yourself in agreement with?

### R v Brown [1994] 1 AC 212

### Lord Templeman

[I]t was said, every person has a right to deal with his body as he pleases. I do not consider that this slogan provides a sufficient guide to the policy decision which must now be made. It is an offence for a person to abuse his own body and mind by taking drugs. Although the law is often broken, the criminal law restrains a practice which is regarded as dangerous and injurious to individuals and which if allowed and extended is harmful to society generally. In any event the appellants in this case did not mutilate their own bodies. They inflicted bodily harm on willing victims

[...]

A sadist draws pleasure from inflicting or watching cruelty. A masochist derives pleasure from his own pain or humiliation. The appellants are middle-aged men. The victims were youths some of whom were introduced to sado-masochism before they attained the age of 21. In his judgment in the Court of Appeal, Lord Lane C.J. said that two members of the group of which the appellants formed part, namely one Cadman and the appellant Laskey:

> "were responsible in part for the corruption of a youth K ... It is some comfort at least to be told, as we were, that K. has now it seems settled into a normal heterosexual relationship. Cadman had befriended K. when the boy was 15 years old. He met him in a cafeteria and, so he says, found out that the boy was interested in homosexual activities. He introduced and encouraged K. in 'bondage affairs.' He was interested in viewing and recording on videotape K. and other teenage boys in homosexual scenes ... One cannot overlook the danger that the gravity of the assaults and injuries in this type of case may escalate to even more unacceptable heights."

The evidence disclosed that drink and drugs were employed to obtain consent and increase enthusiasm. The victim was usually manacled so that the sadist could enjoy the thrill of power and the victim could enjoy the thrill of helplessness. The victim had no control over the harm which the sadist, also stimulated by drink and drugs might inflict. In one case a victim was branded twice on the thigh and there was some doubt as to whether he consented to or protested against the second branding. The dangers involved in administering violence must have been appreciated by the appellants because, so it was said by their counsel, each victim was given a code word which he could pronounce when excessive harm or pain was caused. The efficiency of this precaution, when taken, depends on the circumstances and on the personalities involved. No one can feel the pain of another. The charges against the appellants were based on genital torture and violence to the buttocks, anus, penis, testicles and nipples. The victims were degraded and humiliated sometimes beaten, sometimes wounded with instruments and sometimes branded. Bloodletting and the smearing of human blood produced excitement. There were obvious dangers of serious personal injury and blood infection. Prosecuting counsel informed the trial judge against the protests of defence counsel, that although the appellants had not contracted Aids, two members of the group had died from Aids and one other had contracted an H.I.V. infection although not necessarily from the practices of the group. Some activities involved excrement. The assertion that the instruments employed by the sadists were clean and sterilised could not have removed the danger of infection, and the assertion that care was taken demonstrates the possibility of infection.

[...]

Society is entitled and bound to protect itself against a cult of violence. Pleasure derived from the infliction of pain is an evil thing. Cruelty is uncivilised. I would answer the certified question in the negative and dismiss the appeals of the appellants against conviction.

### Lord Mustill

Leaving aside repugnance and moral objection, both of which are entirely natural but neither of which are in my opinion grounds upon which the court could properly create a new crime, I can visualise only the following reasons.

(1)  Some of the practices obviously created a risk of genito-urinary infection, and others of septicaemia. These might indeed have been grave in former times, but the risk of serious harm must surely have been greatly reduced by modern medical science.

(2)  The possibility that matters might get out of hand, with grave results. It has been acknowledged throughout the present proceedings that the appellants' activities were performed as a pre-arranged ritual, which at the same time enhanced their excitement and minimised the risk that the infliction of injury would go too far. Of course things might go wrong and really serious injury or death might ensue. If this happened, those responsible would be punished according to the ordinary law, in the same way as those who kill or injure in the course of more ordinary sexual activities are regularly punished. But to penalise the appellants' conduct even if the extreme consequences do not ensue, just because they might have done so would require an assessment of the degree of risk, and the balancing of this risk against the interests of individual freedom. Such a balancing is in my opinion for Parliament, not the courts [...]

(3)  I would give the same answer to the suggestion that these activities involved a risk of accelerating the spread of auto-immune deficiency syndrome [AIDS], and that they should be brought within the Act of 1861 in the interests of public health. The consequence would be strange, since what is currently the principal cause for the transmission of this scourge, namely consenting buggery between males, is now legal. Nevertheless, I would have been compelled to give this proposition the most anxious consideration if there had been any evidence to support it. But there is none, since the case for the respondent was advanced on an entirely different ground.

(4)  There remains an argument to which I have given much greater weight. As the evidence in the present case has shown, there is a risk that strangers (and especially young strangers) may be drawn into these activities at an early age and will then become established in them for life. This is indeed a disturbing prospect, but I have come to the conclusion that it is not a sufficient ground for declaring these activities to be criminal under the Act of 1861. The element of the corruption of youth is already catered for by the existing legislation; and if there is a gap in it which needs to be filled the remedy surely lies in the hands of Parliament, not in the application of a statute which is aimed at other forms of wrongdoing. As regards proselytisation for adult sado-masochism the argument appears to me circular. For if the activity is not itself so much against the public interest that it ought to be declared criminal under the Act of 1861 then the risk that others will be induced to join in cannot be a ground for making it criminal.

We will return to *R v Brown* in Chapter 6, where we study it (the law, not the facts!) in more detail.

## ● ● ● Conclusion

In this chapter we have looked at a number of principles that are important in the criminal law.[35] We have also looked at a case study of how some of these principles might be applied in practice. What may have struck you as you worked through the case study is how malleable the different principles are. People may not only have very different views of which principles are the most important in particular contexts (e.g. in *R v Brown* Lord Templeman appeared to place more weight on legal moralism and legal paternalism than Lord Mustill), they may also disagree over how to interpret the demands of particular principles (e.g. both Lord Templeman and Lord Mustill discuss individual autonomy and social welfare, yet reach opposite conclusions!). This demonstrates a simple fact that you should remember throughout the rest of this text: applying these principles is not a mathematical process which results in either a right or a wrong answer. The principles are tools for you to use when analysing and evaluating the law. It is important that you build the confidence and the ability to think critically and form your own opinions. As you do so you will develop your own view on the relative importance of each of the principles and what they require in specific contexts. This will enable you to write strong answers to exam essay and problem questions!

## ● ● ● Self-test questions

1. Using the principles we have studied in this chapter, draw up a bullet point list of arguments for and against each of the following two statements:
   a. 'The ban on smoking cigarettes in public places should be repealed, so that people are free to smoke wherever they wish.'
   b. 'The ban on smoking cigarettes in public places should be extended, so that smoking is a criminal offence wherever it takes place.'
2. 'Any homeowner that has an unsightly or intrusive tree, hedge or other foliage which interferes with their neighbour's enjoyment of their garden should be convicted of a criminal offence.' With reference to the principles of criminal law, discuss the extent to which you agree with this statement.

## ● ● ● Your criminal law toolkit checklist

Having worked through this chapter, you should now have:

✓ An understanding of a range of the most important principles in the criminal law

✓ An awareness of the different opinions of what each of these principles require

✓ An ability to apply these principles to particular examples.

---

[35]The chapter has not attempted to provide an exhaustive list of principles of criminal law. There are other principles that we could have studied. One example is necessitous over-inclusion. This is where it is deemed necessary for a criminal law to be over-inclusive. For example, in order to prevent the use of handguns in committing crimes a criminal offence might be enacted, which prevents all possession of handguns by members of the public.

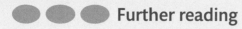 **Further reading**

Ashworth, A. and Zedner, L. (2012) 'Prevention and Criminalization: Justifications and Limits' 15 *New Criminal Law Review* 542.

Chalmers, J. and Leverick, F. (2008) 'Fair Labelling in Criminal Law' 71 *Modern Law Review* 217.

Dennis, I. (2005) 'Reverse Onuses and the Presumption of Innocence: In Search of Principle' *Criminal Law Review* 901.

Horder, J. (1995) 'A Critique of the Correspondence Principle in Criminal Law' *Criminal Law Review* 759.

Husak, D. (2004) 'The Criminal Law as Last Resort' 24 *Oxford Journal of Legal Studies* 207.

Mitchell, B. (1999) 'In Defence of a Principle of Correspondence' *Criminal Law Review* 195.

Murphy, C.C. (2010) 'The Principle of Legality in Criminal Law under the European Convention on Human Rights' *European Human Rights Law Review* 192.

Roberts, P. (1995) 'Taking the Burden of Proof Seriously' *Criminal Law Review* 783.

Simester, A.P. and von Hirsch, A. (2011) *Crimes, Harms, and Wrongs: On the Principles of Criminalisation* Oxford: Hart Publishing.

# 2

# The anatomy of a crime

## Chapter objectives

By the end of this chapter you should have:

- An understanding of how criminal offences are structured
- A basic understanding of the *actus reus*, *mens rea* and substantive defences categories
- An understanding of the requirement that the *actus reus* and *mens rea* of a crime must coincide in time and an ability to apply this to a hypothetical set of facts to discuss whether criminal liability may be established.

 **Introduction**

There are lots of things you might want to know before deciding whether or not I committed theft of the bike. We can divide this information into three categories:

- First, you would probably want to know who the owner of the bike was! Was the bike mine or someone else's? If it was someone else's had I been given permission to use it? Had the bike been abandoned, so that it was ownerless? We can label this category: *actus reus* (which is a Latin expression that means 'guilty act'). The *actus reus* of an offence specifies the conduct that must be proved for an offence to have occurred. So in our example, the *actus reus* of theft requires that the defendant appropriated an item of property that belonged to another person.[1]

- Second, you probably would have several questions about what I was thinking when I took the bike. Was I aware that it wasn't my bike? If so, did I believe that I had the owner's permission to use it? Did I intend to return the bike or to keep it for myself? We can label this category: *mens rea* (which is a Latin expression that means 'guilty mind').[2] The *mens rea* of an offence specifies the state of mind the defendant must have possessed in order to be convicted of the offence. So in our example, the *mens rea* of theft requires that, when the defendant appropriated the property, he did so dishonestly and with an intention to permanently deprive the owner of the item.

- Third, if I knowingly took someone else's bike, you would want to know whether I had some good reason for doing so. Perhaps I was being chased by a knife-wielding student upset at the mark I gave him for his coursework, and I sped off on the bike in order to escape. Or perhaps the Law librarian pointed a gun at my head, marched me outside, and told me to 'steal the bike or else'. In other words, perhaps I acted in self-defence or under duress. We can call this category: substantive defences. When a defendant successfully pleads a substantive defence, he is found not guilty even though he perpetrated the *actus reus* of the offence with the necessary *mens rea*.

So this simple example illustrates how crimes are structured. To establish criminal liability, the prosecution must establish: (1) the *actus reus* of the offence (the conduct element); (2) the *mens rea* of the offence (the mental element) and (3) the absence of a substantive defence. We can sum this up as shown in Figure 2.1.

$$\textbf{Actus reus} \; + \; \textbf{Mens rea} \; - \; \textbf{Substantive defence} \; = \; \textbf{Criminal offence}$$

**Figure 2.1.** The anatomy of a crime

---

[1]See Chapter 8.

[2]The expressions *actus reus* and *mens rea* come from the Latin maxim *actus non facit reum nisi mens sit rea* ('an act does not make a man guilty of a crime, unless his mind also be guilty').

If the prosecution fails to establish either the *actus reus* or the *mens rea*, or if it fails to disprove any substantive defence raised by the defendant, there can be no conviction for the offence.

In this chapter we examine each of these three categories in turn. The objective is to give you a broad understanding of how criminal offences are structured. The chapter will also provide an overview of the rest of this text, to help you understand how the different chapters fit together and relate to one another.

As well as outlining the *actus reus*, *mens rea* and substantive defences categories, the chapter also looks in detail at one fundamental requirement for criminal liability: that the *actus reus* and *mens rea* of an offence coincide. Our discussion of this requirement will introduce us to two other important concepts: continuing acts and the transaction principle.

## Actus reus

The *actus reus* is the conduct element of an offence. The *actus reus* of every crime that we study in this book will consist of one or more of the following components:

- **Behaviour:** the behavioural part of the *actus reus* refers to some action that the defendant must have performed. On a charge of rape, for example, the defendant must have penetrated the victim's vagina, anus or mouth with his penis. For some crimes, no specific behaviour is required: it is enough simply to show that the defendant did something. For example, the *actus reus* of murder requires that the defendant did something that was a cause of the victim's death.

- **Circumstances:** this part of the *actus reus* specifies circumstances that must have existed at the time of the defendant's behaviour. For example, on a charge of rape the victim must not have been consenting. And on a charge of criminal damage, the property that was damaged must have belonged to someone else.

- **Consequences:** this part of the *actus reus* specifies consequences that must have occurred as a result of the defendant's behaviour. For example, the *actus reus* of murder requires proof that the victim died.

---

### EXTRACT

Section 3A of the Road Traffic Act 1988 (below) defines the offence of causing death by careless driving when under the influence of drink or drugs. Read the definition and identify the behavioural, circumstances and consequence components of the *actus reus* of the offence.

### Section 3A Road Traffic Act 1988

### 3A Causing death by careless driving when under influence of drink or drugs.

(1) If a person causes the death of another person by driving a mechanically propelled vehicle on a road or other public place without due care and attention, or without reasonable consideration for other persons using the road or place, and–

　　(a) he is, at the time when he is driving, unfit to drive through drink or drugs [...] he is guilty of an offence.

There are three other points to bear in mind:

- The *actus reus* of an offence will not necessarily have all three components: behaviour, circumstances and consequence. In fact, most offences will not contain one or more of these. For example, the *actus reus* of rape does not have a consequence component, and the *actus reus* of murder does not have a circumstances component.

- A distinction is often drawn between conduct crimes and result crimes:
  - A conduct crime is one whose *actus reus* consists of just a behavioural component. An example is the offence of fraud by false representation. As we'll see in Chapter 8, the *actus reus* of this offence only requires proof that the defendant made a false representation.
  - A result crime is one whose *actus reus* contains a consequence component. So murder is a result crime, since the *actus reus* of murder requires proof that the victim died. All result crimes require proof of causation: the defendant's behaviour must have been a factual and legal cause of the consequence.

- Sometimes, the *actus reus* of an offence will not include any behaviour requirement. Examples include crimes of possession (such as possession of weapons or illegal drugs) and so-called 'state of affairs' crimes (such as being in charge of a motor vehicle when under the influence of drink or drugs[3]).

In Chapter 3, we focus on some general *actus reus* concepts. The three that we study are:

- **Voluntariness:** if the defendant's conduct was involuntary, there can be no *actus reus*
- **Omissions:** a defendant cannot normally be held criminally liable for an omission, that is, a failure to act.
- **Causation:** a defendant can only be held criminally liable for a result crime if his conduct was a factual and legal cause of the specified consequence.

The reason that these three concepts have their own chapter is that they are overarching. One or more of these concepts will be relevant to every specific offence that we study.

## Mens rea

The *mens rea* of an offence specifies requirements which relate to the defendant's thought processes and state of mind at the moment he perpetrated the *actus reus*. For example, on a charge of rape, one of the *mens rea* requirements is lack of a reasonable belief that the victim was consenting. And on a charge of criminal damage, one of the *mens rea* requirements is that the defendant destroyed or damaged the other person's property either intentionally or recklessly. There are a number of different *mens rea* concepts. In Chapter 4, we study two of these in detail – intention and recklessness – and also look more briefly at four others: knowledge; belief; negligence and strict liability. There are also other *mens rea* concepts that we encounter when studying specific offences, such as malice and dishonesty.[4]

For now, it is worth highlighting two general principles which are relevant when considering issues of *mens rea*: ignorance of the criminal law is no defence to a criminal charge; and a commendable motive does not negate *mens rea*. These principles

---

[3]Road Traffic Act 1988, s.4.

[4]The term 'malice' is used in some of the non-fatal offences against the person that we study in Chapter 6. The term 'dishonesty' is used in several of the property offences that we study in Chapter 8.

demonstrate that the term *mens rea* – 'guilty mind' – is in fact misleading if taken literally. A defendant may be found to have had the *mens rea* of an offence even if he had no idea that he was committing a crime and even if he had a commendable motive for his actions. We will examine each of these general principles in turn.

## 1. Ignorance of the criminal law is no defence to a criminal charge

Think back to *R v Brown*, which we looked at in the last chapter. Suppose one of the defendants had said, 'I honestly thought that these activities are legal. I had no idea that I was committing a crime'. If the jury believed him, would this have provided him with a defence? The answer is no. The general principle is that ignorance of the criminal law is no defence to a criminal charge. A defendant cannot escape criminal liability by saying, 'I didn't know that what I was doing was an offence'.

A well-known example is *R v Esop* (1836) 7 C & P 456. The defendant was from Baghdad. He was accused of committing buggery whilst on board a ship docked in St Katharine Docks in London. The court stated that the fact Esop did not realise he was committing a crime was no defence, even though buggery was not a crime in his home country and Esop had no reason to think that he was breaking the law.

A more recent example is *R v Beard* [2007] EWCA Crim 3168. The defendant, Thomas Beard, was convicted of a firearms offence. Police had found 78 cartridges in Beard's caravan; 66 of these contained CS gas, and so they were prohibited ammunition under the Firearms Act 1968. Beard explained that a friend had left the gas cartridges in the caravan several years earlier. Beard thought they were blanks. The prosecution accepted that he did not know they were prohibited ammunition, and did not suggest that he should have known. Although there was a warning on the outside of the box, Beard was illiterate and could not read the label. He did not possess a weapon that could fire the cartridges. He had no intention of ever using them. He had no record of violent crime and expressed genuine remorse. A probation officer said that he posed little risk of reoffending. He was married with two children, one of which was just two weeks old. On appeal against sentence the Court of Appeal sentenced Beard to two years' imprisonment (reduced from the original sentence of five years imposed at trial).

Citing *R v Beard* – as well as several other cases – Andrew Ashworth has argued that the principle that ignorance of the criminal law is no defence is 'a preposterous doctrine, resting on insecure foundations within the criminal law and on questionable propositions about the political obligations of individuals and of the State'.

## EXTRACT

Read the following extract from Ashworth's article. He considers three alternatives to the existing law. What are these? Which is his preferred approach? Why?

### Ashworth, A. (2011) 'Ignorance of the Criminal Law, and Duties to Avoid It' 74 *Modern Law Review* 1

[P]art of my argument is that it is fair and right to expect people to make a reasonable effort to find out what the law is; the other part of my argument [...] is that the State should also have an obligation to provide more information about the criminal law and about changes made to it, thus making the citizen's task easier. To impose this moderate duty on people is not inconsistent with the rule of law, so long as the State discharges its duty to make the criminal law sufficiently accessible.

My provisional conclusion, then, is that there is a fundamental problem of principle with the English ignorance-of-law doctrine. It subjects people to the censure of conviction when they may not have been culpable. It is not suited to protecting individuals from conviction in situations in which it would not be reasonable to expect them to have discovered the criminal prohibition, a failure that contravenes the rule of law and which cannot be justified by reference to any broader 'public interest.' Three ways of responding may be considered. *First*, ignorance of the criminal law could be allowed to negative liability, as part of or on a par with *mens rea*. That was rejected above, on the ground that it is fair and right to expect citizens to acquaint themselves with the criminal law and wrong to give them an incentive to remain ignorant. *Secondly*, ignorance of the law could be treated as a bar to trial, resulting in a stay of proceedings. This would recognise the State's role in the matter, and would of course avoid subjecting the defendant to trial. The Crown Prosecution Service would have guidance to the effect that a person who was reasonably ignorant of or mistaken about the law should not be prosecuted; to prosecute in spite of that guidance would be an abuse of process. However, the State's role would typically not have been so great as in cases of entrapment and of acting on official advice as to the law, and it is questionable whether reasonable ignorance of the law is not more appropriately dealt with by a lay tribunal (magistrates, jury) in the same way as duress and other excusing conditions.

My preference is therefore for a *third* approach: that of introducing a general but circumscribed defence of excusable ignorance of the law. This implies that citizens rightly have duties to try to find out about the criminal law, and these should be linked to the kind of duties of the State advocated by Fuller – notably the duty to give adequate publicity to laws, and particularly to criminal laws. Thus where a new piece of legislation introduces a whole raft of offences, the details of which receive little publicity (as a possible example, the Sexual Offences Act 2003), it may be understandable that an individual remains ignorant of some of the legislative changes, in the sense that there has been nothing to put her or him on notice. In those circumstances the law should recognise excusable ignorance of criminal law as a defence, supporting it by reference to (for example) Gardner's argument that the individual must have 'lived up to expectations in a normative sense.' Thus the defence should be based on an appropriate objective standard – what could reasonably be expected of an individual in the defendant's position – perhaps a little broader than the defence in Germany and Sweden. The grounds of excuse would be negligence-based, what could 'reasonably be expected,' and it would be proper for this to be subject to capacity-based exceptions for those unable to perform this citizen's duty.

On this model the rule of law cuts both ways, being part of the framework that constrains those in positions of public authority by imposing on them duties relating to the way in which they should carry out their legislative functions. There is room for debate about the degree of certainty that is required to fulfil the ideal of the rule of law: that ideal is sometimes expressed as if absolute certainty of definition is achievable and desirable, whereas in practice it is not and the law can be used to guide behaviour even if it does not achieve maximum certainty. Insofar as the criminal law employs both rules and standards, it should strive to ensure that terms such as 'reasonable' or 'dishonest' are supplemented by illustrations or sub-principles that enhance people's ability to use them as a guide.

So the general principle is that ignorance of the criminal law is no defence to a criminal charge. However, Parliament has the ability to create exceptions to this. An example, which we will study further in Chapter 8, can be found in section 2(1)(a) of the Theft Act 1968. This states that a defendant is not guilty of theft if he genuinely believed that he had a legal right to appropriate the property in question – even if his belief was mistaken.

## 2. A commendable motive does not negate mens rea

A second general principle is that a defendant's *mens rea* is not negated by proof that he had a commendable motive. So, for example, if the defendant's wife has an incurable, incapacitating disease, and he eventually gives in to her repeated pleas to have her life ended, he has the *mens rea* of murder.[5] He intentionally killed his wife. His motive does not negate his *mens rea*.

A further illustration of this principle is *R v Smith (John)* [1960] 2 QB 423. The defendant, John Smith, was convinced that his local council was corrupt. Wanting to expose this corruption, Smith offered the town mayor a bribe. He was convicted of a corruption offence. He appealed against his conviction, saying that he simply wanted to expose the mayor. The Court of Appeal rejected his appeal. Smith had the necessary *mens rea* since his intention was to corrupt the mayor. His motive for so doing was irrelevant.

Again, though, whilst a commendable motive does not generally negate *mens rea*, there appear to be exceptions to this principle. In some circumstances it seems that a defendant's motive could be taken into account when determining his intention. We will examine this issue further in Chapter 4.

## Coincidence of *actus reus* and *mens rea*

Having studied general *actus reus* and *mens rea* concepts in Chapters 3 and 4, we then move on in Chapters 5–8 to study the *actus reus* and *mens rea* requirements of a number of specific criminal offences. We study the following four types of offence: homicide; non-fatal offences against the person; sexual offences; and property offences.

For a defendant to be convicted of any of the crimes that we study, all of the *actus reus* and *mens rea* requirements of the relevant offence must be established. Moreover, establishing the *actus reus* and *mens rea* requirements alone is not enough. The prosecution must also prove that they coincided in time. In other words, the defendant must have possessed the necessary *mens rea at the moment* he perpetrated the *actus reus*. So suppose that, as Andrew leaves a crowded lecture theatre, he inadvertently knocks someone's iPad onto the floor. The iPad breaks. When Andrew discovers that the iPad belonged to Robert he is secretly rather pleased, as he has always hated Robert and had been looking for an opportunity to upset him. On these facts Andrew is not guilty of criminal damage. At the moment he caused the damage to the iPad he lacked the necessary *mens rea*.[6] And by the time he subsequently discovered whose iPad it was the *actus reus* had already occurred.

Note that, if the crime in question is a result crime, the crucial point in time is not the moment the relevant consequence occurs but the moment of the defendant's behaviour that caused the consequence. Suppose that Andrew poisons Robert, intending to kill him. The poison is slow-working. A couple of hours after administering the poison Andrew has

---

[5]See *R v Cocker* [1989] Crim LR 740, which we study in Chapter 5.
[6]Inadvertence is insufficient for the *mens rea* of criminal damage: see Chapter 8.

a change of heart. He tells Robert what he has done and rushes him to hospital, but it is too late. Robert dies and Andrew is charged with murder. The relevant moment in time is not when Robert died. It is the time of Andrew's behaviour that caused death, that is, the moment he administered the poison. At this moment he perpetrated the *actus reus* with the necessary *mens rea*. He would therefore be guilty of murder. His subsequent repentance came too late (just as his repentance would come too late if he stabbed Robert to death and then immediately regretted what he had done).[7]

## 1. Continuing acts

Having stated that the *actus reus* and *mens rea* must coincide in time, we now need to look at two specific types of case where this requirement is not so straightforward. The first concerns continuing acts. In *Fagan v Metropolitan Police Commissioner* [1969] 1 QB 439 the defendant, Vincent Fagan, was reverse parking his car. The victim, a police officer named David Morris, was directing him. Fagan reversed the car onto Morris' foot. Morris said, 'Get off, you are on my foot!' to which Fagan replied 'Fuck you, you can wait'. He then turned the ignition off. Several times Morris repeated, 'Get off my foot!' Eventually Fagan said 'okay, man, okay' and moved the car. At trial Fagan was convicted of battery. He appealed against his conviction, arguing that there was no coincidence of *actus reus* and *mens rea*. He claimed: that when he drove onto Morris' foot there was an infliction of force (*actus reus*), but since this was accidental there was no *mens rea*; and, when he subsequently refused to move the car there was *mens rea*, but the force had already been inflicted and so there was no *actus reus*. The Divisional Court dismissed his appeal and upheld the conviction.

### EXTRACT

Read the following extract from the judgment of James J. He draws a distinction between acts which are complete and acts which are continuing. How did he apply this distinction to the facts of Fagan's case?

### *Fagan v Metropolitan Police Commissioner* [1969] 1 QB 439

### James J

For our part we think the crucial question is whether in this case the act of the appellant can be said to be complete and spent at the moment of time when the car wheel came to rest on the foot or whether his act is to be regarded as a continuing act operating until the wheel was removed. In our judgment a distinction is to be drawn between acts which are complete – though results may continue to flow – and those acts which are continuing [...]

It is not necessary that *mens rea* should be present at the inception of the *actus reus*; it can be superimposed upon an existing act. On the other hand the subsequent inception of *mens rea* cannot convert an act which has been completed without *mens rea* into an assault.

[...]

---

[7]Of course, if Andrew had managed to save Robert's life he would not have been guilty of murder, since there would have been no death and therefore no *actus reus*. On these facts, he would be guilty of attempted murder instead.

There was an act constituting a battery which at its inception was not criminal because there was no element of intention but which became criminal from the moment the intention was formed to produce the apprehension which was flowing from the continuing act. The fallacy of the appellant's argument is that it seeks to equate the facts of this case with such a case as where a motorist has accidentally run over a person and, that action having been completed, fails to assist the victim with the intent that the victim should suffer.

So if an act is complete, any subsequent formulation of *mens rea* cannot convert the completed act into a crime. We saw this earlier in the example with Andrew and the iPad; by the time he discovered whose iPad it was the *actus reus* had already occurred.

But if a defendant forms the necessary *mens rea* whilst the act is still continuing, then he may be liable. Crucially, the Divisional Court held that the infliction of force onto Morris' foot was a continuing act, which began when Fagan drove onto it and continued until he drove off. Fagan thus formed the *mens rea* whilst the act was still continuing and so, as Figure 2.2 illustrates, *actus reus* and *mens rea* coincided in time.

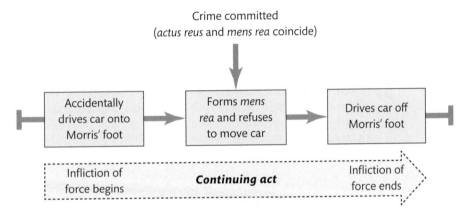

**Figure 2.2.** *Fagan v Metropolitan Police Commissioner* [1969] 1 QB 439

Before moving on, it is worth noting that some commentators have questioned the reasoning in *Fagan v Metropolitan Police Commissioner*. They suggest that a better justification for Fagan's liability can be found in the law on omissions. We will examine this suggestion in the next chapter.

## 2. The transaction principle

Using the concept of a continuing act, it was possible in *Fagan v Metropolitan Police Commissioner* to find a moment in time at which *actus reus* and *mens rea* coincided. Things are different with the transaction principle. The leading case is *Thabo Meli v R* [1954] 1 WLR 228. The defendant was one of four men who formed a plan to kill the victim and make it look like an accident. They invited the victim to a hut and gave him some beer. The men then hit the victim over the head, knocking him unconscious. Mistakenly believing that he was dead, they rolled his body off a low cliff and left him there. The victim died, but medical evidence showed that the cause of death was not the injuries the men inflicted. He died from exposure as a result of being left at the foot of the cliff.

At trial the four men were convicted of murder. Meli appealed against his conviction. He argued that there was no coincidence of *actus reus* and *mens rea*: when he attacked the victim he had the *mens rea* of murder, but the attack was not the cause of death (so no *actus reus*); and there was the *actus reus* when he rolled the body off the cliff since this act caused death, but this act was not performed with an intention to kill since he believed the victim was already dead (so no *mens rea*). His appeal reached the Privy Council, who dismissed the appeal.

## EXTRACT

Read the following extract from the judgment of Lord Reid. Explain, in your own words, the transaction principle Lord Reid advances.

### Thabo Meli v R [1954] 1 WLR 228

### Lord Reid

It is said that two acts were necessary and were separable: first, the attack in the hut; and, secondly, the placing of the body outside afterwards. It is said that, while the first act was accompanied by *mens rea*, it was not the cause of death; but that the second act, while it was the cause of death, was not accompanied by *mens rea* [...]

It appears to their Lordships impossible to divide up what was really one transaction in this way. There is no doubt that the accused set out to do all these acts in order to achieve their plan and as parts of their plan; and it is much too refined a ground of judgment to say that, because they were under a misapprehension at one stage and thought that their guilty purpose had been achieved before in fact it was achieved, therefore they are to escape the penalties of the law.

So the plan of the defendants in *Thabo Meli v R* formed one transaction. Since this transaction was carried out with the *mens rea* of murder, and it was a part of this transaction that caused death, the defendants were guilty of murder. Figure 2.3 illustrates this.

The transaction principle thus groups together a series of actions as one 'transaction'. As long as the *actus reus* is present at one stage of this transaction, and the transaction is carried out with the necessary *mens rea*, the defendant is liable – even if the *actus reus* and *mens rea* do not in fact coincide in time. The transaction principle is therefore an exception to the normal requirement that the *actus reus* and *mens rea* must coincide in time.

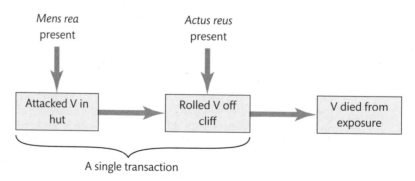

**Figure 2.3.** *Thabo Meli v R* [1954] 1 WLR 228

The transaction principle was also applied in *R v Le Brun* [1992] QB 61.[8] The defendant, John Le Brun, had an argument with his wife in the street outside their house. During the argument he struck her and knocked her unconscious. He then picked her up, in order to move her body inside and hide what he had done, but as he carried her he dropped her. She suffered a fractured skull and died. At trial Le Brun was convicted of manslaughter (since the jury found that he only intended to cause his wife non-serious harm when he struck her). He appealed against his conviction, arguing that there was no coincidence of *actus reus* and *mens rea*: when he struck his wife there was the *mens rea* of manslaughter but not the *actus reus*, since this act did not cause death and when he dropped his wife there was the *actus reus* of manslaughter but not the *mens rea* since it was an accident. The Court of Appeal dismissed his appeal and upheld the conviction.

## EXTRACT

Read the following extract from the judgment of Lord Lane CJ. In what ways does he say the facts of this case are different to *Thabo Meli v R*? Did the transaction principle still apply? Why/why not?

In your opinion, would the outcome in *R v Le Brun* have been different if Le Brun had dropped his wife whilst trying to carry her to hospital?

### *R v Le Brun* [1992] QB 61

#### Lord Lane CJ

However, it will be observed that the present case is different from [*Thabo Meli v R*] in that death here was not the result of a preconceived plan which went wrong [...] Here the death, again assuming the jury's finding to be such as it must have been, was the result of an initial unlawful blow, not intended to cause serious harm, in its turn causing the appellant to take steps possibly to evade the consequences of his unlawful act. During the taking of those steps he commits the *actus reus* but without the *mens rea* necessary for murder or manslaughter. Therefore the *mens rea* is contained in the initial unlawful assault, but the *actus reus* is the eventual dropping of the head on to the ground.

Normally the *actus reus* and *mens rea* coincide in point of time. What is the situation when they do not? Is it permissible, as the prosecution contend here, to combine them to produce a conviction for manslaughter?

[...]

It seems to us that where the unlawful application of force and the eventual act causing death are parts of the same sequence of events, the same transaction, the fact that there is an appreciable interval of time between the two does not serve to exonerate the defendant from

---

[8]A further example is *R v Keane (David)* [2016] EWCA Crim 2018. In this case the defendant punched the victim repeatedly, then pushed him over and stamped on his head. The victim suffered a severe head injury and developed epilepsy. Two-and-a-half years later the epilepsy caused his death. On appeal, defence counsel suggested that the attack should be divided up into: (a) a series of punches; and, (b) the stamp, and that there might therefore not have been coincidence of *actus reus* and *mens rea*. Rejecting this as 'tenuous and artificial' ([27]), the Court of Appeal described the attack as a 'single incident' ([30]). Since the attack caused the victim's subsequent death, and was perpetrated with the necessary *mens rea*, the murder conviction was upheld.

liability. That is certainly so where the appellant's subsequent actions which caused death, after the initial unlawful blow, are designed to conceal his commission of the original unlawful assault.

[...]

In short, in circumstances such as the present, which is the only concern of this court, the act which causes death, and the necessary mental state to constitute manslaughter, need not coincide in point of time.

There are two important points to note from Lord Lane CJ's judgment in *R v Le Brun*. First, the transaction principle applied even though there was no preconceived plan (as there was in *Thabo Meli v R*). Second, the judgment states that actions which are designed to conceal previous unlawful conduct form part of the same transaction. This suggests that subsequent actions which are lawful – such as trying to find medical help – will not be held to be part of the same transaction.

## Substantive defences

In a criminal trial there are two types of defences:

- First, the defendant may seek to defend himself by arguing that the prosecution has failed to prove the *actus reus* and *mens rea* of the offence. For example, a defendant charged with criminal damage might argue that the property was not in fact damaged. A defendant charged with rape might argue that the sexual intercourse was in fact consensual. And a defendant charged with attempted murder might argue that he lacked any intention to kill. Whilst these are all examples of defences, they are not 'substantive defences'. Rather, they are a denial of the *actus reus* or *mens rea* In Chapters 9 and 10, we will look at some specific examples of 'denial of *actus reus*' and 'denial of *mens rea*' defences. In Chapter 9, we examine the law governing intoxicated defendants. It is common for defendants to argue that they were so drunk at the time of the alleged offence that they were incapable of forming the necessary *mens rea*. In Chapter 10, we examine the defences of sane automatism and insanity. Defendants who plead these defences are claiming that they acted involuntarily. These defences therefore constitute a denial of the *actus reus*.

- Substantive defences are different. We study five of these defences in total: necessity; duress by threats; duress of circumstances; prevention of crime and private defence. Substantive defences only apply once the *actus reus* and the *mens rea* of the offence have been established. A defendant who seeks to plead a substantive defence is in effect saying, 'Yes, I perpetrated the *actus reus* with the necessary *mens rea*, but there is a good reason why I should nonetheless be found not guilty'. Perhaps there were circumstances which mean the defendant was justified to do as he did. For example, a surgeon performing a life-saving operation would not be guilty of intentionally wounding his patient. Or perhaps there were circumstances which mean the defendant should be excused for acting as he did, such as where a person steals money because he has a gun pointed to his head. We study the substantive defences in Chapter 11.

## Conclusion

The offences that we will study in Chapters 5–8 all impose punishment on a defendant who has harmed another person or their property. But if the criminal law was limited to just offences like these it would be seriously defective. It needs a broader scope, in two respects:

- **Actions:** The criminal law should seek to prevent crimes as well as punish those who commit them. For this reason, there are a range of crimes – known as 'inchoate offences' – which penalise defendants who have embarked on preparations to commit an offence but not yet done so. We study the inchoate offences in Chapter 12.

- **Actors:** The criminal law should not only punish those who actually commit murders, rapes, thefts and so on. It should also punish those who provide assistance or encouragement to murderers, rapists, thieves and others who commit crimes. We refer to such people as 'accessories'. The final chapter of the text – Chapter 13 – examines the law which determines when a person may be held criminally liable as an accessory.

This completes our overview of how crimes are structured, and of how this text is structured. As you progress through the text, you may find it helpful to refer back to this chapter to remind yourself of how the different topics we study fit together.

## Self-test questions

1. Define each of the following terms: (a) *actus reus*; (b) *mens rea*; (c) substantive defence; (d) conduct crime; (e) result crime; (f) a continuing act; (g) the transaction principle and (h) a denial of *actus reus/mens rea* defence.

2. Andrew and Robert are work colleagues. Andrew feels he is undervalued by his boss, David, and is very angry that Robert, whom he considers less capable and hardworking, has been promoted ahead of him. Andrew arranges to meet them both one evening and sets off in his car, planning to kill them when he arrives. On the way, and through no fault of his own, Andrew is involved in a road accident in which his car knocks over a pedestrian who is killed instantly. By sheer coincidence, the pedestrian happens to be Robert. Andrew is secretly rather pleased: opportunities at work improve, and all murderous thoughts as to David disappear from his mind.

   a. Could Andrew be convicted of murdering Robert? Explain your reasoning.

   b. How would your answer be different if, after the accident, Andrew had climbed out of his car, recognised Robert, pulled out a gun and shot him?

   c. How would your answer be different if: Andrew had seen Robert and deliberately driven into him. Then, thinking that Robert was dead, Andrew had attempted to hide Robert's body but as he did so he dropped Robert on his head. Medical evidence later shows that Robert died from a fractured skull caused by his being dropped on his head.

## The anatomy of a crime checklist

Having worked through this chapter, you should now have:

✓ An understanding of how crimes are structured

✓ An ability to identify the behaviour, circumstances and consequence components of a crime's *actus reus*

✓ An understanding of the general principles of *mens rea*

✓ An understanding of the requirement that *actus reus* and *mens rea* coincide in time

✓ An understanding of the concept of a continuing act and the transaction principle

✓ An understanding of the difference between denial of *actus reus/mens rea* defences and substantive defences.

## Further reading

Arenson, K.J. (2013) '*Thabo Meli* Revisited: The Pernicious Effects of Result-driven Decisions' 77 *Journal of Criminal Law* 41.

Ashworth, A. (2011) 'Ignorance of the Criminal Law, and Duties to Avoid It' 74 *Modern Law Review* 1.

Chan, W. and Simester, A.P. (2011) 'Four Functions of Mens Rea' 70 *Cambridge Law Journal* 381.

Horder, J. (2000) 'The Irrelevance of Motive in Criminal Law' in Horder (ed.) *Oxford Essays in Jurisprudence: Fourth Series*. OUP: Oxford.

# 3

# Key *actus reus* concepts

## Chapter objectives

By the end of this chapter you should have:

- An understanding of the *actus reus* concepts of voluntariness, omissions and causation
- An ability to critically discuss the general rule that there is no criminal liability for omissions and the arguments for and against extending the existing exceptions to this rule
- An ability to critically discuss the case law governing legal causation.

## Introduction

In Chapter 2, we saw that the first step in proving criminal liability is to establish the *actus reus* of the crime in question. In this chapter we focus on three key *actus reus* concepts: voluntariness; omissions and causation. What makes these concepts so important that they deserve their own chapter is that they will be relevant to most of the crimes we study in this text. In other words, they are general concepts. Having a firm understanding of these concepts will help you when you look at the *actus reus* of specific crimes in Chapters 5–8.

The chapter begins with the concept of voluntariness, which we deal with fairly briefly at this stage. We then turn to omissions and causation, which we examine in greater detail.

## Voluntariness

If the defendant's conduct was involuntary, there can be no *actus reus*. The reason is simple: a defendant should not be held responsible for behaviour over which she had no control!

It is important to point out that there are different definitions of voluntariness. Later in the chapter we will see that, in the context of causation, voluntariness has been defined as 'free, deliberate and informed'. Here, however, we are talking about voluntariness in a different sense. There can be no *actus reus* when the defendant's conduct was involuntary, in the sense that she had no control over the movements of her body.

There are many reasons why someone's body might move involuntarily. Suppose you are browsing in the Student Union shop, when I creep up behind you and push you into the wine display. Dozens of bottles of wine are smashed. You are not guilty of criminal damage because there is no *actus reus*. Although it was your body which smashed the bottles, these movements were involuntary.

Another example would be if you are sitting in a crowded lecture theatre when you suffer a sudden, uncontrollable muscle spasm. Your arm jerks outwards and hits the person sitting next to you. You are not guilty of battery because your bodily movements were involuntary. There is no *actus reus*.

One particularly important reason why someone might act involuntarily is known as automatism. What is 'automatism'? Its meaning was considered by the Court of Appeal in *Attorney-General's Reference (No 2 of 1992)* [1994] QB 91. The defendant in this case was a lorry driver. He had set off at 11 am. By 11 pm he had covered 343 miles (having taken regular breaks during the day), when he steered onto the hard shoulder and crashed into a white van that had broken down. Two people were killed. At his trial a psychologist gave evidence that the defendant had been in a condition known as 'driving without awareness'. This condition is caused by repetitive visual stimuli and results in a trance-like state. Although someone in this state will be largely unaware of what is happening, they are still able to steer the vehicle and are usually able to react and return to full awareness when confronted with strong visual stimuli.

At trial the trial judge gave the jury the option of finding that the defendant had been in a state of automatism. The jury acquitted the defendant. The Attorney-General subsequently referred the following question to the Court of Appeal: is the condition driving without awareness capable of amounting to automatism? In his judgment Lord Taylor CJ stated:

> [T]he defence of automatism requires that there was a total destruction of voluntary control on the defendant's part. Impaired, reduced or partial control is not enough.

Since someone who is driving without awareness retains some awareness and some control over their actions, the condition is not capable of amounting to automatism. Automatism requires that the defendant suffered a 'total destruction of voluntary control'. This was confirmed by the Court of Appeal in *R v Coley* [2013] EWCA Crim 223, where Hughes LJ emphasised that acting irrationally is not the same as acting involuntarily:

> 22 [...] The essence of [automatism] is that the movements or actions of the defendant at the material time were wholly involuntary. The better expression is complete destruction of voluntary control [...] Examples which have been given in the past include the driver attacked by a swarm of bees or the man under hypnosis. 'Involuntary' is not the same as 'irrational'; indeed it needs sharply to be distinguished from it.

Applying this, the Court of Appeal held one of the defendants in the case, Colin McGhee, had not acted in a state of automatism. McGhee – who had become disinhibited and aggressive after taking prescription medication and drinking alcohol – had stabbed someone in an off-licence. Hughes LJ explained that someone who is disinhibited has not suffered a total destruction of voluntary control.

If the defendant acted in a state of automatism, the next question to ask is whether it was sane automatism or insane automatism. This distinction is crucial. Sane automatism results in a finding of not guilty, and the defendant is acquitted. But insane automatism results in a finding of not guilty by reason of insanity. If the defendant is found not guilty by reason of insanity the trial judge can order hospitalisation, a supervision order or an absolute discharge.[1] We will look at the law which determines whether automatism was sane or insane in Chapter 10.

So our first *actus reus* concept is voluntariness. If the defendant acted involuntarily, in the sense that she had no control at all over her bodily movements, there can be no *actus reus*!

## Omissions

Our second *actus reus* concept is omissions. There are some crimes which can only be committed by doing an act. Of the offences we will study in this text, one example is (as its name suggests!) unlawful act manslaughter.[2] But many of the other offences that we will study can also be committed by omission, that is, by a failure to act.[3] Examples include murder,[4] gross negligence manslaughter,[5] offences involving bodily harm,[6] battery,[7] criminal damage[8] and fraud.[9]

Before a person can be found to have committed a crime by omission, two things must first be established: (1) that the defendant had a duty to act; and (2) that the defendant

---

[1]Criminal Procedure (Insanity) Act 1964, s.5.
[2]*R v Lowe* [1973] QB 702.
[3]It is also possible to be an accessory to a crime by omission. See Chapter 13.
[4]*R v Gibbins & Proctor* (1918) 13 Cr App R 134.
[5]*R v Adomako* [1995] 1 AC 171.
[6]*R v Gibbins & Proctor* (1918) 13 Cr App R 134.
[7]*DPP v Santana-Bermudez* [2003] EWHC 2908 (Admin) (though there is some uncertainty: see Chapter 6).
[8]*R v Miller* [1983] 2 AC 161.
[9]*R v Rai* [2000] 1 Cr App R 242.

breached this duty. In this section we begin by outlining the situations in which a defend-ant will have a duty to act, and what the defendant's duty will be in these situations.

We will then look at the requirement, in result crimes, to prove that the defendant's breach of duty caused the harm. Finally, we'll look at some situations in which it may be difficult to distinguish between acts and omissions and reflect on the criminal law's reluctance to impose omissions liability.

##  1. When will a defendant have a duty to act?

Generally, there is no criminal liability for omissions. This was made clear by the House of Lords in *R v Miller* [1983] 2 AC 161. So a defendant will not be criminally liable if he stands and watches a stranger drown in the sea, nor if he refuses to call an ambulance for a stranger who has just been beaten up and instead walks off and leaves the victim lying injured on the ground.

However, there are a number of exceptions to the general rule that there is no criminal liability for omissions. In each of the following six situations a defendant may be crimi-nally liable if he is under a duty to act and breaches this duty.

### i. Statutory duty

Some statutes impose a duty to act in certain circumstances. If the defendant fails to act in the manner required by the statute he will breach his duty and may be criminally lia-ble. There are many examples, which include:

- Failure to stop at or report a road traffic accident[10]
- Failure to provide a police officer with a specimen breath test when required to do so[11]
- Failure to disclose information which the defendant knows or believes might assist in the prevention of an act of terrorism[12]
- Allowing the death of a child or vulnerable adult who lives in the same household (also known as 'familial homicide').[13]

### ii. Family relationships

The second exception is family relationships, though as we'll see this exception is actually quite limited in scope.

#### *Parents–children*

Parents have a duty to care for their children. In *R v Gibbins & Proctor* (1918) 13 Cr App R 134 the victim was a seven-year-old girl called Nelly. Nelly lived with Walter Gibbins (her father), Edith Proctor (Gibbins' girlfriend) and Gibbins and Proctor's other children. The other children were all healthy. But no one looked after Nelly. She was kept upstairs alone, away from the other children and starved to death. There was evidence that Proc-tor hated Nelly and had deliberately withheld food from her. Both Gibbins and Proctor were convicted of murder and sentenced to death. Their appeals were dismissed by the Court of Appeal. We will look at what the Court said about Edith Proctor shortly. For now

---

[10]Road Traffic Act 1988, s.170.
[11]Road Traffic Act 1988, s.6.
[12]Terrorism Act 2000, s.38B.
[13]Domestic Violence, Crime and Victims Act 2004, s.5.

our focus is Walter Gibbins. The Court stated that as Nelly's father Gibbins had a duty to care for her. He had breached this duty:

> [Gibbins] lived in the house and the child was his own, a little girl of seven, and he grossly neglected the child. He must have known what her condition was if he saw her, for she was little more than a skeleton. He is in this dilemma; if he did not see her the jury might well infer that he did not care if she died; if he did he must have known what was going on.

So parents have a duty to care for their children. How long does this duty last? For the whole of the child's life? Or until the child reaches independence? The general view, supported by the decision in *R v Shepherd* (1862) 9 Cox CC 123, is that the duty terminates once the child reaches independence.

A further question is whether the duty operates in both directions: do children have a duty to care for their parents? The answer to this question is unclear. Whilst some have argued that children do have a duty to care for their parents,[14] the better view is that children do not automatically have such a duty.[15] A duty would only arise if the child had voluntarily assumed responsibility for their parent (voluntary assumption of responsibility is the third exception to the general rule that there is no criminal liability for omissions, which we'll look at shortly).

### Husband–wife

There will normally be a duty to act between spouses. However, the Court of Appeal's approach in *R v Smith* [1979] Crim LR 251 was to base this duty on a voluntary assumption of responsibility (the third exception to the general rule). In other words, spouses do not owe each other a duty to act simply because they are married. They owe each other the duty because they have voluntarily assumed responsibility for each other. This difference would be significant in a case involving a married couple who have separated. Although they are still married, the fact that they have chosen to separate shows that they are no longer assuming responsibility for one another, and so would no longer owe each other a duty to act.

### Other family relationships

What about other family relationships? Brothers and sisters? Grandparents and grandchildren? Aunts/uncles and nephews/nieces? Cousins? Whatever the relationship, a duty to act will only arise if there has been a voluntary assumption of responsibility. The blood tie will not, in itself, generate a duty to act.

### iii. Voluntary assumption of responsibility

The third exception is voluntary assumption of responsibility. A person may voluntarily assume a legal duty to act.

One obvious way in which a person might assume responsibility for others is through their choice of job. In *Airedale NHS Trust v Bland* [1993] AC 789 the House of Lords stated that doctors have a duty to act in the best interests of their patients. If they fail to act in their patients' best interests they breach their duty and may be criminally liable. Police officers may also be criminally liable for failing to perform their duties as a police officer.[16]

---

[14]See, for example, Ormerod, D. and Laird, K. (2015) *Smith and Hogan's Criminal Law* (14th edn) Oxford: OUP, p78.

[15]See Simester, A.P., Spencer, J.R., Stark, F., Sullivan, G.R. & Virgo, G.J. (2016) *Simester and Sullivan's Criminal Law: Theory and Doctrine* (6th edn) Oxford: Hart Publishing, p76.

[16]*R v Dytham* [1979] QB 722.

There are many other ways of assuming responsibility for someone, besides choosing a job. Think back to *R v Gibbins & Proctor*. We saw that the basis for Walter Gibbins' duty to look after Nelly was the parent–child relationship. But what about Edith Proctor? Nelly was not Proctor's daughter, so on what basis did the Court of Appeal conclude that Proctor owed Nelly a duty to act?

## EXTRACT

Read the following extract from the judgment of Darling J. What facts does he point to in support of the conclusion that Proctor had voluntarily assumed a duty to care for Nelly?

### R v Gibbins & Proctor (1918) 13 Cr App R 134

#### Darling J

The case of Proctor is plainer. She had charge of the child. She was under no obligation to do so or to live with Gibbins, but she did so, and receiving money, as it is admitted she did, for the purpose of supplying food, her duty was to see that the child was properly fed and looked after, and to see that she had medical attention if necessary [...] Here Proctor took upon herself the moral obligation of looking after the children

For further insight into the factors the Courts will consider when deciding whether or not there has been a voluntary assumption of responsibility, we will look at two further cases. The first is *R v Stone & Dobinson* [1977] QB 354. The defendants in this case were John Stone – a 67-year-old man who was partially deaf, almost blind and had low average intelligence and no appreciable sense of smell – and Gwendoline Dobinson – a 43-year-old woman who was Stone's housekeeper and mistress and who also had limited mental capacity. They lived with Stone's son, Cyril, who was 34 years old and mentally subnormal. In 1972 Stone's sister Fanny also came to live with them. Fanny was aged 61 and was anorexic. She was morbidly anxious about putting on weight and so went without proper meals. She would often stay in her room for days at a time.

In the Spring of 1975 the police found Fanny wandering the streets by herself, apparently not knowing where she was. Following this, Stone and Dobinson tried to find Fanny's doctor. But Fanny refused to tell them her doctor's name, and they were unable to find him. In the weeks that followed Fanny's condition deteriorated. By July she was unable to leave her bed. On 19 July a neighbour volunteered to help Dobinson wash Fanny. The neighbour described how Fanny was lying in her own excrement and how much of her body was 'raw'. The neighbour advised Dobinson to contact social services. A few days later Stone and Dobinson went to their local pub. Dobinson told the landlord about Fanny's condition, and the landlord advised her to contact a doctor. Whilst some efforts were made to arrange for a doctor to visit, these efforts were unsuccessful. By 2 August Fanny had died. Stone and Dobinson were convicted of manslaughter for their failure to care for Fanny and arrange medical assistance. They appealed against their convictions, arguing that there was no evidence that they had assumed responsibility for Fanny. The Court rejected their appeals.

**EXTRACT**

> Read the following extract from the judgment of Geoffrey Lane LJ. What facts does he point to in support of the conclusion that the jury were entitled to find that Stone and Dobinson had voluntarily assumed a duty to care for Fanny?

## R v Stone & Dobinson [1977] QB 354

### Geoffrey Lane LJ

The suggestion is that, heartless though it may seem, this is one of those situations where the appellants were entitled to do nothing; where no duty was cast upon them to help, any more than it is cast upon a man to rescue a stranger from drowning, however easy such a rescue might be.

This court rejects that proposition. Whether Fanny was a lodger or not she was a blood relation of the appellant Stone; she was occupying a room in his house; the appellant Dobinson had undertaken the duty of trying to wash her, of taking such food to her as she required. There was ample evidence that each appellant was aware of the poor condition she was in by mid-July. It was not disputed that no effort was made to summon an ambulance or the social services or the police despite the entreaties of Mrs. Wilson [the neighbour] and Mrs. West [the pub landlord]. A social worker used to visit Cyril. No word was spoken to him. All these were matters which the jury were entitled to take into account when considering whether the necessary assumption of a duty to care for Fanny had been proved.

This was not a situation analogous to the drowning stranger. They did make efforts to care. They tried to get a doctor; they tried to discover the previous doctor. The appellant Dobinson helped with the washing and the provision of food. All these matters were put before the jury in terms which we find it impossible to fault. The jury were entitled to find that the duty had been assumed. They were entitled to conclude that once Fanny became helplessly infirm, as she had by July 19, the appellants were, in the circumstances, obliged either to summon help or else to care for Fanny themselves.

As well as illustrating when a duty to act might arise, the judgment in *R v Stone & Dobinson* also reveals something about the standard of care that is expected. When deciding whether or not Stone and Dobinson breached the duty they owed to Fanny, the Court appears to have made no concession for their personal characteristics. Although they both had limited mental capacity, and Stone was partially deaf and almost blind, the Court nonetheless concluded that they had breached the duty they owed to Fanny.

The second case is *R v Sinclair, Johnson & Smith* (1998) 148 NLJ 1353. The three defendants – James Sinclair, Brian Johnson and Ian Smith – were all methadone addicts. Johnson and Smith lived together in a flat owned by Johnson. Johnson knew that Smith used the flat to sell methadone. One day Sinclair went to the flat with the victim – Darren Coleman – to buy some methadone from Smith. They bought the methadone and stayed at the flat to inject themselves. Ten minutes after injection, at about 2:30 pm, Coleman fell unconscious. He never regained consciousness. By 7 am the next morning Coleman was dead.

Sinclair remained with Coleman for the entire period that he was unconscious. But apart from pouring cold water over him and slapping him, he did nothing to help until he called an ambulance at 6:30 am the next morning. At some point between 7 pm and 8 pm

Johnson had also injected Coleman with a saline solution in an effort to restore consciousness. At 11 pm he went to bed and slept until Sinclair woke him at 5 am concerned about Coleman's condition.

At trial Sinclair and Johnson were convicted of manslaughter for their failure to call medical assistance. They appealed, arguing that there was no evidence that they had voluntarily assumed responsibility for the victim. The Court of Appeal started by discussing Brian Johnson.

## EXTRACT

Read the following extract from the judgment of Rose LJ. According to the Court of Appeal, was there any evidence that Johnson had voluntarily assumed responsibility for Coleman? What facts does Rose LJ point to in support of this conclusion?

### *R v Sinclair, Johnson & Smith* (1998) 148 NLJ 1353

#### Rose LJ

So far as Johnson is concerned, there is no English authority in which a duty of care has been held to arise, over a period of hours, on the part of a medically unqualified stranger [...] Johnson did not know the deceased. His only connection with him was that he had come to his house and there taken methadone and remained until he died. Others were coming and going in the meantime. The fact that Johnson had prepared and administered to the deceased saline solutions does not, as it seems to us, demonstrate on his part a voluntary assumption of a legal duty of care rather than a desultory attempt to be of assistance. In our judgment, the facts in relation to Johnson were not capable of giving rise to a legal duty of care and the judge should have withdrawn his case from the jury.

The Court of Appeal then turned to James Sinclair.

## EXTRACT

According to the Court of Appeal, was there any evidence that Sinclair had voluntarily assumed responsibility for Coleman? What facts does Rose LJ point to in support of this conclusion?

### *R v Sinclair, Johnson & Smith* (1998) 148 NLJ 1353

#### Rose LJ

Sinclair was in a different position. The evidence was that he was a close friend of the deceased for many years and the two had lived together almost as brothers. It was Sinclair who paid for and supplied the deceased with the first dose of methadone and helped him to obtain the second dose. He knew that the deceased was not an addict. He remained with the deceased throughout the period of his unconsciousness and, for a substantial period, was the only person with him. In the light of this evidence, there was in our judgment material on which the jury properly directed, could have found that Sinclair owed the deceased a legal duty of care. The judge was therefore correct to leave Sinclair's case to the jury on this aspect.

In spite of this conclusion, Sinclair was not guilty of manslaughter. Although he had breached the duty he owed to his friend, there was insufficient evidence that the breach of duty caused Coleman's death. Even if Sinclair had called an ambulance, it might not have made any difference. The trial judge had misdirected the jury on the issue of causation, and so Sinclair's manslaughter conviction was quashed. (Both Sinclair and Johnson were, however, convicted of drugs offences.)

### iv. Contractual duty

A defendant may have a contractual duty to act. Often this will be a contract of employment. The leading case on contractual duty is *R v Pittwood* (1902) 19 TLR 37. The defendant was a gatekeeper on a railway. He was employed to shut the gate at a level crossing whenever a train was passing, between the hours of 7 am and 7 pm. One day he left the gate open while he went for his lunch. As a result a haycart was struck by a train, and a man was killed. Pittwood was convicted of manslaughter for his failure to shut the gate.

When determining whether a defendant has breached a contractual duty, it is important to look closely at the terms of the contract. For example, Pittwood's contract of employment limited his duty to the hours of 7 am to 7 pm. So if someone else had carelessly left the gate open at 9 pm, and as a result there was an accident ten minutes later, Pittwood would not have been in breach of his contractual duty.

Remember too that:

- **It is always necessary to establish that the defendant breached his duty**. Suppose that an on-duty lifeguard notices that a swimmer is struggling. He reacts immediately and does his best to save the swimmer, but unfortunately the swimmer drowns. Although the swimmer died, the lifeguard is not criminally liable since he fulfilled his contractual duty to make all reasonable efforts to protect the safety of swimmers.

- **The defendant's breach of duty must have caused the harm**. Suppose that the lifeguard had noticed that the swimmer was struggling, but did nothing and sat and watched as the swimmer drowned. The lifeguard unquestionably breached his contractual duty. But whether or not the lifeguard is guilty of a homicide offence will depend on whether it can be shown that his breach of duty was a cause of the swimmer's death. It might be that, even if the lifeguard had done everything he could, the swimmer would still have drowned. If this is the case then, as we'll see shortly, there would be no causal link between the lifeguard's failure to act and the swimmer's death.

### v. Creation of a dangerous situation

The leading case here is *R v Miller* [1983] 2 AC 161. The defendant, James Miller, was homeless. He was squatting in an unoccupied house. One night Miller lit a cigarette and lay down on a mattress in the house. This is his account of what happened next:

I went upstairs into the back bedroom where I've been sleeping. I lay on my mattress and lit a cigarette. I must have fell to sleep because I woke up to find the mattress on fire. I just got up and went into the next room and went back to sleep. Then the next thing I remember was the police and fire people arriving. I hadn't got anything to put the fire out with so I just left it.

Miller was convicted of arson. His conviction was based on his failure to take any steps to put the fire out once he had become aware of it. He appealed against his conviction, arguing that he could not be held criminally liable for his omission. The case reached the House of Lords, who unanimously dismissed the appeal and upheld the conviction. Lord Diplock explained:

> [T]he conduct of the accused that is causative of the result may consist not only of his doing physical acts which cause the fire to start or spread but also of his failing to take measures that lie within his power to counteract the danger that he has himself created [...] I see no rational ground for excluding from conduct capable of giving rise to criminal liability, conduct which consists of failing to take measures that lie within one's power to counteract a danger that one has oneself created, if at the time of such conduct one's state of mind is such as constitutes a necessary ingredient of the offence.

So if a defendant creates a dangerous situation, he has a duty to take steps to counteract the danger he has created.

Before moving on, notice that the duty imposed by *R v Miller* is to take such steps that 'lie within one's power'. So a defendant only breaches this duty if he fails to take steps that lie within his power.

*R v Miller* was applied in a different context by the Court of Appeal in *R v Evans* [2009] EWCA Crim 650. The victim in this case was a 16-year-old girl called Carly Townsend. She lived with her mother Andrea Townsend and her half-sister, 24-year-old Gemma Evans. Although all three women had a history of heroin addiction, Carly was trying to overcome her addiction and had not used heroin for at least three months. In May 2007 Evans bought some heroin from a drug dealer and gave it to Carly. Carly injected herself with it. Both her mother and half-sister were in the house when Carly injected herself with the drugs. Soon afterwards Carly developed symptoms which were consistent with a heroin overdose. But her mother and half-sister decided not to call an ambulance because they were worried that they would get into trouble. So instead they put Carly to bed, hoping that she would get better. By the next morning Carly had died.

At trial Andrea Townsend and Gemma Evans were both convicted of manslaughter for their failure to summon medical help. The trial judge told the jury that they could conclude that Evans had a duty to act since she supplied the heroin. On appeal Evans argued that this was a misdirection, and that supplying the drugs could not give rise to a duty to act. The Court of Appeal rejected this argument and applied the principle from *R v Miller*. Lord Judge CJ stated:

> When a person has created or contributed to the creation of a state of affairs which he knows, or ought reasonably to know, has become life threatening, a consequent duty on him to act by taking reasonable steps to save the other's life will normally arise.

So since Gemma Evans had contributed to the dangerous situation by giving Carly the heroin, she had a duty to take all reasonable steps to save Carly's life. By failing to call an ambulance she had breached this duty. Her breach of duty was a cause of Carly's death, and so her manslaughter conviction was upheld.

Notice two further points about the judgment in *R v Evans*. First, as the extract above indicates, if a defendant has a duty to act arising from the *R v Miller* principle, the duty only begins at the moment that the defendant realised, or ought to have realised, the danger. Second, in *R v Miller* Lord Diplock said that the *R v Miller* principle applies to defendants who created the dangerous situation. In *R v Evans* Lord Judge CJ went further than this, saying that the principle applies to defendants who created, *or contributed to*, the dangerous situation. This extension of the *R v Miller* principle was crucial in *R v Evans*. As we will see later in the chapter, in *R v Kennedy (No 2)* [2007] UKHL 38 the House of Lords held that voluntarily self-injecting drugs breaks the chain of causation. Therefore, Gemma Evans was not a (legal) cause of (i.e. she did not create) the dangerous situation that Carly found herself in, because Carly voluntarily self-injected the drugs.[17] Evans did, however, *contribute* to the dangerous situation by supplying the drugs in the first place. This extension of the *R v Miller* principle has been criticised by Ashworth, who argues that:

> Lord Judge's extension of the *Miller* principle dilutes it to too great a degree, not least because 'all kinds of background acts of facilitation' could now be found to support a duty sufficient for manslaughter liability, expanding both the potential ambit and the uncertainty of the duty-situations.[18]

## ACTIVITY

Johann is a cleaner in a supermarket. He washes the floor around the fish counter, then leaves the floor to dry while he goes to have his lunch. As he is eating his sandwich he realises that he has forgotten to put up the 'Caution: Wet Floor' sign. He decides to finish his sandwich quickly, and then go and put the sign up. When he returns to the fish counter with the sign he finds that Ludwig has already slipped on the wet floor and suffered a broken wrist. It is later discovered that Ludwig slipped after Johann had finished his sandwich, while he was collecting the sign from the cleaning cupboard.

- Apply the principle from *R v Miller* to this scenario. Does Johann fall within the 'creation of a dangerous situation' exception to the general rule that there is no criminal liability for omissions?
- Would your answer be any different if, upon realising that he had forgotten to put the sign up, Johann had immediately stopped eating his sandwich, collected the sign and returned to the fish counter only to find that Ludwig had already slipped and broken his wrist?
- Would any of the other exceptions that we have studied so far apply to Johann?

(Hint: in Johann's case there are two omissions. The first is Johann's initial failure to put the sign up. The second is his failure to stop eating his sandwich and put the sign up. Consider each failure in turn.)

### vi. Continuing acts

Strictly speaking, continuing acts are acts not omissions. So continuing acts are not really an exception to the general rule that there is no criminal liability for omissions, because they are not really omissions! But continuing acts can often seem very similar to omissions, so it is useful to mention them briefly here.

---

[17]To avoid confusion, remember to distinguish between the following: (1) the conduct that gave rise to the duty. In *R v Evans*, a duty arose because Evans gave Carly the heroin; and (2) the conduct that constituted a breach of the duty. In *R v Evans*, it was the failure to call an ambulance that amounted to a breach of the duty, and it was this failure that was held to be a factual and legal cause of Carly's death.

[18]Ashworth, A. (2015) 'Manslaughter by Omission and the Rule of Law' *Criminal Law Review* 563.

In Chapter 2 we looked at the case of *Fagan v Commissioner of Metropolitan Police* [1969] 1 QB 439, the case in which the defendant accidentally drove onto the policeman's foot and then refused to drive off. We saw that the Divisional Court upheld Fagan's battery conviction by applying the continuing acts doctrine. Remember, however, that *Fagan* was decided more than ten years before the House of Lords' decision in *R v Miller*. So at the time of the decision in *Fagan* the principle from *R v Miller* did not exist. If a case like *Fagan* occurred today, many commentators believe that the courts would apply the principle from *R v Miller*, not the continuing acts doctrine. The reasoning would go like this. When Fagan drove onto the policeman's foot he created a dangerous situation. From the moment he realised what he had done he was under a duty to counteract the danger he had created. By failing to drive off the policeman's foot he breached this duty.

If the continuing acts doctrine is not needed to explain the outcome of *Fagan*, does this mean that the doctrine is redundant? No! There are other situations in which the continuing acts doctrine would still apply. An example is *Kaitamaki v R* [1985] AC 147. In this case the defendant admitted having sexual intercourse with the victim. He said that when he penetrated her he genuinely believed that she was consenting. He only became aware that she was not consenting after penetration. But he admitted that once he realised she was not consenting he continued to have sexual intercourse with her and did not withdraw. At first this might look like an omission, a failure to withdraw. But it does not really make sense to talk of having sex by omission. It is more sensible to say that the defendant ignored the victim and continued the positive act of sexual intercourse. This was the reasoning the Privy Council used in upholding his rape conviction. Sexual intercourse is a continuing act, which begins at penetration and continues until withdrawal. The defendant formed the necessary *mens rea* whilst the guilty act was still continuing, and so the *actus reus* and *mens rea* of rape coincided.

## 2. Omissions and causation

In exam problem questions, one mistake students commonly make is to write things like 'Johann would be guilty of an omission' or 'Johann would be guilty of a breach of his duty'. The problem here is that breach of duty is not, in itself, a crime. Establishing that the defendant may be criminally liable for his omission is only the first step. Once you have done this, you will then need to identify the relevant criminal offence (from the ones we will study in Chapters 5, 6, 7 and 8) and determine whether all the *actus reus* and *mens rea* elements of the offence are satisfied.

If the crime in question is a result crime (like murder or gross negligence manslaughter), you will need to discuss whether the defendant's breach of duty was a cause of the harm. As some of the examples we have looked at have illustrated, sometimes a defendant's breach of duty may not have made any difference. For example, suppose that the defendant sees his young daughter get run over by a car. The defendant does nothing to help, and does not call an ambulance. Medical evidence later shows that the girl died within minutes, and that doctors would not have been able to save her. On these facts the defendant breached his duty to his daughter, but the breach was not a cause of her death. Even if he had phoned an ambulance she would still have died. So he will not be guilty of a homicide offence.

There are other offences which can be committed by omission which are not result crimes. Crimes like failing to stop at or report a road traffic accident, or failure to provide a police officer with a specimen breath test when required to do so, have no consequence element and so there is no requirement to prove causation. However, you still need to show that all the other *actus reus* and *mens rea* elements of the crime are satisfied before concluding that the defendant is criminally liable.

BREACH OF DVTY
↓
IDENTIFY RELEVANT *
CRIMINAL OFFENCE
↓
ESTABLISH ACTVS REVS
& MENS REA.

*SOME OFFENCES
HAVE NO CONSEQUENCE
ELEMENT
→ NO REQUIREMENT
TO PROVE CAUSATION.

## 3. Distinguishing between acts and omissions

In most cases deciding whether the defendant's behaviour was an act or an omission will be straightforward. If the defendant points a gun at the victim and pulls the trigger, this is clearly an act. If the defendant stands on a pier and watches as a stranger drowns, this is clearly an omission. But sometimes there can be more difficult cases.

An example is *Airedale NHS Trust v Bland* [1993] AC 789. Tony Bland was a victim of the Hillsborough stadium disaster. Too many fans were allowed onto the terraces to watch an FA Cup semifinal between Liverpool and Nottingham Forest. Tony, who was aged 18 at the time, was crushed. His lungs were crushed and punctured, and as a result the supply of blood to his brain was interrupted. This caused him serious and irreversible brain damage. Tony was left in a persistent vegetative state (PVS). He could not see, hear or feel anything. He could not communicate in any way. And he would never regain consciousness. However, his brain stem, which controls heartbeat, digestion and breathing, continued to operate. In the eyes of the legal and medical world, a person is still alive as long as his brain stem is functioning. So although Tony was in a persistent vegetative state, for legal purposes he was still alive. But to keep him alive he had to be fed through a nasogastric tube.

By the time of this case Tony had been in this condition for three-and-a-half years. The undisputed medical consensus was that there was no prospect of Tony making any recovery from his condition. However, if he continued to receive the same medical care he could be kept alive in the same condition for many years to come. The hospital and Tony's parents decided that no useful purpose was to be served by continuing Tony's medical care. His father said that Tony would not have wanted 'to be left like that'. However, the doctors were concerned that ceasing Tony's medical treatment could constitute a criminal offence. So the hospital applied to the courts for a declaration that medical treatment could be ceased without any crime being committed. The case reached the House of Lords. The first question the House of Lords had to answer was whether ceasing Tony's treatment would be an act or an omission.

(Note: the doctors were not asking for permission to commit euthanasia. They were not seeking to actively bring Tony's life to an end. They were only applying for permission to cease treatment.)

At first this might seem straightforward. Not treating a patient looks like an omission. But it wasn't this easy! One of the things the doctors were asking for permission to do was remove the nasogastric tube that was feeding Tony, and removing a tube looks more like an act than an omission.

---

**EXTRACT**

Read the following extracts from the judgments of Lord Goff and Lord Browne-Wilkinson. Was ceasing Tony's treatment and removing the nasogastric tube an act or an omission? What reasons did they give for their conclusion?

According to Lord Goff, if a stranger had crept into the hospital at night and removed the nasogastric tube that was feeding Tony, would this have been an act or an omission?

### *Airedale NHS Trust v Bland* [1993] AC 789

### Lord Goff

I agree that the doctor's conduct in discontinuing life support can properly be categorised as an omission. It is true that it may be difficult to describe what the doctor actually does as an omission, for example where he takes some positive step to bring the life support to an end. But discontinuation of life support is, for present purposes, no different from not initiating life support in the first place. In each case, the doctor is simply allowing his patient to die in the sense that he is desisting from taking a step which might, in certain circumstances, prevent his patient from dying as a result of his pre-existing condition; and as a matter of general principle an omission such as this will not be unlawful unless it constitutes a breach of duty to the patient. I also agree that the doctor's conduct is to be differentiated from that of, for example, an interloper who maliciously switches off a life support machine because, although the interloper may perform exactly the same act as the doctor who discontinues life support, his doing so constitutes interference with the life-prolonging treatment then being administered by the doctor. Accordingly, whereas the doctor, in discontinuing life support, is simply allowing his patient to die of his pre-existing condition, the interloper is actively intervening to stop the doctor from prolonging the patient's life, and such conduct cannot possibly be categorised as an omission.

### Lord Browne-Wilkinson

The positive act of removing the nasogastric tube presents more difficulty. It is undoubtedly a positive act, similar to switching off a ventilator in the case of a patient whose life is being sustained by artificial ventilation. But in my judgment in neither case should the act be classified as positive, since to do so would be to introduce intolerably fine distinctions. If, instead of removing the nasogastric tube, it was left in place but no further nutrients were provided for the tube to convey to the patient's stomach, that would not be an act of commission. Again, as has been pointed out (*Skegg, Law, Ethics and Medicine* (1984), pp. 169 et seq.) if the switching off of a ventilator were to be classified as a positive act, exactly the same result can be achieved by installing a time-clock which requires to be reset every 12 hours: the failure to reset the machine could not be classified as a positive act. In my judgment, essentially what is being done is to omit to feed or to ventilate: the removal of the nasogastric tube or the switching off of a ventilator are merely incidents of that omission: see *Glanville Williams, Textbook of Criminal Law*, p. 282; *Skegg*, pp. 169 et seq.

So the House of Lords decided that, when taken as a whole, what the doctors were doing was to cease Tony's treatment. Although this did involve some positive acts, like removing the nasogastric tube, ceasing treating is an omission. Having decided that ceasing Tony's treatment would be an omission, the next question was whether the doctors would be criminally liable for this omission. As we saw above, the House of Lords stated that doctors have a duty to act in their patients' best interests. Since Tony no longer had any interest in being kept alive, the House of Lords held that ceasing his treatment would not violate his best interests. Therefore the doctors would not be breaching their duty and so could not be held criminally liable.

The decision in *Bland* involves some difficult distinctions. It is an omission for a doctor to remove a patient's nasogastric tube in order to cease treatment, whereas if a stranger were to remove the tube it is an act. Is it right that the same action can be an act when performed by one person and an omission when performed by someone else? And whilst it was lawful to leave Tony Bland to starve to death in a hospital bed over a period of weeks,[19] it would have been unlawful to end his life immediately by lethal injection.

## 4. Is the scope of omissions liability too narrow?

We have seen that there is normally no criminal liability for omissions. Whilst there are some exceptions to this general rule, they are quite limited in scope. It is worth pausing to

---

[19]The House of Lords' judgment is dated 4 February 1993. Tony died on 3 March that year.

consider whether these exceptions are *too* limited. In many European countries, for example, there is a duty of easy rescue.

In his article 'The Scope of Criminal Liability for Omissions' (below) Andrew Ashworth contrasts the 'conventional view' with the 'social responsibility view'. The conventional view insists 'that the criminal law should be reluctant to impose liability for omissions except in clear and serious cases'. Supporters of the conventional view 'tend to argue that there is moral distinction between acts and omissions'. Performing an act knowing that it will cause harm is morally worse, they argue, than a failure to prevent the same harm. The 'social responsibility view', by contrast, queries whether it is possible to draw such a hard-and-fast distinction. It also emphasises the extent to which we, as citizens, rely and depend on one another. This means that sometimes 'it may be fair to place citizens under obligations to render assistance to other individuals in certain situations'.

## EXTRACT

Read the following extract from Ashworth's article. Summarise the arguments in favour of the 'conventional view'. Summarise the counter-arguments of the 'social responsibility view'. Can you think of any additional arguments for either viewpoint?

Which set of arguments do you find the most convincing?

## Ashworth, A. (1989) 'The Scope of Criminal Liability for Omissions' 105 *Law Quarterly Review* 424

### The conventional view

The conventional view embodies a minimalist stance on criminal liability for omissions. It accepts that criminal law is the sharpest end of a legal structure which aims to ensure both that respect for social values is enforced and that essential social needs are provided for. It therefore accepts criminal liability for such omissions as non-payment of taxes. But it regards it as exceptional, and as requiring special justification, for the criminal law to impose duties to assist other individuals. Apart from special relationships (such as parent–child) and other voluntarily undertaken duties, there should be no criminally enforceable duties to assist others or to perform socially useful acts.

The main buttress is an argument from individual autonomy and liberty. Each person is regarded as an autonomous being, responsible for his or her own conduct. One aim of the law is to maximise individual liberty, so as to allow each individual to pursue a conception of the good life with as few constraints as possible. Constraints there must be, of course, in modern society: but freedom of action should be curtailed only so far as is necessary to restrain individuals from causing injury or loss to others. Setting these outer limits to freedom of action is, however, much more acceptable than requiring certain actions of a citizen, especially at times and in circumstances which may be inconvenient and may conflict with one's pursuit of one's personal goals. To impose a duty to do X at a certain time prevents the citizen from doing anything else at that time, whereas the conventional prohibitions of the criminal law leave the citizen free to do whatever else is wanted apart from the prohibited conduct. Moreover, the criminal law should recognise an individual's choices rather than allowing liability to be governed by chance, and the obligation to assist someone in peril may be thrust upon a chance passer-by, who may well prefer not to become involved at all. If I am driving to a concert 50 miles away which is to feature a soloist who is being heard for the last time in this country, should I be obliged to stop and render assistance to the victims of a road accident in which I was not involved, at the risk of missing part or the whole of the concert? It is no argument to say that such a journey is always open to the possibility of chance happenings, such as engine failure in the car, a road blocked by a fallen tree, and so on, because in the case of the accident victims I am physically free to drive on to my destination whereas the other happenings amount to physical prevention, and render me incapable of reaching my destination on time. Thus it is no argument to say that all arrangements are vulnerable to chance, since the law can strive to minimise its effect and to keep individual choice as wide as possible. There is a choice whether to stop and offer assistance or to continue on my way to the concert, but an offence requiring a citizen to stop and render assistance would effectively foreclose that choice, coercing me to sacrifice the pursuit of my own interests in favour of alleviating the misfortunes of others to whom I have not voluntarily assumed any duty. By its "chance" nature, the incidence of such a duty reduces the predictability of one's obligations and impinges on the liberty to pursue one's conception of the good life. On the conventional view, then, I deserve moral praise if I stop to assist the accident victims and thereby lose the opportunity to attend the (whole) concert, but it does not follow that I deserve blame if I do not stop. Praise may be appropriate for an act of "saintliness" going beyond duty, whereas the duties themselves require only the basic conditions of peaceful co-existence. Stopping to help is part of the morality of aspiration, not the morality of duty.

In thus equating individual autonomy with *negative* liberty (*i.e.* liberty not to do certain acts), the conventional view rejects broad duties to others as paternalistic, and as failing to respect each individual's right to self-determination. Any obligation to help others in peril begs the question of who is to decide what "peril" is. Individuals may choose to engage in amateur boxing or in motor cycle racing, knowing of the high risk of injury but deciding that it is worth the risk in order to enjoy the excitement of the sport. Are these boxers or motor cyclists "in peril"? Few would extend a citizen's obligation to intervene (where it exists) to these cases, probably because the individual's decision to engage in the sport may be assumed to be an informed and settled decision. Self-determination, a value closely entwined with individual autonomy, would be impaired by the intervention of others. But what about the person who decides to commit suicide and jumps from a bridge into the River Thames? Should the passing citizen be obliged to alert the emergency services or, if the conditions are favourable, to mount a rescue attempt? The passing citizen is unlikely to know about the potential suicide's state of mind. It is known that some attempts at suicide proceed from an unbalanced state of mind, and some are merely attempts to draw attention to the person's problems rather than to relinquish life. On the conventional view these possibilities for paternalistic intervention should not be made the basis of any legal duty. If a citizen sees what appears to be an attempted suicide, the citizen's freedom from non-voluntary obligations together with the potential suicide's right to self-determination are sufficient to conclude the case against a duty to intervene.

A third argument looks to the social consequences of the opposite, "social responsibility" view. Its effect in requiring each citizen to offer assistance to others in peril might on the one hand reduce the autonomy and privacy of others in pursuing their own objectives and enjoyment, however dangerous it may appear to others, and might on the other hand make citizens into busybodies who believe that they must be constantly advising others to avoid risk and danger. In other words, it might be too intrusive and too onerous – both tendencies which go against the maximisation of liberty which is the keynote of the conventional view.

Fourthly, there is the argument that the "social responsibility" view is unpractical because it would require each of us to avert or alleviate large numbers of situations which we know about. One strand of this argument calls attention to the problem of setting limits to the individuals duties on the social responsibility view: must I sell my car and my house, live at subsistence level and devote all my surplus earnings and time to preventing so many people from "sleeping rough" in London, or to provide towards the relief of starvation in Africa? In what way do perils of these kinds differ materially from the accident victims or the person who jumps into the River Thames? A second strand of the argument is that the "social responsibility" view may lead to the inculpation of large numbers of people, e.g. all the members of a crowd who witness someone being beaten up by others. It is excesses of this nature, in the depth and breadth of the obligations imposed, which are seen as sufficient to condemn the "social responsibility" view as an unworkable moral or legal standard.

A fifth argument draws strength from the principle of legality: it maintains that citizens are so unaccustomed to thinking in terms of legal duties to act (as distinct from the well-known prohibitions) that it is unfair to impose such burdens except in circumstances which are well-defined and well-publicised. Protagonists might add that few provisions on general liability for omissions attain these standards, and that the obligation to take reasonable steps to assist a person in peril is much too uncertain to meet these standards. The social consequence is likely to be that ignorance of the law is a frequent occurrence, which cannot be good either for society or for the individuals concerned. Wide conceptions of social responsibility must therefore be rejected as a basis for criminal legislation: the conventional view, with its few well-known and voluntarily assumed duties to others, is the preferable approach.

## The individualism of the conventional view doubted

The arguments for the conventional view may appear strong and practical, but they depend on a narrow, individualistic conception of human life which should be rejected as a basis for morality and (although this raises further issues) as a basis for criminal liability. Let us look again at the arguments, in turn.

The first argument, based on individual autonomy and freedom, is altogether too pure. To the extent that the conventional view relies on "social fact" for some of its justifications, it is worth pointing out that rarely is individual autonomy promoted as a supreme value throughout a moral or legal system. For example, paternalistic considerations are taken to outweigh it when imposing a duty to wear a seat belt in the front seat of a car: this restricts individual liberty and self-determination, and it may be justified by reference to the known dangers of travelling without a seat-belt, combined with the relatively large benefit (in the social costs of health care) reaped from such a comparatively minor infringement of freedom of action. Systems of criminal law typically include a wide range of offences which impose duties to act, in relation to taxation, motoring and business activities. However, it is not necessary to turn "social fact" arguments against the conventional view, for its proclaimed principle of individual autonomy is itself unsatisfactory. If individual autonomy is truly a supreme value, then it requires social principles rather than this kind of isolationist individualism in order to secure its fulfilment. Individuals tend to place a high value on interpersonal contacts, relationships, mutual support and the fulfilment of obligations, and a society which values collective goals and collective goods may therefore provide a wider range of worthwhile opportunities for individual development. At the very least, then, there is no inherent logic in arguing from the ideal of individual autonomy to moral and legal principles which regard duties to other citizens *qua* fellow-citizens as prima facie objectionable and exceptional, for that neglects the importance of human interdependence to the realisation of individual autonomy. This is still a far cry from the utilitarian view, since that tends to aggregate people in its calculations and fails to respect each individual as an end in himself or herself. The counter-argument to the conventional view is thus that a duty to co-operate with or to assist others should not be ruled out *ab initio* by an asocial and falsely restricted view of individual autonomy. Moreover, the proposition is not that citizens should be permanently at the beck and call of one another, but that (at the very least) there is a strong case for going beyond the conventional view and, for example, creating a duty to assist a citizen whose life is in peril. This may not maximise the quantity of liberty left to individuals, but it increases the quality of social life.

The second and third arguments for the conventional view establish, however, that limits must be set to the obligations to others if the ideal of individual autonomy is not to be submerged beneath a welter of duties imposed on each person. The resolution of these conflicts of theory and practice is no easy matter, but the "social responsibility" view would at least start from the assumption that duties to others are not necessarily alien to individual autonomy, and would have to reconcile this with the desirability of individuals safeguarding their own interests too. This dilemma, which also underlies the fourth argument for the conventional view, demonstrates the need for principled debate about the extent of social co-operation necessary to realise individual autonomy. Those who advocate "social responsibility" bear the heavy burden of formulating defensible and workable criteria for the imposition of duties to act. Indeed, as the fifth argument showed, attention is also necessary to the promulgation of such rules. In so far as it is true that people do not consider that they have legal duties to assist others, any legislation to introduce such duties must be phrased as precisely as possible, and must be supported by a programme of education and information. These represent considerable challenges for the "social responsibility" view on criminal liability for omissions.

## Causation

Our third *actus reus* concept is causation. In Chapter 2, we saw that crimes which have a consequence element as part of their *actus reus* are known as result crimes. Causation is an essential feature of all result crimes. Whenever a defendant is charged with a result crime a 'causal link' must be shown between the defendant's actions and the specified consequence. To establish a causal link it is necessary to prove both factual causation and legal causation. In this section we look first at factual causation, and then legal causation. This is the order in which you would discuss these issues in an exam problem question answer: begin with factual causation, and if this is present move on to consider legal causation.

### 1. Factual causation

To test for factual causation we use the 'but for' test. This simply asks: but for the defendant's actions, would the consequence have occurred in the same way? If the answer to this question is 'Yes, the consequence would have occurred in the same way without the defendant's actions' there is no factual causation. But if the answer is 'No, the consequence would not have occurred in the same way without the defendant's actions' there is factual causation, and you should move on to consider whether or not legal causation is also present.

The following two cases are helpful examples of the 'but for' test in action.

### EXAMPLE

- In *R v White* [1910] 2 KB 124 the defendant put poison in the victim's drink. The victim had a few sips, but suffered a fatal heart attack before she could drink any more. Medical evidence suggested that the heart attack was unrelated to the poison. So the poisoned drink was not a factual cause of the victim's death. But for the poison, the victim would still have suffered the heart attack and died in the same way.[20]

- In *R v Dalloway* (1847) 2 Cox CC 273 the defendant was riding a horse-drawn cart. He was standing up, not holding the reins. A three-year-old child called Henry ran across the road in front of the horse. One of the wheels of the cart knocked Henry down and killed him. Dalloway was charged with manslaughter. The prosecution argued that his negligent driving had caused Henry's death. The jury concluded that even if Dalloway had been driving carefully he would not have been able to avoid hitting Henry. So there was no factual causation. Dalloway's negligent driving was not a factual cause of Henry's death, because even if Dalloway had been driving carefully Henry would still have been knocked over and killed.

---

[20] Although this meant the defendant had not committed murder (he had not caused the victim's death), he was convicted of attempted murder.

## 2. Legal causation

The 'but for' test sets a very low threshold. As a result, there can be many factual causes of a consequence which are not deserving of criminal liability. Suppose that your lecturer overruns by ten minutes. As a result you miss your bus home and have to walk. While you are walking home your housemate calls you on your mobile to find out where you are. Preoccupied by the phone conversation, you step out in front of a car and are run over. On these facts, both your lecturer and your housemate are factual causes of your death. But for your lecturer overrunning, you would have caught your bus and not been walking home. And but for your housemate phoning you, you would have not been distracted and not stepped out in front of the car.

The role of legal causation is to identify which factual causes should also be regarded as legal causes. In other words, the role of legal causation is to filter out those factual causes which are not deserving of criminal liability. This is what makes legal causation difficult. It is not a dispassionate exercise in logic. As we shall see, questions of legal causation involve difficult moral and policy considerations.

### i. The basic test for legal causation: significant contribution

In *R v Cheshire* [1991] 1 WLR 844 Beldam LJ stated:

> It is not the function of the jury to evaluate competing causes or to choose which is dominant provided they are satisfied that the defendant's acts can fairly be said to have made a significant contribution to the victim's death. We think the word "significant" conveys the necessary substance of a contribution made to the death which is more than negligible.

So the starting point for determining questions of legal causation is to ask whether the defendant's actions made a significant contribution to the relevant consequence. If the contribution made by the defendant's actions was insignificant (in other words, negligible) there is no legal causation. So in our earlier example, the lecturer overrunning and the housemate phoning were not legal causes of your death because neither can be regarded as having made a significant contribution.

Notice one further point about this test: the question is simply whether the defendant's actions made a significant contribution. So you do not have to compare the defendant's actions to other factual causes of the consequence and ask which was the most significant. The question is simply whether the contribution made by the defendant's actions was significant or not. It is possible for more than one factual cause to make a significant contribution. This means that there might be several legal causes of the same consequence, as Beldam LJ explained in *R v Cheshire*:

> [W]e think it is sufficient for the judge to tell the jury that they must be satisfied that the Crown have proved that the acts of the defendant caused the death of the deceased adding that the defendant's acts need not be the sole cause or even the main cause of death it being sufficient that his acts contributed significantly to that result.

Deciding whether or not the defendant's contribution was significant can sometimes involve difficult moral and policy considerations. But questions of legal causation can become even more difficult if there was an intervening act (of a third party, of nature or of the victim herself) or if the victim had characteristics (physical or otherwise) that meant she was particularly susceptible. As we work our way through these issues, we will see that the courts have developed a total of five different principles:

- The voluntariness principle
- The fact of life principle

- The reasonable foreseeability principle
- The operative cause principle
- The thin skull principle.

These principles do not always pull in the same direction. In many situations some of these principles will conflict. Two questions for you to consider as we work our way through the relevant case law are: (1) Where there is conflict between these principles why did the courts choose to apply the principle(s) they did? and (2) Have the courts applied the principles in a coherent and consistent way?

### ii. Intervening acts of a third party

The general principle is that voluntary intervening acts of a third party break the chain of causation. Suppose that Johann stabs Ludwig. As Ludwig lies on the ground, bleeding heavily, Hans walks up and shoots Ludwig dead. Medical evidence shows that, although Ludwig would probably have died from the stab wound, the fatal injury was the bullet wound. On these facts, the stabbing is not a legal cause of Ludwig's death. The chain of causation was broken by Hans' voluntary intervening act.[21]

The voluntariness principle is regarded as extremely important. As Glanville Williams explains in the following extract, the voluntariness principle is grounded in the principle of individual autonomy (which we studied in Chapter 1).

## EXTRACT

Read the following extract. What is the connection between the voluntariness principle and the principle of individual autonomy?

### Williams, G. (1989) 'Finis for Novus Actus?' 48 *Cambridge Law Journal* 391

A person is primarily responsible for what he himself does. He is not responsible, not blameworthy, for what other people do. The fact that his own conduct, rightful or wrongful, provided the background for a subsequent voluntary and wrong act by another does not make him responsible for it. What he does may be a but-for cause of the injurious act, but he did not do it. His conduct is not an imputable cause of it. Only the later actor, the doer of the act that intervenes between the first act and the result, the final wielder of human autonomy in the matter, bears responsibility (along with his accomplices) for the result that ensues.

[...]

The autonomy doctrine, expressing itself through its corollary the doctrine of *novus actus interveniens*, teaches that the individual's will is the autonomous (self-regulating) prime cause of his behaviour. Although this may sound unbelievably metaphysical, the doctrine is supported because it accords with our ideas of moral responsibility and just punishment, and serves social objectives. The first actor who starts on a dangerous or criminal plan will often be responsible for what happens if no one else intervenes; but a subsequent actor who has reached responsible years, is of sound mind, has full knowledge of what he is doing, and is not acting under intimidation or other pressure or stress resulting from the defendant's conduct, replaces him as the responsible actor. Such an intervening act is thought to break the moral connection that would otherwise have been perceived between the defendant's acts and the forbidden consequence.

---

[21]Although Johann would not be guilty of murder, he would be guilty of other crimes: wounding with intent (Offences Against the Person Act 1861, s.18) and perhaps attempted murder.

In *R v Pagett* (1983) 76 Cr App R 279 the defendant, 31-year-old David Pagett, formed a relationship with the victim, 16-year-old Gail Kinchen. After several arguments, Gail, who was six months pregnant, left Pagett and moved back home with her mother and stepfather. Pagett armed himself with a shotgun, tracked Gail down, kidnapped her and took her to a block of flats. Police arrived at the scene and told Pagett to surrender and come out. Eventually Pagett came out, using Gail as a human shield. He fired at the police, and two officers instinctively fired back. Gail was hit three times and died. Pagett and the police officers were unharmed.

At trial Pagett was convicted of the manslaughter of Gail. He appealed, arguing that he was not a legal cause of Gail's death. The policemen's act of firing their guns was, he claimed, an intervening act which broke the chain of causation. The Court of Appeal rejected Pagett's appeal, saying that the policemen's actions were not voluntary and so did not break the chain of causation.

## EXTRACT

Read the following extract from the judgment of Robert Goff LJ. Why were the policemen's actions not voluntary?

What did Robert Goff LJ say the word 'voluntary' should normally be understood to mean in this context?

### *R v Pagett* (1983) 76 Cr App R 279

### Robert Goff LJ

Now the whole subject of causation in the law has been the subject of a well-known and most distinguished treatise by Professors Hart and Honorâ, *Causation in the Law*. Passages from this book were cited to the learned judge, and were plainly relied upon by him; we, too, wish to express our indebtedness to it. It would be quite wrong for us to consider in this judgment the wider issues discussed in that work. But, for present purposes, the passage which is of most immediate relevance is to be found in Chapter XII, in which the learned authors consider the circumstances in which the intervention of a third person, not acting in concert with the accused, may have the effect of relieving the accused of criminal responsibility. The criterion which they suggest should be applied in such circumstances is whether the intervention is voluntary, i.e. whether it is "free, deliberate and informed." We resist the temptation of expressing the judicial opinion whether we find ourselves in complete agreement with that definition; though we certainly consider it to be broadly correct and supported by authority. Among the examples which the authors give of non-voluntary conduct, which is not effective to relieve the accused of responsibility, are two which are germane to the present case, viz. a reasonable act performed for the purpose of self-preservation, and an act done in performance of a legal duty.

There can, we consider, be no doubt that a reasonable act performed for the purpose of self-preservation, being of course itself an act caused by the accused's own act, does not operate as a *novus actus interveniens* [...] Furthermore, in our judgment, if a reasonable act of self-defence against the act of the accused causes the death of a third party, we can see no reason in principle why the act of self-defence, being an involuntary act caused by the act of the accused, should relieve the accused from criminal responsibility for the death of the third party.

[...]

No English authority was cited to us, nor we think to the learned judge, in support of the proposition that an act done in the execution of a legal duty, again of course being an act itself caused by the act of the accused, does not operate as a *novus actus interveniens* [...] Of course, it is inherent in the requirement that the police officer, or other person, must be acting in the execution of his duty that his act should be reasonable in all the circumstances: see section 3 of the Criminal Law Act 1967. Furthermore, once again we are only considering the issue of causation. If intervention by a third party in the execution of a legal duty, caused by the act of the accused, results in the death of the victim, the question whether the accused is guilty of the murder or manslaughter of the victim must depend on whether the necessary ingredients of the relevant offence have been proved against the accused, including in particular, in the case of murder, whether the accused had the necessary intent.

The definition of voluntary as 'free, deliberate and informed' provides a useful explanation for the decision in the old case of *R v Michael* (1840) 9 C & P 356. The defendant wanted to kill her illegitimate baby. She gave the baby's nurse a bottle of poison, telling her that it was the baby's medicine. The nurse decided that the baby did not need any medicine and left the bottle on the mantelpiece. Later, the nurse's five-year-old child took the bottle and gave some to the baby. The baby died and the defendant was convicted of murder. The five-year-old's actions did not break the chain of causation because they were not voluntary. They were not 'free, deliberate and informed'.

A more recent example of the voluntariness principle being applied is *R v Rafferty* [2007] EWCA Crim 1846. Joel Taylor, Joshua Thomas and Andrew Rafferty attacked the victim, 17-year-old Ben Bellamy. Taylor and Thomas punched, kicked and stamped on Ben. On a couple of occasions Ben tried to escape, but Rafferty knocked him over to stop him from running away. Rafferty then left the scene of the attack, taking Ben's debit card with him. After Rafferty had left, Taylor and Thomas carried Ben's unconscious body 100 metres to the sea in Swansea Bay, stripped him naked and drowned him in the water.

Rafferty pleaded guilty to robbery. At trial he was also convicted of the manslaughter of Ben. He appealed against the manslaughter conviction, arguing that the actions of Taylor and Thomas had broken the chain of causation. The Court of Appeal agreed. Quashing the manslaughter conviction the Court held that the actions of Taylor and Thomas were voluntary intervening acts which broke the chain of causation.

Although the principle that voluntary interventions of a third party break the chain of causation is well established, it has not been universally applied. In its controversial decision in *Environment Agency v Empress Car Co (Abertillery) Ltd* [1999] 2 AC 22 ('*Empress*') the House of Lords held that a third party had not broken the chain of causation even though the third party's actions were free, deliberate and informed. The defendant company in *Empress* had attached a tap to a diesel tank in its yard. The tap had no lock. One day a trespasser entered the yard, opened the tap and drained the entire contents of the tank. The contents poured out and flowed into a nearby river. At trial the company was convicted of causing polluting matter to enter controlled waters.[22] The company appealed against its conviction, arguing that its actions (fixing a tap with no lock) were not a legal cause of the pollution. It argued that the trespasser's actions had broken the chain of causation.

---

[22]Water Resources Act 1991, s.85(1).

Read the following extract from the judgment of Lord Hoffmann. What distinction does he draw? According to this distinction, when will the acts of a third party break the chain of causation? When will they not break the chain of causation?

**EXTRACT**

## Environment Agency v Empress Car Co (Abertillery) Ltd [1999] 2 AC 22

### Lord Hoffmann

The true common sense distinction is, in my view, between acts and events which, although not necessarily foreseeable in the particular case, are in the generality a normal and familiar fact of life, and acts or events which are abnormal and extraordinary. Of course an act or event which is in general terms a normal fact of life may also have been foreseeable in the circumstances of the particular case, but the latter is not necessary for the purposes of liability. There is nothing extraordinary or abnormal about leaky pipes or lagoons as such: these things happen, even if the particular defendant could not reasonably have foreseen that it would happen to him. There is nothing unusual about people putting unlawful substances into the sewage system and the same, regrettably, is true about ordinary vandalism. So when these things happen, one does not say: that was an extraordinary coincidence, which negatived the causal connection between the original act of accumulating the polluting substance and its escape. In the context of [this offence], the defendant's accumulation has still caused the pollution. On the other hand, the example I gave of the terrorist attack would be something so unusual that one would not regard the defendant's conduct as having caused the escape at all.

So according to Lord Hoffmann's fact of life principle, the actions of a third party will not break the chain of causation if they were 'a normal and familiar fact of life' – even if the actions were free, deliberate and informed, and even if they were not 'foreseeable in the circumstances of the particular case'.

The outcome of *Empress* has been strongly criticised. The defendant company was lawfully storing oil on its own land. Perhaps the company should have taken greater care and locked the tap. But saying the company should have taken greater care to secure the tank is altogether different from saying that it was a legal cause of the pollution. Suppose a supermarket employee carelessly leaves an open till unattended, allowing a customer to steal £100 from the cash drawer. We might describe the employee as careless, but we would not describe the employee as a thief.[23] The customer's voluntary intervening act breaks the chain of causation. In *Empress* the trespasser made a free, deliberate and informed choice to drain the contents of the tank. The principle of individual autonomy tells us that the trespasser, not the company, should be held responsible for the consequences of the trespasser's voluntary choice.

It has been suggested that the House of Lords in *Empress* was influenced by the policy concern to protect the environment. Its strict approach encourages companies to take more stringent measures to safeguard potentially dangerous and hazardous materials. On this view, the fact of life principle set out by Lord Hoffmann should be confined to

[23]Even if the employee had deliberately left the till open so that someone else could steal from it, we would describe them as an accessory to theft, not as a principal (see Chapter 13).

cases involving environmental protection. This view has been confirmed by the House of Lords in *R v Kennedy (No 2)* [2007] UKHL 38. Lord Bingham stated:

> 15 Questions of causation frequently arise in many areas of the law, but causation is not a single, unvarying concept to be mechanically applied without regard to the context in which the question arises. That was the point which Lord Hoffmann, with the express concurrence of three other members of the House, was at pains to make in *Environment Agency (formerly National Rivers Authority) v Empress Car Co (Abertillery) Ltd* [1999] 2 AC 22. The House was not in that decision purporting to lay down general rules governing causation in criminal law. It was construing, with reference to the facts of the case before it, a statutory provision imposing strict criminal liability on those who cause pollution of controlled waters.

## ACTIVITY

On 28 January 2013 footballer Paul Scholes had his top-of-the-range car stolen from his driveway. The car's windscreen was covered in ice, so Scholes left the engine running to melt the ice while he went back inside his house. While he was inside the thief got into the car and drove off in it.[24] Were Scholes' actions a factual and legal cause of the theft?

### iii. Intervening acts of a medical practitioner

Suppose the defendant injures the victim. The victim receives medical treatment, but the doctor treating her makes a mistake and as a result the victim suffers even greater harm or dies. May the defendant claim that the doctor's error broke the chain of causation?

In situations like this, bad medical treatment will only break the chain of causation in exceptional circumstances. The policy reason for this position is that the victim would not have needed medical treatment had the defendant not injured her. Since the defendant caused the victim to require medical treatment, he can hardly complain about the standard of care she received.

An example is *R v Smith* [1959] 2 QB 35. The defendant, Thomas Smith, was a soldier. He took part in a fight with soldiers from another regiment who were sharing the same barracks. During the fight he stabbed the victim twice. A fellow soldier attempted to carry the victim to the medical station, but tripped over a wire and dropped him. He picked him up, went a little further, then dropped him a second time. When the victim arrived at the medical station the medical officer was already trying to deal with some other serious cases and did not appreciate the seriousness of the victim's condition. Specifically, he did not realise that one of the stab wounds had pierced the victim's lung and caused haemorrhage. As a result he ordered treatment that was inappropriate (artificial respiration) and which might well have affected the victim's chances of recovery. An hour after arriving in the medical station the victim died. One of the issues on appeal was whether the chain of causation had been broken by the bad medical treatment and by the victim being dropped on his way to the medical station.

---

[24]http://news.sky.com/story/1044488/paul-scholes-car-stolen-while-defrosting (accessed 1 March 2013).

## EXTRACT

Read the following extract from the judgment of Lord Parker CJ. Did the bad medical treatment break the chain of causation?

Of the five principles we outlined earlier, which one did Lord Parker CJ apply? In what circumstances will bad medical treatment break the chain of causation?

### *R v Smith* [1959] 2 QB 35

### Lord Parker CJ

It seems to the court that if at the time of death the original wound is still an operating cause and a substantial cause, then the death can properly be said to be the result of the wound, albeit that some other cause of death is also operating. Only if it can be said that the original wounding is merely the setting in which another cause operates can it be said that the death does not result from the wound. Putting it in another way, only if the second cause is so overwhelming as to make the original wound merely part of the history can it be said that the death does not flow from the wound.

[...]

[I]n the opinion of the court, [the facts of the case] can only lead to one conclusion: a man is stabbed in the back, his lung is pierced and haemorrhage results; two hours later he dies of haemorrhage from that wound; in the interval there is no time for a careful examination, and the treatment given turns out in the light of subsequent knowledge to have been inappropriate and, indeed, harmful. In those circumstances no reasonable jury or court could, properly directed, in our view possibly come to any other conclusion than that the death resulted from the original wound. Accordingly, the court dismisses this appeal.

In *R v Smith* the victim died from injuries inflicted by the defendant. But what if the injuries the defendant inflicted were no longer life-threatening by the time of death? In this situation, will bad medical treatment break the chain of causation? This was the issue in *R v Cheshire* [1991] 1 WLR 844.

The defendant, David Cheshire, got into an argument with the victim, Trevor Jeffrey, late one night in a fish and chip shop. Cheshire produced a handgun and shot Jeffrey twice, once in the leg and once in the stomach. Jeffrey was taken to hospital and underwent surgery. Afterwards he developed problems breathing, and so a tracheotomy tube was placed in his windpipe. This tube remained in place for four weeks. A few weeks after the tube had been removed, Jeffrey complained of difficulty breathing. He was seen by a number of doctors, who concluded that the reason for his breathing problems was anxiety attacks. However, Jeffrey's condition deteriorated and (more than two months after the initial shooting) he died. At the time of death the original gunshot wounds were no longer life-threatening.

It was later discovered that Jeffrey's windpipe had narrowed near where the tracheotomy tube had been inserted. This was a rare, but not unknown, side effect of tracheotomies. Jeffrey's windpipe had become so narrow that even a small amount of mucus would block it and cause asphyxiation.

At trial Cheshire was convicted of murder. The issue for the Court of Appeal was whether the doctors' failure to diagnose the reason for Jeffrey's breathing problems broke the chain of causation.

## EXTRACT

Read the following extract from the judgment of Beldam LJ. Did the bad medical treatment break the chain of causation?

According to Beldam LJ, when will bad medical treatment break the chain of causation?

### *R v Cheshire* [1991] 1 WLR 844

### Beldam LJ

[W]hen the victim of a criminal attack is treated for wounds or injuries by doctors or other medical staff attempting to repair the harm done, it will only be in the most extraordinary and unusual case that such treatment can be said to be so independent of the acts of the defendant that it could be regarded in law as the cause of the victim's death to the exclusion of the defendant's acts.

[...]

In a case in which the jury have to consider whether negligence in the treatment of injuries inflicted by the defendant was the cause of death we think it is sufficient for the judge to tell the jury that they must be satisfied that the Crown have proved that the acts of the defendant caused the death of the deceased adding that the defendant's acts need not be the sole cause or even the main cause of death it being sufficient that his acts contributed significantly to that result. Even though negligence in the treatment of the victim was the immediate cause of his death, the jury should not regard it as excluding the responsibility of the defendant unless the negligent treatment was so independent of his acts, and in itself so potent in causing death, that they regard the contribution made by his acts as insignificant.

It is not the function of the jury to evaluate competing causes or to choose which is dominant provided they are satisfied that the defendant's acts can fairly be said to have made a significant contribution to the victim's death. We think the word "significant" conveys the necessary substance of a contribution made to the death which is more than negligible.

In the present case the passage in the summing up complained of has to be set in the context of the remainder of the direction given by the judge on the issue of causation. He directed the jury that they had to decide whether the two bullets fired into the deceased on 10 December caused his death on 15 February following. Or, he said, put in another way, did the injuries caused cease to operate as a cause of death because something else intervened? He told them that the prosecution did not have to prove that the bullets were the only cause of death but they had to prove that they were one operative and substantial cause of death. He was thus following the words used in *Reg. v. Smith* [1959] 2 Q.B. 35.

The judge then gave several examples for the jury to consider before reverting to a paraphrase of the alternative formulation used by Lord Parker C.J. in *Reg. v. Smith*. Finally, he reminded the jury of the evidence which they had heard on this issue. We would remark that on several occasions during this evidence the jury had passed notes to the judge asking for clarification of expressions used by the medical witnesses which showed that they were following closely the factual issues they had to consider. If the passage to which exception has been taken had not been included, no possible criticism could have been levelled at the summing up. Although for reasons we have stated we think that the judge erred when he invited the jury to consider the degree of fault in the medical treatment rather than its consequences, we consider that no miscarriage of justice has actually occurred. Even if more experienced doctors than those who attended the deceased would have recognised the rare complication in time to have prevented the deceased's death, that complication was a direct consequence of the appellant's acts which remained a significant cause of his death. We cannot conceive that, on the evidence given, any jury would have found otherwise.

There is an important difference between *R v Smith* and *R v Cheshire*. In *R v Smith* the physical cause of death was the haemorrhage the defendant inflicted. But in *R v Cheshire* the gunshot wounds were healing at the time of death and were no longer life-threatening. The Court of Appeal nonetheless concluded that the defendant's actions were still operative at the time of death. Simester and Sullivan explain that the doctors' error was an omission.[25] The defendant set in motion a chain of events that culminated in the victim's death. The doctors failed to step in and prevent this series of events, but the victim's death was the direct consequence of the defendant's actions: the shooting resulted in the tracheotomy and the tracheotomy resulted in the narrowing of the windpipe. So even if the gunshot wounds were not an operating cause of death, the defendant's actions were.

It is clear from *R v Cheshire* that bad medical treatment will rarely break the chain of causation. An example of a case in which the chain of causation was broken is *R v Jordan* (1956) 40 Cr App R 152. The defendant, James Jordan, stabbed the victim, Walter Beaumont. Beaumont was taken to hospital and the wound was stitched up. But a few days later Beaumont died. At trial Jordan was convicted of murder and sentenced to death.

Following the trial additional medical evidence became available, which showed that the stab wound had almost healed at the time of death. In order to prevent infection, Beaumont had been given an antibiotic called Terramycin™. After the initial doses Beaumont developed diarrhoea. The doctors concluded that Beaumont was allergic to Terramycin. However, the next day another doctor ordered that administration of the drug be recommenced. Moreover, the amount of the drug the doctor prescribed was 'wholly abnormal'. As a result of being given exceptionally high quantities of a drug he was allergic to, Beaumont contracted pneumonia and died. Quashing Jordan's conviction, the Court of Appeal said that the medical treatment in this case was so bad – the doctor made two errors which were both 'palpably wrong' – that the chain of causation had been broken.

### iv. Intervening acts of the victim

Our starting point here is *R v Roberts* (1971) 56 Cr App R 95. The defendant, Kenneth Roberts, was giving the victim a lift in his car following a party. Here is the victim's account of what happened:

> He just jumped on me. He put his hands up my clothes and tried to take my tights off. I started to fight him off, but the door of the car was locked and I could not find the catch. Suddenly he grabbed me and then he drove off and I started to cry and asked him to take me home. He told me to take my clothes off and, if I did not take my clothes off, he would let me walk home, so I asked him to let me do that. He said, if he did, he would beat me up before he let me go. He said that he had done this before and had got away with it and he started to pull my coat off. He was using foul language […]

---

[25]Simester, A.P., Spencer, J.R., Stark, F., Sullivan, G.R. & Virgo, G.J. (2016) *Simester and Sullivan's Criminal Law: Theory and Doctrine* (6th edn) Oxford: Hart Publishing, p115.

Again, he tried to get my coat off, so I got hold of my handbag and I jumped out of the car. When I opened the door he said something and revved the car up and I jumped out.

The victim suffered concussion and grazing.

At trial Roberts was convicted of assault occasioning actual bodily harm. He appealed against his conviction. The issue for the Court of Appeal was whether the victim's act of jumping from the car had broken the chain of causation.

## EXTRACT

Read the following extract from the judgment of Stephenson LJ. What test does he say must be applied to determine whether an intervening act of the victim breaks the chain of causation?

### *R v Roberts* (1971) 56 Cr App R 95

#### Stephenson LJ

[Defence counsel] was wrong in submitting to this Court that the jury must be sure that a defendant, who is charged either with inflicting grievous bodily harm or assault occasioning actual bodily harm, must foresee the actions of the victim which result in the grievous bodily harm, or the actual bodily harm. That, in the view of this Court, is not the test. The test is: Was it the natural result of what the alleged assailant said and did, in the sense that it was something that could reasonably have been foreseen as the consequence of what he was saying or doing? As it was put in one of the old cases, it had got to be shown to be his act, and if of course the victim does something so "daft," in the words of the appellant in this case, or so unexpected, not that this particular assailant did not actually foresee it but that no reasonable man could be expected to foresee it, then it is only in a very remote and unreal sense a consequence of his assault, it is really occasioned by a voluntary act on the part of the victim which could not reasonably be foreseen and which breaks the chain of causation between the assault and the harm or injury.

The Court concluded that the trial judge had not misdirected the jury and so dismissed Roberts' appeal.

So according to *R v Roberts*, the reasonable foreseeability principle should be applied to determine whether or not an intervening act of the victim breaks the chain of causation. Only actions which are so daft or unexpected that no reasonable person could have been expected to foresee them will break the chain. A subsequent case, *R v Williams & Davis* [1992] 1 WLR 380, provided further guidance. The Court of Appeal in this case said that when applying the reasonable foreseeability test:

The jury should bear in mind any particular characteristic of the victim and the fact that in the agony of the moment he may act without thought and deliberation.

In *R v Roberts* the victim's escape occurred when the defendant assaulted her. What if there is a delay before the victim tries to escape, so that there is time for thought and deliberation? In *R v Tarasov* [2016] EWCA Crim 2278 the two defendants were brothers from Lithuania. They attacked the victim, a Polish man named Pawel Pacholak (PP), at around midnight. Pacholak sustained significant injuries and was bleeding heavily. He fled and locked himself in a first floor bathroom. Over an hour later, fearing a further attack, he climbed out of the bathroom window. The window was small (50 cm by 60 cm), and was 1.54 m off the bathroom floor. Pacholak fell head-first onto the ground below. Shortly afterwards he collapsed and died. At the Tarasov brothers' appeal against conviction, they argued that Pacholak's actions broke the chain of causation. This was rejected by the Court of Appeal. Citing *R v Roberts* and *R v Williams & Davis*, the Court held that the victim's actions were within the range of reasonable responses that might be expected from someone in his situation.

## EXTRACT

Read the following extract from the judgment of Sharp LJ. In 'flight' cases like this one, is there is a requirement that the victim feared immediate attack?

What reasons did Sharp LJ give for the Court's conclusion that Pacholak's actions were reasonably foreseeable?

### R v Tarasov [2016] EWCA Crim 2278

#### Sharp LJ

35 [...] Indeed, the very difficulty of this means of escape, given the size of the window, its height from the floor and the severity of his injuries, was potent evidence in support of the prosecution's case of his state of mind and fear at the time. In our judgment, the mere fact that there may have been a gap between the time when the beating occurred and PP's flight from further assaults through fear was not fatal to the prosecution's case either.

36 We accept that the cases on "flight" to which reference has been made involved "immediacy", in the sense that the assaults and the flight from them were close together in time. However, we can see no logical reason to make this a requirement, provided immediately before the victim sustained the fatal injuries he or she was in fear of being hurt [...]. The length of time that a victim of an assault may hide from an attacker, may be relevant, depending on the facts, as to whether the fear of an immediate assault was still operative on the victim's mind when the attempt to escape was made. But the issue is fact specific: and in our judgment, mere length of time between assault and flight, cannot in and of itself fatally undermine a prosecution of this nature.

37 There was ample evidence to support the safe conclusion that the appellants were the perpetrators of the savage beating which PP had suffered before exiting the window. And it was open to the jury to find that his escape was within the range of reasonable responses to be expected from someone in his situation.

38 The [medical evidence], after all, was that PP had been subjected to a very serious assault which had resulted in very serious injury; multiple blows to the head, five areas of injury to the neck and multiple blows to the body, none of which were caused by the fall. There was scientific blood evidence coupled with CCTV evidence that the assault on PP had started outside [the property] and that it had continued inside in the living room. The fact that PP felt driven to escape through a tiny bathroom window on the first floor, notwithstanding the seriousness of his injuries, in the context of the other evidence in the case, entitled the jury to infer that he was in fear of further attack immediately before he exited the bathroom window, and had avoided going downstairs and out through the front door past "the lion's den" as [prosecuting counsel] put it, where he had already been seriously assaulted.

The approach taken in the 'flight' cases *R v Roberts* and *R v Tarasov* may be contrasted with the approach taken in cases involving self-injection of drugs. During the 2000s a line of cases involving drug abuse caused the Court of Appeal considerable difficulty.[26] All of these involved the same basic facts: the defendant helped the victim to self-inject drugs, the victim suffered an overdose and died. The issue in these cases was whether the defendant's acts of assistance were a factual and legal cause of death.

The issue eventually reached the House of Lords in *R v Kennedy (No 2)* [2007] UKHL 38. The defendant, Simon Kennedy, prepared a dose of heroin for his friend Marco Bosque. Bosque injected himself. Soon after Bosque stopped breathing and died. At trial Kennedy was convicted of the manslaughter of Bosque. He appealed, arguing that his acts of assistance were not a legal cause of death since Bosque's act of self-injection broke the chain of causation.

## EXTRACT

Read the following extract from the judgment of Lord Bingham. Did Bosque's act of self-injection break the chain of causation?

Of the five principles we outlined earlier, which one did Lord Bingham apply?

### *R v Kennedy (No 2)* [2007] UKHL 38

### Lord Bingham

14 The criminal law generally assumes the existence of free will. The law recognises certain exceptions, in the case of the young, those who for any reason are not fully responsible for their actions, and the vulnerable, and it acknowledges situations of duress and necessity, as also of deception and mistake. But, generally speaking, informed adults of sound mind are treated as autonomous beings able to make their own decisions how they will act, and none of the exceptions is relied on as possibly applicable in this case. Thus D is not to be treated as causing V to act in a certain way if V makes a voluntary and informed decision to act in that way rather than another.

[...]

18 [...] The finding that the deceased freely and voluntarily administered the injection to himself, knowing what it was, is fatal to any contention that the appellant caused the heroin to be administered to the deceased or taken by him.

The decision in *R v Kennedy (No 2)* is difficult to reconcile with *R v Roberts*. The House of Lords applied the voluntariness principle, not the reasonable foreseeability principle. Had it applied the reasonable foreseeability principle the outcome may well have been different. It was reasonably foreseeable that Bosque would inject himself with the heroin (in fact, Bosque had asked Kennedy for the heroin saying he wanted it to help him sleep). The House of Lords' conclusion that the chain of causation was broken is thus at odds with the insistence in *R v Roberts* that intervening acts of the victim only break the chain of causation if they are so daft or unexpected that no reasonable person could have foreseen them.

---

[26]*R v Kennedy (No 1)* [1999] Crim. L.R. 65; *R v Richards* [2002] EWCA Crim 3175; *R v Dias* [2002] 2 Cr. App. R. 96; *R v Rodgers* [2003] EWCA Crim 945; *R v Finlay* [2003] EWCA Crim 3868.

There is further confusion as a result of the decision in *R v Dear* [1996] Crim LR 595. The defendant, Dear, and the victim, McAuley, were drinking partners. When Dear's 12-year-old daughter claimed that McAuley had sexually assaulted her, Dear tracked McAuley down and slashed him repeatedly with a Stanley knife. McAuley refused to go to hospital. He wiped the wounds with a towel and put plasters on them, which seemed to stop the bleeding. But two days later he died. Medical evidence revealed that one of the cuts had severed a main artery and that McAuley had died from loss of blood from the multiple wounds. A medical expert said that McAuley would not have died if the wounds had been treated properly. A suicide note was found with McAuley's body and evidence was led that McAuley may have deliberately reopened his wounds.

At trial Dear was convicted of murder. Before the Court of Appeal, one of his grounds of appeal was that McAuley's actions had broken the chain of causation.

## EXTRACT

Read the following extract from the judgment of Rose LJ. Did McAuley's actions break the chain of causation?

Of the five principles we outlined earlier, which one did Rose LJ apply?

### *R v Dear* [1996] Crim LR 595

### Rose LJ

The real question in this case [...] was [...] whether the injuries inflicted by the defendant were an operating and significant cause of the death. It is immaterial whether some other cause was also operating. It would not, in our judgment, be helpful to juries if the law required them [...] to decide causation in a case such as the present by embarking on an analysis of whether a victim had treated himself with mere negligence or gross neglect, the latter breaking but the former not breaking the chain of causation between the defendant's wrongful act and the victim's death [...] The correct approach in the criminal law is [...]: were the injuries inflicted by the defendant an operating and significant cause of death? That question, in our judgment, is necessarily answered, not by philosophical analysis, but by common sense according to all the circumstances of the particular case ... In the present case the cause of the deceased's death was bleeding from the artery which the defendant had severed. Whether or not the resumption or continuation of that bleeding was deliberately caused by the deceased, the jury were entitled to find that the defendant's conduct made an operative and significant contribution to the death.

So in *R v Dear* the Court of Appeal applied neither the reasonable foreseeability principle from *R v Roberts* nor the voluntariness principle from *R v Kennedy (No 2)*. Instead it applied the operating cause principle!

## ACTIVITY

If the Court of Appeal had applied either the reasonable foreseeability principle or the voluntariness principle in *R v Dear*, would the outcome of the case have been different?

In *R v Dear* the wounds inflicted by the defendant were an operating cause of death in a physical sense. Compare this to *R v Dhaliwal* [2006] EWCA Crim 1139. In this case the defendant had abused his wife physically and mentally for a number of years. In February 2005 she committed suicide. Earlier that evening they had had an argument, during which he struck her on the forehead. Although it was this incident which triggered the suicide, psychiatric evidence suggested that the 'overwhelming primary cause' for the suicide 'was the experience of being physically abused by her husband in the context of experiencing many such episodes over a very prolonged period of time'.

The defendant was charged with the manslaughter of his wife, and with inflicting grievous bodily harm on her. At trial the judge held that there was no case to answer. On appeal, the Court of Appeal said that the trial judge's ruling was correct and acquitted the defendant (because, as we shall see in Chapter 6, the psychological harm suffered by the victim fell short of a recognised psychiatric illness). For present purposes, the case is significant because of the following suggestion from Sir Igor Judge P:

> We should however record that, subject to evidence and argument on the critical issue of causation, unlawful violence on an individual with a fragile and vulnerable personality, which is proved to be a material cause of death (even if the result of suicide) would at least arguably, be capable of amounting to manslaughter.

This goes further than *R v Dear*. While Dear's actions were an operating cause of McAuley's death in a physical sense, in the type of case envisaged by Sir Igor Judge P the defendant's actions are an operating cause of death in a psychological sense. Using the operating cause principle in this way would be a strong use of the principle, which could potentially be difficult to reconcile with the reasonable foreseeability and voluntariness principles.

### v. Intervening acts of nature

Although there is little case law on this point in England and Wales, it is generally accepted that the reasonable foreseeability principle applies when determining whether an intervening act of nature broke the chain of causation.[27]

One case which illustrates this is *R v Gowans & Hillman* [2003] EWCA Crim 3935. The defendants robbed the victim, a pizza delivery man. During the robbery they kicked him in the head. As a result he fell into a coma. Over the next few months there was some improvement in the victim's condition. However, he then suffered a serious infection. Within a few days he died. Defence counsel argued that the infection was an intervening act of nature which broke the chain of causation. Rejecting the appeal, the Court of Appeal explained that someone with severe brain injuries is vulnerable to severe and life-threatening infections.

In a similar vein, if a defendant knocks someone unconscious, then leaves her body on the beach below the high tide mark, there will be no break in the chain of causation when the tide comes in and the victim drowns.[28]

### vi. The thin skull principle

Suppose that the victim had some rare and unusual physical condition that made her particularly vulnerable. As a result of this condition, the defendant's actions cause the victim serious harm. Had the victim not had this condition the defendant's actions would not have caused her any harm at all, and the defendant had no way of knowing that the

---

[27]See, for example, Simester, A.P., Spencer, J.R., Stark, F., Sullivan, G.R. & Virgo, G.J. (2016) *Simester and Sullivan's Criminal Law: Theory and Doctrine* (6th edn) Oxford: Hart Publishing, p94.
[28]Cf the New Zealand case *Hart* [1986] 2 NZLR 408.

victim had the condition. In these circumstances, may the defendant argue that there is no legal causation?

It has long been accepted that the answer to this question is no. In terms of physical characteristics, the defendant must take his victim as he finds her. This is known as the thin skull principle. An example is *R v Hayward* (1908) 21 Cox CC 692. Witnesses heard a violent argument between Hayward and his wife. His wife ran out of the house with Hayward chasing her. She collapsed and died. It transpired that she had an abnormal heart condition. A person with this condition could die from a combination of fright, strong emotion and physical exertion. Ridley J held that Hayward was a factual and legal cause of his wife's death. His wife's rare condition did not negate legal causation; Hayward had to take his victim as he found her.

The question which arose in *R v Blaue* [1975] 1 WLR 1411 was whether the thin skull principle should be applied to other, non-physical, characteristics of the victim. The victim in *R v Blaue* was an 18-year-old girl named Jacolyn Woodhead. Jacolyn was a Jehovah's Witness. The defendant, Ronald Blaue, stabbed her four times. One of the stab wounds pierced her lung. An ambulance rushed her to hospital, where she was told that she would die unless she received a blood transfusion. In accordance with her religious beliefs, Jacolyn refused the blood transfusion. She died the next day. The issue for the Court of Appeal was whether Jacolyn's refusal broke the chain of causation.

## EXTRACT

Read the following extract from the judgment of Lawton LJ. On what basis did Blaue's counsel (Mr Comyn) argue that Jacolyn's refusal should break the chain of causation? Why did Lawton LJ reject this?

According to Lawton LJ, does the thin skull principle apply to physical and non-physical characteristics, or just physical ones?

### *R v Blaue* [1975] 1 WLR 1411

#### Lawton LJ

The physical cause of death in this case was the bleeding into the pleural cavity arising from the penetration of the lung. This had not been brought about by any decision made by the deceased but by the stab wound.

Mr. Comyn tried to overcome this line of reasoning by submitting that the jury should have been directed that if they thought the deceased's decision not to have a blood transfusion was an unreasonable one, then the chain of causation would have been broken. At once the question arises – reasonable by whose standards? Those of Jehovah's Witnesses? Humanists? Roman Catholics? Protestants of Anglo-Saxon descent? The man on the Clapham omnibus? But he might well be an admirer of Eleazar who suffered death rather than eat the flesh of swine (2 Maccabees, ch. 6, vv. 18–31) or of Sir Thomas More who, unlike nearly all his contemporaries, was unwilling to accept Henry VIII as Head of the Church in England. Those brought up in the Hebraic and Christian traditions would probably be reluctant to accept that these martyrs caused their own deaths.

As was pointed out to Mr. Comyn in the course of argument, two cases, each raising the same issue of reasonableness because of religious beliefs, could produce different verdicts depending on where the cases were tried. A jury drawn from Preston, sometimes said to be the most Catholic town in England, might have different views about martyrdom to one drawn from the inner suburbs of London. Mr. Comyn accepted that this might be so: it was, he said, inherent in trial by jury. It is not inherent in the common law as expounded by Sir Matthew Hale and Maule J. It has long been the policy of the law that those who use violence on other people must take their victims as they find them. This in our judgment means the whole man, not just the physical man. It does not lie in the mouth of the assailant to say that his victim's religious beliefs which inhibited him from accepting certain kinds of treatment were unreasonable. The question for decision is what caused her death. The answer is the stab wound. The fact that the victim refused to stop this end coming about did not break the causal connection between the act and death.

The policy reasons for this judgment are clear enough: it would be offensive to allow a defendant to stab someone and then accuse them of having unreasonable religious beliefs. However, there are some concerns about the reasoning in *R v Blaue*:

- At first, it appears to be inconsistent with the decision in *R v Roberts*. Lawton LJ refused to assess the reasonableness of Jacolyn's decision not to have a blood transfusion. In *R v Roberts*, on the other hand, the Court of Appeal applied the reasonable foreseeability principle. Stephenson LJ said that if the victim's actions were so daft or unexpected that no reasonable man could have foreseen them they will break the chain of causation. On this approach, Blaue should have had the opportunity to argue that Jacolyn's refusal was so unexpected that it could not have reasonably been foreseen.

  It is possible, however, to reconcile *R v Blaue* and *R v Roberts*. In *R v Roberts* the victim's intervention was an act (jumping out of the car), whereas in *R v Blaue* it was an omission (refusal to have a blood transfusion). The cases can be reconciled by saying that the reasonable foreseeability principle applies to intervening acts of the victim, but not to intervening omissions.

- Although *R v Roberts* can be distinguished, another problem remains. The Court of Appeal in *R v Blaue* did not need to extend the thin skull principle to non-physical characteristics in order to reach the conclusion it did. It could have just applied the operating cause principle. As we saw in the extract from Lawton LJ's judgment, the 'physical cause of death in this case was the bleeding into the pleural cavity arising from the penetration of the lung'. The stab wound was thus an operating cause of death. The case could have been decided on this basis alone without any mention of the thin skull principle.

  The extension of the thin skull principle to non-physical characteristics was not only unnecessary, it is also potentially far too broad. What about a victim who is irrational, neurotic, vindictive or spiteful? Would the thin skull principle still apply? Since the operating cause principle was sufficient to explain the outcome in *R v Blaue*, Lawton LJ's comments about the thin skull principle may be regarded as *obiter dictum* and not binding on future cases.

In the following extract, Andrew Simester criticises the reasoning in *R v Blaue* for similar reasons.

## EXTRACT

### Simester A.P. (2017) 'Causation in (Criminal) Law' 133 *Law Quarterly Review* 416

Understanding omissions as non-interventions means their causal significance runs alongside the direct or indirect chains that they fail to prevent. Contra Hart and Honoré, it follows that an omission cannot constitute a *novus actus interveniens*, in the sense that it cannot break the relevant causal chain – precisely because it is the failure to break that chain which is our ground of complaint. To illustrate, consider another example:

*Antidote*: V is brought to hospital having been poisoned by P. D3, the on-duty doctor, correctly diagnoses V's condition but forgets to administer the standard antidote. V dies of the poison. Had the antidote been administered, V would have recovered.

Of what did V die? The poison. However egregious, D3's omission does not, indeed cannot, break the mechanical causal chain leading to V's death. It cannot break it as a conceptual matter, since it is that very failure to interrupt the causal chain which constitutes D3's omission; one cannot break causal chains by failing to break them. In this case, *both* P and D3 cause V's death. Their contributions are, in effect, concurrent causes.

This explanation is key to understanding the controversial case of *R. v Blaue*. In that case, V, a Jehovah's Witness, was brought to hospital after being stabbed four times by D. Despite having lost a large amount of blood, she refused a blood transfusion on the grounds of her religious beliefs. As she knew she would, V died of blood loss the next day. D appealed his conviction of manslaughter, on the ground that V's refusal to have a blood transfusion was a *novus actus interveniens* that broke the causal chain between the stabbing and V's death. Clearly, the non-transfusion was *one* cause of V's death. Nonetheless, the Court of Appeal ruled that the original wound inflicted by D remained an operating cause of death. Equally clearly, that ruling was correct. We can trace a straightforward, direct causal chain from the stabbing to V's death.

The court should have left the matter there. Alas, it did not. Counsel for D sought to argue that V's refusal of the blood transfusion was an unreasonable one. In effect, counsel sought to recharacterise the causal path to death as indirect, and thus subject to constraints of foreseeability. Misguidedly, the court met that submission on its own terms, responding that:

"It has long been the policy of the law that those who use violence on other people must take their victims as they find them. This in our judgment means the whole man, not just the physical man. It does not lie in the mouth of the assailant to say that his victim's religious beliefs which inhibited him from accepting certain kinds of treatment were unreasonable."

That is not right. There is no legal requirement that we must take a victim's *choices* as we find them. As is well established by cases such as *R. v Roberts*, an intervening reaction by V *does* break the chain of causation where it is extraordinary (or, as was said in *Roberts*, "daft"). Responses by victims, just like other indirect causal interventions, are subject to reasonable foreseeability criteria. And this means that D does not have to bear responsibility for the consequences of V's choices whatever they may be. D must do so only in so far as V's reaction is a reasonably foreseeable possibility.

The truth of the matter is that *Blaue* did not turn at all on whether V's refusal of the transfusion was "daft" or unforeseeable, because the failure to transfuse blood was an omission. As such, the case presented a straightforward, unbroken mechanical chain from stabbing to death. We may wish that the causal chain had been severed. But an omission cannot, by itself, do that. The failure to transfuse, however unreasonable, could only be a concurrent cause of death.

**ACTIVITY**

Johann stabs Ludwig. Although he is bleeding heavily, Ludwig refuses to go to hospital. He says, 'I've seen the news stories about hospital patients catching the MRSA infection. I'd rather go home and look after myself'. He staggers home and wraps towels around the stab wound. Two hours later he dies. Medical evidence shows that the cause of death was substantial loss of blood, and that if Ludwig had gone to hospital his life could have been saved. Is Johann a factual and legal cause of Ludwig's death? Which principle(s) of legal causation would you use to justify your conclusion?

## Conclusion

When answering a problem question, it is sensible to begin by considering whether the *actus reus* of the crime in question can be established. In this chapter we have studied three important *actus reus* concepts. Figure 3.1 provides an overview.

If the problem question you are answering raises the issue of the voluntariness of the defendant's behaviour it is logical to discuss this first, since if the defendant acted involuntarily there can be no *actus reus* and therefore the defendant cannot be guilty of the crime.

If the defendant did act voluntarily, next ask yourself whether the relevant conduct constituted an act or an omission. If it was an omission you will need to consider whether the defendant was under a duty to act and, if so, whether he breached this duty. If the defendant's conduct was an omission and he was not under a duty to act, or he did not breach his duty, there is no *actus reus* and the defendant cannot be guilty of the crime.

If the defendant's conduct was either: (1) an act; or (2) an omission which amounted to a breach of his duty to act, the next step is to work through the *actus reus* requirements of the crime in question. If the crime is a result crime, one of the *actus reus* requirements

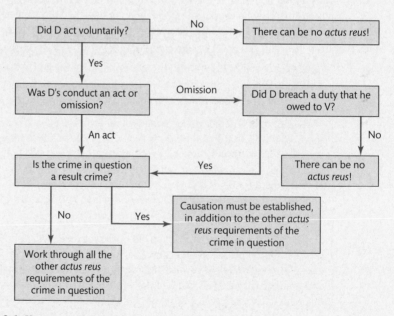

**Figure 3.1.** Key *actus reus* concepts: an overview

will be causation. To establish causation, you should begin with factual causation and, if this is established, then consider legal causation. For legal causation begin with the significant contribution test. If the defendant's actions did make a significant contribution then consider whether there was an intervening act or whether it is necessary to apply the thin skull principle. If there was an intervening act, determine which type of intervening act it was:

- Intervening acts of a third party: apply the voluntariness principle (*R v Pagett*), unless it is a case involving environmental protection where the fact of life principle is likely to apply (*Empress*).
- Intervening acts of a medical practitioner: apply the operating cause principle (*R v Cheshire*), unless the medical treatment was so 'palpably wrong' that it supersedes the defendant's actions (*R v Jordan*).
- Intervening acts of the victim: apply the reasonable foreseeability principle (*R v Roberts*), unless the case has factual similarities to *R v Kennedy (No. 2)* (voluntariness principle) or *R v Dear* (operating cause principle).
- Intervening acts of nature: apply the reasonable foreseeability principle.

Legal causation might seem like a daunting topic, but in fact it offers a good opportunity to showcase your ability to construct legal arguments. For example, when you are considering whether the actions of the victim broke the chain of causation you could write something like: 'The prosecution would use [case name] to argue ..., whereas the defence would use [case name] to argue ... In my opinion the stronger argument is ... because ...' This displays the higher-level skills needed to achieve the best marks!

# Self-test questions

1. Igor is out for an afternoon stroll along the cliff tops with his grown-up daughter Alla. He is so preoccupied composing a text message on his mobile phone that he doesn't notice a rock in the path. He trips over the rock, falls into Alla and knocks her off the path and over the cliff edge. At the last moment Alla manages to grab hold of a branch to stop herself from falling. However, she cannot manage to pull herself up and dangles precariously over the edge. Alla screams for help, but Igor is worried that he might slip and fall himself and so refuses to help.

   Meanwhile Sergei, a passer-by, hears Alla's screams. He runs over, leans down and grabs hold of Alla's sleeve. But just as Sergei is about to pull Alla to safety he recognises that she is his estranged wife (who had repeatedly cheated on him and made his life a misery). He decides not to help her after all, lets go of her sleeve and walks off. A few minutes later Alla loses her grip and falls to her death.

   a. Could Igor be criminally liable for his refusal to help Alla? Was his refusal a factual and legal cause of Alla's death?
   b. Could Sergei be criminally liable for his refusal to pull Alla to safety? Was his refusal a factual and legal cause of Alla's death?
   c. How (if at all) would your answers to (i) and (ii) be different if: Alla had landed on a ledge unharmed; she was very prone to panic and anxiety and, after waiting for more than two hours, concluded that no one would rescue her and so chose to end her suffering by jumping to her death?

2. Wolfgang, Franz and Gustav are members of a band. One day during rehearsals Wolfgang starts to argue with Franz. When Franz says, 'I quit', Wolfgang pushes him

as hard as he can. Franz stumbles backwards and knocks over Gustav (who had been telling the pair to 'Calm down'). Gustav lands awkwardly and suffers a broken arm.

Gustav is taken to hospital. His doctor, Josef, fails to read Gustav's notes properly and as a result prescribes Gustav a painkiller to which he is allergic. Although the dose administered would not have harmed most people, Gustav suffers a violent allergic reaction and dies.

    a.   Could Franz be criminally liable for knocking Gustav over and breaking his arm?

    b.   Were Wolfgang's actions a factual and legal cause of Gustav's death?

3.   Johann, Ludwig, Hans and Felix are housemates. One day Johann decides to play a practical joke on Ludwig (against whom he has a longstanding secret grudge). He says to Hans, 'I'm playing a joke on Ludwig. I've made him a cup of coffee and put salt in it. Could you take it to him?' Hans finds this very amusing and replies, 'Sure, I can't wait to see him drink it!' In fact, Johann has not put salt in Ludwig's coffee, but a large quantity of a potent laxative. To Hans' surprise, Ludwig drinks the entire cup without saying anything about the taste. Shortly afterwards Johann and Hans leave and go to the pub.

Unknown to his housemates, Ludwig suffers from a rare digestive disorder. An hour after drinking the coffee he starts having severe stomach cramps. Felix comes downstairs to find out what is happening. Ludwig asks him to call an ambulance, but Felix just tells him to stop being a wimp, goes back to his bedroom and shuts the door. Twenty minutes later Ludwig manages to call an ambulance himself. He is rushed to hospital, but soon after suffers cardiac arrest and dies.

Medical evidence later suggests that, if an ambulance had been called 20 minutes earlier, there would have been a slim chance that Ludwig could have been saved.

    a.   Were Johann's actions a factual and legal cause of Ludwig's death?

    b.   Could Felix be criminally liable for his failure to call an ambulance?

4.   'The criminal law is right to only impose liability for omissions in exceptional circumstances. Whilst it is possible to justify the existing exceptions to the general rule that there is no criminal liability for omissions, any further extension of these exceptions must be avoided.'

Discuss the extent to which you agree with this statement.

5.   'Questions of legal causation often involve difficult moral and policy assessments of responsibility. In spite of this, the Courts have managed to formulate a clear set of principles of legal causation which produce consistent and justifiable results.'

Discuss the extent to which you agree with this statement.

## Key *actus reus* concepts checklist

Having worked through this chapter, you should now have:

✓ An understanding of the *actus reus* concept of voluntariness

✓ An understanding of the general rule that there is no criminal liability for omissions and the exceptions to this rule

✓ An ability to critically discuss the general rule that there is no criminal liability for omissions and the arguments for and against extending omissions liability

✓ An understanding of the law governing factual causation and legal causation

✓ An ability to critically discuss the case law governing legal causation.

 **Further reading**

Alexander, L. (2002) 'Criminal Liability for Omissions: An Inventory of Issues' in S. Shute and A. Simester (Eds) *Criminal Law Theory: Doctrines of the General Part*. OUP: Oxford.

Ashworth, A. (1989) 'The Scope of Criminal Liability for Omissions' 105 *Law Quarterly Review* 424.

Horder, J. and McGowan, L. (2006) 'Manslaughter by Causing Another's Suicide' *Criminal Law Review* 1035.

Jones, T.H. (2006) 'Causation, Homicide and the Supply of Drugs' 26 *Legal Studies* 139.

Simester, A.P. (2017) 'Causation in (Criminal) Law' 133 *Law Quarterly Review* 416.

# 4

# Key *mens rea* concepts

## Chapter objectives

By the end of this chapter you should have:

- An understanding of the concept of recklessness and an ability to critically discuss the *R v Cunningham* test
- An understanding of the concept of intention and an ability to critically discuss the *R v Woollin* direction
- A basic understanding of the concepts of knowledge, belief, negligence and strict liability
- An understanding of the doctrine of transferred *mens rea*.

## Introduction

This chapter focuses on the two *mens rea* concepts that we will use most frequently in this text: recklessness and intention. The definitions of these two concepts are extremely important. For many of the crimes that we study in this text, recklessness is the minimum level of *mens rea* that is required. So for crimes like malicious wounding, assault occasioning actual bodily harm, assault and battery, the dividing line between recklessness and non-recklessness is also the dividing line between guilt and innocence. Similarly, liability for some of the most serious crimes turns on the absence or presence of intention. The obvious example is murder. To be guilty of murder, a defendant must have intended to kill or cause serious injury. Anything less than intention – even a high degree of recklessness – will not suffice. The same applies to attempted murder and to grievous bodily harm with intent.

So when we define terms like 'intention' or 'recklessness', what we are doing is drawing the boundaries between different offences and between guilt and innocence. This is what makes *mens rea* such an interesting and challenging topic.

We will examine the law on recklessness and intention in detail, evaluating whether there are ways in which the law might be changed and improved. The chapter then briefly outlines some other *mens rea* concepts – knowledge, belief, negligence and strict liability – before finishing by explaining the doctrine of transferred *mens rea*.

## Recklessness

There used to be two different tests for recklessness in the criminal law – the *R v Cunningham* test and the *R v Caldwell* test. But, as we will see, whilst the House of Lords' decision to overrule the *R v Caldwell* test was met with almost unanimous approval there remain some lingering doubts about the *R v Cunningham* test.

### 1. The *R v Cunningham* test for recklessness

In *R v Cunningham* [1957] 2 QB 396 the defendant, Roy Cunningham, was engaged to be married. His future mother-in-law lived next door to an elderly couple called Mr and Mrs Wade. The two houses had originally been one house. When they were converted into two houses, a wall had been built in the cellar to divide it into two. The wall was poorly constructed and consisted of rubble loosely cemented together.

On the night of the offence Cunningham broke into his soon-to-be mother-in-law's house. In the cellar was a coin-operated gas meter. Cunningham ripped the meter off the wall, took some money out and then threw the meter away. Even though the gas stop tap was only two feet away, Cunningham did not turn it off. As a result a large volume of gas escaped. Some of it seeped through the poorly built cellar wall into the Wades' cellar, up into the Wades' house and partially asphyxiated Mrs Wade, who was asleep in her bed.

At trial Cunningham was convicted of an offence under the Offences Against the Person Act 1861.[1] The *mens rea* of this offence required that the defendant acted maliciously. On appeal, Cunningham argued that the trial judge had misdirected the jury on the meaning of maliciously. His appeal was successful and his conviction was quashed. In the course of his judgment Byrne J set out the meaning of recklessness, as well as the meaning of malice.

---

[1]He was convicted of the section 23 offence (maliciously causing Mrs Wade to take a noxious thing and thereby endangering her life).

## EXTRACT

In the following extract, how does Byrne J define malice? How does he define recklessness?

### R v Cunningham [1957] 2 QB 396

#### Byrne J

[Counsel for the defence cited the following cases: *Reg. v Pembliton, Reg. v Latimer* and *Reg. v Faulkner.* In reply, Mr. Snowden, on behalf of the Crown, cited *Reg. v Martin.*]

We have considered those cases, and we have also considered, in the light of those cases, the following principle which was propounded by the late Professor C.S. Kenny in the first edition of his *Outlines of Criminal Law* published in 1902 and repeated at p. 186 of the 16th edition edited by Mr. J.W. Cecil Turner and published in 1952: "In any statutory definition of a crime, malice must be taken not in the old vague sense of wickedness in general but as requiring either (1) An actual intention to do the particular kind of harm that in fact was done; or (2) recklessness as to whether such harm should occur or not (i.e., the accused has foreseen that the particular kind of harm might be done and yet has gone on to take the risk of it). It is neither limited to nor does it indeed require any ill will towards the person injured." The same principle is repeated by Mr. Turner in his 10th edition of Russell on Crime at p. 1592.

We think that this is an accurate statement of the law

---

Today this is known as the *R v Cunningham* test for recklessness. The test has two stages:

- First, did the defendant foresee the risk and choose to take it? The focus here is on what the defendant was thinking at the time. For this reason, you will sometimes see the *R v Cunningham* test referred to as subjective recklessness.

- Second, was the risk a justifiable one to take? Although this part of the test is not stated explicitly in Byrne J's judgment, it is widely accepted. Suppose that a surgeon carries out an operation which has a risk of some side effects. The surgeon satisfies the first stage of the *R v Cunningham* test because he foresaw the risks involved and went ahead and took them. But the potential benefits and the patient's consent mean that the risk was a justified one to take. Therefore, the doctor does not pass the second stage of the test and did not act recklessly.

An example of the *R v Cunningham* test being applied is *R v Stephenson* [1979] QB 695. The defendant, a tramp named Brian Stephenson, had a long history of schizophrenia. One day he went to a large straw stack in a field, made a hollow in the side of the stack, crept into the hollow and tried to go to sleep. He felt cold, so he lit a fire of twigs and straw inside the hollow. The stack caught fire. The fire then spread to a hut containing farming equipment and caused £3,500 worth of damage. Stephenson was charged with arson. At trial a psychiatrist gave evidence that, as a result of his schizophrenia, Stephenson may not have had the same ability to foresee risk as a mentally normal person. It was conceivable, the psychiatrist said, that Stephenson lit the fire to keep himself warm without having appreciated the risk of the straw stack catching fire. In spite of this evidence he was convicted. On appeal, the Court of Appeal quashed his conviction. The first stage of the *R v Cunningham* test requires that the defendant foresaw the relevant risk. Due to his schizophrenia, it was impossible to say beyond reasonable doubt that Stephenson had foreseen the risk of the fire spreading. Therefore he had not acted recklessly.

So the *R v Cunningham* test focuses on one state of mind. It encompasses the defendant who foresees a risk and unjustifiably chooses to take it. The key issue surrounding the *R v Cunningham* test is whether it is too narrow. Are there other states of mind which are also sufficiently culpable to be deemed reckless? This was addressed by the House of Lords in *R v Caldwell*.

## 2. The *R v Caldwell* test for recklessness

In *R v Cunningham* the Court of Appeal explained the meaning of the word 'malice'. As we'll see in Chapter 6, this word is used in a number of offences in the Offences Against the Person Act 1861. It was also used in a number of offences in the Malicious Damage Act 1861, a statute which focused on offences against property. Unlike the Offences Against the Person Act 1861 (which is still in force today), the Malicious Damage Act 1861 was replaced in 1971 by the Criminal Damage Act. As we'll see in Chapter 8, instead of using the word 'malice' the Criminal Damage Act 1971 simply uses the words 'intention' and 'recklessness'. The issue for the House of Lords in *R v Caldwell* [1982] AC 341 was whether the word 'reckless' has the same meaning under the 1971 Act as it did under the 1861 Acts. By a majority of 3–2, the House of Lords held that it did not.[2] The following extract is taken from the leading judgment of Lord Diplock.

### EXTRACT

According to Lord Diplock, recklessness covers a second state of mind in addition to the one encompassed by *R v Cunningham*. What is this second state of mind?

What reasons does Lord Diplock give for saying that recklessness should also encompass this second state of mind?

### *R v Caldwell* [1982] AC 341

#### Lord Diplock

My Lords, the restricted meaning that the Court of Appeal in *Reg. v. Cunningham* had placed upon the adverb maliciously in the Malicious Damage Act 1861 in cases where the prosecution did not rely upon an actual intention of the accused to cause the damage that was in fact done, called for a meticulous analysis by the jury of the thoughts that passed through the mind of the accused at or before the time he did the act that caused the damage, in order to see on which side of a narrow dividing line they fell. If it had crossed his mind that there was a risk that someone's property might be damaged but, because his mind was affected by rage or excitement or confused by drink, he did not appreciate the seriousness of the risk or trusted

---

[2]In his dissenting judgment, Lord Edmund-Davies (with whom Lord Wilberforce agreed) stated that the *R v Cunningham* test should continue to apply to recklessness under the 1971 Act: 'recklessness involves foresight of consequences, combined with an objective judgment of the reasonableness of the risk taken'.

that good luck would prevent its happening, this state of mind would amount to malice in the restricted meaning placed upon that term by the Court of Appeal; whereas if, for any of these reasons, he did not even trouble to give his mind to the question whether there was any risk of damaging the property, this state of mind would not suffice to make him guilty of an offence under the Malicious Damage Act 1861.

Neither state of mind seems to me to be less blameworthy than the other; but if the difference between the two constituted the distinction between what does and what does not in legal theory amount to a guilty state of mind for the purposes of a statutory offence of damage to property, it would not be a practicable distinction for use in a trial by jury. The only person who knows what the accused's mental processes were is the accused himself – and probably not even he can recall them accurately when the rage or excitement under which he acted has passed, or he has sobered up if he were under the influence of drink at the relevant time. If the accused gives evidence that because of his rage, excitement or drunkenness the risk of particular harmful consequences of his acts simply did not occur to him, a jury would find it hard to be satisfied beyond reasonable doubt that his true mental process was not that, but was the slightly different mental process required if one applies the restricted meaning of "being reckless as to whether" something would happen, adopted by the Court of Appeal in *Reg. v. Cunningham*.

My Lords, I can see no reason why Parliament when it decided to revise the law as to offences of damage to property should go out of its way to perpetuate fine and impracticable distinctions such as these, between one mental state and another. One would think that the sooner they were got rid of, the better.

[...]

In my opinion, a person charged with an offence under section 1(1) of the Criminal Damage Act 1971 is "reckless as to whether any such property would be destroyed or damaged if" (1) he does an act which in fact creates an obvious risk that property will be destroyed or damaged and (2) when he does the act he either has not given any thought to the possibility of there being any such risk or has recognised that there was some risk involved and has nonetheless gone on to do it. That would be a proper direction to the jury; cases in the Court of Appeal which held otherwise should be regarded as overruled.

Note that the decision in *R v Caldwell* applied to the Criminal Damage Act 1971, but not to the Offences Against the Person Act 1861. In other words, following the House of Lords' decision we had one test for recklessness in cases involving offences against people,[3] and a different test for cases involving offences against property. This lacked coherence.

So following *R v Caldwell* the word 'reckless' in the Criminal Damage Act 1971 encompassed each of the two states of mind shown in Figure 4.1.

In the extract above Lord Diplock stated that neither of these two states of mind 'seems to me to be less blameworthy than the other'. He pointed out that there might be blameworthy reasons for a person's failure to give any thought to an obvious risk, such as rage or indifference. But a person might also fail to give any thought to an obvious risk for non-blameworthy reasons. *R v Stephenson* is an example. As we saw above, the reason Stephenson did not foresee the risk of the straw stack catching fire was his schizophrenia. Another example is *Elliott v C* [1983] 1 WLR 939. The defendant in this case was a 14-year-old schoolgirl. She was of low intelligence and in a remedial class at school. On the evening

---

[3] A decade later the House of Lords in *R v Savage & Parmenter* [1992] 1 AC 699 confirmed that the *R v Cunningham* test still applied to the crimes contained in the Offences Against the Person Act 1861.

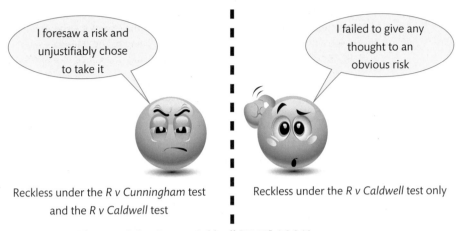

Reckless under the *R v Cunningham* test
and the *R v Caldwell* test

Reckless under the *R v Caldwell* test only

**Figure 4.1.** Recklessness following *R v Caldwell* [1982] AC 341

of the offence she had stayed out all night. At about 5 am she entered a garden shed belonging to the victim, Walter Davies. Inside the shed she found some white spirit, poured this onto the floor and then set fire to it with a match. The shed, which contained tools and paints worth a total of £3,206, was completely burnt down. The defendant was charged with criminal damage. At trial the justices found the following as fact:

- That while the defendant had realised that the contents of the bottle which contained white spirit were possibly inflammable, she had not handled it before and had not appreciated how explosively it would burn.

- That the defendant had given no thought at the time that she started the fire to the possibility of there being a risk that the shed and contents would be destroyed by her actions.

- That in the circumstances this risk would not have been obvious to her or been appreciated by her if she had given thought to the matter.

On the basis of these findings she was acquitted. The prosecutor then appealed to the Divisional Court. On appeal, the issue was the meaning of the word 'obvious' in the *R v Caldwell* test. Did it mean that the risk would have been obvious to the defendant if she had thought about it? Or did it mean obvious to the reasonable man? Allowing the prosecutor's appeal, the Divisional Court held that it meant obvious to the reasonable man. In his judgment Robert Goff LJ voiced his dissatisfaction with the *R v Caldwell* test:

> I [have reached this decision] simply because I believe myself constrained to do so by authority. I feel moreover that I would be lacking in candour if I were to conceal my unhappiness about the conclusion which I feel compelled to reach. In my opinion, although of course the courts of this country are bound by the doctrine of precedent, sensibly interpreted, nevertheless it would be irresponsible for judges to act as automata, rigidly applying authorities without regard to consequences. Where therefore it appears at first sight that authority compels a judge to reach a conclusion which he senses to be unjust or inappropriate, he is, I consider, under a positive duty to examine the relevant authorities with scrupulous care to ascertain whether he can, within the limits imposed by the doctrine of precedent (always sensibly interpreted), legitimately interpret or qualify the principle expressed in the authorities to achieve the result which he perceives to be just or appropriate in the particular case. I do not disguise the fact that I have sought to perform this function in the present case

In spite of this criticism of the *R v Caldwell* test, the House of Lords expressed its approval of the decision by refusing the defendant leave to appeal against her conviction.

So the *R v Caldwell* test classified as reckless all defendants who failed to give any thought to a risk which would have been obvious to the reasonable man – even if the reason for this failure was a non-blameworthy one such as age or mental incapacity.[4] It was not until more than 20 years later, in *R v G & another* [2003] UKHL 50, that the House of Lords overruled *R v Caldwell*. The defendants in *R v G & another* were two boys, aged 11 and 12. They entered the backyard of a Co-op shop in the early hours of the morning. They found some bundles of newspapers, looked at them and then set fire to them using a lighter. Each of them threw some of the lit newspaper under a large plastic wheelie-bin. They then left the yard without putting out the fire. The wheelie-bin caught fire. The fire then spread to another wheelie-bin, then to the shop wall and guttering, then up into the roof space of the shop. Eventually the roof collapsed and the adjoining buildings all caught fire. Approximately £1m worth of damage was caused. The boys were charged with criminal damage of the buildings and with arson.

At trial the boys said they expected the newspapers to extinguish themselves on the concrete floor. It was accepted as a fact that neither of them appreciated that there was any risk whatsoever of the fire spreading in the way that it did. However, applying the *R v Caldwell* test they had acted recklessly. They had failed to give any thought to the risk that the shop would be damaged and this risk would have been obvious to the reasonable man. They were therefore convicted.

Their appeals against conviction reached the House of Lords. The House of Lords unanimously agreed that *R v Caldwell* should be overruled and that the *R v Cunningham* test should apply in all cases of criminal damage. The boys' convictions were accordingly quashed.

## EXTRACT

In the following extract, Lord Bingham gives four reasons why he believed *R v Caldwell* should be overruled. Summarise each of these in your own words. Which of the reasons do you think is the most compelling? Do you disagree with any of Lord Bingham's reasons?

In [37] and [38] Lord Bingham considers the possibility of refining the *R v Caldwell* test instead of overruling it. What were the refinements that had been suggested? Why did Lord Bingham reject them?

### *R v G & another* [2003] UKHL 50

#### Lord Bingham

32 First, it is a salutary principle that conviction of serious crime should depend on proof not simply that the defendant caused (by act or omission) an injurious result to another but that his state of mind when so acting was culpable. This, after all, is the meaning of the familiar rule *actus non facit reum nisi mens sit rea*. The most obviously culpable state of mind is no doubt an intention to cause the injurious result, but knowing disregard of an appreciated and

---

[4]A similar case is *R v Coles* [1995] 1 Cr App R 157, in which the Court of Appeal upheld the trial judge's refusal to admit evidence of the 15-year-old defendant's low mental capacity.

unacceptable risk of causing an injurious result or a deliberate closing of the mind to such risk would be readily accepted as culpable also. It is clearly blameworthy to take an obvious and significant risk of causing injury to another. But it is not clearly blameworthy to do something involving a risk of injury to another if (for reasons other than self-induced intoxication: *R v Majewski* [1977] AC 443) one genuinely does not perceive the risk. Such a person may fairly be accused of stupidity or lack of imagination, but neither of those failings should expose him to conviction of serious crime or the risk of punishment.

33 Secondly, the present case shows, more clearly than any other reported case since *R v Caldwell*, that the model direction formulated by Lord Diplock (see paragraph 18 above) is capable of leading to obvious unfairness. As the excerpts quoted in paragraphs 6–7 reveal, the trial judge regretted the direction he (quite rightly) felt compelled to give, and it is evident that this direction offended the jury's sense of fairness. The sense of fairness of 12 representative citizens sitting as a jury (or of a smaller group of lay justices sitting as a bench of magistrates) is the bedrock on which the administration of criminal justice in this country is built. A law which runs counter to that sense must cause concern. Here, the appellants could have been charged under section 1(1) with recklessly damaging one or both of the wheelie-bins, and they would have had little defence. As it was, the jury might have inferred that boys of the appellants' age would have appreciated the risk to the building of what they did, but it seems clear that such was not their conclusion (nor, it would appear, the judge's either). On that basis the jury thought it unfair to convict them. I share their sense of unease. It is neither moral nor just to convict a defendant (least of all a child) on the strength of what someone else would have apprehended if the defendant himself had no such apprehension. Nor, the defendant having been convicted, is the problem cured by imposition of a nominal penalty.

34 Thirdly, I do not think the criticism of *R v Caldwell* [1982] AC 34 expressed by academics, judges and practitioners should be ignored. A decision is not, of course, to be overruled or departed from simply because it meets with disfavour in the learned journals. But a decision which attracts reasoned and outspoken criticism by the leading scholars of the day, respected as authorities in the field, must command attention. One need only cite (among many other examples) the observations of Professor John Smith [1981] Crim LR 392, 393–396, and Professor Glanville Williams in "Recklessness Redefined" [1981] CLJ 252. This criticism carries greater weight when voiced also by judges as authoritative as Lord Edmund-Davies and Lord Wilberforce in *R v Caldwell* itself, Robert Goff LJ in *Elliott v C* [1983] 1 WLR 939 and Ackner LJ in *R v R (Stephen Malcolm)* 79 Cr App R 334. The reservations expressed by the trial judge in the present case are widely shared. The shopfloor response to *R v Caldwell* may be gauged from the editors' commentary, to be found in Archbold Pleading, Evidence and Practice in Criminal Cases, 41st ed (1982), pp 1009–1010, paras 17–25. The editors suggested that remedial legislation was urgently required.

35 Fourthly, the majority's interpretation of "reckless" in section 1 of the 1971 Act was, as already shown, a misinterpretation. If it were a misinterpretation that offended no principle and gave rise to no injustice there would be strong grounds for adhering to the misinterpretation and leaving Parliament to correct it if it chose. But this misinterpretation is offensive to principle and is apt to cause injustice. That being so, the need to correct the misinterpretation is compelling.

[...]

37 In the course of argument before the House it was suggested that the rule in *R v Caldwell* might be modified, in cases involving children, by requiring comparison not with normal reasonable adults but with normal reasonable children of the same age. This is a suggestion with some attractions but it is open to four compelling objections. First, even this modification would offend the principle that conviction should depend on proving the state of mind of the individual

defendant to be culpable. Second, if the rule were modified in relation to children on grounds of their immaturity it would be anomalous if it were not also modified in relation to the mentally handicapped on grounds of their limited understanding. Third, any modification along these lines would open the door to difficult and contentious argument concerning the qualities and characteristics to be taken into account for purposes of the comparison. Fourth, to adopt this modification would be to substitute one misinterpretation of section 1 for another. There is no warrant in the Act or in the *travaux préparatoires* which preceded it for such an interpretation.

38 A further refinement, advanced by Professor Glanville Williams in his article "Recklessness Redefined" [1981] CLJ 252, 270–271, adopted by the justices in *Elliott v C* [1983] 1 WLR 939 and commented upon by Robert Goff LJ in that case is that a defendant should only be regarded as having acted recklessly by virtue of his failure to give any thought to an obvious risk that property would be destroyed or damaged, where such risk would have been obvious to him if he had given any thought to the matter. This refinement also has attractions, although it does not meet the objection of principle and does not represent a correct interpretation of the section. It is, in my opinion, open to the further objection of over-complicating the task of the jury (or bench of justices). It is one thing to decide whether a defendant can be believed when he says that the thought of a given risk never crossed his mind. It is another, and much more speculative, task to decide whether the risk would have been obvious to him if the thought had crossed his mind. The simpler the jury's task, the more likely is its verdict to be reliable. Robert Goff LJ's reason for rejecting this refinement was somewhat similar: *Elliott v C*, p 950.

39 I cannot accept that restoration of the law as understood before *R v Caldwell* [1982] AC 341 would lead to the acquittal of those whom public policy would require to be convicted. There is nothing to suggest that this was seen as a problem before *R v Caldwell*, or (as noted above in paragraphs 12 and 13) before the 1971 Act. There is no reason to doubt the common sense which tribunals of fact bring to their task. In a contested case based on intention, the defendant rarely admits intending the injurious result in question, but the tribunal of fact will readily infer such an intention, in a proper case, from all the circumstances and probabilities and evidence of what the defendant did and said at the time. Similarly with recklessness: it is not to be supposed that the tribunal of fact will accept a defendant's assertion that he never thought of a certain risk when all the circumstances and probabilities and evidence of what he did and said at the time show that he did or must have done.

Following the decision in *R v G & another*, whenever you come across the word 'reckless' in this text you know that you should apply the *R v Cunningham* test!

## 3. Evaluation of the *R v Cunningham* test

Following the decision in *R v G & another*, David Ibbetson commented:[5]

Caldwell was a terrible decision, and no lawyer will lament its consignment to the scrap-heap of legal history. It introduced into the criminal law an unprincipled distinction between criminal damage and offences against the person. Its mechanical application led to palpably unjust results, particularly where the defendant was young or educationally sub-normal. And as a piece of statutory interpretation it was shoddy, if not downright shocking. Whatever the threshold for the House of Lords to depart from its own previous decisions, it was comfortably satisfied here. Nonetheless, it would be premature simply to breathe a sigh of relief. For all its faults, Caldwell was a

---

[5]Ibbetsen, D. (2004) 'Recklessness Restored' 63 *Cambridge Law Journal* 13.

genuine response to problems which were perceived to exist in the criminal law in the late 1970s, and not all of these have simply disappeared through the effluxion of time.

The problems which Ibbetson refers to are illustrated by *R v Parker* [1977] 1 WLR 600. The defendant, Daryl Parker, had had a bad evening. He had been to a function in London and afterwards caught a train home from King's Cross station. However, he fell asleep on the train and by the time he woke up he had missed his station. He got off the train at the next opportunity, only to be charged the excess fare for travelling beyond his destination. Parker then went to a telephone box outside the station to call a taxi but couldn't get through to the taxi company. Frustrated and angry, Parker slammed the telephone handset down so hard that it smashed. It just so happened that at this moment two police officers were driving past the phone box and saw Parker smash the telephone handset. He was charged with criminal damage.

Importantly, when Parker gave evidence he said, 'It did not occur to me that what I was doing might damage [the telephone]. I was simply reacting to the frustration which I felt.' In other words, Parker claimed that he was so angry that he acted without thinking. He was so angry that the risk of damage to the telephone never crossed his mind.

At trial Parker was convicted of criminal damage. He appealed, arguing that under the *R v Cunningham* test he had not acted recklessly. The first stage of the *R v Cunningham* requires that the defendant foresaw the relevant risk. Parker claimed that, because he had acted in the heat of the moment and without thinking, he had not foreseen the risk of damage to the telephone. The Court of Appeal rejected this argument and upheld his conviction.

## EXTRACT

Read the following extract from the judgment of Geoffrey Lane LJ. How does he describe Parker's thought process at the moment he damaged the telephone?

### *R v Parker* [1977] 1 WLR 600

#### Geoffrey Lane LJ

[Parker] was fully aware that what he was handling was a telephone handset made of Bakelite or some such material. He was well aware that the cradle on to which he admittedly brought down the handset was made of similar material. He was well aware, of course, of the degree of force which he was using – a degree described by Mr. Tager [defence counsel] before us as slamming the receiver down and a demonstration by Mr. Tager, whether wittingly or not, was given of a hand brought down from head-height on to whatever the receiving object was.

In those circumstances, it seems to this court that if he did not know, as he said he did not, that there was some risk of damage, he was, in effect, deliberately closing his mind to the obvious – the obvious being that damage in these circumstances was inevitable. In the view of this court, that type of action, that type of deliberate closing of the mind, is the equivalent of knowledge and a man certainly cannot escape the consequences of his action in this particular set of circumstances by saying, "I never directed my mind to the obvious consequences because I was in a self-induced state of temper."

The key assertion here is that deliberately closing your mind to an obvious risk is equivalent to having foreseen the risk. The reasoning goes as follows: in order to be able to deliberately close your mind to an obvious risk, you must be aware that the risk exists; if you are aware that a risk exists, then you have foresight of it; if you have foresight of a risk and unjustifiably choose to take it, then you are reckless under the *R v Cunningham* test.

There are obvious policy reasons why it would be undesirable to allow a defendant like Parker to escape criminal liability on the basis that he acted angrily and without thinking. But the strained reasoning employed by the Court of Appeal in *R v Parker* suggests that the *R v Cunningham* test is too narrow. The test's insistence that the defendant must have foreseen the relevant risk means that, on a literal interpretation, it excludes defendants like Parker and so is under-inclusive. As Ibbetson has remarked:[6]

> At no time did Parker stop and decide not to think whether there was a risk of causing damage. He simply slammed down the receiver. If we believe that Parker should be convicted, and if we are honest in our use of language, we have no choice but to recognise that the purely subjective analysis of recklessness is not in itself enough.

In the following extract from her article 'The Foresight Saga: The Biggest Mistake of All', Diane Birch evaluates the primacy that the *R v Cunningham* test attaches to a defendant's foresight of risk. She argues that the decision in *R v Parker* is at odds with the *R v Cunningham* test's insistence on foresight of risk, and that sometimes a defendant's attitude may be a better guide to his culpability than whether or not he had a fleeting awareness of risk.

## EXTRACT

Birch argues that the *R v Cunningham* test is based on the 'informed choice' theory. What is the informed choice theory? Why is it difficult to reconcile with the decision in *R v Parker*?

What does Birch argue are the advantages of an attitude-based test for recklessness? What does she say are the obstacles to an attitude-based test?

### Birch, D. (1988) 'The Foresight Saga: The Biggest Mistake of All?' *Criminal Law Review* 4

This takes us to [the assumption in the *R v Cunningham* test] that the presence of foresight is the only legally relevant consideration. In cases where foresight can be established, caring is irrelevant. What if foresight cannot be established, but a reprehensible attitude, such as that D "couldn't care less" what harm he does, is proved? Is that an adequate alternative to foresight?

Two examples suggest that the answer is a qualified "yes". The first concerns a result-crime where D knows all the relevant circumstances from which the reasonable man would have deduced the risk, but claims not to have put two and two together, perhaps in the heat of the moment.

A good example is the pre-*Caldwell* damage case of *Parker*. D, in a temper, banged down a telephone handset onto its cradle. He knew it was made of a lightweight material, and he knew the degree of force he employed, yet he claimed not to have thought about the possibility of

---

[6]Ibbetson, D. (2004) 'Recklessness Restored' 63 *Cambridge Law Journal* 13.

damage until it was too late. He had not "chosen" to run the risk, yet he was convicted. The justifications for this outcome vary subtly on appeal from:

(1) "if he did not know that there was some risk of damage he was deliberately closing his mind to the obvious."

to:

(2) "the knowledge or appreciation of risk of some damage must have entered the defendant's mind, even though he may have suppressed it or driven it out."

Both justifications require a re-appraisal of the "choice" model of recklessness, and both appear to accord primacy to the reprehensible attitude of D in refusing to think through the possible consequences of his actions. The difference is that in (1) this refusal appears to be a substitute for foresight, whereas in (2) it is coupled with the notion that, while D may not have calculated the odds and made a cold-blooded choice, nevertheless he must have experienced at least a flash of awareness.

Those who support the view that foresight alone is the test for [R v Cunningham] recklessness have attempted to square both (1) and (2) with their thesis; the former more half-heartedly than the latter. (1) is explained in terms of foresight not having to be a matter of instantaneous awareness at the time the act is done; it is enough if D has all the relevant knowledge and could easily bring it to the forefront of his mind if he chose to do so. (2) is explained on the ground that the suppression of the appreciation of risk by D is not an operative part of the fault element which must be proved. Rather it is the case that in [R v Cunningham] recklessness generally the flash of awareness is sufficient, whether it is followed by hasty suppression or a more leisurely contemplation of the odds.

Reading these explanations together we conclude that the goalposts have shifted somewhat from the "informed choice" theory, for the information in question may not need to be in the forefront of D's mind at the time, nor need the choice be a meaningful one in the common situation where D acts on the spur of the moment. Indeed in such cases the flash of awareness, if it comes at all, may occur too late, in that he may already be too committed to the action to withdraw from it. To apportion blame in such cases using the detached and reflective language of knowledge of risk and determination to run it rings false, and it is preferable to seek a more appropriate formula. But is it better to express it in terms of awareness (actual or potential) or attitude? Let us look at the second example before answering the question.

The second case is the extreme one where D's attitude was such that he would not have been put off by the risk had it occurred to him. The strong moral ground for convicting once led Professor Williams to suggest that attitude alone might, in such a case, prove recklessness, and in *Kimber* the Court of Appeal appears to have adopted the same stance. D was convicted of indecent assault on a mental patient, having raised the defence of honest belief in consent. He conceded that he could see that the woman was mentally unstable because "she kept mumbling", but nevertheless insisted that he thought she was a willing partner. However he admitted "I was not really interested in her feelings at all." His conviction was upheld, notwithstanding the absence of any proper direction on the defence, because:

> "His own evidence showed that his attitude to her was one of indifference to her feelings and wishes. This state of mind is aptly described in the colloquial expression 'couldn't care less'. In law this is recklessness."

It is possible to explain this statement away on the ground that the point was that D's attitude was relevant only because it was inconsistent with the conclusion he claimed to have reached that his victim was consenting: a view which is supported by the Court's insistence that a direction should have been given to acquit if D was genuinely mistaken. However it is submitted that the truth which surfaces in *Kimber* is more profound, and is one with which many trial judges would, I believe, associate themselves. If the jury believe that D would have done exactly as he did had he been aware of the risk, what does it matter if, at the time of acting, he did not experience the flash of awareness which would have sealed his fate beyond doubt?

A similar situation may arise regarding recklessness as to a result. Suppose that D, to impress his friends, vaults over a seaside breakwater without looking before he leaps. The seashore is crowded with holiday makers and their possessions, and it is entirely predictable that he will land on something or someone and cause damage or injury. He lands on a sunbather and causes painful bruising. A jury might well find it plausible that the thought of causing such harm never entered D's head, but insofar as his conduct suggests the indifference to others of one who "couldn't care less," and who would have jumped even if he had been fully apprised of the risk, they might well itch to convict him. By what moral principle should they be prevented from doing so?

If the answer is none, then we should have a second means of proving recklessness with an equal claim to recognition along with foresight, and perhaps a superior one, because the attitude of D, if it can be proved, may be a more reliable guide to moral fault than a momentary awareness of risk. The difficulty with preferring a test based on attitude alone is the practical one that the English rules of evidence are not geared to such an inquiry, and would stand in the way of using previous instances of D's off-hand or selfish behaviour in order to demonstrate his indifference to others. Awareness as an indicator, though it may be no easier to prove, has at least the virtue of confining itself to the occasion in question. However it cannot be claimed that for this reason alone it must oust all other considerations and stand in the way of a test in which attitude might also play an active role, although one would not think so judging by the majority of textbooks, cases, and even some statutes on criminal law. It may be that the search for a simple formula for this kind of recklessness has triumphed over the need for a comprehensive one. The extension of recklessness in *Caldwell* can be seen as in part an understandable attempt to bridge this gap.

Antony Duff has also argued that we should move away from a test based on foresight of risk (what Duff calls an 'orthodox subjectivist' test) and instead use a test based on attitude. Duff proposes a test based on 'practical indifference'.

## EXTRACT

In the following extract, Duff gives an example involving a bridegroom who forgets his wedding. What does he say this example illustrates?

What does Duff argue is the truth in orthodox subjectivist tests like *R v Cunningham*? What error does he say these tests make?

What does Duff argue is the truth in the *R v Caldwell* test? What error does he say this test made?

## Duff, A. (1990) *Intention, Agency & Criminal Liability.* Blackwell: Oxford, pp163, 165–166

A bridegroom has missed his wedding; he explains to his (ex-)bride that he was in the pub with his friends at the time, and that the wedding just slipped his mind. On the orthodox subjectivist account that explanation should reduce the moral charge against him to one of mere negligence or forgetfulness; his fault is categorically less serious than it would have been had he realized that he was missing his wedding. But his bride would surely (and rightly) be unimpressed by this story: for to forget his wedding (when there was no sudden emergency which might have made even a 'reasonable man' forget his wedding) itself manifests an utter lack of concern for his bride and their marriage. Had he cared at all for her, he *could* not have forgotten their wedding. The fact that he forgot it shows that he did not care; and that lack of concern, as manifested in his conduct, is the fault for which she rightly condemns him.

This shows how I can be indifferent to what I do not notice. What I notice or attend to reflects what I care about; and my very failure to notice something can display my utter indifference to it. Orthodox subjectivist objections to defining recklessness as indifference may reflect the dualist conception of indifference as an occurrent mental state which is quite distinct from conduct, and therefore irrelevant to criminal liability. But once we reject this dualist distinction between attitude and action, and recognize that an agent's actions can manifest her attitudes as well as her intentions, we can explain criminal recklessness in terms of the practical indifference which the agent's actions display; and we can also see that such practical indifference can be displayed both in conscious risk-taking and in her very failure to notice a risk.

[...]

The truth in orthodox subjectivism is that an agent most clearly display her reckless indifference to a risk in consciously creating it, and that her unawareness of a risk often precludes the ascription of such reckless indifference: its error lies in the claim that *only* one who consciously creates a risk can be said to be reckless of that risk – that unawareness of risk must *always* preclude the ascription of recklessness. The truth in *Caldwell* [...] on the other hand, is that the indifference which constitutes recklessness can sometimes be shown in an agent's very failure to notice a risk which her action creates, as well as in her conscious risk-taking. [Its] error lies in [its] suggestion that *any* failure to notice an obvious (and serious) risk created by one's action displays a reckless indifference to that risk: for what matters is not just *that*, but *why*, the agent fails to notice an obvious risk; she is reckless only if she fails to notice it *because* she does not care about it.

So Duff's practical indifference test seeks to rectify both the narrowness of the *R v Cunningham* test (by also encompassing those fail to notice a risk) and the breadth of the *R v Caldwell* test (by only encompassing those who fail to notice a risk as a result of reckless indifference).

## ACTIVITY

Should the test for recklessness be changed to one based on attitude, like Duff's practical indifference test? Can you think of any possible objections to Duff's proposal?

## Intention

In this section we examine the concept of intention. We begin by distinguishing two types of intention: direct intention and oblique intention (sometimes referred to as indirect intention). We then focus on oblique intention, considering: whether the courts' approach differentiates adequately between oblique intention and recklessness; whether it vests too much discretion in the jury; and options for reform.

First, though, a preliminary point. Many students often ask, 'How can we ever know what someone intended? We're lawyers, not mind-readers!' The answer is found in section 8 of the Criminal Justice Act 1967.

---

**EXTRACT**

### Section 8 of the Criminal Justice Act 1967

#### 8 Proof of criminal intent

A court or jury, in determining whether a person has committed an offence,–

(a)  shall not be bound in law to infer that he intended or foresaw a result of his actions by reasons only of its being a natural and probable consequence of those actions; but

(b)  shall decide whether he did intend or foresee that result by reference to all the evidence, drawing such inferences from the evidence as appear proper in the circumstances

---

As paragraph (b) explains, we infer a defendant's intentions 'by reference to all the evidence'. Sometimes this will be straightforward. If Dwayne points a gun at Saalim's head, says 'Say goodbye' and then pulls the trigger, we will have no hesitation in inferring from Dwayne's actions that he intended to kill Saalim. Or, if you spend ten hours a day, seven days a week, revising for your criminal law exam I will have no hesitation in inferring from your actions that your intention is to achieve a good mark in the exam. Of course, there will sometimes be difficult cases. In these cases the jury's job is to look at all the evidence and decide whether they are sure, beyond reasonable doubt, that the intention required for the crime can be inferred.

## 1. Two types of intention: direct intention and oblique intention

We have seen that a defendant acts recklessly when he foresees a risk and unjustifiably chooses to take it. Intention also involves a choice: a choice to bring about a result. So, in the example above, Dwayne intended to kill Saalim because he chose to bring about Saalim's death.

A defendant's choice to bring about a result may take one of two forms:

- The first is where he chooses to bring about a result because he wants it to occur. This is known as direct intention.

- The second is where the defendant may not want the result to occur but acts in the knowledge that it is a virtually certain side effect of his action. This is known as oblique intention.

We will look at each type of intention in turn.

### i. Direct intention

Your direct intention is your aim or objective. In our previous example, Dwayne's objective was to kill Saalim. He hated Saalim and he wanted Saalim to die. So killing Saalim was Dwayne's direct intention.

A useful way of testing whether or not a result was a defendant's direct intention is Antony Duff's 'test of failure'.[7] This test simply asks whether the defendant would have regarded himself as having failed if the result did not occur. If Dwayne had pulled the trigger but Saalim had somehow managed to dodge the bullet, Dwayne would not have killed Saalim and would have regarded this as a failure. We can therefore conclude that killing Saalim was indeed his direct intention.

Duff's success/failure test is helpful in analysing another example. This time Dwayne wants to give Saalim a shock. He sees Saalim sitting in an armchair in his lounge, near to the window. Dwayne picks up a brick and throws it through the window as hard as he can. On these facts, Dwayne had two objectives which were inextricably linked. First, his ultimate objective was to frighten Saalim. If the brick had smashed the window but Saalim had been totally unfazed, Dwayne would have regarded this as a failure. Second, it was also his objective to smash the window. This objective was purely instrumental – Dwayne only wanted to smash the window in order to frighten Saalim – but it was nonetheless his direct intention. Had the brick simply bounced off the window without smashing it, Dwayne would have regarded this as a failure. So smashing the window was also his direct intention.

So a person may directly intend a result either because it is his ultimate objective or for purely instrumental reasons.

Notice one further point, which is illustrated by the following example.

---

**EXAMPLE**

Armed with a sniper rifle, Dwayne is lying in wait for his enemy Saalim (whom he has hated for a long time). Dwayne has never fired a gun before, let alone practised with a sniper rifle. Plus Saalim is a kilometre away, it is windy and Dwayne is so nervous that he cannot hold the rifle steady. He pulls the trigger, doing all he can to try and hit Saalim and kill him. Was it Dwayne's direct intention to kill Saalim? (Hint: remember to apply Duff's success/failure test.)

---

As this example illustrates a person may directly intend a result even if he realises he is very unlikely to succeed.

### ii. Oblique intention

Sometimes you may act not wanting a particular result to occur but knowing that it is virtually certain to do so. Suppose you go to the Student Union bar tonight and spend five hours drinking lager, then wine and then vodka. Your direct intention is not to give yourself a terrible hangover tomorrow. You do not want a hangover, and you will actually be pleasantly surprised if you wake up tomorrow feeling fine. But at the same time you realise that a hangover is the virtually certain consequence of your actions. On these facts, you obliquely intend to have a hangover tomorrow since you realise it is the virtually certain consequence of your actions.

---

[7]Duff, A. (1990) *Intention, Agency & Criminal Liability.* Blackwell: Oxford, p61.

A key point to grasp here is the difference between this example and the earlier one involving Dwayne smashing Saalim's window. The two examples are similar, in that both involve consequences which are inextricably linked. In Dwayne's example smashing the window was inextricably linked to his ultimate objective, frightening Saalim. In the Student Union bar example, tomorrow's hangover is inextricably linked to tonight's heavy alcohol consumption. The difference between them is that Dwayne wanted the window to smash (so smashing the window was his direct intention), whereas you did not want tomorrow's hangover (so having the hangover was your oblique intention).

With this distinction in mind, consider the following example.

**EXAMPLE**

Dwayne is about to stand trial for terrorism offences. A world-renowned lawyer, Saalim, is flying to London to act as prosecutor in Dwayne's case. Saalim has spent months examining the evidence and preparing the case against Dwayne. Dwayne puts a bomb on board the plane that is bringing Saalim to London. Dwayne wants Saalim to die but hopes that, by some miracle, the pilot Tariq will survive. Is killing Saalim Dwayne's direct or oblique intention? Is killing Tariq Dwayne's direct or oblique intention?

Whilst killing Saalim was Dwayne's direct intention (he would have regarded it as a failure had Saalim not been killed), killing Tariq was his oblique intention (he did not want Tariq to die but realised that this was a virtually certain consequence of his actions). This example illustrates why we need a category of oblique intention as well as direct intention. If we only had a category of direct intention Dwayne would be guilty of murdering Saalim, but not Tariq. This would be unacceptable. Even though Dwayne did not desire Tariq's death, he still *chose* to kill Tariq, just as he *chose* to kill Saalim.

In cases involving oblique intention we do not use Duff's success/failure test. Instead we use the following direction, which was set out by the House of Lords in *R v Woollin* [1999] 1 AC 82:

> Where the charge is murder and in the rare cases where the simple direction is not enough, the jury should be directed that they are not entitled to find the necessary intention, unless they feel sure that death or serious bodily harm was a virtual certainty (barring some unforeseen intervention) as a result of the defendant's actions and that the defendant appreciated that such was the case

So a jury are 'entitled to find' oblique intention if two conditions are satisfied: (i) the result in question was a 'virtual certainty' (barring some unforeseen intervention); and (ii) the defendant realised this.

Note the following four points about this direction:

- If either of the two conditions is not satisfied, the jury may *not* find oblique intention.
- If both conditions are satisfied, the jury are *entitled* to find oblique intention but are not obliged to do so. In other words, the jury has some discretion and may decide

that, even though both conditions are satisfied, there was no oblique intention. This was confirmed by the Court of Appeal in *R v Matthews & Alleyne* [2003] EWCA Crim 192.

- The jury should only be given the *R v Woollin* direction if it is necessary to do so, on the basis of the facts of the particular case before them. So in a problem question always begin with direct intention, and only consider oblique intention if it is necessary to do so.

- *R v Woollin* was a murder case, and so the extract above refers to 'death or serious bodily harm'. In cases involving other offences the wording should be adapted accordingly.

## ACTIVITY

Dwayne hides a bomb on a busy high street. Two hours before the bomb is set to explode, he gives a telephone warning to enable the surrounding area to be evacuated. He knows that a bomb disposal squad will attempt to defuse the bomb, and he expects them to succeed. In fact, however, the bomb explodes and a member of the bomb disposal squad is killed.

Afterwards Dwayne states that he expected the publicity generated by the bomb to draw attention to his cause. He explains that he gave the warning because he did not want anyone to suffer injury, since he feared that if this were to happen he would lose public support.

Did Dwayne intend (either directly or obliquely) to kill? How would your answer be different if he had given a deliberately unclear warning just 90 seconds before the bomb was due to explode?

In the remainder of this section we are going to examine the *R v Woollin* direction more carefully. There are two key issues for us to consider: first, whether the *R v Woollin* direction succeeds in drawing a clear dividing line between oblique intention and recklessness; and, second, whether the *R v Woollin* direction is correct to vest some discretion in the jury. Finally, we will look at proposals for reform.

## 2. The distinction between oblique intention and recklessness

So far we have seen that there is an important conceptual distinction between intention and recklessness. A defendant acts intentionally when he chooses to bring about a result, whereas he acts recklessly when he foresees a risk that the result will occur and unjustifiably chooses to take that risk. As we will see in the next chapter, this distinction is particularly important in the law of homicide. Only intention suffices for the *mens rea* of murder. A defendant who recklessly caused death will be convicted of manslaughter, not murder. So the dividing line between intention and recklessness is important because it is also the dividing line between murder and manslaughter. However, devising a definition of oblique intention that clearly distinguishes it from recklessness is far from easy. This is demonstrated by the following example.

## EXAMPLE

Dwayne owns a two-bedroom house, which he shares with his lodger Saalim. Dwayne is behind with his mortgage payments and so decides to set fire to the house and then make an insurance claim. Even though Dwayne does not want Saalim to suffer any harm, he sets fire to the house knowing that Saalim is inside. Saalim is killed in the fire. Did Dwayne: (a) have an oblique intention to kill Saalim; or (b) kill Saalim recklessly if, when he set fire to the house, Dwayne realised:

- there was a 100 per cent chance Saalim would be killed?
- there was a 50 per cent chance Saalim would be killed?
- there was a 90 per cent chance Saalim would be killed?

The first of these three alternatives is straightforward. Dwayne may not have wanted Saalim to die (so killing Saalim was not his direct intention), but he chose to set fire to the house knowing that Saalim's death was an inevitable consequence of his actions. The two conditions in the *R v Woollin* direction are satisfied and a jury would be entitled to find that Dwayne had an oblique intention to kill Saalim.

In the second alternative, by contrast, Saalim's death was far from inevitable. Although there was a 50 per cent chance Saalim would be killed, there was an equal chance he would survive. So what Dwayne did was take an unjustified risk that Saalim would be killed. In other words, he acted recklessly.

So somewhere between the first and second alternatives lies the dividing line between oblique intention and recklessness. The question is, where? The *R v Woollin* direction says that recklessness becomes oblique intention when the risk stops being merely a risk and becomes a virtual certainty. But how likely must a consequence be for it to stop being just a risk and become a virtual certainty? In the third alternative, there was a 90 per cent chance Saalim would be killed. Is something that is 90 per cent likely a virtual certainty, or a grave risk? This is a difficult question, but the answer will determine whether Dwayne is guilty of murder or manslaughter.

This example helps us to understand why some have suggested that the *R v Woollin* direction blurs the dividing line between oblique intention and recklessness. As Sir John Smith explains in the following extract, the cause of this uncertainty is the qualification of the word 'certainty' with the word 'virtual'.

## EXTRACT

### Smith, J.C. (1990) 'A Note on Intention' *Criminal Law Review* 85

[Oblique intention] is intended to apply only to a person [...] who, though [it] is not his purpose [to cause the result in question], knows that he is going to cause that result. He is not merely taking a risk of causing that result. He is going to cause it and he knows it. But because nothing is certain in human affairs successive draftsmen and courts have felt obliged to qualify the [...] definition – he has *no substantial doubt* that the result will happen, he knows that it is *almost* certain, or *virtually* certain, or *morally* certain, to happen, or that it will happen *in the ordinary course of events*. There is a danger that any of these qualifications will be so interpreted as to blur the distinction between intention and recklessness. Once it is conceded that something less than certainty is required, it may be argued that we are into degrees of probability.

The obvious solution, therefore, would be to remove the word 'virtual' from the *R v Woollin* direction. This would produce a clear dividing line between oblique intention (where the consequence was 100 per cent certain to ensue) and recklessness (where the consequence was less than 100 per cent certain). But this clarity could have damaging effects in practice. In his article, Sir John Smith goes on to say that 'My friend, Brian Hogan, quotes *the Guinness Book of World Records* to show that, very occasionally, people have fallen out of planes from great heights and survived'. So think back to our example of Dwayne putting a bomb on board the plane carrying Saalim (the prosecutor) and Tariq (the pilot). We saw earlier that, under the *R v Woollin* direction, Dwayne obliquely intended to kill Tariq. But suppose that the word 'virtual' was removed from the *R v Woollin* direction and that Dwayne had read the *Guinness Book of Records* and was aware that there have been instances of people falling from planes and surviving. Smith explains that Dwayne would then have to be acquitted of murder:

> What of the case where the defendant gives evidence and says that he *did* contemplate the remote possibility, *e.g.* he, a devotee of *the Guinness Book of Records*, was aware of the remote chance that the crew of the doomed aircraft might escape and indeed hoped that they would? It would seem that the judge [...] must direct that jury that, if they thought the defendant might be speaking the truth, they must acquit him of an offence requiring proof of intention.

So, whilst the word 'virtual' in the *R v Woollin* direction might involve some sacrifice of clarity, it can be argued that this is necessary for practical reasons.

## 3. The element of discretion in the *R v Woollin* direction

We saw earlier that the *R v Woollin* direction vests some discretion in the jury. Even if the two conditions in the *R v Woollin* direction are both satisfied, the jury is not obliged to find oblique intention. It is 'entitled' to do so. There are conflicting opinions on whether this element of discretion is appropriate.

### i. Arguments for an element of discretion

In June 2017 a fire broke out at Grenfell Tower, a 24-storey residential block in west London. In the days following the blaze stories emerged of parents being forced to throw their young children from the building to the crowds below. These included the mother of a four-year-old girl who was trapped on the fifth floor, and the mother of a baby who was trapped on the tenth floor. Both children were caught by those on the ground.[8]

Almost 20 years earlier, in a Parliamentary debate on the meaning of intention, Lord Goff had considered a similar, hypothetical, example:[9]

> Let us take this example. A house is on fire. A father is trapped in the attic floor with his two little girls. He comes to the conclusion that unless they jump they will all be burned alive. But he also realises that if they jump they are all likely to suffer serious personal harm. The children are too frightened to jump and so in an attempt to save their lives he throws one

---

[8]White, C. (2017) 'The man who caught a 4-year-old girl from the Grenfell Tower blaze pictured' *Metro* 16 June 2017; 'Baby dropped from 10th floor of Grenfell Tower "caught by man on ground"' *The Telegraph* 14 June 2017. Other, similar, examples have also been reported. For example, in February 2008 a fire broke out in a four-storey building in Ludwigshafen in south-western Germany. A family found themselves trapped at a third-floor window. They threw their nine-month-old daughter out of the window, to a policeman on the ground 40 feet below. Thankfully he managed to catch the girl and she was unharmed. The girl's parents also survived.

[9]Hansard, HL Deb, vol 512, cols 469–470, 6 November 1989.

out of the window to the crowd waiting below and jumps with the other one in his arms. All are seriously injured, and the little girl he threw out of the window dies of her injuries.

Suppose that it was virtually certain that the girl that the father threw from the window would suffer serious injury, and that the father realised this. The two conditions in the *R v Woollin* direction would then be satisfied. Without an element of discretion, it follows that a jury would have to conclude that the father obliquely intended to seriously injure his daughter. But this would be nonsensical. He did not intend for her to suffer serious harm. Serious harm was the very thing that he was trying to save her from!

Another example is the case *R v Steane* [1947] KB 997. The defendant, Anthony Steane, was an English actor (alias: Jack Trevor). He was awarded the Military Cross for his service during World War I. But when World War II broke out he was working in Germany and was immediately arrested. He was asked to broadcast for the Nazis. Initially he refused, but eventually agreed after Gestapo officers beat him badly (one of his ears was partly torn off) and threatened to send his wife and children (who were living in Germany) to a concentration camp. Following the end of the war, Steane was charged with doing acts likely to assist the enemy. At trial he was convicted. He appealed to the Court of Appeal, arguing that he lacked *mens rea*. He said that he had never intended to assist the enemy; he only broadcast in order to save his family. The Court of Appeal allowed his appeal and quashed his conviction. Lord Goddard CJ explained that, because Steane had been under pressure from the enemy, his actions were potentially consistent with either an 'innocent intent' to save his family or a 'guilty intent' to assist the enemy. Unless it could be shown, beyond reasonable doubt, that Steane had acted with a guilty intent to assist the enemy he was entitled to be acquitted.

*R v Steane* was decided many years before the House of Lords formulated the *R v Woollin* direction. But suppose that the *R v Woollin* direction had been in existence at the time *R v Steane* was decided. What would the outcome have been? Steane's actions were virtually certain to provide assistance to the enemy, and he realised this. The two conditions in the *R v Woollin* direction would therefore have been satisfied. Without an element of discretion, a jury would therefore have had to conclude that Steane intended to assist the enemy.

The burning building example and *R v Steane* demonstrate the principal benefit of the element of discretion in the *R v Woollin* direction. As Alan Norrie explains in the following extract, the element of discretion allows juries to make a moral assessment of the defendant's intention. The element of discretion thus acts as a moral safety valve, allowing juries to ensure that non-blameworthy defendants are not inappropriately convicted.

## EXTRACT

### Norrie, A. (1999) 'After *Woollin*' Criminal Law Review 532

These are cases where there is a "moral threshold" such that even though the accused could foresee a result as virtually certain, it is so at odds with his moral conception of what he was doing that it could not be conceived as a result that he intended. While a number of interpretations of *Steane* are possible, it is plausible to argue that at the nub of the case lies a moral gap between what Steane did, broadcasting to assist the enemy, and his purpose, to save his family. In that context, the judges declined to find that he had anything other than an intention to save his family. Yet this was clearly a case where they might have thought that it could be foreseen as virtually certain that assistance to the enemy would either result from the broadcasting, or was a necessary means to Steane's saving his family. It is therefore plausible to see this as a case where [oblique] intent could be established but was not found.

### ii. Arguments against an element of discretion

There is another way of analysing the facts of *R v Steane*. Commenting on the Court of Appeal's reasoning, Glanville Williams wrote:[10]

> [A] more satisfactory way of deciding the case would have been to say that the accused did in law intend to assist the enemy but that duress was a defence.

The argument here is not just that the availability of substantive defences renders the discretionary element in the *R v Woollin* direction unnecessary. It is that issues of justification and excuse are more appropriately addressed in the realm of the substantive defences. As we will see in Chapter 11, the courts have developed tests for defences like duress and self-defence. Each defence also has an accompanying body of case law which provides guidance on how the tests should be applied. By contrast, a jury applying the *R v Woollin* direction is given little guidance on how to exercise its discretion. William Wilson has written:[11]

> Even if the judge chooses to give the [*R v Woollin*] direction, moreover, it should be remembered that this does not foreclose the possibility of a linguistically sophisticated jury saying to themselves "OK, we are entitled to find intention here but we prefer not to. People intend what they set out to achieve. They do not intend the undesired side effects of what they are in business to achieve, particularly where these are inconsistent with the point of the defendant's action". Neither, more importantly, does it foreclose the possibility of a similar jury embarrassing the trial judge by asking for a further direction on this very point. How should a judge respond to such an inquiry? The real weakness of *Woollin* lies in its resounding silence on this issue.

Vesting this discretion in juries, but offering little or no guidance on how the discretion should be exercised, creates uncertainty. It also creates a risk of different juries reaching different verdicts in similar cases. This would infringe the rule of law.

Significantly, in *Re A (Children)(Conjoined Twins: Surgical Separation)* [2001] Fam 147 the Court of Appeal chose not to exercise its discretion under the *R v Woollin* direction. This case involved conjoined twins, Jodie and Mary. The twins were joined at the pelvis. Each had her own brain, heart, lungs and other vital organs, but Mary's heart and lungs were too deficient to oxygenate blood and pump it through her own body. However, the twins shared a common artery, which enabled Jodie's heart to pump the blood she oxygenated through Mary's body. Without an operation separating them it was expected that Jodie's heart would fail within a few months and both would die. On the other hand, if the twins were separated Jodie would have a good chance of survival but Mary would die within minutes. The Court of Appeal had to decide whether it would be lawful for doctors to separate the twins. One of the questions the Court faced was whether, by separating the twins, the doctors would be murdering Mary. This in turn involved the question whether the doctors would be killing Mary intentionally.

By a majority of 2–1, the Court of Appeal held that the doctors would be killing Mary intentionally. The dissenting judge, Robert Walker LJ, acknowledged that the two

---

[10]Williams, G. (1961) *Criminal Law: The General Part* (2nd edn) London: Stevens & Sons, section 18.
[11]Wilson, W. (1999) 'Doctrinal Rationality After *Woollin*' 62 *Modern Law Review* 448.

conditions in the *R v Woollin* direction would be satisfied, but nonetheless concluded that the doctors would lack any intention to kill Mary:

> The proposed operation would not be unlawful. It would involve the positive act of invasive surgery and Mary's death would be foreseen as an inevitable consequence of an operation which is intended, and is necessary, to save Jodie's life. But Mary's death would not be the purpose or intention of the surgery, and she would die because tragically her body, on its own, is not and never has been viable.

By contrast, the majority held that, because the two conditions in the *R v Woollin* direction would be satisfied, the doctors would have an oblique intention to kill Mary. Ward LJ stated:

> The test I have to set myself is that established by [*R v Woollin*]. I have to ask myself whether I am satisfied that the doctors recognise that death or serious harm will be virtually certain, barring some unforeseen intervention, to result from carrying out this operation. If so, the doctors intend to kill or to do that serious harm even though they may not have any desire to achieve that result. It is common ground that they appreciate that death to Mary would result from the severance of the common aorta. Unpalatable though it may be – and Mr Whitfield contends it is – to stigmatise the doctors with "murderous intent", that is what in law they will have if they perform the operation and Mary dies as a result.

Similarly, Brooke LJ said:

> Now that the House of Lords [in *R v Woollin*] has set out the law authoritatively in these terms, an English court would inevitably find that the surgeons intended to kill Mary, however little they desired that end, because her death would be the virtually certain consequence of their acts, and they would realise that for all practical purposes her death would invariably follow the clamping of the common aorta.

Both Ward and Brooke LJJ nonetheless concluded that the doctors would not be guilty of murdering Mary. As we will see in Chapter 11, both held that the doctors would be able to rely on a substantive defence.

Finally, it is worth considering how this approach of Glanville Williams and the majority of the Court of Appeal in *Re A* would apply in the earlier example of the father throwing his daughter from a burning building. Since the father's act of throwing the girl from the window was a factual and legal cause of her death there is the *actus reus* of murder. Moreover, if we remove the discretionary element from the *R v Woollin* direction, the father would have the *mens rea* of murder. He realised that serious injury to his daughter was a virtual certainty, and an oblique intention to cause serious injury is sufficient for the *mens rea* of murder. To avoid being guilty of murdering his daughter, he would therefore need to be able to plead a substantive defence. Two comments can be offered about this:

- As we will see in Chapter 11, the courts have taken quite a restrictive approach to the availability of the substantive defences on murder charges. The father's most obvious defence – duress of circumstances – would be unavailable, since the House of Lords has held that duress is not available as a defence to murder.[12] An alternative might be the defence of necessity, but there is uncertainty as to whether necessity is available as

---

[12]*R v Howe* [1987] AC 417.

a defence to murder either. So the moral safety valve offered by the discretionary element in the *R v Woollin* direction might be necessary after all, at least until changes have been made to the law governing the substantive defences.

- Even if the father could plead a substantive defence, and so be not guilty of murder, there remains the basic fact that it is nonsensical to say that he intended to cause his daughter serious harm when this was the very thing he was trying to save her from!

The second of these points leads us to consider whether there are other respects in which the *R v Woollin* direction might be improved.

## 4. Proposals for reform

The Law Commission considered the definition of intention in the 1990s and again in the 2000s. Here are three of the options it considered – have a think about which you think is best!

### i. Option one: 'in the ordinary course of events'

The first option is found in clause 1(a) of the Law Commission's 1993 Draft Criminal Law Bill. The first limb (i) deals with direct intention. The second limb (ii) deals with oblique intention.

### EXTRACT

Law Commission (1993) No 218 *Legislating the Criminal Code: Offences Against the Person and General Principles* Cm 2370 (1993)

#### Clause 1(a)

[A] person acts −

(a)   "intentionally" with respect to a result when −

(i)  it is his purpose to cause it, or

(ii)  although it is not his purpose to cause it, he knows that it would occur in the ordinary course of events, if he were to succeed in his purpose of causing some other result;

The key points to note about this definition are:

- It used the phrase 'in the ordinary course of events' instead of the phrase 'virtual certainty' because it believed that this wording would be clearer.
- It does not contain a discretionary element. If the conditions in limb (ii) are satisfied the jury must find oblique intention.
- It adds the phrase '[…] if he were to succeed in his purpose of causing some other result'. This was designed to prevent the nonsensical conclusion in the burning building example. If the father succeeds in his purpose of saving his daughter from serious harm, then his daughter will not suffer serious harm in the ordinary course of events. So under this definition the father would not have an oblique intention to cause serious harm to his daughter.

ACTIVITY

Under this definition, would: (a) Steane have had an oblique intention to assist the enemy; and (b) the doctors have had an oblique intention to kill Mary?

### ii. Option two: remove the discretionary element

The second and third options are both found in the Law Commission's consultation paper and final report on the law of homicide.[13] The second option is set out in the consultation paper as follows (limb (1) deals with direct intention and limbs (2) and (3) deal with oblique intention).

EXTRACT

### Law Commission (2005) *A New Homicide Act for England and Wales?* (Law Commission Consultation Paper No 177)

4.62 [...] Subject to the proviso set out below:

a person acts "intentionally" with respect to a result when he or she acts either:

(1)　in order to bring it about, or

(2)　knowing that it will be virtually certain to occur; or

(3)　knowing that it would be virtually certain to occur if he or she were to succeed in his or her purpose of causing some other result.

**Proviso:** a person is not to be deemed to have intended any result, which it was his or her specific purpose to avoid.

4.63 In directing a jury on the meaning of intention, the judge would be required only to refer the jury to the appropriate clause of this definition. There would be no need for a judge to refer jurors to the proviso, except in cases where the particular facts raise the possibility of it being applicable. A Practice Direction to this effect may be sufficient to ensure that this definition will provide a workable, clear, simple definition of intention.

The key points to note about this definition are:

- In *R v Woollin* Lord Steyn stated that 'over a period of 12 years [...] the test of foresight of virtual certainty has apparently caused no practical difficulties. It is simple and clear'. In the light of this, the Law Commission reverted to the phrase 'virtual certainty' instead of 'in the ordinary course of events'.

- It does not contain a discretionary element. If the conditions in limb (2) or (3) are satisfied the jury must find oblique intention.

---

[13]See: Law Commission Consultation Paper No 177 (2005) *A New Homicide Act for England and Wales?* Part 4; and Law Commission No 304 (2006) *Murder, Manslaughter and Infanticide* HC 30, paras 3.9–3.27.

- The proviso is designed to deal with the nonsensical conclusion in the burning building example.
- Unlike the 1993 proposal that we just looked at, this proposal splits the definition of oblique intention into two strands:
  - Limb (3) mirrors the definition of oblique intention found in the 1993 proposal. Limb (3) was felt to be necessary in order to deal with cases of 'conditional oblique intention'. Think back to our example of Dwayne placing a bomb on board the plane carrying Saalim (the prosecutor) and Tariq (the pilot). We saw earlier that Dwayne had an oblique intention to kill Tariq. But suppose that Dwayne knew that the bomb he planted was defective, and only had a 50 per cent chance of exploding. Under the *R v Woollin* direction as it stands today, Dwayne would lack an oblique intention to kill Tariq because Tariq's death is not a virtual certainty. The phrase '[...] if he or she were to succeed in his or her purpose of causing some other result' corrects this. Dwayne knows that, if he succeeds in his purpose of killing Saalim, it is a virtual certainty that Tariq will die too.
  - However, sometimes defendants do not have 'some other result' that they hope to achieve.[14] An example is *R v Woollin* itself. Stephen Woollin lost his temper with his three-month-old son, and threw him onto a hard surface. The child suffered a fractured skull and died. Woollin would fall outside limb (3) because it was not his purpose to cause some other result. For this reason, limb (2) does not contain these extra words. A defendant like Woollin would therefore fall under limb (2).

## ACTIVITY

Would Stephen Woollin be found to have had an intention to kill or cause serious harm to his son under the 1993 proposal?

### iii. Option three: retain the *status quo*

The third option is to codify the existing law. The Law Commission set out this option in its consultation paper.

## EXTRACT

### Law Commission (2005) *A New Homicide Act for England and Wales?* (Law Commission Consultation Paper No 177)

4.69 A codification of the common law would need, first, to refer to the ordinary situation in which a person is to be regarded as acting intentionally. Then it should replicate the [*Woollin*] direction. Finally, the clause relating to the chances of the defendant succeeding in some other purpose should be introduced. The resulting formulation would be as follows:

(1)   A person is to be regarded as acting intentionally with respect to a result when he or she acts in order to bring it about.

---

[14]A point made by Sir John Smith [1998] Crim LR 318.

(2)    In the rare case where the simple direction in clause (1) is not enough, the jury should be directed that:

they are not entitled to find the necessary intention with regard to a result unless they are sure that the result was a virtual certainty (barring some unforeseen intervention) as a result of the defendant's actions and that the defendant appreciated that such was the case.

(3)    In any case where the defendant's chance of success in his or her purpose of causing some other result is relevant, the direction in clause (2) may be expanded by the addition of the following phrase at the end of the clause (2) direction:

or that it would be *if he or she were to succeed in his or her purpose of causing some other result,* and that the defendant appreciated that such was the case.

The key difference between this option and the previous one is that this option retains the discretionary element.

The Law Commission's final report, in 2006, recommended the third option. It argued, first, that the phrase 'virtual certainty' should be retained since it has not caused any significant problems in practice:[15]

4.60 In 1998, Lord Steyn pointed out in *Woollin,* that "over a period of 12 years since *Nedrick,* the test of foresight of virtual certainty has apparently caused no practical difficulties. It is simple and clear …". This raises the question of whether it would be better to use the expression "virtually certain" in a new statutory definition of "intentionally", rather than "in the ordinary course of events". In our view, in light of the observations of Lord Steyn in *Woollin*, it would be preferable to use the tried and tested phrase "knowing that it is virtually certain to occur". The phrase has the advantage of simplicity and it has proved to be workable.

It then argued that the element of discretion should be retained:[16]

3.21 We acknowledge that this approach gives the jury an element of discretion in deciding whether, […] a verdict of […] murder can and should be returned. The result in such cases will not be wholly determined by legal rules governing the meaning of intention. We believe that it is sometimes necessary and desirable that juries should have that element of discretion if the alternative is a more complex set of legal rules that they must apply. It is the price of avoiding complexity.

## ACTIVITY

Do you agree with the Law Commission's recommendation? Or would you favour one of the other two proposals? Or can you construct a better proposal of your own?

---

[15]Law Commission (2005) *A New Homicide Act for England and Wales?* (Consultation Paper No 177).
[16]Law Commission (2006) *Murder, Manslaughter and Infanticide* (No 304) HC 30.

## Other *mens rea* terms

So far in this chapter we have examined recklessness and intention – the two *mens rea* concepts that we will use most frequently in this text – in detail. We will now briefly introduce some other concepts that you will encounter as you study criminal law.

### 1. Knowledge

The *mens rea* concept of knowledge is used in some of the property offences that we will study in Chapter 8 (burglary and fraud) and in the law on accessories (Chapter 13). The word is normally used in relation to circumstances (so we might say, for example, that the defendant knew that his representation was false).

There are two types of knowledge. The first is actual knowledge. This is where someone has formed a belief, and that belief is correct. As the House of Lords stated in *R v Saik* [2006] UKHL 18, 'knowledge means true belief'.

The second type of knowledge is known as wilful blindness. This is where the only reason that the defendant has not yet formed a (correct) belief is because he has deliberately failed to investigate his suspicions. In *Westminster CC v Croyalgrange Ltd* [1986] 1 WLR 674 Lord Bridge explained wilful blindness as follows:

> it is always open to the tribunal of fact, when knowledge on the part of a defendant is required to be proved, to base a finding of knowledge on evidence that the defendant had deliberately shut his eyes to the obvious or refrained from enquiry because he suspected the truth but did not want to have his suspicion confirmed.

### 2. Belief

We will encounter the *mens rea* concept of belief in Chapter 6 (non-fatal offences against the person), Chapter 7 (sexual offences) and Chapter 8 (property offences). Like knowledge, the concept of belief is used primarily in relation to circumstances (so we might say, for example, that the defendant genuinely believed that he had a legal right to the property).

The difference between knowledge and belief is that knowledge cannot be mistaken but a belief can be. Belief must also be distinguished from suspicion. As Beldam LJ explained in *R v Forsyth* [1997] 2 Cr App R 299, a person who believes something has concluded that it is true whereas someone who suspects something has not:

> It is beyond question that even great suspicion is not to be equated with belief [...] The ordinary meaning of belief is the mental acceptance of a fact as true or existing.

### 3. Negligence

A defendant acts negligently if his behaviour falls short of the standard that we would expect of a reasonable person in the same situation. This is an objective test. So unlike intention, knowledge, belief and recklessness, which as we have seen focus on the defendant's state of mind, negligence simply requires an assessment of whether the defendant's conduct lived up to the objective standard of reasonableness.

Although negligence is used in the *mens rea* of a large number of regulatory offences, it is not used in any of the crimes that we study in this text. However, we will study one offence which requires proof of gross negligence: namely, gross negligence manslaughter.

## 4. Strict liability

The term 'strict liability' is used to describe crimes which have one or more *actus reus* requirements that do not have any corresponding *mens rea* requirement. An example is the offence of rape of a child under the age of 13.[17] This crime has two *actus reus* requirements, but only one of these has a corresponding *mens rea* requirement:

- The defendant penetrated the vagina, anus or mouth of the other person. This *actus reus* requirement has a corresponding *mens rea* requirement: the penetration must have been intentional.

- The other person was aged under 13. This requirement does not have a corresponding *mens rea* requirement.[18] A defendant can therefore be convicted of this offence even if he honestly believed the victim was aged 16 and the possibility that she was aged under 13 never crossed his mind.

It is important to understand the difference between crimes of strict liability and crimes of constructive liability. As shown in Figure 4.2, in crimes of constructive liability every *actus reus* requirement does have a corresponding *mens rea* requirement. However,

**Strict liability**

**An example: rape of a child under the age of 13**

| *Actus reus* requirements | *Mens rea* requirements |
|---|---|
| D penetrated the vagina, anus or mouth of another person  ⟶ | Corresponding *mens rea* requirement: The penetration must have been intentional |
| The other person was aged under 13  ⟶ | No corresponding *mens rea* requirement |

**Constructive liability**

**An example: murder**

| *Actus reus* requirements | *Mens rea* requirements |
|---|---|
| D caused the death of the victim  ⟶ | The corresponding *mens rea* requirement specifies a lesser consequence than death: It is sufficient that the defendant intended to cause serious harm to the victim |

**Figure 4.2.** Comparing strict liability and constructive liability

---

[17] Sexual Offences Act 2003, s.5.
[18] *R v G* [2008] UKHL 37.

as we saw in Chapter 1, in crimes of constructive liability one or more of the *mens rea* requirements will specify a lesser consequence or circumstance than the corresponding *actus reus* requirement. The example we looked at in Chapter 1 was murder. The *actus reus* of murder requires that the victim died, but the corresponding *mens rea* requirement states that it is enough that the defendant intended to cause serious harm.

In this text we will study several offences which impose constructive liability, but none which impose strict liability. This does not mean that offences of strict liability are rare. On the contrary, roughly 45 per cent of all criminal offences are crimes of strict liability.[19] For many regulatory offences, such as drink driving and parking tickets, strict liability is commonplace.

(For discussion of the use of strict liability, see Simester, A. (2005) (ed.) *Appraising Strict Liability.* Oxford: OUP.)

## Transferred *mens rea*

Suppose that Dwayne is so upset at his criminal law coursework mark that he decides to kill his lecturer Saalim. He points a gun at Saalim and pulls the trigger, but somehow misses Saalim and instead kills his EU law lecturer Tariq. On these facts Dwayne is guilty of murdering Tariq. It is no defence for Dwayne to say that he did not intend to kill Tariq, because his intention to kill Saalim can be transferred to Tariq. This is known as the doctrine of transferred *mens rea*.[20]

(NB: Sometimes the doctrine is referred to as transferred malice. This is a misleading title, since it applies to any form of *mens rea*, not just malice.)

An example of a case in which the doctrine of transferred *mens rea* was applied is the 2007 murder of 11-year-old Rhys Jones. Rhys was murdered by 16-year-old Sean Mercer. Mercer was a member of a gang in Liverpool called the Croxteth Crew. The killing occurred when Mercer fired three gunshots at the members of a rival gang – the Norris Green gang – across a pub car park. Rhys, who was walking home from football practice, was hit by the second shot and killed. Mercer's intention to kill one of the members of the Norris Green gang was transferred to the actual victim, Rhys.

Note the following three points about the doctrine of transferred *mens rea*:

- It does not only apply to cases of murder. If I throw a stone at your bedroom window intending to smash it, but miss and smash your neighbour's window instead, my intention to smash your window can be transferred to your neighbour's window. So I would be guilty of criminal damage. However, an intention to injure a person cannot be transferred to an intention to damage property (and vice versa). So if I throw a brick at you, but miss and hit your neighbour's window instead, my intention to injure you cannot be transferred to your neighbour's window. Where the doctrine does not apply, you should consider other offences instead. Often it will be possible to charge the defendant with a criminal attempt (e.g. I could be charged with attempted battery of you) and with another full offence which involves recklessness (e.g. I could also be charged with reckless criminal damage of your neighbour's window).

---

[19]See the study completed by Andrew Ashworth and Meredith Blake: Ashworth, A. and Blake, M. (1996) 'The Presumption of Innocence in English Criminal Law' Crim LR 306. The study found that roughly half of the strict liability offences had some form of due diligence defence.

[20]See: *R v Latimer* (1886) 17 QBD 359; *R v Pembliton* (1874) LR 2 CCR 119.

- Be careful to distinguish cases of transferred *mens rea* from two slightly different types of scenario. First, suppose Dwayne wants to kill Saalim. He sees a man across the street and, believing that the man is Saalim, shoots him dead. In fact, it turns out that the man was not Saalim, but Tariq. Here there is no need to apply the doctrine of transferred *mens rea*. Dwayne did not fire his gun at one person and mistakenly hit someone else. He shot the person he intended to shoot: the man on the other side of the street. Dwayne's mistake as to the person's identity does not negate his intention to kill this person. Second, suppose Dwayne plants a bomb on a busy high street. The bomb explodes and kills several people. Here there is no need to apply the doctrine of transferred *mens rea* either. Dwayne did not target the bomb at anyone in particular: he had an indiscriminate intention to kill passers-by.

- In *Attorney-General's Ref (No 3 of 1994)* [1998] AC 245 the defendant stabbed a woman even though he knew that she was (between 22 and 24 weeks) pregnant. Seventeen days later the baby was born premature. The baby lived for 121 days before dying due to the effects of the premature birth. The defendant could not be charged with murder of the foetus, since a foetus is not a 'person in being' for the purposes of the offence of murder (see Chapter 5). Nor was the defendant guilty of murder of the baby, since the doctrine of transferred *mens rea* could not be used to transfer the defendant's intention to seriously injure the woman to the baby. Lord Mustill in the House of Lords explained that this would require 'a double "transfer" of intent: first from the mother to the foetus and then from the foetus to the child as yet unborn'.[21]

## ● ● ●  Conclusion

When answering problem questions, there are three basic steps to addressing issues of *mens rea*. These are set out in the following table, along with some practical advice:

| Three steps | Pointers |
| --- | --- |
| First, identify all of the *mens rea* requirements of the relevant offence. | Use Chapters 5–8 of this text to identify the *mens rea* requirements of the relevant offence. |
| So, for example, the offence of murder has one *mens rea* requirement (an intention to kill or cause serious injury) and the offence of criminal damage has two *mens rea* requirements (the defendant intentionally or recklessly destroyed or damaged the property and the defendant knew that the property belonged to another person or was reckless as to whether it did). | |

---

[21]Before the baby died the defendant had already pleaded guilty to wounding with intent (section 18 of the Offences Against the Person Act 1861: see Chapter 6) and been sentenced to four years' imprisonment. Following the child's death he was charged with murder. The trial judge ruled that the facts could not support a charge of either murder or manslaughter and directed the jury to acquit the defendant. The Attorney-General then referred a point of law of general importance to the appeal courts. The House of Lords held that the defendant had not committed murder, but that the facts were capable of supporting a manslaughter conviction.

| Three steps | Pointers |
|---|---|
| Second, identify the meaning and any applicable legal tests for each of the *mens rea* concepts that are used in the offence definition. | In this chapter we have examined the meaning and legal tests for the *mens rea* concepts that we will encounter most frequently in this text. |
| Third, use the facts of the problem question to assess whether the defendant satisfies each of the *mens rea* requirements. | One of the key skills that problem questions test is the ability to apply the law to factual scenarios. So don't just write something like 'Dwayne acted recklessly on an application of the *R v Cunningham* test'. Make sure that you use the facts of the question to explain your reasoning and justify your conclusion. |

The material that we have covered in this chapter will help you with the second of these three steps. We have examined the meaning of recklessness and the *R v Cunningham* test and the two types of intention and how to test for each of these. We have also looked briefly at the concepts of knowledge, belief, negligence and strict liability, as well as the doctrine of transferred *mens rea*.

That is the end of the first part of the text! In these first four chapters we have looked at the basic principles of criminal law and at the key general *actus reus* and *mens rea* concepts. In part two we move onto specific offences, beginning in Chapter 5 with the law of homicide.

## Self-test questions

1. Dwayne, on his motorcycle on a busy Saturday afternoon, decides it would be fun to speed along a pedestrian precinct. He skilfully avoids many shoppers, but as he speeds round a corner he hits Judy, a small child who had wandered out of a shop. Judy suffers serious injuries. At trial, expert evidence is admitted that Dwayne suffers from a psychiatric condition, one effect of which could be to deprive him of the ability of a normal person to foresee or appreciate the risk of harm inherent in driving as he did. In his evidence Dwayne says that he had not thought about the risk of hurting anyone but that he didn't really care.

   Consider whether Dwayne caused Judy's injuries recklessly. (Hint: try constructing the arguments that the prosecutor would use, and then the arguments that defence counsel would use. Looking at both sets of arguments would you feel sure beyond reasonable doubt that Dwayne acted recklessly?)

2. Alessandro is a famous magician. He plans an illusion in which he will appear to play Russian roulette live on television. The illusion will involve a member of the studio audience spinning the barrel of a six-barrel pistol which will appear to contain one live bullet. Alessandro will then proceed to point the gun at his head and pull the trigger. Alessandro will do this a total of five times, with an additional bullet added before each spin. Alessandro is confident that he can use the power of his incredible mind to prevent his untimely death but, just in case he has an 'off night', the 'bullets' will in fact be duds.

   On the evening of the performance Alessandro's manager Fabio tells Alessandro that the press have been inquiring as to whether he will use real bullets, and adds, 'Wouldn't it be more exciting, and a better story, if we did it for real?' Thinking Fabio is joking, Alessandro says 'No problem'. Unbeknown to Alessandro, Fabio was serious and replaces the duds with real bullets.

During the performance the barrel is spun for the first time, Alessandro pulls the trigger and he survives. This also happens on the second occasion, the third and the fourth. However, tragedy strikes following the final spin of the barrel (which now contains five live bullets and only one empty barrel). Alessandro is killed.

Did Fabio intend to kill Alessandro?

3. Alice wants to kill Beth, who has stolen her boyfriend Charles. She breaks into Beth's house and waits for her. The front door opens. Alice shoots at Beth but misses. Instead, the bullet hits Charles who has followed Beth into the house and is the last person Alice would want to harm. Charles dies.

    Does Alice have the *mens rea* of murder?

    Suppose that, instead of hitting Charles, the bullet smashed a window. Could Alice's intention to shoot Beth be transferred to the window?

4. In *R v G & another* [2003] UKHL 50, Lord Bingham stated: 'I cannot accept that restoration of the law as understood before *R v Caldwell* [1982] AC 341 would lead to the acquittal of those whom public policy would require to be convicted' ([39]).

    Explain and critically discuss Lord Bingham's assertion.

5. In its report (No 304) *Murder, Manslaughter and Infanticide* the Law Commission argued that the *R v Woollin* direction should be retained and codified. The Commission explained that the phrase 'virtual certainty' is simple and has been tried and tested, and that the element of discretion is necessary and desirable.

    Do you agree with the Law Commission's recommendation? Or do you prefer one of the other suggested reform options?

## Key *mens rea* concepts checklist

Having worked through this chapter, you should now have:

✓ An understanding of the concept of recklessness

✓ An ability to critically discuss the *R v Cunningham* test

✓ An understanding of the concept of intention

✓ An ability to critically discuss the *R v Woollin* direction and proposals for reform

✓ A basic understanding of the concepts of knowledge, belief, negligence and strict liability

✓ An understanding of the doctrine of transferred *mens rea*.

## Further reading

Birch, D.J. (1988) 'The Foresight Saga: The Biggest Mistake of All?' *Criminal Law Review* 4.

Chan, W. and Simester, A.P. (2011) 'Four Functions of *Mens Rea*' 70 *Cambridge Law Journal* 381.

Duff, A. (1990) *Intention, Agency & Criminal Liability*. Blackwell: Oxford.

Halpin, A. (1998) 'Definitions and Directions: Recklessness Unheeded' 18 *Legal Studies* 294.

Horder, J. (2006) 'Transferred Malice and the Remoteness of Unexpected Outcomes from Intentions' *Criminal Law Review* 383.

Ibbetson, D. (2004) 'Recklessness Restored' 63 *Cambridge Law Journal* 13.

Kugler, I. (2004) 'Conditional Oblique Intention' *Criminal Law Review* 284.

Law Commission (2005) *A New Homicide Act for England and Wales?* (Consultation Paper No 177) Part 4.

Law Commission (2006) *Murder, Manslaughter and Infanticide* (No 304) HC 30, paras 3.9–3.27.

Norrie, A. (1999) 'After *Woollin*' *Criminal Law Review* 532.

Pedain, A. (2003) 'Intention and the Terrorist Example' *Criminal Law Review* 579.

Smith, J.C. (1990) 'A Note on Intention' *Criminal Law Review* 85.

Wilson, W. (1999) 'Doctrinal Rationality after *Woollin*' 62 *Modern Law Review* 448.

# 5

# Homicide

## Chapter objectives

By the end of this chapter you should have:

- An understanding of the requirements for establishing criminal liability for: (a) murder; (b) unlawful act manslaughter and (c) gross negligence manslaughter
- An understanding of the requirements for establishing the partial defence of loss of control
- An ability to apply the relevant law to a hypothetical set of facts and discuss whether criminal liability may be established for any of the offences listed above and whether the defence of loss of control can be established
- An ability to discuss and evaluate the *mens rea* of murder, the two-tier structure of the law of homicide and the loss of control defence.

## Introduction

In 2016 there were a total of 697 homicides in England and Wales.[1] As we will see in the course of this chapter, there are a wide range of homicides which vary significantly in terms of their heinousness and culpability. There are serial killers, sexually motivated child killers and terrorists. But we will also encounter honour killings, non-intentional deaths which occur during the commission of some other crime, battered women who kill their abusive partners, mercy killers and hapless medics who inadvertently cause death. One of the key questions we will be asking as we work through the chapter will be whether the existing law deals with these different types of killing appropriately. In other words, does the existing law respect the ladder principle (which we studied in Chapter 1)?

The chapter begins by describing the law of murder. It then moves on to the law of manslaughter. There are two categories of manslaughter: voluntary manslaughter and involuntary manslaughter. Voluntary manslaughter is where the defendant satisfies the *actus reus* and *mens rea* of murder but is able to plead a partial defence. There are three partial defences in total. We study two of them in this text.[2] The first is loss of control, which we examine in this chapter. The other is diminished responsibility, which we will study in Chapter 10. Involuntary manslaughter is where the defendant caused the victim's death without the *mens rea* of murder but is nonetheless sufficiently blameworthy to deserve being held criminally liable for the death. There are two forms of involuntary manslaughter: unlawful act manslaughter (sometimes referred to as constructive manslaughter); and gross negligence manslaughter. We study both of these in this chapter. The chapter finishes by outlining the Law Commission's proposals for restructuring the law of homicide.

## Murder

Before examining the definition of murder, it is important to first understand how those convicted of murder are sentenced.

### EXTRACT

### Murder (Abolition of Death Penalty) Act 1965

#### 1 Abolition of death penalty for murder

(1) No person shall suffer death for murder, and a person convicted of murder shall be sentenced to imprisonment for life.

Notice the word 'shall'. The sentencing court has no discretion; a sentence of life imprisonment must be imposed. It is mandatory.

When a sentencing court imposes a sentence of life imprisonment, it must state how many years the defendant must spend in prison before he can be considered for parole. Here the courts must apply the relevant provisions of the Criminal Justice Act 2003.[3]

---

[1] Office for National Statistics *Crime in England and Wales, Year Ending December 2016.* This figure covers the offences of murder, manslaughter, corporate manslaughter and infanticide.

[2] The third partial defence is suicide pact. This is governed by the Homicide Act 1957, s.4.

[3] See s.269 and sch.21.

This Act creates different categories of murder. For each category the statute states a starting point, which is a presumption of how long the defendant should spend in prison before he is eligible for release on parole. This starting point can be adjusted by the sentencing court if there are any aggravating or mitigating features. The starting points are as follows:

- For the most serious category the starting point is a whole life order (i.e. the defendant should never be released).[4] This category applies if the defendant was aged 21 or over at the time of the murder and includes cases where: he killed two or more persons and the killings involved a substantial degree of premeditation or planning, the abduction of the victim or sexual or sadistic conduct; he killed a child and the killing involved either abduction or a sexual or sadistic motive and he killed to advance a political, religious, racial or ideological cause.

- For the next category the starting point is 30 years. This category applies if the defendant was aged 18 or over at the time of the murder and includes cases where: he killed a police officer in the course of his duty; the killing involved a firearm or explosives; the killing was done for financial gain (such as during a robbery or in return for payment) and the killing was racially or religiously aggravated.

- For the next category the starting point is 25 years. This category applies if the defendant was aged 18 or over at the time of the murder and covers cases where the defendant took a knife or other weapon to the scene of the crime and used it to murder the victim.

- For the next category the starting point is 15 years. This category applies to all killings where the defendant was aged 18 or over at the time of the murder which do not fall into one of the previous categories.

- For the final category the starting point is 12 years. This category applies if the defendant was aged under 18 at the time of the killing.

Remember too that if a defendant serves his minimum term and is released, his release is not unconditional. He is released on a life licence. If he subsequently breaks the conditions of his release, or is found to pose a danger to the public, he can be immediately returned to prison.

It is important to understand the sentencing framework for murder in order to be able to evaluate the definition of the offence. As we will see in the following pages, the offence of murder has a broad scope. At one end of the spectrum are serial killers, sexually motivated sadistic murderers and terrorist killings. But at the other end of the spectrum are mercy killers and battered women who kill their abusive spouse. Everyone convicted of murder receives the mandatory life sentence. And for adults, the starting point for the least serious category of murder is 15 years. Many commentators believe that the sentencing framework for murder is too rigid and unjustifiably harsh on some defendants who are convicted of murder. This has resulted in many calls for the mandatory life sentence to be replaced with a discretionary life sentence – or, failing that, a greater range of partial defences to murder.

---

[4]In *Vinter v UK* (app no. 66069/09) the Grand Chamber of the European Court of Human Rights held that, for a life sentence to be compatible with Article 3 of the Convention, there has to be both a possibility of review and a prospect of release. In *R v McLoughlin and another* [2014] EWCA Crim 188 the Court of Appeal subsequently held that the judgment in *Vinter* did not mean that the imposition of whole life orders violates Article 3, since domestic law provides for the possibility of release in exceptional circumstances which render the whole life order no longer justifiable.

With this introduction out of the way, we can now examine how murder has been defined. You may be surprised to discover that there is in fact no statutory definition of the offence. However, case law has established that it has the following four requirements:

1. The victim was a person
2. The victim died
3. The defendant caused the victim's death
4. The defendant intended to kill the victim or cause the victim grievous bodily harm.

(Some definitions of murder also contain the following two requirements:

- The killing must have occurred during the 'Queen's peace'. This simply means that it is not murder to kill an enemy alien during a war.[5] In an exam problem question you can safely assume that the events took place during the Queen's peace and so it will not be necessary to mention this requirement.

- The killing must have been 'unlawful'. This simply means that the defendant is unable to plead any of the substantive defences (which we study in Chapter 11). In an answer to an exam problem question it is best to establish whether the *actus reus* and *mens rea* of murder are satisfied first, and if they are then go on to consider possible defences.)

Numbers 1, 2 and 3 on the list above are *actus reus* requirements. Number 4 is a *mens rea* requirement. We will work through them in turn.

## 1. The victim was a person

The key question here is when does life begin? For the purposes of the criminal law, the courts have held that a foetus becomes a person once it has emerged into the world and has an existence independent of its mother.[6] This means that a defendant who destroys a viable foetus is not guilty of murder or manslaughter. However, there are other offences which might apply, including procuring a miscarriage[7] and child destruction.[8]

It is also important to note that a defendant may be guilty of murder or manslaughter if he attacks a foetus pre-birth, the foetus is born alive but later dies as a result of the injuries sustained in the attack. This was confirmed by the House of Lords in *Attorney-General's Ref (No 3 of 1994)* [1998] AC 245 (which we studied at the end of the previous chapter, in the section on transferred *mens rea*).

## 2. The victim died

The key question here is when does life end? In *Airedale NHS Trust v Bland* [1993] AC 789 (the case involving Tony Bland, a victim of the Hillsborough disaster, which we studied in Chapter 3) the House of Lords held that legally a person is dead once their brain stem is dead (i.e. once they are brain dead).

---

[5] In *R v Adebolajo & another* [2014] EWCA Crim 2779 one of the men who killed Fusilier Lee Rigby in the Woolwich terrorist attack argued that the killing had not taken place under the Queen's peace since it was part of a war with the British Government. Rejecting this argument, the Court explained that the term 'Queen's peace' is concerned with the status of the victim as an enemy alien, and has 'nothing whatsoever' to do with the status of the killer ([33]).
[6] *R v Poulton* (1832) 5 C & P 329.
[7] Offences Against the Person Act 1861, s.58.
[8] Infant Life (Preservation) Act 1929.

### 3. The defendant caused the victim's death

The third requirement is that the defendant's conduct was a factual and legal cause of the victim's death. Here you apply the law governing causation that we studied in Chapter 3.

Note that it is possible to commit murder by act or by omission.[9] If you are answering an exam question which involves an omission, remember that you must show that the defendant breached a duty of care which he owed the victim before considering whether or not the defendant satisfies the *actus reus* of murder (see Chapter 3).

### 4. The defendant intended to kill the victim or cause the victim grievous bodily harm

To establish the *mens rea* of murder the prosecution must show that the defendant either intended to kill the victim or that the defendant intended to cause the victim grievous bodily harm. This was confirmed by the House of Lords in *R v Cunningham* [1982] AC 566.[10]

There are two points to note here:

- The prosecution may establish either direct intention or oblique intention (see Chapter 4 for the distinction between these two types of intention).

- As we will see in the next chapter, the House of Lords has held that grievous bodily harm ('GBH') simply means 'really serious' harm.[11] Examples of GBH include broken bones, injuries causing substantial loss of blood and injuries resulting in lengthy treatment or incapacity.

There has been much discussion of the *mens rea* of murder. This has focused on two important issues. First, it is sufficient to show that the defendant intended to cause the victim GBH. Some have argued that in this respect the *mens rea* of murder is too wide. Someone may satisfy the *mens rea* of murder even though they did not intend to kill and the possibility of the victim dying never crossed their mind. Second, only intention will suffice. Some have argued that in this respect the *mens rea* of murder is too narrow. A defendant who recklessly kills another person lacks the *mens rea* of murder even if he displayed a high degree of recklessness. We will consider each of these issues in turn.

#### i. Intention to cause GBH will suffice for the *mens rea* of murder: is this too wide?

The rule that an intention to cause GBH will suffice for the *mens rea* of murder is known as the 'GBH rule'. Although the GBH rule was reaffirmed by the House of Lords in *R v Cunningham*, there have been cases since then in which it has been criticised. For example, in *Attorney-General's Ref (No 3 of 1994)* [1998] AC 245 Lord Mustill stated:

> My Lords, murder is widely thought to be the gravest of crimes. One could expect a developed system to embody a law of murder clear enough to yield an unequivocal result on a given set of facts, a result which conforms with apparent justice and has a sound intellectual base. This is not so in England, where the law of homicide is permeated by anomaly, fiction, misnomer and obsolete reasoning. One conspicuous anomaly is the [GBH] rule which identifies the [*mens rea* of murder] not only with a conscious intention to kill but also with an intention to cause grievous bodily harm. It is, therefore, possible to commit a murder not only without wishing the death of the victim but without the

---

[9]An example of murder by omission is *R v Gibbins & Proctor* (1918) 13 Cr App R 134, which we studied in Chapter 3.

[10]A different case to the one we studied in the last chapter on recklessness!

[11]*DPP v Smith* [1961] AC 290.

least thought that this might be the result of the assault. Many would doubt the justice of this rule, which is not the popular conception of murder and (as I shall suggest) no longer rests on any intellectual foundation.

The GBH rule was also criticised by Lord Steyn in *R v Powell & English* [1999] 1 AC 1.

## EXTRACT

Read the following extract from Lord Steyn's judgment. What does he identify as the principal justification for the GBH rule? Why does he reject this justification?

What criticisms does Lord Steyn make of the GBH rule?

What amendment does Lord Steyn suggest to the *mens rea* of murder? Do you agree with his proposal?

### *R v Powell & English* [1999] 1 AC 1

### Lord Steyn

In English law a defendant may be convicted of murder who is in no ordinary sense a murderer. It is sufficient if it is established that the defendant had an intent to cause really serious bodily injury. This rule turns murder into a constructive crime. The fault element does not correspond to the conduct leading to the charge, i.e. the causing of death. A person is liable to conviction for a more serious crime than he foresaw or contemplated [...] This is a point of considerable importance. The Home Office records show that in the last three years for which statistics are available mandatory life sentences for murder were imposed in 192 cases in 1994; in 214 cases in 1995; and in 257 cases in 1996. Lord Windlesham, writing with great Home Office experience, has said that *a minority* of defendants convicted of murder have been convicted on the basis that they had an intent to kill: "Responses to Crime," vol. 3 (1996), at 342, n.29. That assessment does not surprise me. What is the justification for this position? There is an argument that, given the unpredictability whether a serious injury will result in death, an offender who intended to cause serious bodily injury cannot complain of a conviction of murder in the event of a death. But this argument is outweighed by the practical consideration that immediately below murder there is the crime of manslaughter for which the court may impose a discretionary life sentence or a very long period of imprisonment. Accepting the need for a mandatory life sentence for murder, the problem is one of classification. The present definition of the mental element of murder results in defendants being classified as murderers who are not in truth murderers. It happens both in cases where only one offender is involved and in cases resulting from joint criminal enterprises. It results in the imposition of mandatory life sentences when neither justice nor the needs of society require the classification of the case as murder and the imposition of a mandatory life sentence.

[...] There is available a precise and sensible solution, namely that a killing should be classified as murder if there is an intention to kill or an intention to cause really serious bodily harm coupled with awareness of the risk of death; 14th Report of the Law Revision Committee on Offences against the Person (1980) (Cmnd. 7844), p.14, para. 31, adopted in the Criminal Code for England and Wales (Law Com. No. 177) (1989), clause 54(1). This solution was supported by the House of Lords Select Committee on Murder and Life Imprisonment, H.L. Paper (1988–1989) No. 78-1, p.25, para.68.

In this extract Lord Steyn describes murder as a constructive crime – in other words, a crime of constructive liability. One of the principles we examined in Chapter 1 was the principle of correspondence. As Figure 5.1 shows, according to this principle the *mens rea* of a

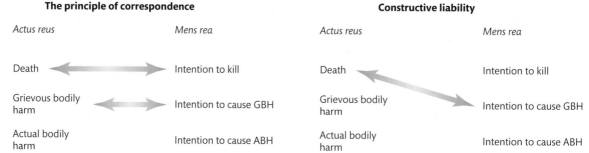

**Figure 5.1.** Murder as a crime of constructive liability

crime should correspond with its *actus reus*. So, applying this to murder, the principle states that the defendant should be shown to have had *mens rea* in relation to death, not merely GBH. The GBH rule violates this, and therefore means that murder is a crime of constructive liability. As Lord Steyn explains, the practical upshot of this is that a defendant may be guilty of murder even though the possibility of the victim dying never occurred to him.

In the following extract the Law Commission also criticises the GBH rule. It goes on to argue that the two-tier structure of our existing law of homicide (murder and manslaughter) is inadequate. As we will see later in the chapter, the Commission proposes a new, three-tier structure.

## EXTRACT

Why does the Law Commission criticise the GBH rule?

The Law Commission suggest that cases which involve a defendant who intended to cause GBH but not kill should be subdivided into two categories: those where the defendant realised that his conduct posed a serious risk of death and those where he did not. According to the Law Commission, where should each of these two subcategories fit in their proposed three-tier structure (top, middle or bottom tier)? What reasons does the Commission give? Do you agree?

### Law Commission (2006) *Murder, Manslaughter and Infanticide (Report No 304) HC 30*

1.17 Under the current law, D is liable for murder not only if he or she kills intentionally but also if he or she kills while intentionally inflicting harm which the jury considers to have been serious. In our view, the result is that the offence of murder is too wide. Even someone who reasonably believed that no one would be killed by their conduct and that the harm they were intentionally inflicting was not serious, can find themselves placed in the same offence category as the contract or serial killer. Here is an example:

D intentionally punches V in the face. The punch breaks V's nose and causes V to fall to the ground. In falling, V hits his or her head on the curb causing a massive and fatal brain haemorrhage.

1.18 This would be murder if the jury decided that the harm that D intended the punch to cause (the broken nose) can be described as 'serious'. Whilst it is clear that a person who kills in these circumstances should be guilty of a serious homicide offence, it is equally clear to the great majority of our consultees that the offence should not be the top tier or highest category offence.

[...]

1.20 The inclusion of all intent-to-do-serious-harm cases within murder distorts the sentencing process for murder. The fact that an offender only intended to do serious harm, rather than kill, is currently regarded as a mitigating factor that justifies the setting of a shorter initial custodial period as part of the mandatory life sentence. On the face of it, this seems perfectly reasonable. However, there is a strong case for saying that when an offence carries a *mandatory* sentence, there should be no scope for finding mitigation in the way in which the basic or essential fault elements come to be fulfilled.

1.21 We have been informed by research, carried out by Professor Barry Mitchell, into public opinion about murder. This shows that the public assumes that murder involves an intention to kill or its moral equivalent, namely a total disregard for human life. The latter may not be evident in a case where someone has intentionally inflicted harm the jury regards as serious, as when D intentionally breaks someone's nose. Indeed, some members of the public regarded deaths caused by intentionally inflicted harm that was not inherently life threatening as being in some sense "accidental".

1.22 Having said that, we do not recommend that killing through an intention to do serious injury should simply be regarded as manslaughter. Manslaughter is an inadequate label for a killing committed with that degree of culpability. In any event, to expand the law of manslaughter still further would be wrong because manslaughter is already an over-broad offence.

1.23 We will be recommending that the intent-to-do-serious-injury cases should be divided into two. Cases where D not only intended to do serious injury but also was aware that his or her conduct posed a serious risk of death should continue to fall within the highest category or top tier offence. This is warranted by the kind of total disregard for human life that such Ds show. They are morally equivalent to cases of intentional killing. Cases where D intended to do serious injury but was unaware of a serious risk of killing should fall (along with some instances of reckless killing) into a new middle tier homicide offence.

### ii. Recklessness will not suffice for the *mens rea* of murder: is this too narrow?

If a defendant lacked any intention to kill or cause GBH, he is not guilty of murder – even if he was reckless as to the possibility of killing the victim. Consider the following example. A terrorist plants a bomb and then contacts the authorities and warns them. He plants a live bomb instead of a fake one – so that the authorities will fear him and listen to him – but he doesn't want the bomb to explode because he fears that he will lose public support if innocent people are killed. He gives the warning some time before the bomb is set to explode, so that the public can be evacuated and a bomb disposal expert can defuse the bomb. However, the bomb explodes and kills the bomb disposal expert. On these facts it was not the defendant's direct intention to kill anyone or cause anyone GBH (he would not have regarded it as a failure if the bomb had been defused and no one had been harmed). Nor was it his oblique intention (serious harm to others was not a virtual certainty since the bomb might have been defused successfully). So notwithstanding the terrorist's disregard for human life, he would be not guilty of murder. His crime would be unlawful act manslaughter (which we study below).

Examples like this well-known 'terrorist example' have led some (including Lord Goff[12]) to suggest that the *mens rea* of murder is too narrow, and should be widened to include those who kill with a high degree of recklessness. In the following extract Andrew Ashworth discusses this proposal.

---

[12] 'The Mental Element in the Crime of Murder' (1988) 104 *Law Quarterly Review* 30.

## EXTRACT

According to Ashworth, what are the arguments for and against widening the *mens rea* of murder to include a high degree of recklessness?

### Ashworth, A. (1990) 'Reforming the Law of Murder'
*Criminal Law Review* 75

It may be argued, however, that there are some reckless killings which ought to be classified as murder, since they show such a high disregard for human life as to be socially and morally equivalent to many intentional killings. It is not difficult to accept the latter proposition, but it is difficult to identify with precision the characteristics of these cases. Perhaps the most frequent example is the terrorist bomber who places a bomb and then gives a warning, despite which death is caused by the ensuing explosion. It was this example and a number of actual cases which led Lord Goff to advocate the adoption in English law of the Scots definition of murder, which goes beyond an intention to kill and labels as murder a killing which displays "such wicked recklessness as to imply a disposition depraved enough to be regardless of the consequences." Glanville Williams has disputed whether all the cases used by Lord Goff would be regarded as "wickedly reckless." A further objection is that its vagueness is such as to transfer too much power to the jury. It is less a rule of law than a rule permitting juries to respond to what they see as the equity of the case. As Sheriff Gordon has written in relation to Scots law: "to say that 'A is guilty of murder when he kills with wicked recklessness' means only 'A is guilty of murder when he kills with such recklessness that he deserves to be treated as a murderer.'"

The question whether to widen the *mens rea* of murder was considered by a House of Lords Select Committee in 1989.[13] In the following extract Ashworth explains why he agreed with the Committee's recommendation that the *mens rea* of murder not be extended to include wicked recklessness.

## EXTRACT

Read the following extract. In light of your list of arguments for and against extending the *mens rea* of murder, do you agree with Ashworth and the Committee that the *mens rea* of murder should not be extended to include wicked recklessness?

### Ashworth, A. (1990) 'Reforming the Law of Murder'
*Criminal Law Review* 75

The Committee decided that "it is neither satisfactory nor desirable to distort [the principle that only intention will suffice for the *mens rea* of murder] in order to deal with the reckless terrorist and other 'wickedly' reckless killers, who will, in any event, be [guilty of manslaughter and] liable to imprisonment for life." This may be seen as a victory for the "rule of law" values of certainty

---

[13]*Report of the Select Committee on Murder and Life Imprisonment* (Session 1988–89, HL Paper 78).

and predictability over the merits of a vague test which would not only allow juries to reflect the subtler shades of moral and social culpability but also invite juries to return verdicts based on a distaste for the defendant's background, allegiance or general activities. Critics were quick to point out this gap between the Committee's proposals and the alleged public view that terrorist killings, even where a warning is given, should be murder. The reply to this is that the definition of the highest crime should not be broadened and loosened when there are many other offences (*e.g.* manslaughter, causing an explosion) to deal condignly with terrorist cases.

Whilst it is true that the terrorist in our example would be guilty of manslaughter and liable to life imprisonment, the Law Commission has argued that a manslaughter conviction would be insufficient. 'A manslaughter verdict', the Commission states, 'is an inadequate label for the offence'[14] (we studied the principle of fair labelling in Chapter 1). The Commission also offers the following two examples of cases where the defendant would be not guilty of murder but a manslaughter conviction would be inadequate.

## EXTRACT

Why would the defendants in the Law Commission's two examples be not guilty of murder?

Do you agree that a manslaughter conviction would be inadequate in these two examples?

### Law Commission (2005) A *New Homicide Act for England and Wales? A Consultation Paper* (Consultation Paper No 177)

EXAMPLE 2: In the small hours of the morning, D, knowing that a dwelling house is occupied by a rival in love, pours petrol through the letter box and sets light to it. The house burns down killing one or more of the sleeping occupants.

EXAMPLE 3: D lifts a large piece of concrete on to the parapet of a bridge over a busy road. He or she waits until a car is just about pass underneath the bridge and then pushes the piece of concrete off the parapet. It crushes to death one of the occupants of the car.

3.45 Suppose that, in both of these examples, the defendant says that his or her intention was simply to give the victims a severe fright but also admits that he or she went ahead despite knowing that it was likely that someone would be killed as a result of his or her action. The defendant says that he or she was not sure this would be the result, however, because (in example 1) the defendant knew the property had an exit at the back and (in example 2) the defendant thought the concrete might miss the car.

3.46 In both examples the defendant's admission is an admission of an exceptionally high degree of fault. At present, if the prosecution wishes to convict the defendant of murder they must at the very least show that the defendant foresaw death as the virtually certain consequence of his or her action. Even then, this only provides the basis for a possible inference

---

[14]Law Commission (2006) *Murder, Manslaughter and Infanticide* (Report No 304) HC 30, para 1.31.

by the jury that the defendant intended to kill or to do serious harm. Yet if one puts on one side this process of inference, there may sometimes be no significant moral difference between foresight of virtual certainty and foresight of high probability as such. So, justice is not served by putting the prosecution to this extra burden of proof.

The Law Commission goes on to argue that cases like these demonstrate a further reason why we need a new three-tier structure for the law of homicide. Under our existing two-tier structure, the terrorist and the defendants in these other two examples fall in the bottom tier (manslaughter). But under the Commission's proposed scheme they would fall in the middle tier, and so would be convicted of a more serious offence than manslaughter.

## Loss of control

The partial defence of loss of control was introduced by the Coroners and Justice Act 2009, replacing the partial defence of provocation. It is called a partial defence because, if successful, it does not result in the defendant being found not guilty of any crime. Instead it reduces the defendant's liability from murder to manslaughter.

Note too that loss of control is a special defence. It is only available on a charge of murder or being an accessory to murder. For all other crimes the fact that the defendant lost his self-control is not a defence (although it may be taken into account when sentencing). This is a common error in exam problem questions: students often make the mistake of discussing the loss of control defence even though the alleged offence is one of the non-fatal offences that we will study in the next chapter.

The requirements for the loss of control defence are set out in section 54 of the Act.

### EXTRACT

#### Coroners and Justice Act 2009

**54 Partial defence to murder: loss of control**

(1) Where a person ("D") kills or is a party to the killing of another ("V"), D is not to be convicted of murder if —

 (a) D's acts and omissions in doing or being a party to the killing resulted from D's loss of self-control,

 (b) the loss of self-control had a qualifying trigger, and

 (c) a person of D's sex and age, with a normal degree of tolerance and self-restraint and in the circumstances of D, might have reacted in the same or in a similar way to D.

[...]

(7) A person who, but for this section, would be liable to be convicted of murder is liable instead to be convicted of manslaughter.

(8) The fact that one party to a killing is by virtue of this section not liable to be convicted of murder does not affect the question whether the killing amounted to murder in the case of any other party to it.

This tells us that the defence has three requirements:

1. The defendant's conduct was the result of a loss of self-control
2. The loss of self-control had a qualifying trigger
3. A person of the defendant's age and sex, with a normal degree of tolerance and self-restraint and in the circumstances of the defendant, might have reacted in the same or in a similar way to the defendant.

Under the old law, the trial judge had to leave the defence of provocation to the jury if there was *any* evidence that the defendant was provoked to lose his self-control, however unlikely the defence was to succeed. This was regarded as unsatisfactory, not least because it created the possibility that an unmeritorious claim might succeed. The 2009 Act therefore requires the trial judge to 'undertake a much more rigorous evaluation of the evidence before the defence [can] be left to the jury'.[15] Section 54(5) states that 'sufficient evidence' must be adduced, which is defined in section 54(6) as evidence on which a jury could reasonably conclude that the defence *might* apply. This requires sufficient evidence to be adduced for all three of the requirements listed above.[16] If there is not sufficient evidence of any of the three requirements, the defence will not be left to the jury. But if there is sufficient evidence of all three requirements, the onus passes to the prosecution to disprove the defence beyond reasonable doubt (s.54(5)).

We will work through the three requirements for the defence in turn.

## 1. The defendant's conduct was the result of a loss of self-control

The first requirement is that the defendant had lost his self-control at the time of the killing. Note two points here:

- The Coroners and Justice Act 2009 does not define the term 'loss of self-control'. In *R v Jewell* [2014] EWCA Crim 414 the Court of Appeal accepted as correct David Ormerod's definition of the term as 'a loss of the ability to act in accordance with considered judgment or a loss of normal powers of reasoning'. In the later case *R v Gurpinar* [2015] EWCA Crim 178, the prosecution criticised this definition, arguing that it is potentially too broad and could include someone who merely loses their temper. Since the issue was not raised by the facts of the case, the Court opted not to discuss it and leave a decision for a future case where the issue arises.
- The question for this part of the defence is *not* whether it was reasonable for the defendant to lose his self-control. Rather, it is a subjective test: did the defendant lose his self-control or not? If so, then the first requirement for the defence is satisfied. If not, then the defence fails.

The question whether the defendant lost his self-control assumes that the defendant possessed powers of self-control to begin with. As Richard Holton and Stephen Shute explain in the following extract, some defendants will not be able to plead loss of control because they lacked the ability to exercise self-control in the first place.

---

[15] *R v Gurpinar* [2015] EWCA Crim 178, [14].

[16] *R v Gurpinar* [2015] EWCA Crim 178, [22]. For the argument that it is inappropriate to require the defendant to adduce 'sufficient evidence' of the last of the three requirements of the defence (the response of the normal person), see Storey, T. (2015) 'Loss of Control: "Sufficient Evidence" (Again)' 79 *Journal of Criminal Law* 154.

**EXTRACT**

What examples do Holton and Shute give of defendants who cannot plead loss of control because they lacked an ability to exercise self-control to begin with? Can you think of any other examples?

### Holton, R. and Shute, S. (2007) 'Self-Control in the Modern Provocation Defence' 27 *Oxford Journal of Legal Studies* 49

The subjective test is far more complex, and far more demanding, than has been generally realized. It requires not simply that agents must kill in response to provocation, but that they must kill *as a result of losing self-control* in response to provocation. We aim to take seriously the idea of loss of self-control. Once we do so, we find that the subjective test provides a substantial hurdle, for the simple reason that only an agent who antecedently possessed self-control can lose it as a result of provocation. To borrow Muddy Water's words, you can't lose what you ain't never had; nor, we might add, can you lose what you have already lost.

Irascibility and drunkenness plausibly fall into the class of characteristics that should result in the defendant failing the subjective test. Irascible agents have never gained self-control, drunks have already lost it.

In order to decide whether the defendant lost his self-control, the jury may take into account any past events that are relevant.[17] So they are not limited to looking just at the events that occurred at the time of the killing: the cumulative impact of past events may be taken into account.

Section 54 of the Coroners and Justice Act 2009 also offers the following guidance for juries trying to decide whether or not the defendant lost his self-control.

**EXTRACT**

### Coroners and Justice Act 2009

#### 54 Partial defence to murder: loss of control

[...]

(2)  For the purposes of subsection (1)(a), it does not matter whether or not the loss of control was sudden.

[...]

(4)  Subsection (1) does not apply if, in doing or being a party to the killing, D acted in a considered desire for revenge.

So the loss of self-control need not have been sudden, but the defendant must not have formed a considered desire for revenge.

Before moving on to the next part of the defence, it is important to consider how the loss of self-control requirement applies in three specific contexts: mercy killings; revenge killings and cases involving domestic abuse.

---

[17]*R v Dawes* [2013] EWCA Crim 322.

### i. Mercy killings

In *R v Cocker* [1989] Crim LR 740 the defendant's wife suffered from an incurable disease. She had become severely incapacitated and repeatedly begged Cocker to kill her. One morning, after deliberately keeping Cocker awake for most of the night, she woke him by clawing his back and demanded that he kill her. Cocker put a pillow over her face and asphyxiated her. He later explained that her pleas to have her life ended had become too much for him. At trial, the trial judge ruled that there was no evidence of provocation and so Cocker pleaded guilty to murder. He then appealed against the trial judge's ruling. The Court of Appeal upheld his murder conviction. The Court explained that Cocker had not suffered a loss of self-control. He was not out of control at the time he killed his wife. He was in full control of himself and had acted calmly and deliberately.

Although *R v Cocker* was a case under the old law, the same principle would apply today. A mercy killer will not be able to plead loss of control unless he suffered a loss of self-control at the time of the killing. This is unlikely to be the case, since the notion of a mercy killing suggests a conscious decision to relieve the victim's suffering. If a mercy killer is to avoid a murder conviction and the mandatory life sentence, the only possible partial defence is therefore diminished responsibility (which also may well not be available, as we'll see in Chapter 10). Some, including Keating and Bridgeman, have accordingly argued for the creation of a partial defence specifically for mercy killers.[18]

### ii. Revenge killings

As we have seen, section 54(4) states that the loss of control defence is unavailable if the defendant 'acted in a considered desire for revenge'. The word 'considered' is important here. The Court of Appeal in *R v Clinton, Parker & Evans* [2012] EWCA Crim 2 approved the following explanation of when section 54(4) applies:

> 129 [...] An act of retribution as a result of a deliberate and considered decision to get your own back, that is one that has been thought about. If you are sure that what the defendant did was to reflect on what had happened and the circumstances in which he found himself and decided to take his revenge [...] that would not have been a loss of self-control as the law requires

So section 54(4) would *not* apply to a defendant who momentarily loses his self-control and acts vengefully, because on these facts the desire for revenge was not 'considered'.

An example (from the old law) of when section 54(4) would apply is *R v Ibrams & Gregory* (1981) 74 Cr App R 154. Ibrams had been bullied and terrorised by his fiancée's former boyfriend – the victim – for some time. Ibrams' friend Gregory had also been targeted. They had contacted the police twice but no effective action had been taken, so they formed a plan. Ibrams' fiancée would get the victim drunk and take him to his bed. She would leave the front door open for Ibrams and Gregory, who would then burst in, attack the victim and break both his legs. They carried out the plan. Following the attack the victim died. Ibrams and Gregory were convicted of murder. The Court of Appeal upheld their murder convictions, ruling that there was no evidence that the defendants had lost their self-control. On the contrary, they had taken time to construct a plan and then carried it out. If a case like this occurred under the new loss of control defence, the outcome would be the same: section 54(4) would apply. The defendants acted in a considered desire for revenge, so the defence would be unavailable.

---

[18]Keating, H. and Bridgeman, J. (2012) 'Compassionate Killings: The Case for a Partial Defence' 75 *Modern Law Review* 697.

### iii. Slow-burn reactions and domestic abuse cases

Under the old law, a defendant could only plead the defence of provocation if his loss of self-control was 'sudden and temporary'.[19] As we have seen, things are different under the new defence. Section 54(2) states that it does not matter whether or not the loss of control was sudden. The reason for this change was to make allowance for slow-burn reactions (where a person's anger and resentment festers and then some time later explodes). The Government explained that slow-burn reactions are associated particularly with domestic abuse cases.[20] The old law's requirement for a 'sudden and temporary' loss of self-control therefore presented an obstacle to battered women who seek to plead this defence after killing their abusive partners.

An important case under the old law which illustrates a slow-burn reaction is *R v Ahluwalia* [1992] 4 All ER 889.[21] The defendant in this case was Kiranjit Ahluwalia. Her family arranged for her to marry the victim, Deepak Ahluwalia, whom she had never previously met. She suffered violence and abuse from the outset of the marriage. After suffering for many years, her husband's violence intensified in January 1989. For example, at Easter that year Ahluwalia was knocked unconscious, suffered a broken tooth, swollen lip and was off work for five days. In addition to this Ahluwalia discovered in March 1989 that her husband was having an affair with a woman he worked with. He would taunt her with this relationship. Despite all of this Ahluwalia wished to hold the marriage together, partly for the sake of their children and partly out of a sense of duty. In fact, in April 1989 her husband left her and Ahluwalia wrote a grovelling letter begging that he come back. On the evening of 8 May 1989 Ahluwalia tried to talk to her husband about their relationship, but he refused and said it was over. He demanded money from her for a telephone bill, and said he would beat her if she did not give him the money the next morning. Ahluwalia went to bed but couldn't sleep, thinking about his threat to beat her the next morning and his insistence that their relationship was over.

A few days earlier Ahluwalia had bought a can of petrol, which she had left outside. At 2:30 in the morning she got up, went downstairs, poured two pints of petrol into a bucket (to make it easier to throw), lit a candle on the gas cooker and carried these things upstairs. She also took an oven glove and a stick. She went into her husband's bedroom, threw in some petrol, lit the stick from the candle and threw it into the room. She then went to her son's bedroom, dressed him and went downstairs. Neighbours who saw her said she looked calm. Her husband died from his injuries.

At trial Ahluwalia was convicted of murder. On appeal, defence counsel produced fresh medical evidence, which showed that Ahluwalia had been suffering from a depressive illness. Since this evidence could potentially form the basis of a defence of diminished responsibility, a retrial was ordered. Before the retrial took place the prosecution accepted a plea of guilty to manslaughter on the grounds of diminished responsibility. Ahluwalia was sentenced to 40 months' imprisonment (the time she had already served) and was released immediately.[22]

Importantly, at Ahluwalia's appeal the Court of Appeal also discussed the defence of provocation. Lord Taylor CJ confirmed that the defence would only apply if the defendant's loss of self-control was 'sudden and temporary', but did add that as long as the loss of control was sudden and temporary it didn't matter if it didn't immediately follow the provocative event:

---

[19]*R v Duffy* [1949] 1 All ER 932.
[20]*Murder, Manslaughter and Infanticide: Proposals for Reform of the Law* (Consultation Paper CP 19/08, 2008).
[21]See also *R v Thornton* [1992] 1 All ER 306.
[22]Her story has since been made into a film, *Provoked* (2006).

We accept that the subjective element in the defence of provocation would not as a matter of law be negatived simply because of the delayed reaction in such cases, provided that there was at the time of the killing a "sudden and temporary loss of self-control" caused by the alleged provocation. However, the longer the delay and the stronger the evidence of deliberation on the part of the defendant, the more likely it will be that the prosecution will negative provocation.

In spite of Lord Taylor CJ's judgment, it remained unlikely that women like Ahluwalia would be able to plead provocation. It was difficult to regard Ahluwalia's actions as a 'sudden and temporary' loss of self-control. She had been lying awake thinking what to do. She went and collected the petrol and other items, lit a candle and then took the items upstairs. All of this suggested thought and planning, which are the antithesis of a 'sudden and temporary' loss of self-control. The Government believed that removing the requirement that the loss of self-control was 'sudden and temporary' would enable more victims of domestic abuse to plead the new loss of control defence.

---

### ACTIVITY

Imagine a case like *R v Ahluwalia* occurred today. In your opinion, would the defendant satisfy this first requirement for the loss of control defence? In other words, did Ahluwalia suffer a loss of self-control?

NB: When answering this question, you may find it helpful to bear in mind the following statement from the Court of Appeal in *R v Clinton, Parker & Evans*:

10 [...] In reality, the greater the level of deliberation, the less likely it will be that the killing followed a true loss of self-control.

---

## 2. The loss of self-control had a qualifying trigger

Under the old law, the subjective limb of the defence of provocation simply required that the defendant lost his self-control in response to things said or done.[23] This was criticised for being both too wide and too narrow:

- It was regarded as too wide because it meant that defendants could seek to plead provocation in cases where the victim's conduct was trivial or blameless. In *R v Doughty* [1986] 83 Cr App R 319, for example, the defendant killed his baby son. He said he lost his self-control because he was fatigued and the baby had cried persistently despite being fed, changed and other attempts made to settle him. The Court of Appeal reduced his conviction from murder to manslaughter on the basis of provocation.

- It was regarded as too narrow because it focused exclusively on one emotion: anger. This was widely regarded as problematic on the basis that it was gender-biased. Men are more likely to lash out in anger than women. Psychiatrists explain that a person is more likely to lose his self-control in response to provocation if the provoker is physically smaller and weaker. If the provoker is stronger the person is less likely to lose his self-control. This is why abused women tend to attack their abusers when they are off-guard.

---

[23]Homicide Act 1957, s.3.

The Coroners and Justice Act 2009 sought to address each of these criticisms of the old law by introducing the requirement that the defendant's loss of control was caused by a qualifying trigger. The qualifying triggers are defined in section 55.

---

**EXTRACT**

## Coroners and Justice Act 2009

### 55 Meaning of *"qualifying trigger"*

(1)   This section applies for the purposes of section 54.

(2)   A loss of self-control had a qualifying trigger if subsection (3), (4) or (5) applies.

(3)   This subsection applies if D's loss of self-control was attributable to D's fear of serious violence from V against D or another identified person.

(4)   This subsection applies if D's loss of self-control was attributable to a thing or things done or said (or both) which —

    (a)  constituted circumstances of an extremely grave character, and

    (b)  caused D to have a justifiable sense of being seriously wronged.

(5)   This subsection applies if D's loss of self-control was attributable to a combination of the matters mentioned in subsections (3) and (4).

---

The first qualifying trigger (in s.55(3)) responds to the concern that the old law was too narrow by creating a qualifying trigger based on fear. It applies where the defendant's loss of self-control was attributable to the defendant's fear of serious violence from the victim. The second qualifying trigger (in s.55(4)) responds to the concern that the old law was too wide by limiting the availability of the defence in cases where the defendant acted in anger. It only applies if the defendant had a justifiable sense of being seriously wronged as a result of things done or said (or both) which constituted circumstances of an extremely grave character. We will look at each of these qualifying triggers in turn. (Note that there is also a third qualifying trigger (in s.55(5)), which applies where the defendant's loss of self-control was attributable to a combination of the other two qualifying triggers.)

### i. D feared serious violence from V against D or another identified person

A defendant who fears serious violence and uses force to defend himself will normally plead the defence of prevention of crime or private defence (which we study in Chapter 11). Defendants will prefer to plead these defences because if successful they result in a complete acquittal, whereas loss of control is only a partial defence. However, as we will see later in the book, prevention of crime and private defence are only available if the amount of force used by the defendant was reasonable. A defendant who is charged with murder and found to have used an excessive amount of force to defend himself will therefore be unable to plead prevention of crime or private defence. Under the old law, such a defendant had no other defence and so would have been guilty of murder.

There were many who believed this to be too harsh. They argued that a defendant who genuinely feared serious violence but used excessive force to defend himself only deserves to be convicted of manslaughter, not murder. Following the changes made by the Coroners and Justice Act 2009, such defendants may now plead loss of control.

Note the following four points about this qualifying trigger:

- The defendant must have feared *serious* violence.
- There only has to be *fear* of serious violence. There is no requirement that violence was actually used.
- The threat of violence need not necessarily have been directed at the defendant. It may have been directed at another identified person. So, for example, the qualifying trigger applies where the defendant fears that his child will suffer serious violence from the victim.
- The threat of violence must emanate from the victim. The defence is unavailable if the defendant fears serious violence from one person (T) but kills someone else (V).

As we have already seen, in practice it was very difficult for women like Kiranjit Ahluwalia to successfully plead the old defence of provocation. The provocation defence not only required that the defendant suffered a 'sudden and temporary' loss of self-control. It also focused exclusively on anger. The Government believed that adding this new qualifying trigger based on fear of serious violence would make the loss of control defence available to victims of domestic abuse. It stated that the defence would apply:[24]

> where a victim of sustained abuse kills his or her abuser in order to thwart an attack which is anticipated but not immediately imminent

However, commentators have pointed out that a qualifying trigger based on fear of serious violence sits uneasily alongside the requirement that the defendant suffered a loss of self-control. In the following extract Susan Edwards explains that there is a tension between the kind of fear suffered by victims of domestic abuse and the law's requirement of a momentary eruption in which the battered woman experiences a loss of self-control.

## EXTRACT

Read the following extract. What characterises the kind of fear that victims of domestic abuse suffer? Why is such fear hard to reconcile with the requirement of a loss of self-control?

According to Edwards, how will this tension likely be resolved? In your opinion, is this satisfactory?

### Edwards, S. (2010) 'Anger and Fear as Justifiable Preludes for Loss of Self-Control', *Journal of Criminal Law* 74(3), 223–241

Instead of an eruptive moment, as is anger, fear is an enduring underlying state. For the abused woman living with and in domestic violence, the state of fear is in the continuous present. Victims of domestic violence do not suffer from general anticipatory fear, i.e. the fear we all might experience when walking unaccompanied at night in a deserted place that we might fall prey to attack. Instead they suffer from an extreme and continuous fear or state of continuous terror. Fear, therefore does not sit comfortably with loss of self-control as an eruptive moment. Fear is a breakdown in control; it is an inability to control circumstances because of an outside

---

[24]Ministry of Justice (2008) *Murder, Manslaughter and Infanticide: Proposals for Reform of the Law* (Consultation Paper CP 19/08).

force rather than an inner eruptive response. It may be accompanied by a state of despair, a feeling of powerlessness and frustration of being robbed of effective agency, but it by no means follows that a person who lives in a state of fear is passive. As Burke noted, 'No passion so effectively robs the mind of all power of acting and reasoning as fear'. In the tenth book of *The Iliad*, the two Greek leaders aimed a spear at the head of a Trojan, 'He stood still and fell into a gibbering terror-his teeth began to chatter in his mouth and he went white with fear ... He burst into tears ... His body was trembling'. Yet the new definition of provocation requires fear, like anger, to result in a loss of self-control which is predicated on a roused state. So, what exactly will that fear-loss of self-control look like? Under the previous defence of provocation, the battered woman's fear was constructed around an habituated toleration of male violence which saps and undermines her will until the victim snaps. As Helena Kennedy once expressed it, 'the final surrender of frayed elastic'. But 'snapping' or 'last straw' articulations of cumulative provocation, and the loss of self-control of battered women, were so expressed as a means of bringing the battered woman within the ambit of anger-provocation-loss of self-control, which hitherto required an immediate response to an act done by the deceased. And to further bolster such an ill-fitting defence the battered woman syndrome typology was developed to emphasise that her fragile mental state was of relevance to capacity arguments.

Such expressions may now be formulated under the defence of fear-loss of self-control, s. 55(3), or anger-loss of self-control under s. 55(4), or both (s. 55(5)). The predicament of Pauline Wyatt sums up this dualism of fear and snapping or breaking, 'I was frightened to death of him ... I couldn't take any more'. It must also be understood that expressions of anger and fear are linguistic devices, and represent attempts by the defendant to negotiate the legal outcome, rather than a true reflection of an underlying inner state. Joanna Bourke writes, 'Fear acquires meaning through cultural language and rites ... Emotions enter the historical archive only to the extent to which they transcend the insularity of individual psychological experience and present the self in the public realm'. A new set of fear descriptors is therefore destined to enter the legal arena and it will be for the courts to identify the evidence that can bear upon it.

### ii. D had a justifiable sense of being seriously wronged as a result of things done or said (or both) which constituted circumstances of an extremely grave character

The second qualifying trigger applies where the defendant had a justifiable sense of being seriously wronged as a result of things done or said (or both) which constituted circumstances of an extremely grave character. As we saw above, the aim of this trigger was to impose some limitations on when defendants who lash out in anger may plead the defence. However, the wording used in section 55(4) has been criticised for being vague.[25] When will a sense of being seriously wronged be justifiable? And what constitutes circumstances of an extremely grave character?

As Figure 5.2 illustrates, when answering an exam problem question there are four steps to work through to decide whether or not this qualifying trigger applies.

The first step is to determine whether the defendant had a sense of being seriously wronged. The Court of Appeal in *R v Clinton, Parker & Evans* explained that this is a subjective test based on the defendant's own perception. So the question is whether the defendant himself believed he had been seriously wronged.

The second step is to determine whether the defendant's sense that he had been seriously wronged was justifiable. The Court of Appeal in *R v Clinton, Parker & Evans* explained that this must be assessed objectively. In *R v Dawes* [2013] EWCA Crim 322 the

---

[25]See, for example, Simester, A.P., Spencer, J.R., Stark, F., Sullivan, G.R. & Virgo, G.J. (2016) *Simester and Sullivan's Criminal Law: Theory and Doctrine* (6th edn) Oxford: Hart Publishing, p401.

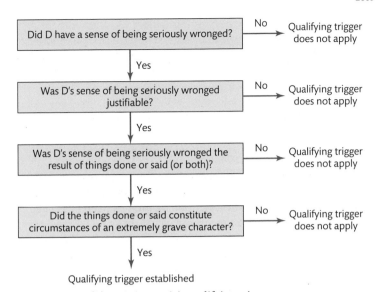

Figure 5.2. An overview of the section 55(4) qualifying trigger

Court of Appeal considered three separate appeals against conviction. Two of these involved the question whether the defendant's sense of being seriously wronged was justifiable. In the first the defendant, Mark Hatter, fatally stabbed his girlfriend following the break-up of their relationship. The Lord Chief Justice stated:

> 65 [...] Dealing with it generally, we agree that the fact of the break-up of a relationship, of itself, will not normally constitute circumstances of an extremely grave character and entitle the aggrieved party to feel a justifiable sense of being seriously wronged.

This suggests that events which form part of the ordinary trials and tribulations of life are unlikely to be sufficient for the purposes of this qualifying trigger. Indeed, the Government stated that this qualifying trigger should only apply in 'situations which go far beyond what anyone could reasonably be expected to deal appropriately with and which may warrant a more sympathetic response in the form of a manslaughter rather than a murder conviction'.[26] One of the examples it gave was where a woman who is raped kills the rapist after he taunts her.

In the other appeal the defendant, Barry Bowyer, and the victim, Gary Suller, knew each other and knew that they were both having a relationship with the same woman, Katie Gilmore. One evening, Bowyer broke into Suller's home in order to commit a burglary. However, Suller returned home. Bowyer claimed that he killed Suller because he lost his self-control in response to Suller attacking him and making provocative comments about Katie Gilmore. The Lord Chief Justice stated:

> 66 [...] The appellant was a self-confessed burglar. He deliberately entered the home of the deceased in order to steal property, to sell it to feed his drug habit. He deliberately targeted the house, taking every precaution to avoid detection. At the very best, he suggests that he just snapped when, following the householder's return, he, the householder, reacted violently to the presence of the burglar in his home and used deliberately insulting remarks about the appellant's girlfriend. To that the somewhat

---

[26]Ministry of Justice (2008) *Murder, Manslaughter and Infanticide: Proposals for Reform of the Law* (Consultation Paper CP 19/08) para 33.

colloquial answer is, "So what"? If either of these men was justified in losing his self-control, it was the deceased. The deceased was entitled to say and do anything reasonable, including the use of force, to eject the burglar from his home. Even taking the appellant's evidence at face value (and we bear in mind that the jury must have rejected it) it is absurd to suggest that the entirely understandable response of the deceased to finding a burglar in his home provided the appellant with the remotest beginnings of a basis for suggesting that he had any justifiable sense of being wronged, let alone seriously wronged.

So whether or not the defendant's sense that he had been seriously wronged was justifiable must be assessed objectively. What is uncertain, however, is whether the defendant's particular circumstances can be taken into account. Imagine the following example (which is based on a case decided under the old law[27]). One evening the defendant, who has strongly held religious beliefs, finds his teenage daughter in her bedroom with a young man. This is in spite of warnings he has given her previously. The defendant is so angry that he lashes out and kills his daughter. On these facts it would seem that the defendant had a sense that he had been seriously wronged. But was this objectively justifiable? The answer to this question may vary depending on whether or not the defendant's strongly held religious beliefs may be taken into account.[28] Yet at present it is unclear whether these beliefs would be considered.

The third step in Figure 5.2 is to ask whether the defendant's sense of being seriously wronged was the result of things done or said (or both). In other words, the defendant's grievance must have been due to some human activity. So if the defendant was extremely upset because his house had been flooded in a freak rain storm, this qualifying trigger would not apply.

The final step is to ask whether the things that were said or done constituted circumstances of an extremely grave character. The Court of Appeal in *R v Clinton, Parker & Evans* confirmed that whether or not the circumstances were extremely grave must be assessed objectively. As with the second step above, it would seem that circumstances will only qualify as extremely grave if they go beyond the ordinary ups and downs of everyday life.

### iii. Restrictions on what may constitute a qualifying trigger

So far we have studied what the qualifying triggers are. But the statute goes on to list three specific things which may *not* amount to a qualifying trigger. These can be found in section 55(6).

---

## EXTRACT

### Section 55(6) of the Coroners and Justice Act 2009

(6)   In determining whether a loss of self-control had a qualifying trigger –

(a)   D's fear of serious violence is to be disregarded to the extent that it was caused by a thing which D incited to be done or said for the purpose of providing an excuse to use violence;

(b)   a sense of being seriously wronged by a thing done or said is not justifiable if D incited the thing to be done or said for the purpose of providing an excuse to use violence;

(c)   the fact that a thing done or said constituted sexual infidelity is to be disregarded.

---

[27]*R v Mohammed* [2005] EWCA Crim 1880.
[28]Of course, the loss of control defence will only apply if the defendant also satisfies the third requirement for the defence, which we study below.

The first two exclusions are relatively straightforward. A defendant may not rely on the fear of serious violence qualifying trigger if he: (1) incited the victim to cause him fear; and (2) did this *in order* to provide himself with an excuse to use violence. So suppose Harold forms a plan. He persistently provokes Peter until Peter reacts violently. Harold then attacks Peter, kills him and says, 'Peter attacked me and I feared for my life'. On these facts, section 55(6)(a) states that Harold may not rely on the fear of serious violence qualifying trigger.

Similarly, a defendant may not rely on the justifiable sense of being seriously wronged qualifying trigger if he: (1) incited the victim to provoke him; and (2) did this *in order* to provide an excuse to use violence. So suppose Harold forms a plan. He persistently irritates Peter until Peter starts shouting gravely provocative comments back. Harold then attacks Peter, kills him and says 'Peter insulted me so gravely that I lost my temper and lashed out'. On these facts, section 55(6)(b) states that Harold may not rely on the justifiable sense of being seriously wronged qualifying trigger.

Whilst these two exclusions are straightforward, it is questionable whether they are in fact necessary. In *R v Dawes* the Lord Chief Justice commented:

> 58 [...] One may wonder (and the judge would have to consider) how often a defendant who is out to incite violence could be said to "fear" serious violence; often he may be welcoming it. Similarly, one may wonder how such a defendant may have a justifiable sense of being seriously wronged if he successfully incites someone else to use violence towards him.

The third exclusion, found in section 55(6)(c), has generated much comment. It states that, where a defendant claims to have had a justifiable sense of being seriously wronged, anything said or done that 'constituted sexual infidelity' must be disregarded. The aim of this provision is to ensure that the loss of control defence is unavailable to men who kill their partners after discovering that they have been unfaithful. The Government explained:

> It is quite unacceptable for a defendant who has killed an unfaithful partner to seek to blame the victim for what occurred. We want to make it absolutely clear that sexual infidelity on the part of the victim can never justify reducing a murder charge to manslaughter.

However, there are several issues regarding the wording of section 55(6)(c):

- Not all cases involving infidelity fall within section 55(6)(c), only those which involve 'sexual' infidelity. So if Harold kills his wife after discovering that she has been having a sexual relationship with another man, section 55(6)(c) would apply. But if Harold kills his wife after discovering that she has been dating another man, but the relationship was not yet a sexual one, it seems that section 55(6)(c) would not apply.

- The word 'infidelity' suggests an ongoing relationship. The relationship need not be a marriage or a civil partnership. It is sufficient that the parties have a mutual understanding.[29] However, the word 'infidelity' means that section 55(6)(c) would not apply if there never was a relationship or if the relationship has already ended. So if a jealous stalker kills the victim when he finds her having sex with another man,[30] section 55(6)(c) would not apply because there was no infidelity: the stalker was not in a

---

[29]*R v Clinton, Parker & Evans* [2012] EWCA Crim 2, [19].
[30]This example is based on the Australian case *R v Stingel* [1990] 171 CLR 312.

relationship with the victim. Or suppose Harold's wife tells him that their marriage is over. The next day Harold returns home to collect some of his belongings and discovers his wife having sex with another man. Section 55(6)(c) would not apply because there was no infidelity: the relationship was over. These are fine and arguably tenuous distinctions.

- Whilst it is clear how a thing that is 'done' can constitute sexual infidelity, it is less obvious how a thing that is 'said' can. If a husband hears his wife say 'I love you' to another man this may be evidence of sexual infidelity, but it does not necessarily 'constitute' it. Moreover, suppose that in the heat of an argument the victim falsely boasts to her spouse that she has had sex with other men simply in order to hurt his feelings. The statement cannot 'constitute' sexual infidelity since it is false, but the fact it is untrue does not mean it will be any less hurtful and provocative. The Court of Appeal in *R v Clinton, Parker & Evans* stated, 'We are required to make sense of this provision'. Saying that it would be illogical for section 55(6)(c) to apply to statements of sexual infidelity which are true but not ones which are false, the Court held that admissions of sexual infidelity (even if untrue) cannot amount to a qualifying trigger. Nor do reports (by others) of sexual infidelity.[31]

These interpretative difficulties have led Andrew Ashworth to describe section 55(6)(c) as having 'more than [its] fair share of obscurities' and as 'little more than a crass attempt to level the playing field'.[32] In a series of interviews conducted by Kate Fitz-Gibbon, professionals working within the criminal justice system also criticised the provision.

## EXTRACT

### Fitz-Gibbon, K. (2013) 'Replacing Provocation in England and Wales: Examining the Partial Defence of Loss of Control' 40 *Journal of Law and Society* 280

Interestingly, however, rather than welcoming the exclusion of such cases from the new partial defence, respondents across all samples interviewed were overwhelmingly critical of this provision in the formulation of the new defence. Legal counsel respondents described the exclusion as 'incredibly convoluted' (UKCounselE) and 'barmy' (UKCounselQ), while one judicial respondent posed that it was 'ill-advised' and 'bad law' (UKJudgeB). Similarly, policy respondents described the sexual infidelity provision as 'very problematic' (UKPolicyA), 'dire' (UKPolicyB), and 'really unnecessary' (UKPolicyC). These criticisms were often based upon respondents' belief that the exclusion of a particular situation was not conducive to good law-making and that it would lead to significant questions surrounding the situations in which the new partial defence would and would not apply. In explaining this perceived problem, a senior member of the English judiciary commented that:

> to try to produce specific subcategories of conduct that couldn't amount to a defence was not good law-making, it was better to lay down the general principles and provide the judicial check mechanism rather than try and carve out an additional specific exception. (UKJudgeA)

This judicial respondent further stated that the exclusion was 'unwise' for two key reasons: it was 'unnecessary' given that traditional sexual infidelity defences had lost favour with juror members

---

[31] *R v Clinton, Parker & Evans* [2012] EWCA Crim 2.
[32] Ashworth, A. (2012) Commentary on *R v Clinton, Parker & Evans* Crim LR 543.

in recent years, and that one should 'never say never' because 'there may be cases of which sexual infidelity forms a part, where a properly directed jury might say on the particular facts of this case we do think there is' an argument for a partial defence to succeed (UKJudgeA).

In agreement, other respondents also considered that there was no need to overtly exclude sexual infidelity, because, where unreasonably used, juries could discount it themselves. As one counsel respondent noted, 'it should be left completely to a jury with the usual directions' (UKCounselQ). In supporting the ability of the jury to adequately assess the individual circumstances of such cases, a policy respondent argued that:

> you have to trust the jury to use its common sense and I think what has happened here is that there has been an over-engineering of the law to try and make sure that juries can't consider certain things (UKPolicyA).

These viewpoints reflect a shared view amongst several respondents interviewed that juries inject an important community value judgement into the evaluation and categorization of differing culpabilities in homicide cases, a judgement that respondents believed should not be overridden by legislation.

The central issue in *R v Clinton, Parker & Evans* was whether section 55(6)(c) applies not only where sexual infidelity is the only element relied on to establish a qualifying trigger, but also where it forms part of the context for another, admissible, qualifying trigger. The defendant in this case was Jon-Jacques Clinton. He and the victim, his wife Dawn Clinton, had been married for almost ten years and had two children together. Two weeks before her death, they separated. Dawn went to live with her parents, but they continued to spend time together with the children as a family. On the day of the killing Clinton, who had been on medication for depression, looked at several websites containing material on suicide. He also logged into Dawn's Facebook account and found photos of her with another man, including some which were sexually explicit. That afternoon Clinton confronted Dawn. She told him that she had had sex with five different men, going into graphic detail. She also noticed that he had been looking at suicide websites and taunted him about this, saying he didn't have the nerve and 'it would have been easier if you had, for all of us'. Clinton then attacked her, striking her with a piece of wood and strangling her. At trial he was convicted of murder. The trial judge ruled that the jury should not be asked to consider the possibility of a defence of loss of control. She explained that, according to section 55(6)(c), Dawn's description of having sex with other men had to be disregarded. Once these remarks were disregarded, all that was left was Dawn's remarks about Clinton not having the nerve to commit suicide. The trial judge held that these remarks alone provided insufficient evidence of circumstances of an extremely grave character and a justifiable sense of being seriously wronged. On appeal, Clinton challenged the trial judge's ruling.

The Court of Appeal held that the trial judge had been wrong not to ask the jury to consider a possible defence of loss of control. It accordingly allowed Clinton's appeal and ordered a retrial. The Court stated that the section 55(6)(c) exclusion only applies where sexual infidelity *on its own* is claimed to constitute a qualifying trigger. Where sexual infidelity arises for consideration in the context of other matters which may constitute a qualifying trigger, the section 55(6)(c) exclusion does not apply. Applying this, the Lord Chief Justice explained that Dawn's remarks about Clinton not having the nerve to commit suicide had to be evaluated in the context of the evidence of Dawn's sexual infidelity.

## EXTRACT

Read the following extract from the judgment of the Lord Chief Justice. What reasons does he give for saying that the section 55(6)(c) exclusion does not apply when the sexual infidelity forms part of the context for another, admissible, qualifying trigger?

### R v Clinton, Parker & Evans [2012] EWCA Crim 2

#### Lord Judge CJ

23 [...] A much more formidable and difficult example would be the defendant who kills her husband when she suddenly finds him having enthusiastic, consensual sexual intercourse with her sister. Taken on its own, the effect of the legislation is that any loss of control consequent on such a gross betrayal would be totally excluded from consideration as a qualifying trigger. Let us for the purposes of argument take the same example a little further. The defendant returns home unexpectedly and finds her spouse or partner having consensual sexual intercourse with her sister (or indeed with anyone else), and entirely reasonably, but vehemently, complains about what has suddenly confronted her. The response by the unfaithful spouse or partner, and/ or his or her new sexual companion, is to justify what he had been doing, by shouting and screaming, mercilessly taunting and deliberately using hurtful language which implies that she, not he, is responsible for his infidelity. The taunts and distressing words, which do not themselves constitute sexual infidelity, would fall to be considered as a possible qualifying trigger. The idea that, in the search for a qualifying trigger, the context in which such words are used should be ignored represents an artificiality which the administration of criminal justice should do without. And if the taunts by the unfaithful partner suggested that the sexual activity which had just been taking place was infinitely more gratifying than any earlier sexual relationship with the defendant, are those insults – in effect using sexual infidelity to cause deliberate distress – to be ignored? On the view of the legislation advanced for our consideration by [counsel for the prosecution], they must be. Yet, in most criminal cases, as our recent judgment in the context of the riots and public order demonstrates, context is critical.

24 We considered the example of the wife who has been physically abused over a long period, and whose loss of self-control was attributable to yet another beating by her husband, but also, for the first time, during the final beating, taunts of his sexual activities with another woman or other women. And so, after putting up with years of violent ill-treatment, what in reality finally caused the defendant's loss of control was hurtful language boasting of his sexual infidelity. Those words were the final straw. [Counsel for the prosecution] invited us to consider (he did not support the contention) whether, on a narrow interpretation of the statutory structure, if evidence to that effect were elicited (as it might, in cross-examination), there would then be no sufficient qualifying trigger at all. Although the persistent beating might in a different case fall within the provisions for qualifying triggers in section 55(4)(a)(b), in the case we are considering, the wife had endured the violence and would have continued to endure it but for the sudden discovery of her husband's infidelity. On this basis the earlier history of violence, as well as the violence on the instant occasion, would not, without reference to the claims of sexual infidelity, carry sufficient weight to constitute a qualifying trigger. Yet in the real world the husband's conduct over the years, and the impact of what he said on the particular occasion when he was killed, should surely be considered as a whole

[...]

39 [...] It may not be unduly burdensome to compartmentalise sexual infidelity where it is the only element relied on in support of a qualifying trigger, and, having compartmentalised it in

this way, to disregard it. Whether this is so or not, the legislation imposes that exclusionary obligation on the court. However, to seek to compartmentalise sexual infidelity and exclude it when it is integral to the facts as a whole is not only much more difficult, but is unrealistic and carries with it the potential for injustice. In the examples we have given earlier in this judgment, we do not see how any sensible evaluation of the gravity of the circumstances or their impact on the defendant could be made if the jury, having, in accordance with the legislation, heard the evidence, were then to be directed to excise from their evaluation of the qualifying trigger the matters said to constitute sexual infidelity, and to put them into distinct compartments to be disregarded. In our judgment, where sexual infidelity is integral to and forms an essential part of the context in which to make a just evaluation whether a qualifying trigger properly falls within the ambit of subsections 55(3) and 55(4), the prohibition in section 55(6)(c) does not operate to exclude it.

Before moving on, it is worth noting three further points. First, commentators have questioned whether section 55(6)(c) is actually necessary. Even if a jealous husband did suffer a loss of self-control in response to discovering his wife's sexual infidelity, he will only be convicted of manslaughter instead of murder on the basis of loss of control if he also passes the final part of the defence: the objective test (which we will study in a moment). In many cases jealous husbands will not pass this test. In fact, Withey notes that the evidence gathered by the Government showed that under the old law jealous men were *not* avoiding murder convictions by claiming provocation.[33]

Second, some have questioned why there is a specific statutory exclusion for cases of sexual infidelity but not for other types of case such as honour killings.[34] Withey discusses this point in the following extract.

### EXTRACT

Read the following extract. Do you agree that honour killings are a 'more worthy' candidate for exclusion than killings in response to sexual infidelity?

What moral message do you think section 55(6)(c) sends out?

### Withey, C. (2011) 'Loss of Control, Loss of Opportunity?' *Criminal Law Review* 263

The public might question why sexual infidelity has been singled out for exclusion. Some might sympathise with a person who receives the mandatory life sentence because they killed their partner upon discovering their adultery. Recent media reports involving celebrity affairs have shown how the public frown on those who cheat on their loved ones. There are perhaps more worthy candidates for exclusion. Few sympathise with those who commit honour killings. In *Mohammed (Faqir)* a Muslim father stabbed his daughter to death having discovered a young man in her bedroom. The defence of provocation could be considered by the jury. There is no

[33]Withey, C. (2011) 'Loss of Control, Loss of Opportunity?' *Criminal Law Review* 263.

[34]See also Clough, A. (2016) 'Honour Killings, Partial Defences and the Exclusionary Conduct Model' 80 *Journal of Criminal Law* 177.

express restriction in the new law for such cases, as there is with sexual infidelity. This does not mean that D who commits an honour killing will be able to rely upon the partial defence; the thing done, the conduct of a daughter, will have to be seriously grave and give a justifiable sense of being seriously wronged. In addition, the objective test will have to be met, which is highly unlikely. By not excluding situations like this from the ambit of the partial defence, Parliament has indirectly sent out a moral message regarding those who resort to killing having discovered sexual infidelity.

Lastly, Horder and Fitz-Gibbon have shown that, when sentencing for murder, the courts have continued to regard evidence of sexual infidelity as capable of amounting to grave provocation that may justify a significantly lower minimum term of imprisonment. They argue that this ignores the spirit of the sexual infidelity exclusion and threatens the integrity of the moral message that section 55(6)(c) was intended to communicate.[35]

## 3. A person of the defendant's age and sex, with a normal degree of tolerance and self-restraint and in the circumstances of the defendant, might have reacted in the same or in a similar way to the defendant

The third requirement for the defence is that a person of the defendant's age and sex, with a normal degree of tolerance and self-restraint and in the circumstances of the defendant, might have reacted in the same or in a similar way to the defendant. This is an objective test. It is designed to stop defendants from pleading loss of control when they have failed to show the level of self-restraint that society is entitled to expect from its members.

We can break the wording of the objective test down into the following four parts.

### i. '... might have reacted in the same or in a similar way to the defendant'

First, note that section 54(1)(c) uses the word 'might'. The question is whether a normal person might have reacted in the same or a similar way to the defendant, not whether a normal person would have done so. Remember too that the burden of proof rests on the prosecution: the prosecution must establish beyond reasonable doubt that a normal person would not have reacted as the defendant did. So if a jury is unsure whether a normal person might have reacted as the defendant did or not, this part of the loss of control defence is satisfied.

Second, note that it is not enough that a normal person might also have lost their self-control in the same situation. The test is whether a normal person might have reacted 'in the same or in a similar way to the defendant'. In other words, might a normal person not only have lost their self-control, but also killed the victim in the same or in a similar way to the defendant?

### ii. 'A person of the defendant's age and sex ...'

The wording of section 54(1)(c) makes it clear that the hypothetical normal person is the same age and gender as the defendant. This is the same as under the old law, as set out by the House of Lords in *R v Camplin* [1978] AC 705. In this case the defendant was a 15-year-old boy. He killed the victim, a middle-aged man named Mohammed Lal Khan,

---

[35]Horder, J. & Fitz-Gibbon, K. (2015) 'When Sexual Infidelity Triggers Murder: Examining the Impact of Homicide Law Reform on Judicial Attitudes in Sentencing' 74 *Cambridge Law Journal* 307.

by splitting his skull with a chapati pan. Camplin said that Khan had sexually assaulted him and that he lost his self-control and lashed out when Khan later laughed at him. The House of Lords held that Camplin should be judged according to the standards of a normal 15-year-old boy, not a normal adult. Lord Diplock explained that 'to require old heads upon young shoulders' would be inconsistent with the rationale of the defence: to make some concession for human frailty.

Why the statute explicitly refers to the defendant's gender is less clear. There is no obvious reason why the level of self-restraint society is entitled to expect should differ according to whether the defendant is male or female. One possible explanation might be that adolescent girls mature more quickly than adolescent boys. If this is correct (and it would require scientific validation), a 15-year-old girl might be expected to show more self-restraint than a 15-year-old boy.

### iii. '... in the circumstances of the defendant ...'

When applying the objective test, the jury should consider the reaction of a normal person 'in the circumstances of the defendant'. There are two types of situation where this will be particularly important:

- Cases which involve a cumulative impact. In such a case the jury may take into account any past events that are relevant. This will be important in order to appreciate the significance of the events at the time of the killing. So, for example, in a case like *R v Ahluwalia* a jury would not only take into account the threats that occurred in the hours before the killing. They would be able to take into account the full history of violence and abuse.

- Cases where the defendant is taunted about a particular characteristic. Where the defendant is taunted about a particular characteristic, the jury should consider the impact on someone with that characteristic. For example, if the victim shouts racist abuse at the defendant, the jury should take into account the defendant's ethnicity. Or if the victim taunts the defendant about his recent release from prison, calling him a jailbird, the jury should take into account the fact that the defendant is an ex-offender.[36] This was confirmed by the Court of Appeal in *R v Asmelash* [2013] EWCA Crim 157. The Court stated that if 'a defendant with a severe problem with alcohol or drugs was mercilessly taunted about the condition, to the extent that it constituted a qualifying trigger, the alcohol or drug problem would then form part of the circumstances for consideration'.[37]

Note also that the Court of Appeal in *R v Clinton, Parker & Evans* held that sexual infidelity may be taken into account when applying the objective test. The statutory exclusion contained in section 55(6)(c) only applies to the second limb of the defence (i.e. whether or not there was a qualifying trigger). In his judgment the Lord Chief Justice commented on the difficulties this may present to juries:

> 32 We must reflect briefly on the directions to be given by the judge to the jury. On one view they would require the jury to disregard any evidence relating to sexual infidelity

---

[36]Sir John Smith wrote: 'Suppose that an old lag, now trying to go straight, is taunted with being "a jailbird". This might be extremely provoking, especially if it reveals his murky past to new friends or employers unaware of it. It really would not make much sense to ask the jury to consider the effect of such provocation on a man of good character' (Smith, J.C. (1993) Commentary on *R v Morhall* Crim LR 957).

[37]This mirrors the position under the old law. In *R v Morhall* [1996] AC 90 the victim taunted the defendant about his glue-sniffing addiction. The House of Lords held that the jury should have been told to consider the effect of the taunts on a person with such an addiction.

when they are considering the second component of the defence, yet, notwithstanding this prohibition, would also require the same evidence to be addressed if the third component arises for consideration. In short, there will be occasions when the jury would be both disregarding and considering the same evidence. That is, to put it neutrally, counter intuitive.

### iv. '... with a normal degree of tolerance and self-restraint ...'

Whilst the general rule is that the jury may take the defendant's circumstances into account, there is one exception. This can be found in section 54(3):

---

## EXTRACT

### Section 54(3) of the Coroners and Justice Act 2009

### 54 Partial defence to murder: loss of control

[...]

(3)  In subsection (1)(c) the reference to *"the circumstances of D"* is a reference to all of D's circumstances other than those whose only relevance to D's conduct is that they bear on D's general capacity for tolerance or self-restraint.

---

So suppose the defendant is particularly hot-headed or short-tempered. The jury should not be instructed to consider whether a normal hot-headed or short-tempered person would have reacted in the same or in a similar way. Individuals who are hot-headed or short-tempered are expected to show a normal level of tolerance and self-restraint. To hold otherwise would dilute the objectivity of the test and undermine its rationale.

Importantly, section 54(3) applies not only to characteristics like hot-headedness and short-temperedness. It also applies to mental abnormalities which impair an individual's capacity for tolerance and self-restraint.[38] So a defendant who has a depressive illness which affects his powers of self-control will still be expected to show a normal level of tolerance and self-restraint notwithstanding his illness. Why does the Coroners and Justice Act 2009 take this strict approach to defendants with mental abnormalities? The reason is to preserve a distinction between the defence of loss of control and the defence of diminished responsibility.

---

## ACTIVITY

Harold has a mental abnormality which impairs his capacity for tolerance and self-restraint. One day, in response to Peter gently teasing him, Harold lashes out violently and kills Peter. Was the predominant cause of Harold's loss of self-control: (a) Peter's provocative words; or (b) Harold's mental abnormality?

---

[38]This was also the position under the old law: see *Attorney-General for Jersey v Holley* [2005] UKPC 23.

DISTINCTION BETWEEN DIMINISHED RESPONSIBILITY & LOSS OF CONTROL

The approach of the existing law is effectively to say that, if the predominant cause of a defendant's loss of self-control was his mental abnormality, then he should plead diminished responsibility, not loss of control.[39] So in our example, since the predominant cause of Harold's loss of self-control was his mental abnormality he should plead diminished responsibility. To take Harold's mental abnormality into account in the objective test for loss of control would blur the distinction between the two defences by encouraging him to plead loss of control.

You may be reading this thinking, why is the distinction between the two defences so important? After all, both are partial defences which lead to the same result – a manslaughter conviction instead of a murder conviction. The reason the distinction matters is the burden of proof. As we have seen, for the loss of control defence the burden of proof rests on the prosecution. The prosecution must disprove the defence beyond reasonable doubt. But for diminished responsibility it is the defendant who bears the burden of proof. The defendant must show, on the balance of probabilities, that he is entitled to the defence. If mental abnormalities which reduce a defendant's powers of self-control could be taken into account in the objective test for loss of control, a defendant like Harold in our example would be able to circumvent the more onerous burden of proof which applies to diminished responsibility by pleading loss of control instead.

## ACTIVITY

- Kiranjit Ahluwalia suffered from a depressive illness and from battered woman syndrome. Both of these conditions reduced her ability to exercise self-control. So, in a case like *R v Ahluwalia*, section 54(1)(c) and section 54(3) tell us that when applying the objective test the long history of violence may be considered but the defendant's reduced powers of self-control may not. With this in mind, do you think a normal person might have reacted in the same or in a similar way to Ahluwalia?
- Looking at your answer to the previous question, and at the other two requirements for the loss of control defence, do you think that if a case like *R v Ahluwalia* occurred today the defendant would be able to plead loss of control? (Your answer to this question will be important in assessing whether the new defence achieves one of its key objectives.[40])

Finally, note that the Court of Appeal has also held that a defendant's voluntary intoxication may not be taken into account when applying the objective test.[41]

---

[39] For criticism of this distinction see Mitchell, B.J., Mackay, R.D. & Brookbanks, W J. (2008) 'Pleading for Provoked Killers: In Defence of *Morgan Smith*' 124 *Law Quarterly Review* 675.

[40] It is also important to point out that there is a 'very real possibility' that, if a case like *R v Ahluwalia* occurred today and the defendant was convicted of murder, the minimum term that would be imposed under the Criminal Justice Act 2003 would be around 20 years' imprisonment. This is nearly double the tariff period of 12 years that Ahluwalia originally received, before the Court of Appeal heard her appeal and ordered a retrial. See Horder, J. & Fitz-Gibbon, K. (2015) 'When Sexual Infidelity Triggers Murder: Examining the Impact of Homicide Law Reform on Judicial Attitudes in Sentencing' 74 *Cambridge Law Journal* 307.

[41] *R v Asmelash* [2013] EWCA Crim 157.

# Unlawful act manslaughter

There is no statutory definition of unlawful act manslaughter. So instead we must look at how it was defined by the House of Lords in *DPP v Newbury & Jones* [1977] AC 500. In this case Lord Salmon stated that a person is guilty of unlawful act manslaughter if:

> he intentionally did an act which was unlawful and dangerous and that act inadvertently caused death.

This tells us that the offence has the following five requirements:

1. The defendant did an act
2. The act was unlawful
3. The act was dangerous
4. The act caused the victim's death
5. The defendant intended to do the act.

(In *R v Dalby* [1982] 1 WLR 425 Waller LJ suggested that there is a further requirement, namely that the unlawful and dangerous act was 'directed at the victim'. However, this is inconsistent with other decisions[42] and was rejected by the House of Lords in *Attorney-General's Reference (No 3 of 1994)* [1998] AC 245.)

Numbers 1, 3 and 4 on the list above are *actus reus* requirements. Number 2 includes both *actus reus* and *mens rea* requirements. Number 5 is a *mens rea* requirement. We will work through them in turn.

## 1. The defendant did an act

In other words, a defendant cannot commit unlawful act manslaughter by omission.[43] So if you are answering an exam problem question on involuntary manslaughter and the defendant's conduct constituted an omission, not an act, this offence will not apply. You should consider gross negligence manslaughter instead.

## 2. The act was unlawful

The second requirement is that the defendant's act was unlawful. Here, the word 'unlawful' has been understood to mean criminal. So it is not enough to show that the defendant's act was a civil wrong. It must have been a criminal offence. An example which illustrates this is *R v Franklin* (1883) 15 Cox CC 163. The defendant was walking along Brighton Pier on a bank holiday Monday when he picked up a 'good sized box' from a refreshments stall and threw it into the sea. The box landed on a swimmer who was swimming underneath the pier and killed him. At trial, the prosecution's case was that the defendant's actions amounted to the tort of trespass to goods. Field J stated that proof of a tort was insufficient to establish liability for unlawful act manslaughter:

> the mere fact of a civil wrong committed by one person against another ought not to be used as an incident which is a necessary step in a criminal case

A more recent example is *R v Lamb* [1967] 2 QB 981. The defendant, Terence Lamb, had acquired a revolver. The revolver had a five-chambered cylinder which rotated when the trigger was pulled. One day the defendant was joking around with his best friend, the

---

[42]Such as *R v Mitchell* [1983] QB 741.
[43]*R v Lowe* [1973] QB 702.

victim Timothy O'Donaghue. He pointed the revolver at O'Donaghue and pulled the trigger. Although there were two bullets in the chambers, neither Lamb nor O'Donaghue expected the gun to fire because neither bullet was in the chamber opposite the barrel. Neither realised that when the trigger was pulled the cylinder would rotate and place a bullet opposite the barrel. O'Donaghue was killed. At trial it was accepted that Lamb had not realised that the gun would fire. Three experts testified that Lamb's mistake was a natural one for somebody who was unfamiliar with firearms. Lamb was nonetheless convicted. Importantly, the trial judge told the jury that it was unnecessary for them to decide whether or not Lamb had committed the crime of assault. Lamb appealed against his conviction, arguing that the judge had misdirected the jury. In the Court of Appeal Sachs LJ held that the act in question must have been a crime:

> It is long settled that it is not in point to consider whether an act is unlawful merely from the angle of civil liabilities.

Lamb's appeal was therefore successful. Without proof that he had committed an assault he could not be convicted of unlawful act manslaughter.

Before moving on, it is important to note two further points:

- Whilst the unlawful act must be a crime, it does not have to be a crime of violence. For example, in a few pages' time we will look at *R v Watson* [1989] 1 WLR 684. In this case the relevant crime was burglary. Another example is *R v Goodfellow* (1986) 83 Cr App R 23, where the relevant crime was criminal damage.

- The prosecution must prove both the *actus reus* and the *mens rea* of the crime in question. So if the relevant offence is battery, the prosecution must establish both the *actus reus* and *mens rea* of battery.

## 3. The act was dangerous

The third requirement is that the act was dangerous. Here we need to consider two issues: first, what test is used to assess dangerousness; and, second, what information may the jury take into account when applying this test?

### i. The test for dangerousness

The courts have developed a legal test which must be applied when deciding whether or not the defendant's unlawful act was dangerousness. One of the most common mistakes students make when answering exam problem questions on unlawful act manslaughter is to apply their own understanding of the word 'dangerous' instead of applying the test the courts have set out.

The first point to note about the test for dangerousness is that it is an objective test. Lord Salmon in *DPP v Newbury & Jones* stated:

> In judging whether the act was dangerous, the test is not did the accused recognise that it was dangerous but would all sober and reasonable people recognise its danger.

So, when applying the dangerousness test, you must focus on what the reasonable person would have foreseen, not on what the defendant himself foresaw. No concession is made for individual characteristics, such as age or mental capacity.[44]

---

[44]This is illustrated by *R v JF & NE* [2015] EWCA Crim 351. JF and NE were both young people (aged 14 and 16 respectively), and JF had an exceptionally low IQ (such that a psychologist said that JF's answers in police interviews should be judged as if he were a six-year-old). The Court of Appeal rejected defence counsel's suggestion that the objective test for dangerousness should be reconsidered, stating that 'the law is clear and well established' and that it is 'for Parliament to determine' whether reform is needed ([33]).

Second, in *R v Church* [1966] 1 QB 59 Edmund Davies J explained that, for the act to qualify as dangerous, the prosecution must show that the reasonable man would have foreseen a risk that the victim would suffer some harm. Importantly, he explained that the reasonable man need not have foreseen a risk of serious harm:

> The unlawful act must be such as all sober and reasonable people would inevitably recognise must subject the other person to, at least, the risk of some harm resulting therefrom, albeit not serious harm.

The scope of the *R v Church* test was considered in *R v JM & SM* [2012] EWCA Crim 2293. In this case the Court of Appeal had to consider whether it is necessary to show that the reasonable man would have foreseen the type of harm that the victim suffered. The victim in *R v JM & SM* was 40-year-old Peter Jopling. He worked at a nightclub as a doorman and was believed to be in good health. One evening the two defendants were ejected from the club and then tried to force their way back in. Jopling was one of the doormen who dealt with them. Shortly after the disturbance Jopling collapsed and died. It was later discovered that he had been suffering from a renal artery aneurysm. The shock and surge in blood pressure triggered by the disturbance had caused the aneurysm to rupture. The two defendants were charged with affray and unlawful act manslaughter.

At trial the judge ruled that, even if the jury decided that the defendants had committed an unlawful act (the offence of affray[45]), there was no evidence on which they could convict the defendants of unlawful act manslaughter. The judge stated that the *R v Church* test for dangerousness is only satisfied if the reasonable man would have foreseen the *type* of harm that the victim suffered. The prosecution appealed against this, arguing that it placed an unwarranted restriction on the scope of the *R v Church* test.

## EXTRACT

Read the following extract from the judgment of Lord Judge CJ. For the dangerousness test must the prosecution prove: (1) that the reasonable man would have foreseen a risk that the victim would suffer the type of injury the victim suffered; or (2) that the reasonable man would have foreseen a risk of some injury (not necessarily the sort of injury the victim actually suffered)?

### R v JM & SM [2012] EWCA Crim 2293

#### Lord Judge CJ

18 [T]he judge misdirected himself when he required the Crown to establish [...] that the reasonable and sober person envisaged in *R v Church* must realise that there was a risk that the unlawful act would cause the sort of physical harm as a result of which the victim died. We agree that such a requirement provided a gloss on the ingredients of this offence which is not justified by the authorities [...] Indeed, the observations at the end of the judgment appear to elevate the requisite risk from an appreciation that some harm will inevitably occur into foresight of the type of harm which actually ensued and indeed the mechanism by which death occurred. Of course, unless the Crown can prove that death resulted from the defendant's unlawful and dangerous act, the case of manslaughter would fail on causation grounds. However a requirement that the bystander must appreciate the "sort" of injury which might occur undermines the "some" harm principle explained in *R v Church*

---

[45]Public Order Act 1986, s.3.

[...]

20 In our judgment, certainly since *R v Church* [1966] 1 QB 59 and *Director of Public Prosecutions v Newbury* [1977] AC 500, it has never been a requirement that the defendant personally should foresee any specific harm at all, or that the reasonable bystander should recognise the precise form or "sort" of harm which did ensue. What matters is whether reasonable and sober people would recognise that the unlawful activities of the defendant inevitably subjected the deceased to the risk of some harm resulting from them.

[...]

22 In our judgment there is evidence from which a jury properly directed could conclude that sober and reasonable people observing events on 12 December 2012 would readily have recognised that all the doormen involved in the effort to control the defendants were at the risk of some harm, and that the fatal injury incurred while it was in progress or in its immediate aftermath while Mr Jopling was still subject to its effects.

23 Accordingly this appeal will be allowed.

The Court also stated that, whilst general stress and anxiety do not amount to harm for the purposes of the *R v Church* test, emotional shock does. This followed the decision in *R v Watson*, which we will look at shortly.

So, to summarise, the test for dangerousness is an objective one. The prosecution must show that the reasonable man would have foreseen a risk that the victim would suffer some harm. No concession is made for an individual's characteristics, such as age or mental capacity, and it is not necessary to show that the reasonable man would have foreseen the precise type of harm that the victim actually suffered. This test has been widely criticised for setting the bar too low, particularly given that unlawful act manslaughter is a homicide offence. The Law Commission, for example, has stated:[46]

1.15 At the less serious end of the involuntary manslaughter spectrum, the law may be too harsh on defendants who kill as a result of an unlawful and dangerous act. The risk of harshness arises when defendants do not realise that the act may cause harm:

EXAMPLE 1: D is seeking to steal a large book from the fourth floor of a library whose windows face on to a busy street. Seeing the librarian coming towards him, D quickly drops the book out of the window. It lands on V's head as she walks underneath the window, killing her.

1.16 D's theft of the book should not be sufficient to convict D of the manslaughter of V even though, in the circumstances, there was an obvious risk of some harm arising from D's action.

## ACTIVITY

- Do you agree that the defendant in the Law Commission's example should not be convicted of manslaughter?
- Do you agree with the Law Commission that the *R v Church* test for dangerousness is too harsh on defendants who do not realise that their unlawful act may cause harm?

---

[46]Law Commission (2005) *A New Homicide Act for England and Wales? A Consultation Paper* (Consultation Paper No 177).

## ii. What information may the jury take into account when applying the dangerousness test?

In some situations there may be particular facts or circumstances which affect the dangerousness of the defendant's act. There are a number of cases in which the courts have set out guidance on when such facts or circumstances may be taken into account.

The first case to consider is *R v Bristow* [2013] EWCA Crim 1540. The victim, Julian Gardner, ran an off-road vehicle repair business from premises on a secluded farm. The four defendants committed a night-time burglary of the business. Gardner interrupted the burglary and attempted to intervene. As the defendants escaped, they drove into Gardner and killed him. At trial the defendants were convicted of unlawful act manslaughter (the unlawful act being the burglary). They appealed against their convictions, arguing that the burglary did not satisfy the *R v Church* test for dangerousness (at least not until one of the defendants started to drive dangerously, which they argued was too late as the prosecution had not proved who ran Gardner over). The Court of Appeal dismissed their appeal.

### EXTRACT

Read the following extract from the judgment of Treacy LJ. At what point in time does he say the dangerousness of the burglary should be assessed: before the defendants embarked on the burglary; when Gardner intervened or when the defendants started to drive dangerously?

What reasons does Treacy LJ give for saying that the burglary satisfied the *R v Church* test for dangerousness?

#### *R v Bristow* [2013] EWCA Crim 1540

#### Treacy LJ

16 The prosecution case [...] was one of unlawful act manslaughter. The unlawful act was alleged to be the burglary of the farm, which was committed as a joint enterprise. Although the Crown could not say who was driving the vehicle or vehicles that had struck Mr Gardner, they asserted that each appellant took part in the burglary and in doing so, in the particular circumstances, foresaw a real possibility that somebody intervening at the scene might suffer harm as a result of the carrying out of the burglary, including harm caused during their escape from the scene. The presence of residential farm buildings would have alerted the appellants to the risk of being caught in the act of burglary, which would result in the need to escape promptly from the scene in vehicles along the single track.

17 In those circumstances a reasonable bystander would, the Crown submitted, recognise the risk of some harm being caused to a person intervening at night, in the dark, in a relatively confined space, where powerful vehicles were involved, and there was only one route of escape from the workshops. In this context, it is worth recording that the jury went on a view of the scene as well as having many still images provided.

[...]

34 This is not a case [...] where the circumstances demonstrating the risk of harm to the occupier of property did not arise until a point during the burglary or at all. Whilst burglary of itself is not a dangerous crime, a particular burglary may be dangerous because of the circumstances surrounding its commission. We consider that the features identified by the Crown, as set out

earlier in this judgment, were capable of making this burglary dangerous when coupled with foresight of the risk of intervention to prevent escape.

35 In those circumstances we consider that the features of this crime were sufficient for the burglary to be capable of being an unlawful act which a reasonable bystander would inevitably realise must subject any person intervening to the risk of some harm resulting

[...]

37 Since the crime to be focussed on was the burglary, we reject Mr Nelson's submission as to the point at which foresight and danger were to be assessed. We consider that on the facts of this case the judge was correct to focus the jury's attention on the period up to the inception of the burglary. It is that question which lies at the very heart of the submissions made on behalf of the appellants, namely the point in time at which foresight and recognition of danger arose. What needed to be considered was the foresight of the participants as they embarked upon the crime, and what, if anything a reasonable bystander would inevitably have recognised as a risk of physical harm to any person intervening.

So in *R v Bristow* the information which demonstrated the dangerousness of the act was available to the defendants before they committed the burglary. The application of the *R v Church* test was therefore based on what the reasonable person would have foreseen at the moment the defendants embarked on the crime. But what if there are special facts or circumstances which only become evident whilst the crime is being committed? This was the issue in *R v Watson* [1989] 1 WLR 684. The defendant, Clarence Watson, broke into the home of an 87-year-old man named Harold Moyler, who had a weak heart. Moyler woke up whilst Watson was in the house. Watson verbally abused him and then escaped. Shortly afterwards Moyler suffered a fatal heart attack. At trial the judge told the jury that, when applying the *R v Church* test, they could take into account information which became available to Watson during the course of the burglary (including the fact that Moyler was frail and elderly). Watson was convicted of unlawful act manslaughter. He appealed against his conviction, arguing that the trial judge had misdirected the jury.

## EXTRACT

According to the following extract from Lord Lane CJ's judgment, had the trial judge misdirected the jury? When applying the *R v Church* test may the jury take into account facts and circumstances which become evident to the defendant?

### *R v Watson* [1989] 1 WLR 684

#### Lord Lane CJ

The judge clearly took the view that the jury were entitled to ascribe to the bystander the knowledge which the appellant gained during the whole of his stay in the house and so directed them. Was this a misdirection? In our judgment it was not. The unlawful act in the present circumstances comprised the whole of the burglarious intrusion and did not come to an end upon the appellant's foot crossing the threshold or windowsill. That being so, the appellant (and therefore the bystander) during the course of the unlawful act must have become aware of Mr. Moyler's frailty and approximate age, and the judge's directions were accordingly correct.

So any relevant facts or circumstances can be taken into account when applying the *R v Church* test if they were available to the defendant before he embarked on the unlawful act or if they became available to him during the unlawful act. But what about facts which only transpire afterwards? This was the issue in *R v Dawson* (1985) 81 Cr App R 150. The victim in this case was a 60-year-old petrol station attendant named Robert Black. Black suffered from heart disease. He was at work one evening when the defendant, Brian Dawson, and two other men attempted to rob the petrol station. They were armed with a replica gun and a pickaxe handle. As they demanded money they saw Black press an alarm button and fled. Shortly afterwards Black suffered a heart attack and died. At trial the three men were convicted of unlawful act manslaughter. They appealed against their convictions. The key issue on appeal was whether the trial judge was right to tell the jury to take into account Black's heart condition when applying the test for dangerousness.

## EXTRACT

Read the following extract from the judgment of Watkins LJ. Was the trial judge correct to tell the jury to take into account Black's heart condition? Why/why not?

### *R v Dawson* (1985) 81 Cr App R 150

### Watkins LJ

[The dangerousness] test can only be undertaken upon the basis of the knowledge gained by a sober and reasonable man as though he were present at the scene of and watched the unlawful act being performed and who knows that, as in the present case, an unloaded replica gun was in use, but that the victim may have thought it was a loaded gun in working order. In other words, he has the same knowledge as the man attempting to rob and no more. It was never suggested that any of these appellants knew that their victim had a bad heart. They knew nothing about him.

A jury must be informed by the judge when trying the offence of manslaughter what facts they may and those which they may not use for the purpose of performing the [dangerousness] test. The judge's direction here, unlike the bulk of an admirable summing-up, lacked that necessary precision and in the form it was given may, in our view, have given the jury an erroneous impression of what knowledge they could ascribe to the sober and reasonable man.

For these reasons we see no alternative to quashing the convictions for manslaughter as unsafe and unsatisfactory. The appeal against the convictions for manslaughter is therefore allowed.

A similar case to *R v Dawson* is *R v Carey* [2006] EWCA Crim 17. The victim, 15-year-old Aimee Wellock, was out with her friends. They were approached by the three defendants, who started acting aggressively. One of the defendants punched Aimee, while one of the other defendants punched one of Aimee's friends. Aimee managed to run away, but then collapsed and died later that night. Unknown to Aimee, she had a severely diseased heart. Her running had caused her heart to stop pumping blood. At trial the defendants were convicted of affray and unlawful act manslaughter (the unlawful act being the affray). They appealed, arguing that the *R v Church* test for dangerousness was not satisfied. The Court of Appeal agreed and quashed the manslaughter convictions (but upheld the convictions for affray). Dyson LJ stated:

37 [...] Even if the affray had caused Aimee to suffer shock as opposed to emotional upset, the affray lacked the quality of dangerousness in the relevant sense. This is

because it would not have been recognised by a sober and reasonable bystander that an apparently healthy 15-year-old (or indeed anyone else present) was at risk of suffering shock as a result of this affray. In our view, this affray was less dangerous in the relevant sense than the attempted robbery of the 60-year-old petrol station attendant in *Dawson*. The risk of that victim suffering shock leading to a heart attack would have been recognised by a sober and reasonable person as more likely than the risk of Aimee suffering shock leading to a heart attack as a result of the affray.

So in both *R v Dawson* and *R v Carey* the victims' heart conditions were not taken into account when applying the *R v Church* test because a reasonable bystander would not have been aware of them.

The final question is whether the jury should take into account any mistaken beliefs held by the defendant. This was the issue in *R v Ball* [1989] Crim LR 730. The defendant allowed the victim, Mrs Green, to store her Land Rover™ on his land. Then one day he sold the vehicle without Mrs Green's consent. When Mrs Green went to Ball's house to ask him to return the Land Rover, the two started to argue. Mrs Green then ran away and, as she was trying to climb over the garden wall, Ball raised his shotgun and shot her. Ball's defence was that he kept live and blank shotgun cartridges together in the pocket of his overall in his house. When he picked up the gun he also grabbed a handful of cartridges. He believed he had only loaded blank cartridges into the gun (the blanks were lighter than the live ones). He said he only fired the gun in order to frighten Mrs Green and had not intended to kill her. The jury accepted Ball's account (which is why he was acquitted of murder). However, the trial judge told the jury that they should not take Ball's mistaken belief into account when applying the *R v Church* test for dangerousness. Ball was accordingly convicted of unlawful act manslaughter. He appealed, arguing that the trial judge had misdirected the jury.

## EXTRACT

Read the following extract from the judgment of Stuart Smith LJ. Was the trial judge correct to tell the jury not to take into account Ball's mistaken belief? Why/why not?

### *R v Ball* [1989] Crim LR 730

#### Stuart Smith LJ

[Counsel for the defendant] submits that the reference to the sober and reasonable man having the same knowledge as the [defendant] and no more, involves the proposition that if that person has a mistaken belief, albeit brought about by his own carelessness, the sober and reasonable man must share that mistaken belief. But in our judgment *Dawson's* case goes no further than showing that the sober and reasonable man must look at the unlawful act to see if it is dangerous and not at peculiarities of the victim.

[…]

Once these matters are established, namely, that the act was both unlawful and that he intended to commit the assaults, the question whether the act is a dangerous one is to be judged not by the appellant's appreciation but by that of the sober and reasonable man, and it is impossible to impute into his appreciation the mistaken belief of the appellant that what he was doing was not dangerous because he thought he had a blank cartridge in the chamber. At that stage the appellant's intention, foresight or knowledge is irrelevant.

So according to *R v Ball* any mistaken beliefs held by the defendant should be disregarded when applying the *R v Church* test. This principle has been criticised on the basis that it could potentially lead to harsh results.[47] The judgment suggests that any mistaken belief held by the defendant should be disregarded, however reasonable the mistake might have been. Suppose Ball had instead purchased a box of blank cartridges, but owing to a mishap at the factory the box also contained some live ones. Ball's mistaken belief that he was firing a blank cartridge would have been entirely justified. Yet following the Court of Appeal's judgment the dangerousness test would be applied on the basis that the reasonable man knew that the cartridge was in fact live.

## 4. The act caused the victim's death

The defendant's unlawful act must have been a factual and legal cause of the victim's death. Here you apply the law governing causation that we studied in Chapter 3.

### ACTIVITY

Harold breaks into Peter's house whilst Peter is asleep upstairs. Peter wakes up, hears sounds from downstairs and realises that there is an intruder. Terrified, he runs out of the house and straight into the road in front of a car that is being driven in excess of the speed limit by Fred. Peter is killed. Was the burglary a factual and legal cause of Peter's death?

## 5. The defendant intended to do the act

The second requirement for this offence was that the act in question was a criminal offence. As we saw earlier, this means that the defendant must satisfy both the *actus reus* and *mens rea* requirements of the relevant crime. Beyond this, the only other *mens rea* requirement of unlawful act manslaughter is that the defendant intended to do the relevant act. In *DPP v Newbury & Jones* Lord Salmon confirmed that it is unnecessary to prove that the defendant knew that the act was unlawful and it is unnecessary to prove that the defendant knew that the act was dangerous. This is why this offence is sometimes referred to as 'constructive manslaughter'. It is possible that a defendant may be guilty of this offence even if he was unaware of any risk that the victim would suffer physical harm (let alone death).

It is also important to note that in *Andrews v DPP* [1937] AC 576 HL Lord Atkin attempted to draw a distinction between two types of act. He said:

There is an obvious difference in the law of manslaughter between doing an unlawful act and doing a lawful act with a degree of carelessness which the Legislature makes criminal.

He explained that a defendant can only be convicted of unlawful act manslaughter if he commits the first type of act (an unlawful act). If a defendant commits the second type of act (a careless lawful act), you should consider gross negligence manslaughter instead.

This distinction is not an easy one. It has been criticised for being unclear and unsustainable (the second type of act is really a subcategory of the first type of act, since a lawful

---

[47]Simester, A.P., Spencer, J.R., Stark, F., Sullivan, G.R. & Virgo, G J. (2016) *Simester and Sullivan's Criminal Law: Theory and Doctrine* (6th edn) Oxford: Hart Publishing, p413.

act which is performed so carelessly as to become criminal is an unlawful act!). Lord Atkin may be understood as saying that where the allegation is of carelessness the defendant should be charged with gross negligence manslaughter, not unlawful act manslaughter. Suppose that Harold is driving his car. He is looking out of the window at the view, fails to notice Peter (a frail old man) crossing the road at a zebra crossing and knocks him over. Peter dies. Since the allegation is that Harold drove carelessly he should be charged with gross negligence manslaughter, not unlawful act manslaughter. On the other hand, suppose Harold had seen Peter and decided it would be fun to scare him by accelerating and driving as close to him as possible without hitting him. Peter is so frightened that he suffers a heart attack and dies. On these facts Harold intentionally committed an unlawful act (assault: see Chapter 6) and so the appropriate offence is unlawful act manslaughter.

## Gross negligence manslaughter

There is no statutory definition of gross negligence manslaughter. So instead we must look at how it was defined by the House of Lords in *R v Adomako* [1995] 1 AC 171. In this case Lord Mackay explained the requirements of gross negligence manslaughter as follows:

> [T]he ordinary principles of the law of negligence apply to ascertain whether or not the defendant has been in breach of a duty of care towards the victim who has died. If such breach of duty is established the next question is whether that breach of duty caused the death of the victim. If so, the jury must go on to consider whether that breach of duty should be characterised as gross negligence and therefore as a crime.

This tells us that gross negligence manslaughter has the following four requirements:

1. The defendant owed the victim a duty of care
2. The defendant breached his duty of care
3. The breach of duty caused the death of the victim
4. The breach of duty should be characterised as gross negligence and therefore as a crime.

Numbers 1 to 3 are *actus reus* requirements. Number 4 is a *mens rea* requirement. We will work through them in turn.

### 1. The defendant owed the victim a duty of care

The first requirement is that the defendant owed the victim a duty of care. Whether such a duty exists is a question of law which the judge must answer, it is not a question of fact for the jury.[48] In general terms, to determine whether or not there is a duty of care you must apply the ordinary principles of the law of tort, specifically, the law of negligence.[49] There are many situations in which a duty of care will arise. Some examples are:

- A doctor owes a duty of care to his patients[50]
- A driver owes a duty of care to other road users[51]

---

[48]This was confirmed by the Court of Appeal in *R v Evans* [2009] EWCA Crim 650.
[49]*R v Adomako* [1995] 1 AC 171.
[50]*R v Adomako* [1995] 1 AC 171.
[51]*Page v Smith* [1996] AC 155.

- An employer owes a duty of care to his employees[52]
- A teacher owes a duty of care to his pupils[53]
- A gatekeeper at a railway crossing owes a duty of care to those who use the crossing[54]
- A prison officer owes a duty to prisoners who are a known suicide risk.[55]

A duty of care was also held to exist in *R v Evans* [2009] EWCA Crim 650, which we studied in Chapter 3. This was the case in which the defendant bought some heroin and gave it to the victim (her half-sister, who was a recovering addict). The defendant owed the victim a duty of care because she had contributed to the dangerous situation the victim was in, and she breached this duty by failing to call for medical assistance. Similar reasoning was also applied in *R v Bowler* [2015] EWCA Crim 849.[56] In this case the victim, W, was interested in masochistic sexual experiences, particularly mummification. The defendant wrapped W in cling film and PVC, had sex with him, then left him. He checked on W half an hour later. W was moving. The defendant left again and didn't return for some time. When he did return, W was lifeless. The defendant was convicted of gross negligence manslaughter. A duty of care arose because W 'was left helpless and in a situation which was obviously dangerous' ([20]), and the defendant breached this duty by failing to monitor and check on W properly.

One question which the courts have had to address is whether a duty of care can exist in cases where the defendant and victim were jointly embarked on an unlawful enterprise. This issue arose in *R v Wacker* [2002] EWCA Crim 1944. The defendant, Perry Wacker, was a lorry driver. He had agreed to help 60 Chinese immigrants enter the UK illegally by hiding them in his lorry. The immigrants got onto the lorry in Holland. They were hidden in a concealed container behind crates of tomatoes. The only ventilation came from a small vent at the front of the container. Before boarding the ferry at Zeebrugge, Wacker closed the air vent in order to reduce the likelihood of detection. The immigrants had been warned that this would happen, but were told the vent would only be closed for a short time. However, Wacker failed to reopen the vent during the ferry crossing. By the time the ferry arrived at Dover more than five hours later, 58 of the immigrants had died of suffocation. At trial, Wacker was convicted on 58 counts of gross negligence manslaughter.

Wacker's appeal focused on whether or not he owed the immigrants a duty of care. In the law of tort there is a principle known as *ex turpi causa*. This principle states that no action can be based on a disreputable cause. It prevents one party from suing another in the law of tort where both were jointly engaged in an unlawful enterprise. The issue for the Court of Appeal was whether the *ex turpi causa* principle also applies to the crime of gross negligence manslaughter. If so, Wacker would not have owed the immigrants a duty of care and so could not be found guilty of gross negligence manslaughter.

[52] *Wilson and Clyde Coal Co v English* [1938] AC 57.

[53] *Wilkin-Shaw v Fuller* [2013] EWCA Civ 410.

[54] *R v Pittwood* (1902) 19 TLR 37.

[55] *R (on the application of the Justice Secretary) v HM Deputy Coroner for the Eastern District of West Yorkshire* [2012] EWHC 1634 (Admin).

[56] See also *R v S* [2015] EWCA Crim 558, in which the defendant S, a gang member, had been given a gun to look after by another member of the gang. S removed the magazine from the handle of the gun, but did not realise that there was still a bullet in the chamber. Whilst showing off, he pointed the gun at his girlfriend and pulled the trigger. The gun fired and his girlfriend was killed. S was acquitted of murder but convicted of gross negligence manslaughter. The duty of care S owed to his girlfriend appeared to be based on the dangerous situation he created by pointing the gun and pulling the trigger without ensuring that it was safe to do so (see [10] of Cranston J's judgment).

**EXTRACT**

Read the following extract from the judgment of Kay LJ. What reasons does he give for saying that Wacker owed the immigrants a duty of care?

Does the *ex turpi causa* principle apply to the crime of gross negligence manslaughter? Why/why not?

## *R v Wacker* [2002] EWCA Crim 1944

### Kay LJ

38 The next question which is posed is whether it is right to say in this case that no duty of care can arise because it is impossible or inappropriate to determine the extent of that duty. We do not accept this proposition. If at the moment when the vent was shut one of the Chinese had said, "You will make sure that we have enough air to survive", the defendant would have had no difficulty understanding the proposition and clearly, by continuing with the unlawful enterprise in the way that he did, he would have been shouldering the duty to take care for their safety in this regard. The question was such an obvious one that it did not need to be posed and we have no difficulty in concluding that in these circumstances the defendant did voluntarily assume the duty of care for the Chinese in this regard. He was aware that no one's actions other than his own could realistically prevent the Chinese from suffocating to death and if he failed to act reasonably in fulfilling this duty to an extent that could be characterised as criminal, he was guilty of manslaughter if death resulted.

39 One further issue merits consideration, namely is it any answer to a charge of manslaughter for a defendant to say, "We were jointly engaged in a criminal enterprise and, weighing the risk of injury or death against our joint desire to achieve our unlawful objective, we collectively thought that it was a risk worth taking"? In our judgment it is not. The duty to take care cannot, as a matter of public policy, be permitted to be affected by the countervailing demands of the criminal enterprise. Thus, in this case, the fact that keeping the vent shut increased the chances of the Chinese succeeding in entering the United Kingdom without detection was not a factor to be taken into account in deciding whether the defendant had acted reasonably or not.

In *R v Willoughby* [2004] EWCA Crim 3365 the Court of Appeal confirmed that the *ex turpi causa* principle does not apply to gross negligence manslaughter. The defendant, Keith Willoughby, owned a pub in Canterbury but had run into financial trouble. He decided to set fire to the pub and asked his friend Derek Drury to help him. One evening the two men went to the pub together, poured petrol inside and ignited it. There was then an explosion, which injured Willoughby and killed Drury. At trial Willoughby was convicted of gross negligence manslaughter. On appeal, Willoughby's counsel argued that Willoughby had not owed Drury a duty of care. He tried to distinguish *R v Wacker* by arguing that in that case the immigrants were in a vulnerable position and Wacker had chosen to assume responsibility for them. By contrast, Willoughby and Drury took part in the unlawful plan as equals.

## EXTRACT

In the following extract what reasons does Rose LJ give for holding that Willoughby did owe Drury a duty of care?

### R v Willoughby [2004] EWCA Crim 3365

#### Rose LJ

20 In the present case, we accept that there could not be a duty in law to look after the deceased's health and welfare arising merely from the fact that the defendant was the owner of the premises. But the fact that the defendant was the owner, that his public house was to be destroyed for his financial benefit, that he enlisted the deceased to take part in this enterprise, and that the deceased's role was to spread petrol inside were, in conjunction, factors which were capable, in law, of giving rise to a duty to the deceased on the part of the defendant. In a very different situation the lorry driver in *R v Wacker* [2003] QB 1207 was held to owe a duty of care to the illegal immigrants he was carrying. The civil law doctrine of *ex turpi causa* was held not to apply in the criminal law.

Lastly, it should be noted that it is possible to commit gross negligence manslaughter by omission. We have already seen three examples: *R v Evans*, *R v Bowler* and *R v Wacker*. In cases which involve an omission it must be shown that the defendant had both: (1) a duty to act (see Chapter 3); and (2) a duty of care under the law of tort (which we have worked through here). So in an exam problem question, you should begin by discussing whether the defendant had a duty to act which he breached. Once you've done this you can then focus on gross negligence manslaughter and discuss whether the defendant owed the victim a duty of care. (In practice, if there was a duty to act there will almost certainly be a duty of care too.)

### 2. The defendant breached his duty of care

The second requirement is that the defendant breached the duty of care he owed to the victim. The standard of care is an objective one: the defendant will breach his duty if he fails to live up to the standard of the reasonable person. If the defendant is performing a skilled activity he will be required to live up to the standard of the reasonable person with that skill. So a driver must live up to the standard of the reasonable motorist, and a doctor must live up to the standard of a reasonable doctor.

These points are illustrated by *R v Adomako*. The defendant in this case, John Adomako, was an anaesthetist. He was part of a team carrying out an eye operation on the victim. During the operation the tube that was supplying oxygen to the victim became disconnected. An expert witness said that Adomako should have noticed this within 15 seconds. But Adomako did not notice the disconnection. Four-and-a-half minutes later an alarm sounded on the blood pressure monitor. Adomako administered some drugs to raise the victim's pulse, but still didn't notice the disconnection. Approximately nine minutes after the original disconnection the victim suffered cardiac arrest and died. Only then did Adomako discover the disconnection. Another expert witness described the standard of care Adomako provided as 'abysmal'.

In his defence, Adomako explained that he was exhausted. The day before he had worked a long shift and had not got to bed until 3:30 am. He was then back on the wards at 7 am. He also said that, although he had some experience of eye operations, he had never acted as the sole anaesthetist in such an operation before. The House of Lords nonetheless upheld his conviction for gross negligence manslaughter. The standard of care for this offence is determined objectively. Adomako therefore had to be judged by the standard of a reasonably competent anaesthetist. If he did not achieve the standard of a reasonably skilled anaesthetist he breached his duty of care to the patient.

### 3. The breach of duty caused the death of the victim

The third requirement is that the breach of duty was a factual and legal cause of the victim's death. Here you apply the law governing causation that we studied in Chapter 3.

In Chapter 3 we saw that the basic test for legal causation is the 'significant contribution' test from *R v Cheshire*. In cases involving medical negligence, the significant contribution test will be satisfied if the defendant's negligence caused the victim to die significantly sooner (in other words, would competent treatment have saved or significantly prolonged the victim's life?).[57]

### 4. The breach of duty should be characterised as gross negligence and therefore as a crime

The final requirement is that the defendant's breach of duty was grossly negligent. Whether or not the breach of duty amounted to gross negligence is a question of fact for the jury to decide. The role of an expert witness is to provide material for juries to evaluate when considering this question. Expert witnesses may also express an opinion on whether the negligence was gross, but if they do the trial judge must make it clear to the jury that they are not bound by the expert's opinion.[58]

In *R v Adomako* Lord Mackay offered the following guidance on how to distinguish gross negligence from mere negligence:

> This will depend on the seriousness of the breach of duty committed by the defendant in all the circumstances in which the defendant was placed when it occurred. The jury will have to consider whether the extent to which the defendant's conduct departed from the proper standard of care incumbent upon him, involving as it must have done a risk of death to the patient, was such that it should be judged criminal [...] The essence of the matter which is supremely a jury question is whether having regard to the risk of death involved, the conduct of the defendant was so bad in all the circumstances as to amount in their judgment to a criminal act or omission.

Lord Mackay conceded that this test involves 'an element of circularity': the defendant's conduct is criminal if it was grossly negligent, and it was grossly negligent if it

---

[57]*R v Bawa-Garba* [2016] EWCA Crim 1841.
[58]*R v Sellu* [2016] EWCA Crim 1716.

deserves to be criminal. The test has also been criticised for being too vague and vesting too much discretion in juries. This, it has been argued, violates the principle of maximum certainty (which we studied in Chapter 1). In fact, in *R v Misra* [2004] EWCA Crim 2375 defence counsel argued that the test is so vague that it violates Article 7 ECHR. Counsel's submissions emphasised the ambiguity and circularity of the test, and claimed that the offence definition fails to give citizens fair warning on what conduct is and isn't prohibited.

## EXTRACT

Read the following extract from the judgment of Judge LJ. Did he agree that the definition of gross negligence manslaughter is vague? Why/why not?

Who do you think is correct: defence counsel or Judge LJ?

### *R v Misra* [2004] EWCA Crim 2375

#### Judge LJ

64. In our judgment the law is clear. The ingredients of the offence have been clearly defined, and the principles decided in the House of Lords in *Adomako*. They involve no uncertainty. The hypothetical citizen, seeking to know his position, would be advised that, assuming he owed a duty of care to the deceased which he had negligently broken, and that death resulted, he would be liable to conviction for manslaughter if, on the available evidence, the jury was satisfied that his negligence was gross. A doctor would be told that grossly negligent treatment of a patient which exposed him or her to the risk of death, and caused it, would constitute manslaughter.

65. After Lord Williams' sustained criticism of the offence of manslaughter by gross negligence, the House of Lords in *Adomako* clarified the relevant principles and the ingredients of this offence. Although, to a limited extent, Lord Mackay accepted that there was an element of circularity in the process by which the jury would arrive at its verdict, the element of circularity which he identified did not then and does not now result in uncertainty which offends against Article 7, nor if we may say so, any principle of common law. Gross negligence manslaughter is not incompatible with the ECHR.

Whatever your view on the vagueness of the test for gross negligence, there is one important restriction. In the extract from Lord Mackay's judgment above, he stated that the defendant's conduct may only be held to constitute gross negligence if it involved a risk of death to the patient. This was reiterated by the Court of Appeal in *R v Singh (Gurphal)* [1999] Crim LR 582. In this case, Schiemann LJ said that the trial judge had been correct to tell the jury that they could only convict the defendant of gross negligence manslaughter if:

A reasonably prudent person in the position of the appellant would have foreseen a serious and obvious risk of death.

Notice that the question is whether the reasonable person would have foreseen the risk of death, not whether the defendant foresaw it.[59] If the defendant did foresee the risk

---

[59] A point confirmed in *R v Mark (Alan James)* [2004] EWCA Crim 2490.

of death the jury might be more inclined to decide that his negligence was gross. But the jury can find that the defendant's negligence was gross even if the risk of death never occurred to the defendant.

Further guidance on this requirement was provided in *R v Rudling* [2016] EWCA Crim 741. The victim was a 12-year-old boy named Ryan Morse. On Thursday 6 December 2012 Ryan was sent home from school unwell. The following morning he was still ill. He was feeling dizzy, his head was aching, and he had vomited twice and had diarrhoea. That afternoon he had diarrhoea again. As his mother was cleaning him up, she noticed that his genitalia were black. She phoned the doctor's surgery and spoke to Dr Rudling. She asked Dr Rudling to come and see Ryan. Her reply was 'No, it's to do with his hormones. Ring up on Monday, we'll fit him in to be seen by a male doctor'. The next day Ryan died of Addison's disease. Dr Rudling was charged with gross negligence manslaughter. The prosecution's case was that Dr Rudling's failure to either immediately visit Ryan at home or call an ambulance was a grossly negligent breach of duty. However, the trial judge accepted defence counsel's submission of no case to answer. The prosecution applied for leave to appeal against the trial judge's decision, arguing that it was not reasonable to conclude that there was no case to answer.

## EXTRACT

Read the following extract from the judgment of Sir Brian Leveson P. According to the Court of Appeal, was it reasonable for the trial judge to conclude that, at the time of the phone call, there was no evidence of an obvious and serious risk of death?

What did the Court say must be distinguished from an obvious and serious risk of death?

### *R v Rudling* [2016] EWCA Crim 741

#### Sir Brian Leveson P

38. The nub of [the prosecution's] argument was that if it is necessary to have a face to face assessment in order to risk manage a patient and assess what might potentially be a life-threatening condition, it is necessarily implicit that there is an obvious and serious risk of death at that time. As he put it, the thrust of [the prosecution's expert witness] Dr Peter's evidence was that a reasonably competent GP would have said to himself/herself "I cannot eliminate the possibility that this child may be suffering from a rare risk to life without the child being seen urgently" and that that equates to an obvious and serious risk of death.

39. In our judgment, that proposition simply does not follow, as is apparent when one focuses on each of the three aspects of this ingredient of the offence of gross negligence manslaughter. At the time of the breach of duty, there must be a risk of death, not merely serious illness; the risk must be serious; and the risk must be obvious. A GP faced with an unusual presentation which is worrying and undiagnosed may need to ensure a face to face assessment urgently in order to investigate further. That may be in order to assess whether it is something serious, to use Dr Peter's expression, which may or may not be so serious as to be life-threatening. A recognisable risk of something serious is not the same as a recognisable risk of death.

40. What does not follow is that if a reasonably competent GP requires an urgent assessment of a worrying and undiagnosed condition, it is necessarily reasonably foreseeable that there is a

risk of death. Still less does it demonstrate a serious risk of death, which is not to be equated with an "inability to eliminate a possibility". There may be numerous remote possibilities of very rare conditions which cannot be eliminated but which do not present a serious risk of death. Further, and perhaps most importantly, a mere possibility that an assessment might reveal something life-threatening is not the same as an obvious risk of death. An obvious risk is a present risk which is clear and unambiguous, not one which might become apparent on further investigation.

41. These distinctions are not a matter of semantics but represent real differences in the practical assessments which fall to be made by doctors. It is clearly of significance that Dr Peter did not in his evidence suggest that the need for a face to face assessment was because of an obvious and serious risk of death at the time of the phone call, either in chief or on any of the three occasions in cross examination when the opportunity to do so arose.

42. Accordingly the Judge's conclusion that there was no evidence upon which a jury could safely find an obvious and serious risk of death at the time of the phone call with Dr Rudling was not only a reasonable one, but in our view obviously correct.

So the prosecution must prove that the reasonably prudent person would have foreseen a serious and obvious risk of death. It is insufficient to prove a risk of something serious, or that the defendant failed to eliminate the possibility of something life-threatening.

Before moving on, it is worth stating that students often forget the 'serious and obvious risk of death' requirement when answering exam problem questions. It is all too easy to discuss whether the defendant's negligence deserves to be categorised as gross negligence, but forget to consider whether the reasonable person in the defendant's position would have foreseen a serious and obvious risk of death.

## ACTIVITY

- Some argue that manslaughter liability should only be imposed on those who foresaw a risk of death and unjustifiably chose to take (i.e. those who were reckless according to the *R v Cunningham* test). They argue that manslaughter liability should not be imposed on someone who (like Adomako) never chose to take a risk that the victim would be killed. Thinking back to the principles of criminal law that we studied in Chapter 1, make a list of arguments for and against imposing manslaughter liability on individuals (like Adomako) whose well-intentioned but hapless conduct causes the death of another person.

- In your opinion, is the offence of gross negligence manslaughter unacceptably broad?

## Proposals for reform: The Law Commission's Homicide Ladder

In its report on the existing law of homicide the Law Commission stated that it had been guided by the ladder principle. The meaning of this principle is set out in the following extract.

**EXTRACT**

In your own words, explain the relevance of the ladder principle to: (1) the existing two-tier structure of the law of homicide; (2) the mandatory life sentence and (3) the partial defences.

## Law Commission (2006) *Murder, Manslaughter and Infanticide* (Law Commission Report No 304) HC 30

1.64 In structuring the general homicide offences we have been guided by a key principle: the 'ladder' principle. Individual offences of homicide should exist within a graduated system or hierarchy of offences. This system or hierarchy should reflect the offence's degree of seriousness, without too much overlap between individual offences. The main reason for adopting the 'ladder' principle is as Lord Bingham has recently put it (in a slightly different context):

> The interests of justice are not served if a defendant who has committed a lesser offence is either convicted of a greater offence, exposing him to greater punishment than his crime deserves, or acquitted altogether, enabling him to escape the measure of punishment which his crime deserves. The objective must be that defendants are neither over-convicted nor under-convicted ...

1.65 The 'ladder' principle also applies to sentencing. The mandatory life sentence should be confined to the most serious kinds of killing. A discretionary life sentence should be available for less serious (but still highly blameworthy) killings.

1.66 Partial defences currently only affect the verdict of murder. This is because a verdict of murder carries a mandatory sentence. That sentence is not appropriate where there are exceptional mitigating circumstances of the kind involved in the partial defences. These mitigating circumstances necessitate a greater degree of judicial discretion in sentencing. The law creates this discretion by means of the partial defences which reduce what would otherwise be a verdict of murder, which carries a mandatory sentence, to manslaughter, which does not. Therefore, our recommended scheme does not extend the application of the partial defences to second degree murder or manslaughter. These offences would permit the trial judge discretion in sentencing and they therefore lack the primary justification for having partial defences.

**ACTIVITY**

Think back to the following four cases and examples that we have studied earlier in this chapter. Under the existing law, would the defendant in each scenario be convicted of murder or manslaughter? Comparing your four answers, to what extent do you think the existing law respects the ladder principle?

- D intentionally punches V in the face. The punch breaks V's nose and causes V to fall to the ground. In falling, V hits his or her head on the curb causing a massive and fatal brain haemorrhage.

- A terrorist plants a bomb and then contacts the authorities and warns them. He plants a live bomb instead of a fake one – so that the authorities will fear him and listen to him

– but he doesn't want the bomb to explode because he fears that he will lose public support if innocent people are killed. He gives the warning some time before the bomb is set to explode, so that the public can be evacuated and a bomb disposal expert can defuse the bomb. However, the bomb explodes and kills the bomb disposal expert.

- *R v Cocker.*
- *R v Ahluwalia.*

The Law Commission has proposed replacing the existing two-tier law of homicide with a three-tier structure.[60] As Figure 5.3 shows, the Law Commission's proposed scheme would have first degree murder at the top, with second degree murder in the middle and manslaughter at the bottom.

| Current law | Law Commission's proposal |
|---|---|
| **Murder**<br>• Intention to kill or to cause GBH<br>*(Mandatory sentence of life imprisonment)* | **First degree murder**<br>• D intended to kill<br>• D intended to do serious injury *and* was aware there was a serious risk of causing death<br>*(Mandatory sentence of life imprisonment)* |
| **Manslaughter**<br>• Voluntary manslaughter (killing with *mens rea* of murder where partial defence applies)<br>• Involuntary manslaughter (culpable killing where D lacked the *mens rea* of murder)<br>*(Discretionary maximum of life imprisonment)* | **Second degree murder**<br>• D intended to do serious injury<br>• D intended to cause some injury or a fear or risk of injury *and* was aware of a serious risk of causing death<br>• Where a partial defence applies to what would have been first degree murder<br>*(Discretionary maximum of life imprisonment)* |
|  | **Manslaughter**<br>• Killing by gross negligence<br>• Killing through a criminal act intending to cause injury or aware of a serious risk of causing injury<br>*(Discretionary maximum of life imprisonment)* |

**Figure 5.3.** The Law Commission's proposed homicide ladder

## ACTIVITY

Look back at the four cases and examples in the previous question. Which offence would the defendant in each scenario be convicted of under the Law Commission's proposed scheme? To what extent does the Law Commission's proposal respect the ladder principle? To what extent does the Law Commission's proposal rectify the problems with the existing law?

(For further evaluation of the Law Commission's proposals, see the sources in the further reading list.)

---

[60]*Murder, Manslaughter and Infanticide* (Report No 304, 2006) HC 30.

# Conclusion

We have covered a lot of material in this chapter. The flow chart in Figure 5.4 shows how you should structure this material when answering an exam problem question.

The first question to ask is whether a person has died and the defendant was a factual and legal cause of death. In other words, are all of the *actus reus* requirements of murder

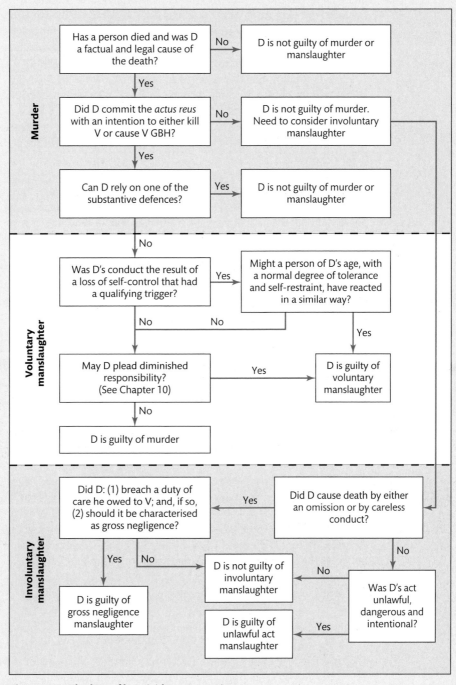

**Figure 5.4.** The law of homicide: an overview

satisfied? If not, then the defendant cannot be guilty of murder or manslaughter. When this is the case in an exam problem question you need to consider other possible offences instead, such as whether the defendant was an accessory to murder (see Chapter 13), whether the defendant is guilty of conspiracy to murder or attempted murder (see Chapter 12) or whether the defendant is guilty of a non-fatal offence (see Chapter 6).

If a person has died and the defendant was a factual and legal cause of death, the next question is whether the defendant had the *mens rea* of murder. If the defendant lacked the *mens rea* of murder you should consider involuntary manslaughter instead. The first issue here will be to decide whether to discuss unlawful act manslaughter or gross negligence manslaughter. To help you decide you should use the distinction Lord Atkin drew in *Andrews v DPP* between unlawful acts and careless lawful acts.

If the defendant had the *mens rea* of murder then, on the face of it, he is guilty of murder. However, before reaching a conclusion you need to consider possible defences. It is best to begin with the substantive defences (see Chapter 11). Since these result in a complete acquittal, defendants will prefer to plead a substantive defence rather than a partial defence. If no substantive defence is available, you should then consider the partial defences instead.

Finally, it is worth pointing out that in some exam questions it will not be possible to answer some of the questions in this flow chart with certainty. For example, it might be debatable whether the defendant had the *mens rea* of murder or not. In this case, your answer should discuss all possible eventualities. So you should write something like, 'If the jury concluded that Harold had the *mens rea* of murder, he would seek to plead the partial defence of loss of control'. After discussing whether Harold's defence of loss of control would succeed or not, you should then write something like, 'On the other hand, if the jury concluded that Harold lacked the *mens rea* of murder involuntary manslaughter would need to be considered instead'. You should then discuss whether Harold satisfies the requirements of the relevant type of involuntary manslaughter.

## Self-test questions

1.　Maeve has worked at the airport check-in desk for many years, and has grown tired of dealing with customer complaints. Rory arrives at the check-in desk ten minutes before his scheduled take-off time. He had left home four hours earlier to catch a train to the airport, but had been held up first by a traffic jam and second by his train being delayed due to signal problems on the train line. Out-of-breath and agitated he insists, 'I need to check in, my flight leaves in ten minutes.' Maeve replies, 'Sorry Sir, you're too late. You'll have to wait for the next available flight.' Annoyed, Rory asks, 'When is the next available flight?' 'Tomorrow morning', Maeve answers, 'and it will cost an extra £150.' 'What?' shouts Rory, 'I am booked on a flight that takes off in ten minutes and I demand that you let me on it.' Frustrated, Maeve responds, 'Don't shout at me. It's your own stupid fault for being late.' At this Rory snaps. He climbs over the check-in desk and attacks Maeve, hitting her repeatedly. Unknown to Rory, Maeve has a weak heart. She suffers a heart attack and dies.

Elsewhere at the airport there is a long queue at the check-in desk for the flight to Athens. Andreas, who has been queuing for almost one-and-a-half hours, is incensed when he sees Thanos arrive and push in at the front of the queue. He immediately marches up behind Thanos and shoves him out of the queue. Thanos stumbles and collides with an elderly passenger named Eleni. Eleni falls over and cracks her head on the hard floor. She later dies in hospital.

Discuss the criminal liability of Rory and Andreas. How (if at all) would your answer be different if, when Eleni arrived at hospital, a junior doctor failed to check her medical records properly and prescribed her a drug to which she was allergic. She died as a result of an allergic reaction to the drug. Had this mistake not been made, she would have made a full recovery.

2. Teenager Leo, who is preparing to go to university in September, goes to his local bank. He intends to ask for a student loan, but also takes a loaded gun with him in case his loan request is refused. He meets with the bank manager, Rasheed, who refuses to lend Leo all the money he asks for. Leo responds by pulling the gun from his pocket, pointing it at Rasheed, and saying, 'In that case, give me £20,000. Now.' Terrified, Rasheed quickly fetches the money from the safe and gives it to Leo. After Leo has left the bank Rasheed suffers a heart attack and dies.

   It is later discovered that although Rasheed was only 41 years old, he suffered from a rare heart condition which meant his heart could not cope with extremely stressful situations.

   Discuss the criminal liability of Leo. How (if at all) would your answer be different in each of the following three situations?
   a. Rasheed was 76 years old and obviously frail. After Leo pointed the gun at him he immediately suffered a fatal heart attack;
   b. Rasheed had refused to give Leo any money and so Leo fired the gun, killing Rasheed instantly. Leo says that he mistakenly thought the gun was unloaded, and that he only pulled the trigger to frighten Rasheed into handing over the money; and
   c. After being refused the bank loan, Leo decided to instead raise the money by setting fire to his car and claiming the insurance money. He asked his friend, George, to help him set fire to the car. However, when they set fire to the car it exploded, killing George.

3. Timothy has campaigned unsuccessfully for more stringent security measures at airports for several years. In order to convince the authorities to listen to him, he plants a live bomb in the airport's check-in area. He telephones the airport's security office three hours before the bomb is set to explode and tells them about the bomb, so that the public can be safely evacuated and the bomb defused. The phone is answered by Jake. Jake wrongly assumes that Timothy's warning is a hoax, and ignores it. Three hours later the bomb explodes and 41 members of the public are killed.

   Timothy states that he did not want anyone to suffer any harm. He says that he used a live bomb, not a fake one, to ensure that the authorities took notice of his campaign.

   Discuss the criminal liability of Timothy and Jake. How (if at all) would your answer be different in each of the following two situations?
   a. Jake immediately arranged for the airport to be evacuated and telephoned a bomb disposal team. After inspecting the bomb the team's leader Clive announced, 'This one looks easy. Leave it to me lads.' As he began to try and defuse the bomb he made an inadvertent error which caused the bomb to explode, killing him and two other members of the team. Had he not made this error the bomb could have been easily defused.
   b. Timothy only gave the telephone warning 20 minutes before the bomb was set to explode. As soon as Jake received the warning he arranged for the airport to be evacuated. In the ensuing panic a five-year-old girl called Daisy was knocked over and killed by a police car being driven by Ravi as she fled from the building. Ravi had been driving to the airport as quickly as he could so that he could help evacuate members of the public.

4. 'Under the existing law of homicide some defendants may only be convicted of manslaughter when a murder conviction would be more appropriate, whilst some other defendants who do not deserve the label "murderer" may be convicted of this offence. Enacting the Law Commission's proposed homicide ladder would rectify this situation.'

Discuss the extent to which you agree with this statement.

5. 'The loss of control defence successfully addresses a number of problems with the old defence of provocation. The new law not only ensures that those who are hot-headed, short-tempered, jealous or possessive no longer escape a murder conviction. It also achieves justice for those who fear serious violence, suffer a slow-burn reaction and endure years of abuse.'

Discuss the extent to which you agree with this statement.

## Homicide checklist

Having worked through this chapter, you should now have:

✓ An understanding of the structure of the law of homicide and the Law Commission's proposal for a new three-tier structure

✓ An ability to critically discuss the existing two-tier structure of the law of homicide and the Law Commission's proposal for a new three-tier structure

✓ An understanding of the requirements of the crime of murder

✓ An ability to critically discuss the *mens rea* of murder

✓ An understanding of the requirements of the loss of control defence

✓ An ability to critically discuss the loss of control defence

✓ An understanding of the requirements of the crime of unlawful act manslaughter

✓ An understanding of the requirements of the crime of gross negligence manslaughter.

## Further reading

Ashworth, A. (2007) 'Principles, Pragmatism and the Law Commission's Recommendations on Homicide Law Reform' *Criminal Law Review* 333.

Ashworth, A. (2015) 'Manslaughter by Omission and the Rule of Law' *Criminal Law Review* 563.

Ashworth, A. & Mitchell, B. (eds) (2004) *Rethinking English Homicide Law*. OUP: Oxford.

Baker, D.J. & Zhao, L.X. (2012) 'Contributory Qualifying and Non-Qualifying Triggers in the Loss of Control Defence: A Wrong Turn on Sexual Infidelity' 76 *Journal of Criminal Law* 254.

Cornford, A. (2016) 'Mitigating Murder' 10 *Criminal Law and Philosophy* 31.

Edwards, S. (2010) 'Anger and Fear as Justifiable Preludes for Loss of Self-Control' 74 *Journal of Criminal Law* 223.

Fitz-Gibbon, K. (2013) 'Replacing Provocation in England and Wales: Examining the Partial Defence of Loss of Control' 40 *Journal of Law and Society* 280.

Herring, J. & Palser, E. (2007) 'The Duty of Care in Gross Negligence Manslaughter' *Criminal Law Review* 24.

Keating, H. & Bridgeman, J. (2012) 'Compassionate Killings: The Case for a Partial Defence' 75 *Modern Law Review* 697.

Law Commission (2005) *A New Homicide Act for England and Wales? A Consultation Paper* (Consultation Paper No 177).

Law Commission (2006) *Murder, Manslaughter and Infanticide* (Report No 304) HC 30.

Lodge, A. (2017) 'Gross Negligence Manslaughter on the Cusp: The Unprincipled Privileging of Harm over Culpability' 81 *Journal of Criminal Law* 125.

Mitchell, B.J., Mackay, R.D. & Brookbanks, W.J. (2008) 'Pleading for Provoked Killers: In Defence of *Morgan Smith*' 124 *Law Quarterly Review* 675.

Norrie, A. (2010) 'The Coroners and Justice Act 2009 – Partial Defences to Murder (1) Loss of Control' *Criminal Law Review* 275.

Nourse, V. (1997) 'Passion's Progress: Modern Law Reform and the Provocation Defense' 106 *Yale Law Journal* 1331.

Reed, A. & Bohlander, M. (eds) (2011) *Loss of Control and Diminished Responsibility: Domestic, Comparative and International Perspectives*. Ashgate Publishing.

Tadros, V. (2006) 'The Homicide Ladder' 69 *Modern Law Review* 601.

Taylor, R. (2007) 'The Nature of "Partial Defences" and the Coherence of (Second Degree) Murder' *Criminal Law Review* 345.

Wilson, W. (2006) 'The Structure of Criminal Homicide' *Criminal Law Review* 471.

Withey, C. (2011) 'Loss of Control, Loss of Opportunity?' *Criminal Law Review* 263.

# 6

# Non-fatal offences against the person

## Chapter objectives

By the end of this chapter you should have:

- An understanding of the requirements for establishing criminal liability for: (a) assault; (b) battery; (c) assault occasioning actual bodily harm; (d) malicious wounding or infliction of grievous bodily harm and (e) wounding or grievous bodily harm with intent

- An understanding of the case law governing consent to injury and consent obtained by fraud

- An ability to apply the relevant law to a hypothetical set of facts and discuss whether criminal liability may be established for any of the offences listed above

- An ability to discuss and evaluate the case law on consent to injury

- An ability to discuss and evaluate the Law Commission's proposed reforms of the non-fatal offences against the person.

# Introduction

There are a large number of non-fatal offences against the person. Many of these are contained in the Offences Against the Person Act 1861 (OAPA). If you flick through the sections of this Act you'll find some offences which you've probably heard of before (like assault with intent to resist arrest (s.38) and solicitation to murder (s.4)), and others which now seem very dated (like not providing apprentices or servants with food whereby life is endangered (s.26) and drivers of carriages injuring persons by furious driving (s.35)).

The first part of this chapter focuses on five of the most significant non-fatal offences. As Figure 6.1 illustrates, these offences are meant to form a ladder with the least serious at the bottom and the most serious at the top. But, as we'll see, it is questionable whether the offences adequately respect the ladder principle.

We're going to start at the bottom of the ladder, with the crimes of assault and battery, and work our way up, finishing with the most serious of the five offences: wounding or GBH with intent.

In the second part of the chapter we explore some difficult issues relating to consent. These are: first, what happens if the defendant fraudulently tricks the victim into consenting to an activity; and, second, when does the criminal law allow individuals to consent to injury? The final part of the chapter examines the Law Commission's proposals for reform of the non-fatal offences against the person.

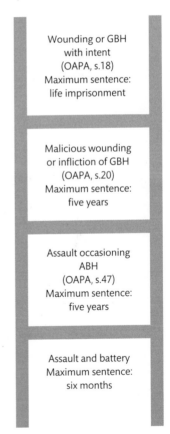

Wounding or GBH
with intent
(OAPA, s.18)
Maximum sentence:
life imprisonment

Malicious wounding
or infliction of GBH
(OAPA, s.20)
Maximum sentence:
five years

Assault occasioning
ABH
(OAPA, s.47)
Maximum sentence:
five years

Assault and battery
Maximum sentence:
six months

**Figure 6.1.** Non-fatal offences against the person: the ladder of offences

# Assault

There is no statutory definition of assault, so instead we must turn to case law. The *actus reus* of the offence was set out by Robert Goff LJ in *Collins v Wilcock* [1984] 1 WLR 1172:

> An assault is an act which causes another person to apprehend the infliction of immediate, unlawful, force on his person

The *mens rea* of the offence was considered in *R v Venna* [1976] QB 421. In this case, the defence argued that only intention will suffice; recklessness, it was claimed, is not enough. The Court of Appeal rejected this, stating:

> We see no reason in logic or in law why a person who recklessly applies physical force to the person of another should be outside the criminal law of assault. In many cases the dividing line between intention and recklessness is barely distinguishable. This is such a case. In our judgment the direction was right in law and this ground of appeal fails.

The crime of assault therefore has the following five requirements:

1. The victim must *apprehend* the infliction of force on his person
2. The victim must apprehend the infliction of *immediate* force
3. The victim must apprehend the infliction of *unlawful* force
4. The defendant's actions must have been the *cause* of the victim's apprehension
5. The defendant must have either: (a) intended to cause the victim to apprehend the infliction of immediate, unlawful force; or (b) been reckless as to whether the victim would be caused to apprehend the infliction of immediate, unlawful force.

Numbers 1 to 4 are *actus reus* requirements. Number 5 is a *mens rea* requirement. We will work through them in turn.

## 1. The victim must *apprehend* the infliction of force on his person

The victim must apprehend the infliction of force on his person. This is the essence of an assault. It is also what distinguishes an assault from a battery. As we shall see shortly, for a battery there must have been contact with the victim's body. But no contact is required for an assault. It is sufficient to show that the victim apprehended the infliction of force.

---

**ACTIVITY**

In which two of the following scenarios is there the *actus reus* of an assault?

- I pull a gun out of my pocket and point it at you. You fear that I am going to shoot you and are terrified.
- I pull a gun out of my pocket and point it at you. Knowing that I am joking, you laugh then turn around and walk away.
- I take my gun out of my pocket and show it to you, saying, 'Don't worry, it isn't loaded'. You think that I am lying and believe that I am going to shoot you.
- I creep up behind you, pull a gun out of my pocket and point it at the back of your head. You are completely unaware of my presence.

---

## 2. The victim must apprehend the infliction of *immediate force*

In *Collins v Wilcock* Robert Goff LJ stated that the victim must apprehend the infliction of *immediate* force. The *Oxford English Dictionary* defines 'immediate' as 'taking effect without delay or lapse of time; done at once; instant'. So this appears to place a strict limitation on the scope of the offence. Taken literally, the victim must believe that the apprehended force will follow instantly, without any delay.

In fact, however, the courts have not applied the immediacy requirement strictly. There are several cases in which the immediacy requirement has been diluted. Take *R v Lewis* [1970] Crim LR 647 as an example. V, Lewis' wife, said that Lewis treated her violently. So she locked their home – a third floor flat – and would not let him in. Lewis shouted threats to her and said he would kill her. V then heard the sound of breaking glass from one of the other rooms in the flat. Thinking that he was breaking into the flat, and fearing what would happen if she stayed in the flat, V then jumped out of the window. The fall broke both her legs. Lewis was charged with maliciously inflicting GBH (OAPA, s.20). Even though Lewis was locked outside the flat, the Court of Appeal held that V had apprehended the infliction of immediate force. This obviously stretches the meaning of immediate.

Similar issues were examined by the House of Lords in *R v Ireland & Burstow* [1998] AC 147. In this judgment the House of Lords considered two cases. The first case concerned Robert Ireland. During a three-month period in 1994 he harassed three women by repeatedly making silent telephone calls to them. Most of the calls were at night. The women suffered psychiatric illness as a result. At trial Ireland was convicted of assault occasioning ABH. His appeal against conviction was dismissed by the Court of Appeal, and reached the House of Lords.

The second case concerned Anthony Burstow. He had had a relationship with the victim, Tracey Sant. When she ended the relationship Burstow refused to accept it and began to harass her. During an eight-month period in 1995 he made both silent and abusive telephone calls to her, he distributed offensive cards in the street where she lived, he frequently turned up at her home and her place of work, he secretly photographed her and her family and he sent a menacing note. As a result of his actions Sant suffered a severe depressive illness. The Court of Appeal dismissed Burstow's appeal against his conviction for malicious infliction of GBH (OAPA, s.20), and he appealed to the House of Lords.

One of the issues the House of Lords had to consider was whether it is possible to commit assault by making silent telephone calls. In the leading judgment, Lord Steyn examined this question in three steps. First, he considered whether it is possible to commit an assault simply by speaking.

## EXTRACT

Read the following extract. According to Lord Steyn, is it possible to commit assault by words alone?

### *R v Ireland & Burstow* [1998] AC 147

### Lord Steyn

Counsel argued that as a matter of law an assault can never be committed by words alone and therefore it cannot be committed by silence. The premise depends on the slenderest authority, namely, an observation by Holroyd J. to a jury that "no words or singing are equivalent to an assault:" *Rex v. Meade and Belt* (1823) 1 Lew. 184. The proposition that a gesture may amount to an assault, but that words can never suffice, is unrealistic and indefensible. A thing said is also a thing done. There is no reason why something said should be incapable of causing an apprehension of immediate personal violence, e.g. a man accosting a woman in a dark alley saying, "Come with me or I will stab you." I would, therefore, reject the proposition that an assault can never be committed by words.

Second, Lord Steyn said that if it is possible to commit an assault by words alone, then it is possible to commit an assault by speaking on a telephone. He commented:

[T]here is no reason why a telephone caller who says to a woman in a menacing way "I will be at your door in a minute or two" may not be guilty of an assault if he causes his victim to apprehend immediate personal violence.

So, third, is it possible to commit an assault by making a silent telephone call? Here is Lord Steyn's answer:

That brings me to the critical question whether a silent caller may be guilty of an assault. The answer to this question seems to me to be "Yes, depending on the facts." It involves questions of fact within the province of the jury

[...]

Take now the case of the silent caller. He intends by his silence to cause fear and he is so understood. The victim is assailed by uncertainty about his intentions. Fear may dominate her emotions, and it may be the fear that the caller's arrival at her door may be imminent. She may fear the *possibility* of immediate personal violence. As a matter of law the caller may be guilty of an assault: whether he is or not will depend on the circumstance and in particular on the impact of the caller's potentially menacing call or calls on the victim.

So whether there is the *actus reus* of assault in cases like these all depends on the response of the victim. If the victim is caused to apprehend the possibility of immediate, unlawful force, there will be the *actus reus* of assault.

## ACTIVITY

In the light of Lord Steyn's judgment, decide whether there is the *actus reus* of an assault in each of the following two scenarios:

- As a prank, a student decides to make a silent telephone call to his European Law lecturer. When the lecturer answers the phone, the student says nothing for a few seconds, then starts breathing heavily down the phone line. Thinking it is a wrong number, the lecturer hangs up and quickly forgets about it.

- As a prank, a student decides to make a silent telephone call to his Criminal Law lecturer. Having just finished reading a particularly gruesome case, the lecturer is already feeling edgy. When he answers the phone and hears nothing but heavy breathing he begins screaming hysterically, 'Who's there?' He quickly locks all the windows and doors, draws the curtains and hides behind the sofa.

Before moving on, there are two further points to note about Lord Steyn's judgment:

- Notice how the judgment stretches the meaning of immediacy. Lord Steyn said that the caller who says 'I will be at your door *in a minute or two*' causes the victim to apprehend immediate force. He also said that a victim might react to a silent telephone call with fear that 'the caller's arrival at her door may be *imminent*'. So according to *R v Ireland & Burstow*, for the crime of assault 'immediate' has a broader meaning than the one found in a dictionary. It means something more like imminent.

- Notice also that Lord Steyn said that the victim may fear the *possibility* of immediate personal force. So it is not necessary for the victim to have believed that the defendant would inflict immediate, unlawful force. It is enough that the victim believed that the defendant might do so. This also gives the *actus reus* of the offence a far broader scope.

Lastly, note that the *Ireland* and *Burstow* cases occurred before Parliament enacted the Protection from Harassment Act 1997. This legislation was introduced specifically to deal with the problem of stalking. So if similar cases occurred today prosecutions could be brought under this Act instead.

## 3. The victim must apprehend the infliction of *unlawful* force

There are a number of reasons why the apprehended force might not be unlawful. First, it might be consensual. For example, suppose Valentina asks her boyfriend Romeo for a hug. When she sees him putting his arms around her she apprehends the infliction of force, but the force is lawful. We consider issues relating to consent in more detail later in the chapter.

Second, the force might be lawful because it is used in self-defence. Suppose I attack you, and you have no choice but to push me backwards and run away. As I see your hands coming towards me I apprehend the infliction of force, but the force is lawful. We study self-defence in Chapter 11.

Third, a lawful occupier may use reasonable force to remove an unwanted trespasser.[1] Suppose Romeo is standing in the doorway of Valentina's flat. Valentina asks him to leave several times, but he refuses, so Valentina pushes him out of the door. As Romeo sees Valentina's hands coming towards him, he apprehends the infliction of force, but the force is lawful.

Fourth, the force might be lawful because it is legally authorised. Suppose a policeman is about to arrest Romeo. When Romeo sees the policeman make a grab for him he apprehends the infliction of force, but the force is lawful.

In all four of these examples there is not the *actus reus* of assault, because in each case the victim does not apprehend the infliction of *unlawful* force.

## 4. The defendant's actions must have been the *cause* of the victim's apprehension

The defendant's actions must have been a factual and legal cause of the victim's apprehension. Here you apply the law governing causation, which we studied in Chapter 3.

## 5. The defendant must have either: (a) intended to cause the victim to apprehend the infliction of immediate, unlawful force; or (b) been reckless as to whether the victim would be caused to apprehend the infliction of immediate, unlawful force

As we saw above, the *mens rea* of assault was set out by the Court of Appeal in *R v Venna* [1976] QB 421. One question which emerged in the years that followed was whether the *Cunningham* definition of recklessness applies here. In *R v Savage & Parmenter* [1992] 1 AC 699 the House of Lords confirmed that *Cunningham* recklessness applies.

---

[1] *R v Day* [2015] EWCA Crim 1646.

# Battery

There is also no statutory definition of battery, so again we must turn to case law. The *actus reus* of the offence was set out by Robert Goff LJ in *Collins v Wilcock* [1984] 1 WLR 1172:

> [A] battery is the actual infliction of unlawful force on another person.

As we saw above, the argument that only intention should be sufficient for the *mens rea* was rejected by the Court of Appeal in *R v Venna*. Recklessness will also suffice.

The offence of battery therefore has the following three requirements:

1. The defendant must have inflicted force on the victim
2. The force must have been unlawful
3. The defendant must have either: (a) intended to inflict unlawful force on the victim; or (b) been reckless as to whether unlawful force would be inflicted on the victim.

Numbers 1 and 2 are *actus reus* requirements. Number 3 is a *mens rea* requirement.

## 1. The defendant must have inflicted force on the victim

As we have seen, no contact is required for an assault. But contact is necessary for a battery. This is the essence of a battery. The defendant must have inflicted force on the victim.

There are four issues we need to consider on this limb of the *actus reus*:

### i. How much force is necessary?

First, how much force is necessary? This question was answered by Robert Goff LJ in *Collins v Wilcock*.

---

**EXTRACT**

Read the following extract from Robert Goff LJ's judgment. Which of the following statements is correct?

a. The force used must have been overpowering.
b. The amount of force must have been significant.
c. Any contact, however slight, is sufficient.

### Collins v Wilcock [1984] 1 WLR 1172

#### Robert Goff LJ

The fundamental principle, plain and incontestable, is that every person's body is inviolate. It has long been established that any touching of another person, however slight, may amount to a battery. So Hold C.J. held in *Cole v. Turner* (1704) 6 Mod. 149 that "the least touching of another in anger is a battery." The breadth of the principle reflects the fundamental nature of the interest so protected. As Blackstone wrote in his *Commentaries*, 17th ed. (1830), vol. 3, p. 120:

> "the law cannot draw the line between different degrees of violence, and therefore totally prohibits the first and lowest stage of it; every man's person being sacred, and no other having a right to meddle with it, in any the slightest manner."

The effect is that everybody is protected not only against physical injury but against any form of physical molestation.

Robert Goff LJ went on to say that such a broad rule must be subject to exceptions. These exceptions are set out in the following extract.

## EXTRACT

Read the extract and compile a list of all the exceptions stated by Robert Goff LJ.

Looking at your list, decide whether there is the *actus reus* of battery in each of the following scenarios:

- It is rush hour on the London Underground. You are waiting on the platform. When a tube train arrives, it is packed full of people. The only way you can squeeze onto the train is by pushing those already onboard backwards.
- Halfway through a lecture your pen runs out. You don't have a spare pen with you, so you tap the person sitting in front of you on the shoulder to ask whether you can borrow one. They ignore you, so you keep tapping them until they eventually turn around.

### *Collins v Wilcock* [1984] 1 WLR 1172

### Robert Goff LJ

But so widely drawn a principle must inevitably be subject to exceptions. For example, children may be subject to reasonable punishment; people may be subjected to the lawful exercise of the power of arrest; and reasonable force may be used in self-defence or for the prevention of crime. But, apart from these special instances where the control or constraint is lawful, a broader exception has been created to allow for the exigencies of everyday life. Generally speaking consent is a defence to battery; and most of the physical contacts of ordinary life are not actionable because they are impliedly consented to by all who move in society and so expose themselves to the risk of bodily contact. So nobody can complain of the jostling which is inevitable from his presence in, for example, a supermarket, an underground station or a busy street; nor can a person who attends a party complain if his hand is seized in friendship, or even if his back is, within reason, slapped: see *Tuberville v. Savage* (1669) 1 Mod. 3. Although such cases are regarded as examples of implied consent, it is more common nowadays to treat them as falling within a general exception embracing all physical contact which is generally acceptable in the ordinary conduct of daily life [...]

Among such forms of conduct, long held to be acceptable, is touching a person for the purpose of engaging his attention, though of course using no greater degree of physical contact than is reasonably necessary in the circumstances for that purpose [...] But a distinction is drawn between a touch to draw a man's attention, which is generally acceptable, and a physical restraint, which is not. So we find Parke B. observing in *Rawlings v. Till* (1837) 3 M. & W. 28, 29, with reference to *Wiffen v. Kincard*, that "There the touch was merely to engage [a man's] attention, not to put a restraint upon his person." Furthermore, persistent touching to gain attention in the face of obvious disregard may transcend the norms of acceptable behaviour and so be outside the exception. We do not say that more than one touch is never permitted; for example, the lost or distressed may surely be permitted a second touch, or possibly even more, on a reluctant or impervious sleeve or shoulder, as may a person who is acting reasonably in the exercise of a duty. In each case, the test must be whether the physical contact so persisted in has in the circumstances gone beyond generally acceptable standards of conduct; and the answer to that question will depend upon the facts of the particular case.

In *Collins v Wilcock* Alexis Collins was accused of assaulting policewoman WPC Wilcock in the execution of her duty.[2] Wilcock was in her police car when she saw Collins walking along a street with another woman who was a known prostitute. They appeared to be soliciting men in the street. Wilcock asked the two women to get into the car so that she could have a word with them. Collins refused to do so, and walked away. Wilcock got out of the car and asked for Collins' name and address. Collins said she didn't want to talk to the police and started to walk away again. Wilcock took hold of Collins' left arm to restrain her. Collins responded by scratching Wilcock's forearm with her fingernails.

At trial Collins was convicted. She appealed to the High Court. The issue in the case was whether Wilcock committed a battery when she took hold of Collins to stop her from walking away. If so, then Wilcock's actions were unlawful and outside the course of her duties as a police officer – which in turn would mean that Collins could not be convicted of assaulting Wilcock *in the execution of her duties*. (It is important to note that Wilcock was not exercising her power of arrest.)

## EXTRACT

In your opinion, did Wilcock's actions fall within any of the exceptions to the rule that any touching is sufficient for a battery? So did Wilcock commit a battery when she took hold of Collins to stop her from walking away?

Now read the following extract to see the conclusion of the High Court!

### *Collins v Wilcock* [1984] 1 WLR 1172

#### Robert Goff LJ

But if a police officer, not exercising his power of arrest, nevertheless reinforces his request with the actual use of force [...] then his act in thereby detaining the other person will be unlawful. [H]is action will constitute a battery.

Having regard to the facts of the present case, we have no doubt that the magistrate framed his question having in mind the act of the woman police officer in taking hold of the defendant's arm to restrain her, which we have held to be a battery and so unlawful.

### ii. Is there an infliction of force if the defendant touches the victim's clothes, not the victim's body?

The short answer is yes. In *R v Thomas* [1985] 81 Cr App R 331 a school caretaker rubbed the bottom of an eleven-year-old pupil's skirt, lifted the skirt, then dropped it again. At no stage did the caretaker touch the girl's body, or try to do so. The Court of Appeal held that a defendant does inflict force on a person by touching the clothes she is wearing.[3] Ackner LJ stated:

> There could be no dispute that if you touch a person's clothes whilst he is wearing them that is equivalent to touching him.

---

[2] *Collins v Wilcock* may be contrasted with the pragmatic decision reached in *McMillan v CPS* [2008] EWHC 1457 (Admin). In this case a police officer led a woman from a property to the street before speaking to her because she was drunk and unsteady on her feet and the garden was on a steep slope. It was held that the force used fell within generally acceptable standards of conduct.

[3] Although his conviction for indecent assault was quashed due to lack of corroborative evidence.

### iii. Can force be inflicted indirectly or using an object?

In Chapter 2, we looked at the case *Fagan v Metropolitan Police Commissioner* [1969] 1 QB 439, the case in which a motorist accidentally drove onto a policeman's foot and then refused to move his car. One of the issues in this case was whether there is a battery when the force is inflicted using an object. In *Fagan*, for example, the force was inflicted through the medium of the defendant's car.

## EXTRACT

Read the following extract from the judgment of James J. Can there be a battery when the force is inflicted using an object?

### *Fagan v Metropolitan Police Commissioner* [1969] 1 QB 439

#### James J

Where an assault involves a battery, it matters not, in our judgment, whether the battery is inflicted directly by the body of the offender or through the medium of some weapon or instrument controlled by the action of the offender. An assault may be committed by the laying of a hand upon another, and the action does not cease to be an assault if it is a stick held in the hand and not the hand itself which is laid on the person of the victim. So for our part we see no difference in principle between the action of stepping on to a person's toe and maintaining that position and the action of driving a car on to a person's foot and sitting in the car whilst its position on the foot is maintained.

In *DPP v K* [1990] 1 WLR 1067 D, a 15-year-old schoolboy, took a boiling tube of sulphuric acid out of a chemistry lesson, without permission, to the school toilets. He said that he wanted to pour some of the acid onto toilet paper to test the reaction. While he was in the toilet cubicle he heard footsteps outside and panicked. He went to one of the hot air hand driers, turned the nozzle upwards and poured the acid into the nozzle. He then went back to his lesson, intending to return and clean the drier later. In the meantime, however, another pupil V went to the toilets to wash his hands. When V turned the drier on the acid was blown onto his face, leaving a permanent scar.

D was charged with assault occasioning ABH (OAPA, s.47). At trial the case was dismissed. The prosecutor appealed, and the case reached the High Court. The Court held that D had inflicted force on V, and so would be guilty of battery if he had acted with the necessary *mens rea*. The key points for our purposes are:

1.  The infliction of force can be through a medium. In this case the force was inflicted via the acid. Similarly, I would commit a battery if I throw my pint of beer over you. And I would commit a battery if I am driving on a rainy day, see you walking on the pavement, and deliberately splash you by driving through a puddle.

2.  The infliction of force can be indirect. In *DPP v K* the defendant did not directly inflict force on the victim. The victim turned the hand drier on himself. The Court said that this was immaterial.

Another example of force being applied indirectly is *Haystead v Chief Constable of Derbyshire* [2000] 3 All ER 890. In this case John Haystead punched his ex-partner Angela in the face whilst she was holding her 12-month-old son Matthew. As a result she dropped Matthew, and he hit his head on the floor. Haystead was not only charged with battery of Angela, but also battery of baby Matthew. At trial he was convicted. He subsequently appealed against his conviction for battery of Matthew. The High Court dismissed his appeal. Haystead had committed battery of Matthew. He indirectly applied force to him by causing Angela to drop him.

### iv. Can you inflict force by doing nothing?

Think back to *Fagan* again. In this case the three members of the Divisional Court unanimously agreed that it is not possible to commit the offence of battery by omission. The majority of the Court nonetheless upheld Fagan's conviction, applying the doctrine of continuing acts.

As we saw in Chapter 3, however, the reasoning in *Fagan* has been questioned. Some have argued that it is possible to commit battery by omission. There is now case law which supports this viewpoint.

In *DPP v Santana-Bermudez* [2003] EWHC 2908 (Admin) policewoman PC Hill approached D in a tube station. She suspected that he was a ticket tout. She informed D that she intended to search him, took him to a supervisor's office and asked him to turn out his pockets. D did so, and placed a number of items on the table, including some syringes without needles. PC Hill then asked, 'Is that everything?' D replied, 'Yes.' She then asked, 'Are you sure?' He said, 'Yes'; She then asked, 'Are you sure that you don't have any needles or sharps on you?' D answered, 'No.' PC Hill then commenced her search. She put two fingers of her left hand into a breast pocket on D's jacket and felt a stinging sensation. She took her fingers out of the pocket and found that her finger had been pierced by a hypodermic needle, which was still hanging from her fingertip. She noticed D smirking. D then took another needle from a pocket on his trousers. PC Hill then said, 'I thought you didn't have any sharps on you', at which D shrugged his shoulders and smirked. Fortunately, although D was HIV positive and had hepatitis C, PC Hill was not infected.

D was charged with assault occasioning ABH. At trial the defence argued that he had not performed a positive act – all he had done was fail to tell the truth. The trial judge agreed, and dismissed the prosecution's case on the basis that battery cannot be committed by omission. The prosecutor appealed against this finding. The issue for Maurice Kay J in the High Court was whether there was any evidential basis for the charge of assault occasioning ABH.

## EXTRACT

Read the following extract from the judgment. When (if at all) may a defendant commit a battery by doing nothing?

### *DPP v Santana-Bermudez* [2003] EWHC 2908 (Admin)

#### Maurice Kay J

10. A great deal of undesirable complexity has bedevilled our criminal law as a result of quasi theological distinctions between acts and omissions. Some of the illogicality is identified in Smith and Hogan, *Criminal Law*, 10th Edition, pages 46 to 52. In my judgment, and without the

need to express oneself in the language of universal principle, the authorities of *Roberts*, *K* and *Miller* support the following proposition: where someone (by act or word or a combination of the two) creates a danger and thereby exposes another to a reasonably foreseeable risk of injury which materialises, there is an evidential basis for the *actus reus* of an assault occasioning actual bodily harm. It remains necessary for the prosecution to prove an intention to assault or appropriate recklessness.

11. In the present case, if (as the court implicitly found) the respondent, by giving PC Hill a dishonest assurance about the contents of his pockets, thereby exposed her to a reasonably foreseeable risk of an injury which materialised, it was erroneous of the court to conclude that there was no evidential basis for the *actus reus* of assault occasioning actual bodily harm [...]

### 2. The force must have been unlawful

As noted above, many applications of force will be lawful. They might have been consensual. They might have been in justifiable self-defence. They might have been a reasonable attempt to remove an unwanted trespasser. They might have been legally authorised (e.g. the police's power of arrest). In all of these situations there is not the *actus reus* of battery because there is not an infliction of *unlawful* force.

### 3. The defendant must have either: (a) intended to inflict unlawful force on the victim; or (b) been reckless as to whether unlawful force would be inflicted on the victim

The *mens rea* of battery was set out by the Court of Appeal in *R v Venna* [1976] QB 421. As was the case with assault, the *Cunningham* definition of recklessness applies here. This was confirmed by the House of Lords in *R v Savage & Parmenter* [1992] 1 AC 699.

## Assault occasioning ABH (actual bodily harm)

Section 47 of the Offences Against the Person Act 1861 states:

Whosoever shall be convicted upon an indictment of any assault occasioning actual bodily harm shall be liable [...] to be imprisoned for any term not exceeding five years.

This tells us that the offence has three requirements:

1. The defendant must have committed an assault
2. The victim must have suffered ABH (actual bodily harm)
3. The assault must have occasioned the ABH.

We will work through these in turn.

### 1. The defendant must have committed an assault

Here the word 'assault' has a different meaning. It is not being used to refer specifically to the crime we studied a few pages ago. Instead, it is being used as a collective term to refer to *both* assault *and* battery. In other words, the first step in establishing liability for this offence is to prove that the defendant committed either an assault or a battery.

If you are answering a problem question and trying to decide whether to establish an assault or a battery, begin by asking yourself whether there was an actual infliction of force or just an apprehension that force would be applied. If there was an infliction of force you should focus on battery. If there was an apprehension of force you should focus on assault. Remember that you need to establish both *actus reus* and *mens rea* of the relevant offence.

 ## 2. The victim must have suffered ABH (actual bodily harm)

The victim must have suffered ABH. There are two issues we need to consider here.

### i. Is ABH limited to physical injuries?

Although the OAPA uses the words 'bodily harm', and although the statute was enacted in 1861 long before the emergence of psychiatry as we know it today, the courts have held that ABH is not limited to physical injuries. In *R v Ireland & Burstow* the House of Lords held that recognised psychiatric illnesses may also amount to ABH.

---

### EXTRACT

The following extract is taken from Lord Steyn's judgment in *R v Ireland & Burstow*. What reasons does he give for interpreting 'bodily harm' to include psychiatric illness?

#### R v Ireland & Burstow [1998] AC 147

#### Lord Steyn

[T]he correct approach is simply to consider whether the words of the Act of 1861 considered in the light of contemporary knowledge cover a recognisable psychiatric injury [...] Bearing in mind that statutes are usually intended to operate for many years it would be most inconvenient if courts could never rely in difficult cases on the current meaning of statutes. Recognising the problem Lord Thring, the great Victorian draftsman of the second half of the last century, exhorted draftsmen to draft so that 'An Act of Parliament should be deemed to be always speaking.' *Practical Legislation* (1902), p. 83; see also Cross, *Statutory Interpretation*, 3rd ed. (1995), p. 51; Pearce and Geddes, *Statutory Interpretation in Australia*, 4th ed. (1996), pp. 90–93. In cases where the problem arises it is a matter of interpretation whether a court must search for the historical or original meaning of a statute or whether it is free to apply the current meaning of the statute to present day conditions. Statutes dealing with a particular grievance or problem may sometimes require to be historically interpreted. But the drafting technique of Lord Thring and his successors have brought about the situation that statutes will generally be found to be of the 'always speaking' variety: see *Royal College of Nursing of the United Kingdom v. Department of Health and Social Security* [1981] A.C. 800 for an example of an 'always speaking' construction in the House of Lords.

The proposition that the Victorian legislator when enacting sections 18, 20 and 47 of the Act of 1861, would not have had in mind psychiatric illness is no doubt correct. Psychiatry was in its infancy in 1861. But the subjective intention of the draftsman is immaterial. The only relevant inquiry is as to the sense of the words in the context in which they are used. Moreover the Act of 1861 is a statute of the 'always speaking' type: the statute must be interpreted in the light of the best current scientific appreciation of the link between the body and psychiatric injury.

[...]

I would hold that 'bodily harm' in sections 18, 20 and 47 must be interpreted so as to include recognisable psychiatric illness.

The decision in *R v Ireland & Burstow* was applied in *R v Dhaliwal* [2006] EWCA Crim 1139. Mrs Dhaliwal committed suicide as a result of the psychological and physical abuse she suffered from her husband over a number of years. Her husband was charged with manslaughter and inflicting GBH, but Judge Roberts at the Central Criminal Court ruled that the case could not proceed to trial because there was no evidence on which a reasonable jury could be satisfied that Mrs Dhaliwal had suffered GBH. The prosecution appealed against this ruling. Medical evidence suggested that the years of abuse had caused Mrs Dhaliwal psychological harm, but not recognised psychiatric illness. So the issue for the Court of Appeal was whether, in the light of *R v Ireland & Burstow*, psychological harm not amounting to recognised psychiatric illness could constitute bodily harm.

## EXTRACT

According to the Court of Appeal, can psychological harm that does not amount to recognised psychiatric illness constitute bodily harm? What reasons did the Court give for its conclusion?

### *R v Dhaliwal* [2006] EWCA Crim 1139

#### Sir Igor Judge

31 Our conclusion can be briefly expressed. The problem which we have to address is whether psychological injury, not amounting to recognisable psychiatric illness, falls within the ambit of bodily harm for the purposes of the 1861 Act [...] [T]he extension sought by the prosecution would introduce a significant element of uncertainty about the true ambit of the relevant legal principles to which the concept of "bodily harm" in the 1861 Act applies, which would be compounded by the inevitable problems of conflicting medical opinion in this constantly developing area of expertise. By adhering to the principle of recognisable psychiatric illness, although some medical experts may be concerned with the way in which the definitions are arrived at, the issue which requires to be addressed can be clearly understood and those responsible for advising the prosecution and defendants can approach their cases with an appropriate degree of certainty.

### ii. How bad must the injuries have been to amount to ABH?

Whether or not a victim's injuries in a particular case amount to ABH is a question of fact to be answered by the jury. The trial judge may offer the jury some guidance on how to approach this task. In *R v Chan-Fook* [1994] 1 WLR 689 Hobhouse LJ explained what trial judges should (and shouldn't!) say to the jury:

['Actual', 'bodily' and 'harm'] are three words of the English language which require no elaboration and in the ordinary course should not receive any. The word "harm" is a synonym for injury. The word "actual" indicates that the injury (although there is no need for it to be permanent) should not be so trivial as to be wholly insignificant.

Similarly, in *R v Donovan* [1934] 2 KB 498 the Court of Appeal stated that to constitute ABH the harm 'need not be permanent, but must, no doubt, be more than merely transient and trifling'. So bruising, grazing and scratches may all potentially be found to amount to ABH.

In *T v DPP* [2003] EWHC 266 Admin the defendant kicked the victim, causing him to temporarily lose consciousness. The defendant was convicted of assault occasioning ABH. The defendant appealed against his conviction, arguing that the victim's loss of consciousness was too short-lived to be able to amount to ABH. The High Court rejected this. It said that a loss of consciousness can amount to ABH since it involves 'an injurious impairment to the victim's sensory functions'.

If a loss of consciousness can amount to ABH, what about cutting off someone's pony-tail? This was the issue in *DPP v Smith* [2006] EWHC 94 (Admin). The victim, Michelle Tether, was the ex-partner of the defendant, Michael Smith. Smith and Tether had had an on-off relationship for five years. In April 2005 Tether went to Smith's house. She went to his bedroom, where he was asleep, and woke him up. He pushed her onto the bed, produced some kitchen scissors, and cut off her ponytail. Smith was charged with assault occasioning ABH, but when the case went to the Magistrates' Court the justices held that there was no case to answer since cutting someone's hair cannot amount to ABH. The prosecution appealed against this finding. The issue for the High Court was whether cutting off someone's ponytail can constitute ABH.

Notice, first of all, that any upset or distress that Tether may have felt was irrelevant. As we saw above, psychological harm cannot amount to ABH unless it is a recognised psychiatric illness – and there was no suggestion that Smith's actions had caused Tether psychiatric illness. The focus was simply on the physical act of cutting off the ponytail.

## EXTRACT

Read the following extract from the Court's judgment. Is cutting off someone's hair capable of constituting ABH? How did the Court justify its conclusion?

### *DPP v Smith* [2006] EWHC 94 (Admin)

#### Sir Igor Judge

In my judgment, whether it is alive beneath the surface of the skin or dead tissue above the surface of the skin, the hair is an attribute and part of the human body. It is intrinsic to each individual and to the identity of each individual. Although it is not essential to my decision, I note that an individual's hair is relevant to his or her autonomy. Some regard it as their crowning glory. Admirers may so regard it in the object of their affections. Even if, medically and scientifically speaking, the hair above the surface of the scalp is no more than dead tissue, it remains part of the body and is attached to it. While it is so attached, in my judgment it falls within the meaning of "bodily" in the phrase "actual bodily harm". It is concerned with the body of the individual victim.

In my judgment, the defendant's actions in cutting off a substantial part of the victim's hair in the course of an assault on her – like putting paint on it or some unpleasant substance which marked or damaged it without causing injury elsewhere – is capable of amounting to an assault which occasions actual bodily harm.

### 3. The assault must have occasioned the ABH

The word 'occasioned' simply means caused. So the assault or battery must have been the factual and legal cause of the actual bodily harm suffered by the victim.

### NB: Must the prosecution prove that the defendant intended to cause/recklessly caused the ABH?

In Chapter 1 we looked at the correspondence principle. According to this principle a defendant should only be convicted of assault occasioning ABH if he at least realised that there was a possibility that his actions would cause ABH. It is an infringement of a defendant's autonomy to hold him responsible for an outcome which he did not foresee.

This issue was examined by the House of Lords in *R v Savage & Parmenter*. The House of Lords had to decide whether the section 47 offence contains a *mens rea* element which corresponds to the *actus reus* requirement that the victim suffered ABH. Lord Ackner stated:

> The verdict of assault occasioning actual bodily harm may be returned upon proof of an assault together with proof of the fact that actual bodily harm was occasioned by the assault. The prosecution are not obliged to prove that the defendant intended to cause some actual bodily harm or was reckless as to whether such harm would be caused

**ACTIVITY**

In the light of *R v Savage & Parmenter*, decide whether the defendant in the following scenario is guilty of assault occasioning ABH:

Romeo is trying to enjoy a quiet drink at his local pub, but his evening is being spoilt by the raucous behaviour of Vincenzo. Romeo gets so frustrated that he throws his pint of beer over Vincenzo. As he does so, the glass slips out of his hand. It hits Vincenzo and smashes, causing a painful bruise and graze. The possibility of the glass slipping out of his hand never crossed Romeo's mind.

The decision in *R v Savage & Parmenter* means that assault occasioning ABH is a crime of constructive liability (see Chapter 1). The only *mens rea* which has to be proved is the *mens rea* necessary to establish an assault (requirement Number 1 above). This means that someone like Romeo can be convicted of assault occasioning ABH even though the possibility of the victim suffering ABH never crossed his mind.

**ACTIVITY**

Can you think of any possible justifications for this example of constructive liability? (Hint: think back to some of the other principles we studied in Chapter 1.)

## Malicious wounding or infliction of GBH (grievous bodily harm)

Section 20 of the Offences Against the Person Act 1861 states:

> Whosoever shall unlawfully and maliciously wound or inflict any grievous bodily harm upon any other person, either with or without any weapon or instrument, shall be guilty of an offence, and being convicted thereof shall be liable […] to imprisonment for a term not exceeding five years.

This tells us that the offence has three requirements:

1. The defendant must have *either* wounded the victim *or* inflicted GBH (grievous bodily harm) on her
2. The wounding or infliction of GBH must have been unlawful
3. The defendant must have acted maliciously.

Numbers 1 and 2 are *actus reus* requirements. Number 3 is a *mens rea* requirement. We will work through them in turn.

## 1. The defendant must have either wounded the victim or inflicted GBH (grievous bodily harm) on her

'Wound' and 'GBH' are two separate terms with different meanings. It only has to be shown that the defendant *either* wounded the victim *or* that he inflicted GBH on her.

The meaning of 'wound' was considered in *C v Eisenhower* [1984] QB 331. The Court held that a wound requires 'a break in the continuity of the whole skin'. So a cut would constitute a wound, but a scratch would not.

Turning next to 'GBH'. This can include broken bones, injuries causing substantial loss of blood and injuries resulting in lengthy treatment or incapacity. As we saw previously, the House of Lords in *R v Ireland & Burstow* held that it can also include recognised psychiatric illness. Sexually transmitted diseases may also amount to GBH. In *R v Dica* [2004] EWCA Crim 1103 the defendant had unprotected sexual intercourse with two women even though he knew he was HIV positive. We'll be looking at this case more closely shortly. For now, the important point to note is that the Court of Appeal held that contracting HIV (or another sexually transmitted disease[4]) can amount to GBH.

### ACTIVITY

- If a sexually transmitted disease can amount to GBH, should non-sexually transmitted diseases also be capable of amounting to GBH?
- Even though he is suffering from tuberculosis, Romeo attends his criminal law lecture. Throughout the lecture he coughs and sneezes repeatedly. Fellow student Valentina subsequently contracts the disease from Romeo. Should Romeo face criminal liability for infecting Valentina? Why/why not?

Whether or not the victim suffered GBH is a question of fact for the jury. The House of Lords in *DPP v Smith* [1961] AC 290 said that a trial judge giving guidance to a jury should tell them to give the words their ordinary meaning:

> I can find no warrant for giving the words "grievous bodily harm" a meaning other than that which the words convey in their ordinary and natural meaning. "Bodily harm" needs no explanation, and "grievous" means no more and no less than "really serious."

---

[4]For example, in *R v Golding* [2014] EWCA Crim 889 the Court of Appeal held that genital herpes can amount to GBH. In his commentary on this case, Laird criticises the Court of Appeal for relying on intuition and argues that greater use of expert evidence is needed when deciding whether a disease constitutes a harm for the purposes of the Offences Against the Person Act 1861 ([2014] Crim LR 687).

When deciding whether a victim's injuries were grievous, may the jury take into account the characteristics of the particular victim? This was the issue in *R v Bollom* [2003] EWCA Crim 2846. The victim in this case was a 17-month-old baby called Alex. She had suffered bruising and abrasions to her body, arms and legs. The injuries were inflicted by Alex's mother's boyfriend, Stephen Bollom. At Bollom's trial the trial judge told the jury that, when deciding whether the harm Alex suffered was grievous, they could take into account Alex's young age. Bollom was subsequently convicted of the section 18 offence of GBH with intent. One of his grounds of appeal was that the trial judge was wrong to tell the jury to take the victim's age into account.

## EXTRACT

Read the following extract from the judgment of Fulford J. What factors may the jury take into account when deciding whether the harm the victim suffered is grievous?

### R v Bollom [2003] EWCA Crim 2846

#### Fulford J

52. Mr Davies, on behalf of the appellant, at paragraph 9 of his Advice and orally before us, submits that the injuries should be assessed without reference to the particular victim. He suggests the age, health or any other particular factors relating to the person harmed should be ignored when deciding whether the injuries amounted to really serious harm. We are unable to accept that proposition. To use this case as an example, these injuries on a 6 foot adult in the fullness of health would be less serious than on, for instance, an elderly or unwell person, on someone who was physically or psychiatrically vulnerable or, as here, on a very young child. In deciding whether injuries are grievous, an assessment has to be made of, amongst other things, the effect of the harm on the particular individual. We have no doubt that in determining the gravity of these injuries, it was necessary to consider them in their real context.

We also need to consider the meaning of the word 'inflict'. There is some confusion here, stemming from the fact that both Lord Mackay in *R v Mandair* [1995] 1 AC 208 and Lord Steyn in *R v Ireland & Burstow* said that 'inflict' does not have the same meaning as 'cause'.[5] What is unclear is how the meaning of the two words differs:

- For both 'cause' and 'inflict' it is not necessary to prove that there was an assault (see *R v Wilson (Clarence)* [1984] AC 242).

---

[5]Lord Mackay stated, 'In my opinion, as I have said, the word "cause" is wider or at least not narrower than the word "inflict"', whilst Lord Steyn stated, 'I am not saying that the words "cause" and "inflict" are exactly synonymous. They are not.'

- For both 'cause' and 'inflict' it is not necessary to prove that there was a direct application of force. In *R v Ireland & Burstow* Anthony Burstow was held to have inflicted GBH on Tracey Sant even though he had not directly applied force to her.

- In *R v Ireland & Burstow* Lord Hope suggested that the difference between 'cause' and 'inflict' is that 'the word "inflicts" implies that the consequence of the act is something which the victim is likely to find unpleasant or harmful.' But this is problematic. Think back to *R v Brown* [1994] 1 AC 212, which we looked at in Chapter 1 (and will be looking at again shortly). Three of the defendants in this case were convicted of malicious wounding. Suppose that some of the others had been charged with maliciously inflicting GBH. On Lord Hope's interpretation of 'inflict', these other defendants would have been acquitted because their victims did not find the injuries unpleasant (on the contrary, in fact). This seems implausible.

So where does this leave us? Until we have some clear explanation of what (if any) difference there is between the terms 'inflict' and 'cause' the most sensible approach is to treat them as synonymous. So to establish an infliction you should simply apply the law governing factual and legal causation.

---

**ACTIVITY**

Decide whether Valentina inflicts GBH on Romeo in the following example:

After several months Romeo finally builds up the courage to ask out Valentina. Valentina replies that she wants to be 'just good friends'. She knows that Romeo is a fragile and sensitive individual who will take this very badly. In fact, he is so crushed that he suffers clinical depression as a result.

---

## 2. The wounding or infliction of GBH must have been unlawful

It is not always unlawful for a person to inflict GBH or wound another person. A person acting in reasonable self-defence would not be acting unlawfully. And as we shall see later in the chapter, a person may lawfully inflict GBH or wound another person in the course of certain lawful activities like surgery, tattooing and sports such as boxing.

## 3. The defendant must have acted maliciously

In the early part of this chapter we saw that, for the purposes of assault, the courts have given the word 'immediate' a very different meaning to the standard dictionary definition. It is a similar story with the word 'malicious'. The *Oxford English Dictionary* defines 'malicious' as 'active ill will or hatred'. For the purposes of the section 20 offence, however, the word has a quite different meaning, which was given to it by the Court of Appeal in *R v Cunningham* [1957] 2 QB 396.

**EXTRACT**

Read the following extract from Byrne J in *R v Cunningham*. What test does he set out to establish malice? Must it be shown that the defendant had ill-feeling or hatred towards the victim?

## *R v Cunningham* [1957] 2 Q.B. 396

### Byrne J

We have considered [the cases cited by counsel], and we have also considered, in the light of those cases, the following principle which was propounded by the late Professor C. S. Kenny in the first edition of his *Outlines of Criminal Law* published in 1902 and repeated at p. 186 of the 16th edition edited by Mr. J. W. Cecil Turner and published in 1952: "In any statutory definition of a crime, malice must be taken not in the old vague sense of wickedness in general but as requiring either (1) An actual intention to do the particular kind of harm that in fact was done; or (2) recklessness as to whether such harm should occur or not (i.e., the accused has foreseen that the particular kind of harm might be done and yet has gone on to take the risk of it). It is neither limited to nor does it indeed require any ill will towards the person injured." The same principle is repeated by Mr. Turner in his 10th edition of *Russell on Crime* at p. 1592.

We think that this is an accurate statement of the law.

A simple example will illustrate how different the *Cunningham* definition of malice is to the dictionary definition. Imagine a surgeon delivering a baby by Caesarian section. To deliver the baby the surgeon must cut through the mother's abdomen. As we've just seen, the cut would be classified as a wound since all layers of the skin are broken. Does the surgeon wound the mother maliciously? If we apply the test from *Cunningham* the answer is yes, since the doctor wounded the mother intentionally. Of course, in everyday conversation we would not use the word 'malice' in this way. When answering a problem question, it is important to remember that your job is not to apply the word in its everyday sense. You must apply the technical, legal meaning given to it by the Court of Appeal in *R v Cunningham*.

(And don't worry, the doctor would not be guilty of the section 20 offence! The mother's consent to the operation means that the wound was not unlawful.)

If you look back at the test from *R v Cunningham* you'll see that it refers to the 'particular kind of harm'. Malice requires either: (1) An actual intention to do the *particular kind of harm* that in fact was done; or (2) That the defendant foresaw that the *particular kind of harm* might be done and yet has gone on to take the risk of it. It is unclear from this what is meant by the 'particular kind of harm'. You might think that, since the *actus reus* of the section 20 offence requires either GBH or wounding, the defendant should only be convicted if he intended or foresaw GBH or wounding. This would be consistent with the correspondence principle. But it is not the position the courts have adopted. Lord Ackner in *R v Savage & Parmenter* stated:

My Lords, I am satisfied that [...] it is quite unnecessary that the accused should either have intended or have foreseen that his unlawful act might cause physical harm of the gravity described in section 20, i.e. a wound or serious physical injury. It is enough that he should have foreseen that some physical harm to some person, albeit of a minor character, might result

In other words, the section 20 offence is a crime of constructive liability (in the same way as assault occasioning ABH). The only *mens rea* requirement is 'malice', and this is satisfied if the defendant either: (1) intended to cause the victim some harm; or (2) was reckless as to whether the victim would suffer some harm.

---

### ACTIVITY

After several months, Romeo finally builds up the courage to ask Valentina out on a date. But she replies 'No chance' and laughs at him. Romeo is so upset that he pushes her. She stumbles backwards, falls and lands awkwardly, breaking her arm. Is Romeo guilty of the section 20 offence?

---

## Wounding or GBH with intent

Section 18 of the Offences Against the Person Act 1861 states:

Whosoever shall unlawfully and maliciously by any means whatsoever wound or cause any grievous bodily harm to any person … with intent … to do some … grievous bodily harm to any person, or with intent to resist or prevent the lawful apprehension or detainer of any person, shall be guilty of an offence, and being convicted thereof shall be liable, … to imprisonment for life …

This tells us that the offence has four requirements:

1.  The defendant must have *either* wounded the victim *or* caused her GBH (grievous bodily harm)
2.  The wounding or causing of GBH must have been unlawful
3.  The defendant must have acted maliciously
4.  The defendant must have *either* intended to cause the victim GBH *or* intended to resist or prevent a lawful arrest.

The first three requirements on this list are identical to the section 20 offence (the only difference is that section 18 uses the word 'cause' instead of 'inflict', but as we've seen this is of no practical significance). The sole difference between the two offences is that section 18 has an additional *mens rea* requirement: the defendant must have either intended to cause the victim GBH or intended to resist or prevent a lawful arrest. In other words, section 18 is an aggravated version of the section 20 offence. The extra *mens rea* requirement makes a very big difference to sentencing. The maximum sentence for the section 20 offence is five years' imprisonment, whereas the maximum sentence for the section 18 offence is life imprisonment.

When answering a problem question, the best approach is therefore to begin with the section 20 offence. If the requirements of this offence are satisfied, you should then ask whether the additional *mens rea* requirement of the section 18 offence is satisfied. If it is, the defendant will be guilty of the aggravated offence (and liable to up to life imprisonment!).

 **Issues relating to consent**

For each of the offences we have looked at, one of the requirements is that the defendant acted unlawfully. As we have seen, there are various reasons why a defendant's actions may not have been unlawful. One possible reason is that the victim consented to the defendant's actions. We now need to look more closely at this concept of consent.

First of all we need to understand an important point. Sometimes a victim might agree to something without having consented. For example, the victim might have lacked mental capacity. So although she agreed to the defendant's actions, she did not consent because she lacked the capacity to do so. Alternatively, the victim might have been pressurised by threats. So although she submitted to the defendant's actions she did not consent because her choice was not a free one.[6] In cases like these there is no *effective* consent.

In this part of the chapter we are going to look at two other types of case in which the victim's consent may not have been effective. First, we will look at cases in which the victim only agreed to the defendant's actions because the defendant deceived her. Second, we will look at how the criminal law regulates when individuals may choose to consent to injury.

## 1. Consent obtained by fraud

For more than a century the courts have held that a victim's consent will only be vitiated (i.e. invalidated) by fraud if the victim was deceived about the nature of the act or the identity of the person. So as long as the deception did not relate to either the nature of the act or the defendant's identity the victim's consent will be deemed effective.

An example is *R v Richardson* [1999] QB 444. The defendant in this case was a dentist named Diana Richardson. On 30 August 1996 she was suspended from practice by the General Dental Council. In spite of this, she continued to treat a number of patients. The mother of two of these patients complained to the police, because she thought Richardson had been under the influence of drink and drugs. The police subsequently discovered that Richardson had been practising whilst disqualified, and she was charged with assault occasioning ABH. The key issue in the case was whether Richardson had committed a battery. This depended on whether the force she had inflicted on her patients had been unlawful, which in turn depended on whether her deception had vitiated her patients' consent.

The prosecution conceded that Richardson had not deceived the patients about the nature of the act. At first you might find this quite surprising. Isn't there an important difference between treatment by a registered dentist and treatment by a suspended dentist? Arguably there is. But the criminal law draws a distinction between the nature of an act and the quality of an act. Whether or not the dentist treating you is registered or suspended is relevant only to the quality of the act. As long as the patients understood that they were receiving dental treatment they understood the nature of the act. There was no suggestion that Richardson had tricked them into believing they were not receiving dental treatment, and so there was no deception as to the nature of the act.

Instead, the prosecution argued that Richardson had deceived the patients about her identity. The prosecution's argument was that a person's identity covers not only their name and who they are, but also their attributes and qualifications. So when Richardson fraudulently failed to tell the patients that she had been suspended, she deceived them as to her identity.

---

[6]This distinction is discussed further in Chapter 7 when we look at the definition of consent found in the Sexual Offences Act 2003.

## EXTRACT

Read the following extract from the Court of Appeals' judgment in *R v Richardson*. Did the Court accept the prosecution's argument? Had Richardson deceived the patients as to her identity?

### *R v Richardson* [1999] QB 444

### Otton LJ

In essence the Crown contended that the concept of the "identity of the person" should be extended to cover the qualifications or attributes of the dentist on the basis that the patients consented to treatment by a qualified dentist and not a suspended one. We must reject that submission. In all the charges brought against the defendant the complainants were fully aware of the identity of the defendant. To accede to the submission would be to strain or distort the everyday meaning of the word identity, the dictionary definition of which is "the condition of being the same."

It was suggested in argument that we might be assisted by the civil law of consent, where such expressions as "real" or "informed" consent prevail. In this regard the criminal and the civil law do not run along the same track. The concept of informed consent has no place in the criminal law. It would also be a mistake, in our view, to introduce the concept of a duty to communicate information to a patient about the risk of an activity before consent to an act can be treated as valid. The gravamen of the defendant's conduct in the instant case was that the complainants consented to treatment from her although their consent had been procured by her failure to inform them that she was no longer qualified to practise. This was clearly reprehensible and may well found the basis of a civil claim for damages. But we are quite satisfied that it is not a basis for finding criminal liability in the field of offences against the person.

## ACTIVITY

- Romeo looks a lot like the footballer Wayne Rooney. Although Valentina does not find Wayne Rooney attractive, she has always dreamt of enjoying the wealthy lifestyle of a footballer's wife and so begins to flirt with Romeo. Although Romeo realises her mistake he does not correct her and, after a few minutes, they kiss. When Valentina realises her mistake she is horrified. She says she would never have kissed Romeo had she known that he was not a wealthy footballer and accuses him of battery. Did Romeo's deception vitiate Valentina's consent?

- Imagine that you were one of Diana Richardson's patients. Which would have been more important to you: to know that you were being treated by Diana Richardson, or to know that you were being treated by a registered dentist? In the light of your answer, critically comment on the rule that only fraud as to the nature of the act or identity of the person vitiates consent.

The rule that only fraud as to the nature of the act or the identity of the person vitiates consent was applied in the 19th-century case *R v Clarence* (1888) 22 QBD 23. Charles Clarence was suffering from the sexually transmitted disease gonorrhoea. Although he knew of his condition, he did not tell his wife Selina. They had sexual intercourse, and shortly afterwards Selina contracted the disease. She said she would not have had sex with her husband had she known of his condition. Clarence was charged with malicious infliction of GBH. At trial he was convicted. On appeal, the conviction was quashed by a majority of nine to four. In response to the suggestion that Selina's consent had been vitiated by fraud, one of the majority, Stephen J, stated:

> The woman's consent here was as full and conscious as consent could be. It was not obtained by any fraud either as to the nature of the act or as to the identity of the agent.

One of the problems with this assertion is that it fails to distinguish between: (1) consent to sexual intercourse; and (2) consent to the risk of infection. As far as (1) is concerned, Stephen J was correct. Selina was not deceived as to the nature of sexual intercourse. Her consent to sexual intercourse was effective. But the prosecution had not alleged non-consensual sex! They had not charged Clarence with rape. They had charged him with malicious infliction of GBH. For this offence, it is (2) that is crucial. Had Selina consented to the risk of harm? Or was her consent to the harm vitiated because her husband had deceived her as to the nature of the harmful act?

In *R v Dica* [2004] EWCA Crim 1103 the Court of Appeal had the opportunity to revisit the decision in *R v Clarence*. The facts of *R v Dica* were similar to *R v Clarence*. Although he knew that he was HIV positive, Mohammed Dica had unprotected sexual intercourse with two women. Both women subsequently contracted HIV. At trial Dica was convicted on two counts of maliciously inflicting GBH. He appealed, arguing that his conviction was inconsistent with the decision in *R v Clarence*.

The Court of Appeal drew the distinction outlined above between consent to sexual intercourse and consent to the risk of infection. The key question, it said, was whether the two women had consented to the risk of infection.

## EXTRACT

Read the following extract from the judgment of Judge LJ. Had the two women consented to the risk of infection? So was the infliction of GBH lawful or unlawful?

### *R v Dica* [2004] EWCA Crim 1103

#### Judge LJ

39. In our view, on the assumed fact now being considered, the answer is entirely straightforward. These victims consented to sexual intercourse. Accordingly, the defendant was not guilty of rape. Given the long-term nature of the relationships, if the defendant concealed the truth about his condition from them, and therefore kept them in ignorance of it, there was no reason for them to think that they were running any risk of infection, and they were not consenting to it. On this basis, there would be no consent sufficient in law to provide the defendant with a defence to the charge under section 20.

Having reached this conclusion, Judge LJ held that *R v Clarence* should be overruled:

31. In our judgment, the reasoning which led the majority in *Clarence* to decide that the conviction under section 20 should be quashed has no continuing application. If that case were decided today, the conviction under section 20 would be upheld.

Shortly after *R v Dica* came the case *R v Konzani* [2005] EWCA Crim 706. Konzani, who was HIV positive, had had unprotected sexual intercourse with three women without telling them that he was HIV positive. Each of them subsequently contracted the virus. At trial he was convicted of malicious infliction of GBH. He appealed against his conviction on two grounds:

1. At trial Konzani's counsel had argued that, by consenting to unprotected sexual intercourse, each of the women had consented to all of the risks associated with unprotected sex, including the risk of contracting HIV. The trial judge rejected this, telling the jury that Konzani could only rely on the women's consent as a defence if their consent had been 'informed and willing'. On appeal, Konzani argued that this was wrong.

2. Konzani's counsel also argued that, even if the three women had not consented to the risk of infection, Konzani genuinely believed that they had. Counsel argued that Konzani's claimed belief in consent should have resulted in an acquittal, even if the belief was unreasonable.

The Court of Appeal examined each of these grounds of appeal.

## EXTRACT

Read the following extract from the judgment of Judge LJ. On the first ground of appeal, did the Court agree that a distinction must be drawn between giving a general consent to the risks of unprotected sexual intercourse and giving an informed consent to the specific risk of contracting HIV? According to the Court, had the three women consented to the risk of contracting HIV from Konzani? Why/why not?

On the second ground of appeal, the Court accepted that a defendant should be acquitted if he genuinely believed the victim had consented to the risk of contracting HIV. According to the Court, did Konzani genuinely believe the three women had consented to the risk of contracting HIV? Why/why not?

### *R v Konzani* [2005] EWCA Crim 706

#### Judge LJ

41. [...] There is a critical distinction between taking a risk of the various, potentially adverse and possibly problematic consequences of sexual intercourse, and giving an informed consent to the risk of infection with a fatal disease. For the complainant's consent to the risks of contracting the HIV virus to provide a defence [...] her consent must be an informed consent. If that proposition is in doubt, we take this opportunity to emphasise it. We must therefore examine its implications for this appeal.

42. The recognition in *R v Dica* of informed consent as a defence was based on but limited by potentially conflicting public policy considerations. In the public interest, so far as possible, the spread of catastrophic illness must be avoided or prevented. On the other hand, the public interest also requires that the principle of personal autonomy in the context of adult non-violent sexual relationships should be maintained. If an individual who knows that he is suffering from the HIV virus conceals this stark fact from his sexual partner, the principle of her personal autonomy is not enhanced if he is exculpated when he recklessly transmits the HIV virus to her through consensual sexual intercourse. On any view, the concealment of this fact from her

almost inevitably means that she is deceived. Her consent is not properly informed, and she cannot give an informed consent to something of which she is ignorant. Equally, her personal autonomy is not normally protected by allowing a defendant who knows that he is suffering from the HIV virus which he deliberately conceals, to assert an honest belief in his partner's informed consent to the risk of the transmission of the HIV virus. Silence in these circumstances is incongruous with honesty, or with a genuine belief that there is an informed consent. Accordingly, in such circumstances the issue either of informed consent, or honest belief in it will only rarely arise: in reality, in most cases, the contention would be wholly artificial.

[...]

44. In deference to Mr Roberts' submission, we accept that there may be circumstances in which it would be open to the jury to infer that, notwithstanding that the defendant was reckless and concealed his condition from the complainant, she may nevertheless have given an informed consent to the risk of contracting the HIV virus. By way of example, an individual with HIV may develop a sexual relationship with someone who knew him while he was in hospital, receiving treatment for the condition. If so, her informed consent, if it were indeed informed, would remain a defence, to be disproved by the prosecution, even if the defendant had not personally informed her of his condition. Even if she did not in fact consent, this example would illustrate the basis for an argument that he honestly believed in her informed consent. Alternatively, he may honestly believe that his new sexual partner was told of his condition by someone known to them both. Cases like these, not too remote to be fanciful, may arise. If they do, no doubt they will be explored with the complainant in cross-examination. Her answers may demonstrate an informed consent. Nothing remotely like that was suggested here. In a different case, perhaps supported by the defendant's own evidence, material like this may provide a basis for suggesting that he honestly believed that she was giving an informed consent. He may provide an account of the incident, or the affair, which leads the jury to conclude that even if she did not give an informed consent, he may honestly have believed that she did. Acknowledging these possibilities in different cases does not, we believe, conflict with the public policy considerations identified in *R v Dica*. That said, they did not arise in the present case.

45. Why not? In essence because the jury found that the complainants did not give a willing or informed consent to the risks of contracting the HIV virus from the appellant. We recognise that where consent does provide a defence to an offence against the person, it is generally speaking correct that the defendant's honest belief in the alleged victim's consent would also provide a defence. However for this purpose, the defendant's honest belief must be concomitant with the consent which provides a defence. Unless the consent would provide a defence, an honest belief in it would not assist the defendant. This follows logically from *R v Brown*. For it to do so here, what was required was some evidence of an honest belief that the complainants, or any one of them, were consenting to the risk that they might be infected with the HIV virus by him. There is not the slightest evidence, direct or indirect, from which a jury could begin to infer that the appellant honestly believed that any complainant consented to that specific risk. As there was no such evidence, the judge's ruling about "honest belief" was correct. In fact, the honest truth was that the appellant deceived them.

In a case like *R v Dica* or *R v Konzani* the defendant can only be convicted if he acted maliciously – which, as we saw above, means that he inflicted the harm intentionally or recklessly. As we saw in Chapter 4, the *Cunningham* test for recklessness asks whether the defendant foresaw the relevant risk and unjustifiably chose to take it. In both *R v Dica* and *R v Konzani* this issue was straightforward, since both defendants were aware of the risk of transmitting the virus and yet chose not to use any protection. But consider the following example:

## ACTIVITY

Romeo is HIV positive but has not yet told Valentina, whom he has been dating for almost a month. When they have sexual intercourse for the first time, Romeo uses a condom. He does not believe it is necessary to tell her that he is HIV positive because he knows that the condom will greatly reduce the risk of transmitting the virus to Valentina. Unfortunately Valentina contracts the virus. Applying the *Cunningham* test, did Romeo act recklessly? In other words, did he foresee the risk of Valentina contracting the virus and did he *unjustifiably* choose to take this risk?

The judgments in *R v Dica* and *R v Konzani* have been criticised by Weait. He points out that, if a person must have known he was HIV positive in order to be found to have acted recklessly, the effect of the decisions could be to dissuade people from having an HIV test and accessing available medical care and treatment. More fundamentally, he argues that the transmission of HIV should be seen first and foremost as a public health issue:[7]

Some commentators, including the present author, have argued that where a person is aware of the risks associated with unprotected sex and has not satisfied him- or herself that a partner is HIV negative (or free from other serious sexually transmitted infections (STIs)) the defence of consent should, in principle, be available. The reason for taking such a position is, primarily, that the transmission of HIV should be seen first and foremost as a public health issue and that everyone, not just those who are HIV positive, has a responsibility for minimising the spread of the virus. To impose criminal liability on those who recklessly transmit HIV or STIs to people who are in a position to protect themselves against infection, and elect not to, sends a message that people are, and should be, entitled to assume that their partners will ensure that transmission does not occur. The very fact that the virus has spread so dramatically in recent years among the sexually active demonstrates that this is simply not the case.

These issues were considered by the Law Commission in its 2015 scoping report on the non-fatal offences against the person.[8] The Commission commented that it 'seems unlikely that anyone, while conscious of a significant risk that he or she is indeed infected with HIV or a serious disease, would deliberately refrain from being tested in order to avoid satisfying the recklessness requirement of the offence under section 20. Such an attitude would combine exceptional legal knowledge with exceptional indifference to one's own health and safety' (para 6.70). As for the argument that the law places responsibility exclusively on those with HIV or STIs to ensure that transmission does not occur, the Commission expressed doubts. For a start, a person would 'have to be naïve in the extreme' to take no responsibility themselves in reliance on the deterrent effect of the criminal law: 'people rely on the existence of the offence of burglary to discourage break-ins and punish them when they occur, but still lock the door to their homes' (para 6.77). More fundamentally, the Commission stated that decriminalising the transmission of

---

[7]Weait, M. (2005) 'Knowledge, Autonomy and Consent: *R v Konzani*' *Criminal Law Review* 763.
[8]We examine the report in detail later in the chapter.

disease would be unfair: 'If two people are confronting the same danger, and one of them is aware of it and the other is not, the primary blame for failing to avoid it must be that of the person who was aware. This must be all the more true when the danger is only to the party who was not aware' (para 6.78). So, whilst stating that there needs to be a wider review of the law governing the transmission of disease, the Commission provisionally recommended preserving the current position.

## 2. Consent to injury

In Germany in 2001 a cannibal named Armin Meiwes posted an advertisement on several websites and chatrooms asking for 'young, well-built men aged 18 to 30 to be slaughtered and then consumed'. Bernd-Juergen Brandes, a 43-year-old computer technician, responded to the advertisement. After selling his car and writing a will, Brandes took a day off work and travelled to Meiwes' house. First, Meiwes cut off Brandes' penis and the two men tried to eat this together. Brandes then allowed Meiwes to stab him to death. Meiwes carved up the body and stored portions of flesh in his freezer. Over the next ten months he ate approximately 20 kilogrammes of the flesh.

Although this is an extreme example, it does raise an important question: when should the criminal law prohibit consensual injury? Figure 6.2 shows the ladder of offences against the person. It is the same as the one at the start of the chapter, except it has an extra rung at the top for murder and manslaughter. As you can see, in England and Wales a defendant who is charged with murder or manslaughter may never rely on the fact the victim consented as a defence.

At the bottom of the ladder are the offences of assault and battery. The House of Lords in *R v Brown* [1994] 1 AC 212 held that a defendant charged with either of these offences may always rely on the fact the victim consented as a defence.

In the middle of the ladder are the section 47, 20 and 18 offences. For these offences, the House of Lords in *R v Brown* held that the consent of the victim is only available as a defence if the injury (ABH/GBH/wounding) occurred in the course of a 'lawful activity'. What we need to do is to examine which activities are lawful activities and which are unlawful activities. We will also consider the approach the courts have taken to deciding whether an activity should be classified as lawful or unlawful.

### i. Unlawful activities

The first unlawful activity is fighting and brawling. In *Attorney-General's Reference (No. 6 of 1980)* [1981] QB 715 the defendant and victim began

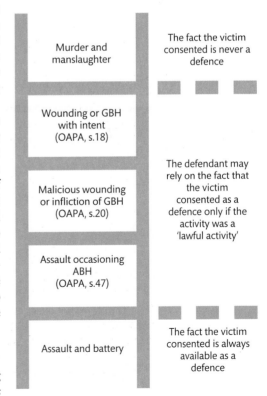

**Figure 6.2.** Non-fatal offences against the person: consent to injury

arguing in the street, and then agreed to have a fist fight. The victim suffered bruises on his face and a bleeding nose. The defendant was charged with assault occasioning ABH. The trial judge told the jury that if both parties consented to the fight then the fight may well be lawful. The defendant was subsequently acquitted. The Attorney-General referred a point of law of general importance to the Court of Appeal: if two people agree to a fight, can one of them rely on the consent of the other as a defence to a charge of ABH/GBH/wounding? The Court of Appeal answered no, stating that 'it is not in the public interest that people should try to cause, or should cause, each other bodily harm for no good reason'. In *R v Brown* the House of Lords agreed with this and confirmed that fighting and brawling is an unlawful activity.

The activity that was in question in *R v Brown* was sado-masochism. A group of homosexual middle-aged men committed acts of violence against each other for sexual pleasure. The acts included: whipping; caning; applying stinging nettles to the genitals; inserting fish hooks into the penis; nailing the scrotum or foreskin to pieces of board and burning the penis with a candle. The activities were carried out in private and had been going on for a number of years. The activities were videoed and the tapes were distributed amongst the members of the group. There was no evidence that any of the men had suffered permanent injury or ever sought medical treatment. The police discovered the group's activities by chance, when investigating other matters. At trial the defendants were convicted of assault occasioning ABH. Three were also convicted of malicious wounding. The case reached the House of Lords. By a majority of 3–2 the Lords decided that sado-masochism (i.e. deliberately causing ABH/GBH/wounding for sexual pleasure) is an unlawful activity and upheld the convictions.

It is important to understand the approach the majority took when deciding whether sado-masochism is a lawful or unlawful activity. They started from the assumption that deliberately causing ABH/GBH/wounding is unlawful, and asked whether there are good policy and public interest reasons for classifying the activity as lawful. For example, Lord Templeman stated:

> [T]he courts have accepted that consent is a defence to the infliction of bodily harm in the course of some lawful activities. The question is whether the defence should be extended to the infliction of bodily harm in the course of sado-masochistic encounters [...]

> The question whether the defence of consent should be extended to the consequences of sado-masochistic encounters can only be decided by consideration of policy and public interest.

And Lord Lowry stated:

> [T]here are prima facie offences against sections 20 and 47 and the next question is whether there is good reason to add sado-masochistic acts to the list of exceptions.

The underlying assumption is that sado-masochism is an unlawful activity. Should the defence of consent be *extended* to sado-masochism? Are there good reasons to *add* sado-masochism to the list of exceptions? This has been described as a 'social utility' model: an activity that deliberately causes ABH/GBH/wounding will only be lawful if it has social utility.

Having set out this approach, the majority then considered whether policy and public interest considerations required sado-masochism to be a lawful activity.

## EXTRACT

Read the following extracts from the judgments of Lord Templeman and Lord Jauncey and make a list of the reasons they gave for deciding that policy and public interest considerations did not require sado-masochism to be a lawful activity.

Look back at the principles we studied in Chapter 1. Try and match each of the reasons given by Lord Templeman and Lord Jauncey to at least one of the principles from Chapter 1.

### *R v Brown* [1994] 1 AC 212

### Lord Templeman

Counsel for the appellants argued that consent should provide a defence to charges under both section 20 and section 47 because, it was said, every person has a right to deal with his body as he pleases. I do not consider that this slogan provides a sufficient guide to the policy decision which must now be made. It is an offence for a person to abuse his own body and mind by taking drugs. Although the law is often broken, the criminal law restrains a practice which is regarded as dangerous and injurious to individuals and which if allowed and extended is harmful to society generally. In any event the appellants in this case did not mutilate their own bodies. They inflicted bodily harm on willing victims [...]

The assertion was made on behalf of the appellants that the sexual appetites of sadists and masochists can only be satisfied by the infliction of bodily harm and that the law should not punish the consensual achievement of sexual satisfaction. There was no evidence to support the assertion that sado-masochist activities are essential to the happiness of the appellants or any other participants but the argument would be acceptable if sado-masochism were only concerned with sex, as the appellants contend. In my opinion sado-masochism is not only concerned with sex. Sado-masochism is also concerned with violence. The evidence discloses that the practices of the appellants were unpredictably dangerous and degrading to body and mind and were developed with increasing barbarity and taught to persons whose consents were dubious or worthless.

A sadist draws pleasure from inflicting or watching cruelty. A masochist derives pleasure from his own pain or humiliation. The appellants are middle-aged men. The victims were youths some of whom were introduced to sado-masochism before they attained the age of 21. In his judgment in the Court of Appeal, Lord Lane C.J. said that two members of the group of which the appellants formed part, namely one Cadman and the appellant Laskey:

"were responsible in part for the corruption of a youth K ... It is some comfort at least to be told, as we were, that K. has now it seems settled into a normal heterosexual relationship. Cadman had befriended K. when the boy was 15 years old. He met him in a cafeteria and, so he says, found out that the boy was interested in homosexual activities. He introduced and encouraged K. in 'bondage affairs.' He was interested in viewing and recording on videotape K. and other teenage boys in homosexual scenes ... One cannot overlook the danger that the gravity of the assaults and injuries in this type of case may escalate to even more unacceptable heights."

The evidence disclosed that drink and drugs were employed to obtain consent and increase enthusiasm. The victim was usually manacled so that the sadist could enjoy the thrill of power and the victim could enjoy the thrill of helplessness. The victim had no control over the harm which the sadist, also stimulated by drink and drugs might inflict. In one case a victim was branded twice on the thigh and there was some doubt as to whether he consented to or protested against the second branding. The dangers involved in administering violence must have been appreciated by the appellants because, so it was said by their counsel, each victim was given a code word which he could pronounce when excessive harm or pain was caused. The efficiency of this precaution, when taken, depends on the circumstances and on the personalities involved. No one can feel the pain of another. The charges against the appellants were based on genital torture and violence to the buttocks, anus, penis, testicles and nipples. The victims were degraded and humiliated sometimes beaten, sometimes wounded with instruments and sometimes branded. Bloodletting and the smearing of human blood produced excitement. There were obvious dangers of serious personal injury and blood infection. Prosecuting counsel informed the trial judge against the protests of defence counsel, that although the appellants had not contracted Aids, two members of the group had died from Aids and one other had contracted an H.I.V. infection although not necessarily from the practices of the group. Some activities involved excrement. The assertion that the instruments employed by the sadists were clean and sterilised could not have removed the danger of infection, and the assertion that care was taken demonstrates the possibility of infection. Cruelty to human beings was on occasions supplemented by cruelty to animals in the form of bestiality. It is fortunate that there were no permanent injuries to a victim though no one knows the extent of harm inflicted in other cases. It is not surprising that a victim does not complain to the police when the complaint would involve him in giving details of acts in which he participated. Doctors of course are subject to a code of confidentiality.

In principle there is a difference between violence which is incidental and violence which is inflicted for the indulgence of cruelty. The violence of sado-masochistic encounters involves the indulgence of cruelty by sadists and the degradation of victims. Such violence is injurious to the participants and unpredictably dangerous. I am not prepared to invent a defence of consent for sado-masochistic encounters which breed and glorify cruelty and result in offences under sections 47 and 20 of the Act of 1861 [...]

Society is entitled and bound to protect itself against a cult of violence. Pleasure derived from the infliction of pain is an evil thing. Cruelty is uncivilised. I would answer the certified question in the negative and dismiss the appeals of the appellants against conviction

### Lord Jauncey

[I]n considering the public interest it would be wrong to look only at the activities of the appellants alone, there being no suggestion that they and their associates are the only practitioners of homosexual sado-masochism in England and Wales. This House must therefore consider the possibility that these activities are practised by others and by others who are not so controlled or responsible as the appellants are claimed to be. Without going into details of all the rather curious activities in which the appellants engaged it would appear to be good luck rather than good judgment which has prevented serious injury from occurring. Wounds can easily become septic if not properly treated, the free flow of blood from a person who is H.I.V. positive or who has Aids can infect another and an inflicter who is carried away by sexual excitement or by drink or drugs could very easily inflict pain and injury beyond the level to which the receiver had consented. Your Lordships have no information as to whether such situations have occurred in relation to other sado-masochistic practitioners. It was no doubt these dangers which caused Lady Mallalieu to restrict her propositions in relation to the public interest to the actual rather than the potential result of the activity. In my view such a restriction is quite unjustified. When considering the public interest potential for harm is just as relevant as actual harm. As Mathew J. said in *Reg. v. Coney*, 8 Q.B.D. 534, 547: "There is, however, abundant authority for saying that no consent can render that innocent which is in fact dangerous." Furthermore, the possibility of proselytisation and corruption of young men is a real danger even in the case of these appellants and the taking of video recordings of such activities suggests that secrecy may not be as strict as the appellants claimed to your Lordships. If the only purpose of the activity is the sexual gratification of one or both of the participants what then is the need of a video recording?

In his dissenting judgment, Lord Mustill took a quite different approach. His starting point was as follows:

> I ask myself, not whether as a result of the decision in this appeal, activities such as those of the appellants should *cease* to be criminal, but rather whether the Act of 1861 (a statute which I venture to repeat once again was clearly intended to penalise conduct of a quite different nature) should in this new situation be interpreted so as to *make* it criminal

In other words, Lord Mustill started from the assumption that sado-masochism is a lawful activity and asked whether there are policy and public interest reasons to make it unlawful. This is the opposite of the majority's approach. It has been described as a 'social disutility' model: deliberately causing ABH/GBH/wounding will only be unlawful if it causes social disutility. We will soon consider which is best: the majority's social utility model or Lord Mustill's social disutility model.

Having set out his starting point, Lord Mustill then explained why he felt policy and public interest reasons did not require sado-masochism to be an unlawful activity.

## EXTRACT

Read the following extract from Lord Mustill's judgment and make a list of the reasons he gave for deciding that policy and public interest considerations did not require sado-masochism to be an unlawful activity.

Look back at the principles we studied in Chapter 1. Try and match each of the reasons given by Lord Mustill to at least one of the principles from Chapter 1.

### *R v Brown* [1994] 1 AC 212

#### Lord Mustill

Leaving aside repugnance and moral objection, both of which are entirely natural but neither of which are in my opinion grounds upon which the court could properly create a new crime, I can visualise only the following reasons.

(1) Some of the practices obviously created a risk of genito-urinary infection, and others of septicaemia. These might indeed have been grave in former times, but the risk of serious harm must surely have been greatly reduced by modern medical science.

(2)  The possibility that matters might get out of hand, with grave results. It has been acknowledged throughout the present proceedings that the appellants' activities were performed as a pre-arranged ritual, which at the same time enhanced their excitement and minimised the risk that the infliction of injury would go too far. Of course things might go wrong and really serious injury or death might ensue. If this happened, those responsible would be punished according to the ordinary law, in the same way as those who kill or injure in the course of more ordinary sexual activities are regularly punished. But to penalise the appellants' conduct even if the extreme consequences do not ensue, just because they might have done so would require an assessment of the degree of risk, and the balancing of this risk against the interests of individual freedom. Such a balancing is in my opinion for Parliament, not the courts [...]

(3)  I would give the same answer to the suggestion that these activities involved a risk of accelerating the spread of auto-immune deficiency syndrome [AIDS], and that they should be brought within the Act of 1861 in the interests of public health. The consequence would be strange, since what is currently the principal cause for the transmission of this scourge, namely consenting buggery between males, is now legal. Nevertheless, I would have been compelled to give this proposition the most anxious consideration if there had been any evidence to support it. But there is none, since the case for the respondent was advanced on an entirely different ground.

(4)  There remains an argument to which I have given much greater weight. As the evidence in the present case has shown, there is a risk that strangers (and especially young strangers) may be drawn into these activities at an early age and will then become established in them for life. This is indeed a disturbing prospect, but I have come to the conclusion that it is not a sufficient ground for declaring these activities to be criminal under the Act of 1861. The element of the corruption of youth is already catered for by the existing legislation; and if there is a gap in it which needs to be filled the remedy surely lies in the hands of Parliament, not in the application of a statute which is aimed at other forms of wrongdoing. As regards proselytisation for adult sado-masochism the argument appears to me circular. For if the activity is not itself so much against the public interest that it ought to be declared criminal under the Act of 1861 then the risk that others will be induced to join in cannot be a ground for making it criminal.

Leaving aside the logic of this answer, which seems to me impregnable, plain humanity demands that a court addressing the criminality of conduct such as that of the present should recognise and respond to the profound dismay which all members of the community share about the apparent increase of cruel and senseless crimes against the defenceless. Whilst doing so I must repeat for the last time that in the answer which I propose I do not advocate the decriminalisation of conduct which has hitherto been a crime; nor do I rebut a submission that a new crime should be created, penalising this conduct, for Mr. Purnell has rightly not invited the House to take this course. The only question is whether these consensual private acts are offences against the existing law of violence. To this question I return a negative response.

[The defendants in *R v Brown* pursued their case to the European Court of Human Rights. The Court unanimously held that there had been no violation of the men's Article 8 right to respect for their private lives: see *Laskey v UK* (1997) 24 EHRR 39.]

As your list of reasons and principles should illustrate, *R v Brown* is a stark example of how people can hold very different views on the role and function of the criminal law. Principles like social welfare, legal paternalism and legal moralism can sometimes conflict very sharply with principles like individual autonomy.

The case also raises questions about the principle of legality: more specifically, whether the decision operated retrospectively.

---

### ACTIVITY

- Imagine that on the day before the defendants in *R v Brown* were arrested someone had asked you whether their activities were criminal. What would you have said?

- To put the previous question slightly differently, which of the following statements would you agree with:

  1. The defendants' activities were criminal from the day the Offences Against the Person Act 1861 became law. The House of Lords in *R v Brown* were simply explaining and applying the meaning that the statute had had for over 100 years.

  2. Before the House of Lords' decision in *R v Brown* it was uncertain whether the defendants' activities were criminal or not. The House of Lords decided that it should be a crime to deliberately inflict ABH/GBH/wounding in the course of sado-masochism and then applied this decision to the defendants.

- If you thought statement 2 was more plausible than statement 1, this suggests that the House of Lords effectively criminalised the defendants' conduct and applied this decision retrospectively. Is this defensible? Could it be justified on the basis that it was a reasonably foreseeable development of the law (see Chapter 1)?

---

It is immaterial that the defendants in *R v Brown* were homosexual; heterosexual sado-masochism that deliberately causes ABH/GBH/wounding is also an unlawful activity. In *R v Emmett* (*The Times* 15 October 1999) the defendant, Stephen Emmett, and his girlfriend, the victim, cohabited. During sexual activity Emmett tied his girl-friend up, put a plastic bag over her head and tied it around her neck, and then per-formed oral sex on her. When he became aware that she was distressed he pulled the bag off her head. It is probable that she lost consciousness. Her eyes became bloodshot, so she went to see her doctor. The doctor found haemorrhages in both her eyes and bruising around her neck. No treatment was prescribed, and after a week her eyes returned to normal. A few weeks later, again during sexual activity, Emmett poured lighter fuel on his girlfriend's breasts and set light to it. She suffered a burn measuring 6 cm by 4 cm. The burn became infected, so she went to see her doctor again. In fact the burn healed fully without any scarring, but the doctor was so alarmed by these two vis-its that he contacted the police. Emmett was arrested and charged with assault occa-sioning ABH. At trial Emmett was convicted following a ruling by the trial judge that the pair were engaged in an unlawful activity and so his girlfriend's consent was not availa-ble as a defence. Emmett's appeal against conviction was dismissed by the Court of Appeal. Pointing to the degree of harm Emmett's girlfriend suffered, and the degree of unpredictability and potential harm, the Court held that the pair had been engaged in an unlawful activity.

So *R v Brown* and *R v Emmett* make it clear that if a defendant deliberately causes a vic-tim ABH/GBH/wounding during sado-masochistic sexual activity he will not be able to rely on the victim's consent as a defence. But what about the following, slightly different scenario:

Although there is a case *R v Donovan* [1934] 2 KB 496 which suggests Romeo could not rely on Valentina's consent as a defence, it must now be read in the light of the judgments in *R v Brown*. In *R v Brown* the House of Lords stated quite clearly that a victim's consent is *always* available as a defence on a charge of assault or battery. So Romeo would be able to rely on Valentina's consent as a defence to a charge of battery. Had he been charged with assault occasioning ABH he would not have been able to rely on Valentina's consent as a defence, since deliberately injuring someone for sexual pleasure is an unlawful activity.

The best way to analyse this situation, it is suggested, is to say that Romeo and Valentina were engaged in sexual intercourse, not sado-masochism. Since sexual intercourse is a lawful activity, the consent of the victim is available as a defence and so Romeo would not be guilty of assault occasioning ABH.

### ii. Lawful activities

In *R v Brown* the House of Lords listed a number of lawful activities. These included: surgery; sports (such as boxing); tattooing and ear-piercing.[11] So, for example, a surgeon who cuts open his patient in order to perform an operation is not guilty of malicious wounding because the consent of the patient is available as a defence. Following the case *DPP v Smith* we can also add having your hair cut to the list of lawful activities. The hairdresser who cuts off your ponytail would not be guilty of assault occasioning ABH because he could rely on your consent as a defence.

Earlier we looked at the case *R v Dica*, in which the defendant had unprotected sexual intercourse with two women without telling them that he was HIV positive. In its judgment the Court of Appeal also discussed the situation where the defendant *does* tell the

---

[9]This situation is based on the case *R v Donovan* [1934] 2 KB 498. Donovan consensually caned a 17-year-old for sexual gratification.

[10]This situation is based on the case *R v Meachen* [2006] EWCA Crim 2414. In this case the victim suffered serious anal injuries. The defendant claimed that the cause of the injuries was him inserting his fingers into the victim's anus with her consent.

[11]Lord Mustill also listed religious mortification. For discussion of this, and religious exorcism, see Hall, H. (2016) 'Exorcism, Religious Freedom and Consent: The Devil in the Detail' 80 *Journal of Criminal Law* 241.

victim that he is HIV positive, the victim consents to unprotected sexual intercourse and subsequently contracts the virus. The Court of Appeal said that this is a lawful activity as long as the couple were not having sex in order to deliberately spread the disease.

## EXTRACT

Read the following extract from the Court's judgment. What reasons did the Court give for saying that sexual intercourse where there is a risk of infection but no desire to pass on the disease is a lawful activity?

## *R v Dica* [2004] EWCA Crim 1103

### Lord Justice Judge

49 [Suppose] one of a couple suffers from HIV. It may be the man: it may be the woman. The circumstances in which HIV was contracted are irrelevant. They could result from a contaminated blood transfusion, or an earlier relationship with a previous sexual partner, who unknown to the sufferer with whom we are concerned, was himself or herself infected with HIV. The parties are Roman Catholics. They are conscientiously unable to use artificial contraception. They both know of the risk that the healthy partner may become infected with HIV. Our second example is that of a young couple, desperate for a family, who are advised that if the wife were to become pregnant and give birth, her long-term health, indeed her life itself, would be at risk. Together the couple decide to run that risk, and she becomes pregnant. She may be advised that the foetus should be aborted, on the grounds of her health, yet, nevertheless, decide to bring her baby to term. If she does, and suffers ill health, is the male partner to be criminally liable for having sexual intercourse with her, notwithstanding that he knew of the risk to her health? If he is liable to be prosecuted, was she not a party to whatever crime was committed? And should the law interfere with the Roman Catholic couple, and require them, at the peril of criminal sanctions, to choose between bringing their sexual relationship to an end or violating their consciences by using contraception?

50 These, and similar risks, have always been taken by adults consenting to sexual intercourse. Different situations, no less potentially fraught, have to be addressed by them. Modern society has not thought to criminalise those who have willingly accepted the risks, and we know of no cases where one or other of the consenting adults has been prosecuted, let alone convicted, for the consequences of doing so.

51 The problems of *criminalising* the consensual taking of risks like these include the sheer impracticability of enforcement and the haphazard nature of its impact. The process would undermine the general understanding of the community that sexual relationships are pre-eminently private and essentially personal to the individuals involved in them. And if adults were to be liable to prosecution for the consequences of taking known risks with their health, it would seem odd that this should be confined to risks taken in the context of sexual intercourse, while they are nevertheless permitted to take the risks inherent in so many other aspects of everyday life, including, again for example, the mother or father of a child suffering a serious contagious illness, who holds the child's hand, and comforts or kisses him or her goodnight.

52 In our judgment, interference of this kind with personal autonomy, and its level and extent, may only be made by Parliament.

There are two remaining lawful activities for us to consider, both of which are contentious. The first is branding. This was considered by the Court of Appeal in *R v Wilson* [1997] QB 47. One day the victim, a woman of 'mature years' named Julie Wilson, went to her husband Alan and asked him to tattoo his name on her breasts. Alan explained that he 'didn't know how to do a tattoo'. Julie replied, 'Well, there must be some way. If you can't do a tattoo, there must be some way [...] I'm not scared of anybody knowing that I love you enough to have your name on my body.' They talked about it some more, and then 'hit on this idea of using a hot knife on her bum'. So Alan heated up a knife and branded a 'W' on Julie's right buttock. A few days later he finished the job and branded an 'A' on her left buttock. He told police, 'It wasn't life threatening, it wasn't anything, it was done for love. She loved me. She wanted me to [...] put my name on her body.' Alan was convicted at trial of assault occasioning ABH. He appealed against his conviction, arguing that Julie's consent should be available to him as a defence.

This case came a couple of years after *R v Brown*. As we have seen, since Julie suffered ABH the fact that she consented is only available as a defence if the injuries occurred in the course of a lawful activity. Applying the approach of the majority in *R v Brown*, the activity should be presumed to be unlawful and good policy and public interest reasons are required for the activity to be classified as lawful. This was the difficulty facing Alan Wilson. What are the good policy and public interest reasons that require branding to be lawful?

In spite of this difficulty, the Court of Appeal allowed Alan Wilson's appeal and quashed the conviction. A number of commentators have questioned whether the Court's reasoning can be reconciled with the House of Lords' judgment in *R v Brown*.

## ACTIVITY

Earlier we saw the different underlying approaches of the majority and Lord Mustill in *R v Brown* (the social utility and social disutility models). According to the doctrine of precedent, should the Court of Appeal in *R v Wilson* have applied the social utility model or the social disutility model?

## EXTRACT

Read the following extract from the judgment of Russell LJ in *R v Wilson*. Did he apply the social utility or social disutility model? (Hint: the clearest indication can be found in the final paragraph.)

Make a list of the reasons Russell LJ gave for saying that *R v Brown* and *R v Wilson* are distinguishable.

### R v Wilson [1997] QB 47

#### Russell LJ

We are abundantly satisfied that there is no factual comparison to be made between the instant case and the facts of either *Rex v. Donovan* [1934] 2 K.B. 498 or *Reg. v. Brown* [1994] 1 A.C. 212: Mrs. Wilson not only consented to that which the appellant did, she instigated it. There was no aggressive intent on the part of the appellant. On the contrary, far from wishing to cause injury to his wife, the appellant's desire was to assist her in what she regarded as the acquisition of a desirable piece of personal adornment, perhaps in this day and age no less understandable than the piercing of nostrils or even tongues for the purposes of inserting decorative jewellery.

In our judgment *Reg. v. Brown* is not authority for the proposition that consent is no defence to a charge under section 47 of the Act of 1861, in all circumstances where actual bodily harm is deliberately inflicted. It is to be observed that the question certified for their Lordships in *Reg. v. Brown* related only to a "sado-masochistic encounter." However, their Lordships recognised in the course of their speeches, that it is necessary that there must be exceptions to what is no more than a general proposition. The speeches of Lord Templeman, at p. 231, Lord Jauncey of Tullichettle, at p. 245, and the dissenting speech of Lord Slynn of Hadley, at p. 277, all refer to tattooing as being an activity which, if carried out with the consent of an adult, does not involve an offence under section 47, albeit that actual bodily harm is deliberately inflicted.

For our part, we cannot detect any logical difference between what the appellant did and what he might have done in the way of tattooing. The latter activity apparently requires no state authorisation, and the appellant was as free to engage in it as anyone else. We do not think that we are entitled to assume that the method adopted by the appellant and his wife was any more dangerous or painful than tattooing. There was simply no evidence to assist the court on this aspect of the matter.

Does public policy or the public interest demand that the appellant's activity should be visited by the sanctions of the criminal law? The majority in *Reg. v. Brown* clearly took the view that such considerations were relevant. If that is so, then we are firmly of the opinion that it is not in the public interest that activities such as the appellant's in this appeal should amount to criminal behaviour. Consensual activity between husband and wife, in the privacy of the matrimonial home, is not, in our judgment, normally a proper matter for criminal investigation, let alone criminal prosecution

Each of the reasons Russell LJ gave for distinguishing *R v Brown* has been carefully scrutinised by Paul Roberts in his case note 'Consent To Injury: How Far Can You Go?' (1997) 113 *Law Quarterly Review* 27. First, Roberts discusses the significance of the fact that Julie Wilson instigated the branding and Russell LJ's statement that Alan Wilson lacked any 'aggressive intent'.

### EXTRACT

## Roberts, P. (1997) 'Consent to Injury: How far can you go?' 113 *Law Quarterly Review* 27

That "an aggressive element" or "hostility" is in law an essential ingredient of an assault was an argument pressed by the appellants in *Brown*, and, in substance, unequivocally rejected by the House (Lord Jauncey of Tullichettle at p. 244; Lord Lowry at p. 254; Lord Mustill at pp. 260–261; Lord Slynn of Hadley at p. 280). Russell L.J.'s assertion that the facts of *Brown* were "truly extreme" is also problematic. Although the *Brown* appellants' idea of recreation might strike many people as bizarre or disgusting, the agreed facts, as they appear from the judgment of Lord Jauncey, were that "the receivers ["victims"] had neither complained to the police nor suffered any permanent injury as a result of the activities of the appellants" (p. 238). Mrs Wilson's scar tissue was, if anything, greater and more permanent disfigurement than any of the excruciating but temporary discomforts inflicted and suffered by the *Brown* defendants; although none of the injuries in either case could properly be described as "serious". What of Russell L.J.'s reliance on the fact that Mrs Wilson herself asked to be branded rather than merely agreeing to it? The question of which participants actually instigated the acts causing injury was not explored in *Brown*, but it is difficult to see how a distinction between instigation and consent could form the basis of a defensible or even workable boundary between lawful and criminal conduct. Victim-precipitation is usually irrelevant to criminal liability, which turns on whether or not the conduct in question is prohibited, not on whether the victim "asked for it". If the "victim's" consent is no answer to criminal liability for causing injury, his or her "instigation" is no answer either; except to expose the victim to possible prosecution for incitement or as an accomplice. Moreover it seems that the facts as well as the law are against [the instigation argument]. Responses to the Law Commission's consultation paper *Consent and Offences Against the Person* (1994) suggest that the sadomasochistic encounters in the *Brown* litigation were more than likely instigated and controlled by the apparently submissive partner, much as Mrs Wilson invited her husband to sign his name on her body (see Law Com. C.P. No. 139, *Consent in the Criminal Law* (1995) para. 10.32). There are no grounds to distinguish *Wilson* from *Brown* here.

Next, Roberts considers Russell LJ's comment that Alan Wilson's motive was to help his wife acquire what she regarded as 'a desirable piece of personal adornment':

### EXTRACT

#### Roberts, P. (1997) 'Consent to Injury: How far can you go?' 113 *Law Quarterly Review* 27

Nor do Russell L.J.'s references to the defendant's "wishes" and "desires" [...], although faithful to the agreed facts, appear to take the Court of Appeal's argument much further. It is well established that "desire" is not to be equated with the "intent" required to prove *mens rea* (*R. v. Moloney* [1985] 1 A.C. 905, at p. 926), and, as the House of Lords recently and emphatically reaffirmed in *R. v. Kingston* [1995] 2 A.C. 355, the defendant's motive is usually irrelevant to his criminal liability. If the defendant did the prohibited act in one of the specified mental states and without a recognised defence, that is enough to establish legal guilt, no matter how innocuous or even laudable his motivation. Mr Wilson, on his own admission, intentionally burned his initials into his wife's flesh with a hot knife. In the absence of a valid "defence" of consent (either a true "defence" or a negation of liability), that admission is sufficient proof that Mr Wilson committed assault occasioning actual bodily harm.

Roberts then examines the analogy Russell LJ drew between Alan Wilson's actions and tattooing.

### EXTRACT

#### Roberts, P. (1997) 'Consent to Injury: How far can you go?' 113 *Law Quarterly Review* 27

It is true that [in *R v Brown*] Lord Templeman and Lord Slynn accepted the legality of tattooing, although without argument and without citing any authority [...] It also seems reasonable to speculate that the pains and dangers incident to amateur branding are not too dissimilar to those inflicted by the amateur tattooist, although, as Russell L.J. himself observed, "there was simply no evidence to assist the court on this aspect of the matter" (p. 128b) [...] But even this narrow point fails to establish a truly satisfactory foundation for the court's decision in *Wilson* [...]

Two points need to be emphasised. First, by setting up a general proposition, hinting at an open list of exceptions, yet failing to specify what they are, *Brown* left the law in a state of considerable uncertainty. At a stroke, an extremely diverse range of injury-causing activities became presumptively unlawful, at least until the courts should determine otherwise. But many of these activities had hitherto been conducted beyond the law's gaze and it is far from easy to predict how the courts will judge them when they fall to be scrutinised. As the Law Commission has recently observed, "The less common minority practices of branding and scarification, which carry considerable risks if not carried out by skilled people in proper safe and hygienic conditions, fall into a grey area which the common law and statute have hardly touched" (*Consent in the Criminal Law*, para. 9.1). The second point to note is that, when it came to creating new exceptions to the general liability rule, the House of Lords in *Brown* declined to make "logical" connections between the defendants' behaviour and lawful forms of body decoration. For although the activities of the *Brown* defendants could arguably be described as "tattooing" and "piercing", or at least as close analogies to these lawful practices, the House recoiled from creating any exception for the particular forms of consensual injury confronting them on that occasion. Lord Jauncey sardonically remarked at p. 246f-g that:

"If it is to be decided that such activities as the nailing by A of B's foreskin or scrotum to a board or the insertion of hot wax into C's urethra followed by the burning of his penis with a candle or the incising of D's scrotum with a scalpel to the effusion of blood are injurious neither to B, C and D nor to the public interest then it is for Parliament with its accumulated wisdom and sources of information to declare them to be lawful."

It therefore seems pertinent to ask whether their Lordships would have looked any more favourably on the activities of amateur branders such as Mr Wilson; and this must be open to doubt. The majority in *Brown* took the view, most clearly expressed by Lord Lowry, that "[a] proposed *general* exemption is to be tested by considering the likely *general* effect" (p. 255h). In deciding against creating an exception to the general liability rule their Lordships consequently took into account the possibility that sadomasochistic encounters might get out of hand, that serious injuries might result, that disease and infection might spread, and that practitioners might corrupt the young and impressionable. Lord Jauncey candidly admitted that "your Lordships have no information as to whether such situations have occurred in relation to other sado-masochistic practitioners" (p. 246b), but the majority preferred to err on the side of caution: "[w]hen considering the public interest potential for harm is just as relevant as actual harm" (p. 246c).

Now these arguments could equally well apply to Mr Wilson's exploits.

Lastly, Roberts examines Russell LJ's underlying approach:

## EXTRACT

### Roberts, P. (1997) 'Consent to Injury: How far can you go?' 113 *Law Quarterly Review* 27

Russell L.J. correctly observed that in *Brown* their Lordships had regard to "public policy" and to "the public interest" in order to determine the legal status of consensually inflicted injury. From this, the Court of Appeal deduced that the crucial question is: "Does public policy or the public interest demand that the appellant's activity should be visited by the sanctions of the criminal law?" In other words, the court began with a presumption of legality and looked for reasons to extend the criminal law to the appellant's activities. In view of the appellant's and his wife's weighty interests in keeping their private lives private, and in the absence of any evidence to suggest that Mrs Wilson actually objected to being branded, Russell L.J. could find no such reasons. The court refused to speculate about the potential for amateur branding to be excessively painful or unpredictably dangerous, since such contingencies did not arise on the facts.

[...]

But this proposition, invoking a presumption of legality in favour of consensual injury, directly contradicts the majority's decision in *Brown* and must therefore be considered *per incuriam*. It propounds the same approach to the relationship between consent and criminal liability that animates Lord Mustill's dissent in *Brown*. Lord Mustill embraced a minimalist principle of criminalization according to which "the state should interfere with the rights of an individual to live his or her life as he or she may choose no more than is necessary to ensure a proper balance between the special interests of the individual and the general interests of the individuals who together comprise the populace at large" (p. 273e-f). His Lordship explicitly observed that his dissenting conclusion flowed from his fundamental disagreement with the majority's approach to determining the proper shape and content of the criminal law: "... if the question were differently stated it might well yield a different answer... . Thus, if I had begun from the same point of departure as my noble and learned friend, Lord Jauncey of Tullichettle, I would have arrived at a similar conclusion; but differing from him on the present state of the law, I venture to differ" (pp. 273, 274). The *Brown* majority rejected Lord Mustill's approach, founded on the value of individual autonomy, preferring instead to adopt a general rule that "the infliction of actual or more serious bodily harm is an unlawful activity to which consent is no answer" (*per* Lord Jauncey, at p. 245), subject, as we have observed, to an open and ill-defined list of exceptions. Russell L.J.'s [approach] would therefore have placed him in the dissenting minority in *Brown*.

[...]

None of the above is intended to cast any doubt on the good sense of Russell L.J.'s judgment, nor on its strong foundation in principle; only its legality is denied. Beyond its ephemeral voyeuristic and entertainment value, *Wilson* is an unremarkable case, but it does valuable service by demonstrating that *Brown* was a regrettable decision that has become an unsatisfactory precedent. In an area of the criminal law which bears upon such controversial subjects as surgical intervention, contact sports (-including boxing), dangerous exhibitions, and traditional religious practices such as circumcision, as well as the minority sexual practices and tattooing and scarification which arose respectively in *Brown* and *Wilson*, it is inconceivable that the Court of Appeal, much less prosecutors and first instance judges, will be able to turn a blind eye to the leading case indefinitely. Nor should they have to. The criminal law is seriously defective when the Court of Appeal feels obliged to go as far as it did in *Wilson* in taking liberties with their Lordships' decisions so that common sense and justice can prevail. The House of Lords will surely have to reconsider *Brown* before too long, and one suspects that Russell L.J. will be amongst those hoping that Lord Mustill gets to write the majority judgment next time.

## ACTIVITY

Look back at your list of the reasons Russell LJ gave in *R v Wilson* for distinguishing *R v Brown*. In the light of Roberts' comments, do you believe the two cases are distinguishable?

The final lawful activity is horseplay (where there is no intention to cause injury). There are three examples of this lawful activity in case law.

> **EXAMPLE**
>
> - The first example is *R v Jones (Terence)* (1986) 83 Cr App R 375. The defendants in this case were six schoolboys aged 14 to 17. They grabbed hold of the first victim, a 14-year-old pupil, threw him about nine to ten feet in the air, and didn't catch him. The victim suffered a ruptured spleen, which had to be removed. The second victim was a 15-year-old pupil. They threw him in the air, didn't catch him, and the victim suffered a broken arm. The defendants were convicted of the section 20 offence of maliciously inflicting GBH. On appeal the Court of Appeal quashed their convictions.
>
> - The second example is *R v Aitken* [1992] 1 WLR 1006. The three defendants in this case were RAF Officers. They were at a party with a number of other officers. Everyone was wearing their fire resistant flying suits. Two of the men fell asleep. As a joke, the others decided to set light to the trouser leg of their fire resistant suits. Both men woke up with a start. Shortly afterwards the party broke up and the defendants left. On their way home, they noticed the victim, Flying Officer Gibson, staggering around drunk. Gibson had been at the party earlier when the two other men had had their trouser legs set alight, so the three defendants decided to set light to Gibson's suit. They did so. Gibson was engulfed in flames. He suffered extremely severe burning; 35 per cent of his body was covered in life-threatening burns. The defendants were convicted of the section 20 offence of maliciously inflicting GBH. On appeal, their convictions were quashed.
>
> - The third example is *R v Richardson & Irwin* [1999] 1 Cr App R 392. The two defendants, Richardson and Irwin, and the victim, Simon Rose, were university students. One night they were at Irwin's student accommodation and started 'bundling'. Irwin then suggested that they hold Rose over the edge of the balcony. There was a tussle, they lifted Rose over the balcony, then accidentally dropped him. He fell approximately twelve feet and suffered serious injuries. The defendants were convicted of the section 20 offence of maliciously inflicting GBH. On appeal the convictions were quashed.

These three cases establish two important points. First, they establish that horseplay is a lawful activity as long as there was no intention to cause injury. This is difficult to justify. The social utility model set out by the majority in *R v Brown* states that activities which cause ABH/GBH/wounding must be presumed to be unlawful, and good policy and public interest reasons are required for them to be classified as lawful. What are the policy and public interest reasons which require that horseplay be classified as a lawful activity? Suggestions that rough and undisciplined play is commonplace in environments like the playground and the locker room, and that it helps people bond and develop camaraderie, seem inadequate. Moreover, to say that horseplay is a lawful activity, but the activities in *R v Brown* were unlawful, appears discriminatory.

You may be thinking to yourself, surely the victims in these cases didn't consent? Surely the schoolboys in *R v Jones (Terence)* didn't consent to being thrown in the air? Surely Flying Officer Gibson didn't consent to being set alight? Surely Simon Rose didn't consent to being held over the balcony? This leads us to the second important point from these three cases. Even if the victim did not consent, the defendant still has a defence if he *genuinely believed* that the victim was consenting. Notice the word 'genuinely'. The belief need not have been a reasonable one; it is sufficient that it was honestly held. In *R v Jones (Terence)* the defendants said that they genuinely believed that the victims were consenting. They thought the victims were taking it as a joke. In *R v Aitken* the defendants said that since Gibson had joined in with setting the other men's trouser legs alight earlier in the evening they genuinely thought that he was consenting to being set alight himself. And in *R v Richardson & Irwin* the defendants said that since tussles were a regular occurrence amongst the group they genuinely believed Rose was consenting to being lifted over the balcony. So in a case involving a lawful activity, the defendant will have a defence to a charge of ABH/GBH/wounding if he genuinely believed that the victim was consenting to the activity, even if that belief was unreasonable and even if the victim was in fact not consenting.

## ACTIVITY

In your opinion, can the case law on horseplay be reconciled with *R v Brown*?

### iii. The social utility or social disutility model?

Earlier we saw that the majority and minority in *R v Brown* took quite different approaches to determining whether an activity which causes injury should be classified as lawful or unlawful. The majority adopted a social utility approach, whereas Lord Mustill's dissenting judgment took a social disutility approach. An important question to consider is which approach is the most appropriate.

## EXTRACT

Read the following extract from David Kell's article 'Social disutility and the law of consent' (1994) 14 *Oxford Journal of Legal Studies* 121. In your own words, summarise the three reasons he gives for favouring the social disutility approach.

Do you agree or disagree with David Kell? Try and use the principles that we studied in Chapter 1 to explain your reasoning.

### Kell D. (1994) 'Social disutility and the law of consent' 14 *Oxford Journal of Legal Studies* 121

[The majority of the House of Lords in *R v Brown*] espoused a social utility model whereby, once injury reached the level of bodily harm, the accused was required to demonstrate that the particular activity was needed in the public interest (social utility), rather than the prosecution having to prove that good reason exists for prohibiting the conduct (social disutility). Yet the public interest underpinning most listed exceptions is yet to be articulated. While at one end of the spectrum are those exceptions clearly serving a valuable social purpose, including reasonable surgical (and dental) interference, necessary for the preservation of life and good health, at the other end are to be found tattooing, ear-piercing, and dangerous sports, such as boxing, where the social purpose served is perhaps less clear

[...]

The social disutility model has a number of attractive advantages. First, by refusing to prohibit conduct unless the State provides cogent reasons, the model is better suited to a modern democratic society which places significant value on individual autonomy. Although autonomy cannot be the only value which the law seeks to enhance and must be balanced against what the Supreme Court of Canada termed 'some larger societal interest', the overriding question should always be 'what justifies the intervention?' The present social utility model often allows this question to be completely evaded. Thus although the House of Lords majority were quite thorough in rejecting the case for an exception for sado-masochistic conduct, the Court of Appeal, in language closer to assertion than reason, was able almost summarily to reject the defendants' appeals, stating: 'What may be "good reason" [i.e. justifying an exception] it is not necessary for us to decide. It is sufficient to say ... that the satisfying of sado-masochistic libido does not come within the category of good reason ...'.

Second, although it is not suggested that it was a motivating force in shaping the present law, the model may actually provide a better explanation for many of the proffered exceptions to the general rule, than does the social utility model that currently holds sway. It may, for instance, be difficult to state why tattooing or ear-piercing are needed in the public interest, but it may be equally difficult to state why the public interest would require their prohibition. And even in the case of the daredevil stuntmen referred to above in [the judgment of the Supreme Court of Canada in *R v Jobidon* [1991] 2 SCR 714], a social disutility approach might be more persuasive than talk of 'socially valuable cultural products'. Of course, for some forms of conduct, for instance public brawling, the choice of model would make no difference. *Jobidon* itself involved an allegedly consensual fight in the parking lot of an Ontario public bar, and the court, employing the language of social utility, was quick to note the social uselessness of such fights. But not only are such consensual fights not required in the public interest (in social utility terms), there are persuasive public policy reasons for prohibiting the conduct (social disutility). Such fights can often lead to injury more serious than intended by the combatants, and to larger, disorderly brawls as supporters join in. Moreover, such combatants if permitted to fight consensually may, on some future occasion, 'too readily find their fists raised against a person whose consent they forgot to ascertain with full certitude'; and, though often not amounting to a legal vitiation of consent, those drawn into such fights often do so more out of fear of being branded a coward than out of a genuine desire to face the aggressor. And one should note also that a social disutility model should not be too radical a change for the judiciary to bear, as evidenced perhaps by occasional judicial slippage into the language of social disutility.

Third, arguably one unfortunate consequence of the social utility model, as advocated by the courts, is an unreasonable distortion of the criterion of 'bodily harm'. In *R v Boyea* [(1992) 156 J.P. 505] in a well-intentioned attempt to liberate the law on consensual, unorthodox sexual conduct from the strictures placed on it in 1934 by the Court of Appeal in *Donovan*, the Court of Appeal sought to refine the definition of bodily harm. After noting that the court ought to take into account changing social attitudes to sexual activities between consenting adults, the court stated:

> As a generality, the level of vigour in sexual congress which is generally acceptable, and therefore the voluntarily accepted risk of incurring some injury, is probably higher now than it was in 1934. It follows ... that the phrase 'transient or trifling' [in the *Donovan* definition] must be understood in the light of conditions in 1992 rather than those of nearly 60 years ago.

The bodily harm criterion represents the level at which the effectiveness of consent is brought into question, under the present law by the accused facing the often difficult task of demonstrating why a particular activity is needed in the public interest. By manipulating the bodily harm criterion the court in *Boyea*, albeit obiter, foreshadowed an approach whereby, in an attempt to avoid such difficulty, injuries (resulting from particular conduct) once considered to fall within the definition are now classified as outside it, thus permitting consent to operate effectively. While any attempt at liberation may be considered a welcome advance on the current state of the law, it is arguable that the bodily harm criterion, perhaps more comfortably positioned as a rigid, rather than a normative, concept, is being asked to bear too much of the weight of reform.

A social disutility model, on the other hand, with greater weight being given to individual autonomy and possessing sufficient flexibility to re-examine, in an appropriate case, the merits of prohibiting (previously-outlawed) conduct in the light of changed social conditions, would remove the need for reform of the law by the more cumbersome, and indirect, means of manipulating the bodily harm criterion.

## The Law Commission's proposals for reform

As part of its 11th programme of Law Reform, the Law Commission was asked by the Ministry of Justice to carry out a scoping exercise as a first step towards reform of the Offences Against the Person Act 1861. The Commission published a scoping consultation paper in November 2014,[12] followed one year later by a scoping report containing its recommendations.[13]

Before examining the Law Commission's proposals, it is useful to begin by looking at the reasons why the Commission felt that reform of the OAPA 1861 is necessary.

### EXTRACT

Read the following extract from the final report. In your own words, list the Commission's criticisms of the OAPA 1861.

(Note: in this extract, and the ones that follow below, the acronym 'SCP' refers to the scoping consultation paper that preceded the final report.)

### Law Commission (2015) *Reform of Offences Against the Person* (No 361) HC 555

#### Definitions of offences

3.3 In the SCP we argued that the drafting of the offences in the 1861 Act is unnecessarily complex, in particular in two respects: there are too many divisions between the offences, and too many divisions within the offences.

(1)    There are often several narrowly defined and highly detailed offences relating to the same subject matter, which could be covered by a single broader offence with fewer elements. For example, there are four offences relating to the misuse of explosives and similar substances (and three more under the Explosives Substances Act 1883).

---

[12]Law Commission (2014) *Reform of Offences Against the Person: A Scoping Consultation Paper* (Consultation Paper No 217).

[13]Law Commission (2015) *Reform of Offences Against the Person* (Law Commission No 361) HC 555.

(2)   In other cases, the same section of the 1861 Act contains a list of different but related detailed situations, leaving doubt about whether the section creates one offence or several. One example is section 18, which arguably creates four offences, covering ten different factual situations. We argue in the SCP that "if there is a common theme to the scenarios listed, the offence should be defined by that common theme. If there is not, the scenarios should be separate offences set out in separate sections."

3.4 We also argued that there is no clear hierarchy among the main offences. At first sight there does appear to be a hierarchy: the offence under section 18 (wounding or grievous bodily harm with intent) is the most serious, the offence under section 20 (malicious wounding or grievous bodily harm) is the middle-ranking offence and the offence under section 47 (assault occasioning actual bodily harm) is the least serious. However, this apparent hierarchy is marred by two facts:

(1)   the maximum sentence for the offences under sections 20 and 47 is the same (5 years);

(2)   the special status given to "wounding" means that the offences are not clearly distinguished by the seriousness of the injury caused: a wound can be quite minor and nevertheless constitute the offence under section 20 or even section 18.

## Unnecessary offences

3.5 There are several offences which are seldom or never encountered in modern conditions and could be considered for abolition. Examples include:

(1)   assaulting a magistrate or other person in the exercise of his duty preserving a wreck;

(2)   impeding a person escaping from a shipwreck;

(3)   not providing apprentices or servants with food;

(4)   exposing children to danger; and

(5)   setting a spring gun, man trap or other engine calculated to destroy life or cause grievous bodily harm.

## Language and style

3.6 Further criticisms of the 1861 Act are that:

(1)   it uses archaic vocabulary, such as "grievous" (to describe a serious injury) and "detainer" (to mean detention);

(2)   it uses words without a clear meaning, such as "maliciously", that have required extensive interpretation by the courts and are sometimes redundant;

(3)   it refers to specific devices and chemicals, such as laudanum, as means of committing offences and is therefore liable to obsolescence as these means fall out of use or further inventions are made;

(4)   it refers to obsolete legal concepts, such as felony, misdemeanour and penal servitude, which have to be re-interpreted by provisions in other statutes; and

(5)   it does not state the penalties for major offences, such as those under sections 47 and 20: these have to be deduced from a chain of interlocking provisions in other statutes.

Having set out these criticisms of the OAPA 1861, the Commission then listed three options:

1.   To say that most ambiguities have been resolved by judicial interpretation and the 1861 Act works well in practice, so there is no pressing practical need for reform;

2. To retain the 1861 Act, but amend it to update its language and abolish any obsolete offences; or

3. To replace the 1861 Act with a comprehensive new statute.

During the consultation phase, the vast majority of consultees favoured the third option. The main arguments advanced by the minority who favoured option one or two were that 'the present system works in practice and that a new statute would be difficult to draft and probably result in further mistakes' (para 3.15). The Law Commission rejected each of these concerns. First, there remain some unresolved ambiguities, and unforeseen ones still sometimes emerge. In addition:

> 3.18 [...] [E]ven assuming that the meaning of the 1861 Act is now settled by judicial decision, it is not apparent on the face of the statute. In effect, the law in this area is the product of 'judicial legislation', accessible only to those lawyers and officials who are experts in the field. From the point of view of that class the law may be clear and the system may work without problems. That however is not good enough. One basic function of law is to inform the public clearly about what conduct is permitted or forbidden, and if it is forbidden what the consequences are. This is not achieved by a statute which is in effect written in code.

As for the argument that a new statute would generate further problems, the Commission pointed out that over the past few decades there have been several drafts of replacement legislation, and none of these generated 'any suggestion of "problems or mistakes" at all comparable to those in the existing Act' (para 3.19).

Having recommended that the 1861 Act should be replaced by a comprehensive, modern statute, the Law Commission then set out its proposed new scheme of offences. In developing this new scheme, the Commission used as its starting point the draft Bill contained in the 1998 Home Office Consultation Paper *Violence: Reforming the Offences Against the Person Act 1861*. Building on this, the 2015 report proposed amending the five offences we have studied in this chapter as set out in Table 6.1.

In its exposition of the proposed offences, the Law Commission addressed a number of issues, including:

- Whether to distinguish between different types of injury, such as shooting, poisoning and stabbing;
- The appropriate hierarchy of offences, having regard to the level of injury suffered and the *mens rea* of the defendant;
- Whether a definition of injury is necessary and, if so, which kinds of mental harm it should include;
- Whether assault and battery should be merged into a single offence; and,
- The rationale for creating an additional offence, called aggravated assault.

(Note that the report did not consider issues relating to consent. The Commission did state, however, that the principle from *R v Brown* that consent is only available as a defence in cases involving a lawful activity would apply to the top three offences in its hierarchy. For aggravated assault, physical assault and threatened assault, the consent of the victim would always be available as a defence.)

**Table 6.1** Proposed reform of offences against the person

| Existing offences | | | Proposed offences | | |
|---|---|---|---|---|---|
| | **Description** | **Maximum sentence** | | **Description** | **Maximum sentence** |
| OAPA 1861, s18 | Wounding or causing grievous bodily harm with intent to cause grievous bodily harm | Life | | Intentionally causing serious injury<br><br>Note: wounding is not included unless the wound is a serious injury | Life |
| OAPA 1861, s20 | Malicious wounding or infliction of grievous bodily harm<br><br>Note: the defendant must intend or be reckless about some harm; not necessarily about a wound or grievous bodily harm | 5 years | | Recklessly causing serious injury<br><br>Note: D must be reckless about the risk of serious injury; wounding is not included unless the wound is a serious injury | 7 years |
| | | | | Intentionally or recklessly causing injury (whether or not by assault)<br><br>Note: D must intend or be reckless about the risk of some injury | 5 years |
| OAPA 1861, s47 | Assault occasioning actual bodily harm<br><br>Note: this includes every assault or battery which in fact causes injury, whether or not the defendant intended or was reckless about injury | 5 years | | Aggravated assault<br><br>Note: includes every physical or threatened assault which in fact causes injury, whether or not D intended or was reckless about injury | 12 months |
| Common law | Battery<br><br>Note: this means actual physical violence, including any unlawful touching however slight. At present, this offence is sometimes used for cases of low-level injuries | 6 months | | Physical assault<br><br>Note: should not be used for cases of low-level injury, as these may be charged as aggravated assault | 6 months |
| Common law | Assault<br><br>Note: this means causing a person to apprehend physical violence, in the same sense as for battery above | 6 months | | Threatened assault | 6 months |

*Source*: Adapted from table at pp200–204 of Law Commission (2015) *Reform of Offences Against the Person* (No 361) HC 555.

---

**EXTRACT**

Read the following extract from the Law Commission's report. In respect of each of the five issues listed above, what did the Law Commission recommend and why?

(Note: in the extracts that follow, the term 'draft Bill' refers to the 1998 draft Bill that the Law Commission took as its starting point.)

## Law Commission (2015) *Reform of Offences Against the Person* (No 361) HC 555

4.15 If we were devising a law of offences of violence from scratch, there would, in very general terms, be a choice between two different approaches.

(1)   In approach 1, the main offences would have external elements defined as the causing of "injury", without distinguishing the type of injury or the means by which it was caused.

(2)   In approach 2, there would be separate offences in which the external elements consisted of causing injuries of different types or by different means: for example, offences of "wounding" and "poisoning".

4.16 Both these approaches are found in other areas of the criminal law.

(1)   Approach 1 is found in the law of homicide. Both murder and manslaughter can consist of causing death by any means: shooting, strangling, drowning, poisoning etc.

(2)   Approach 2 is found in property offences. Theft, robbery and handling stolen goods are all distinct offences, though all involve dishonest interference with another's property interests. In addition, there are offences of fraud and cheat, each describing a particular means of dishonest property interference.

4.17 The 1861 Act does not consistently follow either approach.

(1)   The offence under section 18 was based on an older offence covering only wounding and shooting. It can now consist of either wounding or causing grievous bodily harm by any means.

(2)   Some forms of the section 18 offence involve causing grievous bodily harm "with intent to resist or prevent the lawful apprehension or detainer of any person". This does not restrict the kind of harm or the means by which it is caused, but does require highly specific circumstances.

(3)   The offence under section 20 can consist of either wounding or "inflicting" grievous bodily harm. Infliction was once thought to mean a direct forcible injury such as an assault. It is now recognised as being wider than this, and can cover indirect injuries such as the transmission of infection. There now seems to be little if any distinction between "inflict" in section 20 and "cause" in section 18. This offence, like that under section 18, would therefore appear to cover injuries of any kind (provided they are serious enough) caused by any means.

(4)   In the offence under section 47, the actual bodily harm must be occasioned by an assault (or a battery).

...

4.25 The options for reform are broadly as follows:

(1)   adopt the scheme of the draft Bill (approach 1): general injury offences only;

(2)   create particularised offences of causing injury by wounding, poisoning, maiming etc, but have no general injury offence (approach 2); or

(3)   retain a mixture, as at present: some detailed offences – wounding, choking, etc – and one or more residual general offences.

4.26 The first option has the advantage of being a clear, streamlined and readily understandable scheme. As argued in the SCP, there is just one offence of murder and one of manslaughter, which do not distinguish between different means of causing death. These offences are readily understood by the public and would not be improved or made more accessible by being divided into separate offences of causing death by stabbing, shooting, poisoning and so on. Exactly the same reasoning is applicable to causing non-fatal injuries.

4.27 The second option did not have any support from consultees. It would also be impractical, as human inventiveness will always extend to new ways of causing injury.

4.28 The main argument for the third option is that some means of causing injury, such as poisoning and the use of explosives, rightly attract an especially high level of public disapproval. It is therefore just that people who are guilty of them are labelled appropriately, and where necessary given a higher sentence. This argument needs to be considered separately under the head of labelling and that of appropriate punishment.

4.29 In our view the scheme of the draft Bill meets the requirement for appropriate labelling, because it is possible to charge an offence of administering substances capable of causing injury or causing danger by explosives together with one of the general injury offences.

4.30 The draft Bill also meets the sentencing needs in the most serious cases. The need for punishment is strongest when there is either an intention to cause death or an intention to cause serious injury. In a case involving poisoning or explosives the current offence of attempted murder (which would be unaltered by the recommendations), and the proposed offence of intentionally causing serious injury under the draft Bill (and therefore the offence of attempting to do so), all carry a maximum life sentence. These charges, with or without a charge of causing danger by drugs or explosives, fully meet the need for adequate punishment.

4.31 When there is no intention to cause death or serious injury, the main reason for public disapproval of the acts involving poisons or explosives is that the defendant was acting in a dangerously irresponsible way. Adequate punishment for this is achieved by charging an offence of causing danger by drugs or explosives together with that of recklessly causing serious injury, or intentionally or recklessly causing injury, as the case may be.

4.32 For these reasons, we favour the first option, which is to follow the scheme of the draft Bill.

4.33 We recommend that any new statute governing crimes of violence should follow the scheme of the draft Bill by providing for one or more general offences of causing injury, rather than offences of causing injury of particular types or by particular means

...

4.35 The levels of harm distinguished by the present law and practice are as follows:

(1)    "Grievous bodily harm" – the 1861 Act contains two offences of "grievous bodily harm" (sections 18 and 20), and variants of this phrase are found in some other offences such as those relating to explosives and poisons. The offences under sections 18 and 20 can also consist of "wounding".

(2)    "Actual bodily harm" – section 47 distinguishes those assaults that occasion "actual bodily harm". However, the maximum sentence is five years, the same as for section 20.

(3)    Low level harm – in practice, and following CPS charging standards, assaults causing low level harms are usually charged as [assault or battery] though technically they fall within the scope of the section 47 offence.

4.36 In the SCP we criticised this as not providing a clear hierarchy of seriousness. That is, in principle there is a distinction between serious harm (sections 18 and 20) and less serious harm (section 47). However, this distinction is blurred because:

(1)    the offences under sections 18 and 20 can be committed by wounding, without causing serious harm; and

(2)    the distinction is not reflected in sentencing, as the maximum sentences for sections 20 and 47 are the same.

...

4.43 The main distinction in the present law is between "grievous bodily harm" and "actual bodily harm". The draft Bill preserves this distinction, modernising the language to read "serious injury" and "injury".

4.44 Assuming that some distinction of degrees of injury is desirable, the next question is whether distinguishing between "serious injury" and "injury" is sufficiently precise. As pointed out in the SCP, the word "serious" is ambiguous, as it can mean either "really serious", that is to say of exceptional gravity, or "sufficient to be taken seriously", that is to say more than minor. To avoid ambiguity, it might be best for the offences under clauses 1 and 2 to be defined using wording making clear that the offences must involve an exceptionally grave injury. This would have the effect of preserving the test in the present law, which describes grievous bodily harm as being "really serious".

4.45 We recommend using the hierarchy of injury offences in the draft Bill, distinguishing between serious or severe injuries and injury in general.

## Grading by level of injury intended or foreseen

4.46 An important question discussed in the SCP is whether offences should generally require that the defendant intended or foresaw the same level of injury as that described in the external elements of the offence. For example, if an offence involves causing serious injury, should the requirement be that the defendant intended or foresaw serious injury, or only that the defendant intended or foresaw any injury?

4.47 In Chapter 3 of the SCP we discussed the general principle and explained the differences between the possible positions:

(1) Some offences conform to the "correspondence principle". In these offences, the level of harm that D must intend or foresee in any given offence is the same as the level of harm defined in the external element of the offence. This is the position in battery: D must intend or be reckless about the possible touching of the victim, and that touching must occur.

(2) Others are offences of "constructive liability". In these, it is accepted that, once D intends or foresees a basic level of harm, he or she may also be held to blame for any greater degree of harm that results. An example is murder, where D is guilty if he or she kills, despite only intending to cause grievous bodily harm.

(3) There are also offences of "ulterior intent", where D must intend a consequence that need not occur in fact: for example, assault with intent to rob, where no actual robbery need take place. Following that discussion, we addressed the choice between these approaches as applied to the injury offences under the 1861 Act and the draft Bill.

## Current law

4.48 In the 1861 Act:

(1) the section 18 offence requires:

    (a) grievous bodily harm or wounding;
    (b) with intent either to cause grievous bodily harm or "to resist or prevent the lawful apprehension or detainer of any person";

(2) the section 20 offence requires:

    (a) grievous bodily harm or wounding;
    (b) with intent or recklessness as to some harm;

(3) the section 47 offence requires:

    (a) assault (or battery) occasioning actual bodily harm;
    (b) with the necessary intent or recklessness for assault or battery.

4.49 The second and third offences are offences of "constructive liability" in the sense defined above. The first offence is more complicated, and combines elements from all three approaches:

(1)   It can consist of causing grievous bodily harm, with intent to do grievous bodily harm. In this form, it conforms to the correspondence principle.

(2)   It can consist of wounding, with intent to do grievous bodily harm. This is an offence of both constructive liability (the defendant need not intend or foresee a wound) and ulterior intent (the wound that actually occurs need not amount to grievous bodily harm).

(3)   It can consist of wounding or grievous bodily harm, with intent to resist or prevent arrest or detention. Again this is an offence of both constructive liability (the word "maliciously" implies that the defendant must intend or foresee some harm, but no more) and ulterior intent (the attempt to resist or prevent arrest or detention may be unsuccessful).

...

4.97 In conclusion, the arguments [in favour of constructive liability] do not shake our belief that the correspondence principle is correct in principle and should be the default position, though there may be reasons for departing from it in particular instances. In a previous report, we mentioned the argument that, if any factor is important enough to make the difference between guilt and innocence, awareness of that factor or of the possibility of it should in principle be an element of the offence. Otherwise potential defendants will not know whether they are committing the offence, and the requirement of fair warning is not met. The alternative, namely constructive liability, accepts the fault element for a lower level but related offence on the argument that D knew that he or she was doing "something wrong". This is in effect a reversion to the Victorian concept of malice in "the old vague sense of wickedness in general".

4.98 As concerns the injury offences that we are considering, the scheme of the draft Bill, which reflects the correspondence principle, will enable prosecutors to choose levels of offence that more effectively reflect the wrong that occurred. At the same time, it will not weaken the protection given by the current law, as the disputed cases [where serious injury occurs, but is not intended or foreseen], will continue to carry a maximum sentence of five years.

4.99 We recommend using the hierarchy of offences in the draft Bill, in which the offence of recklessly causing serious injury is only committed if the defendant is aware of the risk that his or her conduct will cause serious injury.

...

4.123 We agree with the conclusion of a majority of consultees that a definition [of injury] is required. The terms "grievous bodily harm" and "actual bodily harm", vague though they are in themselves, are hallowed by usage and the boundaries have been clarified judicially. The word "injury" is comparatively straightforward, but is not generally understood as including mental harm of any kind (other than perhaps harm resulting from brain damage). Clarification of the kind of mental harm covered is certainly required, whatever boundary is decided upon.

4.124 On the substantive question of what kinds of mental harm to include, the main problem is one of drawing clear boundaries. There may be some merit in extending injury beyond the boundaries of recognised psychiatric harm. However, in medical practice the distinction between psychiatric harm and other undesirable psychological conditions is reasonably clear, and the courts do not appear to have experienced difficulty in applying it. There is far less clarity in distinguishing treatable psychological conditions from unpleasant but normal states of mind such as shock, distress and feelings of depression, as the difference is often one of degree rather than kind.

4.125 Another point is that the new offences do not require any kind of physical attack, but include every possible means of causing injury. This is a further reason for caution. There is a case for criminalising a physical attack which causes any kind of harm, however remote from physical injury. There is also a case for criminalising any act that causes a physical or related injury. But allowing the offence to cover purely psychological means of causing purely psychological harm goes too far. A statutory code primarily concerned with offences of violence should not cover examples such as causing depression by dismissing a person from employment or ending a relationship, and we have not been able to devise a test for distinguishing these from more deserving examples such as inducing depression by systematic domestic abuse. This last example will however often be caught by section 76 of the Serious Crime Act 2015, which makes it an offence to engage in controlling or coercive behaviour towards a person in an intimate or family relationship which "causes [V] serious alarm or distress which has a substantial adverse effect on [V]'s usual day-to-day activities".

4.126 We recommend that the definition of mental injury should have the same limits as the existing law, namely recognised psychiatric conditions.

...

5.16 Though the offences of assault and battery are distinct, in many (possibly most) cases they occur together. That is, where D makes a frontal attack on V, V will see the attack coming (so D has committed assault), and D in fact hits V (so D has committed battery). The two exceptional cases are:

(1)    assault without battery: D threatens V, or swings a fist at V but misses;

(2)    battery without assault: D hits V from behind, or while V is asleep.

5.17 Nevertheless we adhere to the view in the SCP that assault and battery are fundamentally different wrongs, particularly since assault includes threatening behaviour such as telephone calls that need not form the opening stage of an intended attack: it is enough that V apprehends that an attack will take place in the near future. The complexity of the draft clauses in both the 1998 draft Bill and its predecessors, and the wide variations among them, testify to the difficulty of embodying both forms of behaviour in a single concept.

...

5.46 ... Section 47 [assault occasioning ABH] performs two different functions.

(1)    In its original context, it did not create a separate offence: it was simply a provision about the sentencing powers for assault, to the effect that a somewhat higher sentence (originally three years) was available if the assault caused bodily harm than if it did not. That is why the offence still does not require any intention to cause bodily harm, or foresight of bodily harm.

(2)    In current practice, it is the offence of choice for some quite significant injuries. This is consistent with the fact that the sentencing powers extend to five years, the same as for the section 20 offence.

It is because there is significant strain between these two functions that the first function has in current practice been largely removed from section 47 and taken over by [assault and battery].

## Offence of aggravated assault?

5.47 One solution would be to separate these two functions. The [intentionally or recklessly causing injury offence], triable either way, would continue to cover the causing of injury of any level by any means, provided that it was intentional or reckless. There would also be a separate offence triable only in a magistrates' court, covering cases where D causes injury by assault or battery, whether the injury was foreseen or not. We suggest that it should be called "aggravated assault".

## Advantages

5.48 This would have the advantages that the lesser offence is not wholly covered by the greater and that there is a clear distinction between the two: one offence is confined to intentional or reckless injuries, while the other includes inadvertent injuries. The new offence of aggravated assault would also provide an adequate label for D's conduct and avoid alienating victims by telling them that their injuries are minor.

5.49 As explained, the formal distinction between the two injury offences is that the [intentionally or recklessly causing injury offence] requires intention or recklessness as to the causing of injury, while aggravated assault would not (though it would require intention or recklessness as to the underlying assault or battery). In practice, aggravated assault would be used for three types of cases:

(1)   cases involving low level injuries – black eyes, split lips, bruising, abrasions – which are currently charged as [assault or battery] following the charging standard; the charging standard would accordingly be amended to refer to aggravated assault ...

(2)   cases where, currently, the prosecution brings a charge under section 47 but seeks to keep the case in the magistrates' court, because the facts are at the lower end of the range for that offence and the expected sentence is within the power of that court (up to 12 months, if our recommendation below is accepted); and

(3)   cases involving injuries of any level where it is impossible to prove intention or recklessness as to causing injury.

In the first two types of case, D will often in fact have intended or been reckless about the risk of some injury; but if aggravated assault is charged there will be no need to prove this.

5.50 In short, the new offence would be used to cover both the more serious cases now prosecuted as [assault or battery] and the less serious offences now prosecuted under section 47 (assault occasioning actual bodily harm). As argued above, this would have the advantage of keeping these cases in the magistrates' courts: at present a considerable proportion of cases under section 47 are tried in the Crown Court but receive sentences which would have been within the power of a magistrates' court ...

## Disadvantages

5.51 In the SCP we criticised the offence under section 47 for its failure to respect the correspondence principle:

In short, here is an offence popularly known as "ABH", of which the main distinguishing feature is the causing of bodily harm. Yet, for the purpose of assessing how far D is to blame, D's state of mind about bodily harm is ignored. Juries may find this confusing, and the offence appears both lopsided and misdescribed.

5.52 The proposed offence of aggravated assault would be open to the same theoretical criticism. However, the main injustice involved in the section 47 offence is that a purely accidental consequence, of which D need have no awareness at all, appears to be the central feature of the offence and increases the possible sentence from six months to five years. In the proposed offence of aggravated assault, the assault would be the central feature of the offence and the injury caused would be mainly relevant as an aggravating factor, with limited consequences for sentencing. Significantly, some consultees who in general favoured following the correspondence principle thought that a limited degree of constructive liability was acceptable at the lower end of the scale of offences.

In the following extract, Matthew Gibson discusses the Law Commission's proposals.

**EXTRACT**

> Which aspects of the proposals does Gibson support, and why? Which does he express concern about, and why?
>
> (Note: in this extract Gibson refers to the Law Commission's proposed offences of intentionally causing serious injury, recklessly causing serious injury and intentionally or recklessly causing injury as offences 1, 2 and 3 respectively.)

### Gibson, M. [2016] 'Getting Their "Act" Together? Implementing Statutory Reform of Offences Against the Person' *Criminal Law Review* 597

#### Reflecting wrongdoing #1: offences 1, 2 and 3

[...]

The modernisation of language in the form of "serious injury" and "injury", along with the removal of words like "inflict", "bodily" and "occasioning", represents an important updating of relevant terms. To be sure, "serious injury" and "injury" are readily understandable to the public as descriptions of harm. Like "wounding", "grievous bodily harm" and "actual bodily harm", they are condemnatory in tone, conveying the idea that it is wrong – and illegal – to cause such outcomes. This recognition of the actual harm caused is particularly important for the victims of these offences. Nonetheless, some might lament the loss of the current harm descriptions for the moral resonance they create in the public imagination. There is no denying that "wounding", "grievous bodily harm" and "actual bodily harm" (along with the abbreviations "GBH" and "ABH") are distinctly evocative. As Gardner states, they contain a "moral clarity which makes them accessible to the ordinary people who must be guided by them." Consequently, it must be wondered whether the pursuit of textual certainty justifies the removal of all morally loaded harm-phrasing from offences against the person. These debates also have fair labelling implications on conviction. The descriptions "serious injury" and "injury" may not sufficiently distinguish the harmful outcome caused. For instance, Horder remarks that:

> "Someone who deliberately breaks another's nose in punching him hard is lumped together in the same offence category—intentionally causing serious injury – as someone who deliberately saws another's leg off, puts out a victim's eyes, severs his spine or castrates him."

Has the scoping report missed an opportunity to variegate outcomes in these more detailed ways? Ultimately, there is the concern that particularism in offence outcomes encourages technical arguments over whether D's conduct falls within the relevant crime. The desire to avoid these strategies by describing more general – if morally sterilised – harms is understandable. Similarly, the absence in offences 1, 2 and 3 of any mention of how D has brought about the harmful outcome alludes to the practical difficulties of discerning between different modes of responsibility – for example, stabbing, cutting or piercing. This is a continuation of the status quo: ss.18, 20 and 47 are also silent on this matter.

[...]

Overall, in defining conduct, the new hierarchy presents a simple and logical ladder of harms across offences 1, 2 and 3. It is therefore more intelligible to practitioners and the public.

However, in some respects, the revised scheme of harms perpetuates existing problems. In particular, the scoping report is vague about the boundary between "serious injury" and "injury". Of course, some degree of overlap in classifying harms is inevitable. However, the scoping report could have been clearer on this distinction. For example, it notes that the word "serious" remains ambiguous, before debating – without resolving – whether it might be preferable for offences 1 and 2 to require "exceptionally grave injury". That extra layer of definition would have better delimited the severity of physical or mental suffering that isolates offences 1 and 2 from offence 3. It is therefore regrettable that the scoping report does not provide more precision on how "serious" should be understood, especially given that demand for precision on this issue is longstanding. At the moment, assuming the split between "serious injury" and "injury" mimics the actus rei divide between ss.18/20 and 47, the problems of overlap, fair warning and fair labelling that have long stalked the law may well persist. The uncertainty created by this gap would need addressing by CPS guidance, keeping in mind the point in *Bollom* that assessment of an injury's seriousness must take into account the effect of the harm on the particular individual.

Notwithstanding these criticisms, offences 1 and 2 should be welcomed for containing requirements of fault (intention or recklessness, respectively, as to causing serious injury) which directly track the harm proscribed by those crimes (serious injury). This satisfies the correspondence principle: there is no constructive liability. This is surely good for fair warning. Moreover, fault corresponds with punishment. Offence 1 – which can only be committed intentionally – contains a higher sentence (life imprisonment) than that in offence 2 (seven years) which can only be committed recklessly. Such sentencing features are a vast improvement on those in ss.18 and 20 where neither necessarily accorded with D's conduct or culpability. Unfortunately, that rule is not adhered to in offence 3. Here, the sentence (five years) is the same irrespective of D's mens rea (intention or recklessness as to causing injury). As Eriera comments:

"This is not obviously rational. The greater seriousness of intentionally caused injury as compared with recklessly caused injury ought to be reflected in a difference in the maximum sentence available."

Consequently, it might be doubted whether convicting intentional and reckless wrongdoers under the same offence amounts to fair labelling. Offence 3 now also houses those individuals who cause serious harm which is neither intended nor foreseen – under the OAPA such situations are governed by s.20 due to the imposition of constructive liability. The scoping report reveals that the CPS argued in its response to the SCP that serious injuries, however caused, ought to be labelled as such under offence 2 – and not offence 3. However, the Commission submits that this view presupposes that offence 3 is the "new" s.47 – effectively, a minor provision which theoretically deals with all injuries, however insignificant. In fact, as explained in the scoping report, offence 3 will only cover the more serious injuries falling within s.47 due to the proposed creation of a new assault-based crime ("aggravated assault") which will deal with s.47's less serious injury cases.

## Reflecting wrongdoing #2: aggravated assault, physical assault and threatened assault

The scoping report maintains assault and battery as separate offences, albeit relabelled as "threatened assault" and "physical assault", respectively. The actus rei of these crimes reflect their common law roots: applying force to, or causing an impact on, the body or another (physical assault); and causing another to think that any such force or impact is or may be imminent (threatened assault). Interestingly, "assault" conjures up a particular mode of responsibility which, when combined with the adjectives "physical" or "threatened", implies the harmful outcome with which these offences are concerned. This sharpens understanding of the requisite outcomes more clearly than the singular labels "assault" and "battery". Moreover, continued use of "assault" retains a moral as well as factual sense of the harms involved in these revised crimes. These references to mode of responsibility and moral character stand in stark contrast to their absences in offences 1, 2 and 3. Such observations confirm that the different harms prohibited by assault and battery will now be more accurately conveyed to the public as matters of fair warning. They will also be more fully captured on conviction. Both crimes can be committed intentionally or recklessly, with conviction for either resulting in a maximum sentence of six months' imprisonment. Whilst these sentencing arrangements are the same as under current law, the fairness of drawing parity of punishment between physical and threatened assault has been questioned.

Meanwhile, above the two assault offences, but below offence 3, the scoping report introduces a brand new crime: aggravated assault. Unlike the continuation of the blurred boundary between "serious injury" and "injury", this substantially minimises any overlap between "injury" and "physical assault" – a problem which affects the parallel offences of s.47 and battery. The offence requires intention or recklessness as to an initial physical or threatened assault which goes onto cause "some injury". In existing law, harm amounting to "some injury" – that is, minor injury – is often mis-labelled: it can be under-charged as common assault (which does not recognise that any injury has been caused) or over-charged as ABH (which technically includes all minor injuries). If minor harms were to be charged under a crime of "aggravated assault", the offence description would more precisely criminalise D according to the harm caused – there would be no under- or over-charging. One type of harm that will be difficult to fit under aggravated assault is disease transmission. As with s.47, this difficulty arises because of the need for a base offence of physical or threatened assault. Infection is not normally passed on via these forms of conduct.

A particularly noteworthy feature of aggravated assault is its imposition of constructive liability: mens rea is not needed in relation to causing "some injury". Nonetheless, the scoping report defends this breach of the correspondence principle. Unlike ss.47 and 20, the base offence remains the central focus of D's conduct, with the subsequent injury acting only as an aggravating characteristic. That characteristic is labelled on conviction and represented through a proportionate rise in maximum sentence – from six months for the base crime to twelve months in its aggravated form. The offence is triable summarily only, a factor which would save inordinate time and money. This is because many of the minor harms currently charged under s.47 would instead be tried in the magistrates' courts. At present, such cases are often tried in the Crown Court despite the eventual punishment being one which would have come within the powers of the magistrates' courts.

Others have suggested that the Law Commission's proposals place too much emphasis on the correspondence principle. For example, Jackson and Storey argue for a 'moderate' form of constructive liability so that a defendant's liability reflects the level of harm he caused the victim.[14] They give the example of a domestic argument, in which D1 aims to slap his partner, X, hard across the face, intending to injure her. However, X ducks out of the way and D1 instead slaps their 3-year-old child, V, who was sitting behind X on the kitchen table. V is knocked to the floor and suffers a broken arm. Under the current law, D1 could be charged with maliciously inflicting GBH, since he had an intention to cause X some harm (which can be transferred to V[15]). Under the Law Commission's proposals,

[14]Jackson, A. and Storey, T. (2015) 'Reforming Offences Against the Person: In Defence of 'Moderate' Constructivism' 79 *Journal of Criminal Law* 437.
[15]See the discussion of transferred *mens rea* in Chapter 4.

if D1 did not intend or foresee serious injury, the relevant offence would be intentionally or recklessly causing injury. Jackson and Storey argue that convicting D1 of this offence 'would fail to reflect the fact that serious injury (a broken arm) had been caused to the victim'. In a similar vein, Demetriou writes:[16]

> '[I]t has to be acknowledged that the criminal law is not solely concerned with D's culpability and fault. The criminal law is also concerned with the harm suffered by V. Recent developments, such as the introduction of the Criminal Injuries Compensation Scheme and of the Victim's Impact Statement, pay particular attention to V's harm and highlight his enhanced role within the criminal justice system (CJS). Allowing D to 'get away' with a lesser crime because he did not foresee the full extent of the injuries that he in fact caused, runs counter to the growing victim focus approach adopted by the CJS.'

## ACTIVITY

For the Law Commission's response to the concerns expressed by Jackson and Storey, and Demetriou, refer back to paragraphs 4.97–4.98 in the extract from its report above. In your opinion, do the Law Commission's proposals place too much emphasis on the correspondence principle?

## Conclusion

In the first part of this chapter we looked at five of the most significant non-fatal offences against the person. In the second and third parts of the chapter we analysed these offences from two perspectives. We examined the case law that governs consent to injury, considering the coherence and consistency of these cases and evaluating the majority (social utility) and minority (social disutility) approaches in *R v Brown*. We then examined the Law Commission's proposals for reform, including why the Commission concluded that reform is necessary and the thinking behind its proposed new scheme. For each of these two topics there is a corresponding essay title in the self-test questions that follow below.

Turning to problem questions, something that some students find difficult is integrating the material from the first two parts of the chapter. To help with this, Figure 6.3 sets out a four-step guide. The first step is to determine the level of injury the victim suffered: this will allow you to identify the relevant offence. Next, putting any issues related to consent to one side, you should work through all the other requirements of the offence. If these are satisfied, the third step is to ask whether the victim consented to the activity and, if so, whether the victim's consent is available as a defence. If the victim did not consent, then the final step is to ask whether the defendant genuinely believed the victim was consenting to the activity and, if so, whether his belief in consent in available as a defence.

---

[16]Demetriou, S. (2016) 'Not Giving Up the Fight: A Review of the Law Commission's Scoping Report on Non-fatal Offences Against the Person' 80 *Journal of Criminal Law* 188.

**Step one: Determine the level of injury the victim suffered in order to identify the relevant offence**

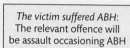

*The victim suffered no injuries, or only trivial or insignificant injuries:*
The relevant offence will be either assault or battery. This depends on whether there was an actual infliction of force (battery) or force was only apprehended (assault)

*The victim suffered ABH:*
The relevant offence will be assault occasioning ABH

*The victim suffered GBH or wounding:*
Begin with the s.20 offence of malicious wounding or infliction of GBH. If this is established then consider whether the aggravating *mens rea* requirement needed for the s.18 offence of wounding or GBH with intent is present

**Step two: Putting any possible defence of consent or belief in consent to one side for a moment, decide whether all of the other requirements of the relevant offence are established**

If all the other requirements of the relevant offence are established, go to step three

If all of the other requirements of the relevant offence are not established, the defendant is not guilty of the offence.
[Consider whether there are other offences that might be applicable]

**Step three: Did the victim consent to the activity?**

Consent here means effective consent (Did the victim have the capacity to consent? Was the victim pressurised by threats? Was the consent vitiated by fraud?)

If there was not effective consent, go to step four.

If there was effective consent, decide whether the victim's consent is available as a defence:
- Assault and battery: Victim's consent always available as a defence
- ABH/GBH/wounding: Victim's consent only available as a defence if injury occurred during a lawful activity
If victim's consent is available as a defence, the defendant is not guilty.
If it is not available, the defendant is guilty.

**Step four: Did the defendant genuinely believe the victim was consenting to the activity?**

If not, the defendant is guilty of the offence.

If the defendant did genuinely believe the victim was consenting, decide whether his belief in consent is available as a defence:
- Assault and battery: Genuine belief in consent always available as a defence.
- ABH/GBH/wounding: Genuine belief in consent only available as a defence if injury occurred during a lawful activity.
If the genuine belief in consent is available as a defence, the defendant is not guilty.
If it is not available, the defendant is guilty.

**Figure 6.3.** Non-fatal offences against the person: how to approach problem questions

●● ● ● **Self-test questions**

1. Romeo and Valentina have been dating for a month when Valentina declares, 'I love you'. In fact, she says she loves Romeo so much that she asks him to give her a love bite as a sign of his affection. Romeo obliges and gives Valentina a love bite on her neck.

   The next day Romeo posts a picture of the love bite on Facebook with the message 'Look what I did LOL'. When Valentina sees it she feels so humiliated that she reports the love bite to the police.

   Discuss Romeo's criminal liability.

2. After a couple of days Valentina's love bite becomes infected and very painful. She goes to her local doctors' surgery. Her normal doctor is fully booked, so reluctantly she agrees to see Dr Dario instead. When she is called, Valentina is surprised at how young Dr Dario is. She explains that she had been hoping to see a more experienced doctor, but he reassures her by saying, 'Don't worry, I have several years' experience. I just look younger than I am'. On hearing this, Valentina relaxes and lets Dr Dario examine her. In fact, Dr Dario has only just qualified and this is his first week in his first job. When Valentina discovers this, she is outraged. She says she would never have let Dr Dario examine her had she known how inexperienced he was.

   Discuss Dr Dario's criminal liability.

3. Later that year Romeo and Valentina are reconciled, get back together, and after a few months get engaged. On the night before the wedding it is Romeo's stag party. Romeo's best man, Vincenzo, decides that he should mark the occasion by playing a joke on Romeo. He waits until Romeo has had a few drinks, then asks some of the other partygoers to hold Romeo down while he shaves off Romeo's eyebrows.

   The next morning Vincenzo is surprised at how angry Romeo is. When Valentina discovers what has happened she is so distraught that she telephones the police.

   Discuss Vincenzo's criminal liability.

4. When Vincenzo arrives home from picking up his best man's suit on the morning of the wedding, he is shocked to find two policemen waiting for him by his front door. When they explain that Valentina has filed a complaint, Vincenzo panics. He pushes one of the policemen out of the way and begins to run away. The policeman falls backwards and cracks his head on the pavement. His colleague chases Vincenzo and arrests him. The policeman's head injury requires stitches.

   Discuss Vincenzo's criminal liability.

5. At no point during their relationship has Romeo told Valentina that he is HIV positive. On their wedding night they have sexual intercourse together for the first time. Romeo does not wear a condom, and Valentina contracts the virus. Romeo subsequently claims that Valentina consented to the risk of contracting the virus by agreeing to have unprotected sex and by promising in her wedding vows to love Romeo 'for better, for worse, for richer, for poorer, in sickness and in health'.

   Discuss Romeo's criminal liability.

6. 'The case law on consent to injury is completely unsatisfactory. It is impossible to reconcile a number of the leading decisions, and the social utility model advocated by the majority in *R v Brown* [1994] 1 AC 212 is inappropriate.'

   How far (if at all) do you agree with this statement?

7. 'There is no need to amend the law governing non-fatal offences against the person. Whilst some of the language used in the Offences Against the Person Act 1861 is admittedly archaic, its meaning has been clarified through judicial interpretation. Moreover, the Law Commission's proposals for reform would merely create a new set of difficulties, including an undue emphasis on the correspondence principle.'

How far (if at all) do you agree with this statement?

## Non-fatal offences against the person checklist

Having worked through this chapter, you should now have:

✓ An understanding of the requirements of the crimes of assault and battery

✓ An understanding of the requirements of the crime of assault occasioning ABH

✓ An understanding of the requirements of the crimes of malicious wounding or infliction of GBH and wounding or GBH with intent

✓ An understanding of when a victim's consent will be vitiated by fraud

✓ An understanding that on a charge involving ABH/GBH/wounding the consent of the victim will only be available as a defence if the injury occurred in the course of a lawful activity and the ability to state which activities are lawful and which are unlawful

✓ An ability to critically discuss the existing case law on which activities are lawful and which are unlawful

✓ An ability to compare the social utility and social disutility models and discuss which is the most appropriate.

✓ An ability to critically discuss the Law Commission's proposed reforms of the non-fatal offences against the person.

## Further reading

Anderson, J. (2014) 'The Right to a Fair Fight: Sporting Lessons on Consensual Harm' 17 *New Criminal Law Review* 55.

Cooper, S. and James, M. (2012) 'Entertainment – The Painful Process of Rethinking Consent' *Criminal Law Review* 188.

Cowan, S. (2014) 'Offenses of Sex or Violence? Consent, Fraud, and HIV Transmission' 17 *New Criminal Law Review* 135.

Demetriou, S. (2016) 'Not Giving Up the Fight: A Review of the Law Commission's Scoping Report on Non-Fatal Offences Against the Person' 80 *Journal of Criminal Law* 188.

Gibson, M. (2016) 'Getting Their "Act" Together? Implementing Statutory Reform of Offences Against the Person' *Criminal Law Review* 597.

Hall, H. (2016) 'Exorcism, Religious Freedom and Consent: The Devil in the Detail' 80 *Journal of Criminal Law* 241.

Jackson, A. and Storey, T. (2015) 'Reforming Offences Against the Person: In Defence of "Moderate" Constructivism' 79 *Journal of Criminal Law* 437.

Kell, D. (1994) 'Social Disutility and the Law of Consent' 14 *Oxford Journal of Legal Studies* 121.

Law Commission (2015) *Reform of Offences Against the Person* (Law Commission No 361) HC 555.

Roberts, P. (1997) 'Consent to Injury: How Far Can You Go?' 113 *Law Quarterly Review* 27.

Spencer, J. (2004) 'Liability for Reckless Infection: Part One' 154 *New Law Journal* 384.

Spencer, J. (2004) 'Liability for Reckless Infection: Part Two' 154 *New Law Journal* 448.

Spencer, J. (2004) 'Retrial for Reckless Infection' 154 *New Law Journal* 762.

Tolmie, J. (2012) 'Consent to Harmful Assaults: The Case for Moving Away from Category Based Decision Making' *Criminal Law Review* 656.

Weait, M. (2004) '*Dica*: Knowledge, Consent and the Transmission of HIV' 154 *New Law Journal* 826.

Weait, M. (2005) 'Knowledge, Autonomy and Consent: *R v Konzani*' *Criminal Law Review* 763.

Weait, M. (2005) 'Criminal Law and the Sexual Transmission of HIV: *R v Dica*' 68 *Modern Law Review* 121.

# 7

# Sexual offences

## Chapter objectives

By the end of this chapter you should have:

- An understanding of the requirements for establishing criminal liability for: (a) rape; (b) assault by penetration; (c) sexual assault and (d) causing a person to engage in sexual activity without consent
- An ability to apply the relevant law to a hypothetical set of facts and discuss whether criminal liability may be established for any of the offences listed above
- An ability to discuss and evaluate the section 74 definition of consent, the conclusive and evidential presumptions contained in sections 76 and 75 and the change to the *mens rea* of rape introduced by the Sexual Offences Act 2003.

# Introduction

In 1977 in England and Wales there were a total of 1,015 reported rapes. Of these reports, 324 resulted in rape convictions.[1] In the years that followed there was a continuing steady increase in the number of rapes reported each year, such that in 2016 police recorded a total of 39,335 rapes.[2] However, the number of rape convictions did not increase at the same rate. In the 12 months from April 2015 to March 2016, the Crown Prosecution Service prosecuted more than 4,600 defendants for rape, securing 2,689 convictions.[3]

Many factors have been identified as contributing to this reduction in the proportion of recorded rapes resulting in convictions, including:

- Evidential difficulties and the burden of proof (many cases are often one person's word against another's)
- Rules on the admission of evidence relating to the complainant's previous behaviour
- Complainants withdrawing from the process (often as a result of fear or because they felt they were not being believed)[4]
- Public attitudes towards sexual violence (e.g. research published in 2005 by Amnesty International reported that a third of people in the UK believe that a woman is partially or totally responsible for being raped if she has behaved in a flirtatious manner)[5]
- So-called 'rape myths', such as the perception that 'true rapes' involve rape by a stranger, occur outdoors, involve violence or threats of violence and normally result in physical injuries, and the belief that a woman can always withhold consent however drunk she is.[6]

It has also been suggested that concern about the number of convictions could itself become counter-productive if it leads to other important priorities being neglected, particularly the support and care of victims.[7]

---

[1]Kelly, L., Lovett, J. & Regan, L. (2005) *A Gap or a Chasm? Attrition in Reported Rape Cases* Home Office Research Study 293.

[2]Office for National Statistics (2017) *Crime in England and Wales: Year Ending December 2016.*

[3]Crown Prosecution Service (2016) *Violence Against Women and Girls: Crime Report 2015-2016.*

[4]One of the most distressing parts of complainants' experiences within the criminal justice system is cross-examination. An empirical study of the questions asked during cross-examination of rape complainants suggests that, in spite of the reforms that have been implemented in recent decades to improve the criminal justice response for rape complainants, when it comes to cross-examination little has changed in the past 50 years. The study concludes that complainants still find cross-examination to be distressing and demeaning, and this is understandable given the tactics employed by defence lawyers (Zydervelt, S., Zajac, R., Kaladelfos, A. & Westera, N. (2017) 'Lawyers' Strategies for Cross-examining Rape Complainants: Have We Moved Beyond the 1950s?' 57 *British Journal of Criminology* 551).

[5]Office for Criminal Justice Reform (2006) *Convicting Rapists and Protecting Victims – Justice for Victims of Rape: A Consultation Paper.*

[6]Temkin, J. (2010) '"And Always Keep A-Hold of Nurse, for Fear of Finding Something Worse": Challenging Rape Myths in the Courtroom' 13 *New Criminal Law Review* 710. For a contrasting view, see Reece, H. (2013) 'Rape Myths: Is Elite Opinion Right and Popular Opinion Wrong?' 33 *Oxford Journal of Legal Studies* 445 and Gurnham, D. (2016) 'Victim-Blame as a Symptom of Rape Myth Acceptance? Another Look at How Young People in England Understand Sexual Consent' 36 *Legal Studies* 258.

[7]A point made by *The Stern Review* (Home Office (2010) *The Stern Review: A report by Baroness Vivien Stern CBE of an independent review into how rape complaints are handled by public authorities in England and Wales*). See also Carline, A. & Gunby, C. (2017) 'Rape Politics, Policies and Practice: Exploring the Tensions and Unanticipated Consequences of Well-Intended Victim Focused Measures' 56 *Howard Journal of Crime and Justice* 34.

In this chapter we focus primarily on the offence of rape. The definition of this offence was given an overhaul by the Sexual Offences Act 2003. A new, statutory definition of consent was introduced, presumptions were created to structure and guide juries' decision-making and the *mens rea* of the offence was changed. One of the objectives of these changes was to increase the number of rape convictions. We will examine the Act's definition of rape and evaluate the changes it made.

Once we have worked through the offence of rape we will then look at three other serious sexual offences: assault by penetration; sexual assault and causing a person to engage in sexual activity without consent. Like the offence of rape, these three offences all target forms of non-consensual sexual activity.

 ## Rape

The offence of rape is defined by section 1 of the Sexual Offences Act 2003:

---

### EXTRACT

### Section 1 of the Sexual Offences Act 2003

**1 Rape**

(1) A person (A) commits an offence if –

    (a) he intentionally penetrates the vagina, anus or mouth of another person (B) with his penis,

    (b) B does not consent to the penetration, and

    (c) A does not reasonably believe that B consents.

(2) Whether a belief is reasonable is to be determined having regard to all the circumstances, including any steps A has taken to ascertain whether B consents.

(3) Sections 75 and 76 apply to an offence under this section.

(4) A person guilty of an offence under this section is liable, on conviction on indictment, to imprisonment for life.

---

This tells us that the offence has four requirements:

1. The defendant penetrated the vagina, anus or mouth of the victim with his penis

2. The victim did not consent to the penetration

3. The defendant intentionally penetrated the victim's vagina, anus or mouth with his penis

4. The defendant lacked a reasonable belief that the victim was consenting to the penetration.

Numbers 1 and 2 are *actus reus* requirements. Numbers 3 and 4 are *mens rea* requirements. We will work through them in turn.

### 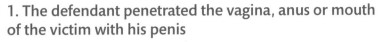 1. The defendant penetrated the vagina, anus or mouth of the victim with his penis

The first requirement for the offence of rape is that the defendant penetrated the vagina, anus or mouth of the victim with his penis. It follows from this requirement that:

- Only men can commit rape, since the offence is limited to penetration with a penis. But whilst women cannot commit rape as principals, they can be convicted of being accessories to rape. They can also commit the other sexual offences we will study later in this chapter.
- Both men and women can be the victims of rape, since the offence includes anal and oral penetration as well as vaginal penetration.

Section 79 of the Sexual Offences Act 2003 also tells us the following:

---

**EXTRACT**

## Section 79 of the Sexual Offences Act 2003

### 79 Part 1: general interpretation
(1) The following apply for the purposes of this Part.
(2) Penetration is a continuing act from entry to withdrawal.
(3) References to a part of the body include references to a part surgically constructed (in particular, through gender reassignment surgery).

[...]

---

Subsection (3) means that female-to-male transsexuals can be convicted of rape, since the offence covers penetration with a surgically constructed penis. It also means that male-to-female transsexuals can be vaginally raped.

Subsection (2) tells us that penetration is a continuing act, which begins on entry and does not end until withdrawal. So suppose the victim consents to the initial penetration, but during sexual intercourse she withdraws her consent and asks the defendant to stop. If the defendant chooses to ignore her and fails to withdraw he commits rape. At the moment he refuses to withdraw there is coincidence of *actus reus* (non-consensual penetration) and *mens rea* (no belief that the victim is consenting).

For centuries the criminal law stated that a husband could not be convicted of raping his wife. This was based on the outdated notion that, by entering into a marriage, a wife consented to sexual intercourse for the duration of the marriage. Shockingly, it was not until the 1990s that this notion was firmly rejected.[8] Today, a husband can be convicted of raping his wife.

---

[8] *R v R* [1992] 1 AC 599 HL.

**2. The victim did not consent to the penetration**

The second *actus reus* requirement is that the penetration was non-consensual.

It is important to begin by stating that whether or not the victim consented is a question that must be answered by looking at the victim's state of mind. In *R v Malone* [1998] 2 Cr App R. 447 CA the victim was a 16-year-old girl. At the time the defendant had sexual intercourse with her she was very drunk. She said that, although she had not attempted to resist, the sex was non-consensual. She said she had been too drunk to resist. At trial the defendant was convicted of rape. On appeal his counsel argued that a defendant should not be convicted of rape if the victim failed to demonstrate or communicate her lack of consent. The Court of Appeal rejected this argument. Roch LJ explained that the issue is whether or not the victim was consenting, not whether or not the victim demonstrated her lack of consent:

> The *actus reus* of rape is an act of sexual intercourse with a woman who at the time of the act of sexual intercourse does not consent to that act of sexual intercourse. There is no requirement that the absence of consent has to be demonstrated or that it has to be communicated to the defendant for the *actus reus* of rape to exist.

However, this does not mean that the victim not communicating her lack of consent is completely irrelevant. Although it is not relevant to the *actus reus* of rape, it might be one of the factors a jury takes into account when applying the *mens rea* requirement that the defendant lacked a reasonable belief in consent. We'll look at the *mens rea* in detail below.

The concept of consent is central to all of the offences we will study in this chapter. But whilst it is an extremely important concept, it is also very difficult to define.

In 2000 the Home Office published a review of the old law on sexual offences,[9] in which it emphasised how important it is to define consent clearly.

## EXTRACT

Read the following extract from the review. Why did the Home Office say it is important to define consent clearly? These reasons are based on which of the principles we studied in Chapter 1?

### Home Office (2000) *Setting the Boundaries: Reforming the law on sex offences*

2.7.3 It is vitally important that in this most private and difficult area of sexual relationships the law should be as clear as possible so that the boundaries of what is acceptable, and of criminally culpable behaviour, are well understood. This understanding is essential for all those involved in the criminal justice system in practicing and interpreting the law (and we had evidence that it was not always well understood even by professionals). It is important for society as a whole for sexual relationships to be based on mutual respect and understanding.

2.7.4 This led us to the inescapable conclusion that it was vital for the law on rape and sexual assault to be, as far as possible, set out in statute so that it was accessible and available to all. The complexity of the common law on consent, and the uncertainty caused by differing decisions, were not helpful to the criminal justice system or to the wider community. There will always be a continuing role for the common law to develop as cases raise new issues over time, but the key principles of the meaning of consent should be set out clearly in the law for all to see.

---

[9]Home Office (2000) *Setting the Boundaries: Reforming the law on sex offences*.

The review went on to state that:

> 2.10.3 [...] Clarifying the meaning of consent in statute would enable judges to be able to explain what the law said and for juries to understand just what is meant by consent. It would also enable Parliament to consider and recommend what should and should not form acceptable standards of behaviour in a modern society [...]

As we examine the provisions which resulted from these recommendations (sections 74 to 76 of the Sexual Offences Act 2003), ask yourselves whether they achieve these objectives. Have they clarified the meaning of consent so that judges can explain the law and juries understand it? In these sections has Parliament clearly specified what behaviour is acceptable and distinguished it from behaviour that is unacceptable and prohibited?

Sections 74 to 76 of the 2003 Act contain a definition of consent (section 74) and two sets of presumptions (sections 75 and 76). We will work through these three sections in reverse order, because this is the order in which you would consider them when answering a problem question.

### i. Section 76: conclusive presumptions

In a problem question, you should begin by asking yourself whether section 76 applies. Section 76 states:

---

**EXTRACT**

## Section 76 Sexual Offences Act 2003

### 76 Conclusive presumptions about consent

(1) If in proceedings for an offence to which this section applies it is proved that the defendant did the relevant act and that any of the circumstances specified in subsection (2) existed, it is to be conclusively presumed—

  (a) that the complainant did not consent to the relevant act, and

  (b) that the defendant did not believe that the complainant consented to the relevant act.

(2) The circumstances are that—

  (a) the defendant intentionally deceived the complainant as to the nature or purpose of the relevant act;

  (b) the defendant intentionally induced the complainant to consent to the relevant act by impersonating a person known personally to the complainant.

---

The word 'conclusive' means that these presumptions cannot be rebutted by the defendant. So if *either* of the two circumstances listed in subsection (2) existed, the conclusion must be that the victim did not consent to the penetration *and* that the defendant lacked a reasonable belief in consent. In other words, if the defendant intentionally penetrated the vagina, anus or mouth of the victim with his penis and either of the circumstances listed in subsection (2) existed, he is guilty of rape.

So what are the two circumstances in which section 76 applies?

*The defendant intentionally deceived the victim as to the nature or purpose of the relevant act*

The first is that the defendant intentionally deceived the victim as to the nature or purpose of the relevant act. The leading case here is *R v Jheeta* [2007] EWCA Crim 1699. As this case illustrates, it is not enough that the defendant intentionally deceived the victim. The defendant must have intentionally deceived the victim as to the nature or purpose of vaginal, anal or oral penetration.

The victim met the defendant, Harvinder Singh Jheeta, at college. They became friends and started a sexual relationship. Consensual sex took place, usually in hotel rooms booked by Jheeta. After a few months the victim started receiving threatening text messages and phone calls, containing comments like 'We are going to kidnap you', 'We are going to convert you', 'We are going to kill you'. She thought that the messages were from other Muslim students at the college and confided in Jheeta. He reassured her and said he would protect her. In fact, he was the one responsible for the messages. Eventually, the victim said she wanted to tell the police. Jheeta said that he would go to the police and make a complaint on her behalf. She agreed. Soon afterwards the victim received a text message from a PC Ken, who said he was in charge of her case. She received regular text messages from PC Ken. But PC Ken did not exist; Jheeta was the one sending the messages. PC Ken was later replaced by PC Bob and then by PC Thomas. Again, both of these figures were fictitious and Jheeta was the one sending the messages.

During this time the victim never suspected Jheeta. But she had grown tired of their relationship, and on several occasions tried to break it off. Each time she did so, she would receive a text message from one of the police officers telling her that Jheeta had tried to kill himself and that she should take care of him. She was even told that if she did not sleep with Jheeta she would be fined for causing him distress. Each time she complied and had sex with the defendant in a hotel room.

In March 2006 the victim went to the police, and Jheeta was arrested. When interviewed, he said that the reason for his scheme was that he had been worried that the victim was going off him. He also made an important concession. He said that, although the victim had been willing to have sexual intercourse with him for the entire period of their relationship, the text messages ensured that the intercourse was more frequent than would otherwise have been the case.

Jheeta was charged with rape. He accepted his lawyer's advice to plead guilty, but subsequently appealed claiming that his lawyer had explained the law to him incorrectly. In its judgment the Court of Appeal considered how section 76 should be interpreted.

**EXTRACT**

Read the following extract from the judgment of Sir Igor Judge. When will section 76(2)(a) apply? Did section 76(2)(a) apply in *R v Jheeta*? Why/why not?

### *R v Jheeta* [2007] EWCA Crim 1699

### Sir Igor Judge

23 [...] [S]ection 76 raises presumptions conclusive of the issue of consent, and thus where intercourse is proved, conclusive of guilt. They therefore require the most stringent scrutiny.

24 In our judgment the ambit of section 76 is limited to the "act" to which it is said to apply. In rape cases the "act" is vaginal, anal or oral intercourse. Provided this consideration is constantly borne in mind, it will be seen that section 76 (2)(a) is relevant only to the comparatively rare cases where the defendant deliberately deceives the complainant about the *nature or purpose* of one or other form of intercourse. No conclusive presumptions arise merely because the complainant was deceived in some way or other by disingenuous blandishments of or common or garden lies by the defendant. These may well be deceptive and persuasive, but they will rarely go to the nature or purpose of intercourse. Beyond this limited type of case, and assuming that, as here, section 75 has no application, the issue of consent must be addressed in the context of section 74.

[...]

28 With these considerations in mind, we must return to the present case. On the written basis of plea the appellant undoubtedly deceived the complainant. He created a bizarre and fictitious fantasy which, because it was real enough to her, pressurised her to have intercourse with him more frequently than she otherwise would have done. She was not deceived as to the nature or purpose of intercourse, but deceived as to the situation in which she found herself. In our judgment the conclusive presumption in section 76 (2)(a) had no application, and counsel for the appellant below were wrong to advise on the basis that it did.

As these paragraphs explain, this was not the end of the story in *R v Jheeta*. Where the conclusive presumptions don't apply you must go on to consider whether the evidential presumptions apply. And where (as in *R v Jheeta*) the evidential presumptions don't apply either you must go on and apply section 74's definition of consent. So we will be returning to *R v Jheeta* when we examine section 74.

The Court of Appeal in *R v Jheeta* also discussed the facts of another case called *R v Linekar* [1995] QB 250. Linekar promised to pay a prostitute £25 if she had sexual intercourse with him. He never intended to pay her. Clearly Linekar deceived the prostitute, but did he deceive her as to the nature or purpose of sexual intercourse? The Court of Appeal in *R v Jheeta* said that he did not:

27 [...] Linekar deceived the prostitute about his intentions. He undoubtedly lied to her. However she was undeceived about either the nature or the purpose of the act, that is intercourse. Accordingly the conclusive presumptions in section 76 would have no application.

So if a case like *R v Linekar* occurred today, whether or not the prostitute consented to sexual intercourse would have to be decided by applying the section 74 definition of consent.

Case law has also established that section 76(2)(a) would *not* apply in the following four situations:

- Where the defendant deceives the victim as to their gender. In *R v McNally* [2013] EWCA Crim 1051 the female defendant pretended to be male. Believing the defendant was male, the victim consented to oral sex. The Court of Appeal stated that 76(2)(a) did not apply (although, as we'll see shortly, the defendant's conviction for the section 2 offence of assault by penetration was upheld, applying section 74).

- Where the victim has stated that she will only consent to sexual intercourse if the defendant uses a condom, but he does not use one. In *Assange v Swedish Prosecution Authority* [2011] EWHC 2849 (Admin) the High Court held that, whilst such conduct is deceptive, the deception does not relate to the nature of sexual intercourse. Again, section 74 should be applied instead.

- Where the victim has stated that she will only consent to sexual intercourse if the defendant withdraws before ejaculating, but after penetration he refuses to withdraw and ejaculates inside her. In *R (F) v Director of Public Prosecutions* [2013] EWHC 945 (Admin) the High Court assumed that such a case would fall outside section 76(2)(a) and instead applied section 74.

- Where the defendant has unprotected sex with the victim without telling her that he is HIV positive. In the previous chapter we studied the decision in *R v Dica* [2004] EWCA Crim 1103. We saw that in a situation like this there is no consent to the risk of infection, but there is consent to sexual intercourse. So whilst the defendant might be guilty of maliciously inflicting GBH, he is not guilty of rape.[10]

(We will look at the first three of these cases in greater detail below.)

So far we have seen six situations in which section 76(2)(a) would not apply. Our next case, *R v Williams* [1923] 1 KB 340, is an example of when it would apply. The defendant in this case, Owen Williams, was a choirmaster. He was giving the 16-year-old victim singing lessons. During their second lesson Williams told her that her breathing was not right. He told her to lie down, removed some of her clothes and climbed on top of her. He said: 'It is quite all right; do not worry. I am going to make an air passage. This is my method of training. Your breathing is not quite right and I have to make an air passage to make it right'. The victim believed him and made no attempt to resist. She did not know that he was having sexual intercourse with her. Williams was convicted of rape and his conviction was upheld by the Court of Appeal. The Court held that the sexual intercourse was non-consensual. The victim had given her consent to a medical procedure, but had not given her consent to sexual intercourse.

These events took place in 1922, long before the Sexual Offences Act 2003. But they are a useful illustration of the rare and unusual circumstances in which section 76(2)(a) would apply. Williams intentionally deceived the victim as to the nature of the act. He tricked her into believing that it was a medical procedure when in fact it was sexual intercourse.

In *R v Williams* there was deception as to the 'nature' of sexual intercourse. Our next three cases focus instead on 'purpose'. Before we turn to them, note first of all that none of these cases was actually a rape case (the defendant and victim did not have sexual intercourse in any of them). In spite of this, all three are still relevant since they give us further guidance on when section 76(2)(a) will apply.

The first case is *R v Green* [2002] EWCA Crim 1501. The defendant in this case was a doctor. He misled a number of male teenage patients into believing that they had potential impotency or infertility problems, and carried out bogus investigations which involved touching the victims' genitals and requiring them to masturbate so that he could take a sample. The case itself occurred before the Sexual Offences Act 2003, but if a similar case occurred today section 76(2)(a) would apply.[11] The victims were deceived as to the purpose of the activities. They believed the activities were for a medical purpose, when in fact they were for the defendant's sexual gratification.

The second case is *R v Devonald* [2008] EWCA Crim 527. The defendant, 37-year-old Stephen Devonald, had a 16-year-old daughter. His daughter had been dating a 16-year-old boy. When the boy decided to end the relationship, Devonald decided to seek revenge.

---

[10]Confirmed in *R v B* [2006] EWCA Crim 2945.
[11]Confirmed in *R v Jheeta* [2007] EWCA Crim 1699.

He went onto the Internet, pretended to be a 20-year-old female named 'Cassey', and struck up an online relationship with his daughter's ex-boyfriend. Pretending to be Cassey, he convinced the boy to masturbate twice in front of a web cam. His plan was to embarrass and humiliate the boy. It seems that he intended to place a video of the boy masturbating on the Internet.

After the trial judge ruled that section 76(2)(a) could apply to the facts of this case, Devonald pleaded guilty to the section 4 offence of causing a person to engage in sexual activity without consent (which we'll study more closely below). He subsequently applied to the Court of Appeal for leave to appeal against his conviction, arguing that the trial judge had been wrong to rule that section 76(2)(a) might apply.

## EXTRACT

Read the following extract from the judgment of Leveson LJ. According to the Court of Appeal, was the trial judge right to rule that section 76(2)(a) might apply? Had the victim been deceived as to the purpose of the act of masturbation?

### *R v Devonald* [2008] EWCA Crim 527

#### Leveson LJ

7 [...] The learned judge ruled that it was open to the jury to conclude that the complainant was deceived as to the purpose of the act of masturbation. We agree. On the facts, as we have described them, it is difficult to see how the jury could have concluded otherwise that the complainant was deceived into believing that he was indulging in sexual acts with, and for the sexual gratification of, a 20-year-old girl with whom he was having an on line relationship. That is why he agreed to masturbate over the sex cam. In fact, he was doing so for the father of his ex girlfriend who was anxious to teach him a lesson doubtless by later embarrassing him or exposing what he had done. It is an inevitable inference that it is for that reason that the applicant changed his plea to guilty when the judge so ruled. Miss Howell has over focussed on the phrase "nature of the act", which undoubtedly was sexual but not on its purpose, which encompasses rather more than the specific purpose of sexual gratification by the defendant in the Act of masturbation. In our judgment, this ruling was correct and there is no grounds for challenging the basis on which the applicant changed his plea. This application is therefore refused.

The Court of Appeal in *R v Devonald* also confirmed that section 76(2)(a) applies in cases like *R v Green*, but does not apply in cases like *R v Linekar*.

## EXTRACT

In the following extract from Leveson LJ's judgment, how does he distinguish *R v Linekar* from *R v Green* and *R v Devonald*?

In your opinion, is this distinction satisfactory?

### R v Devonald [2008] EWCA Crim 527

#### Leveson LJ

7 [...] In relation to those charges in *Green* in which the victim masturbated himself, it was not suggested that he was unaware what he was doing: he believed, however, that the purpose of the act was linked to a medical examination. The distinction with cases such as *Linekar* is that the purpose of "the act" was consensual sexual intercourse between complainant and defendant. The fact that agreement was obtained by promise of money (or any other blandishment) merely identifies a secondary motive for that agreement.

The third case – which also has quite extraordinary facts – is *R v B* [2013] EWCA Crim 823. The defendant, B, had been in a sexual relationship with the victim for five years. In 2009 he created a false profile on Facebook, calling himself Grant. 'Grant' then contacted the victim, developed a relationship with her and persuaded her to send him topless photos of herself. Having received the photos, 'Grant' threatened to send the photos to the victim's employer and to publish them online unless she performed sexual acts over the Internet. The victim told the defendant what had happened (not realising that the defendant was in fact Grant). The defendant said she should lure Grant to a meeting and that he would go in her place to confront Grant. After the supposed meeting, the defendant told the victim that he had killed Grant. The defendant then created a second false Facebook profile, this time calling himself Chad. 'Chad' contacted the victim, said that he was Grant's friend, knew what Grant had done, and that he had the topless photos and would send them to her employer if she did not perform further sexual acts over the Internet. Reluctantly, she complied.

Eventually the victim went to the police and told them what had happened. The defendant was charged with the section 4 offence of causing a person to engage in sexual activity without consent (the same offence as in *Devonald*). The trial judge ruled that the defendant's deception fell within section 76(2)(a), and the jury convicted. The defendant appealed, arguing that *R v Devonald* could be distinguished and that the trial judge should have held that the case fell outside the conclusive presumptions.

#### EXTRACT

Read the following extract from the judgment of Hallett LJ. Did the facts of *R v B* fall within section 76(2)(a)? Why/why not?

According to Hallett LJ, what was the defendant's purpose for forcing the victim into performing the relevant acts? What did the victim believe to be the purpose of the acts? Is the case distinguishable from *R v Devonald*?

### R v B [2013] EWCA Crim 823

#### Hallett LJ

19 There is no definition of the word *purpose* in the Act. It is a perfectly ordinary English word and one might have hoped it would not be necessary to provide a definition. It has been left to the courts and academics to struggle with its meaning in the context of a sexual act. We say 'struggle' advisedly

because it may not be straightforward to ascertain the *purpose* of a sexual act. Those engaging in a sexual act may have a number of reasons or objectives and each party may have a different objective or reason. The Act does not specify whose *purpose* is under consideration. There is, therefore, a great danger in attempting any definition of the word *purpose* and in defining it too widely. A wide definition could bring within the remit of section 76 situations never contemplated by Parliament.

20 We shall, therefore, simply apply the normal rules of statutory construction and echo what was said in *Jheeta*. Where, as here, a statutory provision effectively removes from an accused his only line of defence to a serious criminal charge it must be strictly construed. We respectfully adopt the approach of the court in *Jheeta*. If there is any conflict between the decisions in *Jheeta* and *Devonald*, we would unhesitatingly follow *Jheeta*. Thus, it will be a rare case in which section 76 should be applied.

21 Is this one of those rare cases? [Counsel for the prosecution] reminded the court of the extent of the deception and the affect upon the complainant. It was not unlike the extent and effect of the deception in *Jheeta*. Just as in *Jheeta*, this appellant undoubtedly deceived his girlfriend in a cruel and despicable way. However, the fact that there was a catalogue of deception of an unpleasant kind begs the question as to whether it was deception as to *purpose* so as to trigger the operation of section 76. We have our doubts.

22 The complainant was never asked what her purpose or understanding of the purpose of the act was and the appellant's purpose seems far from clear. His accounts varied but the most likely explanation, as the prosecution argued, was some kind of perverted sexual gratification. The complainant knew full well what she was being asked to do and what she did in fact do, namely perform a sexual act for the benefit of the camera. She could have been in no doubt that the motive was at least in part sexual gratification. If so, on one view, even if one were to extend the definition of *purpose* to include the appellant's intention, as has been suggested, there is here no evidence going to the issue of deceit as to his purpose.

23 Further, we see force in [counsel for the defence's] submission that if reliance was to be placed on section 76, which effectively withdrew the accused's only line of defence, it was incumbent upon the judge to identify the evidence which went to the issue of "deceit as to purpose". Here there was no such analysis, and the jury were never directed that the word had a restricted meaning – see *Jheeta*. They were not informed that deceit as to what some commentators have called "peripheral matters" was not enough.

24 For those reasons we are troubled by the way in which the prosecution put their case and by the way in which it was left to the jury. We understand how prosecuting counsel and the judge may have thought that the decision in *Devonald* applied and appeared to support reliance on section 76. However, as we have indicated, reliance upon section 76 in this case, on these facts and this evidence, was misplaced. The prosecution needed to look no further than the provisions of Section 74. It provides that "a person consents if he agrees by choice and has the freedom and capacity to make that choice". If the complainant only complied because she was being blackmailed, the prosecution might argue forcefully she did not agree by choice.

## ACTIVITY

- In this section we have looked at ten cases on the scope of section 76(2)(a): *R v Jheeta*; *R v Linekar*; *R v McNally*; *Assange v Swedish Prosecution Authority*; *R (F) v Director of Public Prosecutions*; *R v Dica*; *R v Williams*; *R v Green*; *R v Devonald*; and *R v B*. Place each case in the correct column of the following table. For each case, include a one-sentence summary of why section 76(2)(a) would or wouldn't apply.

| Cases where section 76(2)(a) would apply | Cases where section 76(2)(a) would not apply |
|---|---|
|  |  |

- Using the table you have just completed, decide whether section 76(2)(a) would apply in the following two scenarios:
  - Lawrence says to his secretary, a single mother named Mandy: 'I'm going to fire you unless you have sex with me.' Mandy does not want to have sex with Lawrence but reluctantly agrees. In fact, Lawrence had intended all along to fire Mandy whether or not she had sex with him. The next day he fires her.
  - Lawrence, who is unemployed, has a celebrity girlfriend named Mandy. One day he initiates sexual intercourse with Mandy without telling her that he is filming it. The next day he says to her: 'Pay me £10,000 or I'll put the video on the Internet.'

*The defendant intentionally induced the victim to consent to the relevant act by impersonating a person known personally to the victim*

The second situation in which the conclusive presumptions apply is set out in section 76(2)(b). It is where the defendant intentionally induced the victim to consent to the relevant act by impersonating a person known personally to the victim.

Before discussing section 76(2)(b), it is helpful to first look at an important case from the 1990s: *R v Elbekkay* [1995] Crim LR 163. Elbekkay was staying the night with the victim and her boyfriend (who had been living together for 18 months). Elbekkay and the victim's boyfriend had fallen asleep in the lounge, while the victim was sleeping in the bedroom. During the night the victim was woken up by someone moving on her bed. Assuming it was her boyfriend, she said, 'I love you'. She then felt herself being penetrated. Twenty seconds later they kissed. At this point the victim realised that something was not quite right. She opened her eyes and, seeing that it was Elbekkay not her boyfriend, punched him and ran into the lounge. Elbekkay was charged with rape.

At the time of this case it was accepted that a man committed rape if he had sex with a woman by impersonating her husband. The issue in *R v Elbekkay* was whether this should be extended to include impersonation of a long-term partner. The trial judge issued the following ruling:

I now have to consider whether in 1994 at a time when a wife is no longer under a duty to submit to intercourse with her husband, whether there is such a fundamental difference between a wife agreeing to sexual intercourse with her husband and a fiancé or girlfriend agreeing to sexual intercourse with their regular partner that the law should hold that the consent of the wife, if obtained by fraud, is no consent but the consent of the others is still consent in law. I am bound to say, after careful consideration

I can find no justification for so finding. It would be wholly contrary to modern attitudes and values at which the law should seek to reflect where possible. It would also very seriously curtail or interfere with the right of women to choose, understanding the true facts, whether to participate or not in the act of sexual intercourse.

Following this ruling Elbekkay was convicted of rape. He appealed against his conviction to the Court of Appeal, arguing that the trial judge's ruling was wrong.

## EXTRACT

Read the following extract from the judgment of McCowan LJ. Did the Court of Appeal decide that the trial judge's ruling was right or wrong? What reasons did McCowan LJ give for his decision?

### R v Elbekkay [1995] Crim LR 163

#### McCowan LJ

We wholly agree [with the trial judge's ruling]. Indeed, we think it would be extraordinary for us to come to any other conclusion in 1994. How could we conscientiously hold that it is rape to impersonate a husband in the act of sexual intercourse, but not if the person impersonated is merely, say, the long-term, live-in lover, or in the even more modern idiom, the "partner" of the woman concerned?

The vital point about rape is that it involves the absence of consent. That absence is equally crucial whether the woman believes that the man she is having sexual intercourse with is her husband or another.

Importantly, the final sentence of this extract appears to be open-ended. It refers to 'another', and so does not seem to be limited to impersonation of a husband or long-term partner. It therefore supports the following principle: if the victim is having sex with X, but believes she is having sex with Y, then she is not consenting to sex with X. We can refer to this as the *R v Elbekkay* principle.

There are three points to note about the *R v Elbekkay* principle:

- If the principle applies you must then go on and consider whether the defendant had the necessary *mens rea*. In other words, the *R v Elbekkay* principle alone does not determine guilt. It only determines whether or not the victim consented to sexual intercourse with the defendant.

- The *R v Elbekkay* principle applies to the defendant's identity, not to the defendant's attributes and qualifications. In the previous chapter we looked at the case *R v Richardson* [1999] QB 444 (the case of the suspended dentist), and saw that fraud as to attributes does not vitiate consent. *R v Richardson* would also apply here.

- McCowan LJ's judgment used the word 'believes'. So the *R v Elbekkay* principle only applies if the victim *believes* she is having sexual intercourse with Y but in fact is having sex with X. It would not apply if the victim has a lower degree of certainty than 'belief'. For example, it would not apply if the victim is unsure whether she is having sex with X or Y, or if the victim hopes she is having sex with Y but suspects that she is actually having sex with X.

## ACTIVITY

Decide whether the *R v Elbekkay* principle would apply in each of the following two situations:

- Miles is attracted to wealthy men. One evening he meets Lawrence at a nightclub. Lawrence tells Miles that he is a successful businessman. Miles is impressed and begins to flirt with Lawrence. Later that evening they have sexual intercourse. In fact, Lawrence is a poorly paid cleaner.

- Lawrence looks a lot like the famous actor Brad Pitt. He goes to a nightclub and meets Mandy, who is a massive Brad Pitt fan. They begin chatting and, after a while, go to Lawrence's hotel room and have sexual intercourse. Mandy says that she thought it was unlikely that the man she had sex with was Brad Pitt, but had desperately hoped that it was.

Now that we have a firm understanding of the *R v Elbekkay* principle we can turn to section 76(2)(b). At first sight, it might appear that section 76(2)(b) simply enshrines the *R v Elbekkay* principle in statute. But in fact section 76(2)(b) is narrower than the *R v Elbekkay* principle in two important respects:

- The statute refers specifically to impersonation. The *R v Elbekkay* principle, on the other hand, does not require any impersonation. In fact, Elbekkay did not impersonate his victim's boyfriend. He did not dress up like the victim's boyfriend, or try to sound like the victim's boyfriend. What he did was exploit the situation. The victim assumed it was her boyfriend on the bed, and Elbekkay took advantage of this. So the *R v Elbekkay* principle is broader than section 76(2)(b) in that it is not limited to cases involving impersonation; it also applies where the victim has made a mistake and the defendant has taken advantage of this.

- The statute refers specifically to impersonation of a person known personally to the victim. So if the defendant deceives the victim by intentionally impersonating Brad Pitt, the case will fall outside section 76(2)(b) (assuming, of course, that the victim does not know Brad Pitt personally!). The *R v Elbekkay* principle, on the other hand, is not limited in this way. As we saw above, McCowan LJ said that the principle applies if the victim mistakenly believes that she is having sexual intercourse with 'her husband *or another*'.

So where does this leave us? In a problem question you should begin by asking whether section 76(2)(b) applies. If it does, then you should use the conclusive presumptions. If it does not apply, this does not mean that *R v Elbekkay* is irrelevant. You may still use the judgment from *R v Elbekkay* when interpreting the general definition of consent in section 74 (which we will look at shortly).

We have now looked at each of the circumstances in which the conclusive presumptions apply. As we have seen, section 76 has quite a narrow scope. In the following extract Karl Laird suggests that this should be welcomed.

## EXTRACT

What reasons does Laird give for welcoming the narrow scope of the conclusive presumptions? Do you agree that this is welcome?

### Laird, K. (2014) 'Rapist or Rogue? Deception, Consent and the Sexual Offences Act 2003' *Criminal Law Review* 492

[T]he applicability of s.76 has been reduced to vanishing point. This, it is submitted, is to be welcomed. No injustice will be done to C [the victim] given that the issue of her consent can still be considered under s.74 and it is fairer to D, as the conclusive presumptions will not apply. Given the now limited scope of s.76, prosecuting counsel have no option but to place reliance upon s.74 in circumstances where D has deceived C. This is an advantage from the prosecution's perspective, given that s.76 is only applicable in cases where D *intentionally* deceived C. Section 74 does not, prima facie, contain the same restriction. It is not surprising that the judiciary have evinced a preference for reliance upon s.74 over s.76. The presumptions in s.76 are conclusive and so once established all but ensure D will be convicted (provided it is proven that he performed the relevant act). Given that this is the case, reliance upon s.74 at least permits D to mount a defence and so avoids the issue of whether any subsequent conviction violates the presumption of innocence enshrined in art.6 of the ECHR.

#### ii. Section 75: evidential presumptions

An evidential presumption is one which the defendant has the opportunity to rebut. The evidential presumptions are governed by section 75.

### EXTRACT

### Section 75 Sexual Offences Act 2003

#### 75 Evidential presumptions about consent

(1)  If in proceedings for an offence to which this section applies it is proved—

  (a)  that the defendant did the relevant act,

  (b)  that any of the circumstances specified in subsection (2) existed, and

  (c)  that the defendant knew that those circumstances existed,

  the complainant is to be taken not to have consented to the relevant act unless sufficient evidence is adduced to raise an issue as to whether he consented, and the defendant is to be taken not to have reasonably believed that the complainant consented unless sufficient evidence is adduced to raise an issue as to whether he reasonably believed it.

(2)  The circumstances are that—

  (a)  any person was, at the time of the relevant act or immediately before it began, using violence against the complainant or causing the complainant to fear that immediate violence would be used against him;

  (b)  any person was, at the time of the relevant act or immediately before it began, causing the complainant to fear that violence was being used, or that immediate violence would be used, against another person;

  (c)  the complainant was, and the defendant was not, unlawfully detained at the time of the relevant act;

  (d)  the complainant was asleep or otherwise unconscious at the time of the relevant act;

  (e)  because of the complainant's physical disability, the complainant would not have been able at the time of the relevant act to communicate to the defendant whether the complainant consented;

  (f)  any person had administered to or caused to be taken by the complainant, without the complainant's consent, a substance which, having regard to when it was administered or taken, was capable of causing or enabling the complainant to be stupefied or overpowered at the time of the relevant act.

(3)    In subsection (2)(a) and (b), the reference to the time immediately before the relevant act began is, in the case of an act which is one of a continuous series of sexual activities, a reference to the time immediately before the first sexual activity began.

So if the prosecution proves, beyond reasonable doubt, that one of the six circumstances listed in subsection (2) existed, *and* the defendant knew that it existed, then it will be presumed that:

- The victim did not consent, and
- The defendant lacked a reasonable belief in consent.

The defendant can rebut the first presumption by producing some evidence that the victim did in fact consent. And he can rebut the second presumption by producing some evidence that he did in fact have a reasonable belief that the victim was consenting. Whether or not the defendant has produced sufficient evidence is a matter for the trial judge. It seems that relatively little evidence needs to be produced in order to rebut the presumptions.[12] Often, the defendant's own testimony will be sufficient.

If the defendant rebuts the first presumption the prosecution must then prove, beyond reasonable doubt, that the victim did not consent. And if he rebuts the second presumption the prosecution must then prove, beyond reasonable doubt, that the defendant lacked a reasonable belief in consent.

Figure 7.1 presents an overview of this, quite complicated, process.

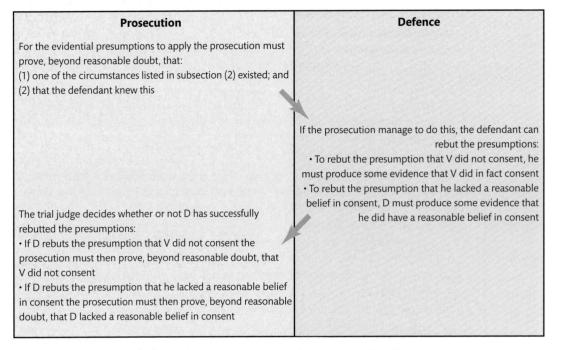

**Figure 7.1.** The process for determining whether the evidential presumptions apply

---

[12]See the extract below from Gunby, Carline and Beynon's article 'Alcohol-related Rape Cases: Barristers' Perspectives on the Sexual Offences Act 2003 and Its Impact on Practice'.

So what are the six circumstances in which the evidential presumptions might apply?

The first three situations, found in paragraphs (a)–(c), deal with the use or threat of immediate violence and unlawful detention. We studied the meaning of the word 'immediate' in the previous chapter, and saw that the courts have interpreted it to mean 'imminent'. Although this is a fairly broad interpretation, the word 'immediate' means that the evidential presumptions would not apply where, for example, the defendant says something like, 'Have sex with me or I'll beat you up tomorrow'.

Paragraph (a) applies where violence, or the threat of violence, is used against the victim. Notice that it needn't be the defendant himself who uses or threatens violence. It is enough that the defendant knew that another person was using or threatening violence. So if Lawrence is a member of a gang which attacks the victim, and during the attack Lawrence has sexual intercourse with the victim, the evidential presumptions will apply even if it was the other gang members that used violence, not Lawrence.

Paragraph (b) applies where violence, or the threat of violence, is not used against the victim, but against someone else. For example, paragraph (b) would apply if Lawrence, armed with a gun, says to the victim, 'Have sex with me or I'll shoot your friend'. And again, paragraph (b) will apply even if it is someone else that uses or threatens violence, not the defendant. So if Lawrence's fellow gang member grabs hold of the victim's friend and says 'Have sex with Lawrence or I'll shoot your friend', the evidential presumptions will apply.

Paragraph (c) applies where the victim was unlawfully detained (and the defendant was not). So it would apply where the defendant kidnaps the victim and has sexual intercourse with her whilst she is being held hostage.

At this point you might be wondering whether evidential presumptions are really necessary in these sorts of situations. Surely if the defendant was using or threatening violence against the victim or one of the victim's friends or family members, or if the victim was being unlawfully detained, a jury would readily conclude that the victim was not freely consenting to sexual intercourse and that the defendant lacked a reasonable belief in consent? Is the extra complexity created by the evidential presumptions really justified?

Much the same applies to the fourth situation, found in paragraph (d). This deals with victims who were asleep or unconscious at the relevant time. A sleeping or unconscious person is unable to consent to sexual intercourse. They lack the capacity to do so. So surely in a situation like this a jury would readily conclude that the victim was not consenting and that the defendant lacked a reasonable belief in consent. In fact, as Temkin and Ashworth state in the following extract,[13] it is difficult to see why a defendant who has sexual intercourse with a sleeping or unconscious victim should be given the opportunity to rebut the presumptions at all:

> [I]t has always been the law that consent must be present at the time of the sexual act. This means that consent is necessarily regarded as absent once it is proved beyond doubt that C was asleep or unconscious at the time sexual intercourse took place. If the absence of consent is not conclusively presumed in these situations, as it was at common law, then the law is being taken backwards rather than forwards.

The fifth situation, found in paragraph (e), is where the victim is unable to communicate whether or not she is consenting as a result of physical disability.

---

[13]Temkin, J. and Ashworth, A. (2004) 'The Sexual Offences Act 2003 – (1) Rape, Sexual Assaults and the Problems of Consent' *Criminal Law Review* 328 at 337.

The sixth situation, found in paragraph (f), is where the victim was given a substance, without her consent, which was capable of causing or enabling her to be stupefied or overpowered. There are a number of points to note about this paragraph:

- The substance must have been given to the victim without her consent. So if the victim consumed the substance voluntarily, paragraph (f) will not apply.

- It need not be the defendant that gives the substance to the victim. But remember, the defendant must have known that the circumstance existed. So the defendant must at least have known that the victim had been given the substance.

- It is not enough that the substance is capable of causing the victim to become disinhibited. The substance must have been capable of causing the victim to be overpowered or stupefied.

- Strangely, the statute does not require that the victim was actually overpowered or stupefied. Instead, it focuses on the potential effect of the substance. It is enough that the substance was *capable* of causing or enabling the victim to be stupefied or overpowered. So the evidential presumptions will apply if the substance was capable of having this effect, even if it did not in fact do so.

- To assess whether the substance was capable of having this effect, you must have regard to 'when it was administered or taken'. Suppose the defendant buys the victim a glass of wine and falsely tells her it is non-alcoholic. If this is the victim's first drink of the night the wine is unlikely to be capable of causing the victim to be overpowered or stupefied. But if the defendant knows that the victim has already drunk several shots of vodka and is feeling quite drunk, then the wine may well be capable of causing her to be overpowered or stupefied.

As with the previous paragraphs you might wonder why paragraph (f) only results in evidential presumptions, not conclusive ones. If the defendant knew that the victim had been given an overpowering or stupefying substance against her will, and consent is about freedom to choose, why should he have an opportunity to argue that the victim did in fact consent to sexual intercourse and that he did in fact have a reasonable belief in consent? Temkin and Ashworth state:

> [I]f the stupefying effect is established, it is questionable whether D should be able to argue that C nevertheless consented to the subsequent sexual act and that the drug or alcohol did not in fact prevent her from consenting. Can freedom and capacity to make a choice really exist in any meaningful sense in this situation?

## ACTIVITY

Decide whether the evidential presumptions would apply in the following situation:

Lawrence, Mandy and Miles are at a bar. Lawrence has liked Mandy for some time, but she has never shown any interest in him. Mandy has already had several glasses of wine when Lawrence says to Miles, 'I dare you to spike her drink'. Miles does so. Later that evening Mandy has sexual intercourse with Lawrence. The next day Mandy says that she only had sex with Lawrence because she was really drunk, and would never have done it if she'd been sober.

Would your answer be any different if Lawrence had only mentioned the 'dare' as a joke, did not realise that Miles had taken it seriously and spiked Mandy's drink and by the time he had sexual intercourse with Mandy had completely forgotten all about it?

We have now worked through the conclusive and evidential presumptions. Before moving on to look at the general definition of consent, it is worth pausing for a moment to reflect. Earlier we saw that the Sexual Offences Act 2003 was intended to escape the complexity of the old law, set out clear principles governing consent and explain in an accessible manner what should and should not form acceptable standards of behaviour. Do sections 75 and 76 achieve these objectives?

In their article 'Alcohol-related Rape Cases: Barristers' Perspectives on the Sexual Offences Act 2003 and Its Impact on Practice' (2010) 74 *Journal of Criminal Law* 579, Clare Gunby, Anna Carline and Caryl Beynon report the findings of their interviews with a total of 14 barristers with experience of prosecuting and defending rape cases. One of the things they asked the barristers about was how the evidential presumptions operate in practice and whether they feel they have been successful.

## EXTRACT

Read the following extract and produce a bullet point list of the key findings from the study.

Looking at your list of findings, assess whether sections 75 and 76 achieve their identified objectives.

### Gunby, C., Carline, A. and Beynon, C. (2010) 'Alcohol-related Rape Cases: Barristers' Perspectives on the Sexual Offences Act 2003 and Its Impact on Practice' 74 *Journal of Criminal Law* 579

### 3. Barristers' perspectives on the 'consent presumptions'

As previously noted, the consent presumptions were introduced in an attempt to 'strike the right balance' between the complainant and the defendant and to '… send a clear signal to the public about the circumstances in which sexual activity is likely to be wrong' and will therefore 'encourage genuine victims to bring cases to court'. Academic opinion, however, has been far less positive about the introduction of the presumptions, and the decision to construct s. 75 as an exhaustive list has been subject to criticism. Barristers were therefore asked to comment on the frequency of presumption use at trial […]

### Presumption frequency and rebuttal evidence

Considering the heavy workload of the barristers interviewed, one would perhaps assume that the majority of advocates would have had experience with cases in which the presumptions had arisen. In fact, very few had worked on cases in which either the evidential or conclusive presumptions had been incorporated into a trial. Indeed, when asked about the application of the presumptions there was unanimous agreement that they were 'rarely' (barrister 9) used and that they may intentionally be 'side-tracked' (barrister 10) and 'circumvented' (barrister 14) in cases. Indeed, one barrister talked about physical violence having been a feature of a rape they defended but commented that the judge had intentionally avoided using the violence presumption (s. 75(2)(a) and (b)). There was a general consensus that those involved in rape cases – the prosecutor, barrister and judge alike – would try to avoid using the presumptions as much as possible. Barrister 1 argued that 'judges try very hard now to keep their presumptions to a minimum … [and] tend to have broadly similar view [to the barristers] which is don't overload the jury with either too many counts or too much law'. It was argued that judges did not like the presumptions due to the perception that they amounted to the judge 'trespassing into the jury's ... domain' (barrister 2). Furthermore, it was argued that the presumptions complicated the trial process and overloaded the jury with additional, and complicated, legal concepts. Again, in light of jurors' perceived difficulties with applying and following legal directions and definitions, this is perhaps unsurprising: '... I think judges shy away from them [the presumptions] ... because they want ... I think they're reaching for clarity and making things straightforward for the jury' (barrister 10). These findings again reflect the conclusions of the Home Office stocktake that suggested the conclusive and evidential presumptions had infrequently been utilised thus far, and have consequently had little impact on the prosecution of rape cases.

When asked their opinions on the presumptions, certain barristers argued that they were patronising and that it was not necessary for them to have been specifically written into the law. Indeed, barrister 3 stated, 'I think all the presumptions do is state the ... obvious ... I don't see sometimes how all these very clever amendments to very good old-fashioned laws make the system any better'. Whilst several advocates disagreed with this viewpoint and felt that it was useful to have a set list of circumstances in which consent was likely to have been absent, these barristers still suggested that jurors would be intelligent enough to realise that if someone was detained, asleep or threatened with violence, they would be unlikely to have consented to the intercourse. For example, barrister 4 argued:

> You know, do people need to have pointed out to them that ... she's not really giving consent ... that if he's spiked her drink ... that she's not really consenting? I don't think people are that daft really, you know, that they have to be given a definitive list ... did they really need it pointing out to them?

Certain advocates also felt the presumptions swung the balance too far in favour of the prosecution and had been specifically included for the purpose of increasing the conviction rate. However, when asked about the amount of evidence necessary to rebut the evidential presumptions barristers generally agreed it was 'not a lot' (barrister 9) and that 'I can't think of a case in which ... an evidential burden wouldn't be discharged by a defendant' (barrister 8). The defendant's own testimony or ability to 'float the contrary possibility' (barrister 10) and suggest that sex was consensual, was often perceived sufficient. This finding provides empirical support for Finch and Munro's speculation that the amount of evidence necessary to rebut the evidential presumptions may not be substantial.

[...]

Overall, there was a general consensus, especially amongst the more experienced barristers, that the presumptions have not only been overwhelmingly unsuccessful: 'I don't think they've helped in the slightest' (barrister 3) and 'I don't think that presumptions really have that much impact on the whole thing' (barrister 12); but also that they are considered to be somewhat of an obstacle and something to be avoided, as opposed to a measure which has helped to achieve justice.

### iii. Section 74: the general definition of consent

In situations where:

- neither the conclusive nor the evidential presumptions apply or
- the evidential presumptions apply, but the defendant has rebutted them

you will need to apply section 74's definition of consent in order to determine whether or not the victim consented. Section 74 states the following.

## Section 74 Sexual Offences Act 2003

### 74 "Consent"

For the purposes of this Part, a person consents if he agrees by choice, and has the freedom and capacity to make that choice.

---

This is a very abstract definition. What is clear, however, is that sometimes a victim might agree to sexual intercourse but not be consenting. There is only consent if the victim agreed *by choice*, had the *capacity* to be able to choose, and had sufficient *freedom* to make that choice.

There is case law which gives us some guidance on how section 74 should be interpreted. These cases address the following three themes: the distinction between 'real consent' and 'mere submission'; deception and capacity to consent.

*The distinction between 'real consent' and 'mere submission'*

Even before the 2003 Sexual Offences Act the courts had made it clear that there is a distinction between 'real consent' and 'mere submission'. In *R v Olugboja* [1982] QB 320 the defendant Olugboja and his friend Lawal met the victim Jayne (aged 16) and her friend Karen (aged 17) at a disco. The men offered the girls a lift home, but instead of taking them home drove in the opposite direction and took them to a bungalow. Olugboja entered the bungalow but both girls refused to go inside and started to walk off. Lawal followed them in the car. After an argument the girls got back in. There was another argument, Karen got out of the car, but Lawal drove off with Jayne, parked the car and raped her.

Lawal then drove Jayne back to the bungalow, picking Karen up on the way. The defendant was asleep on the sofa. It was obvious that Jayne had been crying. Lawal dragged Karen into a bedroom, leaving Olugboja and Jayne alone in the living room. Olugboja told Jayne that he was going to have sex with her. Jayne told him what Lawal had done and asked him to leave her alone, but he told her to take off her trousers. Afraid, she did as he said. He then pushed her onto the sofa and had sex with her. She did not struggle or resist. She did not scream or cry for help.

At trial Olugboja was convicted of rape. He appealed against his conviction, arguing that for rape there must have been violence, or a threat of violence, or fraud. He claimed that he had not used violence or threatened violence, and so his conviction should be quashed. This argument was rejected by the Court of Appeal and Olugboja's rape conviction was upheld.

In the following extract from the judgment of the Court, Dunn LJ makes several important statements about the concept of 'consent'. Make a list of these statements.

### R v Olugboja [1982] QB 320

#### Dunn LJ

Although 'consent' is an equally common word it covers a wide range of states of mind in the context of intercourse between a man and a woman, ranging from actual desire on the one hand to reluctant acquiescence on the other. We do not think that the issue of consent should be left to a jury without some further direction. What this should be will depend on the circumstances of each case. The jury will have been reminded of the burden and standard of proof required to establish each ingredient, including lack of consent, of the offence. They should be directed that consent, or the absence of it, is to be given its ordinary meaning and if need be, by way of example, that there is a difference between consent and submission; every consent involves a submission, but it by no means follows that a mere submission involves consent: *per* Coleridge J. in Reg. v. Day, 9 C. & p. 722, 724 [...] In addition to the general direction about consent which we have outlined, the jury will probably be helped in such cases by being reminded that in this context consent does comprehend the wide spectrum of states of mind to which we earlier referred, and that the dividing line in such circumstances between real consent on the one hand and mere submission on the other may not be easy to draw. Where it is to be drawn in a given case is for the jury to decide, applying their combined good sense, experience and knowledge of human nature and modern behaviour to all the relevant facts of that case.

---

### ACTIVITY

Lawrence and Mandy have been married for 13 years. One Friday night Lawrence suggests that they have sexual intercourse. Although Mandy does not want to have sex, she does so because she knows from experience that Lawrence will sulk for the entire weekend if she does not. Looking at the guidance provided by Dunn LJ, does Mandy consent to sexual intercourse or merely submit?

---

The distinction between 'real consent' and 'mere submission' was applied in *R v Kirk* [2008] EWCA Crim 434.[14] The victim in this case was a 13-year-old girl who had run away from home. Hungry, she went for help to the minicab office where the defendant (a family member) worked, even though the defendant had abused her in the past. He offered to give her £3.25 in exchange for sexual intercourse. She agreed. She later explained, 'I was very hungry and needed to eat so I went to [the defendant's place of work] [...] All I can say is that I ended up having sex with [him] for £3.25. I used the money to buy food'. The defendant was convicted of rape, and on appeal the conviction was upheld by the Court of Appeal. The Court explained that the victim had submitted to sexual intercourse, but not consented to it.

Sometimes applying the distinction between 'real consent' and 'mere submission' could be difficult.

---

[14]See also *R v Doyle* [2010] EWCA Crim 119, in which the Court of Appeal referred to the distinction between 'reluctant but free exercise of choice on the one hand, especially in the context of a long term and loving relationship, and unwilling submission to demand in fear of more adverse consequences from refusal on the other' ([21]).

- A woman has committed a serious crime. She has been arrested. The police officer in charge of her case says he will drop all charges if she has sexual intercourse with him. She agrees. Does she consent to sexual intercourse? Or merely submit?
- Would your answer be any different if the woman had not committed the crime and had been wrongly accused? Would your answer be any different if the woman had been arrested for a minor motoring offence, not a serious crime?

At the end of the extract from Dunn LJ's judgment in *R v Olugboja* above, he said that questions like these should be answered by juries employing 'their combined good sense, experience and knowledge of human nature and modern behaviour'. Is it satisfactory to vest this much discretion in juries, or should juries be given more guidance on the distinction between 'real consent' and 'mere submission'? There are concerns here regarding the principle of maximum certainty. There are also concerns about consistency. Will different juries reach the same verdict in cases with similar facts?[15]

*Cases involving deception*

Some cases involving deception will fall under the conclusive presumptions set out in section 76. But as we saw above, the circumstances listed in section 76 are quite limited in scope. There are many instances of deception which will fall outside of the conclusive presumptions. In these cases, whether or not the victim consented must be determined using section 74's definition of consent.

We have already seen some examples of cases involving deception which fell outside the scope of section 76. The first was *R v Jheeta*: the case involving the defendant who deceived the victim by sending a series of threatening text messages. As the conclusive presumptions did not apply, the Court of Appeal used the section 74 definition of consent to determine whether the victim consented to sexual intercourse.

EXTRACT

Read the following extract from the judgment of Sir Igor Judge. Was the sexual intercourse consensual? Why/why not?

## R v Jheeta [2007] EWCA Crim 1699

### Sir Igor Judge

29 We are being asked to examine the safety of convictions for rape where the appellant pleaded guilty. He did so on the basis of plea which accepted the accuracy of his admissions in interview with the police, and in particular did not question his unequivocal admission that there were occasions when sexual intercourse took place when the complainant was not truly

---

[15]For an alternative, categories-based, approach see the article by Rebecca Williams on the further reading list.

consenting. This is entirely consistent with his acknowledgement that he persuaded the complainant to have intercourse with him more frequently than otherwise, and the persuasion took the form of the pressures imposed on her by the complicated and unpleasant scheme which he had fabricated. This was not a free choice, or consent for the purposes of the 2003 Act. In these circumstances we entertain no reservations that on some occasions at least the complainant was not consenting to intercourse for the purposes of section 74, and that the appellant was perfectly well aware of it. His guilty plea reflected these undisputed facts. Accordingly the appeal against conviction is dismissed.

In terms of the wording used in section 74, the reasoning in this extract focuses on the victim's *freedom* to choose. This approach is rooted in the principle of individual autonomy (see Chapter 1). Individuals have the right to choose how to live their lives. In *R v Jheeta* the victim's autonomy – her freedom to choose – had been so undermined by the defendant's 'complicated and unpleasant scheme' that it could not be said that she had consented to sexual intercourse. On many occasions she had not agreed to sex by choice.

Similar reasoning has been employed in subsequent cases. In *R v McNally* [2013] EWCA Crim 1051 the defendant, 17-year-old Justine McNally, met the 16-year-old victim through the social networking game Habbo. At the time they were aged 13 and 12 respectively. McNally used a male avatar named Scott. Over the next three-and-a-half years the victim's friendship with 'Scott' developed. McNally arranged to travel to London to visit the victim shortly after the victim's 16th birthday. When she arrived McNally was wearing gothic clothing and a strap-on dildo under her trousers. During the visit the victim consented to oral sex. Over the following months McNally visited again, and the victim again consented to oral sex and to digital penetration. After the victim discovered that McNally was not in fact 'Scott', but was actually a girl, McNally was charged with the section 2 offence of assault by penetration (which we study below). At trial McNally was convicted. She appealed, arguing that a deception as to gender cannot vitiate consent. The Court of Appeal rejected her appeal. Leveson LJ explained:

> 26 Thus while, in a physical sense, the acts of assault by penetration of the vagina are the same whether perpetrated by a male or a female, the sexual nature of the acts is, on any common sense view, different where the complainant is deliberately deceived by a defendant into believing that the latter is a male. Assuming the facts to be proved as alleged, M chose to have sexual encounters with a boy and her preference (her freedom to choose whether or not to have a sexual encounter with a girl) was removed by the defendant's deception.

Our next case, *Assange v Swedish Prosecution Authority* [2011] EWHC 2849 (Admin), concerned an incident involving WikiLeaks co-founder Julian Assange. Assange was accused of committing four offences whilst he was in Sweden to give a lecture. He left Sweden, unaware that an arrest warrant had been issued against him. A European Arrest Warrant was subsequently issued. After a district judge ruled that he should be extradited from England to Sweden, Assange appealed to the High Court against the extradition order. One of the issues the Court had to address was whether the alleged incidents in Sweden also amounted to criminal offences under English law. The relevant incident for our purposes involved a victim, AA, who only consented to sexual intercourse with Assange on the basis that he would use a condom. It was alleged that Assange had either not used a condom, or used a condom but had torn it. Applying the section 74 definition of consent, the Court held that, if proved, Assange's conduct would amount to rape.

A further example of the application of section 74 is *R (F) v Director of Public Prosecutions* [2013] EWHC 945 (Admin). The victim in this case married the defendant in an Islamic ceremony. He was abusive from the outset of the marriage. The victim was adamant that she did not want to become pregnant. She was unable to take the contraceptive pill, for medical reasons, and the defendant did not like using a condom, so their agreed method of contraception was withdrawal. On one occasion, the defendant penetrated the victim with consent but shortly afterwards told her that he would be coming inside her 'because you are my wife and I'll do it if I want'. He ejaculated before she could do anything to stop him. She later became pregnant. The victim made a formal complaint to the police, but the Director of Public Prosecutions (DPP) decided not to prosecute on the basis that, even if the victim's account could be proved, there was no realistic prospect of conviction. The victim sought judicial review of the DPP's decision. The High Court held that the defendant's actions, if proved, amounted to rape and therefore ordered that the DPP's decision should be reviewed.

## EXTRACT

According to the following extract from the judgment of Lord Judge CJ, why was the sexual intercourse not consensual?

### *R (F) v Director of Public Prosecutions* [2013] EWHC 945 (Admin)

### Lord Judge CJ

26 In law, the question which arises is whether this factual structure can give rise to a conviction for rape. Did the claimant consent to this penetration? She did so, provided, in the language of section 74 of the 2003 Act, she agreed by choice, when she had the freedom and capacity to make the choice. What the *Assange* case 108(44) LSG 17 underlines is that "choice" is crucial to the issue of "consent", and indeed we underline that the statutory definition of consent provided in section 74 of the 2003 Act applies equally to section 1(1)(c) as it does to section 1(1)(b). The evidence relating to "choice" and the "freedom" to make any particular choice must be approached in a broad common sense way. If before penetration began the interested party had made up his mind that he would penetrate and ejaculate within the claimant's vagina, or even, because "penetration is a continuing act from entry to withdrawal" (see section 79(2) of the 2003 Act) he decided that he would not withdraw at all, just because he deemed the claimant subservient to his control, she was deprived of choice relating to the crucial feature on which her original consent to sexual intercourse was based. Accordingly her consent was negated. Contrary to her wishes, and knowing that she would not have consented, and did not consent to penetration or the continuation of penetration if she had any inkling of his intention, he deliberately ejaculated within her vagina. In law, this combination of circumstances falls within the statutory definition of rape.

In her discussion of *R v McNally*, *Assange v Swedish Prosecution Authority* and *R (F) v Director of Public Prosecutions*, Alex Sharpe argues that the courts have drawn a distinction between 'active deception' (which is capable of vitiating consent[16]) and 'non-disclosure of information' (which is not capable of doing so). She argues that this distinction 'lacks a convincing basis for setting the parameters of criminal liability'.

---

[16] In *R v McNally*, Leveson LJ explained that 'some deceptions (such as, for example, in relation to wealth) will obviously not be sufficient to vitiate consent' ([25]).

## EXTRACT

In the following extract Sharpe sets out four hypothetical scenarios, which she uses to illustrate her argument that the distinction between active deception and non-disclosure of information is flawed. In Sharpe's opinion, what flaws do these scenarios expose? Do you agree?

### Sharpe, A. (2016) 'Expanding Liability for Sexual Fraud Through the Concept of "Active Deception": A Flawed Approach' 80 *Journal of Criminal Law* 28

### Hypothetical scenarios (A–D)

(A)   D, aware V would not have consented to sex had D disclosed his HIV+ status, had sex with V.

(B)   D, aware V would not have consented to sex had D disclosed his HIV+ status, lied when asked and then had sex with V.

(C)   D, aware V would not have consented to sex had D disclosed his HIV+ status, had sex with V. Sexual intercourse was unprotected and D was not on ART (anti-retroviral treatment).

(D)   D, aware V would not have consented to sex had D disclosed his HIV+ status, lied when asked and then had sex with V. D was on ART, had a very low viral load, and used a condom.

### Justifications for the distinction

[...]

[A]pplication of the [active deception – non-disclosure of information] distinction would lead to convictions in scenarios B and D, but not A and C. I would argue that such outcomes, ones that follow the line of reasoning exhibited in the cases discussed, contradict any claim that the distinction satisfactorily distributes defendants in terms of moral culpability. In all four scenarios, the defendant was unwilling to disclose his HIV+ status and was aware that sex was conditional on his *not* being HIV+. In this regard, the scenarios are not distinguished by an intent/recklessness divide. That is, none of the scenarios involve *only* risk-taking. Two differences between scenarios B and D, and scenarios A and C, are that in scenarios B and D the victim is proactive in asking about the defendant's HIV status and the defendant lies. However, in relation to the culpability question, only lying is relevant. Of course, lying is a more active form of deception than non-disclosure. But this does not, of itself, demonstrate greater culpability. Indeed, I would suggest that while the defendant in scenario B may be more morally culpable than the defendant in scenario A, it is certainly not the case that active deception in scenario D is more morally culpable than non-disclosure in scenario C. This is because in scenario D lying needs to be considered in relation to other features of the scenario.

The specific features that ought to be valued here are that the defendant is (i) on anti-retroviral drugs and has a low viral load and (ii) used a condom. While the defendant's actions might be viewed as unethical, they do demonstrate a quite different relation to risk and harm, one that might be viewed as lessening culpability. Certainly, in scenario C, the defendant exposes the victim to a significant risk of serious harm, whereas in scenario D, though the defendant lies, the risk of harm to which the victim is exposed is minimal. Moreover, while the defendant in scenario C is highly likely to be aware of a serious risk of harm to the victim, the defendant in scenario D is likely to be aware of the exceptionally low risk of transmission of the virus. It is true in scenario D, that while lying might not be motivated by a desire to have sex, the defendant is aware of the absence of consent. However, this is true in all four scenarios. What is problematic is the fact that the defendant who took responsibility for his own sexual health, practised safe sex and who accordingly exhibited some degree of care and concern toward the 'victim', is more likely to be convicted of a sexual offence under the judicial distinction under consideration. This appears to me to be intuitively wrong. Reasoning by analogy in this way suggests that the assumption that active deception necessarily involves a greater breach of trust than non-disclosure is misplaced, at least in some plausible cases. As Ashworth has reminded us, 'the act-omission distinction should not be used as a cloak for avoiding the moral issues.'

We have one final case involving a deception left to consider: *R v Linekar* (the case involving the defendant who had no intention to pay the prostitute). This case occurred under the old law and so the section 74 definition of consent was not yet in existence. How would section 74 apply to a case like *R v Linekar* today? Did Linekar's deception so undermine the prostitute's freedom to choose that it cannot be said that she agreed to sexual intercourse by choice?

In his article 'Mistaken Sex', Jonathan Herring argues that a defendant like the one in *R v Linekar* should be convicted of rape.

## EXTRACT

### Herring, J. (2005) 'Mistaken Sex' *Criminal Law Review* 511

The main point to note [about section 74's definition of consent] is the emphasis on the notion of agreement. The focus is not just on the victim and whether she said yes or no; but rather on both parties and seeking to ascertain whether there had been an agreement, a meeting of the minds between them. The complainant's version of what happened will not be restricted legally to her either saying yes or no to sexual intercourse, but the jury will be required to take a broader view of how the parties understood their sexual activity and reach a conclusion as to whether there was a sufficient co-operation to amount to an agreement. I would suggest that the use of agreement enables the court to develop an approach in line with the arguments made in this article. In particular it makes it easier to argue that if one party knows the other is mistaken over an issue which is an essential prerequisite to their consent then the parties do not agree.

[...]

[Some] argue that as the prostitute agreed to have sexual intercourse for £25 the harm to her when the defendant ran off after sex without paying can be valued at £25. In other words, if a deception over such a 'small' sum is sufficient to induce her to consent the wrong done to her is very minor. The error here is to see the only loss in *Linekar* as to the money she was not paid and to ignore the fact that here sexual autonomy had been infringed. A victim of theft or obtaining property by deception is not harmed in the same way as a person who accidentally loses property of the same value. The harm in *Linekar* was the interference of her right to choose with whom and under what conditions to have sexual intercourse and not just the loss of £25.

### Conclusion

In the past it was said:

> [A] male [may] make promises that will not be kept, ... indulge in exaggeration and hyperbole, or ... assure any trusting female that ... the ugly frog is really the handsome prince. Every man is free, under the law, to be a gentleman or a cad.

But we should no longer be in an age when the "gentle art of seduction" is revered and praised; when women or men are sexual objects to be prised open by whatever means comes to hand. It should no longer be enough just to ask did the complainant say "yes" in relation to the proposed sexual activity. Now the values that should underpin our sexual offences law are those of mutual respect, reciprocity, connection and honesty. If we respect sexual integrity and the importance of being able to choose with whom to have sexual partners then the choice must be one that is free from coercion and fraud. A man who has sexual intercourse with another knowing that that person would not be agreeing to the activity if s/he knew the truth is using that person for his own ends. It is the "sheer use of another person". It should be rape.

## ACTIVITY

- Imagine that a case with identical facts to *R v Linekar* occurred today. You are the prosecutor. Construct the outline of your argument that the victim did not consent to sexual intercourse.

- Now imagine you are defence counsel. Construct the outline of your argument that the victim did consent to sexual intercourse.

- Now imagine that you are a member of the jury in the case. Looking at the arguments for the prosecution and defence, would your conclusion be that the victim did or did not consent?

- Consider the following scenario: Lawrence and Mandy have been seeing each other for six months. Lawrence has decided to end the relationship tonight, but decides not to tell Mandy until after they have had sexual intercourse. They have dinner together at Mandy's flat. At the end of the meal Lawrence takes Mandy's hand, looks into her eyes and says 'I love you'. They kiss, and then go to the bedroom and have sexual intercourse. Afterwards Lawrence gets dressed, says 'Sorry Mandy, I don't want to see you anymore', and leaves. Mandy is devastated. She says she would never have had sex with Lawrence if she had known he was going to break up with her.

  According to Herring's proposal, should Lawrence be convicted of rape? Do you agree with Herring?

What makes situations like *R v Linekar* particularly difficult is the all-or-nothing nature of the decision. Under the old law there was an offence of procuring sexual intercourse with a woman by false representations (maximum sentence: two years' imprisonment).[17] A situation like the one in *R v Linekar* was a straightforward example of this offence.[18] But the 2003 Act abolished this offence and did not replace it.[19] So today the defendant in *R v Linekar* has either committed rape or he has committed no sexual offence at all. Temkin and Ashworth observe:[20]

> [I]t appears that, when a court is deciding whether a particular deception or threat is sufficient to negative ostensible consent, it is effectively deciding between conviction of a serious offence and a complete acquittal. There is no lesser offence, no middle way [... so] the vague terms of s74 now assume a heightened importance.

---

[17] Sexual Offences Act 1956, s.3. The maximum sentence was set out in Part II of the Second Schedule to the Act.

[18] This offence was not left to the jury in *R v Linekar*, but when quashing the defendant's rape conviction the Court of Appeal stated that, 'If anything, the appellant was guilty of an offence under section 3 of the Act of 1956'.

[19] For an argument that a similar offence should be created today, see: Laird, K. (2014) 'Rapist or Rogue? Deception, Consent and the Sexual Offences Act 2003' *Criminal Law Review* 492.

[20] Temkin, J. and Ashworth, A. (2004) 'The Sexual Offences Act 2003 – (1) Rape, Sexual Assaults and the Problems of Consent' *Criminal Law Review* 328 at 346.

Before moving on, remember that the principle from *R v Elbekkay* may be used when interpreting section 74's definition of consent. We examined this principle in detail above. So if the case involved impersonation of someone the victim did not know personally, or if it involved the defendant taking advantage of a case of mistaken identity, the *R v Elbekkay* principle can be applied.

### Capacity to consent

As well as freedom to choose, section 74 also states that the victim must have had the capacity to be able to choose. We are going to examine three reasons why a victim might have lacked the capacity to be able to choose: mental disorder; age and intoxication.

The first reason is mental disorder. In *R v Cooper* [2009] UKHL 42 the defendant, Gary Cooper, befriended the victim – a 28-year-old woman with a history of serious mental disorders – gave her crack cocaine and then made her perform oral sex on him. The victim said she did as he asked because she feared violence. Cooper was convicted of an offence under the Sexual Offences Act 2003.[21] He appealed against his conviction, arguing that the woman understood what oral sex was and so did not lack the capacity to consent. The House of Lords rejected this. Baroness Hale explained:

> [T]he case law on capacity has for some time recognised that, to be able to make a decision, the person concerned must not only be able to understand the information relevant to making it but also be able to "weigh [that information] in the balance to arrive at [a] choice".

So when deciding whether a victim had the capacity to consent, a jury should not only consider whether she was able to understand the relevant information but also whether she was capable of weighing up this information in order to make a decision. The jury in Cooper's case decided that, although the victim knew what oral sex was, the fear that she had experienced as a result of her mental disorder meant that she had lacked the capacity to agree by choice.

The second reason a victim might have lacked the capacity to consent is age. For the offence of rape, the law does not specify a particular age at which individuals acquire the capacity to consent to sexual intercourse. Whether a child had the capacity to be able to agree to sexual intercourse by choice is instead a question of fact, to be answered in a particular case by assessing the child's level of maturity and understanding. This is illustrated by *R v Robinson* [2011] EWCA Crim 916. The events in this case took place in the 1990s, and did not come to light until years later. The defendant, Sean Robinson, was charged with the rape of his girlfriend's daughter, ZK. Over time Robinson had formed a close relationship with ZK. At the age of 11 or 12 she would go round to his flat and play computer games with him. On one occasion ZK got into bed with her mother and Robinson and he touched her legs under the cover. When they were in the car together Robinson would kiss and stroke her leg. He began showing her pornographic films when they were at his flat. Gradually, this developed into a fuller sexual relationship. They first had sexual intercourse when ZK was aged 12. The relationship continued for three years. When ZK was asked whether or not she consented on the first occasion they had sexual intercourse, she replied: 'I did not ask the defendant not to, I did not move to stop him. He reassured me that it was okay. I did not make it plain to him that I didn't want to. There was no occasion when I said that I didn't want him to do it.'

---

[21]Sexual Offences Act 2003, section 30 (sexual activity with a person with a mental disorder impeding choice).

At trial Robinson was convicted of rape. He appealed against his conviction, arguing that the trial judge should not have allowed the rape charge to go to the jury since there was no evidence of rape. The evidence, he claimed, showed that the sexual intercourse was consensual and ZK was a willing participant. The Court of Appeal rejected Robinson's appeal and upheld the conviction.

### EXTRACT

Read the following extract from the judgment of Elias LJ. For the purposes of rape, could a 12-year-old child consent to sexual intercourse? What reasons did Elias LJ give for saying that there was evidence that ZK had not consented?

## R v Robinson [2011] EWCA Crim 916

### Elias LJ

21 Grooming is not a term of art, but it suggests cynical and manipulative behaviour designed to achieve a particular sexual objective. Not all relationships with underage children can fairly be characterised as involving grooming, although many will. But even where they can, the fact of grooming plainly does not necessarily vitiate consent. Many a seducer achieves his objectives with the liberal and cynical employment of gifts, insincere compliments and false promises. But such manipulative and deceitful methods could not be relied upon to establish a lack of consent whenever the seduction was successful. The situation will often be no different where the complainant is under age. But where the exploitation is of a girl who is of an age where she does not, or may not, have the capacity to understand the full significance of what she is doing, and in particular, where, as here, there was evidence of acquiescence or acceptance rather than positive consent, we think that, as the judge found, it would be open to the jury to conclude that the complainant, perhaps out of embarrassment or some other reason, had in reality unwillingly gone along with the acts which she did not in fact wish to engage in.

[...]

23 The only question we have to decide is whether, in view of this girl's age, and having regard to the passages in her interview and when she gave evidence, there was sufficient evidence from which the jury could infer a lack of consent. We are satisfied that the judge was right to say that there was. As Galbraith emphasises, the judge should not usurp the jury's functions by withdrawing the case from them. Some 12-year-olds plainly do not have the capacity to consent. Whilst this young girl did not fall into that category, in our judgment there was evidence on which a jury was entitled to find that her immaturity, coupled with the evidence of acquiescence rather than enthusiastic consent, particularly in the context of what could be perceived as grooming, meant that there was no proper consent.

R v Robinson was followed by the Court of Appeal in R v Ali (Yasir Ifran) [2015] EWCA Crim 1279. The defendants in this case targeted young girls, often from troubled backgrounds, whom they befriended and groomed for sexual purposes. One of the 29 counts concerned the defendant Ali's sexual relationship with a 15-year-old girl, SS. At trial, the defence submitted that there no was evidence on which a reasonable jury could convict because SS did not at any stage assert that she had not consented. The trial judge rejected this submission, stating that 'it seems to me that there is evidence on which a jury would be entitled to find that her immaturity, coupled with the evidence of acquiescence rather than enthusiastic consent, particularly in the context of what could be perceived as grooming, meant that there was no proper consent on her part' ([39]). Ali was subsequently convicted of rape, and appealed against his conviction. The Court of Appeal rejected the appeal, holding that since there were 'credible competing submissions as to whether there had been true consent' the issue of consent had properly been left to the jury ([65]).

## EXTRACT

Read the following extract from the judgment of Fulford LJ. In cases involving grooming, why might a victim's apparent consent not in fact have been real consent?

### *R v Ali (Yasir Ifran)* [2015] EWCA Crim 1279

### Fulford LJ

57 One of the consequences when vulnerable people are groomed for sexual exploitation is that compliance can mask the lack of true consent on the part of the victim. As the judge directed the jury in the summing up in this case, where there is evidence of exploitation of a young and immature person who may not understand the full significance of what he or she is doing, that is a factor the jury can take into account in deciding whether or not there was genuine consent

[...]

58 Although, as Elias LJ observed [in *R v Robinson*], grooming does not necessarily vitiate consent, it starkly raises the possibility that a vulnerable or immature individual may have been placed in a position in which he or she is led merely to acquiesce rather than to give proper or real consent. One of the consequences of grooming is that it has a tendency to limit or subvert the alleged victim's capacity to make free decisions, and it creates the risk that he or she simply submitted because of the environment of dependency created by those responsible for treating the alleged victim in this way. Indeed, the individual may have been manipulated to the extent that he or she is unaware of, or confused about, the distinction between acquiescence and genuine agreement at the time the incident occurred.

Before moving on, it is worth pointing out that, even if a defendant is not guilty of rape, there are other crimes which might apply if he had sexual intercourse with a child. For example, sections 5 to 8 of the Sexual Offences Act 2003 contain crimes which apply to sexual activity with children aged under 13, and sections 9 and 10 contain crimes which apply where the child was aged under 16.

The third reason a victim might lack the capacity to be able to choose to agree to sexual intercourse is intoxication. If the victim was so drunk that she passed out, and the defendant was aware of this, then there will be an evidential presumption that she did not consent (section 75(2)(d)). Similarly, if the defendant is aware that the victim was involuntarily given an overpowering or stupefying substance there will be an evidential presumption that she did not consent (section 75(2)(f)). But what about cases where the presumptions don't apply? And cases where the defendant manages to rebut the presumptions?

The leading case is *R v Bree* [2007] EWCA Crim 804. Benjamin Bree, aged 25, was visiting his brother Michael, who was a student at Bournemouth University. Benjamin and Michael went out for the evening with Michael's girlfriend, Holly, and Michael's flatmate M, the eventual victim. They each consumed a lot of alcohol. M drank two pints of cider and between four and six drinks of vodka and Red Bull. Benjamin drank two pints of lager before he too moved on to vodka and Red Bull. Michael and Holly left first. Benjamin and M left soon after. CCTV footage showed them returning to her flat arm-in-arm. Once inside, M vomited in the shower in her room. Benjamin looked after her. He washed her hair. M could not remember having her hair washed, but did remember someone asking her where she kept her shampoo. There were different accounts of what happened next.

- Here is M's account. She said that she must have become unconscious. After being asked for shampoo, her next memory was of lying on her bed. Benjamin was on top of her, with his mouth and tongue on and in her vagina. In her statement she said: 'I did nothing or said anything in response. I felt as if I wasn't in my body. I hadn't recovered significantly from how I felt in the bathroom, and I didn't know how long his mouth was in my vagina. I remember his fingers in my vagina. I could just feel this. I don't know where his head was. The next thing I recall is his coming close by my face and asking if I had a condom. I said no.' She didn't want to have sex, but said that she had not said this to Benjamin. In her statement she said: 'I knew I didn't want this but I didn't know how to go about stopping it.' To try and avoid sexual intercourse she turned over and curled up in a ball facing the wall. Although his penis was withdrawn for a while, he penetrated her again. She had no idea how long intercourse lasted. When it ended she was still facing the wall. Afterwards Benjamin asked if she wanted him to stay, and she said 'no'. In her mind she thought 'get out of my room', although she did not actually say it.

- Here is Benjamin's account. Benjamin said that M was in a much better state after being sick. He gave her her pyjamas. He said that he left the room and had a cigarette while she put them on. CCTV footage confirmed that he did leave the building for five minutes. When he returned, she was sitting on the edge of her bed. He started to stroke her. M seemed to welcome this, and it went from being stroking of a comforting nature to sexual touching. She did nothing to stop him. He put the top of his fingers inside the waistband of her pyjama trousers, and she did nothing to discourage him. He pulled the trousers down slightly, and then she removed them altogether. He said that they then had 'brief sex'. While they were having sex she asked whether he had a condom. He said no and asked whether she had one. She replied no. She was concerned about having unprotected sex, and so he stopped. He did not ejaculate. He went to the bathroom, washed his face, and asked M whether she wanted him to stay the night. She said no, and he left.

Importantly, during the trial the prosecution accepted that M had not lost consciousness. The gaps in her memory were not because she was unconscious; they were due to an alcohol-induced 'blackout' (excessive alcohol consumption can result in impaired memory and recollection).[22]

---

[22]The fact that excessive alcohol consumption can cause impaired memory and recollection means that it is important to distinguish between absence of memory and absence of consent. This was emphasised in *R v Tambedou* [2014] EWCA Crim 954, in which the Court of Appeal held that the fact that the victim could not recall whether or not she consented was not, in itself, sufficient reason to withdraw the case from the jury. There was ample evidence relevant to the question whether she had had the capacity to consent to go before a jury.

The key issue in the case was whether or not M consented to sexual intercourse. The prosecution argued that, even though M never lost consciousness, she had not consented to sexual intercourse. By contrast, Benjamin insisted that, although M may have become less inhibited because she was intoxicated, she was lucid enough to be able to consent to sexual intercourse and she did in fact consent.

At trial Benjamin was convicted of rape. The Court of Appeal subsequently quashed the conviction because of a number of defects in how the trial judge directed the jury. In its judgment the Court sought to clarify the meaning of 'capacity' in cases like this one.

## EXTRACT

Read the following extract from the judgment of Sir Igor Judge. Does a disinhibited person still have the capacity to consent? Can a conscious person ever lack the capacity to consent?

### R v Bree [2007] EWCA Crim 804

### Sir Igor Judge

26 In cases which are said to arise after voluntary consumption of alcohol the question is not whether the alcohol made either or both less inhibited than they would have been if sober, nor whether either or both might afterwards have regretted what had happened, and indeed wished that it had not. If the complainant consents, her consent cannot be revoked. Moreover it is not a question whether either or both may have had very poor recollection of precisely what had happened. That may be relevant as to the reliability of their evidence. Finally, and certainly, it is not a question whether either or both was behaving irresponsibly. As they were both autonomous adults, the essential question for decision is, as it always is, whether the evidence proved that the defendant had sexual intercourse with the complainant without her consent.

[...]

34 In our judgment, the proper construction of section 74 of the 2003 Act, as applied to the problem now under discussion, leads to clear conclusions. If, through drink (or for any other reason) the complainant has temporarily lost her capacity to choose whether to have intercourse on the relevant occasion, she is not consenting, and subject to questions about the defendant's state of mind, if intercourse takes place, this would be rape. However, where the complainant has voluntarily consumed even substantial quantities of alcohol, but nevertheless remains capable of choosing whether or not to have intercourse, and in drink agrees to do so, this would not be rape. We should perhaps underline that, as a matter of practical reality, capacity to consent may evaporate well before a complainant becomes unconscious. Whether this is so or not, however, is fact-specific, or more accurately, depends on the actual state of mind of the individuals involved on the particular occasion.

35 Considerations like these underline the fact that it would be unrealistic to endeavour to create some kind of grid system which would enable the answer to these questions to be related to some prescribed level of alcohol consumption. Experience shows that different individuals have a greater or lesser capacity to cope with alcohol than others, and indeed the ability of a single individual to do so may vary from day to day. The practical reality is that there are some areas of human behaviour which are inapt for detailed legislative structures. In this context, provisions intended to protect women from sexual assaults might very well be conflated into a

system which would provide patronising interference with the right of autonomous adults to make personal decisions for themselves.

36 For these reasons, notwithstanding criticisms of the statutory provisions, in our view the 2003 Act provides a clear definition of "consent" for the purposes of the law of rape, and by defining it with reference to "capacity to make that choice", sufficiently addresses the issue of consent in the context of voluntary consumption of alcohol by the complainant. The problems do not arise from the legal principles. They lie with infinite circumstances of human behaviour, usually taking place in private without independent evidence, and the consequent difficulties of proving this very serious offence.

One of the criticisms of the judgment in *R v Bree* is that it gives insufficient guidance on the meaning of 'capacity'. The reason that juries need more detailed guidance is because different people have very different understandings of what capacity means. This is illustrated by research done by Emily Finch and Vanessa Munro. They conducted a number of mock rape trials, and recorded each jury's deliberations in order to gain an insight into the reasoning employed by the (mock) jurors. The facts were similar to those in *R v Bree*. The following extract reports Finch and Munro's findings on the different understandings of 'capacity'.

## EXTRACT

### Finch, E. and Munro, V. (2006) 'Breaking Boundaries? Sexual Consent in the Jury Room' 26 *Legal Studies* 303

Given that the complainant experienced a high level of intoxication across all the trials in this study – while conscious and able to communicate, she was confused, having trouble walking, slurring her words, and the defendant admitted that she was largely unresponsive as he undressed her – it is perhaps not surprising to find that most jurors concluded that she did not consent to intercourse, since she lacked the capacity to do so under s 74. As one juror expressed this view, 'when he was undressing her, she was a floppy doll. There's no sign of consent there at all, it's, you know, just a lifeless thing' (Jury M). It is important to point out, however, that even in this situation, that view was not shared by everyone. A number of participants indicated that the complainant, so long as she remained conscious, retained the capacity to exercise a choice. Coupling this with a view that the non-consenting complainant had a responsibility to express her dissent to intercourse, such jurors commented, 'why could she not say no, I mean hang on a minute, my arms aren't moving, fine, but why can't you say no, keep on saying no' (Jury G), or similarly 'even though her whole body was slumped, she was still slurring. She could still speak. Even if she was slumped, she could still have said no' (Jury N).

These minority views testify to the way in which the concept of capacity under s 74, when applied to concrete cases, can lead to disparate results, depending on the extent to which jurors adopt a minimalist understanding of it as requiring little more than mere consciousness. Equally, however, the fact that there was a general consensus of outcome on the question of capacity, such that consent was not found, should not be thought to suggest too much interpretive unanimity amongst those jurors who supported this majority conclusion. Indeed, it was apparent from the deliberations that such jurors did not in fact share any common standard by which to judge this issue, whether across the different trials, across different juries or even within the same jury. Some participants, for example, adopted an approach to determining capacity to consent that compelled them to examine the complainant's state during the entire evening. By contrast, others invoked a broader perspective, taking into account factors such as the complainant's normal drinking habits and her likely level of alcohol tolerance. At the same time, other jurors adopted a far narrower time frame, focusing only on her responsiveness to the defendant at the time of intercourse, and attributing different emphases to factors such as her ability to communicate, her ability to weigh up options or her ability to make a decision reflecting her sober preferences.

While in the specific context of the present study, these differential tests rarely led to divergent conclusions, it is clear that this may not have been the case had the scenario involved a less intoxicated complainant. Some jurors, who adopted a highly rationalist understanding, for example, expressed the view that *any* intoxication would necessarily vitiate capacity under s 74. As one juror explained: 'When it's consent by choice and when you've got freedom and capacity to make consent, surely when you're drunk it eliminates that? How can you give consent when you're drunk?' (Jury A). By contrast, other jurors, who focused on communicative or cognitive ability, suggested that someone who was heavily intoxicated (albeit to a lesser extent than the present complainant) could retain a relevant capacity.

In addition, it was suggested that the issue of capacity would become more complex in these less extreme situations because the complainant may be deemed to have capacity for some acts but not for others, and so the significance of the decision to consent to intercourse would itself need to be considered. As one juror put it, 'it's not as simple ... to be able to decide because maybe she was enjoying the physical sensation, the physical act, but not emotionally' (Jury B). This is significant, of course, because it highlights the extent to which including the requirement that the complainant has capacity to make a choice, in the absence of guidance as to what level of consciousness, communication or self-awareness this requires, creates a malleable and unpredictable legal test. What's more, it suggests that in such situations, jurors' views about the level of responsibility an individual ought to take for his/her social and sexual behaviour may prove to be determinative.

Despite this marked divergence in the jurors' interpretations of s 74, what was also clear in the present study was the extent to which participants themselves seemed (paradoxically) confident in their understanding of the law. During their deliberations, mock jurors frequently seized on the statutory language and deployed it in support of their conclusions. Thus, for example, one juror commented, 'the thing that struck me was that in order for her to have consented, it meant that she had the choice and she had to be ... she had to have made her choice and had the freedom to make that choice. I don't think that she was in a situation to have done that' (Jury I). Likewise, another noted, 'the whole thing is her capacity to make any sort of judgement. I mean, that's, from my point of view, where it all hangs because she didn't have the freedom and capacity to make any sort of rational judgement whatsoever' (Jury U). This suggests that participants found the terms used in the s 74 definition to be familiar ones that they could work with. But while we generally applaud law that is user-friendly in this way, in this context, it is submitted that there is cause for caution. After all, as discussed, the fact that freedom, choice and capacity are terms whose meaning is within everyone's understanding does not entail that everyone understands those terms to mean the same thing, either in the abstract or in specific cases. Thus, the familiarity of the terms may itself be problematic since it presents the illusion of greater consensus in the jury room, and in the legal tests that are applied therein, than in fact exists.

Alongside these findings about the way in which participants responded to, interpreted and applied the s 74 provision, there is one further insight into the operation of the 2003 Act that emerged from this study. Across the different jury deliberations, it was apparent that the introduction of the requirement that the complainant agree by choice in circumstances of capacity and freedom, while predicted to promote a more proactive and communicative understanding of sexuality, did little to prevent some jurors from continuing to presume consent in the absence of positive dissent. The statements cited above from jurors who concluded that the complainant retained the capacity to consent, despite intoxication, testify to this, since these jurors moved on to assert that failing to dissent in a context in which the complainant was capable of so doing constituted agreement to intercourse. Significantly, moreover, these jurors were far from isolated in taking this approach. Indeed, while some jurors read the terms of s 74 as requiring something 'active rather than passive' (Jury S), as 'saying that consent isn't just being there and not saying no' (Jury Q), many others did not concur, or at least did not allow this to prevent them from taking a different line. Thus, a number of jurors operated from the opposite direction, commenting, for example: 'I think maybe that's why she consented, because she didn't say anything' (Jury B), or 'in order to not consent you have to ... she has to actually make it clear that she has not consented' (Jury I).

Although the jurors who took this latter approach did not all require evidence of dissent to take the form of physical resistance, there were some participants who insisted that, even in the case of a heavily intoxicated complainant, they would expect to find some evidence of struggle to establish non-consent. As one juror put it, 'a woman's got to cooperate with a man to be able to do it, to have intercourse, unless he thumps her or what, and he didn't – there was no bruising on her body anywhere. I would say she was probably drunk but at the same time she more or less consented' (Jury I). These comments testify to the tenacity of the force requirement in the popular understanding of rape, but their existence is particularly disconcerting here, since the jurors were specifically advised during medical evidence in the trial that lack of complainant injury does not necessarily contra-indicate rape. And while it is true that such comments, when voiced, were sometimes met with stark rebukes from fellow jurors, it is significant that the basis for this did not appear to lie in anything provided by the s 74 definition itself.

Overall, then, while the limitations of the study's method, and the fact that it involved a relatively small sample (168 mock jurors), must be borne in mind, the deliberations undertaken in response to the rape scenarios do indicate considerable support for the concerns raised above by critics of the 2003 Act. Of course, it might be argued that the new legislation has brought some improvements – in the absence of a specific direction to consider capacity and freedom, for example, jurors may have been more inclined to consider that a heavily intoxicated complainant had consented. That said, what is clear is that the s 74 definition did not do all that might have been hoped, either for the complainant or the juror, in the present study, partly as a result of stereotypical views about 'appropriate' gender roles, but partly also because of the vagueness of its central definitional terms.

This extract raises concerns about both the clarity of the law and consistency of its application. The lack of guidance given by the Court of Appeal in *R v Bree* does little to ease these concerns.

## 3. The defendant intentionally penetrated the victim's vagina, anus or mouth with his penis

The first of the two *mens rea* requirements is that the penetration was intentional. In cases where the *actus reus* of rape has been established this *mens rea* requirement will almost inevitably be satisfied too. It is very difficult, if not impossible, to imagine how a defendant could penetrate the victim's vagina, anus or mouth with his penis through carelessness or by accident!

## 4. The defendant lacked a reasonable belief that the victim was consenting to the penetration

Under the old law the *mens rea* of rape was lack of a genuine belief in consent.[23] So if the defendant genuinely believed the victim was consenting he could not be convicted of rape, however unreasonable his belief in consent. This was heavily criticised. When the Government introduced the Sexual Offences Act 2003 it changed the *mens rea* to lack of a reasonable belief in consent. As the following extract from the 2002 Home Office document *Protecting the Public* explains, it was hoped that this change would increase the conviction rate.

### EXTRACT

Home Office (2002) *Protecting the Public: Strengthening Protection Against Sex Offenders and Reforming the Law on Sexual Offences* (Cm 5668)

33 We will also be modifying the test of mistaken belief in relation to non-consensual offences. The current defence of an "honest" belief in consent means that no crime is committed when a person is forced against their will to have sexual intercourse with a person who can convince the court that they "honestly" interpreted their protestations or actions as consent to sex, however unreasonable such a belief might be. We believe the difficulty in proving that some defendants did not truly have an "honest" belief in consent contributes in some part to the low rate of convictions for rape. This in turn leads many victims, who feel that the system will not give them justice, not to report incidents or press for them to be brought to trial.

34 We will therefore alter the test to include one of reasonableness under the law. This will make it clear that, where the prosecution can prove that there is reasonable room for uncertainty about whether someone was consenting and that the defendant did not take reasonable action in the circumstances to ensure that the other person was willing to take part in the sexual acts, he will commit an offence. "Reasonable" will be judged by reference to what an objective third party would think in the circumstances. The jury would however have to take into account the actions of both parties, the circumstances in which they have placed themselves and the level of responsibility exercised by both. The jury would also expect, where relevant, to take account of the circumstances in which the accusation or revelation is delivered (including any media involvement) and the time that has elapsed.

When answering an exam problem question, it is important to remember that the conclusive and evidential presumptions set out in sections 76 and 75 also apply here. If the conclusive presumptions apply, the defendant will automatically be held to satisfy this *mens rea* requirement. If the evidential presumptions apply, you will need to consider whether the defendant can rebut the presumption by producing some evidence that he had a reasonable belief in consent.

Where the presumptions don't apply (or have been rebutted), you should work through this *mens rea* requirement in two steps:

- First, you should ask, 'Did the defendant believe that the victim was consenting?' In Chapter 4 we saw that to believe something you must have mentally accepted it as being true. So a defendant does not believe the victim is consenting if he isn't sure whether she is consenting or not and decides to carry on anyway.

---

[23]*DPP v Morgan* [1976] AC 182 (HL).

- If so, you should ask, 'Was the defendant's belief in consent reasonable?' When answering this question, remember that section 1(2) of the Act states, 'Whether a belief is reasonable is to be determined having regard to all the circumstances, including any steps A has taken to ascertain whether B consents'.

If the answer to either of these questions is no, the defendant lacked a reasonable belief in consent.

One issue the courts have had to address is whether mental illness may be taken into account when assessing whether a defendant's belief in consent was reasonable. In *R v B* [2013] EWCA Crim 3 the defendant was a paranoid schizophrenic. His condition caused him to hold delusional beliefs. A psychiatrist stated that the defendant thought he had sexual healing powers and that the reason he had sexual intercourse with the victim (his partner) in spite of her objections might have been because he thought it would be good for her. At trial the defendant was convicted of rape. The Court of Appeal dismissed his appeal against his conviction. Hughes LJ explained that a delusional belief in consent is, by definition, not a reasonable belief:

> 35 If [...] the defendant's delusional beliefs could have led him to believe that his partner consented when she did not, we take the clear view that such delusional beliefs cannot in law render reasonable a belief that his partner was consenting when in fact she was not. The Act does not ask whether it was reasonable (in the sense of being understandable or not his fault) for the defendant to suffer from the mental condition which he did. Normally no doubt, absent at least fault such as self-induced intoxication by drink or drugs, the answer to that in the case of acute illness such as this defendant seems to have suffered will be that it is reasonable. What the answer would be if the condition were an anti-social, borderline or psychopathic personality disorder may be more problematic. But the Act asks a different question: whether the belief in consent was a reasonable one. A delusional belief in consent, if entertained, would be by definition irrational and thus *un*reasonable, not reasonable.

Hughes LJ went on to say that defendants like the one in *R v B* should instead seek to plead insanity (which we study in Chapter 10) – and if the defence of insanity is unavailable then the defendant's mental illness should be taken into account when sentencing. He also emphasised that he was *not* saying that a defendant's mental illness should never be taken into account when assessing whether a defendant's belief in consent was reasonable. He explained that evidence of mental illness could be relevant in some, limited, circumstances:

> 41 It does not follow that there will not be cases in which the personality or abilities of the defendant may be relevant to whether his positive belief in consent was reasonable. It may be that cases could arise in which the reasonableness of such belief depends on the reading by the defendant of subtle social signals, and in which his impaired ability to do so is relevant to the reasonableness of his belief. We do not attempt exhaustively to foresee the circumstances which might arise in which a belief might be held which is not in any sense irrational, even though most people would not have held it. Whether (for example) a particular defendant of less than ordinary intelligence or with demonstrated inability to recognise behavioural cues might be such a case, or whether his belief ought properly to be characterised as unreasonable, must await a decision on specific facts. It is possible, we think,

that beliefs generated by such factors may not properly be described as irrational and might be judged by a jury not to be unreasonable on their particular facts. But once a belief could be judged reasonable only by a process which labelled a plainly irrational belief as reasonable, it is clear that it cannot be open to the jury so to determine without stepping outside the Act.

As we have seen, the change to the *mens rea* introduced by the 2003 Act was designed to increase the conviction rate. But from the outset critics doubted whether it was capable of having this effect.[24] Of particular concern is the invitation, in section 1(2), to have regard to 'all the circumstances' when assessing the reasonableness of the defendant's belief.

## EXTRACT

The following extract is from an article written by Temkin and Ashworth. What sorts of things do they think a jury might take into account when having regard to 'all the circumstances'. Why does this worry them?

### Temkin, J. and Ashworth, A. (2004) 'The Sexual Offences Act 2003 – (1) Rape, Sexual Assaults and the Problems of Consent' *Criminal Law Review* 328

The broad reference to "all the circumstances" is an invitation to the jury to scrutinise the complainant's behaviour to determine whether there was anything about it which could have induced a reasonable belief in consent. In this respect the Act contains no real challenge to society's norms and stereotypes about either the relationship between men and women or other sexual situations, and leaves open the possibility that those stereotypes will determine assessments of reasonableness. Is B's sexual history to be taken to be a relevant part of the circumstances? In answer to a question raised in Committee, the Minister agreed that the section "should focus the court's attention on what is happening at the time of the offence" and "should make the previous sexual history of the complainant far less relevant." But this does not seem to reflect the natural meaning of the words "*all* the circumstances," which contain no limitation to circumstances existing at the time of the event in question. Further, it is true that s.1(2) requires consideration of "any steps A has taken to ascertain whether B consents," however, if A enquires about consent; B says no, but A concludes that B's "no" is tantamount to "yes," is his culturally engendered belief to be regarded as reasonable or not? In deciding what it is "relevant" to consider, what is to prevent the influence of stereotypes about B's dress, B's frequenting of a particular place, an invitation to have a drink, and so forth?

The mock trials conducted by Finch and Munro allow us to assess whether the concerns expressed by Ashworth and Temkin are justified.

---

[24]In 2006, the Home Office reported that there was little evidence that the 2003 Act had resulted in a greater number of convictions for rape: see Home Office (2006) *Sexual Offences Act 2003: A stocktake of the effectiveness of the Act since its implementation.*

**EXTRACT**

### Finch, E. and Munro, V. (2006) 'Breaking Boundaries? Sexual Consent in the Jury Room' 26 *Legal Studies* 303

[I]n the absence of specific guidance to the contrary, jurors often interpreted the notion of 'reasonable in all the circumstances' extremely broadly, taking into account not only factors about the defendant, about 'the way he thought' (Jury E) and about whether he felt remorse (Jury T), but also about 'the whole situation, the party, the drinking and so on' (Jury R). As one juror put it: 'you might think yeah, that is very unreasonable but from his point of view you might think it's not as unreasonable and the fact that she is at a party, she does look and appear to be drunk, she hasn't told him no, and from the other person's point of view it might look like he's not being unreasonable' (Jury E). These statements are significant because they illustrate the extent to which, on the invitation to consider 'all the circumstances', jurors effectively deduced sexual consent (or at least the defendant's reasonable belief therein) from other, often unrelated, events that lacked any temporal correspondence with intercourse.

The introduction of these wider circumstantial factors is problematic because it allows scope for juror reliance on inferences extrapolated from surrounding circumstances, even when those circumstances bore no necessary relevance to the evaluation of consent between the parties themselves. In addition, moreover, it generates an opportunity for the introduction into the jury room of a range of (ill-founded) views about 'appropriate' socio-sexual interaction, either on the basis that they are shared by jurors who are assessing the signals sent out by the complainant's conduct, or on the basis that the jurors, while not sharing these views themselves, nonetheless consider that they may have been harboured by the defendant and so may be relevant to the question of his reasonableness. The references made in the previous quotes to 'the party and the drinking' clearly allude to these background social conventions, but in a number of the jurors' comments this linkage is made far more explicit. Thus, for example, one juror argued that had the complainant 'gone upstairs' *with* the defendant at the party (rather than on her own), the defendant could have reasonably taken from this that she was consenting to intercourse (Jury Q), while another suggested that this belief would have been reasonable if the complainant had 'been drinking all night, and flirting with him' (Jury E). In both these contexts, of course, jurors have tapped into highly dubious, but widely supported, social conventions which indicate that women who drink or flirt with men, or who take steps to initiate some intimacy, cannot complain when men take this behaviour to imply a willingness to engage in intercourse thereafter.

The extent to which jurors relied on these questionable stereotypes to afford leniency to the defendant within the confines of the present study was noteworthy. Indeed, even the fact that the complainant had been passive during intercourse was deemed, by some jurors, to be sufficient to support the defendant's claim to reasonable belief. As one juror put it, 'I don't think him having made all the advances and having to undress her is as important an issue ... because it's not unusual for one party to be more into it than the other, it's never 50:50% I would have thought and women are often sort of coy in these circumstances ... and he might have thought that as well' (Jury E). Similarly, another juror commented, 'her lack of showing consent, I think on that alone, you know, you could understand him reasonably thinking it was a sign of consent' (Jury C); and another added: 'I think from the fact that she was able to speak, albeit incoherently ... that it was reasonable for him to think that if she'd wanted to say no, she could have done' (Jury E).

It should be noted that in some juries, when these views were raised, they were challenged by other jurors, often through reliance on the wording of the statute. Thus, as one juror commented, 'I don't think the defendant ascertained sufficiently whether she was willing to consent, he didn't ask, he took some potentially token gestures as consent' (Jury M). This supports the claim alluded to in previous discussion that the requirement under the 2003 Act to consider the steps taken by the defendant to ascertain consent will counter these questionable interpretations, both of consent and of reasonableness. However, as noted above, the overall tenor of the jury deliberations in the present study did not bear this out. Indeed, it was apparent that jurors who adopted this line of thinking were rarely moved by the counters of their peers. The following exchange in Jury P reflects this most clearly:

> '1: Why … how do you think if you were in that event or just in the situation that he saw … how do you think he saw consent? How do you think he ascertained that she was giving consent?
>
> 3: Well she didn't say no.
>
> 1: Because she didn't say no?
>
> 7: She wasn't paralytically unconscious was she?'

This suggests that the positive impact of requiring a defendant to take proactive steps to ascertain consent may be substantially undermined by a permission under the 2003 Act to take account of all the circumstances, especially where the 'good sense' of the jury is relied upon to determine the relevance of dubious social conventions indicating that passivity can reasonably be equated with consent.

The findings of Finch and Munro's study were echoed by an Australian study conducted by Larcombe *et al.* In this study, the researchers held eleven focus group discussions with three sets of participants: professionals working in the sexual assault sector; legally trained professionals; and, community members. These participants expressed dissatisfaction with legal definitions of rape that require proof that the defendant lacked a reasonable belief in consent.

## EXTRACT

Larcombe, W., Fileborn, B., Powell, A., Hanley, N. and Henry, N. (2016) '"I Think it's Rape and I Think He Would be Found Not Guilty": Focus Group Perceptions of (un)Reasonable Belief in Consent in Rape Law' 25 *Social & Legal Studies* 611

Across [sexual assault professionals, legal professionals and general community members], we found that a definition of rape that turns on whether the accused may have had a reasonable belief in consent is perceived as biased in favour of the defendant. Reasonable belief in consent was also perceived to enable jury members to apply assumptions and expectations about reasonable sexual conduct and inferred or continuing consent that many of our participants personally rejected. Whilst there was no agreement among our participants about what sexual consent is or how it can be inferred or established, it was expected that at least some jury members would think that it was reasonable for a person to believe that consent was present when a former sexual partner does not protest or resist. This was perceived to impose an unreasonable expectation on the victim of a sexual assault to unequivocally communicate non-consent. As a result, the law was perceived to lag behind these participants' own understandings of rape and to undermine conceptions of affirmative consent. Further law reform was suggested to restrict or abolish the reasonable belief defence or to ensure that a person accused of rape who claimed that they believed in consent should have to testify to their actions and submit to questioning about the grounds for any such belief.

## Assault by penetration

The offence of assault by penetration is defined by section 2 of the Sexual Offences Act 2003.

---

**EXTRACT**

### Section 2 of the Sexual Offences Act 2003

**2 Assault by penetration**

(1)   A person (A) commits an offence if –

    (a)   he intentionally penetrates the vagina or anus of another person (B) with a part of his body or anything else,

    (b)   the penetration is sexual,

    (c)   B does not consent to the penetration, and

    (d)   A does not reasonably believe that B consents.

(2)   Whether a belief is reasonable is to be determined having regard to all the circumstances, including any steps A has taken to ascertain whether B consents.

(3)   Sections 75 and 76 apply to an offence under this section.

(4)   A person guilty of an offence under this section is liable, on conviction on indictment, to imprisonment for life.

---

This tells us that the offence has five requirements:

1.   The defendant penetrated the vagina or anus of the victim with a part of his body or anything else

2.   The penetration was sexual

3.   The victim did not consent to the penetration

4.   The defendant intentionally penetrated the vagina or anus of the victim

5.   The defendant lacked a reasonable belief that the victim was consenting to the penetration.

Numbers 1 to 3 are *actus reus* requirements. Numbers 4 and 5 are *mens rea* requirements. We will work through them in turn.

### 1. The defendant penetrated the vagina or anus of the victim with a part of his body or anything else

Rape was limited to penetration with a penis. This offence is broader. It covers penetration of the vagina or anus (but not the mouth) with other parts of the body (like a finger) or anything else (like a bottle). The offence can be committed by both men and women.

The offence might also be used where the evidence shows that the victim's vagina or anus was penetrated, but it is uncertain whether or not the penetration was with a penis (perhaps because the victim was unconscious).

## 2. The penetration was sexual

The term 'sexual' is an important one. It is used not only in the definition of this offence, but also the section 3 definition of sexual assault and the section 4 definition of causing a person to engage in sexual activity without consent, which we will study shortly.

The term is defined in section 78 of the Sexual Offences Act 2003.

---

### EXTRACT

### Section 78 of the Sexual Offences Act 2003

**78 'Sexual'**

For the purposes of this Part (except section 71), penetration, touching or any other activity is sexual if a reasonable person would consider that—

(a) whatever its circumstances or any person's purpose in relation to it, it is because of its nature sexual, or

(b) because of its nature it may be sexual and because of its circumstances or the purpose of any person in relation to it (or both) it is sexual.

---

A jury deciding whether a particular activity was sexual or not should begin with section 78(a). Section 78(a) states that if an activity was, 'because of its nature', sexual the defendant's purpose is irrelevant. In other words, some activities are intrinsically sexual, even if the defendant's purpose was not a sexual one. An example of an activity which is intrinsically sexual is oral sex.

If the activity in question was not intrinsically sexual the jury must turn instead to section 78(b). The correct approach to this paragraph was set out by the Court of Appeal in *R v H* [2005] EWCA Crim 732:

- First, the jury must consider whether, 'because of its nature', the activity *may* be sexual. An activity which is incapable of being regarded as sexual by reasonable people cannot be made sexual because of the defendant's purpose.

- If the activity may be sexual the jury must consider the surrounding circumstances and the defendant's purpose and decide whether, in this particular instance, it was in fact sexual.

So, for example, suppose that the defendant spanked a 12-year-old girl on the buttocks. Spanking is not intrinsically sexual. Some parents spank their children to tell them off. So section 78(a) does not apply. Turning to section 78(b), spanking may be sexual (as some of the cases studied in the previous chapter illustrated!). So the surrounding circumstances and the defendant's purpose would need to be considered. In *R v Court* [1989] AC 28 (HL) the defendant worked in a shop. Whilst working in the shop he pulled a 12-year-old girl onto his lap and spanked her. He later blamed his actions on a 'buttock fetish'. Taking this into account, it is clear that his actions would be deemed 'sexual' for the purposes of section 78.

## ACTIVITY

It is a Saturday afternoon on a busy high street. Lawrence is armed with a knife. He walks up to a young woman named Mandy, points the knife at her, and says, 'Strip naked or else'. Terrified, Mandy strips naked. Lawrence later says that he did it to humiliate Mandy. Applying the test set out in section 78, were Lawrence's actions sexual?

How (if at all) would your answer be different in each of the two following situations?

- Lawrence forced Mandy to strip naked in private and took photos of her. He sold the photos to an adult website, and kept a copy of one of the pictures for himself.
- Mandy was not a young woman, but an 86-year-old pensioner.

### 3. The victim did not consent to the penetration

This part of the offence is the same as for the offence of rape. So sections 74–76 which we looked at previously also apply here.

### 4. The defendant intentionally penetrated the vagina or anus of the victim

As for the offence of rape, it is difficult to imagine how the penetrative act could be anything other than intentional. So this *mens rea* requirement will always be straightforward.

### 5. The defendant lacked a reasonable belief that the victim was consenting to the penetration

Like the offence of rape, the second *mens rea* requirement for this offence is lack of a reasonable belief in consent. Everything we said about the lack of reasonable belief test when examining rape also applies here.

## Sexual assault

The offence of sexual assault is defined by section 3 of the Sexual Offences Act 2003.

## EXTRACT

### Section 3 of the Sexual Offences Act 2003

**3 Sexual assault**

(1)  A person (A) commits an offence if –
   (a)  he intentionally touches another person (B),
   (b)  the touching is sexual,
   (c)  B does not consent to the touching, and
   (d)  A does not reasonably believe that B consents.

(2) Whether a belief is reasonable is to be determined having regard to all the circumstances, including any steps A has taken to ascertain whether B consents.

(3) Sections 75 and 76 apply to an offence under this section.

(4) A person guilty of an offence under this section is liable –

    (a) on summary conviction, to imprisonment for a term not exceeding 6 months or a fine not exceeding the statutory maximum or both;

    (b) on conviction on indictment, to imprisonment for a term not exceeding 10 years.

This tells us that the offence has five requirements:

1. The defendant touched the victim
2. The touching was sexual
3. The victim did not consent to the touching
4. The defendant intentionally touched the victim
5. The defendant lacked a reasonable belief that the victim was consenting to the touching.

Numbers 1 to 3 are *actus reus* requirements. Numbers 4 and 5 are *mens rea* requirements. We will work through them in turn.

## 1. The defendant touched the victim

The two previous offences both involved penetration. Sexual assault is much broader. It only requires sexual touching. So, for example, it would apply where the defendant fondled the victim. It is also the offence that would apply in a situation like the famous 'Mormon sex in chains case' (which was the subject of the 2010 movie *Tabloid*). In this case the alleged victim – a male Mormon missionary – claimed that the female perpetrator had chained him to a bed and had non-consensual sexual intercourse with him. On these facts the woman could not be convicted of rape (only men can commit rape) or assault by penetration (she did not penetrate the man's anus), so the relevant offence would be sexual assault.

Some guidance on the meaning of 'touching' can be found in section 79(8). This gives a non-exhaustive list of actions which amount to a 'touching'.

### EXTRACT

### Section 79(8) of the Sexual Offences Act 2003

(8) Touching includes touching—

    (a) with any part of the body,

    (b) with anything else,

    (c) through anything,

      and in particular includes touching amounting to penetration.

So 'touching' includes touching someone with an object (paragraph (b)) and touching someone through their clothes (paragraph (c)). The Court of Appeal has also held, in *R v H* [2005] EWCA Crim 732, that touching the clothes someone is wearing (without any contact with the person's body) constitutes a touching for the purposes of this offence.

## 2. The touching was sexual

We studied the meaning of sexual when looking at the offence of assault by penetration. Everything we said there also applies here.

If there was touching of a non-sexual nature you should instead consider the offences against the person (which we studied in the previous chapter).

## 3. The victim did not consent to the touching

This part of the offence is the same as for the offence of rape. So sections 74–76 which we looked at previously also apply here.

## 4. The defendant intentionally touched the victim

The touching must have been intentional. We studied the meaning of intention in Chapter 4. Reckless, negligent or accidental touching falls outside the offence of sexual assault.

## 5. The defendant lacked a reasonable belief that the victim was consenting to the touching

Like the offence of rape, the second *mens rea* requirement for this offence is lack of a reasonable belief in consent. Everything we said about the lack of reasonable belief test when examining rape also applies here.

# Causing a person to engage in sexual activity without consent

The offence of causing a person to engage in sexual activity without consent is defined by section 4 of the Sexual Offences Act 2003.

---

**EXTRACT**

Section 4 of the Sexual Offences Act 2003

**4 Causing a person to engage in sexual activity without consent**

(1)    A person (A) commits an offence if–

    (a)  he intentionally causes another person (B) to engage in an activity,

    (b)  the activity is sexual,

    (c)  B does not consent to engaging in the activity, and

    (d)  A does not reasonably believe that B consents.

(2)    Whether a belief is reasonable is to be determined having regard to all the circumstances, including any steps A has taken to ascertain whether B consents.

(3)    Sections 75 and 76 apply to an offence under this section.

(4)  A person guilty of an offence under this section, if the activity caused involved–

    (a)  penetration of B's anus or vagina,

    (b)  penetration of B's mouth with a person's penis,

    (c)  penetration of a person's anus or vagina with a part of B's body or by B with anything else, or

    (d)  penetration of a person's mouth with B's penis,
       is liable, on conviction on indictment, to imprisonment for life.

(5)  Unless subsection (4) applies, a person guilty of an offence under this section is liable–

    (a)  on summary conviction, to imprisonment for a term not exceeding 6 months or to a fine not exceeding the statutory maximum or both;

    (b)  on conviction on indictment, to imprisonment for a term not exceeding 10 years.

This tells us that the offence has five requirements:

1.  The defendant caused the victim to engage in an activity
2.  The activity was sexual
3.  The victim was not consenting to the activity
4.  The defendant intentionally caused the victim to engage in the activity
5.  The defendant lacked a reasonable belief that the victim was consenting to the activity.

Numbers 1 to 3 are *actus reus* requirements. Numbers 4 and 5 are *mens rea* requirements. We will work through them in turn.

## 1. The defendant caused the victim to engage in an activity

This offence may be used where the defendant did not penetrate or touch the victim. Examples include where the defendant forces the victim to masturbate and where a female defendant forces the victim to penetrate her.

For this first requirement, a causal link must be established between the defendant's actions and the victim's participation in the activity. As we saw in Chapter 3, to establish a causal link it is necessary to show both factual and legal causation.

It is possible to commit this offence by words alone. There is also no requirement that the defendant was present when the victim engaged in the activity. For example, in *R v Devonald* [2008] EWCA Crim 527 (the case we studied earlier in which the defendant tricked his daughter's ex-boyfriend into masturbating in front of a web cam) the defendant was convicted of causing the victim to engage in sexual activity without consent, even though he was not in the room when the victim masturbated.

## 2. The activity was sexual

We studied the meaning of sexual when looking at the offence of assault by penetration. Everything we said there also applies here.

## 3. The victim was not consenting to the activity

This part of the offence is the same as for the offence of rape. So sections 74–76 which we looked at previously also apply here.

### 4. The defendant intentionally caused the victim to engage in the activity

We studied the meaning of intention in Chapter 4. Both direct and oblique intention will suffice.

### 5. The defendant lacked a reasonable belief that the victim was consenting to the activity

Like the offence of rape, the second *mens rea* requirement for this offence is lack of a reasonable belief in consent. Everything we said about the lack of reasonable belief test when examining rape also applies here.

## Conclusion

As we have seen, the conclusive and evidential presumptions introduced by the Sexual Offences Act 2003 have made the process for assessing a defendant's guilt quite complex. The flow chart in Figure 7.2 is designed for you to use when attempting the self-test questions below. It focuses on the offence of rape, and is designed to help you structure your answers correctly. It begins by asking whether the defendant intentionally penetrated the victim's vagina, anus or mouth with his penis (combining the first of the offence's *actus reus* and *mens rea* requirements). It then works through the remaining *actus reus* requirement (absence of consent) and the remaining *mens rea* requirement (lack of a reasonable belief in consent).

**ACTIVITY**

Using this flow chart as your starting point, can you adapt it to create similar charts for the other three offences we have studied?

## Self-test questions

1.  It is Friday night. Rebecca and Paula are having a night out at the pub.

    After they've had a few drinks Rebecca spots Norman, who looks a lot like the famous footballer David Beckham, across the bar. She builds up the courage to talk to him and introduces herself, saying, 'I've been a huge fan of yours for years'. Norman has been mistaken for David Beckham lots of times before, but does not correct Rebecca. Instead he smiles at her and offers to buy her a drink. She replies, 'I shouldn't really, I'm already feeling quite drunk', but Norman convinces her to have a vodka and orange. Unbeknown to Rebecca, Norman asks the barman to make it a double vodka. After finishing their drinks Norman and Rebecca go to the car park, where they have sexual intercourse in Norman's dilapidated Ford Escort.

    Meanwhile Paula meets Nigel. They start talking, and Nigel soon offers to buy Paula a drink. Although Paula has already had several glasses of wine, she asks Nigel for a double vodka. When they've finished their drinks Nigel invites Paula back to his

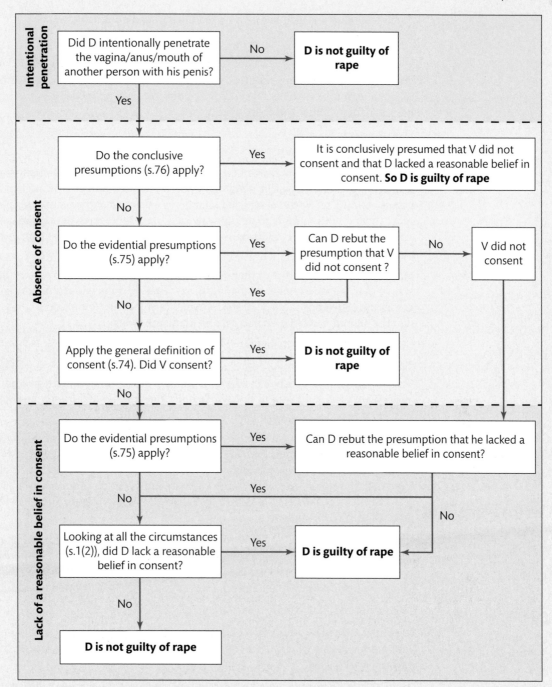

**Figure 7.2.** The offence of rape: an overview

nearby hotel room. Paula agrees. By the time they get to Nigel's room Paula has started to feel dizzy and sick, and so she lies down on Nigel's bed. Nigel climbs on top of her and has sexual intercourse with her.

The next day Paula has little recollection of what happened in Nigel's room. All she remembers is thinking 'Leave me alone, I want to go home'. Nigel says that, although

Paula was quiet and had her eyes closed during sexual intercourse, she did not ask him to stop.

Discuss the criminal liability of Norman and Nigel.

Would your answer be any different if Paula had fallen asleep while Nigel was having sexual intercourse with her, Nigel did not notice at first, and when he did notice he hesitated for a moment and then withdrew?

2. Over the years Rose has made a lot of money by seducing celebrities, having sexual intercourse with them and then selling her story to the press.

   When Rose discovers that members of the local Premier League football team are having a night out at a nearby nightclub she decides to go along. At the nightclub she begins chatting to Wayne, a married man who is also one of the team's star players. After flirting with him for some time she says, 'Let's go somewhere more private'. They go to Wayne's hotel room and have sexual intercourse. The next day Rose contacts several national tabloid newspapers and sells her story for £5,000.

   Wayne is horrified, and says that he would never have had sex with Rose had he known that she would sell her story. Rose says that she only had sex with Wayne for the money. She adds that she despises men who cheat on their partners and hopes that the tabloid headlines embarrass and humiliate Wayne.

   Discuss Rose's criminal liability.

   Suppose, instead, that Rose had been a prostitute. She only sold her story because Wayne had offered to pay her £1,000 if she had sexual intercourse with him, but afterwards Wayne refused to pay her saying, 'I never had any intention of paying you'. How would your answer be different in this situation?

3. Dr Jones works as a gynaecologist in a hospital. When Vera, one of her patients, arrives for her appointment Dr Jones tells Vera that she needs to take a sample from her to order to diagnose her condition. Dr Jones explains that to take the sample she has to insert a smear brush into Vera's vagina. Vera gives her permission. In fact, Dr Jones did not need to take the sample to diagnose Vera's condition. She collected the sample for her own personal sexual gratification.

   One of the other doctors at the hospital, Dr Jekyll, discovers that Dr Jones has been misleading her patients. Dr Jekyll threatens to report Dr Jones to the hospital management unless she has sexual intercourse with him. Terrified at the possibility of losing her job, Dr Jones reluctantly agrees and they have sexual intercourse.

   Discuss the criminal liability of Dr Jones and Dr Jekyll.

   How (if at all) would your answer be different if Dr Jones had taken the sample from Vera not for sexual gratification, but for some private research she was conducting into cervical cancer?

4. 'The Sexual Offences Act 2003 successfully modernises the offence of rape. It contains a clear and unambiguous definition of consent. The introduction of conclusive and evidential presumptions not only provide a simple and straightforward mechanism for structuring jury's decision-making, but also clearly communicate forms of unacceptable sexual behaviour. And the change in the *mens rea* helps secure convictions by preventing defendants from being able to rely on dubious social conventions and stereotypes.'

   Discuss the extent to which you agree with this statement.

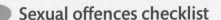

## Sexual offences checklist

Having worked through this chapter, you should now have:

✓ An understanding of the requirements of the crime of rape

✓ An understanding of the requirements of the crime of assault by penetration

✓ An understanding of the requirements of the crime of sexual assault

✓ An understanding of the requirements of the crime of causing a person to engage in sexual activity without consent

✓ An understanding of the conclusive and evidential presumptions and the general definition of consent contained in sections 74 to 76 of the Sexual Offences Act 2003 and an ability to critically discuss whether these provisions achieve their stated objectives

✓ An understanding of the change to the *mens rea* of rape introduced by the 2003 Act and an ability to critically discuss whether this change has helped secure an increase in the conviction rate for rape.

## Further reading

Finch, E. and Munro, V. (2006) 'Breaking Boundaries? Sexual Consent in the Jury Room' 26 *Legal Studies* 303.

Firth, G. (2011) 'Not an Invitation to Rape: The Sexual Offences Act 2003, Consent and the Case of the "Drunken" Victim' 62 *Northern Ireland Legal Quarterly* 99.

Gunby, C., Carline, A. and Beynon, C. (2010) 'Alcohol-related Rape Cases: Barristers' Perspectives on the Sexual Offences Act 2003 and Its Impact on Practice' 74 *Journal of Criminal Law* 579.

Herring, J. (2005) 'Mistaken Sex' *Criminal Law Review* 511.

Home Office (2010) *The Stern Review: A report by Baroness Vivien Stern CBE of an independent review into how rape complaints are handled by public authorities in England and Wales.*

Laird, K. (2014) 'Rapist or Rogue? Deception, Consent and the Sexual Offences Act 2003' *Criminal Law Review* 492.

Larcombe, W., Fileborn, B., Powell, A., Hanley, N. and Henry, N. (2016) '"I Think it's Rape and I Think He Would be Found Not Guilty": Focus Group Perceptions of (un)Reasonable Belief in Consent in Rape Law' 25 *Social & Legal Studies* 611.

Rumney, P.N.S. and Fenton, R.A. (2008) 'Intoxicated Consent in Rape: *Bree* and Juror Decision-making' 71 *Modern Law Review* 279.

Sharpe, A. (2016) 'Expanding Liability for Sexual Fraud through the Concept of 'Active Deception': A Flawed Approach' 80 *Journal of Criminal Law* 28.

Tadros, V. (2006) 'Rape Without Consent' 26 *Oxford Journal of Legal Studies* 515.

Temkin, J. and Ashworth, A. (2004) 'The Sexual Offences Act 2003 – (1) Rape, Sexual Assaults and the Problems of Consent' *Criminal Law Review* 328.

Wallerstein, S. (2009) '"A Drunken Consent Is Still Consent" – Or Is It? A Critical Analysis of the Law on a Drunken Consent to Sex Following *Bree*' 73 *Journal of Criminal Law* 318.

Williams, R. (2008) 'Deception, Mistake and Vitiation of the Victim's Consent' 124 *Law Quarterly Review* 132.

# 8

# Property offences

## Chapter objectives

By the end of this chapter you should have:

- An understanding of the requirements for establishing criminal liability for: (a) theft; (b) robbery; (c) burglary; (d) fraud and (e) criminal damage
- An ability to apply the relevant law to a hypothetical set of facts and discuss whether criminal liability may be established for any of the offences listed above
- An ability to discuss and evaluate the case law on appropriation and dishonesty within the law of theft.

 **Introduction**

In this chapter we study five property offences: theft; robbery; burglary; fraud and criminal damage. Of the different types of offences that we study in this text, these offences are by far the most prevalent. According to police-recorded crime figures, these five offences were committed a total of more than 3.4 million times during 2016.[1] That is nearly 400 times every hour! This compares to a total of 1.1 million offences of violence against the person and 116,012 sexual offences.

The chapter begins by examining the law governing theft. Of the five property offences listed above, theft is the most common. The police recorded a total of 1.8 million thefts during 2016.[2] The definition of theft is therefore very important, because it is applied many times every day. Yet as we will see, the way in which the offence has been defined by the courts has been heavily criticised. This criticism has focused on two concepts in particular – appropriation and dishonesty. We will explore these criticisms so that you can evaluate whether or not they are justified.

After examining theft in detail, we will then work through the offences of robbery, burglary, fraud and criminal damage.

**Theft**

The offence of theft is defined by section 1 of the Theft Act 1968:

> **EXTRACT**
>
> ## Section 1 of the Theft Act 1968
>
> ### 1 Basic definition of theft
>
> (1)  A person is guilty of theft if he dishonestly appropriates property belonging to another with the intention of permanently depriving the other of it; and "thief" and "steal" shall be construed accordingly

This tells us that the offence has five requirements:

1.   The item in question was property
2.   The property belonged to another person
3.   The defendant appropriated the property
4.   The defendant had an intention to permanently deprive the other person of the property
5.   The defendant acted dishonestly.

Numbers 1, 2 and 3 are *actus reus* requirements. Numbers 4 and 5 are *mens rea* requirements. We will work through them in turn.

---

[1]Office for National Statistics (2017) *Crime in England and Wales, Year Ending December 2016.*
[2]Compared to 55,824 robberies, 404,282 burglaries, 641,539 fraud offences and 556,077 criminal damage offences.

**1. The item in question was property**

The first requirement is that the item was property. Property is defined in section 4(1):

> **EXTRACT**
>
> ### Section 4(1) of the Theft Act 1968
>
> **4 "Property"**
>
> (1)  "Property" includes money and all other property, real or personal, including things in action and other intangible property.

Some of the terms used in this definition require some explanation:

- The first is real property. Put simply, real property means buildings and land. Notice, however, that section 4(2) goes on to state that land can only be stolen in certain circumstances. These include: where the defendant is a trustee and commits a breach of confidence by appropriating the land (s.4(2)(a)); where the defendant is a trespasser and appropriates an item by severing it from the land (e.g. a garden shed or fence) (s.4(2)(b)); and, where a tenant removes a fixture or structure from the place he is renting (e.g. wall panelling) (s.4(2)(c)).

- The second term which requires some explanation is personal property. Any property that is not real property is personal property. So banknotes, furniture and a flat-screen TV are all examples of personal property.

- The third term is intangible property. Most property – like banknotes, furniture and a flat-screen TV – is tangible. It has a physical existence, so you can touch it and pick it up (if it isn't too big or too heavy!). But some property does not have a physical existence (e.g. a copyright). It is intangible.

- The fourth term – things in action – is an example of intangible property. A thing in action is a property right that cannot be asserted physically (since the property has no physical existence) but which can be enforced by legal action. An example is a debt. Suppose Derek owes Aubrey £50. Aubrey's right to the money is an item of property. It is a thing in action which can be enforced in the courts. Other examples of things in action are patents, copyrights and shares in a company.

It should be clear from this that the section 4(1) definition of property has a broad scope. It encompasses real property and personal property. It encompasses tangible property and intangible property. It includes things in action.

The definition also includes illegal drugs. In *R v Smith* [2011] EWCA Crim 66 the Court of Appeal held that the fact that property is possessed unlawfully does not mean that it falls outside the definition. The defendant, Michael Smith, arranged to meet a man called Chesterfield Jordan to buy £50 worth of heroin from him. When they met Smith beat Jordan up and took the heroin without paying for it. Smith was charged with theft of the heroin. He argued that the heroin did not fall within the section 4 definition because Jordan's possession of the drug was illegal. The Court of Appeal rejected this argument. It explained that to decide otherwise would result in anarchy:

> Carried to its logical conclusion, the argument would suggest that the drug-misusing community is permitted to conduct itself in the context of what would otherwise be

theft from each other with impunity. The public interest would hardly be secured by the inevitable public warfare which would ensue.

However, despite the breadth of section 4, there are some things which are not included in the definition of property:

- The first is electricity. A person cannot be charged with stealing electricity. Instead, section 13 of the Theft Act 1968 creates a specific offence of dishonestly using electricity. Note also that, whilst electricity is not property for the purposes of theft, gas and water are. So a person can be guilty of stealing gas or water.

- The second is services. Things like a bus ride or a train journey are not property for the purposes of theft. So if Derek goes to a hairdresser's and has his haircut, but never has any intention of paying, he cannot be guilty of stealing the haircut. In a situation like this another property offence should be used instead.[3]

- The third is confidential information. In *Oxford v Moss* (1978) 68 Cr App R 183 the defendant was a university student named Paul Moss. Before his exams took place Moss somehow managed to get hold of one of the exam papers. He read it, and then put it back where it belonged. Moss was charged with theft of confidential information. The issue for the Divisional Court was whether confidential information constitutes property for the purposes of theft. The Court held that it does not.

In the vast majority of problem questions deciding whether or not the item was property will be straightforward. Occasionally, however, there are borderline cases. In these instances you will need to consider whether or not the case involves property in greater detail.

The first borderline case involves wild mushrooms, flowers, fruit and foliage. These cases are governed by section 4(3).

## EXTRACT

According to this subsection, a person can only be guilty of stealing wild mushrooms, flowers, fruit or foliage in what circumstances?

### Section 4(3) of the Theft Act 1968

(3)   A person who picks mushrooms growing wild on any land, or who picks flowers, fruit or foliage from a plant growing wild on any land, does not (although not in possession of the land) steal what he picks, unless he does it for reward or for sale or other commercial purpose.

For purposes of this subsection "mushroom" includes any fungus, and "plant" includes any shrub or tree.

The second borderline case involves wild creatures. These cases are governed by section 4(4).

---

[3]In Derek's case the offence of fraud by false representation could apply. By asking the hairdresser to cut his hair Derek impliedly represented that he would pay for the service and this was a false representation of his intentions (see the discussion of this offence later in the chapter). Another possible offence is making off without payment (which can be found in section 3 of the Theft Act 1978).

## EXTRACT

According to this subsection, when can a person be found guilty of stealing a wild creature? Can you think of an example of when section 4(4) might apply?

## Section 4(4) of the Theft Act 1968

(4) Wild creatures, tamed or untamed, shall be regarded as property; but a person cannot steal a wild creature not tamed nor ordinarily kept in captivity, or the carcase of any such creature, unless either it has been reduced into possession by or on behalf of another person and possession of it has not since been lost or abandoned, or another person is in course of reducing it into possession.

The third borderline case is human body parts. In *R v Kelly* [1999] QB 621 the defendant, Anthony Kelly, was an artist. He asked another man named Neil Lindsay, who worked as a junior technician at the Royal College of Surgeons, to give him a number of body parts from the college. These included three heads, six arms (or parts of an arm) and ten legs (or parts of a leg). Kelly used these to make casts, some of which were exhibited in an art gallery. Kelly and Lindsay were convicted of theft of the body parts. On appeal, one of the issues for the Court of Appeal was whether the body parts were property under the section 4 definition.

## EXTRACT

Read the following extract from the judgment of Rose LJ. Is the general rule: that a corpse (or a part of a corpse) is property or that a corpse (or a part of a corpse) is not property? What are the exceptions to this general rule?

Were the body parts that Kelly and Lindsay took property or not?

## *R v Kelly* [1999] QB 621

### Rose LJ

We return to the first question, that is to say whether or not a corpse or part of a corpse is property. We accept that, however questionable the historical origins of the principle, it has now been the common law for 150 years at least that neither a corpse nor parts of a corpse are in themselves and without more capable of being property protected by rights [...]

If that principle is now to be changed, in our view, it must be by Parliament, because it has been express or implicit in all the subsequent authorities and writings to which we have been referred that a corpse or part of it cannot be stolen.

To address the point as it was addressed before the trial judge and to which his certificate relates, in our judgment, parts of a corpse are capable of being property within section 4 of the Theft Act 1968 if they have acquired different attributes by virtue of the application of skill, such as dissection or preservation techniques, for exhibition or teaching purposes [...]

Furthermore, the common law does not stand still. It may be that if, on some future occasion, the question arises, the courts will hold that human body parts are capable of being property for the purposes of section 4, even without the acquisition of different attributes, if they have a use or significance beyond their mere existence. This may be so if, for example, they are intended for use in an organ transplant operation, for the extraction of DNA or, for that matter, as an exhibit in a trial

Since the decision in *R v Kelly* the Court of Appeal has held, in *Yearworth and others v North Bristol NHS Trust* [2010] QB 1, that frozen sperm stored in a sperm bank constitutes property. In this case, six men who had been diagnosed with cancer provided samples of semen before starting chemotherapy in case they wanted to father children in the future. However, as a result of the defendant's negligence, the semen perished. The men brought a civil action for negligence. One of the issues for the Court of Appeal was whether the sperm was property which belonged to the men. The Court held that it was. Importantly, the Court queried the traditional common law approach that was applied in *R v Kelly*. Instead of applying the principles outlined in *R v Kelly*, the Court emphasised that the sperm was the product of the men's bodies and that the sole purpose for which they had ejaculated it was so that it could be stored and later used for their benefit. The Court thus concluded that 'for the purposes of their claims in negligence, the men had ownership of the sperm which they ejaculated'. This suggests that in future cases the courts will be more willing to decide that people have property rights in their bodily parts and products.

## 2. The property belonged to another person

The second requirement for the offence of theft is that the property belonged to another person. The word 'belong' is defined in section 5(1) of the Theft Act 1968:

### EXTRACT

### Section 5(1) of the Theft Act 1968

#### 5 "Belonging to another"

(1) Property shall be regarded as belonging to any person having possession or control of it, or having in it any proprietary right or interest (not being an equitable interest arising only from an agreement to transfer or grant an interest).

To fully grasp the significance of this definition, it is important to understand the following two points:

- Section 5(1) gives the word belong a far broader meaning than ownership. For the purposes of the offence of theft, property can belong to someone other than the actual owner. Section 5(1) says that property belongs to anyone who has 'possession or control' of the property and to anyone that has 'any proprietary right or interest' in it. As we saw earlier in *R v Smith*, the person's possession of the property does not have to be lawful. Smith was guilty of stealing the heroin from Jordan even though Jordan's possession of the drug was unlawful.

  (Notice that there is one exception contained in the brackets at the end of section 5(1): property does not belong to somebody who only has an equitable interest arising only from an agreement to transfer or grant an interest. This is quite a specific exception which is best explained using an illustration. Suppose that Derek agrees to sell his car to Aubrey. Under the contract of sale Derek is due to transfer the car to Aubrey in one week's time. But a few days later, before ownership is transferred, Derek sells the car to somebody else. Although Aubrey had an equitable interest in Derek's car, arising from the contract of sale, the car did not belong to Aubrey for the purposes of theft.)

● Since the section 5(1) definition is broader than ownership, it follows that property can belong to more than one person at a time. Suppose Derek lends Rodney his iPad. Rodney takes it to the pub with him, and is showing Mickey a video on YouTube when someone snatches the iPad from Mickey's hands and runs off with it. In this scenario the iPad belonged to Mickey (he had control of it), Rodney (he had possession of it) and Derek (as owner, he had proprietary rights in it).

One question which the courts have had to address is whether property can belong to someone even though they are unaware that the property exists! This question arose in *R v Woodman* [1974] QB 754. A company called English China Clays owned a factory. In 1970 the business closed down and the factory shut. At this time there was a large quantity of scrap metal on the factory site, so English China Clays sold this scrap metal to the Bird Group of companies. People from the Bird Group came to the factory site and removed most of the scrap metal. They left some of the scrap metal behind because it was difficult to access, and they decided that it was not worth the cost of recovering it. After this English China Clays put a barbed wire fence around the site and put up a number of signs saying things like 'Private Property', 'Keep out' and 'Trespassers will be prosecuted'. The site then wound down and remained disused for two years.

In 1973 the defendant, George Woodman, turned up at the site in a van. He helped himself to all of the scrap metal that had been left behind (weighing more than one tonne). At trial he was convicted of stealing the scrap metal from English China Clays. He appealed, arguing that the scrap metal did not belong to English China Clays. The Court of Appeal agreed that English China Clays no longer had *ownership* of the scrap metal. The key question, in terms of the section 5(1) definition, was whether they had *possession or control* of it.

## EXTRACT

Read the following extract from the judgment of Lord Widgery CJ. Did English China Clays have possession or control of the scrap metal? What reasons does Lord Widgery CJ give for the decision?

### *R v Woodman* [1974] QB 754

#### Lord Widgery CJ

We have formed the view without difficulty that [...] there was ample evidence that English China Clays were in control of the site and had taken considerable steps to exclude trespassers as demonstrating the fact that they were in control of the site, and we think that in ordinary and straightforward cases if it is once established that a particular person is in control of a site such as this, then prima facie he is in control of articles which are on that site.

[...]

So far as this case is concerned, arising as it does under the Theft Act 1968, we are content to say that there was evidence of English China Clays being in control of the site and prima facie in control of articles upon the site as well. The fact that it could not be shown that they were conscious of the existence of this or any particular scrap iron does not destroy the general principle that control of a site by excluding others from it is prima facie control of articles on the site as well.

Following *R v Woodman* another question has arisen: when will property be regarded as abandoned and ownerless? The issue of abandonment was considered in *Ricketts v Basildon Magistrates' Court* [2010] EWHC 2358 (Admin). In the early hours of the morning Robert Ricketts went to two charity shops. At the first shop, which belonged to the British Heart Foundation, he took some bags that had been left outside by donors. At the second shop, which belonged to Oxfam, he took some bags of items which had been placed in bins at the rear of the shop. Ricketts said that he had planned to sell the items he had taken at a car boot sale. He was charged with theft. At Ricketts' committal hearing he argued that there was no evidence that was capable of supporting a charge of theft. The Magistrates' Court rejected this claim and committed Ricketts to the Crown Court to stand trial. Ricketts then sought judicial review of the Magistrates' decision. The issue for the court was whether there was any evidence that the bags that Ricketts took belonged to another person.

## EXTRACT

In the following extract from the Court's judgment, Wyn Williams J looks at each charge of theft in turn. First, he considers the alleged theft of the bags from outside the British Heart Foundation shop. Had these bags been abandoned? If not, whom did they belong to for the purposes of the offence of theft?

He then considers the alleged theft of the bags from the rear of the Oxfam shop. Had these bags been abandoned? If not, whom did they belong to for the purposes of the offence of theft?

### *Ricketts v Basildon Magistrates' Court* [2010] EWHC 2358 (Admin)

#### Wyn Williams J

12 In my judgment it cannot be said that the British Heart Foundation acquired possession of the items or assumed control of them or even acquired a proprietary interest in them simply by virtue of the fact that they were left in close proximity to the shop.

13 However, it is clearly the case, in my judgment, that it was open to the court to infer that the items had not been abandoned. The obvious inference on the bare facts before the justices was that persons unknown had intended the goods to be a gift to the British Heart Foundation. Those persons had an intention to give; they had also attempted to effect delivery. Delivery would be complete, however, only when the British Heart Foundation took possession of the items. Until that time, although the unknown would-be donor had divested himself of possession of the items, he had not given up his ownership of the items [...]

14 In my judgment the above analysis shows that it was open to the court to conclude that there was evidence from which a court could properly determine that the property belonged to another at the time of appropriation by the claimant. That being the case, in my judgment, the claimant was properly committed on that charge for trial. It will obviously be a matter for the prosecution to consider how best to frame the indictment when the claimant is actually indicted in the Crown Court.

15 I turn to the charge alleging theft from Oxfam since it is somewhat different on the facts. The claimant admits that the items taken from Oxfam were items which had been placed in bins in close proximity to the rear of the shop. In my judgment, it would be open to a court to infer either that would-be donors had placed the items in the bins for receipt by Oxfam or that employees of Oxfam had placed the items in the bins for onward disposal by the local authority. This analysis assumes of course that the bins belonged to or were controlled by Oxfam, which is not presently disputed.

16 Upon that assumption it would be open to a court to infer that Oxfam had taken delivery of the items once placed within the bins. Alternatively, it could infer that Oxfam had taken possession of the items and had then placed them in the bins for disposal. Either way, Oxfam were in possession of the items at the time of the appropriation by the claimant.

17 I am also of the view that it would be open to the court to conclude that the bins were controlled by Oxfam even if this is disputed. The bins were in close proximity to the rear of the premises. That of itself, in my judgment, raises a permissible inference, in the absence of any other evidence, that the bins were under the control of Oxfam. In any event, if the prosecutor so chooses he or she can allege in the indictment in the Crown Court that the property belongs to a person unknown. That cannot be objectionable for the reasons I have given earlier in this judgment.

So in Ricketts' case none of the bags had been abandoned. Similarly, when you put your bin bags full of rubbish outside your house on collection day you do not abandon them. You put them outside your house so that an authorised refuse collector can come and collect them. By placing them outside, you are not inviting all-comers to rummage through your rubbish and help themselves to anything they like. In other words, until your bin bags are collected you continue to exercise some rights over them. You have not abandoned the bin bags, because you have not relinquished all of your rights over them. This is the test for whether property has been abandoned: has the owner intentionally relinquished all of her rights over the property?

There is also an important distinction between property that is lost and property that has been abandoned. Suppose that Derek drops his wallet in the high street while he is out shopping. Later that day, when he realises, he goes back to the high street and searches for his wallet but cannot find it. Reluctantly, he admits defeat and gives up the search. In this scenario Derek has lost his wallet but has not abandoned it because he did not intentionally relinquish all of his rights over it.

The next question to consider is whether the owner of an item of property can be guilty of stealing his own property. This was the issue in *R v Turner (No 2)* [1971] 1 WLR 901. The defendant, Frank Turner, took his car to Arthur Brown's garage for repairs. When Brown told Turner that the car was ready to be collected Turner said that he would pick the car up and pay for the repairs the following day. That evening Brown parked the car on a street outside the garage but kept the key in his office. The next day the key was still there but the car had disappeared. Turner had taken the car away using a spare key. He was charged with theft of the car and was convicted at trial. He subsequently appealed, arguing that he could not be guilty of theft since the car belonged to him and not to Brown. The Court of Appeal dismissed Turner's appeal and upheld his conviction.

Whilst most commentators agree that the outcome in *R v Turner (No 2)* was the correct one, the reasoning has been strongly criticised.[4] In order to understand this criticism, it is helpful to compare *R v Turner (No 2)* with another case, *R v Meredith* [1973] Crim LR 253. Meredith left his car parked in a street while he went to watch a football match. The car was causing an obstruction, so the police removed it and took it to a police pound. After the match had finished Meredith sneaked into the police pound and surreptitiously removed the car. Two days later the police caught up with him and charged him with theft of the car from the police. In the Crown Court Judge Da Cunha held that Meredith could not be convicted of theft, since the police had no right to retain possession of the car. Had Meredith reported to the police station as he should have done he would have had to choose whether to pay the fine or face prosecution. However, whichever of these he chose, the police would have had to return the car to him. Since the police had no right to retain possession of the car, Meredith could not be guilty of stealing the car from them.

So Turner was guilty of stealing his car from Arthur Brown, but Meredith was not guilty of stealing his car from the police. The key to reconciling these cases is a right known as a lien. A lien is a right to retain possession of an item of property until payment has been received. In Turner's case Arthur Brown had a lien. He had a right to retain possession of Turner's car until Turner paid for the repairs. By contrast, in Meredith's case the police had no lien. They had no right to retain possession of Meredith's car. The crucial difference between the cases is thus that in *R v Turner (No 2)* there was a lien whereas in *R v Meredith* there was not. Unfortunately, however, the trial judge in *R v Turner (No 2)* told the jury that it was irrelevant whether Brown had had a lien or not. Yet in spite of this the Court of Appeal upheld Turner's conviction.

One further point to note from the decisions in *R v Turner (No 2)* and *R v Meredith*: whether or not an item of property belongs to someone for the purposes of theft can depend on who it was that appropriated the property! We have seen that in *R v Meredith* when Meredith was charged with theft the car was held not to belong to the police. But suppose that a stranger had crept into the police pound and taken the car, not Meredith. On these facts the stranger would be guilty of stealing the car from the police, because the police would have a right to retain possession against the stranger. So whether or not the car belonged to the police for the purposes of theft depends on who the alleged thief is! This highlights how important it is in problem questions to clearly identify the particulars of the alleged offence before embarking on your analysis.

Finally, note that sections 5(3) and 5(4) deal with two specific scenarios:[5]

### EXTRACT

### Sections 5(3) and 5(4) of the Theft Act 1968

(3)  Where a person receives property from or on account of another, and is under an obligation to the other to retain and deal with that property or its proceeds in a particular way, the property or proceeds shall be regarded (as against him) as belonging to the other.

---

[4]See, for example, Simester, A.P., Spencer, J.R., Stark, F., Sullivan, G.R. & Virgo, G.J. (2016) *Simester and Sullivan's Criminal Law: Theory and Doctrine* (6th edn), Oxford: Hart Publishing, p515–516, and Ormerod, D. & Laird, K. (2015) *Smith and Hogan's Criminal Law* (14th edn) Oxford: OUP, p919–920.
[5]Section 5(2) also deals with a specific scenario: cases involving trusts with no individual beneficiary with an equitable interest in the trust (e.g. a charitable trust).

(4)   Where a person gets property by another's mistake, and is under an obligation to make restoration (in whole or in part) of the property or its proceeds or of the value thereof, then to the extent of that obligation the property or proceeds shall be regarded (as against him) as belonging to the person entitled to restoration, and an intention not to make restoration shall be regarded accordingly as an intention to deprive that person of the property or proceeds.

For section 5(3) to apply the obligation to deal with the property in a particular way must be a legal, not merely a moral, obligation.[6] An example would be where Rodney gives his housemate Derek money to pay the gas bill, but instead Derek goes to the pub and spends the money on expensive drinks. On these facts Derek had a legal obligation to deal with the money or its proceeds 'in a particular way', and so for the purposes of theft the money is regarded as belonging to Rodney.[7]

Section 5(4) deals with property received by mistake. Like section 5(3), the obligation to return the property must be a legal, not merely a moral, obligation.[8] An example of when section 5(4) would apply is where Derek receives his wages and realises that he has been overpaid by £100. Although the money is now in Derek's bank account he has an obligation to repay his employers and so if he dishonestly decides to keep the money he commits theft.[9]

## 3. The defendant appropriated the property

The third requirement for the offence of theft is that the defendant appropriated the property. The word 'appropriates' is defined in section 3(1):

> ### EXTRACT
>
> ### Section 3(1) of the Theft Act 1968
>
> ### 3 "Appropriates"
>
> (1)   Any assumption by a person of the rights of an owner amounts to an appropriation, and this includes, where he has come by the property (innocently or not) without stealing it, any later assumption of a right to it by keeping or dealing with it as owner.

The key words are the opening ones: an appropriation is 'any assumption by a person of the rights of an owner'. These words have generated a series of four important House of Lords cases, which focus on two questions: Is it enough to show an assumption of any of the rights of an owner, or is it necessary to show an assumption of all of the rights of an owner? And, can there be an appropriation if the owner consented to the assumption of the rights? We will look at each of these questions in turn.

---

[6]*R v Foster* [2011] EWCA Crim 1192.

[7]*Davidge v Bunnett* [1984] Crim LR 297. Whether or not the parties intended to create a legal obligation is a question of fact. So, for example, if our example involved members of the same family section 5(3) may well not apply since family members would presumably not intend to create a legally binding arrangement: see *R v Cullen* (1974, unreported, no 968/c/74).

[8]*R v Gilks* [1972] 1 WLR 1341.

[9]See *Attorney-General's Reference (No 1 of 1983)* [1985] QB 182.

### i. Is it enough to show an assumption of any of the rights of an owner, or is it necessary to show an assumption of all of the rights of an owner?

The owner of an item has numerous rights. For example, an owner has the right to use the item, the right to sell the item and the right to destroy it. For this reason ownership is often described as a bundle of rights. The first question which the House of Lords has had to consider is whether, in order to establish an appropriation, it is necessary to show that the defendant assumed *all* of these rights or whether it is sufficient that he assumed *any* of these rights.

This question was first considered in *R v Morris* [1984] AC 320. This case involved two separate appeals, one from David Morris and the other from James Burnside. The case involved the switching of price labels in supermarkets (the case occurred in the days before barcodes!). Morris had entered a supermarket and swapped the price labels on two products so that he would be charged a lower price for the item he wished to buy. At the checkout he paid the lower price, and was then arrested. The only difference in Burnside's case was that he was arrested at the checkout but before he had paid for the item. Both men were convicted of theft and both appealed, arguing that there was no appropriation. The case reached the House of Lords.

---

**EXTRACT**

Read the following extract from the judgment of Lord Roskill. For an appropriation, is it enough to show an assumption of any of the rights of an owner? Or is it necessary to show an assumption of all of the rights of an owner?

### *R v Morris* [1984] AC 320

#### Lord Roskill

Mr. Denison [counsel for the defendants] submitted that the phrase in section 3(1) "any assumption by a person of *the rights*" (my emphasis) "of an owner amounts to an appropriation" must mean any assumption of "*all* the rights of an owner." Since neither respondent had at the time of the removal of the goods from the shelves and of the label switching assumed *all* the rights of the owner, there was no appropriation and therefore no theft. Mr. Jeffreys for the prosecution, on the other hand, contended that *the* rights in this context only meant *any* of the rights. An owner of goods has many rights – they have been described as "a bundle or package of rights." Mr. Jeffreys contended that on a fair reading of the subsection it cannot have been the intention that every one of an owner's rights had to be assumed by the alleged thief before an appropriation was proved and that essential ingredient of the offence of theft established.

My Lords, if one reads the words "the rights" at the opening of section 3(1) literally and in isolation from the rest of the section, Mr. Denison's submission undoubtedly has force. But the later words "any later assumption of a right" in subsection (1) and the words in subsection (2) "no later assumption by him of rights" seem to me to militate strongly against the correctness of the submission. Moreover the provisions of section 2(1)(a) also seem to point in the same direction. It follows therefore that it is enough for the prosecution if they have proved in these cases the assumption by the respondents of any of the rights of the owner of the goods in question

This decision means that the concept of appropriation has a wide scope. It was not necessary for the prosecution to show that Morris and Burnside had assumed all of the rights of an owner. It was enough that they had assumed any of the rights of an owner. It is an owner's right to fix a price label to a supermarket item, so by switching the price labels Morris and Burnside assumed this right. Switching the labels therefore amounted to the *actus reus* of theft. Moreover, since Morris and Burnside had the *mens rea* of theft when they switched the labels the offence was complete at this moment. It did not matter that they had not left the shop with the items. Nor did it matter that Burnside had not yet paid the lower price at the checkout. Both men were guilty of theft as soon as they switched the labels.

The decision in *R v Morris* was controversial. It has been described as 'depressing',[10] 'obviously wrong'[11] and 'at variance with the plain words of the statute'.[12] Yet in the subsequent case *DPP v Gomez* [1993] AC 442 a majority of the House of Lords held that the decision in *R v Morris* was correct on this point.[13] On behalf of the majority, Lord Keith stated:

> In my opinion Lord Roskill was undoubtedly right when he said [...] that the assumption by the defendant of any of the rights of an owner could amount to an appropriation within the meaning of section 3(1), and that the removal of an article from the shelf and the changing of the price label on it constituted the assumption of one of the rights of the owner and hence an appropriation within the meaning of the subsection

We will examine the implications of this in more detail shortly.

### ii. Can there be an appropriation if the owner consented to the assumption of the rights?

The second question the House of Lords has had to consider is whether an action can amount to an appropriation if the owner consented to it. The first case in which this was addressed was *Lawrence v MPC* [1972] AC 626. An Italian man named Eugenio Occhi arrived at Victoria Station on his first visit to England. He spoke little English. The defendant, Alan Lawrence, was a taxi driver. Occhi showed Lawrence a piece of paper with an address written on it. Lawrence said it was very far away and very expensive. Occhi got into the taxi, gave Lawrence £1 and then held his wallet open while Lawrence took another £6 from it. Lawrence then drove Occhi to the address. The correct fare was less than £1. At trial Lawrence was convicted of theft of the £6. He appealed, arguing that he had not appropriated the £6 because Occhi had allowed him to take it. The issue for the House of Lords was whether an action can amount to an appropriation if it was consensual.

---

[10]Spencer, J. (1984) 'Theft – Appropriation and Consent' 43 *Cambridge Law Journal* 7, 10.

[11]Ormerod, D. & Laird, K. (2015) *Smith and Hogan's Criminal Law* (14th edn) Oxford: OUP, p893.

[12]Simester, A.P., Spencer, J.R., Stark, F., Sullivan, G.R. & Virgo, G.J. (2016) *Simester and Sullivan's Criminal Law: Theory and Doctrine* (6th edn) Oxford: Hart Publishing, p534.

[13]In his dissenting judgment Lord Lowry stated: '"the rights" may mean "*all* the rights," which would be the normal grammatical meaning, or (less probably, in my opinion) "*any* rights" [...] Still looking at section 3(1), I point out that "any later assumption of a right to it" (that is, a right to the property) amounts to an appropriation of a right to it and that normally "a right to it" means a right *to* the property and not a right *in* it' (emphasis original).

## EXTRACT

According to the following extract from the judgment of Viscount Dilhorne, can there be an appropriation if the owner consented to the assumption of the rights?

### *Lawrence v MPC* [1972] AC 626

### Viscount Dilhorne

Prior to the passage of the Theft Act 1968, which made radical changes in and greatly simplified the law relating to theft and some other offences, it was necessary to prove that the property alleged to have been stolen was taken "without the consent of the owner" (Larceny Act 1916, section 1 (1)).

These words are not included in section 1 (1) of the Theft Act, but the appellant contended that the subsection should be construed as if they were, as if they appeared after the word "appropriates." Section 1 (1) reads as follows:

"A person is guilty of theft if he dishonestly appropriates property belonging to another with the intention of permanently depriving the other of it; and 'thief' and 'steal' shall be construed accordingly."

I see no ground for concluding that the omission of the words "without the consent of the owner" was inadvertent and not deliberate, and to read the subsection as if they were included is, in my opinion, wholly unwarranted. Parliament by the omission of these words has relieved the prosecution of the burden of establishing that the taking was without the owner's consent. That is no longer an ingredient of the offence.

[...]

That there was appropriation in this case is clear. Section 3 (1) states that any assumption by a person of the rights of an owner amounts to an appropriation. Here there was clearly such an assumption

Following the judgment in *Lawrence v MPC* the position was clear. Just over a decade later, however, things were complicated by the House of Lords' decision in *R v Morris*. In his judgment in this case Lord Roskill discussed whether or not the honest shopper appropriates items when she takes them off the supermarket shelf and places them in her trolley. The prosecutor in the case argued that this does amount to an appropriation. In response Lord Roskill stated:

With the utmost respect, I cannot accept this statement as correct. If one postulates an honest customer taking goods from a shelf to put in his or her trolley to take to the checkpoint there to pay the proper price, I am unable to see that any of these actions involves any assumption by the shopper of the rights of the supermarket. In the context of section 3(1), the concept of appropriation in my view involves not an act expressly or impliedly authorised by the owner but an act by way of adverse interference with or usurpation of those rights. When the honest shopper acts as I have just described, he or she is acting with the implied authority of the owner of the supermarket to take the goods from the shelf, put them in the trolley, take them to the checkpoint and there pay the correct price, at which moment the property in the goods will pass to the shopper for the first time. It is with the consent of the owners of the supermarket, be that consent express or implied, that the shopper does these acts and thus obtains at least control if not actual possession of the goods preparatory, at a later stage, to obtaining the property in them upon payment of the proper amount at the checkpoint. I do not think that section 3(1) envisages any such act as an "appropriation," whatever may be the meaning of that word in other fields such as contract or sale of goods law.

Lord Roskill's comments contradicted the decision in *Lawrence v MPC*. In *Lawrence v MPC* the House of Lords had said that it is irrelevant whether or not the owner consented to the action. The sole question is whether the defendant assumed the rights of an owner. But in the passage from *R v Morris* above Lord Roskill says that an action cannot amount to an appropriation if it was 'expressly or impliedly authorised by the owner'. Importantly, however, Lord Roskill's comments were *obiter dicta* since the owner of the property in *R v Morris* had not consented to the act in question (swapping price labels). In *Lawrence v MPC*, by contrast, Viscount Dilhorne's comments were part of the *ratio decidendi* of the case, since Occhi had consented to Lawrence taking the money from his wallet.

This conflict between *Lawrence v MPC* and *R v Morris* was resolved by the House of Lords in *DPP v Gomez* [1993] AC 442. The defendant in this case, Edwin Gomez, was assistant manager of an electrical goods shop. He formed a plan with his friend Jit Ballay. Ballay placed an order for £7,950 worth of goods and paid using a stolen building society cheque. When Gomez went to his manager to ask him to authorise the transaction he told his manager that he had checked with the bank that the cheque was acceptable and that the cheque was 'as good as cash'. A few days later Ballay collected the goods and Gomez helped him load them into his car. Shortly afterwards Ballay placed a second order – this time for £9,250 worth of goods – and Gomez did the same thing again. Later the bank returned the two cheques and informed the shop manager that they were stolen. At trial Gomez was convicted on two counts of theft. He appealed, arguing that there had been no appropriation since the shop manager had consented to the goods being handed over. The case reached the House of Lords. The majority judgment was delivered by Lord Keith (Lord Lowry dissented).

## EXTRACT

Read the following extract from the judgment of Lord Keith. Did he follow *Lawrence v MPC* or *R v Morris*?

Following *DPP v Gomez*, can there be an appropriation if the owner consented to the assumption of the rights?

### *DPP v Gomez* [1993] AC 442

#### Lord Keith

The actual decision in *Morris* was correct, but it was erroneous, in addition to being unnecessary for the decision, to indicate that an act expressly or impliedly authorised by the owner could never amount to an appropriation [...] *Lawrence* makes it clear that consent to or authorisation by the owner of the taking by the rogue is irrelevant. The taking amounted to an appropriation within the meaning of section 1(1) of the Act of 1968. *Lawrence* also makes it clear that it is no less irrelevant that what happened may also have constituted the offence of obtaining property by deception under section 15(1) of the Act.

The decision in *Lawrence* was a clear decision of this House upon the construction of the word "appropriate" in section 1(1) of the Act, which had stood for 12 years when doubt was thrown upon it by obiter dicta in *Morris*. *Lawrence* must be regarded as authoritative and correct, and there is no question of it now being right to depart from it.

In his dissenting judgment, Lord Lowry argued that the majority's decision was at odds with the basic meaning of 'appropriate':

The ordinary and natural meaning of "appropriate" is to take for oneself, or to treat as one's own, property which belongs to someone else. The primary dictionary meaning is "take possession of, take to oneself, especially without authority," and that is in my opinion the meaning which the word bears in section 1(1). The act of appropriating property is a one-sided act, done without the consent or authority of the owner. And, if the owner consents to transfer property to the offender or to a third party, the offender does not appropriate the property, even if the owner's consent has been obtained by fraud

Lord Lowry then went on to examine the 1966 report of the Criminal Law Revision Committee (CLRC),[14] on which the Theft Act 1968 was based. He explained that the Committee had intended the word 'appropriation' to mean an unauthorised usurpation of another's property rights. This was designed to maintain a distinction between the offence of theft and the offence of obtaining property by deception (which, as we'll see later in the chapter, has since been replaced by the offence of fraud – but the point still applies). The majority, however, declined to consider the CLRC's report. Lord Keith stated that to do so would serve 'no useful purpose'.

So following *DPP v Gomez* the answers to our two questions are clear. It is not necessary to show that the defendant assumed all of the rights of an owner. Nor is it necessary to show that the assumption of the rights was non-consensual. This means that the legal test for an appropriation is quite straightforward. The question is simply: did the defendant assume any of the rights of an owner (regardless of consent)?

But whilst the decision in *DPP v Gomez* produces clarity, it has been heavily criticised for a number of other reasons. The first reason is that it defines the concept of appropriation too broadly. The second is that it collapses the distinction between theft and deception/fraud offences. The third is that theft now encompasses many situations which should be regarded as criminal attempts. And finally, it produces a conflict between the civil and criminal laws. We will look at each of these criticisms of *DPP v Gomez* in turn.

### The breadth of the definition of an appropriation

Following the House of Lords' decision in *DPP v Gomez* Sir John Smith commented that the decision 'reduces the *actus reus* of theft almost to vanishing point'.[15] Suppose that Aubrey decides to buy an expensive bottle of champagne to impress the guests at his dinner party. He goes to the supermarket, finds the alcohol aisle and picks up the most

---

[14]*Theft and Related Offences* (1966) Cmnd 2977.
[15]Smith, J.C. (1993) 'Commentary on *R v Gomez*' *Criminal Law Review* 305, 306.

expensive bottle he can find. Meanwhile another shopper, Derek, has decided to steal a bottle of champagne from the same supermarket. Derek enters the store, walks to the alcohol aisle and picks up the most expensive bottle of champagne he can find. On these facts, both Aubrey and Derek have committed an appropriation. By picking the bottle up they assumed a right of an owner. Following *DPP v Gomez*, it is not necessary to assume *all* of the rights of an owner, and it is irrelevant that the supermarket gives its consent to shoppers picking items up. So in both Aubrey's case and Derek's case there is the *actus reus* of theft. They both appropriated property belonging to another.

The fact that there is the *actus reus* of theft in Aubrey's case illustrates just how broad the definition of appropriation is. Aubrey had not done anything that was wrongful or that caused harm to the supermarket. In fact, he was going to pay for the champagne! For his conduct to amount to the *actus reus* of theft is very difficult to reconcile with the harm principle (see Chapter 1), which states that only harmful wrongdoing should be criminalised.

In fact, if we focus solely on their conduct, Derek did nothing different to Aubrey. He picked a bottle of champagne up off the shelf, just as Aubrey did. Yet Derek is guilty of theft, because at the moment he picked the bottle up he had the *mens rea* of theft. In this sense, the decision in *DPP v Gomez* renders theft little more than a thought crime. A defendant like Derek can be guilty of theft, even though his conduct is no different from that of other citizens, simply on the basis of his guilty mind at the time.

### The distinction between the offence of theft and the offence of fraud

Think back to the facts of *DPP v Gomez*. At first, it looks like a straightforward example of a deception/fraud offence. Gomez lied to the shop manager in order to trick him into handing over the goods. Yet Gomez was convicted not of a deception offence but theft, and the House of Lords upheld this conviction. The Lords acknowledged that the result of this was a significant overlap between the offences of theft and obtaining property by deception (note that the offence of obtaining property by deception has now been replaced by the offence of fraud – but the same point still applies). This overlap between theft and the deception/fraud offences has been criticised by a number of commentators. One example is Christopher Clarkson's piece 'Theft and Fair Labelling'.

## EXTRACT

Read the following extract from Clarkson's commentary. Think back to the principles we studied in Chapter 1. Which of these principles is Clarkson's argument based on? What reasons does Clarkson give for the importance of this principle?

According to Clarkson, what are the key differences between theft and deception/fraud offences? Why does fair labelling require this distinction?

### Clarkson, C. (1993) 'Theft and Fair Labelling' 56 *Modern Law Review* 554

The House of Lords in *DPP v Gomez* has largely collapsed the distinction between theft and obtaining property by deception by holding that an authorised act can amount to an appropriation. Lord Keith (with whom three other Lords agreed) makes no argument for this extraordinary conclusion other than to say that Lawrence is a "clear decision" which has "stood for 12 years" and that "there is no question of it now being right to depart from it." [...]

Criminal offences should accurately describe the prohibited conduct as far as possible. English law has chosen to reject the plea for a single offence of homicide. Even those arguing for the abolition of the mandatory life sentence for murder would retain the separate offences of murder and manslaughter. Similarly, arguments for abandoning the distinction between rape and indecent assault and replacing them with a broad offence of sexual assault have been resisted. The reasons for this are clear. Offences should be structured, labelled and punished to reflect the extent of wrongdoing and/or harm involved. Criminal offences are categorised for symbolic reasons. It is to communicate the differing degrees of rejection or unacceptability of different types of conduct. Such symbolic messages are not conveyed by the creation of broad morally uninformative labels such as "unlawful homicide." Further, such broadly defined offences increase the discretionary powers of the law enforcement agencies and the judges in sentencing, and infringe what Ashworth has called "the principle of maximum certainty." Increased efforts to control or structure such discretionary powers would be thwarted by the introduction of over-broad substantive offences.

Turning to the property offences, all of which share the same concern, namely, the protection of a variety of interests in property, English law has sought to maintain clear distinctions between the various offences in an effort to mark the different wrongs and harms involved therein. For example, robbery, burglary and handling stolen goods are clearly differentiated for obvious reasons. The various offences of deception are perhaps most clearly related to theft. In both theft and obtaining property by deception, the owner has lost property to another – but it is the method of losing such property that marks the moral distinction between the two.

[...]

The paradigmatic theft involves a surreptitious or forcible taking, while deception offences involve a confrontation and a participation by the victim in the loss of the property. With theft, the owner is generally helpless against such a taking. If interrupted there is a risk of violence. With the typical obtaining, the victim has a real opportunity to prevent the commission of the crime. With greater alertness he or she might not have been deceived. He or she has agreed to part with the property. In our society, where mutual transactions based on trust are valued and encouraged, the wrong of *deceiving* another into parting with property is a distinctive wrong – quite different in quality from the paradigmatic theft. Shute and Horder are right to conclude that whereas "the thief makes war on a social practice from the outside, the deceiver is the traitor within."

[...]

Parliament has enacted separate penalties for theft (seven years) and obtaining by deception (ten years), underlining the moral distinction between the two [the penalty for fraud is also ten years]. It is lamentable that the majority in *Gomez* should have brazenly ignored this [...] Urgent statutory reform is imperative. A new definition of theft or appropriation is called for. In devising a new formula, the legislature needs to keep firmly in mind the necessity for clear differentiation between morally distinguishable offences and a definition of theft should be devised that is consistent with the theft paradigm

On this view, the House of Lords in *DPP v Gomez* should have held that there can only be an appropriation if the assumption of the owner's rights took place without the owner's consent. Cases in which the owner was tricked into consenting should be prosecuted using the deception (or, today, fraud) offences.

However, not all commentators agree with this criticism of the decision in *DPP v Gomez*. In the following extract from his provocatively titled note 'Thief or Swindler: Who

Cares?' Peter Glazebrook argues that it is mistaken to try and draw a 'trivial and morally irrelevant' distinction between theft and deception/fraud offences.

What reasons does Glazebrook give for rejecting the argument that a distinction should be drawn between theft and the deception/fraud offences?

### Glazebrook, P. (1991) 'Thief or Swindler: Who Cares?' 50 *Cambridge Law Journal* 389

[In *Lawrence v MPC* the House of Lords] held that though property had been, or might have been, obtained by deception the crook could still be convicted of theft for there was nothing in the definition of stealing in section 1 of the 1968 Act that required the courts to make the trivial and morally irrelevant distinction between someone who dishonestly appropriated another's property by stealth, and one who did so by deceit. The crook is as dishonest in the one case as the other, and the gain to him, and the loss to his victim, is exactly the same. In plain English, a person who obtains another's property by deception appropriates property belonging to another – indeed he plainly misappropriates it – and in *Lawrence* the House of Lords ruled emphatically that the courts should not write into the Theft Act restrictive or qualifying words that are not there. It would certainly be bizarre if a defendant who appropriated property he had received because the transferor had made a mistake to which the defendant had not contributed were guilty of theft (as he is: s. 5(4)), but was not guilty if the property had come to him because of a mistake which he had deliberately induced.

What is more, it may be either difficult to decide, or the merest matter of chance, whether the crook had resorted to deception in order to get his sticky mits on to the property he coveted. In *Lawrence* it would have been as difficult as it would have been pointless to set about deciding whether the travel-weary and English-less Signor Occhi had been deceived by taxi-driver Lawrence into believing that it was so very much more than a Sabbath day's journey from Victoria Station, SW1, to Ladbroke Grove, W10, that the authorised fare was more than £6 rather than less than £1 (1969 money), or whether Signor Occhi was just too bemused to know what exactly was happening as Lawrence helped himself to the notes in his wallet.

Whose argument do you find most compelling: Clarkson's or Glazebrook's? Was the House of Lords in *DPP v Gomez* right to say that cases involving consensual appropriations may be prosecuted as theft?

*The distinction between theft and criminal attempts*

Not only does the offence of theft overlap with the deception/fraud offences. It also now encompasses much conduct that you might expect would be regarded as a criminal attempt. Think back to the earlier example involving Derek. He decides to steal a bottle of champagne from a supermarket. He walks into the store, goes to the alcohol aisle, picks the most expensive bottle he can find off the shelf, then turns around and starts walking to the exit. But before he reaches the exit Derek is stopped by a store detective. As we saw earlier, on these facts Derek committed theft as soon as he picked the bottle up. As soon as he picked the bottle up he appropriated property belonging to another, and at the moment he did so he had the *mens rea* of theft.

In the eyes of many commentators this outcome is counter-intuitive. Following the decision in *DPP v Gomez*, for example, Sir John Smith commented, 'Acts which common sense would regard as attempts or merely preparatory acts are the full offence of theft'.[16] On this view, Derek should at most be convicted of attempted theft (whether he is guilty of attempted theft would depend on whether he had gone beyond mere preparation – see Chapter 12). A conviction for the full offence of theft is not a fair reflection of what actually happened. In fact, suppose that Derek had not been stopped by a store detective but instead had simply changed his mind before leaving the shop and put the bottle back on the shelf. Since his change of heart occurred after he picked the bottle up (i.e. after the offence was already complete), he would still be guilty of the full offence of theft even though he never got so far as to try and leave the shop without paying!

Sometimes this criticism (the theft–criminal attempts distinction) and the previous one (the theft–deception/fraud offences distinction) apply simultaneously. An example is *R v Morris*. James Burnside switched the price labels on two items. His plan was to deceive the checkout operator into charging him a lower price for the item he wanted. But the plan was unsuccessful. He was arrested at the checkout before he was able to pay the lower price for the item. Intuitively, this looks like an (unsuccessful) attempt to obtain property by deception (or, today, an attempt to commit fraud). Yet he was not convicted of attempting to obtain property by deception. He was convicted of the full offence of theft!

### The relationship between the criminal law and the civil law

So far we have studied three of the four major House of Lords cases on the meaning of appropriation. There is one final one for us to consider: *R v Hinks* [2001] 2 AC 241. This case also involved a consensual appropriation, but there was one significant difference to the earlier cases of *Lawrence v MPC* and *DPP v Gomez*. In *DPP v Gomez* the shop manager was deceived into selling the goods. This deception meant that the contract of sale was voidable. In other words, Gomez and Ballay only acquired *defeasible* title. Similarly in *Lawrence v MPC* the contract between Lawrence and Occhi was voidable, and so Lawrence only acquired defeasible title. So in both *Lawrence v MPC* and *DPP v Gomez* the victims could recover the property that had been stolen from them. But things were different in *R v Hinks*. In this case the defendant, Karen Hinks, acquired *indefeasible* title. In other words, the property that she was alleged to have stolen was hers to keep. The question for the House of Lords was whether someone can be convicted of theft when, under the civil law, the property is theirs to keep.

Karen Hinks was a 38-year-old woman who was friendly with a 53-year-old man named John Dolphin. Dolphin was of limited intelligence, with a below-average IQ. A psychiatrist described him as naïve and trusting with no idea of the value of his assets or the ability to calculate their value. In the words of Lord Steyn, the prosecution case was that Hinks 'had taken Mr Dolphin for as much as she could get'. Between April and November 1996 Dolphin withdrew a total of £60,000 and deposited it in Hinks' bank

---

[16]Smith, J.C. (1993) 'Commentary on *R v Gomez*' *Criminal Law Review* 305, 306.

account. During the summer Dolphin was going to his building society almost every day, making the maximum daily withdrawal of £300. Employees of the building society said that during these visits Hinks would do most of the talking and would interrupt if Dolphin tried to say anything. By the end of November Dolphin had lost most of his savings, and his inheritance from his father.

At trial, Hinks was convicted of theft of the £60,000, and of a TV that Dolphin had given her. Importantly, however, the psychiatrist accepted that although Dolphin was naïve and trusting he understood the concept of ownership and was capable of making a gift. So under the civil law Dolphin's transfer of property to Hinks was a valid gift. Hinks therefore appealed, arguing that since she had acquired indefeasible title to the property she had not appropriated it. By a majority of 3–2, the House of Lords dismissed her appeal.[17] Lord Steyn delivered the judgment on behalf of the majority.

## EXTRACT

In the following extract from Lord Steyn's judgment he responds to some of the arguments Hinks' counsel gave for saying that she had not appropriated the property. What were these arguments?

What reasons did Lord Steyn give for rejecting these arguments?

### R v Hinks [2001] 2 AC 241

#### Lord Steyn

Counsel for the appellant submitted in the first place that the law as expounded in *Gomez* and *Lawrence* must be qualified to say that there can be no appropriation unless the other party (the owner) retains some proprietary interest, or the right to resume or recover some proprietary interest, in the property. Alternatively, counsel argued that "appropriates" should be interpreted as if the word "unlawfully" preceded it. Counsel said that the effect of the decisions in *Lawrence* and *Gomez* is to reduce the actus reus of theft to "vanishing point" (see *Smith & Hogan, Criminal Law*, 9th ed (1999), p 505). He argued that the result is to bring the criminal law "into conflict" with the civil law. Moreover, he argued that the decisions in *Lawrence* and *Gomez* may produce absurd and grotesque results. He argued that the mental requirements of dishonesty and intention of permanently depriving the owner of property are insufficient to filter out some cases of conduct which should not sensibly be regarded as theft. He did not suggest that the appellant's dishonest and repellent conduct came within such a category. Instead he deployed four examples for this purpose, namely:

(1) S makes a handsome gift to D because he believes that D has obtained a First. D has not and knows that S is acting under that misapprehension. He makes the gift. There is here a motivational mistake which, it is submitted, does not avoid the transaction. (*Glanville Williams, Textbook of Criminal Law*, 1st ed (1978), p 788.)

(2) P sees D's painting and, thinking he is getting a bargain, offers D £100,000 for it. D realises that P thinks the painting is a Constable, but knows that it was painted by his sister and is worth no more than £100. He accepts P's offer. D has made an enforceable contract and is entitled to recover and retain the purchase price. (*Smith & Hogan, Criminal Law*, pp 507–508.)

---

[17]Lords Hutton and Hobhouse dissented.

(3)  A buys a roadside garage business from B, abutting on a public thoroughfare; unknown to A but known to B, it has already been decided to construct a bypass road which will divert substantially the whole of the traffic from passing A's garage. There is an enforceable contract and A is entitled to recover and retain the purchase price. The same would be true if B *knew* that A was unaware of the intended plan to construct a bypass road. (Compare Lord Atkin in *Bell v Lever Bros Ltd* [1932] AC 161, 224.)

(4)  An employee agrees to retire before the end of his contract of employment, receiving a sum of money by way of compensation from his employer. Unknown to the employer, the employee has committed serious breaches of contract which would have enabled the employer to dismiss him without compensation. Assuming that the employee's failure to reveal his defaults does not affect the validity of the contract, so that the employee is entitled to sue for the promised compensation, is the employee liable to be arrested for the theft the moment he receives the money? (Glanville Williams, "Theft and Voidable Title" [1981] Crim LR 666, 672.)

My Lords, at first glance these are rather telling examples. They may conceivably have justified a more restricted meaning of section 3(1) than prevailed in *Lawrence* [1972] AC 626 and *Gomez* [1993] AC 442. The House ruled otherwise and I am quite unpersuaded that the House overlooked the consequences of its decision. On the facts set out in the examples a jury could possibly find that the acceptance of the transfer took place in the belief that the transferee had the right in law to deprive the other of it within the meaning of section 2(1)(a) of the Act. Moreover, in such cases a prosecution is hardly likely and if mounted, is likely to founder on the basis that the jury will not be persuaded that there was dishonesty in the required sense. And one must retain a sense of perspective. At the extremity of the application of legal rules there are sometimes results which may seem strange. A matter of judgment is then involved. The rule may have to be recast. Sir John Smith has eloquently argued that the rule in question ought to be recast. I am unpersuaded. If the law is restated by adopting a narrower definition of appropriation, the outcome is likely to place beyond the reach of the criminal law dishonest persons who should be found guilty of theft. The suggested revisions would unwarrantably restrict the scope of the law of theft and complicate the fair and effective prosecution of theft. In my view the law as settled in *Lawrence* and *Gomez* does not demand the suggested revision. Those decisions can be applied by judges and juries in a way which, absent human error, does not result in injustice.

Counsel for the appellant further pointed out that the law as stated in *Lawrence* [1972] AC 626 and *Gomez* [1993] AC 442 creates a tension between the civil and the criminal law. In other words, conduct which is not wrongful in a civil law sense may constitute the crime of theft. Undoubtedly, this is so. The question whether the civil claim to title by a convicted thief, who committed no civil wrong, may be defeated by the principle that nobody may benefit from his own civil *or* criminal wrong does not arise for decision. Nevertheless there is a more general point, namely that the interaction between criminal law and civil law can cause problems: compare J Beatson and A P Simester, "Stealing One's Own Property" (1999) 115 LQR 372. The purposes of the civil law and the criminal law are somewhat different. In theory the two systems should be in perfect harmony. In a practical world there will sometimes be some disharmony between the two systems. In any event, it would be wrong to assume on a priori grounds that the criminal law rather than the civil law is defective. Given the jury's conclusions, one is entitled to observe that the appellant's conduct should constitute theft, the only available charge. The tension between the civil and the criminal law is therefore not in my view a factor which justifies a departure from the law as stated in *Lawrence* and *Gomez*. Moreover, these decisions of the House have a marked beneficial consequence. While in some contexts of the law of theft a judge cannot avoid explaining civil law concepts to a jury (e.g. in respect of section 2(1)(a)), the decisions of the House of Lords eliminate the need for such explanations in respect of appropriation. That is a great advantage in an overly complex corner of the law.

The decision in *R v Hinks* is very controversial. Sir John Smith reacted to the decision by saying that it 'is contrary to common sense. It is absurd that a person should be guilty of stealing property which is his and in which no one else has any legal interest whatsoever'.[18] Similarly, Beatson and Simester commented:[19]

> Property offences are designed to protect property rights. Unlike crimes such as assault, the rights being protected are necessarily rooted in the civil law. Remove dependence on the law of property, and property offences have no rationale. To hold otherwise is not merely to put the cart before the horse, but to motorise it

However, there were others who defended the decision. In the following extract Stephen Shute responds to the criticisms advanced by Beatson and Simester.

## EXTRACT

According to Shute, what is the flaw in Beatson and Simester's argument?

Why, in Shute's opinion, does *R v Hinks* not result in an 'unacceptable' conflict between the civil and criminal laws?

### Shute, S. (2002) 'Appropriation and the Law of Theft' *Criminal Law Review* 445

Beatson and Simester argue, in other words, that *Hinks* forces us to choose between abandoning a well-founded principle of civil law and divorcing property offences from their underlying rationale. Since each alternative is highly unattractive *Hinks* must, they conclude, have been wrongly decided. But, despite its ingenuity, this argument is mistaken. It is, as we have already seen, false to assume that, if the law allows a property offence to be committed without a property right having been infringed, then the link between property offences and property rights will necessarily have been broken. Beatson and Simester's error arises because they fail to see that even without breaching a recognised proprietary right the criminalised act may nonetheless have had a *tendency* to undermine property rights, either directly by attacking the interests that they protect, or indirectly by weakening an established system of property rights and so threatening the public good that that system represents. In either case the justification for criminalising the act may still be the protection of property rights, even though in this instance no property right has been violated.

For this reason there is no necessary threat to the underlying rationale of property offences if the law of theft is extended to cover otherwise unimpeachable transfers. Nor is there a threat to that rationale if a crime committed in these circumstances is able to "trump" the normal civil law rules thus rendering an otherwise valid transfer voidable. In fact, the law of property has long since acknowledged such a possibility. It does so by giving legal effect to the principle that "no-one may benefit from his own wrong". The principle is both limited in its application and relatively weak: first, it applies only where there has been a "wrong"; second, even where there has been a wrong, the principle is often redundant because the wrong itself will generate a cause of action that is, on its own, sufficient to strip the wrongdoer of

[18]Smith, J.C. (2001) 'Commentary on *R v Hinks*' *Criminal Law Review* 163, 164.
[19]Beatson, J. and Simester A.P. (1999) 'Stealing One's Own Property' 115 *Law Quarterly Review* 372.

his benefit; third, the principle is of limited weight and hence may easily be overridden or excluded by other considerations; fourth, even where operative, the principle usually works by estopping a wrongdoer from relying on the wrongful transaction rather than by creating a new cause of action in some other party; and, fifth, even when not outweighed, the principle need not require that the wrongdoer be stripped of all the benefits he obtained from his wrongdoing: a partial restitution may be all that is required to meet its demands. That said, however, the "no benefit principle" comes into its own when a criminal wrong has been committed which is not based on a civil law wrong. In these circumstances, driven by a criminal law wrong but not by a civil law wrong, the principle can result in a thief such as Hinks being stripped of (at least some of) the benefits obtained through her wrongdoing. When this happens the civil law is, in a sense, required to "yield" to the criminal law: if it had not been for the criminal wrong no restitution would have been possible. But this is not an indication of an unacceptable conflict between the civil and the criminal law. Nor is it an indication that there has been a "serious distortion" of the law of property. Rather, it is an indication that both the criminal law and the law of property have (wisely) chosen to give legal effect to an important moral proposition.

The next extract is taken from an essay that Simester co-authored with Sullivan a few years after Shute's article was published. In it, they again criticise the decision in *R v Hinks* and respond to the arguments advanced by Shute.

## EXTRACT

Make a list of Simester and Sullivan's criticisms of the decision in *R v Hinks*.

What reasons do Simester and Sullivan give for rejecting the arguments of those who (like Shute) have defended the decision in *R v Hinks*?

### Simester, A.P. and Sullivan, G.R. (2005) 'On the Nature and Rationale of Property Offences' in R.A. Duff and Stuart P. Green (eds) *Defining Crimes: Essays on the Special Part of the Criminal Law*. Oxford: OUP, 168–195

[In *Hinks*] the House of Lords was prepared to put the criminal law directly at odds with the civil law concerning the rules of ownership. D was convicted of stealing cheques and money from V. It was accepted that the property passed from V to D by way of gifts valid at civil law; so that, in civil law, D owned the money she stole. How, then, had she stolen it? Because, apparently, within the domain of criminal law, title to the money remained with V at the point of the theft. One may concede that, in the circumstances, it was dishonest of D to solicit and accept the gifts. (V was said to be a gullible man of somewhat limited intelligence.) Yet even if we acknowledge D's dishonesty, how, at one and the same time, could title to the money be vested in D under civil law yet remain with V for the purposes of the criminal law? One might defend this possibility by arguing that the policies and protected interests of the civil and criminal laws can diverge: the civil law may be concerned primarily with certainty and the security of transactions, whereas the criminal law may be more concerned with the protection of the vulnerable and the punishment of dishonesty. Hence, in the civil law, property could be vested in D while still belonging to V, for the purposes of the criminal law, in order to convict D of theft. *Hinks*, in effect, invents a new category of property that can be owned solely by one person at civil law and owned simultaneously by another person at criminal law. The criminal law property right will trump the civil law right, at least in criminal proceedings held to determine whether D stole from V when acquiring a valid title to the property.

The disruptive potential of this possibility may be illustrated by an example discussed in *Hinks* itself. Suppose D sells his roadside petrol station to V, without disclosing that planning permission has been granted for the building of a bypass road – which, when built, will divert most of the traffic. The contract would be valid under English law; there was no special relationship between the parties, no duress or undue influence, no misrepresentation. Yet a majority of the House of Lords was prepared to accept that, if dishonest, D could have stolen the consideration he receives.

The argument has so far been made that it is in the nature and rationale of the law of theft to protect the proprietary status quo, a status quo consisting of the proprietary rights recognised by civil law. *Hinks* turns this on its head, placing the criminal law in opposition to the civil law where acquisitions of property through indefeasible civil law transaction contravene community standards of honesty. While the academic response to *Hinks* has been predominantly hostile, the decision has its defenders. In the eyes of its supporters, its major merit is the very lack of subjugation of the criminal law to the civil law that has been argued for here. The decision has been perceived as a wedge whereby communitarian and public values of the criminal law (as assumed) can militate against the private and commercial concerns of the civil law. Which, of course, they can, in specified targeted contexts such as consumer protection legislation. But not by the law of theft. If the behaviour in *Hinks* was wrong, it was a wrong of exploitation. It was not the wrong of stealing.

For those who criticise the decision, one ground of complaint is the deployment of the concept of dishonesty to segregate non-criminal from criminal transactions. And it is, we think, undesirable for rule of law reasons that this amorphous and vague concept should bear very significant weight.

In the final two sentences of this extract Simester and Sullivan highlight the important role that the concept of dishonesty now plays in the offence of theft. Since appropriation has been defined so broadly – reducing the *actus reus* of theft almost to vanishing point – in most theft cases the defendant's liability will hinge on whether or not he acted dishonestly. As we shall see shortly, however, many are concerned about giving the concept of dishonesty such a pivotal role.

### iii. Summary: examples of appropriations

In our discussion so far we have seen a number of examples of appropriations:

- Taking money from someone
- Swapping price labels
- Picking an item up
- Taking delivery of goods
- Accepting a gift.

Offering to sell an item of property is also an appropriation: *R v Pitham & Hehl* (1976) 65 Cr App R 45.

A further example of an appropriation is found in the second half of section 3(1):

## EXTRACT

### Section 3(1) of the Theft Act 1968

#### 3 "Appropriates"

(1) Any assumption by a person of the rights of an owner amounts to an appropriation, and this includes, where he has come by the property (innocently or not) without stealing it, any later assumption of a right to it by keeping or dealing with it as owner.

So keeping or dealing with an item as its owner amounts to an appropriation, including where you came by the property innocently. So suppose Derek borrows Aubrey's lawn mower. Aubrey says to 'bring it back tomorrow'. After cutting his grass Derek decides that he would like to keep the mower. The next day he doesn't return the mower as promised. Instead he leaves the mower in his garden shed and hopes that Aubrey will forget having lent it to him. On these facts Derek has appropriated the mower since he kept it 'as owner'.[20]

Although appropriation is very broadly defined, section 3 does set out two restrictions on the concept's scope. The first is found in the words 'without stealing it' in section 3(1). A person can appropriate the same item multiple times until he steals it. But once he has stolen it there can be no further appropriations. You cannot keep restealing the same item again and again! So suppose Derek finds an iPhone on the pavement. He is in a rush to catch a train, so decides to pick the phone up and try and discover its owner later that day. While he is on the train he takes the phone out of his pocket and looks through the address book to try and discover the owner. But by the time he gets home Derek has decided to keep the phone for himself. That evening he uses the phone to make a call and to read the news online. On these facts Derek steals the phone when he decides to keep it for himself. There were multiple appropriations prior to this: picking the phone up off the pavement; putting it in his pocket; looking through the address book. But using the phone to make a call and to read the news were not appropriations because by then Derek had already stolen the phone.

The second restriction on the scope of appropriation is found in section 3(2):

## EXTRACT

### Section 3(2) of the Theft Act 1968

(2) Where property or a right or interest in property is or purports to be transferred for value to a person acting in good faith, no later assumption by him of rights which he believed himself to be acquiring shall, by reason of any defect in the transferor's title, amount to theft of the property

---

[20]Compare the decision in *Broom v Crowther* (1984) 148 JP 592. The defendant purchased a stolen theodolite. When he discovered it was stolen he kept the theodolite for another week until it was seized by the police. He told the police that once he had discovered it was stolen he had merely left the theodolite sitting in his bedroom whilst he decided what to do with it. The Divisional Court held that there had been no appropriation and quashed his theft conviction. Although he had kept the theodolite, the Court said he had not kept it 'as owner' since he had only had it for a few days while he pondered what to do.

So suppose Derek has stolen Aubrey's lawn mower and then sells the stolen mower to Mike. When he buys the mower, Mike has no idea that it is stolen. A week later, however, Mike discovers that the mower is stolen. Section 3(2) states that any subsequent assumption by Mike of the rights of an owner will not amount to theft since Mike purchased the mower in good faith. However, note that: (i) section 3(2) only applies where the item was 'transferred for value' – it would not apply if Derek gave Mike the lawn mower as a gift; and (ii) the section 3(2) exemption would not apply if Mike sold the mower on to someone else without telling them that it was stolen – on these facts he could be convicted of fraud (which we study below).

## 4. The defendant had an intention to permanently deprive the other person of the property

We can now turn to the *mens rea* of theft. The first of the two *mens rea* requirements is that the defendant had an intention to permanently deprive the other person of the property. When applying this *mens rea* requirement to the facts of a problem question, remember the following points:

- It is a *mens rea* requirement, not an *actus reus* one. The question is whether the defendant intended to permanently deprive the other person of the property, not whether the other person was in fact permanently deprived of the property. This means that a defendant may satisfy this *mens rea* requirement even if the owner recovers the property.

- Intention here means direct or oblique intention (see Chapter 4).

- The test is whether the defendant intended to permanently deprive the other person of the property, not whether the defendant intended to gain personally. Section 1(2) states, 'It is immaterial whether the appropriation is made with a view to gain, or is made for the thief's own benefit'. So if Derek takes Rodney's lecture notes and throws them on a camp fire, Derek satisfies this *mens rea* requirement even though he made no personal gain. It is enough that he intended to permanently deprive Rodney of the lecture notes.

- The test is whether the defendant intended to permanently deprive the other person of the property, not whether the defendant intended to cause the other person permanent deprivation. Suppose Derek goes to his local supermarket to buy a tin of baked beans. When he picks them off the shelf he does not intend to cause the supermarket permanent deprivation since he intends to pay for the beans. But he does intend to permanently deprive the supermarket of the beans, since he intends to take them home and eat them. The fact that he intended to pay for them does not negate this part of the *mens rea*. It is taken into account when assessing whether the defendant acted dishonestly.

- The test is item specific: did the defendant intend to permanently deprive the other person of that specific item of property? If the defendant took an item, the fact that he intended to replace it with an equivalent item does not negate this part of the *mens rea*. Rather, it is taken into account when assessing whether the defendant acted dishonestly. This is illustrated by *R v Velumyl* [1989] Crim LR 299. The defendant borrowed over £1,000 from a safe at work. He did so without authority and in breach of company rules. He said that he had intended to return the same amount the following week. The Court of Appeal nonetheless held that he satisfied this *mens rea* requirement since he did not intend to return the same notes and coins that he took. The fact that he intended to repay the money was relevant to dishonesty, but not to whether he intended to permanently deprive his employer of the money. The test is item specific. Another example would be if you drink a bottle of your housemate's milk, intending to buy him a replacement bottle later in the day.

## ACTIVITY

With these points in mind, decide whether Derek satisfies this part of the *mens rea* in each of the following three scenarios:

- Derek is on a train journey with Rodney. Derek is bored, so to amuse himself he picks up Rodney's wallet and throws it out of the train window. Derek does not expect the wallet to ever be found, but to his astonishment Rodney gets it back a few days later after a dog-walker finds it and posts it to him.
- Derek notices that Rodney rarely uses his iPod, so decides to sell it on eBay (figuring that Rodney will never even notice that it has gone). He places the item on eBay, but a few hours before the sale is due to close he changes his mind and withdraws the iPod from sale.
- Derek borrows Rodney's van. He tells Rodney that he only needs to drive 'a few miles', but in fact he travels over one hundred miles in it. Before returning the keys to Rodney Derek goes to the petrol station and replaces the petrol he used.

Occasionally a defendant may have what is known as a conditional intention. In other words, he intends to permanently deprive the other person of an item only if some condition is satisfied (often the condition will be that the item turns out to be valuable!). In such cases it is especially important to take care when wording the particulars of the alleged offence. This is illustrated by *R v Easom* [1971] 2 QB 315. In this case the defendant, John Easom, picked up a handbag in a cinema, looked through it, decided that there was nothing worth stealing inside and put the handbag back. At trial he was convicted of theft of 'one handbag, one purse, one notebook, a quantity of tissues, a quantity of cosmetics and one pen'. On appeal the Court of Appeal quashed the conviction. At no point had Easom intended to permanently deprive the owner of her handbag. His plan had been to look through the handbag and put it back. Nor had Easom intended to permanently deprive the owner of a purse, or a notebook, or any of the other items listed. Whatever he had intended to take (presumably, money), he hadn't found. If the charge had been worded slightly differently, however, Easom's conviction would not have been quashed. It is sufficient for the offence of theft to establish a conditional intention, and when Easom first picked up the handbag he had a conditional intention to steal its contents (the condition being that the contents turned out to be desirable to him). So if Easom had been charged with 'theft of the contents of the handbag' the conviction would have stood.

Now imagine a slightly different scenario. This time the defendant picks up a handbag intending to steal anything that he can find inside that is valuable. But it turns out that the handbag is empty. On these facts the defendant cannot be charged with theft of the contents of the handbag, since there were no contents inside for him to appropriate! Instead he would be guilty of attempted theft (we will study attempts and impossibility in Chapter 12).

So the test for this *mens rea* requirement is whether the defendant intended to permanently deprive the other person of the property. If the answer is yes, this requirement is satisfied. But if the answer is no, this is not the end of the matter. Section 6(1) states that, even if the defendant lacked such an intention, he will still satisfy this *mens rea* requirement in two situations:

---

**EXTRACT**

## Section 6(1) of the Theft Act 1968

### 6 "With the intention of permanently depriving the other of it"

(1)   A person appropriating property belonging to another without meaning the other permanently to lose the thing itself is nevertheless to be regarded as having the intention of permanently depriving the other of it if his intention is to treat the thing as his own to dispose of regardless of the other's rights; and a borrowing or lending of it may amount to so treating it if, but only if, the borrowing or lending is for a period and in circumstances making it equivalent to an outright taking or disposal.

---

The wording of section 6(1) is not terribly clear. In fact, John Spencer commented that it 'sprouts obscurities at every phrase'![21] Figure 8.1 sets out the structure of section 6(1).

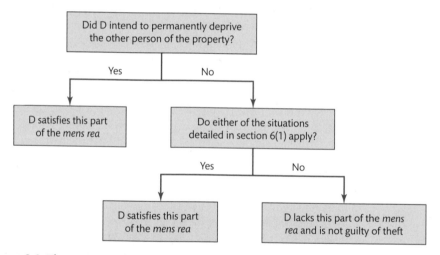

**Figure 8.1.** The structure of section 6(1)

The two situations which are described in section 6(1) are: the defendant intended to treat the thing as his own to dispose of regardless of the other's rights and the defendant intended to borrow the item, but the borrowing was equivalent to an outright taking or disposal. We will consider each in turn.

### i. The defendant intended to treat the thing as his own to dispose of regardless of the other's rights

As a result of its unclear wording, there is some uncertainty over the breadth of the first limb of section 6(1). But before looking at this uncertainty, let's begin with some examples of when this limb would definitely apply.

---

[21]Spencer, J. (1977) 'The Metamorphosis of Section 6 of the Theft Act' *Criminal Law Review* 653.

The first example is set out in section 6(2), which states:

> **EXTRACT**
>
> ## Section 6(2) of the Theft Act 1968
>
> (2)  Without prejudice to the generality of subsection (1) above, where a person, having possession or control (lawfully or not) of property belonging to another, parts with the property under a condition as to its return which he may not be able to perform, this (if done for purposes of his own and without the other's authority) amounts to treating the property as his own to dispose of regardless of the other's rights.

Suppose Derek takes Rodney's expensive watch and pawns it for £500. Derek plans to use the money to buy some shares on the Stock Exchange. He is confident that in just one month he will make £1,000 profit, and plans to then buy the watch back and return it to Rodney. On these facts Derek does not intend to permanently deprive Rodney of the watch, and so we need to determine whether section 6(1) applies. Section 6(2) states that section 6(1) will apply if the defendant parts with property under a condition as to its return which he may not be able to perform. So, since there was no guarantee that Rodney's watch would still be available or that Derek would be able to make enough money to buy the watch back, he must be deemed to have had an intention to treat the watch as his own to dispose of regardless of Rodney's rights. Derek therefore satisfies this part of the *mens rea* of theft.

The second example is *R v Raphael* [2008] EWCA Crim 1014. The victim, Gbemi Adeosun, wanted to sell his car. Pretending to be interested in buying the car the defendant, Jermaine Raphael, arranged a meeting with Adeosun. At the meeting Adeosun was attacked and Raphael drove off in the car. He later phoned Adeosun and offered to sell the car back to him for £500. At trial Raphael was convicted of robbery. As we'll see later in the chapter, to establish robbery the prosecution must prove that there was a theft. Raphael appealed against his robbery conviction, arguing that there had been no theft since he had not intended to permanently deprive Adeosun of the car. The Court of Appeal rejected the appeal. The Court held that the case fell within the first limb of section 6(1):

> [47] The express language of s 6 specifies that the subjective element necessary to establish the mens rea for theft includes an intention on the part of the taker "to treat the thing as his own to dispose of regardless of the other's rights". In our judgment it is hard to find a better example of such an intention than an offer, not to return Adeosun's car to him in exactly the same condition it was when it was removed from his possession and control, but to sell his own property back to him, and to make its return subject to a condition or conditions inconsistent with his right to possession of his own property

So pawning an item and demanding a ransom for the return of an item both fall within the first limb of section 6(1).[22] The judgment in *R v Fernandes* [1996] 1 Cr App R 175 suggests that other situations may also fall within the first limb of section 6(1). The defendant, Roland Fernandes, was a solicitor. He was experiencing severe financial

---

[22] *R v Raphael* may be contrasted with *R v Waters* [2015] EWCA Crim 402, in which the defendants (Sian Waters and Kareem Wasiu) took a mobile phone from the alleged victims (Saskia Voigt and Rhys Faoud) and said they would only return it if the victims first persuaded another person (Dale Holloway) to come and speak to them. At trial the defendants were convicted of robbery. On appeal, Jackson LJ stated that '… if the condition attached to the return of the item … can readily be fulfilled and may be fulfilled in the near future, the jury may well conclude that intention to deprive has not been made out' ([18]). Since the jury might have thought Dale Holloway could be found in the near future, and therefore it was likely that the phone would be rapidly returned to its owner, the convictions were quashed.

difficulties, so he took £20,000 out of the bank account which contained his clients' money and invested it in a firm of licensed backstreet money-lenders. He intended to return the money, but before he could do so it disappeared. At his trial the judge directed the jury to consider whether the first limb of section 6(1) applied. The jury found Fernandes guilty of the theft of his clients' money. Fernandes appealed, arguing that section 6(1) did not apply to the facts of the case and that the trial judge should not have mentioned it to the jury. This was rejected by the Court of Appeal. Auld LJ stated:

> We consider that section 6 may apply to a person in possession or control of another's property who, dishonestly and for his own purpose, deals with that property in such a manner that he knows he is risking its loss.
>
> In the circumstances alleged here, an alleged dishonest disposal of someone else's money on an obviously insecure investment, we consider that the judge was justified in referring to section 6

So, according to *R v Fernandes*, the first limb of section 6(1) is not limited to situations where an item has been pawned or a ransom demanded for an item's return.[23] Its scope is broader than this.

The breadth of section 6(1) was also considered in *R v Mitchell* [2008] EWCA Crim 850. This case involved a carjacking. The defendant, Walter Mitchell, was one of five men in a car being chased by police. Mitchell's car, a Subaru, crashed. The men got out of the crashed car and went to a BMW that was parked nearby. The victim, Mrs Davis, was sitting in the BMW talking on her phone. The men used metal bars to smash the car windows, then dragged Mrs Davis out of the car and drove off in it. A couple of hours later the BMW was discovered a few miles away with the engine running, doors open and hazard lights flashing. The men had abandoned the BMW and taken another car. At trial Mitchell was convicted of robbery of the BMW. As we noted earlier, to establish robbery it is necessary to first prove that there was a theft. Mitchell appealed against his robbery conviction, arguing that he had not stolen the BMW since he had not had an intention to permanently deprive Mrs Davis of the BMW. The issue for the Court of Appeal was whether the case fell within the first limb of section 6(1).

## EXTRACT

Read the following extract from the judgment of Rix LJ. Did Mitchell's case fall within section 6(1)? No
Why/why not?

According to Rix LJ, should section 6(1) be interpreted broadly or narrowly? What examples does he give of situations in which section 6(1) would apply?

### *R v Mitchell* [2008] EWCA Crim 850

#### Rix LJ

[28] In our judgment the facts of this case simply do not support a case to go before a jury of theft and therefore robbery of the BMW. The BMW was plainly taken for the purposes of a getaway. There was nothing about its use or subsequent abandonment to suggest otherwise.

---

[23]In *DPP v SJ* [2002] EWHC 291 (Admin) the High Court held that a defendant who snatched the victim's headphones from him, snapped them and then gave them back fell within the first limb of section 6(1), citing *R v Fernandes* in support of this conclusion.

Indeed, its brief use and subsequent abandonment show very clearly what was the obvious *prima facie* inference to be drawn from its taking which was that the occupants of the Subaru needed another conveyance that evening. We therefore consider that the judge erred in being beguiled by s 6 into leaving this count of robbery to the jury.

[29] [... T]he purpose of s 6 is not greatly to widen the requirement of s 1's intention permanently to deprive. A slightly broader definition of that intention is there provided in order to deal with a small number of difficult cases which had either arisen in the past under the common law or might arise in the future where, although it might be hard to put the matter strictly in terms of an intention permanently to deprive, in the sense of meaning the owner permanently to lose the thing itself, nevertheless something equivalent to that could be obtained through the intention to treat the thing as his own to dispose of, regardless of the other's rights, remembering Professor Smith's Oxford English dictionary use of the words "to dispose of". Thus, the newspaper taken but only returned on the next day when it is out of date, or a ticket which had been used, or a cheque which is paid, or something which has been substantially used up or destroyed, or something which would only be returned to its owner subject to a condition, all these are the sorts of examples to be found in the jurisprudence which discusses s 6. All of these cases are of ready equivalence to an intention permanently to deprive. None of them go any way towards extending the scope of s 6 to a case, however violent, of the taking of a car for the purposes of its brief use before being abandoned with its lights on. It must be remembered of course that a car with its licence plates on, left on the road, is utterly unlike a bundle of newspapers which have disappeared from a newsagents shop to a place where they would not be found.

*[handwritten margin note: examples where s 6 apply]*

So while Mitchell may have intended the treat the BMW as his own, he did not intend to treat the BMW as his own *to dispose of*.[24] The car was only driven a short distance, and when Mitchell abandoned it he did nothing to prevent it being returned to its owner (e.g. he did not hide the car or remove the number plates).[25]

Given the reasoning in *R v Mitchell*, the broad interpretation of section 6(1) in *DPP v Lavender* [1994] Crim LR 297 must now be doubted. Melvyn Lavender took two doors from one council property and used them to replace damaged doors at another council property. The High Court held that he had stolen the two doors. The Court said that the case fell within the first limb of section 6(1) since Lavender had shown an intention to treat the doors as his own. It is impossible to reconcile this with the Court of Appeal's insistence in *R v Mitchell* that section 6(1) should only apply in situations which are equivalent to the owner permanently losing the property. The council did not lose the two doors in *DPP v Lavender* – the doors were simply moved from one council property to another!

---

[24]Note that section 12 of the Theft Act 1968 creates an offence of taking a motor vehicle without authority, which is designed for situations like joyriding where the perpetrators lack an intention to permanently deprive the owner of the car.

[25]See also *R v Vinall* [2011] EWCA Crim 2652, in which the defendants attacked the victim and took his bike. The bike was later found abandoned at a bus stop half a mile away. The Court of Appeal emphasised that the *actus reus* and *mens rea* must coincide in time. On the facts, the case against the defendant could be constructed in one of two ways: the defendants could have been said to have appropriated the bike either when they took it or when they abandoned it. If the alleged theft occurred when the bike was abandoned, the defendants must be shown to have had the necessary intention at this moment. If the alleged theft occurred when the bike was taken, the fact that they later abandoned the bike may be used *as evidence* to prove that they intended to treat the bike as their own to dispose of at the moment they took it. Since the defendants in this case had been charged with robbery, it was important to identify the precise moment at which the alleged theft occurred in order to decide whether force was used before or at the time of the theft (see the discussion of robbery below).

### ii. The defendant intended to borrow the item, but the borrowing was equivalent to an outright taking or disposal

The second situation in section 6(1) is where the defendant intended to borrow the item and the borrowing was equivalent to an outright taking or disposal.

The leading case is *R v Lloyd* [1985] QB 829. The defendant, Sidney Lloyd, worked as chief projectionist in a cinema. For a number of months Lloyd secretly removed films from the cinema and, with the help of two co-conspirators, made large numbers of pirate copies. The process was rapid, so that the films were never out of the cinema for more than a few hours. Lloyd and his co-conspirators then sold the pirate copies. At trial Lloyd was convicted of conspiracy to steal. Lloyd appealed against his conviction, arguing that the case did not involve theft since he only borrowed the films from the cinema. The issue for the Court of Appeal was whether the case fell within the second limb of section 6(1).

## EXTRACT

Read the following extract from the judgment of Lord Lane CJ. What test does he set out for whether a borrowing falls within the second limb of section 6(1)?

Did Lloyd's actions fall within the second limb of section 6(1)? Why/why not?

Lord Lane CJ gives two examples of situations which would fall within the second limb of section 6(1). What are these?

### *R v Lloyd* [1985] QB 829

#### Lord Lane CJ

Borrowing is ex hypothesi not something which is done with an intention permanently to deprive. This half of the subsection, we believe, is intended to make it clear that a mere borrowing is never enough to constitute the necessary guilty mind unless the intention is to return the "thing" in such a changed state that it can truly be said that all its goodness or virtue has gone: for example *Reg. v. Beecham* (1851) 5 Cox C.C. 181, where the defendant stole railway tickets intending that they should be returned to the railway company in the usual way only after the journeys had been completed. He was convicted of larceny. The judge in the present case gave another example, namely, the taking of a torch battery with the intention of returning it only when its power is exhausted.

That being the case, we turn to inquire whether the feature films in this case can fall within that category. Our view is that they cannot. The goodness, the virtue, the practical value of the films to the owners has not gone out of the article. The film could still be projected to paying audiences, and, had everything gone according to the conspirators' plans, would have been projected in the ordinary way to audiences at the Odeon Cinema, Barking, who would have paid for their seats. Our view is that those particular films which were the subject of this alleged conspiracy had not themselves diminished in value at all. What had happened was that the borrowed film had been used or was going to be used to perpetrate a copyright swindle on the owners whereby their commercial interests were grossly and adversely affected in the way that we have endeavoured to describe at the outset of this judgment. That borrowing, it seems to us, was not for a period, or in such circumstances, as made it equivalent to an outright taking or disposal. There was still virtue in the film

**ACTIVITY**

In *R v Mitchell* Rix LJ stated that a defendant who borrows a newspaper and then returns it the following day when it is out of date falls within section 6(1) ([29]). Do you agree?

There is one issue regarding the *R v Lloyd* test that is unclear. Suppose that the owner of the property had the item for a specific purpose. When deciding whether all the goodness or virtue has gone from the item, may the jury take this purpose into account? For example, if the defendant takes someone's wedding dress the day before the wedding and then returns it the day after, has all the goodness or virtue gone from the dress?[26]

**ACTIVITY**

- Think back to *Oxford v Moss* (the case involving the student who read his exam paper before the exam). Imagine that you were the prosecutor in the case and that, instead of charging Moss with theft of confidential information (which, as we saw earlier, is not property), you charged him with theft of the exam paper. Using section 6(1), can you construct an argument that he should be convicted?

- Now imagine that you are Moss' defence counsel. How would you argue that Moss should be acquitted of the charge of theft of the exam paper?

## 5. The defendant acted dishonestly

The second *mens rea* requirement is dishonesty. A partial definition of dishonesty can be found in section 2. It is a partial definition because it does not tell us what dishonesty *is*. Rather, it lists three mind-sets which are *not* dishonest. These three beliefs are listed in subsection (1):

**EXTRACT**

### Section 2 of the Theft Act 1968

### 2 "Dishonestly"

(1)  A person's appropriation of property belonging to another is not to be regarded as dishonest–

    (a)  if he appropriates the property in the belief that he has in law the right to deprive the other of it, on behalf of himself or of a third person; or

    (b)  if he appropriates the property in the belief that he would have the other's consent if the other knew of the appropriation and the circumstances of it; or

    (c)  (except where the property came to him as trustee or personal representative) if he appropriates the property in the belief that the person to whom the property belongs cannot be discovered by taking reasonable steps.

(2)  A person's appropriation of property belonging to another may be dishonest notwithstanding that he is willing to pay for the property

---

[26]Herring, J. (2016) *Criminal Law: Text, Cases, and Materials* (7th edn) Oxford: OUP, p516.

When answering a problem question you should begin with section 2. If the defendant held one of the three beliefs listed in section 2(1) he was not dishonest and is not guilty of theft. But if section 2 does not apply then you need to apply the objective standards of ordinary decent people to determine whether or not the defendant was dishonest.[27] We will look at this test in a moment. But first, notice two other points about section 2:

- When applying section 2(1), the question is whether the defendant genuinely held the belief, not whether the belief was a reasonable one. If the belief was genuine section 2(1) applies even if the belief was unreasonable.

- Section 2(2) states that a defendant may be found to have acted dishonestly even if he was willing to pay for the property. Suppose that Derek owns a signed photo of John Lennon. Aubrey wants to buy it from Derek, but Derek refuses to sell. Aubrey knows that it is worth £500. One day, when Aubrey is at Derek's flat having dinner, Aubrey sneaks into Derek's bedroom and finds the photo. He pockets the photo and replaces it with a cheque for £500. Section 2(2) makes it clear that Aubrey could be found to have acted dishonestly even though he was willing to pay for the photo.

---

**ACTIVITY**

The defendant in each of the following three scenarios is not dishonest under section 2(1). One defendant falls under section 2(1)(a), one falls under section 2(1)(b) and the other falls under section 2(1)(c). Match the defendants to the correct subsection:

- When Rodney goes to the kitchen to have his breakfast he finds that there is no milk for his cereal and cup of tea. Rather than go to the shop, he helps himself to some of Albert's milk thinking that Albert will not mind.   (b)

- Derek finds a £20 note on the floor in the middle of the market. He looks around to see if anyone is searching for it, but no one is. Concluding that it will be impossible to discover the owner he decides to keep it for himself. (c)

- Mike works in a fast-food restaurant. Every now and then during the day he helps himself to some chips from the fryer. Mike's understanding is that employees are entitled to do this, but in fact they are not.   (a)

---

If section 2 does not apply, the jury must apply the common law test for dishonesty instead. From 1982 until 2017, the test that was used was the one from *R v Ghosh* [1982] QB 1053. The following extract, from the judgment of Lord Lane CJ, explains the thinking behind the *R v Ghosh* test.

---

**EXTRACT**

Lord Lane CJ began by rejecting a 'purely objective' test for dishonesty. What reasons did he give for rejecting such a test? What example did he use to illustrate the problems with a purely objective test?

Lord Lane CJ then rejected one type of subjective test for dishonesty. What reasons did he give for this? What examples did he use to illustrate the problems with such a test?

Having rejected these two alternatives, Lord Lane CJ then set out the *R v Ghosh* test. What was this test?

---

[27] See *Ivey v Genting Casinos* [2017] UKSC 67, which we examine further below.

## R v Ghosh [1982] QB 1053

### Lord Lane CJ

This brings us to the heart of the problem. Is "dishonestly" in section 1 of the Theft Act 1968 intended to characterise a course of conduct? Or is it intended to describe a state of mind? If the former, then we can well understand that it could be established independently of the knowledge or belief of the accused. But if, as we think, it is the latter, then the knowledge and belief of the accused are at the root of the problem.

Take for example a man who comes from a country where public transport is free. On his first day here he travels on a bus. He gets off without paying. He never had any intention of paying. His mind is clearly honest; but his conduct, judged objectively by what he has done, is dishonest. It seems to us that in using the word "dishonestly" in the Theft Act 1968, Parliament cannot have intended to catch dishonest conduct in that sense, that is to say conduct to which no moral obloquy could possibly attach. This is sufficiently established by the partial definition in section 2 of the Theft Act itself. All the matters covered by section 2 (1) relate to the belief of the accused. Section 2 (2) relates to his willingness to pay. A man's belief and his willingness to pay are things which can only be established subjectively. It is difficult to see how a partially subjective definition can be made to work in harness with the test which in all other respects is wholly objective.

If we are right that dishonesty is something in the mind of the accused (what Professor Glanville Williams calls "a special mental state"), then if the mind of the accused is honest, it cannot be deemed dishonest merely because members of the jury would have regarded it as dishonest to embark on that course of conduct.

So we would reject the simple uncomplicated approach that the test is purely objective, however attractive from the practical point of view that solution may be.

There remains the objection that to adopt a subjective test is to abandon all standards but that of the accused himself, and to bring about a state of affairs in which "Robin Hood would be no robber": *Reg. v. Greenstein* [1975] 1 W.L.R. 1353. This objection misunderstands the nature of the subjective test. It is no defence for a man to say "I knew that what I was doing is generally regarded as dishonest; but I do not regard it as dishonest myself. Therefore I am not guilty." What he is however entitled to say is" I did not know that anybody would regard what I was doing as dishonest." He may not be believed; just as he may not be believed if he sets up "a claim of right" under section 2 (1) of the Theft Act 1968, or asserts that he believed in the truth of a misrepresentation under section 15 of the Act of 1968. But if he *is* believed, or raises a real doubt about the matter, the jury cannot be sure that he was dishonest.

In determining whether the prosecution has proved that the defendant was acting dishonestly, a jury must first of all decide whether according to the ordinary standards of reasonable and honest people what was done was dishonest. If it was not dishonest by those standards, that is the end of the matter and the prosecution fails.

If it was dishonest by those standards, then the jury must consider whether the defendant himself must have realised that what he was doing was by those standards dishonest. In most cases, where the actions are obviously dishonest by ordinary standards, there will be no doubt about it. It will be obvious that the defendant himself knew that he was acting dishonestly. It is dishonest for a defendant to act in a way which he knows ordinary people consider to be dishonest, even if he asserts or genuinely believes that he is morally justified in acting as he did. For example, Robin Hood or those ardent anti-vivisectionists who remove animals from vivisection laboratories are acting dishonestly, even though they may consider themselves to be morally justified in doing what they do, because they know that ordinary people would consider these actions to be dishonest.

So the *R v Ghosh* test had two stages. First, having regard to the defendant's conduct and his state of mind, was he dishonest according to the standards of reasonable and honest people? If so, did he realise that what he was doing was dishonest by those standards?

The *R v Ghosh* test was heavily criticised, for a number of reasons. John Spencer argued that the test was too convoluted: a claim encapsulated by the title of his commentary, 'What the Jury Thinks the Defendant Thought the Jury Would Have Thought'. He also argued that the effect of the *R v Ghosh* test was to allow defendants to set standards of behaviour.

## EXTRACT

Spencer drew a distinction between two types of question. What was this distinction? Why did Spencer argue that it was inappropriate to answer the second type of question by reference to what the defendant believed?

### Spencer, J. 'Dishonesty: What the Jury Thinks the Defendant Thought the Jury Would Have Thought' (1982) 41 *Cambridge Law Journal* 222

In other words, the jury must first decide what they think of the defendant's behaviour, and then decide what the defendant would have thought the jury would think of it, had the matter crossed his mind. Clearly, intelligence tests for juries will soon be needed.

At the root of all this confusion is a failure to recognise an elementary fact: that the concept of dishonesty involves not one question, but two. First, there is the question what the accused thought and intended. Did he really intend to repay the money? Did he really believe that a cheque was coming from Canada to enable him to do so? This is a question of primary fact, properly within the province of the jury, and to this extent dishonesty is obviously a question of the defendant's state of mind. Secondly, there is an evaluative question: given that he so thought and intended, was it honest to do as he did? Here, by contrast, dishonesty is a qualification of the defendant's conduct. This question, surely, must be for the court to decide, applying its own and not the defendant's standards. Such evaluative questions are in essence questions of law, for all we call them questions of 'secondary fact' when, as here, juries are made to answer them. It is a case of setting standards of behaviour, and we cannot possibly allow the defendant to set his own, even to the attenuated extent the Court of Appeal in *Ghosh* allows. By letting him say 'I'm sorry, I thought society tolerated till-dipping, or cheating bookmakers, or fiddling the N.H.S.,' we are letting him advance what is in effect a mistake of law as a defence. For the courts to take their criminal law from the man on the Clapham omnibus is one thing; to take it from the man accused of stealing it is quite another.

Suppose, for example, that at the first stage of the *R v Ghosh* test a jury decided that there were three different views of what honesty required in a given situation, all of which are commonly held by ordinary and honest members of society (views X, Y and Z). It followed that, at the second stage, a defendant might claim that he was aware of view X, but not views Y and Z.[28] Perhaps the defendant believed so strongly that his own view (view X) was correct that he was oblivious to the fact that other members of society held different views. It followed that, contrary to the assertion of Lord Lane CJ, the *R v Ghosh* test could have resulted in Robin Hood being found to have not acted dishonestly. As Edward Griew argued:

---

[28]Halpin, A. (1996) 'The Test for Dishonesty' *Criminal Law Review* 283.

A person may defend his attack on another's property by reference to a moral or political conviction so passionately held that he believed (so he claims) that 'ordinary' decent members of society would regard his conduct as proper, even laudable. If the asserted belief is treated as a claim to have been ignorant that the conduct was 'dishonest' by ordinary standards (and it has been assumed that it might be so treated), and if the jury think (as exceptionally they might) that the belief may have been held, *Ghosh* produces an acquittal. The result is remarkable. Robin Hood must be a thief even if he thinks the whole of the right-thinking world is on his side.[29]

The decision in *R v Ghosh* also meant that there were different legal tests for dishonesty in civil and criminal law. In the civil law, the test is whether the defendant's conduct is dishonest according to the standards of ordinary, decent people.[30] There is no requirement that the defendant realised that his conduct was dishonest according to those standards. In *Ivey v Genting Casinos* [2017] UKSC 67 the Supreme Court queried why the word 'dishonesty' should mean different things in different types of legal proceedings:

> 63 … [T]here can be no logical or principled basis for the meaning of dishonesty (as distinct from the standards of proof by which it must be established) to differ according to whether it arises in a civil action or a criminal prosecution. Dishonesty is a simple, if occasionally imprecise, English word. It would be an affront to the law if its meaning differed according to the kind of proceedings in which it arose. It is easy enough to envisage cases where precisely the same behaviour, by the same person, falls to be examined in both kinds of proceeding.

The Supreme Court's judgment in this case therefore considered whether *R v Ghosh* should be overruled. The claimant, Phil Ivey, was a professional gambler. He won £7.7m at Crockfords Club casino playing the card game Punto Banco. Ivey used a technique called edge-sorting, which involves identifying tiny differences in the patterns on the back of playing cards to increase the chances of winning. To enable him to deploy this technique, Ivey had deceived the croupier into rotating playing cards of a certain value before putting them back into the dealing shoe, so that he could identify them the next time they were dealt. After reviewing the CCTV footage, Crockfords refused to pay the winnings. Ivey sued. It was accepted that Ivey genuinely believed that what he had done was not cheating but 'legitimate gamesmanship'. The case reached the Supreme Court. One of the issues the Court addressed was whether Ivey had acted dishonestly.

## EXTRACT

In *R v Ghosh* Lord Lane CJ said that Robin Hood and anti-vivisectionists would be found to be dishonest using the *R v Ghosh* test. In the following extract, does Lord Hughes agree? Why/why not?

Lord Hughes also cites *R v Gilks*, a case in which a man was given £100 too much by a bookmaker. He realised the mistake but kept the money anyway, saying that it would be wrong to keep an overpayment from a grocery store but bookmakers are fair game. Lord Hughes states that a person like Gilks would not have been found to have been dishonest using the *R v Ghosh* test. Why? And why does Lord Hughes describe such an outcome as problematic?

---

[29]Griew, E. (1985) 'Dishonesty: The Objections to *Feely* and *Ghosh*', *Criminal Law Review* 341.
[30]See the judgments of Lord Nicholls in *Royal Brunei Airlines Sdn Bhd v Tan* [1995] 2 AC 378 and Lord Hoffmann in *Barlow Clowes International Ltd v Eurotrust International Ltd* [2005] UKPC 37.

What does Lord Hughes say is the correct test for dishonesty? According to Lord Hughes, will this test result in the man who travels on a bus without realising that he is meant to pay (because he is from a country where public transport is free) being held to be dishonest? Why/why not?

In [57] Lord Hughes lists a number of problems with the *R v Ghosh* test. Explain each of these criticisms in your own words (using your answers to the previous questions where relevant). According to Lord Hughes, which of these criticisms is the 'principal objection' to the second limb of the *R v Ghosh* test?

## *Ivey v Genting Casinos* [2017] UKSC 67

### Lord Hughes

53. [D]ishonesty is itself primarily a jury concept, characterised by recognition rather than by definition. Most of the Theft Act 1968 offences required dishonesty without any elaboration of its meaning: section 15 (dishonestly obtaining property by deception) was a prime example and the Fraud Act 2006, which replaces this and other Theft Act offences, adopts the same form. There are in section 2 of the Theft Act 1968 limited rules relating to when appropriation is *not* to be regarded as dishonest (claim of right, belief in consent of owner, belief that owner cannot be found) and a specific provision that it may be dishonest despite a willingness to pay for the goods, but these were designed to reflect existing rules of law, they apply only to appropriation, and they do not alter the underlying principle that dishonesty is not defined. This reflects the view of the Criminal Law Revision Committee that dishonesty was a matter to be left to a jury; it said at para 39 that 'Dishonesty is something which laymen can easily recognise when they see it'. That is not to suggest that there is not room for debate at the fringes whether particular conduct is dishonest or not, but the perils of advance definition would no doubt have been greater than those associated with leaving the matter to the jury. Over the succeeding half century, whilst there have undoubtedly (and inevitably) been examples of uncertainty or debate in identifying whether some conduct is dishonest or not, juries appear generally to have coped well with applying an uncomplicated lay objective standard of honesty to activities as disparate as sophisticated banking practices (for example *R v Hayes* [2015] EWCA Crim 1944) and the removal of golf balls at night from the bottom of a lake on a private golf course (*R v Rostron* [2003] EWCA Crim 2206).

54. A significant refinement to the test for dishonesty was introduced by *R v Ghosh* [1982] QB 1053. Since then, in criminal cases, the judge has been required to direct the jury, if the point arises, to apply a two-stage test. Firstly, it must ask whether in its judgment the conduct complained of was dishonest by the lay objective standards of ordinary reasonable and honest people. If the answer is no, that disposes of the case in favour of the defendant. But if the answer is yes, it must ask, secondly, whether the defendant must have realised that ordinary honest people would so regard his behaviour, and he is to be convicted only if the answer to that second question is yes.

...

57. Thirty years on, however, it can be seen that there are a number of serious problems about the second leg of the rule adopted in *Ghosh*.

(1) It has the unintended effect that the more warped the defendant's standards of honesty are, the less likely it is that he will be convicted of dishonest behaviour.

(2) It was based on the premise that it was necessary in order to give proper effect to the principle that dishonesty, and especially criminal responsibility for it, must depend on the actual state of mind of the defendant, whereas the rule is not necessary to preserve this principle.

(3)   It sets a test which jurors and others often find puzzling and difficult to apply.

(4)   It has led to an unprincipled divergence between the test for dishonesty in criminal proceedings and the test of the same concept when it arises in the context of a civil action.

(5)   It represented a significant departure from the pre-Theft Act 1968 law, when there is no indication that such a change had been intended.

(6)   Moreover, it was not compelled by authority. Although the pre-*Ghosh* cases were in a state of some entanglement, the better view is that the preponderance of authority favoured the simpler rule that, once the defendant's state of knowledge and belief has been established, whether that state of mind was dishonest or not is to be determined by the application of the standards of the ordinary honest person, represented in a criminal case by the collective judgment of jurors or magistrates.

58. The principal objection to the second leg of the *Ghosh* test is that the less the defendant's standards conform to what society in general expects, the less likely he is to be held criminally responsible for his behaviour. It is true that *Ghosh* attempted to reconcile what it regarded as the dichotomy between a 'subjective' and an 'objective' approach by a mixed test. The court addressed the present objection in this way, at p 1064:

'There remains the objection that to adopt a subjective test is to abandon all standards but that of the accused himself, and to bring about a state of affairs in which "Robin Hood would be no robber": *R v Greenstein* [1975] 1 WLR 1353. This objection misunderstands the nature of the subjective test. It is no defence for a man to say "I knew that what I was doing is generally regarded as dishonest; but I do not regard it as dishonest myself. Therefore I am not guilty". What he is however entitled to say is "I did not know that anybody would regard what I was doing as dishonest". He may not be believed; just as he may not be believed if he sets up "a claim of right" under section 2(1) of the Theft Act 1968, or asserts that he believed in the truth of a misrepresentation under section 15 of the Act of 1968. But if he is believed, or raises a real doubt about the matter, the jury cannot be sure that he was dishonest.'

And a little later the court added that upon the test which it was setting:

'In most cases, where the actions are obviously dishonest by ordinary standards, there will be no doubt about it. It will be obvious that the defendant himself knew that he was acting dishonestly. It is dishonest for a defendant to act in a way which he knows ordinary people consider to be dishonest, even if he asserts or genuinely believes that he is morally justified in acting as he did. For example, Robin Hood or those ardent anti-vivisectionists who remove animals from vivisection laboratories are acting dishonestly, even though they may consider themselves to be morally justified in doing what they do, because they know that ordinary people would consider these actions to be dishonest.'

59. Even if this were correct, it would still mean that the defendant who thinks that stealing from a bookmaker is not dishonest (as in *R v Gilks* [1972] 1 WLR 1341 – see para 73 below) is entitled to be acquitted. It is no answer to say that he will be convicted if he realised that ordinary honest people would think that stealing from a bookmaker is dishonest, for by definition he does not realise this. Moreover, the court's proposition was not correct, because it is not in the least unusual for the accused not to share the standards which ordinary honest people set for society as a whole. The acquisitive offender may, it is true, be the cheerful character who frankly acknowledges that he is a crook, but very often he is not, but, rather, justifies his behaviour to himself. Just as convincing himself is frequently the stock in trade of the confidence trickster, so the capacity of all of us to persuade ourselves that what we do is excusable knows few bounds. It cannot by any means be assumed that the appropriators of animals from laboratories, to whom the court referred in *Ghosh*, know that ordinary people would consider their actions to be

dishonest; it is just as likely that they are so convinced, however perversely, of the justification for what they do that they persuade themselves that no one could call it dishonest. There is no reason why the law should excuse those who make a mistake about what contemporary standards of honesty are, whether in the context of insurance claims, high finance, market manipulation or tax evasion. The law does not, in principle, excuse those whose standards are criminal by the benchmarks set by society, nor ought it to do so. On the contrary, it is an important, even crucial, function of the criminal law to determine what is criminal and what is not; its purpose is to set the standards of behaviour which are acceptable. As it was put in *Smith's Law of Theft* 9th ed (2007), para 2.296: '... the second limb allows the accused to escape liability where he has made a mistake of fact as to the contemporary standards of honesty. But why should that be an excuse?'

60. It is plain that in *Ghosh* the court concluded that its compromise second leg test was necessary in order to preserve the principle that criminal responsibility for dishonesty must depend on the actual state of mind of the defendant. It asked the question whether 'dishonestly', where that word appears in the Theft Act, was intended to characterise a course of conduct or to describe a state of mind. The court gave the following example, at p 1063, which was clearly central to its reasoning:

> 'Take for example a man who comes from a country where public transport is free. On his first day here he travels on a bus. He gets off without paying. He never had any intention of paying. His mind is clearly honest; but his conduct, judged objectively by what he has done, is dishonest. It seems to us that in using the word 'dishonestly' in the Theft Act 1968, Parliament cannot have intended to catch dishonest conduct in that sense, that is to say conduct to which no moral obloquy could possibly attach.'

But the man in this example would inevitably escape conviction by the application of the (objective) first leg of the *Ghosh* test. That is because, in order to determine the honesty or otherwise of a person's conduct, one must ask what he knew or believed about the facts affecting the area of activity in which he was engaging. In order to decide whether this visitor was dishonest by the standards of ordinary people, it would be necessary to establish his own actual state of knowledge of how public transport works. Because he genuinely believes that public transport is free, there is nothing objectively dishonest about his not paying on the bus. The same would be true of a child who did not know the rules, or of a person who had innocently misread the bus pass sent to him and did not realise that it did not operate until after 10.00 in the morning. The answer to the court's question is that 'dishonestly', where it appears, is indeed intended to characterise what the defendant did, but in characterising it one must first ascertain his actual state of mind as to the facts in which he did it. It was not correct to postulate that the conventional objective test of dishonesty involves judging only the actions and not the state of knowledge or belief as to the facts in which they were performed. What is objectively judged is the standard of behaviour, given any known actual state of mind of the actor as to the facts.

...

74. These several considerations provide convincing grounds for holding that the second leg of the test propounded in *Ghosh* does not correctly represent the law and that directions based upon it ought no longer to be given. The test of dishonesty is as set out by Lord Nicholls in *Royal Brunei Airlines Sdn Bhd v Tan* and by Lord Hoffmann in *Barlow Clowes* [...] When dishonesty is in question the fact-finding tribunal must first ascertain (subjectively) the actual state of the individual's knowledge or belief as to the facts. The reasonableness or otherwise of his belief is a matter of evidence (often in practice determinative) going to whether he held the belief, but it is not an additional requirement that his belief must be reasonable; the question is

whether it is genuinely held. When once his actual state of mind as to knowledge or belief as to facts is established, the question whether his conduct was honest or dishonest is to be determined by the fact-finder by applying the (objective) standards of ordinary decent people. There is no requirement that the defendant must appreciate that what he has done is, by those standards, dishonest.

75. Therefore in the present case, if, contrary to the conclusions arrived at above, there were in cheating at gambling an additional legal element of dishonesty, it would be satisfied by the application of the test as set out above. The judge did not get to the question of dishonesty and did not need to do so. But it is a fallacy to suggest that his finding that Mr Ivey was truthful when he said that he did not regard what he did as cheating amounted to a finding that his behaviour was honest. It was not. It was a finding that he was, in that respect, truthful. Truthfulness is indeed one characteristic of honesty, and untruthfulness is often a powerful indicator of dishonesty, but a dishonest person may sometimes be truthful about his dishonest opinions, as indeed was the defendant in *Gilks*. For the same reasons which show that Mr Ivey's conduct was, contrary to his own opinion, cheating, the better view would be, if the question arose, that his conduct was, contrary to his own opinion, also dishonest.

So the test for dishonesty is now as follows. First, the jury must determine the defendant's state of mind, including his knowledge or belief of relevant facts. Here, all genuinely held beliefs must be considered. Second, bearing in mind the defendant's state of mind, the jury must decide whether his conduct was dishonest according to the standards of ordinary, decent people.[31] Unlike the *R v Ghosh* test, there is no requirement that the defendant realised that his conduct was dishonest by those standards.

The judgment in *Ivey v Genting Casinos* addresses the problems with the *R v Ghosh* test outlined above. The same test is now used in both the civil and the criminal law, the test is less convoluted than the *R v Ghosh* test, and a defendant may no longer rely on his own passionately held beliefs to claim that he was unaware that his conduct was dishonest according to the standards of ordinary people. However, other concerns remain. In its judgment, the Supreme Court stated that 'it is an important, even crucial, function of the criminal law to determine what is criminal and what is not; its purpose is to set the standards of behaviour which are acceptable' ([59]). At the same time, the Court said that dishonesty is 'characterised by recognition rather than by definition … Dishonesty is something which laymen can easily recognise when they see it' ([53]). This know-it-when-you-see-it approach seems to assume a shared, objective standard of honesty in society. Although Lord Hughes acknowledged that there may be 'room for debate at the fringes whether particular conduct is dishonest or not' ([53]), research by Stefan Fafinski and Emily Finch suggests that in fact values vary widely from person to person and across different socio-economic groups, cultures and locations. Titled 'The Honesty Lab', Fafinski and Finch's study presented

---

[31]In *R v Hayes* [2015] EWCA Crim 1944 the Court of Appeal held that, in cases in which the defendant works in a particular industry, the test is still whether the defendant was dishonest according to the standards of reasonable and honest people. It is not whether he was dishonest according to the standards of that industry. As the Court remarked, 'Not only is there is no authority for the proposition that objective standards of honesty are to be set by a market, but such a principle would gravely affect the proper conduct of business. The history of the markets have shown that, from time to time, markets adopt patterns of behaviour which are dishonest by the standards of honest and reasonable people; in such cases, the market has simply abandoned ordinary standards of honesty' ([32]).

more than 15,000 people with 50 potentially dishonest scenarios.[32] For many of the scenarios there was little consensus.[33] For example:

(a)  43 per cent believed it was dishonest for a carer to try to persuade an elderly person to leave them something after their death;

(b)  37 per cent said it was dishonest not to tell a shop assistant they had undercharged them;

(c)  49 per cent of people thought it dishonest to knowingly watch a pirate DVD;

(d)  58 per cent thought it dishonest to download music for free on the Internet.

In cases like these a test based on the standards of ordinary, decent people generates uncertainty, since ordinary, decent people may hold different views of what honesty requires. Uncertainty can then create further problems. Richard Glover's discussion of the grounding of the *MSC Napoli* in January 2007 provides a useful example.[34] The *MSC Napoli* was a container ship which suffered a serious structural failure when it was on its way from Antwerp to South Africa. The ship was deliberately grounded off Branscombe Bay in south Devon. The ship had a cargo of 2,318 containers; 105 of these were washed overboard, and 37 of these were washed up onto the beach. In the days that followed large crowds of up to 1,000 people at a time went to the beach and took items that had been washed up. Although unambiguous statements were made that unauthorised removal of items from the beach would be theft, no one was arrested or charged with the offence. In the following extract Glover discusses whether the uncertainty surrounding the meaning of dishonesty may have contributed to this.

## EXTRACT

Glover argues that it is possible that the people who took items from the beach would not be found by a jury to have acted dishonestly. What reasons does he give for this?

What does Glover argue were the consequences of the uncertainty surrounding the meaning of dishonesty in the Branscombe Bay incident?

### Glover, R. (2010) 'Can Dishonesty Be Salvaged? Theft and the Grounding of the *MSC Napoli*' 74 *Journal of Criminal Law* 53

It seems probable that a court [...] would have found that the conduct of the 'salvors' was dishonest by the standards of reasonable and honest people. However, it is also possible, to envisage a local court not coming to this conclusion [...] It was evident from the mixed views on the *Napoli* incident represented in the media, and notably in some of the 'blogs' attached to newspaper stories on the web, that there was not a common understanding as to the honesty or dishonesty of the 'looting' on Branscombe beach.

[...]

---

[32]www.dishonestylab.com (accessed 11 July 2013).

[33]'How 80% think it's OK to steal from work as study reveals our wavering moral compass', *Daily Mail*, 7 September 2009.

[34]Glover, R. (2010) 'Can Dishonesty Be Salvaged? Theft and the Grounding of the *MSC Napoli*' 74 *Journal of Criminal Law* 53.

[T]he 'salvors' could conceivably argue that it was regarded as 'normal practice' in that area to 'loot and plunder' wrecks and, accordingly, whether it was private or commercial property their actions were not dishonest according to the 'standards of reasonable and honest people'. Indeed, one person suggested as much:

> There is a decent wreck every 25 years ... I don't regard it as stealing. We're cleaning up the beach as far as I am concerned.

Another commented:

> If we hadn't rescued them, they would have ended up in the sea and useless. I feel we are not stealing them, we are helping the authorities clear them up.

It is evident that the police were confronted with an uncertain legal position in relation to the concept of dishonesty. On the beach they faced 'the hordes of modern Robin Hoods' and because of the uncertain state of the law it was unclear whether they could, as a matter of law, be properly described as dishonest. The behaviour of the 'salvors' may have appeared *prima facie* dishonest, but a jury or court, particularly a local one, was entitled not to regard it as such, just as they were entitled to find Robin Hood not dishonest. Griew believed that one of the consequences of uncertainty was that there were longer trials because defendants had little to lose 'trying their luck' by pleading not guilty and hoping that the dishonesty element of theft would not be proved. However, the converse is what appears to have happened in relation to the *Napoli* incident. The police opted not to 'try their luck' in arresting or charging 'salvors' because, in the absence of a clear definition of dishonesty, they could not be confident that a court would regard the 'salvors' as dishonest. When this lack of certainty about theft is coupled with confusion about the application of salvage law it is, perhaps, not surprising that the police were hesitant to act.

This same uncertainty may also explain, at least in part, why so many people descended on Branscombe beach, despite warnings that removing items from the beach would be theft. It was genuinely unclear whether people would be regarded as dishonest and so commit the offence of theft. That is, as the law was vague, people lacked sufficient *ex ante* direction as to what amounted to dishonest behaviour. It seems likely that that this was exacerbated by police inaction. Consequently, the 'salvors' continued with their activities and caused serious disruption to the local community. For example, roads were blocked and the local school was forced to close for two days because buses could not get through. Some 'salvors' travelled considerable distances (from Bradford, Liverpool, Manchester and further afield) to participate in the 'salvage' and had it been clear that their activities were dishonest it seems at least possible that they would not have done so.

By failing to give individuals a clear indication of what conduct does and does not constitute the offence of theft, it might be argued that the uncertainty surrounding the meaning of dishonesty also violates the principle of maximum certainty (see Chapter 1). Plus, there is a real possibility that different juries considering cases with similar facts will arrive at different verdicts. Such inconsistency undermines the rule of law.

What makes these objections all the more important is the central role that the concept of dishonesty plays in the offence of theft. As we have seen, the *actus reus* of theft has been defined very broadly. In practice, the vast majority of cases will hinge on whether or not the defendant acted dishonestly. For such a key part of the offence to be governed by a test that lacks clear definition is unsatisfactory.

# Robbery

The offence of robbery is defined by section 8 of the Theft Act 1968:

> **EXTRACT**
>
> ## Section 8 of the Theft Act 1968
>
> ### 8 Robbery
>
> (1) A person is guilty of robbery if he steals, and immediately before or at the time of doing so, and in order to do so, he uses force on any person or puts or seeks to put any person in fear of being then and there subjected to force.

This tells us that the offence has four requirements:

1. The defendant committed theft
2. The defendant used force on any person or put or sought to put any person in fear of being then and there subjected to force
3. The defendant used force, or put or sought to put someone in fear of being subjected to force, immediately before committing theft or at the time of doing so
4. The defendant used force, or put or sought to put someone in fear of being subjected to force, in order to commit theft.

Number 1 requires proof of the *actus reus* and *mens rea* of theft. If the offence of theft is established you can then move on to the second, third and fourth requirements. Numbers 2 and 3 are *actus reus* requirements. Number 4 is a *mens rea* requirement. We will work through them in turn.

## 1. The defendant committed theft

Robbery is an aggravated form of theft. So in order to establish robbery you must first prove that the defendant committed theft. If any of the *actus reus* or *mens rea* requirements for theft are absent then the defendant cannot be convicted of robbery.

An example is *R v Skivington* [1968] 1 QB 166. The defendant, Jim Skivington, had his wife's authority to go to her employer and collect her wages. Skivington went to his wife's employer's offices. He produced a knife and said, 'I want the money, I want the money'. When asked what money, he replied, 'My wife's wages'. The assistant manager handed some money over and Skivington left. The Court of Appeal held that Skivington had not committed robbery since there had been no theft. Skivington genuinely believed he had a legal right to the money and so was not dishonest under section 2(1)(a) of the Theft Act 1968. (In effect, Skivington had been charged with the wrong offence. He should have been charged with an offence against the person (see Chapter 6), not robbery.)

The broad meaning given to appropriation in the law of theft means that robbery also has a broad scope. In *Corcoran v Anderton* (1980) 71 Cr App R 104 the two defendants, Christopher Corcoran and Peter Partington, tried to snatch the victim's handbag. They crept up behind her, hit her in the back and tugged at her handbag. She screamed, fell over and let go of the bag. When she screamed the defendants panicked and ran away without the handbag. The Divisional Court upheld their robbery convictions. It did not matter that they had not escaped with the handbag. When they grabbed hold of the bag and tugged it they appropriated it. So this was not an attempted robbery. The offence of theft was complete and so the defendants were guilty of the full offence of robbery.

## 2. The defendant used force on any person or put or sought to put any person in fear of being then and there subjected to force

To satisfy this *actus reus* requirement the defendant must either: (i) have actually used force on another person; or (ii) have put someone in fear of being then and there subjected to force or sought to do so. Notice that the force or threat need not be used against the victim of the theft. A bank robber who threatens to shoot a customer commits robbery even though the person he threatens to use force against is not the person he is stealing from.

### i. The defendant used force on any person

Two questions arise here. Must the force have been applied directly to the other person's body? And, how much force is necessary?

The first of these questions was addressed in *R v Clouden* [1987] Crim LR 56. The defendant came up behind the victim, pulled her shopping basket out of her hand and ran off with it. The Court of Appeal upheld his conviction for robbery. Although the prosecution must show that the defendant used force on the victim, it is not necessary to show that the force was applied directly to the victim's body. It was sufficient that Clouden had used force on the shopping basket, which in turn had caused force to be applied to the victim's body.

The other question – how much force is necessary? – was considered in *R v Dawson & James* (1976) 64 Cr App R 170. The two defendants, Anthony Dawson and Anthony James, and a third man (who was never caught), approached the victim. Two of them began to push the victim from side to side. While he was off balance the third man took the victim's wallet from his pocket. At trial Dawson and James were convicted of robbery. On appeal, the defendants argued that they had not used a sufficient amount of force for the offence of robbery. The Court of Appeal rejected this. Lawton LJ stated that they jury had been entitled to conclude that force had been used.

When we studied non-fatal offences against the person in Chapter 6 we saw that any contact, however slight, qualifies as force for the purposes of battery. But for the purposes of robbery the word 'force' has a slightly narrower meaning. Applications of force which are trivial or insignificant will not suffice. Suppose that Derek is a pickpocket. He takes Rodney's wallet from Rodney's trouser pocket. On these facts Derek probably makes some physical contact with Rodney (perhaps indirectly, via Rodney's clothing). But this will not amount to a use of force for the purposes of robbery. This was confirmed by the High Court in *P v DPP* [2012] EWHC 1657 (Admin). The defendant in this case snatched the victim's cigarette. The defendant was convicted of robbery and appealed, arguing that she had not used force on the victim. The High Court allowed the appeal and replaced the robbery conviction with a conviction for theft. Mitting J explained:

> [15] [...] This case falls squarely on the side of pickpocketing and such like, in which there is no direct physical contact between thief and victim. It cannot be said that the minimal use of force required to remove a cigarette from between the fingers of a person suffices to amount to the use of force on that person. It cannot cause any pain

unless, perhaps, the person resists strongly, in which case one would expect inevitably that there would be direct physical contact between the thief and victim as well. The unexpected removal of a cigarette from between the fingers of a person is no more the use of force on that person than would be the removal of an item from her pocket. This offence is properly categorised as simple theft

So there must have been more than an insignificant amount of force used. Even so, robbery still encompasses a wide range of defendants – from defendants who use weapons and serious violence to those who push a person in order to take their hand-bag or wallet.

### ii. The defendant put or sought to put any person in fear of being then and there subjected to force

Even if the defendant did not use force on another person, he may still be guilty of rob-bery if he put or sought to put any person in fear of being then and there subjected to force. The wording of the statute makes it clear that it is not necessary to show that the other person was actually scared or intimidated by the threat. It is enough that the defendant sought to put the person in fear of being subjected to force. Note also the importance of the words 'then and there'. The threat must be an immediate one.

---

### ACTIVITY

Does Derek satisfy this part of the *actus reus* of robbery in the following four scenarios:

- Derek says to Rodney, 'I'm going to beat you up unless you give me £10 right away'.
- Derek says to Rodney, 'If you don't give me £10 I'll be back next week to beat you up'.
- Rodney and Cassandra are sitting together on a park bench when Derek walks up to them and says to Cassandra, 'I'm going to beat Rodney up unless you give me £10 right away'.
- Cassandra is sitting on a park bench when Derek walks up to her and says, 'Give me £10 or I'm going to go and find Rodney and beat him up'. (Rodney is at home watching TV.)

---

### 3. The defendant used force, or put or sought to put someone in fear of being subjected to force, immediately before committing theft or at the time of doing so

This *actus reus* requirement focuses on when the force or threat of force occurred. The force or threat must have occurred 'immediately before' or 'at the time of' the theft. If the force or threat occurred after the theft was already complete there is no robbery. So if Derek steals something from a market stall and is then chased by a policeman, he does not commit robbery if he pushes people out of his way as he tries to escape (though he would be guilty of battery: see Chapter 6).

In *R v Hale* (1978) 68 Cr App R 415 the Court of Appeal considered the words 'at the time of' the theft. The defendant, Robert Hale, and his accomplice McGuire knocked on the door of the victim Mrs Carrett. When she opened the door they forced their way in. Hale put his hand over Mrs Carrett's mouth while McGuire went upstairs to search. McGuire then came downstairs with a jewellery box and asked where the rest was. All three then went upstairs and Mrs Carrett was asked where her money was. Hale and

McGuire then each went to use the toilet and, before leaving, tied up Mrs Carrett and put socks in her mouth. At trial Hale was convicted of robbery. On appeal Hale argued that the theft was complete as soon as the jewellery box had been seized. The force that was used (tying up Mrs Carrett) therefore occurred, he said, after the theft was already complete.

## EXTRACT

In the following extract, Eveleigh LJ applies the continuing acts doctrine (see Chapter 2). Was the theft complete as soon as the jewellery box was seized? If not, when was the theft complete?

Was Mrs Carrett tied up at the time of the theft or after the theft was complete?

### *R v Hale* (1978) 68 Cr App R 415

#### Eveleigh LJ

To say that [an appropriation] is over and done with as soon as [the thief] lays hands upon the property, or when he first manifests an intention to deal with it as his, is contrary to common-sense and to the natural meaning of words. A thief who steals a motor car first opens the door. Is it to be said that the act of starting up the motor is no more a part of the theft?

In the present case there can be little doubt that if the appellant had been interrupted after the seizure of the jewellery box the jury would have been entitled to find that the appellant and his accomplice were assuming the rights of an owner at the time when the jewellery box was seized. However, the act of appropriation does not suddenly cease. It is a continuous act and it is a matter for the jury to decide whether or not the act of appropriation has finished. Moreover, it is quite clear that the intention to deprive the owner permanently, which accompanied the assumption of the owner's rights was a continuing one at all material times. This Court therefore rejects the contention that the theft had ceased by the time the lady was tied up. As a matter of common-sense the appellant was in the course of committing theft; he was stealing.

There remains the question whether there was robbery. Quite clearly the jury were at liberty to find the appellant guilty of robbery relying upon the force used when he put his hand over Mrs. Carrett's mouth to restrain her from calling for help. We also think that they were also entitled to rely upon the act of tying her up provided they were satisfied (and it is difficult to see how they could not be satisfied) that the force so used was to enable them to steal. If they were still engaged in the act of stealing the force was clearly used to enable them to continue to assume the rights of the owner and permanently to deprive Mrs. Carrett of her box, which is what they began to do when they first seized it.

## 4. The defendant used force, or put or sought to put someone in fear of being subjected to force, in order to commit theft

This is a *mens rea* requirement. The force or threat of force must have been used in order to steal. So suppose that Derek gets into a fight with Roy. Derek punches Roy and knocks him to the ground. Derek then notices that Roy's wallet has fallen out of his pocket, so he picks it up and walks off with it. Whilst Derek has committed theft and an offence against the person, he is not guilty of robbery because he did not punch Roy in order to steal from him.

 **Burglary**

The offence of burglary is defined by section 9 of the Theft Act 1968. As you'll see from the following extract, there are in fact two different types of burglary – section 9(1)(a) burglary and section 9(1)(b) burglary:

---

**EXTRACT**

### Section 9 of the Theft Act 1968

### 9 Burglary

(1)  A person is guilty of burglary if–

    (a)  he enters any building or part of a building as a trespasser and with intent to commit any such offence as is mentioned in subsection (2) below; or

    (b)  having entered any building or part of a building as a trespasser he steals or attempts to steal anything in the building or that part of it or inflicts or attempts to inflict on any person therein any grievous bodily harm.

(2)  The offences referred to in subsection (1) (a) above are offences of stealing anything in the building or part of a building in question, of inflicting on any person therein any grievous bodily harm, and of doing unlawful damage to the building or anything therein.

(3)  A person guilty of burglary shall on conviction on indictment be liable to imprisonment for a term not exceeding–

    (a)  where the offence was committed in respect of a building or part of a building which is a dwelling, fourteen years;

    (b)  in any other case, ten years.

---

This tells us that each type of burglary has five requirements:

1.  The defendant entered a place
2.  The place the defendant entered was a building or a part of a building
3.  The defendant entered the building or part of a building as a trespasser
4.  The defendant was knowingly or recklessly trespassing
5.  Either: (a) the defendant intended to commit one of the specified offences at the time of entry (s.9(1)(a) burglary); or (b) after entering the building the defendant committed one of the specified offences or attempted to do so (s.9(1)(b) burglary).

In a problem question, it is best to begin by working through the first four requirements since these are the same for both types of burglary. Numbers 1, 2 and 3 are *actus reus* requirements. Number 4 is a *mens rea* requirement. If these are satisfied you can then move on to the final requirement, which is where you distinguish between section 9(1)(a) burglary and section 9(1)(b) burglary.

### 1. The defendant entered a place

The first *actus reus* requirement is that the defendant entered a building or a part of a building. The key issue here is what constitutes an entry.

It is generally accepted that a defendant may use an instrument to enter. So, for example, if Aubrey leaves his office window open and Derek uses a pole with a hook on the end to reach inside and pick up Aubrey's key ring and keys, Derek may be held to have entered Aubrey's office. Arguably, a defendant may also enter using an innocent agent. So if Derek tells his young son Damien to enter a sweet shop, pick up a chocolate bar and run straight out of the shop with it, Derek may be held to have entered the building through the innocent agency of his son.

Prior to the Theft Act 1968 the law stated that a defendant had entered a building if any part of his body, however small, had gone inside. So merely inserting a fingertip was enough for an entry.[35] In *R v Collins* [1973] QB 100 the Court of Appeal had to consider whether the same rule applied under the 1968 Act. Edmund Davies LJ set out the facts of this quite exceptional case.

(As you read the facts, bear in mind that at the time of *R v Collins* section 9(1)(a) burglary included entry of a building as a trespasser with intent to commit rape.[36])

## EXTRACT

### *R v Collins* [1973] QB 100

#### Edmund Davies LJ

This is about as extraordinary a case as my brethren and I have ever heard either on the bench or while at the bar [...] Let me relate the facts. Were they put into a novel or portrayed on the stage, they would be regarded as being so improbable as to be unworthy of serious consideration and as verging at times on farce. At about 2 o'clock in the early morning of Saturday, July 24, 1971, a young lady of 18 went to bed at her mother's home in Colchester. She had spent the evening with her boyfriend. She had taken a certain amount of drink, and it may be that this fact affords some explanation of her inability to answer satisfactorily certain crucial questions put to her at the trial.

She has the habit of sleeping without wearing night apparel in a bed which is very near the lattice-type window of her room. At one stage in her evidence she seemed to be saying that the bed was close up against the window which, in accordance with her practice, was wide open. In the photographs which we have before us, however, there appears to be a gap of some sort between the two, but the bed was clearly quite near the window.

At about 3.30 or 4 o'clock she awoke and she then saw in the moonlight a vague form crouched in the open window. She was unable to remember, and this is important, whether the form was on the outside of the window sill or on that part of the sill which was inside the room, and for reasons which will later become clear, that seemingly narrow point is of crucial importance.

The young lady then realised several things: first of all that the form in the window was that of a male; secondly that he was a naked male; and thirdly that he was a naked male with an erect penis. She also saw in the moonlight that his hair was blond. She thereupon leapt to the conclusion that her boyfriend, with whom for some time she had been on terms of regular and frequent sexual intimacy, was paying her an ardent nocturnal visit. She promptly sat up in bed, and the man descended from the sill and joined her in bed and they had full sexual intercourse. But there was something about him which made her think that things were not as they usually

---

[35]*R v Davis* (1823) Russ & Ry 499.
[36]This strand of section 9(1)(a) burglary was removed by the Sexual Offences Act 2003 and replaced with a new offence of trespass with intent to commit a sexual offence (section 63 of the 2003 Act).

were between her and her boyfriend. The length of his hair, his voice as they had exchanged what was described as "love talk," and other features led her to the conclusion that somehow there was something different. So she turned on the bed-side light, saw that her companion was not her boyfriend and slapped the face of the intruder, who was none other than the defendant. He said to her, "Give me a good time tonight," and got hold of her arm, but she bit him and told him to go. She then went into the bathroom and he promptly vanished.

The complainant said that she would not have agreed to intercourse if she had known that the person entering her room was not her boyfriend. But there was no suggestion of any force having been used upon her, and the intercourse which took place was undoubtedly effected with no resistance on her part.

The defendant was seen by the police at about 10.30 later that same morning. According to the police, the conversation which took place then elicited these points. He was very lustful the previous night. He had taken a lot of drink, and we may here note that drink (which to him is a very real problem) had brought this young man into trouble several times before, but never for an offence of this kind. He went on to say that he knew the complainant because he had worked around her house. On this occasion, desiring sexual intercourse – and according to the police evidence he added that he was determined to have a girl, by force if necessary, although that part of the police evidence he challenged – he went on to say that he walked around the house, saw a light in an upstairs bedroom, and he knew that this was the girl's bedroom. He found a step ladder, leaned it against the wall and climbed up and looked into the bedroom. He could see through the wide-open window a girl who was naked and asleep. So he descended the ladder and stripped off all his clothes, with the exception of his socks, because apparently he took the view that if the girl's mother entered the bedroom it would be easier to effect a rapid escape if he had his socks on than if he was in his bare feet. That is a matter about which we are not called upon to express any view, and would in any event find ourselves unable to express one.

Having undressed, he then climbed the ladder and pulled himself up on to the window sill. His version of the matter is that he was pulling himself in when she awoke. She then got up and knelt on the bed, she put her arms around his neck and body, and she seemed to pull him into the bed. He went on:

> "I was rather dazed because I didn't think she would want to know me. We kissed and cuddled for about 10 or 15 minutes and then I had it away with her but found it hard because I had had so much to drink."

At trial Collins was convicted of section 9(1)(a) burglary. He appealed, arguing that he had not entered the building as a trespasser. The case reached the Court of Appeal.

The facts of *R v Collins* need to be considered in two stages: had he committed burglary before the girl invited him into the room and did he commit burglary when he accepted her invitation to enter the room. We will look at the second of these soon. For now, we are concerned with whether Collins had committed burglary before the girl invited him into the room. In his judgment Edmund Davies LJ said that a defendant can only be convicted of burglary if there has been an 'effective and substantial entry'. Since it was uncertain whether any part of Collins' body had entered the building whilst he was kneeling on the window sill (and, even if some part had, it was uncertain whether the jury would have regarded this as 'effective and substantial'), it had not been established that he had entered the building prior to being invited in.

In subsequent cases, however, the Court of Appeal has diluted the 'effective and sub-stantial entry' test that it set out in *R v Collins*. In *R v Brown* [1985] Crim LR 212 the defendant, Vincent Brown, was standing outside a shop window. He lent through the window to rummage around for goods, so that the top half of his body was inside the shop. Commenting on the 'effective and substantial entry' test, the Court of Appeal said that the word substantial does not assist. The test should simply be whether the entry was effective, which in the case of Brown it was. However, following *R v Brown* came the case *R v Ryan* [1996] Crim LR 320, which casts doubt upon the requirement that the entry must have been effective. The defendant, Lee Ryan, put his head and arm inside the window of a house and became stuck. He had to be removed by the fire brigade. The Court of Appeal rejected Ryan's appeal against his burglary conviction, saying that the jury had been entitled to conclude that Ryan had entered the house. It did not matter that he had become stuck and unable to steal anything. It is hard to see how Ryan's entry could be described as effective!

So the current position is uncertain. Commentators have suggested that the 'effective entry' test should be interpreted broadly and understood as a *de minimis* rule, so that it only excludes insignificant or negligible entries (such as a fingertip),[37] or that we should simply discard the 'effective entry' test and return to the pre-1968 rule that a defendant enters a building if any part of his body, however small, has gone inside.[38]

## 2. The place the defendant entered was a building or a part of a building

The word 'building' includes garden sheds, greenhouses and farm outbuildings (such as stables or barns). Section 9(4) states that it also includes inhabited vehicles and vessels:

> **EXTRACT**
>
> ### Section 9(4) of the Theft Act 1968
>
> (4)  References in subsections (1) and (2) above to a building, and the reference in subsection (3) above to a building which is a dwelling, shall apply also to an inhabited vehicle or vessel, and shall apply to any such vehicle or vessel at times when the person having a habitation in it is not there as well as at times when he is.

So a caravan or a houseboat would qualify as a building while someone is living there (even if that person is away at the time).[39] However, a caravan or houseboat that is only used for holidays will only qualify as a building during the holidays and not at other times.

To constitute a building, a structure must have some degree of permanence. This can be illustrated by contrasting the following two cases:

- *B and S v Leathley* [1979] Crim LR 314: B and S stole goods from a freezer container in a farmyard. The container was sitting on railway sleepers and had not been moved for more than two years. It had lockable doors, was connected to an independent

---

[37]Simester, A.P., Spencer, J.R., Stark, F., Sullivan, G.R. & Virgo, G.J. (2016) *Simester and Sullivan's Criminal Law: Theory and Doctrine* (6th edn) Oxford: Hart Publishing, p597.

[38]Ormerod, D. & Laird, K. (2015) *Smith and Hogan's Criminal Law* (14th edn) Oxford: OUP, p1080.

[39]For example, in *R v Coleman* [2013] EWCA Crim 544 the defendant was convicted of burglary from a narrow boat on the Grand Union Canal that was used as a dwelling.

electricity supply and was intended to remain in place for the foreseeable future. The Crown Court at Carlisle held that the container was a building, commenting that it was 'a structure of considerable size and intended to be permanent or at least to endure for a considerable time'.

- *Norfolk Constabulary v Seekings and Gould* [1986] Crim LR 167: this case concerned two articulated lorry trailers that were being used as temporary storage space during building redevelopment by a supermarket. The trailers had been left on their wheels. An electric cable supplied power to each trailer. Steps were used for access and entry was made by unlocking the trailer shutters. The trailers had been in use for a year. The Crown Court at Norwich held that the trailers were not buildings. The distinction with *B and S v Leathley* seems to have been that, since the trailers still rested on their own wheels, they were vehicles, not buildings.

Sometimes a defendant might have had permission to be in some parts of a building but not others. An example is a hotel. Hotel guests have permission to be in communal areas and in their own rooms, but not the rooms of other guests. So if Derek sneaks into another guest's room he enters a separate part of the building as a trespasser.

In *R v Walkington* [1979] 1 WLR 1169 the defendant, Terence Walkington, entered a Debenhams store shortly before it was due to close. A store detective was monitoring him and followed him to an unattended till area. The till area was in the middle of a three-sided counter. Walkington moved into the till area, looked in the till (which he found was empty) and turned around to leave when he was stopped by the store detective. At trial, Walkington was convicted of section 9(1)(a) burglary. He appealed, arguing that he had not entered a separate part of the building.

## EXTRACT

Read the following extract from the judgment of Geoffrey Lane LJ. Was there sufficient evidence for the jury to conclude that the till area was a separate part of the building. Why/why not?

### *R v Walkington* [1979] 1 WLR 1169

#### Geoffrey Lane LJ

One really gets two extremes, as it seems to us. First of all you have the part of the building which is shut off by a door so far as the general public is concerned, with a notice saying "Staff Only" or "No admittance to customers." At the other end of the scale you have for example a single table in the middle of the store, which it would be difficult for any jury to find properly was a part of the building into which the licensor prohibited customers from moving.

Here, it seems to us, there was a physical demarcation. Whether it was sufficient to amount to an area from which the public were plainly excluded was a matter for the jury. It seems to us that there was ample evidence on which they could come to the conclusion (a) that the management had impliedly prohibited customers entering that area and (b) that this particular defendant knew of that prohibition. Whether the jury came to the conclusion that the prosecution made out their case was a matter for them, but there is no dispute that the judge, in those two careful passages which I have read, left the matter fairly and correctly to the jury.

### 3. The defendant entered the building or part of a building as a trespasser

Whether or not the defendant was trespassing is a question of civil law. A trespasser is someone who enters without legal authorisation. The most common form of legal authorisation is the permission of the owner (or other occupiers such as the owner's family). Legal authorisation can also take other forms (such as a police search warrant).

If the defendant enters the building with the owner's permission but the owner later revokes this permission, the defendant must leave within a reasonable length of time. Should the defendant fail to leave within a reasonable length of time, he will be trespassing. Note, however, that to be guilty of burglary section 9(1) states that the defendant must have *entered* the building or part of a building as a trespasser. Suppose that Aubrey invites Derek into his house, but ten minutes later demands that Derek leave immediately. Derek procrastinates and leaves the house as slowly as he can. On his way out he steals a hat from the hat rack in the hallway. On these facts Derek may be trespassing at the moment he steals the hat, but he will not be guilty of burglary as he did not *enter* the building as a trespasser.[40]

The concept of trespass has raised two issues: mistaken authorisation and exceeding permission.

#### i. Mistaken authorisation

If the defendant received permission to enter, but the permission was based on some fundamental mistake, the defendant is trespassing. Think back to *R v Collins*. Earlier we saw that Collins had not committed burglary before the girl invited him into her bedroom. Now we need to ask whether he committed burglary when he accepted her invitation to enter the room. The girl's invitation to enter the room was based on her mistake as to Collins' identity: she thought Collins was her boyfriend. Mistakes as to a person's identity are regarded as fundamental and so Collins' permission to enter the room was void. He therefore entered as a trespasser. (As we'll see in a moment, however, he was not guilty of burglary as he lacked the necessary *mens rea*.)

A defendant's permission to enter may also be invalidated by fraud or deception. So if Derek pretends to be an employee of the electricity board, and Aubrey invites him into his house to read the electricity meter, Derek's permission to enter Aubrey's house is invalidated by his deception.

#### ii. Exceeding permission

If a defendant has permission to enter, but exceeds this permission, he is a trespasser. A simple example is where Aubrey invites Derek, an electrician, to enter his house in order to gain access to the garage where the electricity meter is housed – but when Aubrey is not looking Derek sneaks upstairs and goes to sleep in one of the bedrooms. In this example, Derek was invited into Aubrey's house for a specified purpose. Derek exceeded this purpose and thus exceeded his permission to enter.

What about where the defendant's permission to enter was a general permission, not a permission that was limited to a specified purpose? Is it possible to exceed a general permission to enter? In *R v Jones & Smith* [1976] 1 WLR 672 the defendants, John Jones and Christopher Smith, went to the house of Smith's father Arthur and took two TVs. At trial, they were convicted of section 9(1)(b) burglary. On appeal, they argued that they had

---

[40]Unless it can be established that the hallway is a separate part of the building, so that after being told to leave Derek entered a separate part of the building as a trespasser.

not entered the building as trespassers because Arthur Smith had given his son a general permission to enter the house at any time. The Court of Appeal rejected this argument and upheld the convictions. Commenting that 'When you invite a person into your house to use the staircase you do not invite him to slide down the banisters',[41] James LJ explained that it is possible to exceed a general permission to enter.

The decision in *R v Jones & Smith* means that the emphasis in the offence of burglary is very much on the defendant's guilty mind rather than manifest illegality. This gives the offence a very broad scope. Following *R v Jones & Smith* a shoplifter who enters a supermarket in order to steal an expensive bottle of champagne enters in excess of his permission to enter. He is therefore a trespasser and is guilty of burglary. Moreover, as we'll see in a moment, the shoplifter is guilty of section 9(1)(a) burglary as soon as he enters the supermarket with the intention to steal. So he is guilty of the full offence of burglary even if, having entered, he has a change of heart before he gets to the alcohol aisle, turns around and walks out empty-handed.

## 4. The defendant was knowingly or recklessly trespassing

Think back to *R v Collins* once again. We have seen that the girl's permission to Collins to enter the room was void because she had made a mistake as to his identity. Collins therefore entered the room as a trespasser. However, Edmund Davies LJ stated that a defendant can only be convicted of burglary if he knew he was trespassing or was reckless as to whether he was trespassing. Arguably, Collins believed he had permission to be in the bedroom, yet the judge at his trial failed to direct the jury to consider whether Collins satisfied this *mens rea* requirement. As a result the Court of Appeal allowed Collins' appeal and quashed his conviction.

So a defendant can only be convicted of burglary if he was knowingly or recklessly trespassing. We studied the meaning of these *mens rea* concepts in Chapter 4.

## 5. Either: (a) the defendant intended to commit one of the specified offences at the time of entry (s.9(1)(a) burglary); or (b) after entering the building the defendant committed one of the specified offences or attempted to do so (s.9(1)(b) burglary)

The first four requirements are the same for both types of burglary. Once you have established that all four are satisfied, the final part of the offence requires you to distinguish between section 9(1)(a) and section 9(1)(b) burglary. When answering a problem question, it is sensible to begin with section 9(1)(a).

### i. Section 9(1)(a) burglary

To prove section 9(1)(a) burglary you must establish that, at the moment he entered the building or part of the building as a trespasser, the defendant intended to commit one of the following three offences:

- Theft
- Infliction of GBH (this means the offence found in section 18 of the Offences Against the Person Act 1861)
- Criminal damage.

---

[41]*per* Scrutton LJ in *The Carlgarth* [1927] p93.

So, burglary is actually a broader offence than most people realise. It not only encompasses the person who enters a building or part of a building as a trespasser intending to steal, but also the person who enters with an intention to cause someone inside GBH and the person who enters with an intention to cause unlawful damage to property that is inside.

Note also that the key moment in time is the moment the defendant enters the building. It is at this moment that the defendant must have intended to commit theft, GBH or criminal damage. As long as the defendant entered with the necessary intention, he is guilty of section 9(1)(a) burglary – even if he changed his mind once inside and did not carry out the offence. Conversely, if the defendant only formed the intention after he had already entered, he is not guilty of section 9(1)(a) burglary. In this situation you need to consider section 9(1)(b) burglary instead.

### ii. Section 9(1)(b) burglary

A defendant commits section 9(1)(b) burglary if, having entered a building or part of a building as a trespasser, he commits one of the following offences whilst inside:

- Theft
- Attempted theft
- Infliction of GBH (here this means either the offence found in section 18 of the Offences Against the Person Act 1861 or the offence found in section 20)
- Attempted infliction of GBH.

(Notice that, although criminal damage is one of the offences listed for section 9(1)(a) burglary, it is not on the list for section 9(1)(b) burglary.)

Unlike section 9(1)(a) burglary, the moment at which section 9(1)(b) burglary is committed is not the moment of entry. It is the moment at which the defendant commits (attempted) theft or (attempted) infliction of GBH. So for section 9(1)(b) burglary it is not necessary to show that the defendant intended to commit one of these offences when he entered the building. It is enough to show that he committed one of them once he was inside.

# Fraud

Before the introduction of the Fraud Act 2006 this area of the criminal law was governed by a total of eight different deception offences:

- Obtaining property by deception (s.15 Theft Act 1968)
- Obtaining a money transfer by deception (s.15A Theft Act 1968)
- Obtaining a pecuniary advantage by deception (s.16 Theft Act 1968)
- Obtaining services by deception (s.1 Theft Act 1978)
- Procuring the execution of a valuable security by deception (s.20(2) Theft Act 1968)
- Securing the remission of a liability by deception (s.2(1)(a) Theft Act 1978)
- Inducing a creditor to wait for or forgo payment by deception (s.2(1)(b) Theft Act 1978)
- Obtaining an exemption from or abatement of liability by deception (s.2(1)(c) Theft Act 1978).

In 2002 the Law Commission published a report which criticised the complexity of this range of deception offences. The following extract is taken from this report:

**EXTRACT**

The Law Commission states that the overly particular list of 'overlapping but distinct' deception offences had 'undesirable consequences'. What were these undesirable consequences?

## Law Commission (2002) *Fraud* (Law Commission Report No 276) Cm 5560

### The need for simplification and rationalisation

3.10 At present, there is a multitude of overlapping but distinct statutory offences which can be employed in fraud trials. As Griew noted:

> No one wanting to construct a rational, efficient law of criminal fraud would choose to start from the present position. The law ... is in a very untidy and unsatisfactory condition. The various offences are not so framed and related to each other as to cover, in a clearly organised way and without doubt or strained interpretation, the range of conduct with which the law should be able to deal.

3.11 Arguably, the law of fraud is suffering from an "undue particularisation of closely allied crimes". Over-particularisation or "untidiness" is undesirable in itself, but it also has undesirable consequences.

3.12 First, it allows technical arguments to prosper. When the original Theft Act deception offences were first proposed by the CLRC in their Eighth Report, this problem was foreseen by a minority of the committee members:

> To list and define the different objects which persons who practise deception aim at achieving is unsatisfactory and dangerous, because it is impossible to be certain that any list would be complete. Technical distinctions would also inevitably be drawn – as they have been drawn under [the Larceny Act] 1916 s 32 – between conduct which did and which did not fall within the list.

3.13 The minority who took this view were in favour of a single deception offence, which would not define the offence by reference to the nature of the victim's loss or the relationship between that loss and the defendant's corresponding gain:

> The essence of the offence would be dishonestly using deception for the purpose of gain ... What particular type of gain the offender may aim at getting for himself or somebody else at the expense of his victim should be of no account except for the purpose of sentence.

3.14 They were echoing the sentiments of Lord Hardwicke:

> Fraud is infinite, and were a court once to ... define strictly the species of evidences of it, the jurisdiction would be cramped, and perpetually eluded by new schemes which the fertility of man's invention would contrive.

3.15 However, the majority of the committee took the view that it would be wrong to introduce a general offence. This disagreement was resolved by a compromise. The CLRC recommended two specific offences and a general offence which would carry a limited sentence of two years. This compromise did not find favour with Parliament, and a somewhat complex legislative history ensued. The proposed general offence was not adopted, and the present array of specific offences developed over subsequent years.

3.16 Nonetheless, the views of the minority who had advocated the general offence were found by Lord Goff in *Preddy* to have been "prescient". This was a mortgage fraud case. The defendants made false representations when applying for loans to buy property, and they were charged with obtaining property by deception. Although this is one of the most general deception offences, Lord Goff came to the reluctant conclusion that their actions fell outside it. The rest of the House agreed.

3.17 The difficulty lay in the nature of the property which the defendants obtained. The mortgage lenders provided the defendants with loans by making transfers from their accounts to the defendants' accounts. As Lord Goff explained, the resulting credit balances in the defendants' accounts were choses in action which had never belonged to anyone but the respective defendants. While the lenders had corresponding decreases in their respective accounts, at no time had they had any form of proprietary interest in the defendants' credit balances. Therefore these balances had never been property "belonging to another", for the purposes of section 15 of the Theft Act 1968.

3.18 In reaching this conclusion, Lord Goff considered the CLRC Eighth Report, and the subsequent legislative history. He made it clear that, in his view, the CLRC minority had been right to advocate a single deception offence. It is, perhaps, unsurprising that he reached this view. The defence argument in *Preddy* exploited the very elements of section 15 which the CLRC minority saw as irrelevant to the definition of fraud: the nature of the loss, and the relationship between the loss and the illegitimate gain.

3.19 *Preddy* was not the only case of its kind. It was only the most significant of a long string of highly technical cases involving deception offences: *Duru, Halai, King, Mitchell, Manjdadria,* and *Mensah Lartey and Relevy.* Each of these defendants argued that the particular consequences which he had brought about by deception fell outside the definition of the offence with which he was charged. By relying on a range of specific fraud offences, defined with reference to different types of consequence, the law is left vulnerable to technical assaults.

3.20 The second difficulty that arises from over-particularisation is that a defendant may face the wrong charge, or too many charges. Some of the cases cited in the previous paragraph would have been less problematic had the defendant been charged with a different offence. In *Mensah Lartey and Relevy* the defendants were charged with conspiring and attempting to procure the execution of a valuable security. The prosecution accepted in the Court of Appeal that they should have been charged with conspiring or attempting to obtain property by deception (although, since *Preddy*, section 15 would not have helped either). In *Duru* and *Mitchell*, the deceptions resulted in banks making out cheques in the defendants' favour. They were charged with obtaining property by deception, when the correct charge was procuring the execution of a valuable security.

3.21 This problem is not confined to cases which are wrongly prosecuted under one *deception* offence rather than another. In *Gomez* the defendant was the assistant manager of a shop. He deceived the manager into giving a customer goods in exchange for cheques which the defendant knew to be stolen. He was charged with theft. The case went to the House of Lords, because of an ambiguity in the concept of "appropriation" in theft. Four of their Lordships upheld the conviction, but Lord Lowry gave a powerful dissenting speech, and the issue has continued to cause difficulty. In fact, the argument need not have arisen in that case: the defendant would not have been able to raise it if he had been charged with obtaining property by deception, and he would have been squarely convicted on the agreed facts. It is not clear why the prosecutors chose to persist with bringing a theft charge. Perhaps they were aware of potential legal or factual problems that might arise if the wrong deception offence were charged. They may simply have been insufficiently familiar with the deception offences. In either event, a clear general deception offence might have enabled them to charge an offence which more comfortably reflected the conduct alleged, even though it also fell within the legal definition of theft.

3.22 A similar situation arose recently in *Vincent*. The defendant was charged with the offence of making off without payment. He had stayed in two hotels and left without paying the full bill. He argued that he had made arrangements to pay the bills "when he could", so that by the time he left there was no expectation that he would pay for the services at that point, and therefore payment "on the spot" was not required or expected. The trial judge directed the jury that this was only a defence if the agreement to defer payment was made in good faith by both parties, so it was no defence if the agreement had been brought about by fraud or deception. The Court of Appeal quashed the resultant convictions, stating that this direction was incorrect: even if the agreement was brought about by fraud, it still meant that the defendant was not expected to pay when he left, so he could not be guilty of making off without payment. The court stated that to catch this fraud a different offence would need to be charged, such as obtaining services by deception. Again, had the right charge been selected, much legal argument could have been avoided.

3.23 We do not argue that all the Theft Act offences could or should be combined into one. The fewer there are, however, the easier it is for prosecutors to choose the right one, thus decreasing the likelihood of mistakes. At present, in order to avoid mistakes, prosecutors may take the "belt and braces" approach. In Law Com No 228 we recognised that this practice brings its own problems:

> We are ...very conscious that there has been much criticism of the length and complexity of fraud trials ... [A]lthough much of the criticism was directed to the procedure in criminal trials, there was legitimate criticism of the substantive law in substantial fraud cases, which led to trials of excessive length and to perceptions of injustice. We are concerned to discover if it is possible to reduce the length and complexity of trials by simplifying the law, while always ensuring that the defendant is fully protected.

3.24 The over-particularisation of fraud offences can result in indictments made complex by the charging of alternative offences. A clearer, simpler law of fraud would make it easier for prosecutors to pursue one correct charge, which in turn would give fraud trials greater focus and structure.

Following the Law Commission's report the deception offences were replaced with a single offence of fraud, created by the Fraud Act 2006. Section 1 of the Act explains that the offence of fraud can be committed in three different ways:[42]

## EXTRACT

## Section 1 of the Fraud Act 2006

### 1 Fraud

(1) A person is guilty of fraud if he is in breach of any of the sections listed in subsection (2) (which provide for different ways of committing the offence).

---

[42]Since all three are types of a single offence, there is no need for the prosecution to prove which one the defendant committed as long as the jury is sure that he did commit one of them. This means that it will not matter if the evidence establishes that fraud was committed in a different way to the one alleged by the prosecution.

(2)   The sections are–

    (a)  section 2 (fraud by false representation),

    (b)  section 3 (fraud by failing to disclose information), and

    (c)  section 4 (fraud by abuse of position).

(3)   A person who is guilty of fraud is liable–

    (a)  on summary conviction, to imprisonment for a term not exceeding 12 months or to a fine not exceeding the statutory maximum (or to both);

    (b)  on conviction on indictment, to imprisonment for a term not exceeding 10 years or to a fine (or to both).

We will look at each type of fraud in turn.

# Fraud by false representation

Fraud by false representation is defined by section 2 of the Fraud Act 2006:

## EXTRACT

### Section 2 of the Fraud Act 2006

### 2 Fraud by false representation

(1)   A person is in breach of this section if he–

    (a)  dishonestly makes a false representation, and

    (b)  intends, by making the representation–

        (i)   to make a gain for himself or another, or

        (ii)  to cause loss to another or to expose another to a risk of loss.

This tells us that fraud by false representation has four requirements:

1.   The defendant made a false representation

2.   The defendant knew that the representation was, or might be, untrue or misleading

3.   The defendant intended, by making the false representation, to make a gain for himself or another or to cause loss to another or to expose another to a risk of loss

4.   The defendant acted dishonestly.

Number 1 is an *actus reus* requirement. Numbers 2, 3 and 4 are *mens rea* requirements. We will work through them in turn.

## 1. The defendant made a false representation

The sole *actus reus* requirement is that the defendant made a false representation. Subsections 2(2)–(5) provide further guidance on what constitutes a false representation. We will look at each subsection in turn.

The definition of false that is found in section 2(2)(a) is wider than you might have expected:

So representations are not only false when they are factually untrue. They are also false if they are factually true but nonetheless misleading. Suppose that Derek is a salesman in an electrical goods shop. Mike is interested in buying an LCD TV. When Mike asks Derek, 'Is this model a good one?' Derek replies, 'We haven't had a single bad review or dissatisfied customer'. Although factually true, this statement could be regarded as misleading if the shop has not received any customer feedback (good or bad) on that model, or if the shop has not yet sold any of that particular model.

Section 2(3) explains that a representation may be of fact, law or a person's state of mind:

### EXTRACT

## Section 2(3) of the Fraud Act 2006

(3)   "Representation" means any representation as to fact or law, including a representation as to the state of mind of–

    (a)  the person making the representation, or

    (b)  any other person.

### ACTIVITY

Which of the following representations is an example of: (a) a representation of fact; (b) a representation of law; (c) a representation of the state of mind of the person making the representation and (d) a representation of the state of mind of another person?

- Rodney says to Cassandra, 'I really want to marry you'
- Rodney tells Derek, 'Cassandra wants to marry me!'
- Dereks says to Rodney, 'It is unlawful to be married to two people at the same time'.
- Rodney says to Derek, 'I am not married'.

Section 2(4) states:

**Section 2(4) of the Fraud Act 2006**

(4)   A representation may be express or implied.

There are several examples of implied representations in the case law:

- Someone who pays with a cheque accompanied by a cheque guarantee card impliedly represents that he has the bank's authority to do so: *MPC v Charles* [1977] AC 177. Since the bank had withdrawn Charles' authority to use his chequebook and cheque guarantee card his implied representation was false.
- Similarly, some who pays by credit card impliedly represents that he has the bank's authority to do so: *R v Lambie* [1982] AC 449. The bank had told the defendant to return her credit card because she had exceeded her credit limit. So her implied representation that she had authority to use the credit card was false.
- Someone who orders food in a restaurant impliedly represents that they intend to pay for the food at the end of their meal: *DPP v Ray* [1974] AC 370.
- Someone who takes a taxi impliedly represents that they have the money to pay the fare at the end of the journey: *R v Waterfall* [1970] 1 QB 148.
- Someone who books his driving theory test impliedly represents that he will turn up to sit the test himself: *DPP v Idrees* [2011] EWHC 624 (Admin). In this case the defendant had failed his driving theory test 15 times, so on the 16th attempt he arranged for someone else to sit the test in his place. He was convicted of fraud by false representation and his appeal against conviction was dismissed by the High Court.
- Someone who returns an item to a shop asking for a refund impliedly represents that the returned item is the one that was originally purchased: *R v Hoxhalli* [2016] EWCA Crim 724. In this case the defendant purchased a shirt online from Topshop. She then took the dispatch note and a similar shirt, from a different retailer, into a local Topshop store and asked for a refund, which she received. She was convicted of fraud by false representation, and her appeal against conviction was rejected by the Court of Appeal.

Although most of these cases were decided before the Fraud Act 2006, they will still be followed today.

Another case involving an implied representation was *R v Silverman* (1988) 86 Cr App R 213.[43] The defendant, Michael Silverman, was the manager of a plumbing and

---

[43]See also *R v Wenman* [2013] EWCA Crim 340.

central heating firm. The victims – two sisters aged in their 60s who lived together in a maisonette – had employed Silverman's company to do work for them for 15 years. They had come to trust him. He told them that the boiler in the maisonette needed to be replaced and that the whole property needed to be rewired. He quoted them a figure of £2,875 for the new boiler and £20,000 plus VAT to rewire the property. These figures were grossly excessive, but because the sisters trusted him they employed him to do the work and paid him. At trial Silverman was convicted of a deception offence. He appealed, arguing that there had not been a false representation: he said how much he would charge to do the work and he was paid the amount he quoted.

## EXTRACT

Read the following extract from the judgment of Watkins LJ. Had Silverman made a false representation? If so, what was it?

Suppose that Aubrey needs a plumber. He looks online and finds the details of a local plumber, Derek. Derek gives Aubrey a ridiculously expensive quote, but because Aubrey is gullible he employs Derek to do the work. When Derek is finished he charges Aubrey the amount he quoted. In the light of *R v Silverman*, did Derek make a false representation?

### *R v Silverman* (1988) 86 Cr App R 213

#### Watkins LJ

Mr. Hopmeier, who appeared below and appears here for the appellant, has argued, first, that the appellant made no representations to the complainants. He has not shrunk from conceding that the appellant was dishonest. He has submitted that the appellant quoted the sisters for the work to be done but that it was open to them either to accept or reject the quotation upon such advice as they might seek and perhaps in the light of tenders by others, and that the appellant was in much the same position as anyone else who is asked to quote for work to be done. He has argued that it is a dangerous concept to introduce into the criminal law that an excessively high quotation amounts to a false representation [...]. In certain circumstances that submission may we think be well founded. But whether a quotation amounts to false representation must depend upon the circumstances.

It seems clear to us that the complainants, far from being worldly wise, were unquestionably gullible. Having left their former home, they relied implicitly upon the word of the appellant about their requirements in their maisonette. In such circumstances of mutual trust, one party depending upon the other for fair and reasonable conduct, the criminal law may apply if one party takes dishonest advantage of the other by representing as a fair charge that which he but not the other knows is dishonestly excessive.

[...]

There was material for a finding that there had been a false representation although it is true that the appellant had said nothing at the time he made his representations to encourage the sisters to accept the quotations. He applied no pressure upon them, and apart from mentioning the actual prices to be charged was silent as to other matters that may have arisen for question in their minds.

[...]

Here the situation had been built up over a long period of time. It was a situation of mutual trust and the appellant's silence on any matter other than the sums to be charged were, we think, as eloquent as if he had said: "What is more, I can say to you that we are going to get no more than a modest profit out of this."

It is also possible to make a representation by omission, if the defendant is under a duty to pass on the relevant information.[44] In *R v Rai* [2000] 1 Cr App R 242 the defendant, Thomas Rai, had applied to the council for a grant to install a downstairs bathroom in the home of his elderly mother. The application was successful and he was awarded a grant of nearly £10,000. But before the building work started his mother died. Rai did not inform the council of his mother's death, and so the council went ahead and installed the downstairs bathroom. At trial Rai was convicted of a deception offence and this was upheld by the Court of Appeal. Another example of a representation by omission would be if Derek is filling in a car insurance application online and leaves blank the box which asks for details of previous speeding offences even though he has received two speeding tickets in the past year.

Finally, section 2(5) plugs a gap that existed in the previous law. Under the old deception offences, only people could be deceived. Machines could not be. The offences therefore did not apply in cases where a defendant entered false information into a machine and there was no other human involvement. An example would be where Derek gains access to Aubrey's online banking account and transfers money from Aubrey's account to his own. Section 2(5) of the Fraud Act 2006 now states:

## EXTRACT

### Section 2(5) of the Fraud Act 2006

(5)  For the purposes of this section a representation may be regarded as made if it (or anything implying it) is submitted in any form to any system or device designed to receive, convey or respond to communications (with or without human intervention).

So when Derek transfers the money from Aubrey's account to his own he impliedly represents that he is the account holder (or has the account holder's authority). Since this representation is false there is the *actus reus* of fraud.

Before moving on, it is worth emphasising that the only *actus reus* requirement of this type of fraud is that the defendant made a false representation. In particular, it is not necessary to show that the defendant actually gained anything as a result of the false representation, nor that the victim lost anything. As David Ormerod explains in the following extract, this is quite different to the old deception offences.

## EXTRACT

In the following extract Ormerod explains that, whilst the old deception offences were 'result crimes', fraud is a 'conduct crime'. What questions does Ormerod say this raises? How would you answer these questions?

What are the practical difficulties that Ormerod says result from fraud being a conduct crime?

---

[44] *Government of UAE v Allen* [2012] EWHC 1712 (Admin).

## Ormerod, D. (2007) 'The Fraud Act 2006 – Criminalising Lying?' *Criminal Law Review* 193

Section 2 of the Act is the broadest form of the fraud offence and hence likely to be the most frequently charged. The *actus reus* requires only that a person made a false representation, and the *mens rea* is satisfied by proof that he knew the representation was or might be false, and that he acted dishonestly, with intent to gain or cause loss. Classic examples of conduct caught will be false representations on mortgage application forms, life insurance forms, etc. The offence is also designed to criminalise dishonest "phishing" on the internet.

Before scrutinising individual elements, it is worth emphasising how dramatic is the shift from a result-based deception to a conduct-based representation offence. Under the old law D's conduct had to deceive V thereby causing V to do whatever act was appropriate to the charge-transferring property, executing a valuable security, etc. Under section 2, there is no need to prove a result of any kind or that an alleged victim or indeed any person believed any representation or acted on it; or, crucially, that the accused succeeded in making a gain or causing a loss by his representation. The effect is that D may be liable even though V knows that D's statement is false or V would have acted in the same way even if he had known of the falsity. The new offence has no requirement that V's property interests are damaged (temporarily or permanently), nor even that V's property interests are imperilled; it is sufficient that D intends to cause loss or make a gain. It is wider than conspiracy to defraud since a lone actor can be guilty without even prejudicing anyone's economic interests. This wholly inchoate offence appears to criminalise lying.

Should lying be a sufficient basis for criminal liability? What is the wrong which D performs which warrants the criminal sanction? It is not one derived from intentionally harming V's interests directly – there need be no such harm. Similarly, it is not one of potentially damaging V's interests. The wrong seems to be the act of lying or misleading with intent to gain or cause loss; the harm might be construed as one of destabilising society's processes of property and financial transfers. Even if this is sufficient to warrant criminalisation, is it properly called fraud? Classic definitions such as that from Stephen J. include, even at their widest, an element of intent to deceive which is much narrower than an intention to gain.

The absence of any loss direct or potential to V's interests may make the evaluation of the degree of blameworthiness and appropriate punishment very difficult. If D has typed an impressive high yield investment prospectus into his computer and emailed it, he seems to have breached section 2. What sentence is appropriate? The representation might have made millions of pounds from gullible investors, or been universally treated as irritating spam and deleted.

This shift has other serious practical implications. Obviously, the offence is complete earlier – on the making of the representation. In some instances section 2 might also catch conduct committed later in time-if, after D, a motorist, has with honest mind filled his fuel tank and the entire proprietary interest in the petrol has passed to him, he then falsely represents to V, the cashier, that it will be paid for by D's company, he breaches section 2. Although the "start" date of offending may be more difficult to specify when drafting particulars, this is unlikely to be material in most cases. A further effect is that V, formerly cast in a leading role in proving the causal effect of D's deception, now becomes an optional extra. With liability complete on D's representation being made, no specific victim(s) need to be identified. No doubt prosecutors will still commonly prefer to call a victim to testify about the circumstances of the representation, but technically, all that matters is that D acted with the intention to gain or cause loss; the potential effect of the false representation need not be proved. As with the deception offences it replaced, there will be overlap with theft in cases in which the false representation enables D to 'appropriate' V's property, even if with V's consent, as in *Gomez*. Of course, section 2 goes further by criminalising, D who lies with the intent that V lend him property which D intends to return unaltered

### 2. The defendant knew that the representation was, or might be, untrue or misleading

The first *mens rea* requirement is found in section 2(2)(b):

> **EXTRACT**
>
> ## Section 2(2)(b) of the Fraud Act 2006
>
> (2)  A representation is false if–
>
> [...]
>
>     (b)  the person making it knows that it is, or might be, untrue or misleading.

Notice that this requirement is not limited to knowledge that the representation was untrue or misleading. It is enough to show that the defendant knew that the representation *might be* untrue or misleading.

At the same time, remember that only knowledge will suffice. Less stringent *mens rea* concepts such as belief or suspicion are not enough. Moreover, it is not enough that the reasonable man would have known that the representation was or might be untrue or misleading. As McCombe LJ explained in *R v Augunas* [2013] EWCA Crim 2046:

> What is required is that the accused person knows that the representation is, or might be, misleading. It is not enough that a reasonable person might have known this; what matters is the accused person's actual knowledge. In our judgment, it not good enough for the prosecutor to satisfy the jury that the accused ought to have appreciated that the representation made by him was or might be untrue or misleading, nor is it enough that the circumstances must have given rise to a reasonable suspicion that the representation was, or might be, untrue or misleading.

### 3. The defendant intended, by making the false representation, to make a gain for himself or another or to cause loss to another or to expose another to a risk of loss

As we saw earlier, the *actus reus* of fraud does not contain any requirement that the defendant actually made a gain or caused a loss. However, for this part of the *mens rea* it must be shown that the defendant *intended*, by making the false representation, to make a gain, cause a loss or expose another to a risk of loss. The meaning of the words 'gain' and 'loss' is explained in section 5:

> **EXTRACT**
>
> ## Section 5 of the Fraud Act 2006
>
> ### 5 "Gain" and "loss"
>
> (1)  The references to gain and loss in sections 2 to 4 are to be read in accordance with this section.

(2)  "Gain" and "loss"–

   (a)  extend only to gain or loss in money or other property;

   (b)  include any such gain or loss whether temporary or permanent;

   and "property" means any property whether real or personal (including things in action and other intangible property).

(3)  "Gain" includes a gain by keeping what one has, as well as a gain by getting what one does not have.

(4)  "Loss" includes a loss by not getting what one might get, as well as a loss by parting with what one has.

Three important points emerge from section 5:

- Section 5(2)(a) states that the intended gain or loss must have been in money or other property. This is a point which students sometimes forget in the pressure of an exam, particularly when answering problem questions which involve a defendant who lies in order to trick someone into having sexual intercourse with him. Suppose that Derek says to his girlfriend Raquel, 'I love you and I want to marry you'. He only says this so that she will have sex with him. He does not mean it and intends to break up with her the next day. On these facts Derek has knowingly made a false representation, but he is not guilty of fraud because what he intended to gain (sexual intercourse) is not property. (To decide whether Derek has committed a sexual offence, read Chapter 7.)

- Section 5(2)(b) states that the intended gain or loss can be either temporary or permanent. This means that lying to someone in order to get them to lend you property can constitute fraud. Suppose that Derek asks to borrow Aubrey's sports car. Derek tells Aubrey that his own car has broken down and he is running late for an urgent meeting but, in fact, Derek's car has not broken down and he does not have a meeting to attend. He just fancies going for a drive in a sports car. On these facts Derek intends to make a temporary gain of property (Aubrey's sports car).

- The meaning of the word 'gain' is wider than just acquiring something and the meaning of the word 'loss' is wider than just parting with something. Section 5(3) says that gain also includes keeping what one already has, and section 5(4) says that loss also includes not getting what one might get. So suppose that Derek has recently graduated from university. He uses his out-of-date NUS card to get a student discount at the cinema. Here he intends to make a gain (keeping some money that he would otherwise have had to part with) and he intends to cause the cinema a loss (since they don't receive money they might have got).

Lastly, notice one other important point. The defendant must intend to make the gain or cause the loss by making the false representation. In other words, the defendant must expect that his false representation will *cause* the anticipated gain or loss. Whether this causal link exists is a question of fact for the jury.[45]

---

[45]*R v Gilbert* [2012] EWCA Crim 2392.

## ACTIVITY

- Think back to *R v Linekar* (this was the case we studied in Chapter 7 on sexual offences, in which the defendant falsely stated that he intended to pay a prostitute for sexual intercourse). Suppose that Linekar was charged with fraud. Could the prosecution argue that Linekar intended to make a gain for himself? Could the prosecution argue that Linekar intended to cause a loss to the prostitute?
- Derek has a job interview. He is in desperate need of income, so during the interview he lies about his A level grades and past experience. He figures that he will work so hard when he starts the job that his lies won't matter. Does Derek satisfy this part of the *mens rea* of fraud?

### 4. The defendant acted dishonestly

Note that the partial definition of dishonesty found in section 2(1) of the Theft Act 1968 does not apply here. So in all cases the standards of ordinary and decent people will be used to decide whether the defendant acted dishonestly. We studied this test above, in our examination of the offence of theft.

## Fraud by failing to disclose information

Fraud by failing to disclose information is defined by section 3 of the Fraud Act 2006:

### EXTRACT

**Section 3 of the Fraud Act 2006**

**3 Fraud by failing to disclose information**

A person is in breach of this section if he–

(a) dishonestly fails to disclose to another person information which he is under a legal duty to disclose, and

(b) intends, by failing to disclose the information–

   (i) to make a gain for himself or another, or

   (ii) to cause loss to another or to expose another to a risk of loss

This tells us that fraud by failing to disclose information has three requirements:

1. The defendant failed to disclose to another person information which he was under a legal duty to disclose
2. The defendant intended, by failing to disclose the information, to make a gain for himself or another or to cause loss to another or to expose another to a risk of loss
3. The defendant acted dishonestly.

Number 1 is an *actus reus* requirement. Numbers 2 and 3 are *mens rea* requirements. We will work through them in turn.

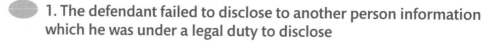

### 1. The defendant failed to disclose to another person information which he was under a legal duty to disclose

The *actus reus* of fraud by failing to disclose information is that the defendant was under a legal duty to disclose information to another person but failed to do so. The offence is thus targeted at deception by silence.

Whether or not there is a legal duty to disclose information is determined by the civil law.[46] Examples of when a duty exists include the duty of solicitors and estate agents to disclose information to their clients and the life insurance applicant's duty to tell the insurance company about his heart condition.

### 2. The defendant intended, by failing to disclose the information, to make a gain for himself or another or to cause loss to another or to expose another to a risk of loss

The offence of fraud by false representation had this same *mens rea* requirement. Everything we said about this requirement previously also applies here.

### 3. The defendant acted dishonestly

This is also the same as for fraud by false representation, which we studied above.

## Fraud by abuse of position

Fraud by abuse of position is defined by section 4 of the Fraud Act 2006:

> **EXTRACT**
>
> Section 4 of the Fraud Act 2006
>
> **4 Fraud by abuse of position**
>
> (1) A person is in breach of this section if he–
>
>   (a) occupies a position in which he is expected to safeguard, or not to act against, the financial interests of another person,
>
>   (b) dishonestly abuses that position, and
>
>   (c) intends, by means of the abuse of that position–
>
>     (i) to make a gain for himself or another, or
>
>     (ii) to cause loss to another or to expose another to a risk of loss.

This tells us that fraud by abuse of position has four requirements:

1. The defendant occupied a position in which he was expected to safeguard, or not act against, the financial interests of another person
2. The defendant abused that position

---

[46] *R v Razoq* [2012] EWCA Crim 674.

3.  The defendant intended, by abusing that position, to make a gain for himself or another or to cause loss to another or to expose another to a risk of loss

4.  The defendant acted dishonestly.

Numbers 1 and 2 are *actus reus* requirements. Numbers 3 and 4 are *mens rea* requirements. We will work through them in turn.

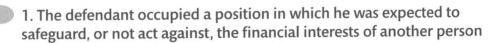

## 1. The defendant occupied a position in which he was expected to safeguard, or not act against, the financial interests of another person

The first *actus reus* requirement is that the defendant occupied a position in which he was expected to safeguard, or not act against, the financial interests of another person. A deliberate decision was made that the statute should not contain any further guidance on the types of positions that are covered by the offence, in order to maximise flexibility. As the following extract from the Law Commission makes clear, relationships where one party owes the other a fiduciary duty are covered. But it is not limited to fiduciary relationships. The offence could potentially also apply where the defendant has a moral, but not a legal, obligation to safeguard another person's financial interests.

### EXTRACT

Read the following extract from the Law Commission's 2002 report on fraud. What examples does it give of: (i) relationships that will be covered by the offence; and (ii) relationships that might be?

In a trial, whose responsibility is it to decide whether this *actus reus* requirement is satisfied?

### Law Commission (2002) *Fraud* (Law Commission Report No 276) Cm 5560

7.38 The necessary relationship will be present between trustee and beneficiary, director and company, professional person and client, agent and principal, employee and employer, or between partners. It may arise otherwise, for example within a family, or in the context of voluntary work, or in any context where the parties are not at arm's length. In nearly all cases where it arises, it will be recognised by the civil law as importing fiduciary duties, and any relationship that is so recognised will suffice. We see no reason, however, why the existence of such duties should be essential. This does not of course mean that it would be entirely a matter for the fact-finders whether the necessary relationship exists. The question whether the particular facts alleged can properly be described as giving rise to that relationship will be an issue capable of being ruled upon by the judge and, if the case goes to the jury, of being the subject of directions.

The types of position that fall within fraud by abuse of position were considered by the Court of Appeal in *R v Valujevs* [2014] EWCA Crim 2888. The defendants in this case were unlicensed gangmasters. They supplied agricultural work, transport and accommodation to individuals who had come to the UK from Latvia and Lithuania. The defendants' strategy was to create 'debt bondage'. To this end, they required the workers to take up their offer of accommodation as a condition of finding work for them. They then charged grossly excessive rent, causing the workers to default on their payments. The defendants then imposed fines, which they deducted from the workers' wages. They were charged with several offences, including fraud by abuse of position. The trial judge held that there was no case to answer on the charge of fraud by abuse of position, on the basis of respect for commercial freedom. The prosecution appealed against this ruling.

## EXTRACT

Read the following extract from the judgment of Fulford LJ. Section 4(1)(a) refers to a position in which a person is expected to safeguard, or not to act against, the financial interests of another person. According to Fulford LJ, does the word 'expected' refer to: (a) the expectation of the potential victim; (b) the expectation of the defendant; or, (c) the expectation of the reasonable person?

The Court of Appeal held that there was evidence that the defendants occupied a position in which they were expected to safeguard, or not to act against, the financial interests of the victims. What facts did Fulford LJ point to in reaching this conclusion?

Fulford LJ also outlined some situations in which the section 4 offence would not apply. What were these? According to Fulford LJ, why should the section 4 offence not apply in these situations?

### R v Valujevs [2014] EWCA Crim 2888

### Fulford LJ

37 In this case, the relevant acts of the gangmasters that are relied on by the prosecution have been set out in the draft amended count, namely that the defendants allegedly "withheld earnings, charged inflated rental payments and imposed unwarranted financial penalties". As described above, it is prohibited in the licensing standards to withhold or to threaten to withhold the whole or part of any payment due to a worker for any work they have done on account of "any matter within the control of the licence holder". In our view, at the very least, it is open to the jury on the evidence to decide that these defendants had gone beyond merely supplying workers and instead they had assumed control of and/or responsibility for collecting the wages of the workers or they controlled the amounts that the workers would be allowed to retain at the moment the wages were handed over. On either basis, the prosecution are able to contend that the defendants had taken on the obligation of paying the wages of the workers, and it is inherent in that commitment that the wages received by the workers will not be reduced by unwarranted financial penalties or deductions, unlawful demands for the repayment of suggested fines, or artificially inflated rental payments. (The prosecution does not rely on any other statutory/regulatory provision or any contractual term to establish an obligation by these defendants to pay the workers' wages without reductions.)

38 The duty not to withhold payment due to a worker has been imposed as part of an enforceable scheme to regulate the activities of gangmasters who provide labour, and in our judgment the prosecution is entitled to suggest that on this basis the relevant defendant "occupies a position in which he is expected to safeguard, or not to act against, the financial interests of another person" for the purposes of section 4. Put otherwise, having assumed responsibility for collecting the wages for a worker, or by exercising control over the wages that would be received by a worker at the point they are received, there is a clear expectation that the worker will receive them without a reduction in the form of (i) unwarranted financial penalties or deductions, (ii) unlawful demands for the repayment of suggested fines, or (iii) artificially inflated rental payments.

39 ... [These] three alternatives ought to be listed as separate particulars within the count as examples of how the defendants breached the obligation not to withhold wages. The jury will need to be directed that they can only convict if they all agree on at least one of the particulars.

40 We stress, we have focused on the regulatory scheme that applies to gangmasters and whether or not the approach taken on this appeal will apply in future cases as regards others who, in different roles, take on the responsibility for collecting the wages of a worker, employed or self-employed, is not for this court to determine.

41 Although the statute does not provide any assistance on the issue, in our view the "expectation" in section 4 of the 2006 Act is an objective one. It is for the judge to assess whether the position held by the individual is capable of being one "in which he is expected to safeguard, or not to act against, the financial interests of another person". If it is so capable, it will be for the jury thereafter to determine whether or not they are sure that was the case. It would be untenable to suggest that the expectation should be that of either the potential victim (the test would, in all likelihood, be too low) or the defendant (the test is likely to be set too high). Therefore, this is an objective test based on the position of the reasonable person.

[...]

43 The prosecution has relied on other forms of questionable financial behaviour on the part of the defendants as part of its reliance on section 4 of the 2006 Act, such as the general device of charging excessive sums for rent, withholding work in order to ensure that the worker in question was indebted to the gangmaster, or lending money to workers for which claims are later made for repayment (as opposed to deducting sums from wages). In our judgment, potentially reprehensible behaviour of this kind falls outside the financial interests of a person the gangmaster could properly be expected to safeguard or not to act against. Individuals do not commit a criminal offence under section 4 of the 2006 Act if they seek rental payments in excess of the market rate and gangmasters are not under an obligation to provide employment for those seeking work. Gangmasters are entitled to ask for repayment of moneys that they have lent to workers. Although we recognise that these can be difficult situations, the individual is able to look for accommodation or employment elsewhere and we are unpersuaded that this suggested behaviour on the part of the defendants arguably provides the basis for inclusion as particulars of a section 4 of the 2006 Act offence. In this critical sense we agree with the judge in the court below that to establish an abuse of position for the purposes of section 4 of the 2006 Act it is necessary for the prosecution to demonstrate a breach of a fiduciary duty, or a breach of an obligation that is akin to a fiduciary duty. This can conveniently be described, for instance, as a breach of trust or a breach of a privileged position in relation to the financial interests of another person. Section 4 does not apply to those who simply supply accommodation, goods, services or labour, whether on favourable or unfavourable terms and whether or not they have a stronger bargaining position. Therefore, the fact that an individual is a gangmaster who offers work or accommodation on particular terms, or lawfully requests the repayments of debts incurred by workers, does not ipso facto involve the abuse of a relevant position as regards the financial interests of another person.

44 We therefore concur with the conclusion of the judge that section 4 should not apply in "the general commercial area where individuals and businesses compete in markets of one kind or another, including labour markets, and are entitled to and expected to look after their own interests". We repeat, the critical factor in this case is that there is evidence that the defendants arguably assumed control of, and responsibility for, collecting the wages of the workers, or they controlled the wages at the moment that they were paid over, and the fact that they were acting as gangmasters merely provided the vital context relied on by the prosecution in which that role was assumed.

So fraud by abuse of position does not apply to those who supply accommodation, goods, services or labour on unfavourable terms simply by virtue of their stronger bargaining position. According to the Court of Appeal, what was crucial in *R v Valujevs* was that there was evidence that the defendants had either assumed responsibility for collecting the workers' wages or exercised control over the wages that they would receive. In the following extract, Jennifer Collins criticises this 'restrictive reading' of the fraud by abuse of position offence.

### EXTRACT

## Collins, J. (2016) 'Fraud by Abuse of Position and Unlicensed Gangmasters' 79 *Modern Law Review* 354

If identification of control or responsibility over monies is an attempt to identify the strongest basis for a relevant position of trust, the point arises that there are other strong reasons for leaving fraud by abuse of position to a jury in cases involving vulnerable migrant workers. Workers who are charged exorbitant rent or who are in debt bondage to intermediaries in the labour market are highly dependent upon those intermediaries. Their status in the labour market is nothing short of precarious. It is implausible that such individuals 'are entitled to and expected to look after their own interests', as Fulford LJ suggests. From this position of precariousness, ought there not to be an expectation that the source of this status must safeguard, or not act against, the vulnerable party's financial interests? Notably the workers in *Valujevs* were migrant workers, and thus part of a group of individuals who labour lawyers have noted 'are made particularly vulnerable by law' itself. Virginia Mantouvalou has identified 'exclusion from labour inspections, minimum wage and maximum working hours' legislation' as examples of ways in which the law creates vulnerability. Ought the criminal law to afford special protection using fraud by abuse of position to persons who are vulnerable to exploitation because of the rules of a legal system? The concern is that the potential for the section 4 offence to be read in this way is significantly impeded by the reasoning in *Valujevs*.

### 2. The defendant abused that position

The second *actus reus* requirement is that the defendant abused that position. We have just seen that, in *R v Valujevs*, there were three ways in which the defendants might have abused their position: imposing unwarranted financial penalties; making unlawful demands for the repayment of suggested fines; and, requiring artificially inflated rental payments. Beyond this, however, there is relatively little guidance since (as with the word 'position') a deliberate choice was made to maximise flexibility by not defining the word 'abuse'. All that the statute does tell us – in section 4(2) – is that a defendant can abuse his position by inaction:

### EXTRACT

## Section 4(2) of the Fraud Act 2006

(2)  A person may be regarded as having abused his position even though his conduct consisted of an omission rather than an act.

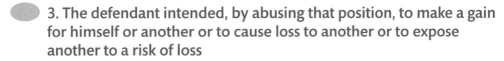

3. The defendant intended, by abusing that position, to make a gain for himself or another or to cause loss to another or to expose another to a risk of loss

The offence of fraud by false representation had this same *mens rea* requirement. Everything we said about this requirement previously also applies here.

### 4. The defendant acted dishonestly

This is also the same as for fraud by false representation, which we studied above.

## Criminal damage

The offence of criminal damage is defined by section 1(1) of the Criminal Damage Act 1971:

---

**EXTRACT**

### Section 1(1) of the Criminal Damage Act 1971

**1 Destroying or damaging property.**

(1)   A person who without lawful excuse destroys or damages any property belonging to another intending to destroy or damage any such property or being reckless as to whether any such property would be destroyed or damaged shall be guilty of an offence.

---

This tells us that criminal damage has six requirements:

1.   The defendant destroyed or damaged an item
2.   The item was property
3.   The property belonged to another person
4.   The defendant intentionally or recklessly destroyed or damaged the property
5.   The defendant knew that the property belonged to another person or was reckless as to whether it did
6.   The defendant lacked a lawful excuse.

Numbers 1, 2 and 3 are *actus reus* requirements. Numbers 4 and 5 are *mens rea* requirements. Number 6 is a defence which is peculiar to criminal damage offences. We will work through them in turn.

### 1. The defendant destroyed or damaged an item

The first *actus reus* requirement is that the defendant destroyed or damaged an item. The word 'destroyed' is relatively straightforward. Something that has been destroyed has ceased to exist. The case law has therefore focused on the word 'damage'.

Whether or not an item has been damaged is a question of fact for the jury. Although the trial judge may withdraw a case from the jury if there is no evidence that the item was damaged, the courts have interpreted the word 'damage' broadly. This means that, in practice, in most cases there will be sufficient evidence to leave the question whether an item has been damaged to the jury.

The case law shows that the courts have tended to apply two considerations when determining whether or not there is evidence that an item has been damaged. The first is whether the usefulness of the item was impaired (either permanently or temporarily). In *R v Fiak* [2005] EWCA Crim 2381 the defendant, Engin Fiak, had been arrested for drink-driving and for assaulting a police officer. At the police station he was placed in a cell and given a new, unused mattress, a clean, dry blanket and a pillow. While in his cell Fiak placed the blanket in the toilet and then flushed it repeatedly. As a result his own cell, as well as two others and the adjoining passage, were flooded. The water which caused the flooding was clean and the cell floor was waterproof. However, the blanket was rendered unusable until it was cleaned and dry and the cells had to be cleaned before they could be used again. At trial, Fiak was convicted of criminal damage of the blanket and his cell. He appealed, arguing that there was no evidence that either item had been damaged.

## EXTRACT

Read the following extract from the judgment of Sir Igor Judge. He refers to two authorities. What is the test that these two authorities set out?

Applying this test to the facts of Fiak's case, in the opinion of the Court had the blanket and cell been damaged?

### *R v Fiak* [2005] EWCA Crim 2381

#### Sir Igor Judge

The issue in relation to criminal damage can be summarised very simply. Mr Belger [defence counsel] argued that there was no evidence that either the blanket or the cells were damaged. He suggested that clean water had flooded onto a waterproof floor, and that in the process the blanket was made wet by clean water. The blanket would have been reusable when dry. Cleaning up a wet cell floor does not constitute damage to the cell itself. However widely interpreted "damage" may be for the purposes of the Criminal Damage Act 1971, a wet blanket and a wet cell floor fall outside any sensible definition. The argument of course assumes that the absence of any possible contamination or infection from the lavatory itself, and the confident expectation that there would be none.

In the 1971 Act, hardly surprisingly, the word "damage" itself is not further defined. The Concise Oxford Dictionary explains damage as "harm or injury impairing the value or usefulness of something ...". We need refer to only two authorities. The first is *Morphitis v Salmon* [1990] Crim LR 48, where the transcript of Auld J's judgment reads:

"The authorities show that the term "damage" for the purpose of this provision, should be widely interpreted so as to conclude not only permanent or temporary physical harm, but also permanent or temporary impairment of value or usefulness."

This analysis was approved in *R v Whiteley* [1991] 93 CAR 25 where, after a comprehensive examination of the authorities, Lord Lane CJ summarised their effect.

"Any alteration to the physical nature of the property concerned may amount to damage within the meaning of the section. Whether it does so or not will depend on the effect that the alteration has had upon the legitimate operator (who for convenience may be referred to as the owner) ... where ... the interference ... amounts to an impairment of the value or usefulness of the [property] to the owner, then the necessary damage is established."

Applying these principles to the present case, while it is true that the effect of the appellant's actions in relation to the blanket and the cell were both remediable, the simple reality is that the blanket could not be used as a blanket by any other prisoner until it had been dried out (and, we believe, also cleaned) and the flooded cells remained out of action until the water was cleared. In our judgment it is clear that both sustained damage for the purposes of the 1971 Act. There plainly was a case to answer.

Another case in which an item's usefulness was found to have been impaired is *Cox v Riley* (1986) 83 Cr App R 54. In this case, the defendant deliberately deleted the program from a printed circuit card that operated a computerised saw. On appeal, the Divisional Court upheld the defendant's conviction for criminal damage. His actions had rendered the saw inoperable and meant that time and money would need to be expended to reprogram the card. This case may be contrasted with the decision of the Divisional Court in *Drake v DPP* [1994] RTR 411.[47] The issue in this case was whether wheel clamping damages a car by rendering it unusable. The Court held that wheel clamping does not constitute damage. Laws J drew a distinction between adding something to an object and interfering with an object's integrity:

[T]here must be some intrusion into what, in the course of argument, Mann LJ described as the "integrity of the object in question". There was no such intrusion here. There was nothing which, as a matter of ordinary language, could sensibly be regarded as damage to the car. Certainly the wheel clamp was applied to it. I do not, for my part, believe that a court could properly have held that this application amounted to "damage"

## ACTIVITY

Derek removes a part from the engine of Aubrey's sports car. Without this part the engine will not start. Has Derek damaged the car?

The second consideration the courts have applied is whether time and money will be required to remedy the defendant's actions. We have just seen that this was one of the reasons why the circuit card was held to have been damaged in *Cox v Riley*. Other examples include:

## EXAMPLE

- *Hardman v Chief Constable of Avon and Somerset* [1986] Crim LR 330: the defendants were campaigners for nuclear disarmament. On the 40th anniversary of the Hiroshima bombing they painted paintings on a pavement. They used water-soluble paint so that, in time, the paintings would wash away. Their criminal damage convictions were upheld by the Crown Court at Bristol. In order to remove the paintings immediately the local authority had to use high-pressure water jets, which caused expense and inconvenience.

---

[47]See also *Lloyd v DPP* [1992] RTR 215.

- *Roe v Kingerlee* [1986] Crim LR 735: the defendant smeared mud and graffiti on the walls of a police cell. The Divisional Court held that this was capable of constituting criminal damage. The Court emphasised that the damage need not be permanent and added that it had cost £7 to clean the cell.
- *Seray-Wurie v DPP* [2012] EWHC 208 (Admin): the defendant lived in a private residential estate. The management company for the estate put up two parking notices. The defendant wrote on these notices using a black marker pen. The High Court upheld his criminal damage conviction, saying that it would cost £90 to remove the writing from the signs.

If the nature of the item in question is such that the defendant's actions do not need to be remedied, there will be no damage. So, in *Morphitis v Salmon* [1990] Crim LR 48 the Divisional Court held that a scratch on a scaffolding bar was incapable of amounting to damage. The scratch did not impair the item's usefulness, and scaffolding bars are frequently scratched during ordinary use. Similarly, if the defendant's actions can be remedied with little effort and at no expense there will be no damage. In *A (A Juvenile) v R* [1978] Crim LR 689 the defendant spat on a police officer's raincoat. Streeter J in Kent Crown Court explained that this was incapable of constituting damage:

> [Spitting at a garment] could be an act capable of causing damage. However, one must consider the specific garment which has been allegedly damaged. If someone spat upon a satin wedding dress, for example, any attempt to remove the spittle might in itself leave a mark or stain [...] An article might also have been rendered "inoperative" if, as a result of what happened, it had been taken to dry cleaners. However, in the present case, no attempt had been made, even with soap and water, to clean the raincoat, which was a service raincoat designed to resist the elements

### 2. The item was property

At the start of this chapter we saw how section 4 of the Theft Act 1968 defines property for the purposes of the offence of theft. Section 10(1) of the Criminal Damage Act 1971 contains a similar, but not identical, definition for the offence of criminal damage:

### EXTRACT

## Section 10(1) of the Criminal Damage Act 1971

### 10 Interpretation

(1)  In this Act "property" means of a tangible nature, whether real or personal, including money and–

(a)  including wild creatures which have been tamed or are ordinarily kept in captivity, and any other wild creatures or their carcasses if, but only if, they have been reduced into possession which has not been lost or abandoned or are in the course of being reduced into possession; but

(b)  not including mushrooms growing wild on any land or flowers, fruit or foliage of a plant growing wild on any land.

For the purposes of this subsection "mushroom" includes any fungus and "plant" includes any shrub or tree.

The most important difference between this definition and the one found in the Theft Act 1968 is that, while the Theft Act's definition encompassed tangible and intangible property, section 10(1) is limited to tangible property. So a defendant cannot be guilty of criminally damaging something intangible like a copyright.

Two other differences between this definition and the one found in the Theft Act 1968 are:

- Section 10(1) encompasses land. So a defendant can be guilty of criminally damaging land, whereas section 4(2) of the Theft Act 1968 states that land can only be stolen in certain circumstances.
- According to section 10(1), a defendant cannot be guilty of criminally damaging wild mushrooms, flowers, fruit or foliage. By contrast, section 4(3) of the Theft Act 1968 states that these can be stolen if they are picked for sale or another commercial purpose.

Given the similarities between the two definitions, it may sometimes be possible to apply by analogy the case law on the meaning of property for the purposes of theft to the offence of criminal damage.

## 3. The property belonged to another person

To be guilty of the basic criminal damage offence the property must have belonged to another person. (As we'll see shortly, things are different for aggravated criminal damage. For the aggravated offence there is no requirement that the property belonged to someone else.)

The word 'belong' is defined in section 10(2), with further specific situations dealt with in sections 10(3) and 10(4):

### EXTRACT

#### Sections 10(2)–10(4) of the Criminal Damage Act 1971

(2) Property shall be treated for the purposes of this Act as belonging to any person–

    (a) having the custody or control of it;

    (b) having in it any proprietary right or interest (not being an equitable interest arising only from an agreement to transfer or grant an interest); or

    (c) having a charge on it.

(3) Where property is subject to a trust, the persons to whom it belongs shall be so treated as including any person having a right to enforce the trust.

(4) Property of a corporation sole shall be so treated as belonging to the corporation notwithstanding a vacancy in the corporation.

This is very similar to the definition of 'belong' in section 5(1) of the Theft Act 1968. As with the offence of theft, section 10(2) makes it clear that in criminal damage cases belonging is a broader concept than ownership. Property belongs to anyone who has 'custody or control' of the item, anyone with 'any proprietary right or interest' in the item and anyone who has a 'charge' over the item. It follows that, for the offence of criminal damage, property can belong to more than one person at a time. Moreover, it is possible for the owner of an item to be guilty of criminal damaging it if someone else has a proprietary right (such as a lien) over the item.

## 4. The defendant intentionally or recklessly destroyed or damaged the property

The first *mens rea* requirement is that the defendant destroyed or damaged the property either intentionally or recklessly. We studied these *mens rea* concepts in Chapter 4. It is worth emphasising that, following the House of Lords' decision in *R v G & another* [2003] UKHL 50, it is the *R v Cunningham* test for recklessness that applies.

## 5. The defendant knew that the property belonged to another person or was reckless as to whether it did

The second *mens rea* requirement is that the defendant knew that the property belonged to another person or was reckless as to whether it did. It follows that if the defendant genuinely believed that the property that he was damaging was his own, he is not guilty of criminal damage. This is illustrated by *R v Smith* [1974] QB 354. The defendant, David Smith, began renting a flat in 1970. With the landlord's permission, he installed some electric wiring for stereo equipment and put up roofing material, wall panels and laid floorboards. Unbeknown to Smith, when he installed the roofing, wall panels and floorboards they became part of the house and so became the landlord's property. Two years later Smith moved out of the flat. Before leaving, he damaged the roofing, wall panels and floorboards in order to recover the electric wiring he had installed. He was subsequently arrested for criminal damage. When interviewed by police Smith said, 'Look, how can I be done for smashing my own property. I put the flooring and that in, so if I want to pull it down it's a matter for me.' At trial the judge told the jury that Smith's belief that the property he damaged belonged to him was no defence. He was subsequently convicted, and appealed. The Court of Appeal allowed his appeal and quashed his conviction. James LJ explained:

> Construing the language of section 1(1) we have no doubt that the *actus reus* is "destroying or damaging any property belonging to another." It is not possible to exclude the words "belonging to another" which describes the "property." Applying the ordinary principles of mens rea, the intention and recklessness and the absence of lawful excuse required to constitute the offence have reference to property belonging to another. It follows that in our judgment no offence is committed under this section if a person destroys or causes damage to property belonging to another if he does so in the honest though mistaken belief that the property is his own, and provided that the belief is honestly held it is irrelevant to consider whether or not it is a justifiable belief.

### ACTIVITY

Derek has been charged with the criminal damage of property belonging to Aubrey. Derek genuinely believed that the property belonged to him, but this belief was an utterly unreasonable one to have held. Does Derek satisfy this part of the *mens rea*?

## 6. The defendant lacked a lawful excuse

A defendant who is charged with criminal damage can rely on any of the substantive defences that we will study in Chapter 11. In addition, section 5 of the Criminal Damage Act 1971 sets out two 'lawful excuses':

> ## EXTRACT
>
> ## Section 5 of the Criminal Damage Act 1971
>
> ### 5 "Without lawful excuse"
>
> [...]
>
> (2) A person charged with an offence to which this section applies, shall, whether or not he would be treated for the purposes of this Act as having a lawful excuse apart from this subsection, be treated for those purposes as having a lawful excuse–
>
>    (a) if at the time of the act or acts alleged to constitute the offence he believed that the person or persons whom he believed to be entitled to consent to the destruction of or damage to the property in question had so consented, or would have so consented to it if he or they had known of the destruction or damage and its circumstances; or
>
>    (b) if he destroyed or damaged or threatened to destroy or damage the property in question or, in the case of a charge of an offence under section 3 above, intended to use or cause or permit the use of something to destroy or damage it, in order to protect property belonging to himself or another or a right or interest in property which was or which he believed to be vested in himself or another, and at the time of the act or acts alleged to constitute the offence he believed–
>
>      (i) that the property, right or interest was in immediate need of protection; and
>
>      (ii) that the means of protection adopted or proposed to be adopted were or would be reasonable having regard to all the circumstances.
>
> (3) For the purposes of this section it is immaterial whether a belief is justified or not if it is honestly held.
>
> (4) For the purposes of subsection (2) above a right or interest in property includes any right or privilege in or over land, whether created by grant, licence or otherwise.

These lawful excuses are not available as a defence to other crimes such as assault or battery. They are unique to criminal damage.

The first lawful excuse, found in section 5(2)(a), applies where the defendant honestly believed that the owner of the property was consenting to the property damage or would have consented had they known about it. An example is *Jaggard v Dickinson* [1981] 2 WLR 118. Beverley Jaggard had been out drinking for the evening. At 10:45 pm she took a taxi to her friend's house. Her friend, who lived at number 67, had given her permission to treat the house as her own. Jaggard got out of the taxi and went to what she thought was her friend's house, but in fact was number 35. Finding that she was locked out she attempted to gain entry by smashing a window in the hallway, and then went to the back door and managed to get inside by smashing another window. It was found as fact that Jaggard had genuinely believed that she was breaking into her friend's house (which was identical in outward appearance to number 35), and that Jaggard's mistake was the result of voluntary intoxication.

At trial, Jaggard was convicted of criminal damage. On appeal, the Divisional Court quashed her conviction. Mustill J explained that, according to section 5(3), the lawful excuses are concerned with what the defendant genuinely believed – even if the belief was mistaken, was unreasonable and was the result of voluntary intoxication:

> It seems to us that the court is required by section 5(3) to focus on the existence of the belief, not its intellectual soundness; and a belief can be just as much honestly held if it is induced by intoxication, as if it stems from stupidity, forgetfulness or inattention

Given that Jaggard genuinely believed that the house belonged to her friend, and that her friend would have consented to her breaking in, she was entitled to rely on the lawful excuse contained in section 5(2)(a).

The second lawful excuse, found in section 5(2)(b), applies where the defendant damaged property in order to protect his own or someone else's property. For this lawful excuse to be available, the defendant must have: (i) damaged the property 'in order to' protect his or someone else's property; (ii) genuinely believed that the property was 'in immediate need of protection' and (iii) genuinely believed that the steps he took to protect the property were 'reasonable having regard to all the circumstances'. The test for numbers (ii) and (iii) is entirely subjective. In *Unsworth v DPP* [2010] EWHC 3037 (Admin) the defendant Jacqueline Unsworth was caught cutting down her neighbour's conifer trees (which were 10–12 feet tall). She explained that she cut them down to protect her right to light in her kitchen and that the lack of light had caused her to become depressed. The Divisional Court confirmed that the test for numbers (ii) and (iii) is 'exclusively a test of the defendant's belief' ([7]). They do not require any objective assessment of the defendant's belief.

However, things are different for number (i). In spite of the apparently subjective wording of sections 5(2) and 5(3), the courts have injected some objectivity. This is illustrated by *R v Hill & Hall* (1989) 89 Cr App R 74. The defendants in this case, Valerie Hill and Jennifer Hall, lived near a US naval base in west Wales. One day they were found in possession of a hacksaw blade, which they said they intended to use to cut part of the perimeter fence of the base. The reason they gave was because they believed the naval base was used to monitor the movements of Russian submarines and so was a prime target for a retaliatory, or even pre-emptive, Russian nuclear strike. Any such attack would devastate the area, including the defendants' homes. So the defendants said that they wanted to compromise the security of the naval base by cutting the perimeter fence, in the hope that this might force the US to relocate the naval base elsewhere.

At trial Hill and Hall were convicted of possessing a hacksaw blade with intent to commit criminal damage.[48] On appeal, the Court of Appeal held that the defendants could not rely on the section 5(2)(b) lawful excuse.

## EXTRACT

In the following extract Lord Lane CJ outlines a two-stage approach to deciding whether the section 5(2)(b) lawful excuse is available. What are these two stages?

Having distinguished the two stages, why was Hill unable to rely on the lawful excuse?

### *R v Hill & Hall* (1989) 89 Cr App R 74

### Lord Lane CJ

There are two aspects to this type of question. The first aspect is to decide what it was that the applicant, in this case Valerie Hill, in her own mind thought. The learned judge assumed, and so do we, for the purposes of this decision, that everything she said about her reasoning was true. I

---

[48]Criminal Damage Act 1971, s.3.

have already perhaps given a sufficient outline of what it was she believed to demonstrate what is meant by that. Up to that point the test was subjective. In other words one is examining what is going on in the applicant's mind.

Having done that, the judges in the present cases – and the judge particularly in the case of Valerie Hill – turned to the second aspect of the case, and that is this. He had to decide as a matter of law which means objectively, whether it could be said that on those facts as believed by the applicant, snipping the strand of the wire, which she intended to do, could amount to something done to protect either the applicant's own home or the homes of her adjacent friends in Pembrokeshire.

He decided, again quite rightly in our view, that that proposed act on her part was far too remote from the eventual aim at which she was targeting her actions to satisfy the test.

It follows therefore, in our view, that the judges in the present two cases were absolutely right to come to the conclusion that they did so far as this aspect of the case is concerned, and to come to that conclusion as a matter of law, having decided the subjective test as the applicants wished them to be decided.

The second half of the question was that of the immediacy of the danger. Here the wording of the Act, one reminds oneself, is as follows: She believed that "the property ... was in immediate need of protection."

Once again the judge had to determine whether, on the facts as stated by the applicant, there was any evidence on which it could be said that she believed there was a need of protection from immediate danger. In our view that must mean evidence that she believed that immediate action had to be taken to do something which would otherwise be a crime in order to prevent the immediate risk of something worse happening. The answers which I have read in the evidence given by this woman (and the evidence given by the other applicant was very similar) drives this Court to the conclusion, as they drove the respective judges to the conclusion, that there was no evidence on which it could be said that there was that belief.

So unlike numbers (ii) and (iii) which are entirely subjective, the test for number (i) 'has both a subjective and an objective aspect'.[49] Not only must the defendant's reason for destroying or damaging the property have been to protect his own (or someone else's) property (subjective), the destruction or damage must also have been capable of protecting the property in question (objective). The court decided that this objective requirement was not satisfied in *R v Hill & Hall*. Note also that Lord Lane CJ emphasised that, even though number (ii) is subjective, the defendant must still produce some supporting evidence to demonstrate that he did in fact believe the property was in immediate need of protection. Hill and Hall had failed to produce any evidence that they did indeed believe that this was the case.

## ACTIVITY

The decision in *R v Hill & Hall* is controversial, for it seems hard to reconcile with the subjective wording of the statute. Can you think of any policy reasons for the decision?

---

[49]*Unsworth v DPP* [2010] EWHC 3037 (Admin), [11].

# Aggravated criminal damage

The offence of aggravated criminal damage is defined by section 1(2) of the Criminal Damage Act 1971:

---

**EXTRACT**

## Section 1(2) of the Criminal Damage Act 1971

### 1 Destroying or damaging property.

[...]

(2)  A person who without lawful excuse destroys or damages any property, whether belonging to himself or another–

(a)  intending to destroy or damage any property or being reckless as to whether any property would be destroyed or damaged; and

(b)  intending by the destruction or damage to endanger the life of another or being reckless as to whether the life of another would be thereby endangered;

shall be guilty of an offence.

---

This tells us that aggravated criminal damage has five requirements:

1.  The defendant destroyed or damaged an item
2.  The item was property
3.  The defendant intentionally or recklessly destroyed or damaged the property
4.  The defendant intended, by the destruction or damage, to endanger the life of another or was reckless as to whether the life of another would be thereby endangered
5.  The defendant lacked a lawful excuse.

Numbers 1 and 2 are *actus reus* requirements. Numbers 3 and 4 are *mens rea* requirements. Number 5 is a defence which is peculiar to criminal damage offences. We will work through them in turn.

## 1. The defendant destroyed or damaged an item

This is the same as for the basic criminal damage offence, which we studied above.

## 2. The item was property

The word 'property' has the same meaning as for the basic criminal damage offence, which we studied above. Notice that for aggravated criminal damage there is no requirement that the property belonged to another person; the defendant may commit the aggravated offence by damaging his own property.

## 3. The defendant intentionally or recklessly destroyed or damaged the property

This is the same as for the basic criminal damage offence, which we studied above.

## 4. The defendant intended, by the destruction or damage, to endanger the life of another or was reckless as to whether the life of another would be thereby endangered

This *mens rea* requirement is the aggravating factor which makes this such a serious offence (punishable by up to life imprisonment[50]). Notice that there is no corresponding *actus reus* requirement; there is no need to show that anyone's life was in fact endangered. What must be shown is that the defendant intended, by the destruction or damage, to endanger the life of another or that he was reckless as to whether the life of another would be thereby endangered. Intention and recklessness have the meanings that we studied in Chapter 4. Note in particular that recklessness here means *R v Cunningham* recklessness.[51]

In *R v Steer* [1987] 3 WLR 205 the defendant, Dennis Steer, armed himself with an automatic rifle and went to the home of his former business partner, David Gregory, against whom he bore a grudge. When Gregory and his wife looked out of their bedroom window, Steer fired a shot at the window and then another one at the front door. No one was hurt. The prosecution accepted that Steer had not intended to hurt Gregory or his wife, but contended that Steer had been reckless as to whether their lives would be endangered. At trial Steer was convicted of aggravated criminal damage. He appealed, emphasising that section 1(2)(b) of the Criminal Damage Act 1971 states 'intending *by the destruction or damage* to endanger the life of another or being reckless as to whether the life of another would be *thereby* endangered'. In other words, the property damage must be the means by which the defendant intends to endanger life or foresees life being endangered. Steer argued that in his case this requirement was not satisfied since it was not the damage he caused (a broken window) that endangered life, rather it was the bullet from the rifle shot. The case reached the House of Lords. The House of Lords accepted Steer's argument and quashed his conviction for aggravated criminal damage. Lord Bridge explained:

> Under both limbs of section 1 of the Act of 1971 it is the essence of the offence which the section creates that the defendant has destroyed or damaged property. For the purpose of analysis it may be convenient to omit reference to destruction and to concentrate on the references to damage, which was all that was here involved. To be guilty under subsection (1) the defendant must have intended or been reckless as to the damage to property which he caused. To be guilty under subsection (2) he must additionally have intended to endanger life or been reckless as to whether life would be endangered "by the damage" to property which he caused. This is the context in which the words must be construed and it seems to me impossible to read the words "by the damage" as meaning "by the damage or by the act which caused the damage." Moreover, if the language of the statute has the meaning for which the Crown contends, the words "by the destruction or damage" and "thereby" in subsection (2)(b) are mere surplusage. If the Crown's submission is right, the only additional element necessary to convert a subsection (1) offence into a subsection (2) offence is an intent to endanger life or recklessness as to whether life would be endangered simpliciter.

> It would suffice as a ground for dismissing this appeal if the statute were ambiguous, since any such ambiguity in a criminal statute should be resolved in favour of the defence. But I can find no ambiguity. It seems to me that the meaning for which the respondent contends is the only meaning which the language can bear.

---

[50]Criminal Damage Act 1971, s.4.
[51]*R v G & another* [2003] UKHL 50.

**5. The defendant lacked a lawful excuse**

The lawful excuses contained in section 5(2) are not available on a charge of aggravated criminal damage. So for this offence, the term 'lawful excuse' simply means any of the substantive defences that we will study in Chapter 11.

 ## Conclusion

Well done for making it to the end of the chapter! Much of the material we have worked through is quite detailed and technical. This technicality means that it is very important, when answering problem questions, to take extra care to be precise. For every possible offence that you consider, always take care to begin by clearly stating the following particulars:

| Information | Why it is important |
|---|---|
| Who the defendant is | Whether or not an item of property belongs to someone can depend on who is alleged to have stolen it. |
| | For example, the car did not belong to the police in *R v Meredith* because Meredith was the defendant. If anyone else had been accused of stealing the car it would have belonged to the police! |
| Which crime or crimes the defendant may have committed | Several of the property offences overlap, so it is important to clearly state which offence you are focusing on. |
| | For example, there are subtle differences between section 9(1)(a) and section 9(1)(b) burglary, so it is important to say which one you are discussing. |
| Which of the defendant's actions you are focusing on | The moment at which the offence was committed can be critical, so it is important to identify which of the defendant's actions constituted the offence. |
| | For example, to establish robbery it is necessary to show that the defendant used force immediately before or at the time of the theft. This means that you need to identify exactly when the theft occurred. |
| What the item of property is | When there is more than one possible way of describing the item in question you need to select the most appropriate description. |
| | For example, we saw how in *R v Easom* the wording of the charge was vital, and resulted in an acquittal instead of a conviction. We also saw in *Oxford v Moss* that the defendant was charged with theft of confidential information, which is not property. Arguably things might have been different had he been charged with theft of the exam paper. |
| Who the victim of the offence was | Where the property might have belonged to several people at once, it is important to state which person the defendant is accused of stealing from. |
| | For example, we saw in *Ricketts v Basildon Magistrates' Court* that the defendant could not be convicted of theft from the British Heart Foundation shop but could be convicted of theft from the donor of the items. |

Often it is possible to give all of this information in one short, concise sentence, such as: 'Derek would be charged with robbery of the handbag from Cassandra by wrenching it from her grasp'. Clarifying the particulars of the offence in this way at the outset can help ensure that you avoid errors later on.

Something else that students sometimes find confusing when studying this topic is the overlap between different offences. A common question is: 'Should I discuss every offence that might apply or just select one?' To answer this it is helpful to distinguish two types of situation:

- Sometimes a defendant can only be guilty of one offence if it can first be shown that he committed another (ulterior) offence. For example, a defendant can only be convicted of robbery if he committed theft. And a defendant can only be convicted of section 9(1)(b) burglary if he committed theft (or attempted theft) or infliction of GBH (or attempted infliction of GBH). In these instances, it is sensible to establish liability for the ulterior offence first, then move on to discuss the other offence.

- Sometimes two offences simply overlap. Of the offences we have studied in this chapter, this is most likely to occur with theft and fraud. When this happens, begin with the offence that you think is the most appropriate (bearing in mind not only the principle of fair labelling, but also the fact that a prosecutor is likely to charge the offence that he thinks is most likely to result in a conviction). If liability for this offence is established, it is still worth mentioning the alternative offence but you can deal with it more briefly.

 **Self-test questions**

1. The following events take place at Golfers' Paradise (a private golf club):
   a. Jack (a club member) arranges to play a round of golf with his friend Arnold (a former member who decided not to renew his membership). The club charges non-members a fee of £30 to play a round, so when they arrive Arnold shows the club caretaker, Gary, his old membership card hoping that Gary will not notice that it has expired. Gary does not notice, and so does not charge Arnold the £30 fee.

      Before teeing off they go to the club shop and look at the golfing magazines. Even though there is a sign saying 'Please do not read the magazines until they have been paid for', Jack picks up one of the magazines and reads three articles from it before returning it to the shelf without paying for it. Meanwhile Arnold notices a voucher for free trolley hire in one of the other magazines. He rips it out, places the magazine back on the shelf without paying for it and then takes the voucher to the counter and says, 'I have a voucher for free trolley hire'. Club assistant Tony had not seen Arnold rip the voucher out of the magazine, and so accepts it. While Tony is outside getting a trolley, Arnold sees some bottles of water behind the counter. He realises he has not brought anything to drink during his round, so leans over the counter and helps himself to a bottle of water. While he is leaning over the counter he notices a box of chocolate bars under the till. He takes one of those too, and then quickly hides the bottle of water and chocolate bar in his golf bag. Tony then returns with a trolley. Arnold takes it, and he and Jack embark on their round of golf.

      Discuss the criminal liability of Arnold and Jack.

   b. Nick and Greg are halfway through their round of golf. Nick suggests, 'How about we make it more interesting? Whoever loses the next hole pays the winner £10'.

Greg agrees. Nick hits his tee shot into a bunker. He is so frustrated that he strikes his golf trolley (which he has hired from the golf club for the day) with his golf club. This scratches the trolley and causes a small dent.

As he walks up the fairway Nick notices two lost golf balls in the long grass. When he picks them up he looks at them and sees the words 'Property of Golfers' Paradise Golf Club'. Nick looks around, sees that no one is watching and then quickly puts the balls in his golf bag.

When they have both finished the hole Nick asks Greg, 'How many shots did you take?' Greg replies, 'Six'. Nick says, 'In that case, I win. I only took five'. In fact, unbeknown to Greg, Nick had taken seven shots. Greg takes a £10 note from his wallet and gives it to Nick.

Discuss the criminal liability of Nick. How (if at all) would your answer be different if there had been nothing written on the two lost golf balls?

c.   Lee has just finished his round of golf. A week earlier he had left one of his golf clubs – his driver – at the clubhouse by mistake. He decides to go to the clubhouse to ask whether anyone has found it and handed it in. On his way he walks past Phil, and notices a driver in Phil's golf bag that looks just like his own. Convinced that it belongs to him, Lee says to Phil, 'Where did you get that driver?' Phil answers, 'I bought it last year on holiday in the US.' Lee replies, 'Rubbish, that's mine and you know it'. He pushes Phil to the floor, takes the driver out of Phil's bag and walks off with it. In fact, Phil was telling the truth; the driver was not the one Lee had lost.

Lee goes to the clubhouse bar and decides to play on the quiz machine. However, instead of inserting a £1 coin he inserts a foreign coin that he has left over from his summer holiday which is the same size and shape as a £1 coin. When Lee gets an answer wrong he is so annoyed that he kicks the machine, causing a dent.

Lee then orders some food from the club restaurant. When he places his order he intends to eat his meal and then sneak out without paying. However, once he has finished eating he changes his mind, pays for his meal and goes home.

Meanwhile two other golfers – Sergio and Martin – go to the clubhouse bar where they are served by barman Darren, who is good friends with both of them. Darren hands them their drinks and says, 'These drinks are free of charge. Enjoy!' even though the bar manager Colin had earlier warned him to stop giving out free drinks.

Discuss the criminal liability of Lee and Darren.

2.  'The decisions of the House of Lords in *R v Gomez* [1993] AC 442 and *R v Hinks* [2001] 2 AC 241 were unsatisfactory and problematic, for a number of reasons. By contrast, the decision of the Supreme Court in *Ivey v Genting Casinos* [2017] UKSC 67 to overrule *R v Ghosh* [1982] QB 1053 is to be applauded.'

Discuss the extent to which you agree with this statement.

## Property offences checklist

Having worked through this chapter, you should now have:

✓  An understanding of the offence of theft
✓  An ability to critically discuss the case law on appropriation
✓  An ability to critically discuss the test for dishonesty

✓ An understanding of the offence of robbery

✓ An understanding of the offence of burglary and the difference between section 9(1)(a) and section 9(1)(b) burglary

✓ An understanding of the offence of fraud and the difference between fraud by false representation, fraud by failing to disclose information and fraud by abuse of position

✓ An understanding of the offences of criminal damage and aggravated criminal damage.

## Further reading

Ashworth, A. (2002) 'Robbery Re-assessed' *Criminal Law Review* 851.

Clarkson, C. (1993) 'Theft and Fair Labelling' 56 *Modern Law Review* 554.

Edwards, I. (2009) 'Banksy's Graffiti: A Not-so-simple Case of Criminal Damage?' 73 *Journal of Criminal Law* 345.

Gardner, J. (1998) 'Property and Theft' *Criminal Law Review* 35.

Griew, E. (1985) 'Dishonesty: The Objections to *Feely* and *Ghosh*' *Criminal Law Review* 341.

Glazebrook, P. (1991) 'Thief or Swindler: Who Cares?' 50 *Cambridge Law Journal* 389.

Glover, R. (2010) 'Can Dishonesty Be Salvaged? Theft and the Grounding of the *MSC Napoli*' 74 *Journal of Criminal Law* 53.

Halpin, A. (1996) 'The Test for Dishonesty' *Criminal Law Review* 283.

Ormerod, D. (2007) 'The Fraud Act 2006 – Criminalising Lying?' *Criminal Law Review* 193.

Pace, P.J. (1985) 'Burglarious Trespass' *Criminal Law Review* 716.

Shute, S. (2002) 'Appropriation and the Law of Theft' *Criminal Law Review* 445.

Simester, A.P. and Sullivan, G.R. (2005) 'On the Nature and Rationale of Property Offences' in R.A. Duff and S.P. Green (eds) *Defining Crimes: Essays on the Special Part of the Criminal Law*. Oxford: OUP.

# 9

# Intoxication

## Chapter objectives

By the end of this chapter you should have:

- An understanding of the case law that applies to defendants who were intoxicated at the time of their alleged offence
- An ability to apply the relevant law to a hypothetical set of facts and discuss whether criminal liability may be established
- An ability to critically discuss whether involuntary intoxication should be available as a substantive defence.

# Introduction

A large proportion of violent crime is committed by intoxicated defendants. Research has consistently found that in at least 40 per cent of all violent incidents the victim believed the offender was under the influence of alcohol. In 2015–16, for example, there were 491,000 violent incidents in which the victim believed the offender was under the influence of alcohol. This constituted 40 per cent of all the violent incidents that year. The same year, there were also 237,000 violent incidents in which the victim believed the offender was under the influence of drugs (19 per cent of all the violent incidents that year).[1] The law that we study in this chapter is therefore of great practical importance.

If you are answering a problem question which involves an intoxicated defendant, the first question to ask yourself is: why is the defendant adducing evidence of his intoxication? There are two possible reasons.

First, he might be using the fact he was intoxicated in order to argue that he lacked the *mens rea* of the offence he has been charged with. The defendant might say something like, 'I was so drunk that I had no awareness of what I was doing' or, 'I was so drunk that I was incapable of forming any intention to injure him'. A couple of real-life examples can be given to illustrate this: (1) a nurse is so drunk that she mistakes a baby for a log of wood, and puts the baby on the fire. The nurse could claim that she lacked the *mens rea* of murder since she never formed an intention to kill or seriously injure the baby; (2) the victim is lying in the defendant's bed, but the defendant is so drunk that he mistakenly thinks the man is a theatrical dummy and stabs the victim to death. The defendant could claim that he lacked the *mens rea* of murder since he did not know he was stabbing a person and so never formed an intention to kill or cause serious injury.[2]

There is a second reason why a defendant might adduce evidence of his intoxication. He might claim that his intoxication caused in him a mistaken belief which should form the basis of a substantive defence. For example, he might say something like, 'I was so drunk that I thought the victim was going to attack me, so I pushed him over to defend myself'.

In this chapter we will look at each of these two reasons in turn. The majority of the chapter will focus on the first reason, since this is more common in practice and has generated the most case law. Before we turn to these two reasons, however, it is important to begin by noting that the law that we study in this chapter only applies to defendants who were intoxicated at the time of the alleged offence. In one of the appeals considered in *R v Coley* [2013] EWCA Crim 223 the defendant had been abusing alcohol for roughly six years. He would have spells where he would drink heavily and would then stop drinking abruptly. This had resulted in episodes of alcohol-induced psychosis, which involved hearing voices and having hallucinations. A few days before the alleged offence he had stopped drinking. So at the time of the offence he was not intoxicated, but was suffering psychotic symptoms. Although the defendant's mental condition was the result of voluntary intoxication, the Court of Appeal held that the case law on intoxication did not apply since the defendant was not intoxicated at the time of the offence. In cases like this one you should instead consider the mental condition defences, which we study in the next chapter.

---

[1] Office for National Statistics (2017) *Overview of Violent Crime and Sexual Offences.*
[2] Both examples are mentioned by Lord Denning in his judgment in *Attorney-General of Northern Ireland v Gallagher* [1963] AC 349.

 ## Denial of *mens rea*

The first reason a defendant may adduce evidence that he was intoxicated is in order to deny that he possessed the necessary *mens rea* at the time of the offence. It is important to begin by noting that if the defendant *did* possess the *mens rea* of the offence, he may not seek to escape liability by arguing that he only formed the *mens rea* because he was intoxicated. In *R v Sheehan* [1975] 1 WLR 739 Geoffrey Lane LJ stated:

> Indeed, in cases where drunkenness and its possible effect upon the defendant's *mens rea* is an issue, we think that the proper direction to a jury is, first, to warn them that the mere fact that the defendant's mind was affected by drink so that he acted in a way in which he would not have done had he been sober does not assist him at all, provided that the necessary intention was there. A drunken intent is nevertheless an intent.

So if an intoxicated defendant satisfies both the *actus reus* and *mens rea* of an offence it is never a defence for him to say, 'I wouldn't have done it if I'd been sober'. He will be convicted, unless he can plead one of the mental condition or substantive defences we study in the next two chapters.[3]

### 1. The distinction between voluntary and involuntary consumption

If a defendant claims that he did not possess the necessary *mens rea* as a result of intoxication, you first need to determine whether he consumed the intoxicating substance voluntarily or not. Two examples of involuntary consumption would be where: Mahmood is deceived and does not realise he is consuming the substance (e.g. Farooq spiked Mahmood's drink); and Mahmood is compelled to consume the substance (e.g. because Farooq points a gun at him and threatens to shoot him if he does not).

A strict view is taken of what constitutes involuntary consumption. In *R v Allen* [1988] Crim LR 698 the defendant drank his friend's home-made wine. The defendant believed the wine only contained low levels of alcohol. In fact, it contained high levels. The Court of Appeal held that the defendant had consumed the alcohol voluntarily. His mistake as to the level of alcohol the wine contained did not render his consumption involuntary.

**ACTIVITY**

> Mahmood goes to a party. At the bar he asks for a glass of non-alcoholic fruit punch. Due to a mix-up he is actually given a glass of alcoholic fruit punch. Mahmood drinks the punch. Does he consume the alcohol voluntarily?

We will look at cases involving voluntary consumption first.

### 2. Drinking with intent

If the defendant consumed the substance voluntarily, the next question to ask is whether the defendant was consuming the intoxicating substance in order to give himself the courage to carry out a crime he was planning to commit. In other words, was the defendant drinking with intent? This was the issue in *Attorney-General of Northern Ireland v*

---

[3]Or loss of control (in a homicide case) or a lawful excuse (in a criminal damage case).

Gallagher [1963] AC 349. The defendant, Patrick Gallagher, decided to kill his wife. He bought a knife and a bottle of whisky. He drank most of the bottle and then attacked his wife with the knife. At trial he was convicted of murder. He appealed, arguing that he was so drunk at the time of the killing that he had been incapable of forming the *mens rea* of murder. The appeal reached the House of Lords.

## EXTRACT

Read the following extract from the judgment of Lord Denning. Could Gallagher use the fact he was intoxicated to argue that he lacked the *mens rea* of murder? Why/why not?

### *Attorney-General of Northern Ireland v Gallagher* [1963] AC 349

#### Lord Denning

My Lords, I think the law on this point should take a clear stand. If a man, whilst sane and sober, forms an intention to kill and makes preparation for it, knowing it is a wrong thing to do, and then gets himself drunk so as to give himself Dutch courage to do the killing, and whilst drunk carries out his intention, he cannot rely on this self-induced drunkenness as a defence to a charge of murder, nor even as reducing it to manslaughter. He cannot say that he got himself into such a stupid state that he was incapable of an intent to kill [...] The wickedness of his mind before he got drunk is enough to condemn him, coupled with the act which he intended to do and did do.

So, in cases of drinking with intent, the defendant may not use evidence of his intoxication to claim he lacked the necessary *mens rea* at the time of the offence.

## 3. Consumption for medicinal purposes

If the defendant consumed the substance voluntarily, but was not drinking with intent, the next question to ask is whether the consumption was for medicinal purposes. If the consumption was for medicinal purposes, you must decide whether the defendant foresaw a risk that the drug would render him aggressive and dangerous and chose to take it. In other words, you must decide whether consumption of the drug was *reckless* (using the *R v Cunningham* test that we studied in Chapter 4). If the consumption *was* reckless, the case will be treated no differently to one involving voluntary consumption of alcohol or recreational drugs. But if the consumption was *not* reckless, the defendant will be deemed to have been involuntarily intoxicated.

An example is *R v Bailey* [1983] 1 WLR 760. John Bailey's girlfriend left him for another man, Mike Harrison. Armed with an iron bar, Bailey went to Harrison's house. The two men sat down and discussed the matter over a cup of tea. When Bailey got up to leave he said he had lost his glove down the side of the chair he was sitting on. Harrison bent over to search for it. While Harrison's back was turned, Bailey struck him on the head with the iron bar. Harrison's head wound required ten stitches. At trial, Bailey was convicted of wounding with intent.[4] He appealed against his conviction. Bailey was a

---

[4]Offences Against the Person Act 1861, s.18.

diabetic. There was evidence that earlier in the evening he had failed to take sufficient food after taking his normal dose of insulin. He claimed that, as a result, he had suffered an episode of hypoglycaemia at the time of the attack and was completely unaware of what he was doing. Since Bailey had taken the insulin for medicinal purposes, the Court of Appeal had to decide whether or not Bailey's consumption of the insulin was reckless. Griffiths LJ stated:

> It is common knowledge that those who take alcohol to excess or certain sorts of drugs may become aggressive or do dangerous or unpredictable things, they may be able to foresee the risks of causing harm to others but nevertheless persist in their conduct. But the same cannot be said without more of a man who fails to take food after an insulin injection. If he does appreciate the risk that such a failure may lead to aggressive, unpredictable and uncontrollable conduct and he nevertheless deliberately runs the risk or otherwise disregards it, this will amount to recklessness. But we certainly do not think that it is common knowledge, even among diabetics, that such is a consequence of a failure to take food and there is no evidence that it was known to this appellant. Doubtless he knew that if he failed to take his insulin or proper food after it he might lose consciousness, but as such he would only be a danger to himself unless he put himself in charge of some machine such as a motor car, which required his continued conscious control.

Since Bailey's consumption of the insulin was not reckless, he was deemed to have been involuntarily intoxicated. As we will see below, in cases involving involuntary intoxication you simply ask whether or not the defendant possessed the necessary *mens rea* at the time of the offence. Looking at the facts of Bailey's case – particularly the fact that he armed himself with the iron bar beforehand – the Court of Appeal held that he possessed the necessary *mens rea* at the moment he attacked Harrison. His appeal was therefore dismissed.

A second example is *R v Hardie* [1985] 1 WLR 64. Paul Hardie lived with his partner, Jeanette, and his daughter, Tonia. His relationship with Jeanette had broken down and she insisted that he move out. Hardie did not want to leave, but on the day of the offence he packed a suitcase. In a distressed state, Hardie found an eight-year-old bottle of Valium™ (which was out-of-date) in the bathroom cabinet. He had never taken Valium before. He took one pill to calm his nerves. It did not have much effect, so later he took two more. Jeanette said to him, 'Take as many as you like, they are old stock and will do you no harm', so he took another two. Shortly afterwards he fell into a deep sleep. That evening Hardie (who was showing signs of intoxication) set fire to a wardrobe in a bedroom in the flat. At trial he was convicted of arson. He appealed against his conviction, arguing that he could not remember starting the fire and had been intoxicated at the time. The Court of Appeal held that Hardie's consumption of the Valium was not reckless. Parker LJ explained:

> In the present instance the defence was that the Valium was taken for the purpose of calming the nerves only, that it was old stock and that the appellant was told it would do him no harm. There was no evidence that it was known to the appellant or even generally known that the taking of Valium in the quantity taken would be liable to render a person aggressive or incapable of appreciating risks to others or have other side effects such that its self-administration would itself have an element of recklessness.

Like Bailey, Hardie was therefore deemed to have been involuntarily intoxicated. Unlike Bailey, however, the Court of Appeal held that it had not been proved beyond reasonable doubt that Hardie had the necessary *mens rea* when he started the fire. His conviction was therefore quashed.

## 4. The distinction between basic intent crimes and specific intent crimes

So far we have looked at cases involving drinking with intent and non-reckless consumption of a drug for medicinal purposes. Next we look at cases involving: reckless consumption of a medicinal drug; and, by far the most common type of scenario, voluntary consumption of alcohol or recreational drugs. The same rules apply to both these types of cases because, as we saw earlier, reckless consumption of a medicinal drug is treated no differently to voluntary consumption of alcohol or recreational drugs.

The leading case here is *DPP v Majewski* [1977] AC 443. The defendant, Robert Majewski, was involved in a pub fight. At trial he was convicted on three counts of assault occasioning ABH and three counts of assaulting a police officer in the execution of his duty. Majewski said that he had taken a mixture of drugs and alcohol that evening and as a result had 'completely blanked out'. He therefore claimed that he had not formed the necessary *mens rea*. His appeal against conviction reached the House of Lords.

The House of Lords' decision in *DPP v Majewski* sought to strike a balance between two competing sets of concerns. On the one hand, there is the concern based on the principle of individual autonomy (see Chapter 1) that people should not be convicted of a crime if they did not possess the necessary *mens rea*. On the other hand, there is the concern based on social welfare (see Chapter 1) that defendants should not be able to escape criminal liability on the basis that their own self-induced intoxication rendered them unable to form *mens rea*. Social welfare requires that people are deterred from voluntarily consuming intoxicating substances which render them aggressive and dangerous.

The House of Lords' decision was effectively an uneasy compromise between these two sets of concerns. The House of Lords drew a distinction between crimes of basic intent and crimes of specific intent. For specific intent crimes (which tend to be the more serious offences), a defendant can only be convicted if he possessed the necessary *mens rea* at the time of the offence. So for specific intent crimes the defendant may argue that he was unable to form *mens rea* as a result of his own voluntary intoxication.

For basic intent crimes, however, things are different. A defendant who is charged with a basic intent crime may not use the fact he was voluntarily intoxicated to claim that he lacked *mens rea*. Lord Elwyn-Jones LC explained:

> If a man of his own volition takes a substance which causes him to cast off the restraints of reason and conscience, no wrong is done to him by holding him answerable criminally for any injury he may do while in that condition. His course of conduct in reducing himself by drugs and drink to that condition in my view supplies the evidence of *mens rea*, of guilty mind certainly sufficient for crimes of basic intent.

The crimes Majewski had been charged with were crimes of basic intent. He was therefore unable to argue that his intoxication left him unable to form *mens rea*, and his convictions were upheld.

The decision in *DPP v Majewski* means that the distinction between crimes of specific intent and crimes of basic intent is crucial. Unfortunately, however, the House of Lords did not clearly explain the difference between the two categories. In his judgment, Lord

Elwyn-Jones LC explained the difference by citing the following extract from Lord Simon's judgment in *R v Morgan* [1976] AC 182:

> By 'crimes of basic intent' I mean those crimes whose definition expresses (or, more often, implies) a *mens rea* which does not go beyond the *actus reus*. The *actus reus* generally consists of an act and some consequence. The consequence may be very closely connected with the act or more remotely connected with it: but with a crime of basic intent the *mens rea* does not extend beyond the act and its consequence, however remote, as defined in the *actus reus*. I take assault as an example of a crime of basic intent where the consequence is very closely connected with the act. The *actus reus* of assault is an act which causes another person to apprehend immediate and unlawful violence. The *mens rea* corresponds exactly. The prosecution must prove that the accused foresaw that his act would probably cause another person to have apprehension of immediate and unlawful violence, or would possibly have that consequence, such being the purpose of the act, or that he was reckless as to whether or not his act caused such apprehension.

So, on this view, basic intent crimes are ones in which the *mens rea* 'does not go beyond the *actus reus*'. Specific intent crimes, by contrast, are ones in which the *mens rea* does go beyond the *actus reus*. An example is burglary under section 9(1)(a) Theft Act 1968. As we saw in the previous chapter, the *actus reus* of burglary is simply entry of a building (or part of a building) as a trespasser. The *mens rea* of section 9(1)(a) burglary goes beyond this, since it requires proof of an ulterior intention to commit theft, inflict GBH or damage property.

This explanation works for some offences. As Lord Simon explains in the extract above, it works for assault (a basic intent crime). It also works for burglary (a specific intent crime).[5] But it doesn't work for some other offences. For example, in *DPP v Majewski* Lord Elwyn-Jones confirmed that murder is a crime of specific intent.[6] Yet the *mens rea* of murder does not extend beyond the *actus reus*. In fact, as we saw in Chapter 5, the *mens rea* does not even extend as far as the *actus reus*! It is sufficient for the *mens rea* of murder to show that the defendant had an intention to cause serious injury.

An alternative explanation of the distinction between basic intent crimes and specific intent crimes was offered by Lord Simon in his judgment in *DPP v Majewski*:

> [A] crime of specific intent requires something more than contemplation of the prohibited act and foresight of its probable consequences. The *mens rea* in a crime of specific intent requires proof of a purposive element.

This 'purposive element' explanation was also used by the Court of Appeal in *R v Heard* [2007] EWCA Crim 125. But it too is problematic. It also fails to explain why murder is a crime of specific intent. We saw in Chapter 5 that a defendant satisfies the *mens rea* of murder if he had a direct or oblique intention to kill or cause serious injury. Foresight of death or GBH as virtually certain is sufficient; it need not have been the defendant's purpose to cause death or GBH. The same also applies to GBH/wounding with intent.[7] This is a crime of specific intent,[8] yet it is sufficient to show that the defendant obliquely intended to cause GBH.

---

[5] *R v Durante* [1972] 1 WLR 1612.
[6] See also *Attorney-General of Northern Ireland v Gallagher* [1963] AC 349.
[7] Offences Against the Person Act 1861, s.18.
[8] *Bratty v Attorney-General of Northern Ireland* [1963] AC 386.

In the absence of a satisfactory explanation of the difference between specific intent and basic intent crimes, the safest course of action is to follow existing precedents and produce a list of which crimes have been held to fall in which category. The following table accordingly categorises all of the offences that we study in this text:

| Basic intent crimes | Specific intent crimes |
|---|---|
| Involuntary manslaughter[9]<br>Wounding or infliction of GBH[10]<br>Assault occasioning ABH[11]<br>Battery[12]<br>Assault[13]<br>Rape[14]<br>Assault by penetration[15]<br>Sexual assault[16] | Causing a person to engage in sexual activity without consent[17]<br>Murder[18]<br>Wounding or causing GBH with intent[19]<br>Theft[20]<br>Robbery[21]<br>Burglary[22] |

(Not listed in this table are: (1) fraud: this, it is suggested, is a crime of specific intent since it requires proof of an ulterior intention; and (2) criminal damage: it has been suggested that whether criminal damage (and aggravated criminal damage) is a crime of basic or specific intent depends on whether the prosecutor in the particular case alleges intentional or reckless damage.[23])

So the distinction between basic intent crimes and specific intent crimes was developed by the House of Lords in *DPP v Majewski* to reconcile the competing demands of the principle of autonomy and the principle of social welfare. For specific intent crimes – which tend to be the more serious – a defendant can only be convicted if it is shown that he possessed the necessary *mens rea* at the time of the offence. For basic intent crimes, by contrast, the defendant may not use the fact that he was voluntarily intoxicated to argue that he lacked *mens rea*.

Lastly, notice that a defendant who cannot be convicted of a specific intent crime because he lacked *mens rea* may be convicted of a basic intent crime instead. So if Mahmood attacks Wasim and kills him, but was too drunk to have formed the *mens rea* of murder, Mahmood may be convicted of the basic intent crime of involuntary manslaughter instead.

---

[9]*Attorney-General of Northern Ireland v Gallagher* [1963] AC 349.
[10]*DPP v Majewski* [1977] AC 443.
[11]*DPP v Majewski* [1977] AC 443.
[12]*DPP v Majewski* [1977] AC 443.
[13]*DPP v Majewski* [1977] AC 443.
[14]Based on the logic of the decision in *R v Heard* [2007] EWCA Crim 125.
[15]Based on the logic of the decision in *R v Heard* [2007] EWCA Crim 125.
[16]*R v Heard* [2007] EWCA Crim 125.
[17]Based on the logic of the decision in *R v Heard* [2007] EWCA Crim 125.
[18]*Attorney-General of Northern Ireland v Gallagher* [1963] AC 349; *DPP v Majewski*.
[19]*Bratty v Attorney-General of Northern Ireland* [1963] AC 386.
[20]*Ruse v Read* [1949] 1 KB 377.
[21]Based on the fact it is an aggravated form of theft.
[22]*R v Durante* [1972] 1 WLR 1612.
[23]See Ormerod, D. and Laird, K. (2015) *Smith and Hogan's Criminal Law* (14th edn) Oxford: OUP, 363. Cf *R v Coley* [2013] EWCA Crim 223.

Mahmood has been at the pub for several hours, drinking heavily. He begins to argue with his friend Wasim. The argument gets heated and Mahmood hits Wasim on the head with his beer bottle. Wasim suffers a deep wound which requires stitches. Medical evidence later shows that, at the moment he struck Wasim, Mahmood was so drunk that he was incapable of forming *mens rea*. Use the table of basic and specific intent offences above to decide which crime Mahmood would be convicted of.

## 5. Involuntary intoxication

In the vast majority of cases the defendant will have voluntarily consumed alcohol or recreational drugs and the *DPP v Majewski* rules will apply. But what about those cases where the defendant consumed the intoxicating substance involuntarily? Or where the defendant became intoxicated inadvertently after consuming drugs for medicinal purposes?

In such cases, you do not need to apply the *DPP v Majewski* rules on basic and specific intent crimes. Instead, you simply ask whether or not the defendant possessed the necessary *mens rea* at the time of the offence in question. An example is *R v Kingston* [1995] 2 AC 355. The defendant, Barry Kingston, was involved in a dispute with his business partners. They employed a man named Kevin Penn to obtain information which could be used to discredit Kingston. Penn knew that Kingston had paedophilic tendencies. Penn invited a 15-year-old boy to his flat and gave him a drink containing sedatives. The boy later said that he remembered nothing in between sitting on the bed in Penn's flat and waking up the next morning. When Kingston arrived at Penn's flat Penn gave him a cup of coffee. Unbeknown to Kingston, the coffee was drugged. Later, Penn showed Kingston the boy naked on his bed. Kingston engaged in sexual acts with the boy, which Penn photographed and recorded.

At trial Kingston was convicted of a sexual offence and sentenced to five years' imprisonment. His appeal against conviction reached the House of Lords. Kingston did not deny that he had the necessary *mens rea* at the time he assaulted the victim. Rather, he argued that he only formed the *mens rea* because he had involuntarily consumed drugs which caused him to become disinhibited. He therefore argued that the courts should create a new substantive defence titled 'involuntary intoxication'. The Court of Appeal accepted this argument and quashed Kingston's conviction. But this decision was overturned by the House of Lords, who unanimously rejected the proposed new defence.

Read the following extract from the judgment of Lord Mustill. What (a) theoretical and (b) practical reasons does he give for rejecting a substantive defence of involuntary intoxication?

What specific concern does Lord Mustill express about the lack of a defence of involuntary intoxication?

## *R v Kingston* [1995] 2 AC 355

### Lord Mustill

To recognise a new defence of this type would be a bold step [...] I suspect that the recognition of a new general defence at common law has not happened in modern times. Nevertheless, the criminal law must not stand still, and if it is both practical and just to take this step, and if judicial decision rather than legislation is the proper medium, then the courts should not be deterred simply by the novelty of it. So one must turn to consider just what defence is now to be created. The judgment under appeal implies five characteristics.

1. The defence applies to all offences, except perhaps to absolute offences. It therefore differs from other defences such as [loss of control] and diminished responsibility.

2. The defence is a complete answer to a criminal charge. If not rebutted it leads to an outright acquittal, and unlike [loss of control] and diminished responsibility leaves no room for conviction and punishment for a lesser offence. The underlying assumption must be that the defendant is entirely free from culpability.

3. It may be that the defence applies only where the intoxication is due to the wrongful act of another and therefore affords no excuse when, in circumstances of no greater culpability, the defendant has intoxicated himself by mistake (such as by shortsightedly taking the wrong drug) [...]

4. The burden of disproving the defence is on the prosecution.

5. The defence is subjective in nature. Whereas [loss of control] and self-defence are judged by the reactions of the reasonable person in the situation of the defendant, here the only question is whether this particular defendant's inhibitions were overcome by the effect of the drug. The more susceptible the defendant to the kind of temptation presented, the easier the defence is to establish.

My Lords, since the existence or otherwise of the defence has been treated in argument at all stages as a matter of existing law the Court of Appeal had no occasion to consider the practical and theoretical implications of recognising this new defence at common law, and we do not have the benefit of its views. In their absence, I can only say that the defence appears to run into difficulties at every turn. In point of theory, it would be necessary to reconcile a defence of irresistible impulse derived from a combination of innate drives and external disinhibition with the rule that irresistible impulse of a solely internal origin (not necessarily any more the fault of the offender) does not in itself excuse although it may be a symptom of a disease of the mind: *Attorney-General for South Australia v. Brown* [1960] A.C. 432. Equally, the state of mind which founds the defence superficially resembles a state of diminished responsibility, whereas the effect in law is quite different. It may well be that the resemblance is misleading, but these and similar problems must be solved before the bounds of a new defence can be set.

On the practical side there are serious problems. Before the jury could form an opinion on whether the drug might have turned the scale witnesses would have to give a picture of the defendant's personality and susceptibilities, for without it the crucial effect of the drug could not be assessed; pharmacologists would be required to describe the potentially disinhibiting effect of a range of drugs whose identity would, if the present case is anything to go by, be unknown; psychologists and psychiatrists would express opinions, not on the matters of psychopathology familiar to those working within the framework of the Mental Health Acts but on altogether more elusive concepts. No doubt as time passed those concerned could work out techniques to deal with these questions. Much more significant would be the opportunities for a spurious defence. Even in the field of road traffic the "spiked" drink as a special reason for not disqualifying from driving is a regular feature. Transferring this to the entire range of criminal offences is a disturbing prospect. The defendant would only have to assert, and support by the evidence of well-wishers, that he was not the sort of person to have done this kind of thing, and to suggest an occasion when by some means a drug might have been administered to him for the jury to be sent straight to the question of a possible disinhibition. The judge would direct the jurors that if they felt any legitimate doubt on the matter – and by its nature the defence would be one which the prosecution would often have no means to rebut – they must acquit outright, all questions of intent, mental capacity and the like being at this stage irrelevant.

My Lords, the fact that a new doctrine may require adjustment of existing principles to accommodate it, and may require those involved in criminal trials to learn new techniques, is not of course a ground for refusing to adopt it, if that is what the interests of justice require. Here, however, justice makes no such demands, for the interplay between the wrong done to the victim, the individual characteristics and frailties of the defendant, and the pharmacological effects of whatever drug may be potentially involved can be far better recognised by a tailored choice from the continuum of sentences available to the judge than by the application of a single yea-or-nay jury decision. To this, there is one exception. The mandatory life sentence for murder, at least as present administered, leaves no room for the trial judge to put into practice an informed and sympathetic assessment of the kind just described. It is for this reason alone that I have felt any hesitation about rejecting the argument for the respondent. In the end however I have concluded that this is not a sufficient reason to force on the theory and practice of the criminal law an exception which would otherwise be unjustified. For many years mandatory sentences have impelled juries to return merciful but false verdicts, and have stimulated the creation of partial defences such as [loss of control] and diminished responsibility whose lack of a proper foundation has made them hard to apply in practice. I do not think it right that the law should be further distorted simply because of this anomalous relic of the history of the criminal law.

All this being said, I suggest to your Lordships that the existing work of the Law Commission in the field of intoxication could usefully be enlarged to comprise questions of the type raised by this appeal, and to see whether by statute a merciful, realistic and intellectually sustainable solution could be newly created. For the present, however, I consider that no such regime now exists, and that the common law is not a suitable vehicle for creating one.

So if a defendant was involuntarily intoxicated, the sole question is did he possess the necessary *mens rea* or not. If he did, the fact that he would not have committed the crime had he been sober is no defence.

Since the decision in *R v Kingston* there has been much discussion of whether or not the law should recognise a substantive defence of involuntary intoxication. In the following extract Sullivan argues that, in certain limited circumstances, involuntary intoxication should constitute a defence.

## EXTRACT

According to Sullivan, when should involuntary intoxication be available as a substantive defence? What reasons does Sullivan advance in support of this?

## Sullivan, G. R. (1996) 'Making Excuses' in A. Smith and G. Sullivan (eds) *Harm and Culpability.* Oxford: OUP, 131–152

Nonetheless, there may have been principled reasons sufficient for the House of Lords to have upheld, rather than reversed, the Court of Appeal. An opportunity may have been missed for creative yet appropriate judicial law-making. Whether a defence should have been provided in *Kingston* depends, it will be argued, on conditions which may, or may not, have been present on the facts of that case. As stated already, disinhibition falling short of automatism cannot *of itself* excuse. But if such a condition arose blamelessly and induced conduct which would not otherwise have occurred, this will attenuate to some extent the culpability of the agent. That culpability would be further attenuated, it will be claimed, if, until the incident in question, the defendant had abstained from practising his paedophilia.

All we know of the defendant in *Kingston* is that he was a homosexual with paedophiliac predilections. The formative influences of sexual preference are obscure. In terms of orientation, our sexuality is something that we have rather than something we have made. If we are dealt a card marked for paedophilia, the most that can be asked of us is that we do not put it into play. The card cannot be surrendered and it would be a barbarity to punish for mere possession. Requiring forbearance in a matter so pervasive and unpredictable as sexual expression is to require a great deal, notwithstanding that the protection of a vulnerable class must always be the overriding concern. If a person of paedophiliac inclinations does not practise his paedophilia, he is entitled to that full dignity and respect which is due to all law-abiding citizens. Indeed, he may claim particular credit for sustaining a non-criminal status. If on a particular occasion he becomes blamelessly disinhibited by drugs and loses self-control when confronted with that temptation he otherwise avoids and resists, it is not obvious that the public interest requires him to suffer the total forfeit of credit which a conviction for a stigmatic offence entails.

The particularity of facts such as those related above renders the consequentialist claims of individual and general deterrence uncompelling. Retributivist claims are less clearly settled. It has already been suggested that his blameless state of disequilibrium must count in his favour, even if only as mitigation. It will be argued more fully below that mitigation may be upgraded to excuse if, until this particular occasion, the defendant had refrained from paedophiliac practices. However, were he a practising paedophile his conduct would not constitute an arguably condonable lapse from a standard he was able otherwise to sustain. Then, at most, he would be a candidate for mitigation. If he is, on the basis outlined above, a candidate for an acquittal, he may yet deservedly be convicted if the conduct for which he claims excuse was very grave, for example a killing. We are dealing with uncompelled conduct perpetrated with *mens rea*. In such cases previous good conduct and a blameless state of disequilibrium may be insufficient to outweigh the culpability evinced by a heinous wrong. We are not dealing with excusatory claims which, if made out, invariably sustain a plea for acquittal. It may depend on what it is the defendant has done.

In essence, this paper attempts to found the claim, adumbrated above, that involuntarily intoxicated persons of previous good character and others in similar cases can, if particular conditions be met, be excused for certain crimes. First, however, we should note the view taken by the House of Lords in *Kingston* that such cases are adequately treated by way of mitigation. This standpoint coheres with the unequivocal opinion of Lord Mustill that a conviction for a serious offence need not entail descriptively or prescriptively that the defendant was in any sense at fault. He endorsed a decision of the Privy Council to the effect that an undercover policeman acting with the knowledge and consent of his superiors and without recourse to entrapment or conduct to the prejudice of third parties would be guilty of trafficking in drugs notwithstanding that the 'trafficking' (carrying drugs out of the jurisdiction) was done solely in the interests of law enforcement. It follows that an involuntarily intoxicated person could at most hope for some degree of mitigation – the policeman's conduct seemed justified whereas the cases we are concerned with fall, at most, to be excused.

By contrast with the House of Lords, the view taken here is that a conviction for a stigmatic offence is a sanction in its own right and that sanctions should be confined to the blameworthy. The non-conviction of the blameless should be a pervasive principle of substantive criminal law limited only by the need to theorize and practise criminal law as a system of rules and by the exigencies of forensic practicability. Those limitations entail that many 'normal' life narratives cannot afford grounds of excuse, however exculpatory the force of the narrative may be. But other accounts, not currently represented in standard defences, can be brought within the framework of substantive criminal law. If it can be done it should be done in order to diminish the incidence of unnecessary criminal convictions.

In its 2009 report *Intoxication and Criminal Liability* the Law Commission examined this issue. The following extract details the Law Commission's conclusions.

## EXTRACT

According to the Law Commission, should there be a defence of involuntary intoxication? What reasons did the Commission give for its recommendation?

In your opinion, should there be a defence of involuntary intoxication?

### Law Commission (2009) *Intoxication and Criminal Liability* (Law Commission Report No 314) Cm 7526

4.1 It is trite law that, if D commits the external element of an offence with the required fault, then, subject to any defence he or she might have, D is liable for that offence.

4.2 In this Part we address the question whether D should be *excused* from liability, if his or her commission of an offence's external element with the required fault has been proved or admitted, on the basis that:

(1)   D's state of involuntary intoxication reduced D's inhibitions to such an extent that, although D was acting voluntarily and with the required fault, he or she could not resist the temptation to commit the offence charged; or

(2)   D's state of involuntary intoxication blurred D's moral vision to the extent that, although D acted with the required fault, appreciated what he or she was doing and could have acted otherwise, D did not appreciate the true moral gravity of his or her behaviour.

4.3 As the law stands, involuntary intoxication is not an excuse. Intoxication induced by the surreptitious act of a third party, for example, is irrelevant to the question of D's criminal liability if D acts with the fault required for liability, even if he or she would not have acted in that way if sober.

[...]

4.9 If created, a defence of reduced inhibitions or blurred moral vision would be relied on by D only in cases where it has been proved to the criminal standard that D committed the external element of the offence charged with the required fault. In our view, however, reduced inhibitions or blurred moral vision should have the effect, to a greater or lesser extent, of simply reducing the degree of blame that can be attached to D. In other words, evidence of involuntary intoxication in such cases should operate in the same way as do many (other) mitigating factors which were beyond D's power to control, such as a violent upbringing giving rise to an inability to control angry outbursts. With any like factor, D's involuntary intoxication may well justify a reduced sentence should he or she be convicted of an offence.

4.10 The justification given for the contrary position adopted by the Court of Appeal in *Kingston* was its view that "the purposes of the criminal law are not served" by holding D liable when "the inhibition which the law requires has been removed by the clandestine act of a third party". This approach accords with Professor Sullivan's (subsequently expressed) view that the law should take cognisance of D's lack of blameworthiness in such cases when attributing criminal liability. However, we are unable to perceive any sufficient reason for elevating the mitigating factor of reduced inhibitions or blurred perception of morality caused by involuntary intoxication to the status of a new defence that would entirely negative D's criminal liability.

4.11 Another argument which might be raised in support of a complete defence of involuntary intoxication is that, as some other extraneous mitigating acts – duress by threats and duress of circumstances – already have the effect of completely excusing D's otherwise proven liability (albeit with some exceptions), so involuntary intoxication should similarly entitle D to an absolute acquittal.

4.12 Such an argument is sustainable only insofar as reduced inhibitions or blurred perceptions of morality may properly be regarded as analogous to the existing excusatory defences. There are, however, stark differences between the mere fact of reduced inhibitions or blurred perceptions of morality induced by involuntary intoxication and the duress defences. To rely on duress by threats, D must reasonably have believed, as a result of a threat, that death or serious injury would result if the offence was not committed; and it must be the case that a reasonable person (with D's relevant characteristics) would have committed the offence in those circumstances. Acting with fault but in a disinhibited or less morally aware state caused by surreptitiously administered drugs is far removed from the negation of culpability implicit in the defence(s) of duress.

4.13 There are, moreover, other extraneous circumstances which mitigate the culpability of the offender without affecting his or her criminal liability. For example, the fact that D was provoked into committing an offence is irrelevant to D's liability, regardless of how grievous the provocation was, unless D is charged with murder. Provocative acts do not as a general rule affect D's liability, but are taken into consideration by the court only when passing sentence. It would be extremely difficult to justify a general excusatory defence of reduced inhibitions, obviating all liability, when it is accepted that the most grotesque acts of provocation cannot excuse liability for even relatively minor crimes.

4.14 The closest analogy with an existing complete defence is perhaps with insanity (of a temporary kind). However, the law does not permit the simple fact of blurred moral vision or moral disinhibition to amount to insanity in law.

4.15 There are also sound public policy reasons for rejecting a complete defence of reduced inhibitions or blurred moral vision founded on involuntary intoxication.

4.16 First, we agree that a defence of this sort would be too easy for the accused to manufacture. This would give rise to the very "disturbing prospect" that the defence would be spuriously raised in any case where there was evidence that the accused was intoxicated at the time the offence was committed, particularly when it is remembered that so many offences of violence are committed under the influence of alcohol.

4.17 After all, D would need to do no more than call witnesses to say that he or she acted out of character, and give evidence, perhaps bolstered by similar evidence from his associates, that alcohol or some other drug must have been added to his (alcoholic or non-alcoholic) drink, causing his inhibitions to be reduced to the level at which he could no longer resist engaging in the offence. As Lord Mustill noted, the defence would be one which the Crown would often have no means of rebutting, and D would be entitled to an acquittal if it was reasonably possible that the defence was true.

4.18 Reversing the burden of proof, that is, placing a legal obligation on D to prove the defence on the balance of probabilities, would make it more difficult for the defence to succeed. However, given the ease with which D would be able to fabricate evidence, the low standard of proof D would have to meet, and the problems the Crown would face in rebutting that evidence, there would still be considerable scope for successful reliance on an unmeritorious defence that allows culpable individuals to avoid all liability.

4.19 Secondly, the defence would be entirely subjective. The question would be whether D's personal inhibitions or moral compass, which ordinarily discourage D from committing the type of offence charged, were undermined as a result of involuntary intoxication to the extent that D should not be liable for that offence, even though D acted with the fault required for liability. There could be no "reasonable person" limb to the test because reasonable people do not have a latent disposition to commit crimes. For example, if the facts of *Kingston* were to recur, the jury would have to determine the inherent strength of D's particular sexual disposition towards adolescent boys and whether the degree to which he was affected by the intoxicant (the nature of which may be unknown) caused him, through his irresistible impulse or blurred awareness of morality, to commit an offence he would not otherwise have committed. It is questionable whether these are matters which expert witnesses would be able to throw much light on and, in the absence of relevant expert testimony, it is difficult to see how the jury could be expected to determine the question.

4.20 Thirdly, the stronger the accused's underlying but latent antisocial disposition, the easier it would be to rely successfully on the defence. If D has strong antisocial tendencies which can be kept under control when sober, but not when intoxicated, it would be relatively easy for D to demonstrate that the reduction in his or her inhibitions from the consumption of alcohol or some other drug is what caused the antisocial conduct on the occasion in question. The sole remaining issue would be whether or not the consumption was voluntary. Public safety requires that the strength of D's disposition to engage in antisocial conduct should not make it easier for D to claim a complete excuse for any crime committed in consequence.

4.21 Fourthly, if an excusatory defence were to be created for the situation where D's inhibitions are removed by an act for which he or she is not responsible, there would be little reason why the law should not recognise a general character based excusatory defence for any inherent condition or "irresistible impulse" for which D is equally not responsible. For example, if D's urge to commit sexual offences against children is so great that he cannot withstand it, then logic would require that he too should be able to rely on the excuse of "insufficient inhibition" in relation to any sexual offence he commits against a child. Indeed, if D has a disposition to behave in an antisocial way on account of the way he or she was raised during his or her formative years, again a matter beyond D's control, arguably there should also be an excuse from liability for that reason.

4.22 There may well be an argument for introducing a general defence of diminished responsibility or provocation, or a broader defence of insanity, but these are matters beyond our present remit. In the absence of any such radical reform of the criminal law it would be illogical and anomalous to create a specific defence for persons whose inhibitions were affected by involuntary intoxication.

4.23 In summary, the fact that the accused was involuntarily intoxicated at the time he or she committed the offence should normally be regarded as a mitigating factor, but it should not be elevated to the level of an excuse which would prevent any liability from attaching.

4.24 We agree with the view of Lord Mustill that: the interplay between the wrong done to the victim, the individual characteristics and frailties of the defendant, and the pharmacological effects of whatever drug may be potentially involved can be far better recognised by a tailored choice from the continuum of sentences available to the judge.

4.25 The law is clear in the light of the House of Lords' judgment in *Kingston* and, given our agreement with their Lordships' reasoning and approach, we make no recommendation for reform in this respect.

## 6. Summary

The flow chart in Figure 9.1 presents an overview of the case law we have studied on defendants who adduce evidence of their intoxication in order to claim that they lacked the *mens rea* of an offence.

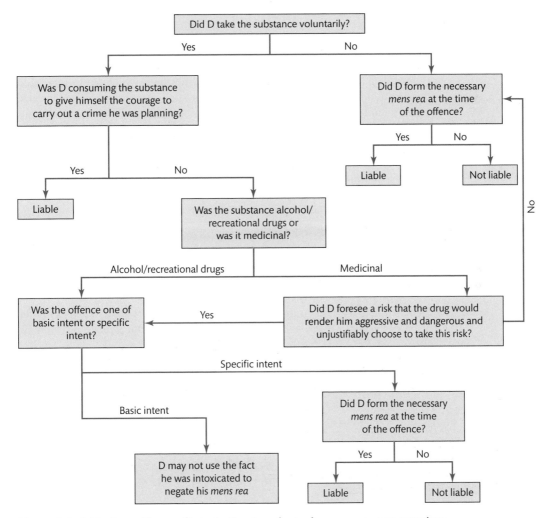

**Figure 9.1.** Adducing evidence of intoxication in order to deny *mens rea*: an overview

 **Basis of a defence**

The introduction to this chapter explained that there are two reasons why a defendant might adduce evidence that he was intoxicated. We can now turn to the second of these reasons: the defendant may claim that his intoxication caused in him a mistaken belief which should form the basis of a substantive defence.

An example is *R v O'Grady* [1987] QB 995. The defendant, Patrick O'Grady, had spent the day drinking with his friend Eddie McCloskey. O'Grady had consumed a large quantity of cider. McCloskey stayed the night at O'Grady's flat. O'Grady said that he was woken up the next morning by a bang on the head. He said he felt blood running down, and saw McCloskey standing next to him holding a piece of glass. The two men fought, and McCloskey was killed. A post mortem revealed that McCloskey had suffered serious wounds to the face as well as injuries to his hands, a fractured rib, severe bruising to the head, brain, neck and chest and a fractured spine. O'Grady claimed that he had acted in self-defence. He told police: 'I did not want to kill him. I wanted him alive, not dead. I had no enmity to him. If I had not hit him I would be dead myself.'

O'Grady was charged with murder. At trial, the jury acquitted him of murder but convicted him of manslaughter. He appealed against his conviction. The case reached the Court of Appeal. The issue on appeal was whether a mistaken belief caused by voluntary intoxication may be taken into account when applying the test for self-defence.[24] Lord Lane CJ stated:

> We have come to the conclusion that where the jury are satisfied that the defendant was mistaken in his belief that any force or the force which he in fact used was necessary to defend himself and are further satisfied that the mistake was caused by voluntarily induced intoxication, the defence must fail [...] There are two competing interests. On the one hand the interest of the defendant who has only acted according to what he believed to be necessary to protect himself, and on the other hand that of the public in general and the victim in particular who, probably through no fault of his own, has been injured or perhaps killed because of the defendant's drunken mistake. Reason recoils from the conclusion that in such circumstances a defendant is entitled to leave the Court without a stain on his character.

So where a defendant mistakenly believes he needs to use force to defend himself, and this mistake was the result of voluntary intoxication, he will be unable to plead self-defence. If the belief was *not* mistaken, or if the belief was *not* the result of voluntary intoxication, the defendant may still plead self-defence and the legal test (which we study in Chapter 11) must be applied in the normal way.

It is important to note that the principle from *R v O'Grady* applies whether the defendant has been charged with a crime of basic intent or a crime of specific intent. Lord Lane CJ said:

> We do not consider that any distinction should be drawn on this aspect of the matter between offences involving what is called specific intent, such as murder, and offences of so called basic intent, such as manslaughter.

This has been criticised, with commentators arguing that the *R v O'Grady* principle should only apply to basic intent crimes. The reason for this is best explained by contrasting the following two cases:

- *R v Hatton* [2005] EWCA Crim 2951: the defendant, Jonathan Hatton, met the victim, Richard Pashley, in a nightclub. During the evening Hatton consumed over 20 pints of

---

[24]We study this test in Chapter 11.

beer and Pashley told people (falsely) that he was an officer in the SAS. The two men went back to Hatton's flat. The next morning Pashley was found dead, having been battered to death with a sledgehammer. Hatton's counsel wished to argue that Hatton's intoxicated state had led him to mistakenly believe that Pashley was an SAS soldier attacking him with a sword. The Court of Appeal followed *R v O'Grady* and held that Hatton could not found a defence of self-defence on a mistaken belief caused by voluntary intoxication. His murder conviction was accordingly upheld.

- *R v Lipman* [1970] 1 QB 152: the defendant, Robert Lipman, and the victim, Claudie Delbarre, both took LSD. Lipman said that in his LSD 'trip' he descended to the centre of the earth and was attacked by snakes, which he fought. In fact, during the LSD trip Lipman killed Delbarre by asphyxiating her (cramming eight inches of bed sheet into her mouth). As we saw earlier in the chapter, since murder is a specific intent crime it must be proved that the defendant acted with the necessary *mens rea*. At trial Lipman argued that he had not formed an intention to kill or seriously injure a human being since he believed he was attacking a snake. The jury accepted this, and so he was convicted of the basic intent crime of manslaughter instead. The Court of Appeal subsequently held that this was correct.

If we contrast *R v Hatton* and *R v Lipman*, Hatton was convicted of murder whereas Lipman was convicted of manslaughter. This seems to place too much weight on the content of the defendant's intoxication-induced belief. Both men killed their victim because they mistakenly believed they were under attack. It is strange that such importance should be attached to whether, in their intoxicated state, they believed they were being attacked by an SAS soldier or a snake. This could be rectified by saying that the *R v O'Grady* principle only applies to basic intent crimes. Hatton would then have been able to rely on his mistaken belief when responding to the murder charge. This would have meant that, if the jury accepted his defence of self-defence, he would have been convicted of the basic intent crime of manslaughter instead – achieving parity with *R v Lipman*.

## Conclusion

Intoxication is commonly referred to as a defence. This is actually misleading.[25] For a start, the law on intoxication does not provide an escape route to defendants who acted with the necessary *mens rea*. As we saw at the start of the chapter, the courts have applied the principle that 'A drunken intent is nevertheless an intent'. In fact, the courts have held that in three situations a defendant may be convicted of a crime even though he did *not* have the necessary *mens rea* at the time of the offence:

- D is charged with a basic intent crime and had voluntarily consumed alcohol or recreational drugs.
- D is charged with a basic intent crime and had recklessly consumed medicinal drugs.
- D had been drinking with intent.

In this chapter we have also seen that: there is no substantive defence for involuntarily intoxicated defendants; and defendants who mistakenly use force to defend themselves as a result of voluntary intoxication may not plead self-defence.

---

[25]Simester, A. P. (2009) 'Intoxication is Never a Defence' *Criminal Law Review* 3.

Instead of thinking of intoxication as a defence, when you answer an exam problem question you should begin by asking why the defendant wishes to adduce evidence of his intoxication. If it is in order to deny that he possessed the necessary *mens rea*, you should consider the effect of his intoxication as part of your discussion of the *mens rea* of the offence. On the other hand, if he wishes to claim that his intoxication caused in him a mistaken belief which should form the basis of a substantive defence, you should consider the effect of his intoxication as part of your discussion of the relevant substantive defence. Try to avoid referring to intoxication as a defence in its own right because it is not!

## Self-test questions

1. Law students Mahmood, Farooq and Priya attend a networking event for aspiring solicitors. The event is sponsored by a leading law firm and has a free bar. Even though Mahmood is currently taking prescription medication for a chest infection, and was warned by his doctor not to mix the drugs with alcohol, he drinks several glasses of wine in quick succession. He becomes irritable. When he sees trainee solicitor Wasim flirting with Priya he picks up an empty wine bottle and hits Wasim on the head with it. Wasim suffers a deep gash which requires stitches. In the resulting mêlée Farooq – who had been drowning his sorrows after receiving his latest coursework mark – pushes over Abdul. Abdul lands awkwardly and suffers a broken arm.

   Mahmood and Farooq both claim that at the time of the brawl they were so intoxicated that they were completely unaware of what they were doing.

   Discuss the criminal liability of Mahmood and Farooq.

2. During happy hour at your local pub the following events take place:
   a. Imran offers to buy teetotaller Zainab a drink. Although Zainab has always detested Imran and considered him extremely sleazy, she accepts and asks him for an orange juice. Unbeknown to Zainab, Imran asks the barman to add a double shot of vodka. Zainab drinks the juice without realising it contains alcohol. She becomes disinhibited. A short time later Imran tells a dirty joke. Zainab is so disgusted that she picks up her empty glass and throws it at him. Imran suffers a scratch and a painful bruise. Zainab later says she would not have thrown the glass had her drink not been spiked.
   b. Suresh drinks several double shots of whisky. Earlier in the day his work colleague Vikram embarrassed him in a meeting in front of their boss. Having resolved to get revenge, Suresh drank the whisky in order to build up the courage to go and beat Vikram up. After leaving the pub Suresh returns to the office, finds Vikram and punches him in the face. Vikram suffers a black eye. Suresh later claims that he has no recollection of that evening.
   c. Over the course of several drinking games Anwar drinks a large quantity of alcohol. Before arriving at the pub he had also taken recreational drugs. When he leaves the pub he is so intoxicated that when he sees Rasheed walking towards him he mistakenly believes that Rasheed is a Roman gladiator about to attack him. Anwar pushes Rasheed over, kicks him repeatedly and then runs away. Rasheed later dies from his injuries. Anwar says that, in his intoxicated state, he genuinely believed Rasheed would have killed him if he hadn't defended himself.

Discuss the criminal liability of: (a) Zainab; (b) Suresh and (c) Anwar.

How (if at all) would your answer be different if Anwar had believed that Rasheed was a fire-breathing dragon, not a Roman gladiator?

3. 'The lack of a substantive defence for involuntarily intoxicated defendants results in unjust convictions. This is demonstrated by *R v Kingston* [1995] 2 AC 355. Parliament should create such a defence as a matter of urgency.'

Discuss the extent to which you agree with this statement.

## Intoxication checklist

Having worked through this chapter, you should now have:

✓ An understanding of the case law that applies when a defendant uses the fact he was intoxicated to claim he lacked *mens rea*

✓ A knowledge of which crimes are basic intent crimes and which are specific intent crimes

✓ An ability to critically discuss whether or not involuntary intoxication should be a substantive defence

✓ An understanding of the case law that applies to defendants whose intoxication causes them to mistakenly act in self-defence.

## Further reading

Crosby, C. (2010) 'Culpability, *Kingston* and the Law Commission' 74 *Journal of Criminal Law* 434.

Law Commission (2009) *Intoxication and Criminal Liability* (Law Commission Report No 314) Cm 7526.

Simester, A. P. (2009) 'Intoxication is Never a Defence' *Criminal Law Review* 3.

Smith, R. and Clements, L. (1995) 'Involuntary Intoxication, the Threshold of Inhibition and the Instigation of Crime' 46 *Northern Ireland Legal Quarterly* 210.

Sullivan, G. R. (1994) 'Involuntary Intoxication and Beyond' *Criminal Law Review* 272.

Sullivan, G. R. (1996) 'Making Excuses' in A. Smith and G. Sullivan (eds) *Harm and Culpability*. Oxford: OUP.

Williams, R. (2013) 'Voluntary Intoxication – a Lost Cause?' 129 *Law Quarterly Review* 264.

# 10

# Mental condition defences

## Chapter objectives

By the end of this chapter you should have:

- An understanding of the requirements for establishing the mental condition defences of sane automatism, insanity and diminished responsibility

- An ability to apply the relevant law to a hypothetical set of facts to determine whether any of these mental condition defences can be established

- An ability to critically discuss the changes made to the diminished responsibility defence by the Coroners and Justice Act 2009.

# Introduction

In this chapter we study three defences which we have already encountered briefly earlier in the text. What the three have in common is that they all concern the mental condition of the defendant. The first two – which were mentioned briefly in Chapter 3 – are sane automatism and insanity. Although we refer to them as defences, they are different in nature from the substantive defences that we study in the next chapter. Substantive defences apply when the *actus reus* and *mens rea* of a crime have been established. By contrast, sane automatism and insanity are both best understood as a denial of the *actus reus*. Defendants who plead one of these defences are denying that they acted voluntarily – which, as we saw in Chapter 3, is one of the core *actus reus* concepts. In other words, they are denying that they had the necessary mental capacity for criminal responsibility.

The third defence that we study in this chapter is diminished responsibility, which was mentioned briefly in the chapter on homicide. To some extent, diminished responsibility overlaps with the defence of insanity. The chapter will set out the requirements for a defence of diminished responsibility and explain the differences between this defence and insanity. We will also look in detail at the changes that were made to the diminished responsibility defence by the Coroners and Justice Act 2009 and evaluate them.

# Sane automatism

If a defendant successfully pleads the defence of sane automatism he is found not guilty. The defence has three requirements:

1. The defendant suffered a total destruction of voluntary control
2. The defendant's condition was caused by an external factor
3. The defendant's condition was not induced by voluntary intoxication.

We will work through these requirements in turn. We will also look at the situation where the defendant's condition was caused by a combination of sane automatism and voluntary intoxication.

## 1. The defendant suffered a total destruction of voluntary control

We studied the meaning of automatism in Chapter 3. We saw there that the Court of Appeal has held that it means a total destruction of voluntary control.[1]

## 2. The defendant's condition was caused by an external factor

Chapter 3 explained that, if the defendant suffered a total destruction of voluntary control, the next question to ask is whether this was caused by an external or an internal factor. The defence of sane automatism is only available if the defendant's condition was caused by an external factor. If the cause was an internal factor, you should instead consider the defence of insanity (and, in murder cases, the defence of diminished responsibility).

For example, in *R v Coley* [2013] EWCA Crim 223 the defendant, 17-year-old Scott Coley, entered his neighbour's house (with whom he was previously on good terms) clad

---

[1] *Attorney-General's Reference (No 2 of 1992)* [1994] QB 91; *R v Coley* [2013] EWCA Crim 223.

in a balaclava and carrying a Rambo knife. He attacked the victim, stabbing him repeatedly and causing life-threatening injuries. Coley was a regular user of strong cannabis. He played violent video games and on the evening of the offence had watched the action movie *xXx* and smoked cannabis. Three psychiatrists stated that Coley had probably suffered a brief psychotic episode induced by the cannabis. They also said that it was possible that he was acting out the role of a character in a video game. At trial he was convicted of attempted murder. On appeal the Court of Appeal held that the defence of insanity was unavailable to Coley because his condition had been caused by an external, not an internal, factor (smoking cannabis).

The distinction between external and internal factors is a difficult one, as the following two pairs of cases illustrate. The first pair of cases involves two diabetics. In *R v Quick* [1973] QB 910 the defendant, William Quick, was a nurse. He was charged with assaulting a patient. Quick was diabetic. On the day of the offence he had taken insulin as normal but ate little food thereafter. As a result he suffered hypoglycaemia (i.e. low blood sugar levels). At trial the trial judge ruled that this evidence supported a defence of insanity, not a defence of sane automatism. Following this Quick changed his plea to guilty[2] and appealed, arguing that the trial judge's ruling was incorrect. The Court of Appeal agreed, holding that the cause of Quick's condition was the injection of insulin, which amounted to an external factor. The appropriate defence was therefore sane automatism. Lawton LJ stated:

> In this case Quick's alleged mental condition, if it ever existed, was not caused by his diabetes but by his use of the insulin prescribed by his doctor. Such malfunctioning of his mind as there was, was caused by an external factor and not by a bodily disorder in the nature of a disease which disturbed the working of his mind. It follows in our judgment that Quick was entitled to have his defence of automatism left to the jury and that Bridge J.'s ruling as to the effect of the medical evidence called by him was wrong.

Quick's conviction was therefore quashed. But compare *R v Quick* to *R v Hennessy* [1989] 1 WLR 287. The defendant, Andrew Hennessy, was also a diabetic. He was charged with motoring offences. He claimed that at the time of the offences he was in a hyperglycaemic state (i.e. too much blood sugar). He explained that this was because – as a result of stress, anxiety and depression – he had failed to take his proper dose of insulin. The trial judge ruled that this amounted to a claim of insanity, not sane automatism. Following this Hennessy changed his plea to guilty and appealed, arguing that the trial judge's ruling was incorrect. The Court of Appeal rejected the appeal and held that the appropriate defence in Hennessy's case was insanity.

## EXTRACT

Read the following extract from the judgment of Lord Lane CJ. How does he distinguish the decision in *R v Quick*?

According to Lord Lane CJ, can stress, anxiety and depression amount to external factors? Why/why not?

---

[2]At the time of the case a finding of not guilty by reason of insanity resulted in compulsory detention in a special hospital.

## R v Hennessy [1989] 1 WLR 287

### Lord Lane CJ

Thus in Quick's case the fact that his condition was, or may have been due to the injections of insulin, meant that the malfunction was due to an external factor and not to the disease. The drug it was that caused the hypoglycaemia, the low blood sugar. As suggested in another passage of the judgment of Lawton L.J. (at p. 922G–H), hyperglycaemia, high blood sugar, caused by an inherent defect, and not corrected by insulin is a disease, and if, as the defendant was asserting here, it does cause a malfunction of the mind, then the case may fall within [the insanity defence].

[...]

In our judgment, stress, anxiety and depression can no doubt be the result of the operation of external factors, but they are not, it seems to us, in themselves separately or together external factors of the kind capable in law of causing or contributing to a state of automatism. They constitute a state of mind which is prone to recur. They lack the feature of novelty or accident [...] It does not, in our judgment, come within the scope of the exception of some external physical factor such as a blow on the head or the administration of an anaesthetic.

Hennessy's conviction – and his two-year suspended prison sentence – were therefore upheld.

So in *R v Quick* the cause of the defendant's condition was the injection of insulin: an external factor. In *R v Hennessy*, by contrast, the defendant had not injected himself with anything. The diabetes simply ran its course. The diabetes was therefore the cause, and diabetes is an internal factor. This is a fine distinction! Both Quick and Hennessy were responsible for mismanaging their diabetes. Whilst their mismanagement took a different form in each case, it seems strange that this difference should result in such radically different legal outcomes.

Also important in cases involving diabetics is the principle that the defence of sane automatism is unavailable if there was prior fault on the defendant's part. In *R v Clarke* [2009] EWCA Crim 921 the defendant, 49-year-old Trevor Clarke, had suffered from diabetes for 30 years. One day when he was driving he began to experience warning signs (sweating, tremor, anxiety) that he was about to suffer a hypoglycaemic episode. He ignored them and continued driving. When the hypoglycaemic episode began Clarke started driving erratically, eventually veering off the road. The car hit two children. The younger one, a four-year-old, was killed. The defence of sane automatism was unavailable to him because he had an awareness of his deteriorating condition and yet continued driving.

The second pair of cases is *R v Burgess* [1991] 2 QB 92 and *R v T* [1990] Crim LR 256. In *R v Burgess* the defendant, Barry Burgess, was in love with his neighbour Katrina Curtis – but she just wanted to be friends. One evening they were watching videos together. Katrina fell asleep. While she was sleeping Burgess hit her on the head with a bottle and then grabbed her by the throat. She cried out. He appeared to come to his senses and showed great remorse over what had happened. Medical evidence suggested that Burgess had been sleepwalking. At trial, the trial judge ruled that Burgess' condition was caused by an internal factor and so the appropriate defence was insanity, not sane automatism. Burgess was found not guilty by reason of insanity. He appealed, arguing that the trial judge's ruling was incorrect. The Court of Appeal rejected his appeal. Lord Lane CJ held that Katrina rejecting Burgess' advances did not amount to an external factor. The cause of his condition was internal:

> One can perhaps narrow the field of inquiry still further by eliminating what are sometimes called the "external factors" such as concussion caused by a blow on the head. There were no such factors here. Whatever the cause may have been, it was an "internal" cause. The possible disappointment or frustration caused by unrequited love is not to be equated with something such as concussion.

But whilst both *R v Hennessy* and *R v Burgess* insist that the ordinary stresses and disappointments of life cannot amount to an external factor, something that is exceptionally traumatic can. In *R v T* the defendant took part in a robbery three days after having been raped. At the time of the offence she was in a dissociative state. The rape was held to constitute an external factor, and she was able to plead a defence of sane automatism.

## 3. The defendant's condition was not induced by voluntary intoxication

The defence of sane automatism is unavailable if the defendant's condition was induced by voluntary intoxication. For example, we saw a few pages ago that in *R v Coley* the defendant was unable to plead insanity because his condition was caused by an external factor. The Court of Appeal held that Coley was also unable to plead sane automatism because his condition was induced by his voluntary consumption of cannabis.

If the defendant was voluntarily intoxicated, you should instead apply the law that we studied in the previous chapter on intoxication. So suppose the defendant voluntarily consumes two bottles of wine and ends up so drunk that he falls over and smashes a valuable ornament. He cannot plead sane automatism, even if he was so drunk that he was completely unable to control his bodily movements when he smashed the ornament, because his condition was the result of his own voluntary intoxication. The case would instead be governed by the principles set out in *DPP v Majewski* [1977] AC 443.

## 4. Sane automatism and voluntary intoxication

What is the position if the defendant's condition was the result of a combination of: (i) voluntary intoxication; and (ii) another external factor that was not self-induced? This issue arose in *R v Stripp* (1978) 69 Cr App R 318. The defendant, David Stripp, had been out drinking with his fiancée. At the end of the evening Stripp caught the last bus home. The next anyone saw of him was in the bus station, where he was found fast asleep on the lower floor of a double-decker bus. Stripp got off the bus and said he wanted to go home. He then climbed into a single-decker bus and drove off in it. Stripp drove the bus for half a mile. He failed to control it properly and left a trail of destruction behind him. At trial Stripp was convicted of a number of driving offences. He appealed, arguing that he had acted in a state of automatism. He claimed that on the original bus journey the bus had swerved causing him to bang his head. This bang, he said, left him concussed. The Court of Appeal held that, in a case where the defendant was both concussed and voluntarily intoxicated, the jury must determine whether the concussion or the intoxication was the dominant cause of the defendant's condition. If it was concussion, he may plead sane automatism. If it was voluntary intoxication, the law that we studied in the previous chapter should be applied.

The Court of Appeal in *R v Stripp* also commented *obiter* on another, similar situation. Suppose Dale is so drunk that he falls over and bangs his head. As a result of concussion he is left completely unaware of what he is doing. Whilst in this state he runs into Mildred and knocks her over. Mildred suffers a broken arm. Medical evidence shows that the dominant cause of Dale's unawareness was his concussion. Could Dale plead sane automatism? Or would the defence be unavailable on the basis that his concussion was caused by his voluntary intoxication? The Court of Appeal in *R v Stripp* suggested that, in a case like this, sane automatism is available as a defence. Whilst defendants may not plead the defence when their condition was induced by voluntary intoxication (as in *R v Coley*), in a case like Dale's the link between his unawareness and his intoxication was too remote for this principle to apply.

## Insanity

In a criminal trial, a person's sanity might be relevant for one of two reasons. First, the defendant may claim that he was insane at the time he committed the offence in question. Second, the defendant may claim that he is insane at the time of the trial and as a result is unfit to be tried. We do not examine the second of these in this text, since it is more a matter of procedure than of substantive criminal law. Instead, we focus on the first situation: where the defendant seeks to establish a defence on the grounds that he was insane at the time of the offence.

As we saw in Chapter 3, a defendant who successfully pleads the defence of insanity is found not guilty by reason of insanity. If the defendant is found not guilty by reason of insanity the trial judge can order hospitalisation, a supervision order or an absolute discharge.[3] The requirements for the defence of insanity were set out by the House of Lords in *M'Naghten's case* (1843) 10 C & F 200:

> [W]e have to submit our opinion to be, that the jurors ought to be told in all cases that every man is to be presumed to be sane, and to possess a sufficient degree of reason to be responsible for his crimes, until the contrary be proved to their satisfaction; and that to establish a defence on the ground of insanity, it must be clearly proved that, at the time of the committing of the act, the party accused was labouring under such a defect of reason, from disease of the mind, as not to know the nature and quality of the act he was doing; or, if he did know it, that he did not know he was doing what was wrong.

As this extract suggests, the defence of insanity has a reversed burden of proof. This was confirmed by the House of Lords in *Woolmington v DPP* [1935] AC 462. So a defendant who pleads insanity must prove, on the balance of probabilities, that the requirements for the defence are established.

*M'Naghten's case* tells us that the defence has three requirements:

1. The defendant was suffering from a disease of the mind
2. The defendant's disease of the mind caused a defect of reason
3. As a result of the defect of reason, the defendant either: (i) did not know the nature and quality of the act he was doing; or (ii) did not know that what he was doing was wrong.

These requirements are known as the *M'Naghten* rules. We will work through them in turn. We will then look briefly at two specific types of case: those where the defendant was both voluntarily intoxicated and suffering from a disease of the mind; and those where the defendant was suffering from an alcohol-induced disease of the mind.

---

[3]Criminal Procedure (Insanity) Act 1964, s.5.

## 1. The defendant was suffering from a disease of the mind

The first requirement is that the defendant was suffering from a disease of the mind. 'Disease of the mind' is a legal concept, not a medical one.[4] So whilst medical evidence is necessary,[5] whether or not the defendant was suffering from a disease of the mind is a question of law. It is important to remember this, because as we shall see a doctor would regard some of the courts' rulings on insanity as very strange indeed!

The principal restriction on what constitutes a disease of the mind is that it must arise from a factor that is internal to the defendant. So, as we saw earlier in the chapter, if a defendant receives a bang on the head and suffers concussion the appropriate defence is sane automatism, not insanity, because his condition was caused by an external factor. Similarly, if the defendant's condition arose from the administration of an anaesthetic or from the injection of insulin (as in *R v Quick*) the appropriate defence is sane automatism, not insanity.

Aside from this restriction, the concept disease of the mind is very wide indeed. The leading case is *R v Sullivan* [1984] AC 156. The defendant, Patrick Sullivan, was an epileptic. He would suffer one or two seizures a week. One day he suffered a seizure whilst he was visiting an elderly neighbour, Mrs Killick. During the seizure he attacked Mr Payne, an elderly man who was also visiting. Sullivan was charged with maliciously inflicting GBH.[6] At trial, Sullivan initially pleaded not guilty. His counsel led evidence that the attack occurred during an epileptic seizure. However, the trial judge ruled that the relevant defence was insanity, not sane automatism. Following this ruling Sullivan chose to plead guilty to assault occasioning ABH (in order to avoid being found not guilty by reason of insanity[7]). He then appealed against the trial judge's ruling. On appeal, the key issue was whether the appropriate defence was sane automatism or insanity. The case reached the House of Lords.

### EXTRACT

Read the following extract from the judgment of Lord Diplock. How does he define a 'disease of the mind'?

To qualify as a disease of the mind, must the condition be a form of brain disease? Must the condition be permanent?

What is the rationale underlying Lord Diplock's definition of disease of the mind?

### *R v Sullivan* [1984] AC 156

#### Lord Diplock

I agree [...] that "mind" in the *M'Naghten Rules* is used in the ordinary sense of the mental faculties of reason, memory and understanding. If the effect of a disease is to impair these faculties so severely as to have either of the consequences referred to in the latter part of the rules, it matters

---

[4]*R v Sullivan* [1984] AC 156.

[5]Section 1 of the Criminal Procedure (Insanity and Unfitness to Plead) Act 1991 states that the evidence of at least two medical practitioners is required for a verdict of not guilty by reason of insanity.

[6]Offences Against the Person Act 1861, s.20.

[7]At the time of the case a finding of not guilty by reason of insanity resulted in compulsory detention in a special hospital.

not whether the aetiology, of the impairment is organic, as in epilepsy, or functional, or whether the impairment itself is permanent or is transient and intermittent, provided that it subsisted at the time of commission of the act. The purpose of the legislation relating to the defence of insanity, ever since its origin in 1800, has been to protect society against recurrence of the dangerous conduct. The duration of a temporary suspension of the mental faculties of reason, memory and understanding, particularly if, as in Mr. Sullivan's case, it is recurrent, cannot on any rational ground be relevant to the application by the courts of the *M'Naghten Rules*, though it may be relevant to the course adopted by the Secretary of State, to whom the responsibility for how the defendant is to be dealt with passes after the return of the special verdict of "not guilty by reason of insanity."

[...]

My Lords, it is natural to feel reluctant to attach the label of insanity to a sufferer from psychomotor epilepsy of the kind to which Mr. Sullivan was subject, even though the expression in the context of a special verdict of "not guilty by reason of insanity" is a technical one which includes a purely temporary and intermittent suspension of the mental faculties of reason, memory and understanding resulting from the occurrence of an epileptic fit. But the label is contained in the current statute, it has appeared in this statute's predecessors ever since 1800. It does not lie within the power of the courts to alter it. Only Parliament can do that. It has done so twice; it could do so once again.

Sympathise though I do with Mr. Sullivan, I see no other course open to your Lordships than to dismiss this appeal.

So the term 'disease of the mind' is not restricted to diseases of the brain. It encompasses any condition which impairs the defendant's faculties of reason, memory or understanding, regardless of whether the impairment is permanent or temporary. As a result, the House of Lords held that the relevant defence in *R v Sullivan* was indeed insanity. Sullivan's conviction – and his sentence of three years' probation with a medical supervision order – were therefore upheld.

In practice, then, the legal meaning attached to the term 'disease of the mind' can lead to peculiar outcomes. Epileptics may be regarded as insane. As we saw earlier in the chapter, other examples include: a diabetic who fails to take his proper dose of insulin and consequently suffers hyperglycaemia (*R v Hennessy*); and, a person who commits an offence whilst sleepwalking (*R v Burgess*). A further example is *R v Kemp* [1957] 1 QB 399. The defendant, Albert Kemp, attacked his wife during the night with a hammer. Kemp was a man of good character and he and his wife were a devoted couple. Kemp said that he had no memory of the attack. Medical evidence showed that he was suffering from arteriosclerosis (hardening of the arteries). The medical experts believed that this disease led to a congestion of blood in his brain, which caused a complete or partial loss of consciousness when he attacked his wife. Devlin J ruled that the relevant defence was insanity. He explained that the term 'disease of the mind' is not limited to diseases of the brain. It encompasses any condition which causes a malfunctioning of the mind:

> The law is not concerned with the brain but with the mind, in the sense that "mind" is ordinarily used, the mental faculties of reason, memory and understanding. If one read for "disease of the mind" "disease of the brain," it would follow that in many cases pleas of insanity would not be established because it could not be proved that the brain had been affected in any way, either by degeneration of the cells or in any other way. In my judgment the condition of the brain is irrelevant and so is the question of whether the condition of the mind is curable or incurable, transitory or permanent.

There is no warranty for introducing those considerations into the definition in the *McNaghten Rules*. Temporary insanity is sufficient to satisfy them. It does not matter whether it is incurable and permanent or not.

As a result Kemp was found not guilty by reason of insanity.

 ## 2. The defendant's disease of the mind caused a defect of reason

The second requirement is that the defendant's disease of the mind caused a defect of reason. To establish a defect of reason, it must be shown that the defendant's powers of reasoning were impaired.

In *R v Clarke* [1972] 1 All ER 219 the defendant, May Clarke, went to a supermarket. She placed the items she wished to buy in her shopping basket but, at some point before she reached the checkout, she took three items (butter, coffee and mincemeat) out of her basket and put them into her handbag. She was charged with theft. She explained that she had been experiencing various domestic problems and was also feeling unwell. She said that things had been getting on top of her, which had left her feeling depressed and had been causing her to act absent-mindedly. At trial a psychiatrist testified that depression can cause absent-mindedness. The trial judge ruled that Clarke was raising a defence of insanity. As a result she chose to plead guilty. On appeal the Court of Appeal held that the trial judge's ruling was incorrect. Ackner J explained that Clarke was not claiming that she had suffered a defect of reason, and so was not raising a plea of insanity. She was simply denying that she had formed the *mens rea* of theft. The Court accordingly quashed the conviction.

### EXTRACT

According to the following extract from Ackner J's judgment, why was Clarke not claiming that she had suffered a defect of reason?

### *R v Clarke* [1972] 1 All ER 219

#### Ackner J

The *M'Naghten Rules* relate to accused persons who by reason of a disease of the mind are deprived of the power of reasoning. They do not apply and never have applied to a momentary failure by someone to concentrate. The picture painted by the evidence was wholly consistent with the appellant being a woman who retained her ordinary powers of reason, but who was momentarily absentminded or confused and acted as she did by failing to concentrate properly on what she was doing and by failing adequately to use her mental powers.

 ## 3. As a result of the defect of reason, the defendant either: (i) did not know the nature and quality of the act he was doing; or (ii) did not know that what he was doing was wrong

The third requirement for the defence is that the defendant *either*: (i) did not know the nature and quality of the act he was doing; *or* (ii) did not know that what he was doing was wrong. Proof of either of these will suffice.

### i. The defendant did not know the nature and quality of the act he was doing

To establish that he did not know the nature and quality of the act he was doing, the defendant must prove that he had no appreciation of the physical aspects of his conduct. Here are three examples:

> ## EXAMPLE
>
> - The defendant who was in a state of automatism. An example would be *R v Sullivan*, where the defendant suffered an epileptic seizure and had no awareness of what was happening.
> - The defendant who, as a result of a delusion, believed he was performing an act that was fundamentally different to the reality. For example, he thought he was slaying a dragon when in fact he was killing a human being.
> - The defendant who had no understanding of the consequences of his act. The jurist Stephen gave the example of a person who cut off the head of a man who is asleep because he thought 'it would be great fun to see him looking for it when he woke up'.[8]

Requiring the defendant to prove that he had no appreciation of the physical aspects of his conduct means that the term 'nature and quality of the act' has a limited scope. Suppose that Dale is schizophrenic. As a result of a schizophrenic delusion, he believes he has been ordered to kill Mildred. He carries out these orders. Dale will be unable to prove that he did not know the nature and quality of his act because he was aware that he was killing a human being.

### ii. The defendant did not know that what he was doing was wrong

If the defendant did know the nature and quality of his act, he may still have a defence of insanity if he can prove that he did not know that what he was doing was wrong. The question which has arisen here is whether in this context wrong means illegal or immoral. In other words, may a defendant plead insanity if he knows he is breaking the law but believes it is the right thing to do in the circumstances?

This question was considered in *R v Windle* [1952] 2 QB 826. The defendant, Francis Windle, was married to an older woman. The marriage was an unhappy one. His wife often spoke about committing suicide and there was evidence that she was certifiably insane. Windle frequently discussed his home life with his work colleagues, until one day one of them said to him, 'Give her a dozen aspirins'. The next day he gave his wife 100 aspirins. The medical evidence suggested that Windle believed that killing his wife was an act of kindness, but that he knew it was illegal. The trial judge therefore ruled that there was no evidence of insanity, and Windle was convicted of murder (and sentenced to death). On appeal, the Court of Appeal ruled that 'wrong' in the *M'Naghten* rules simply means illegal. Lord Goddard CJ stated:

> In the opinion of the court there is no doubt that in the *McNaghten* rules "wrong" means contrary to law and not "wrong" according to the opinion of one man or of a number of people on the question whether a particular Act might or might not be justified. In the present case, it could not be challenged that the appellant knew that what he was doing was contrary to law, and that he realized what punishment the law provided for murder.

---

[8]Stephen, J. F. (1883) *A History of the Criminal Law of England* (vol II), p166.

Windle's appeal was therefore dismissed.

The decision in *R v Windle* has been criticised.[9] Think back to our example in which owing to a schizophrenic delusion Dale believes he has been ordered to kill Mildred. As long as he realises that killing Mildred is illegal, Dale will be unable to plead insanity – even if his schizophrenia caused him to have a deluded belief that killing Mildred was the right thing to do. In spite of this criticism, the decision in *R v Windle* was confirmed by the Court of Appeal in *R v Johnson* [2007] EWCA Crim 1978.

### 4. Insanity and voluntary intoxication

If at the time of the offence the defendant was both voluntarily intoxicated and suffering from a disease of the mind it is likely that the courts will adopt a similar approach to *R v Stripp*, that is the question will be whether the predominant cause of the defendant's condition was his voluntary intoxication or his disease of the mind. If it was his voluntary intoxication, the law on intoxication that we studied in the previous chapter will apply.[10] If it was his disease of the mind, the defendant may plead insanity and the *M'Naghten* rules will apply.[11]

### 5. Alcohol-induced insanity

Here we are dealing with a slightly different scenario to the previous one. The defendant is not voluntarily intoxicated at the time of the offence. Instead, the defendant is suffering from a condition which was caused by the consumption of alcohol (e.g. the defendant is a heavy drinker; after deciding to stop drinking he suffers withdrawal symptoms including hallucinations). Here it is open to the defendant to plead insanity.[12] The *M'Naghten* rules will apply as normal.

## Diminished responsibility

In Chapter 5 we studied the law of homicide. We saw that there are three special partial defences to murder. We studied one of these – loss of control – in Chapter 5. We now turn to one of the others: diminished responsibility.[13] Studying diminished responsibility here (instead of in the homicide chapter) allows us to compare and contrast it to the defence of insanity.

There are a number of important differences between insanity and diminished responsibility. Two of these are:

- Insanity is a general defence, whereas diminished responsibility is a special defence. Diminished responsibility is only available as a defence on a charge of murder.

- A defendant who establishes a defence of insanity is found not guilty by reason of insanity. A defendant who establishes a defence of diminished responsibility, by contrast, is not guilty of murder but is guilty of (voluntary) manslaughter.

---

[9]Mackay, R.D. (2009) 'Righting the Wrong? – Some Observations on the Second Limb of the *M'Naghten* Rules' *Criminal Law Review* 80.
[10]For an example, see *R v Lipman* [1970] 1 QB 152 (which we studied in Chapter 9).
[11]*R v Burns* (1973) 58 Cr App R 364.
[12]*R v Davis* (1881) 14 Cox CC 563.
[13]The third partial defence – suicide pact – is not covered in this text.

There is also a difference in the scope of the defences, as we will see shortly.

The defence of diminished responsibility is defined by section 2 of the Homicide Act 1957. This section was amended significantly by the Coroners and Justice Act 2009.[14] As we work through the test for the defence we will examine the changes introduced by the 2009 Act and evaluate their impact.

As amended, section 2 states:

---

**EXTRACT**

## Section 2 of the Homicide Act 1957

### 2 Persons suffering from diminished responsibility

(1)  A person ("D") who kills or is a party to the killing of another is not to be convicted of murder if D was suffering from an abnormality of mental functioning which –
  (a)  arose from a recognised medical condition,
  (b)  substantially impaired D's ability to do one or more of the things mentioned in subsection (1A), and
  (c)  provides an explanation for D's acts and omissions in doing or being a party to the killing.

(1A) Those things are –
  (a)  to understand the nature of D's conduct;
  (b)  to form a rational judgment;
  (c)  to exercise self-control.

(1B) For the purposes of subsection (1)(c), an abnormality of mental functioning provides an explanation for D's conduct if it causes, or is a significant contributory factor in causing, D to carry out that conduct.

(2)  On a charge of murder, it shall be for the defence to prove that the person charged is by virtue of this section not liable to be convicted of murder.

(3)  A person who but for this section would be liable, whether as principal or as accessory, to be convicted of murder shall be liable instead to be convicted of manslaughter.

(4)  The fact that one party to a killing is by virtue of this section not liable to be convicted of murder shall not affect the question whether the killing amounted to murder in the case of any other party to it.

---

From this section we learn that: the defence of diminished responsibility is available to both the actual killer and accessories (s.2(1); s.2(3)); and the defence of diminished responsibility has a reversed burden of proof. The defendant must prove, on the balance of probabilities, that the defence is established (s.2(2)).[15]

---

[14]Section 52.

[15]The Court of Appeal has rejected the claim that the reverse burden of proof violates the presumption of innocence and Article 6(2) ECHR: *R v Lambert; R v Ali; R v Jordan* [2002] QB 1112; *R v Foye* [2013] EWCA Crim 475. In the latter case the Court explained that: (1) whilst the defence must prove the requirements for diminished responsibility, the prosecution still bears the burden of proving the *actus reus* and *mens rea* of murder; and (2) the defence concerns the inner workings of the defendant's mind, and in many cases it may be practically impossible for the prosecution to disprove beyond reasonable doubt an assertion that the defendant was suffering from diminished responsibility. In particular, the defendant might refuse to submit to, or cooperate with, a medical examination.

Section 2(1) also tells us that the defence has four requirements:

1. The defendant was suffering from an abnormality of mental functioning.
2. The defendant's abnormality of mental functioning arose from a recognised medical condition.
3. The defendant's abnormality of mental functioning substantially impaired his ability to do one of the things listed in subsection (1A).
4. The defendant's abnormality of mental functioning provides an explanation for the defendant's participation in the killing.

All four of these requirements must be satisfied for the defence to apply. We will work through them in turn. We will then look at two specific types of difficult case: ones where the defendant wishes to plead diminished responsibility on the grounds of alcoholism; and ones where the defendant was suffering from an abnormality of mental functioning caused by a recognised medical condition but was also voluntarily intoxicated.

## 1. The defendant was suffering from an abnormality of mental functioning

The first requirement is that the defendant was suffering from an abnormality of mental functioning. In *R v Byrne* [1960] 2 QB 396 Lord Parker CJ explained that 'abnormal' means:

> a state of mind so different from that of ordinary human beings that the reasonable man would term it abnormal.

Although *R v Byrne* was a case decided under the old law, the guidance offered by Lord Parker CJ can still be used today (though you might wonder how much assistance it actually provides!).

The old law used the term 'abnormality of mind'. The Law Commission reported that psychiatrists had criticised this because 'abnormality of mind' was not a psychiatric term:[16]

> 5.111 [T]he definition has not been drafted with the needs and practices of medical experts in mind, even though their evidence is crucial to the legal viability of any claim of diminished responsibility. 'Abnormality of mind' is not a psychiatric term, so its meaning has had to be developed by the courts from case to case.

The Law Commission stated that the term 'abnormality of mental functioning' is 'preferred by psychiatrists' and so recommended that this be used instead.[17]

In order to plead diminished responsibility, the defendant must produce some medical evidence that he was suffering from an abnormality of mental functioning. If he fails to produce at least some relevant medical evidence the trial judge will not leave the defence to the jury. For example, in *R v Bunch* [2013] EWCA Crim 2498 the defendant, Martin Bunch, was convicted of murder. At trial he wished to argue diminished responsibility on the grounds of alcoholism, but called no medical evidence as to whether he was an alcoholic. The only evidence on this matter came from an expert prosecution witness, who stated that in her opinion there was no evidence of alcohol dependency. The trial judge accordingly refused to leave the defence of diminished responsibility to the jury. The defendant subsequently appealed. The issue for the Court of Appeal was whether the trial judge had been right to refuse to leave the defence to the jury.

---

[16]Law Commission (2006) *Murder, Manslaughter and Infanticide* (Report No 304) HC 30.
[17]Law Commission (2006) *Murder, Manslaughter and Infanticide* (Report No 304) HC 30, para 5.114.

## EXTRACT

Read the following extract from the judgment of Holroyde J. May a defendant plead diminished responsibility if he produces no medical evidence that he was suffering from an abnormality of mental functioning?

If the defendant produces medical evidence that he was suffering from an abnormality of mental functioning, must the jury accept this evidence?

## *R v Bunch* [2013] EWCA Crim 2498

### Holroyde J

11 The judge held, in our view correctly, that the amendment of section 2 by the 2009 Act did not diminish the authority of cases such as *Byrne* [1960] 2 QB 396 and *Dix* 74 Cr App R 306, in which it was held that medical evidence, though not in terms required by section 2 of the Act, was "a practical necessity" if the defence was to succeed, because the onus was on the defendant. The judge quoted from a passage at paragraph 19-83 of the current edition of Archbold in which the learned editors say, in our view correctly:

"... it will be for the jury to decide whether the accused was suffering from an abnormality of mental functioning, whether this arose from a medical condition, whether it substantially impaired his ability to do one of the three things mentioned in subsection (1A) and whether it caused, or was a significant contributory factor in causing the defendant to carry out the killing. Medical evidence will, however, be relevant to all these issues, particularly the first three (as to the second, it will be critical). As before ... it is submitted that the jury will not be bound to accept the medical evidence if there is other material before them which, in their good judgment, conflicts with it and outweighs it."

As this extract emphasises, whether or not a defendant was suffering from an abnormality of mental functioning is for the jury to decide. But whilst the jury is not bound to accept the medical evidence, it may only choose to depart from it if there is some material which conflicts with it and outweighs it. This is illustrated by *R v Brennan* [2014] EWCA Crim 2387. In this case the defendant, who had a history of personality and mental health issues, stabbed the victim to death. At trial he raised the defence of diminished responsibility. The expert witness called by the defence gave evidence that, in her opinion, the defendant satisfied all the requirements for diminished responsibility. The expert called by the prosecution did not disagree with this assessment. Yet the jury rejected the defendant's plea of diminished responsibility and convicted him of murder. On appeal, the Court of Appeal quashed the murder conviction and substituted a conviction for manslaughter. Emphasising that juries must base their conclusions on the evidence, Davis LJ stated: 'Where there simply is no rational or proper basis for departing from uncontradicted and unchallenged expert evidence then juries may not do so.'

It is also important to point out that juries will often be faced with conflicting expert evidence. In *R v Brown* [2011] EWCA Crim 2796, for example, the defence's expert witness stated that the defendant was suffering from an adjustment disorder which caused an abnormality of mental functioning, whilst the prosecution's expert witness rejected the diagnosis of an adjustment disorder and stated that there was no abnormality of mental functioning. As Nicola Wake remarks:[18]

---

[18]Wake, N. (2012) 'Psychiatry and the New Diminished Responsibility Plea: Uneasy Bedfellows?' 76 *Journal of Criminal Law* 122.

The jury are therefore left with the unenviable task of deciding between the competing views of reputable medical experts.

One of the principal objectives of the changes to diminished responsibility was to improve the clarity of the law.[19] In the following extract Louise Kennefick discusses whether the new law achieves this objective, in the light of the roles of expert evidence and jury decision-making:

## EXTRACT

In Kennefick's opinion, does the new law achieve its objective of greater clarity? Why/why not?

### Kennefick, L. (2011) 'Introducing a New Diminished Responsibility Defence for England and Wales' 74 *Modern Law Review* 750

There is another line of argument which suggests that, as ideal as a trial by jury may seem, in more difficult cases, particularly involving expert evidence, the jury is simply unable to deal with the questions put before it. So rather than usurping the role of the jury, the expert is assisting the jury in coming to a decision; bringing its own complications. It is impossible to get inside the mind of the individual at the time of the offence, even for psychiatrists, therefore juries are being asked to base their decision on opinion, which usually involves choosing between two differing views.

In *R v Cannings*, Judge LJ goes so far as to warn that '... if the outcome of the trial depends exclusively or almost exclusively on a serious disagreement between distinguished and reputable experts, it will often be unwise, and therefore unsafe, to proceed.' This is largely due to the fact that as psychiatrists give opinion evidence, it is likely that one expert's opinion of the facts will differ from the other. However, place this argument in the hands of the jury, and further difficulties arise. Juries will be quite unfamiliar with the technical language used by forensic psychiatrists, and as Blom-Cooper and Morris point out, this can be bewildering, not least when it is presented for many hours, and over many days.

It appears, therefore, that the question as to who decides what in terms of the mental condition and criminal responsibility of the accused remains unclear, despite the goal of clarification underpinning the new law. What is clear, however, is that the system in place, which sees psychiatrists testifying in relation to responsibility, and juries attempting to decipher complicated psychiatric terminology, results in ambiguity, inconsistency and thus arguably unfair treatment of the mentally disordered offender.

## 2. The defendant's abnormality of mental functioning arose from a recognised medical condition

The second requirement for a defence of diminished responsibility is that the defendant's abnormality of mental functioning arose from a 'recognised medical condition'. This is another important change from the previous law. The old law stated:

> Where a person kills or is a party to the killing of another, he shall not be convicted of murder if he was suffering from such abnormality of mind (whether arising from a

---

[19]The Law Commission, for example, stated: 'The definition of "diminished responsibility" should be modernised, so that it is both clearer and better able to accommodate developments in expert diagnostic practice' (Law Commission (2006) *Murder, Manslaughter and Infanticide* (Report No 304) HC 30, para 5.107).

condition of arrested or retarded development of mind or any inherent causes or induced by disease or injury) as substantially impaired his mental responsibility for his acts and omissions in doing or being a party to the killing.

In other words, under the old law the defendant's abnormality of mind must have arisen 'from a condition of arrested or retarded development of mind or any inherent causes or induced by disease or injury'. This requirement was criticised for being both outdated and lacking any grounding in a medical diagnosis. In its 2006 report on the old law the Law Commission stated:[20]

> 5.111 [...] [D]iagnostic practice in diminished responsibility cases has long since developed beyond identification of the narrow range of permissible 'causes' of an abnormality of mind stipulated in the bracketed part of the definition. In any event, the stipulated permissible causes have never had an agreed psychiatric meaning. The outmoded stipulation of permissible causes has become as much a hindrance as a help. As Dr Madelyn Hicks put it to us:
>
>> [A]ttempting to specify the cause of mental disorders ... is irrelevant [and] misleading, and in fact there are almost always multiple causes stemming from the interaction between genetic vulnerability and life events.

For this reason, the new law uses the term 'recognised medical condition' instead of stipulating a list of permissible causes. The requirement of a recognised medical condition ensures that any successful plea of diminished responsibility is grounded in a medical diagnosis. It also enables the law to keep pace with changes in medicine and accommodate developments in diagnostic practice.

It is important to note, however, that the requirement of a recognised medical condition is potentially very broad. For a start, it is not limited to psychiatric illnesses. It could also encompass physical and psychological conditions. So, for example, diabetics and epileptics have recognised medical conditions. Other examples of medical conditions listed in the World Health Organization (WHO)'s International Statistical Classification of Diseases include: unhappiness; irritability and anger; suspiciousness and marked evasiveness; pyromania; paedophilia; sado-masochism and kleptomania.[21]

The WHO's International Statistical Classification of Diseases also lists acute intoxication. Based on this, the defendant in *R v Dowds* [2012] EWCA Crim 281 argued that voluntary acute intoxication is a recognised medical condition which may form the basis of a successful plea of diminished responsibility. The defendant in this case, Stephen Dowds, was not an alcoholic and did not have an alcohol dependency. He was a binge drinker, who drank heavily but only drank when he chose to do so. One weekend, he stabbed his partner to death whilst heavily intoxicated. The trial judge ruled that the defence of diminished responsibility was unavailable to him, since he was voluntarily intoxicated. He was therefore convicted of murder. On appeal, he argued that the trial judge's ruling was incorrect. Pointing to the fact that acute intoxication appears in the WHO's list of medical conditions, Dowds' counsel argued that defendants should be allowed to plead diminished responsibility on the basis of voluntary acute intoxication. The Court of Appeal rejected this argument. Hughes LJ stated:

> 40 [...] It is enough to say that it is quite clear that the reformulation of the statutory conditions for diminished responsibility was not intended to reverse the well established rule that voluntary acute intoxication is not capable of being relied upon to found diminished responsibility. That remains the law. The presence of a "recognised

---

[20]Law Commission (2006) *Murder, Manslaughter and Infanticide* (Report No 304) HC 30.
[21]See *R v Dowds* [2012] EWCA Crim 281, [31].

medical condition" is a necessary, but not always a sufficient, condition to raise the issue of diminished responsibility.

This reaffirms the stance taken under the old law that voluntary intoxication may not form the basis of a successful plea of diminished responsibility.[22] But Hughes LJ's statement that a recognised medical condition 'is a necessary, but not always a sufficient' condition raises the question whether there are other conditions which the courts may rule cannot provide a basis for a defence of diminished responsibility. Nicola Wake has accordingly commented:[23]

> [T]he rationale for including the "recognised medical condition" requirement was "to ensure a greater equilibrium between the law and medical science" (*R v Brown (Robert)* [2011] EWCA Crim 2796 at [23]; Law Commission, *Murder, Manslaughter and Infanticide*, Law Com. Report No. 304 (2006) para. 5.114). The idea that the courts will be required to determine which recognised medical conditions are valid for the purposes of the partial defence is inimical to this aim.

## ACTIVITY

Look back at the examples of medical conditions listed in the WHO's International Statistical Classification of Diseases. Do you think the courts might rule that any of these cannot form the basis of a plea of diminished responsibility? Which ones? Why?

Whilst the term 'recognised medical condition' is potentially very broad, it is also important to note that it could exclude some defendants who might have been able to plead diminished responsibility under the old law. As Louise Kennefick explains in the following extract, one possible example is the mercy killer who – whilst not suffering from a recognised medical condition – kills his terminally ill partner under great stress.

## EXTRACT

In the following extract Kennefick refers to the 'benign conspiracy' that sometimes occurred under the old law. What was the benign conspiracy? Will it still be possible under the new law?

In your opinion, should the law be flexible enough to allow for benign conspiracies?

### Kennefick, L. (2011) 'Introducing a New Diminished Responsibility Defence for England and Wales' 74 *Modern Law Review* 750

Thus, in practice, it is likely that psychiatric classificatory systems will play a more central role in establishing the existence of a recognised medical condition resulting in an abnormality of mental functioning. Of course, most diagnoses by experts under the original definition would have had some recognised medical basis. The new wording, however, makes this requirement essential, so in that respect, it clarifies the law. But this change in definition may have more far-reaching consequences than initially anticipated. Accepting that it has not yet been interpreted by the

---

[22]See, for example, *R v Fenton* (1975) 61 Cr App R 261.
[23]Wake, N. (2012) 'Diminished Responsibility and Acute Intoxication: Raising the Bar?' 76 *Journal of Criminal Law* 197.

courts, the term 'recognised medical condition', as it stands, has the effect of narrowing the defence of diminished responsibility by excluding those disorders which may no longer or may not yet be accepted internationally as 'medical conditions'.

The original definition had progressed to the point where it was interpreted by the courts to show leniency to a 'highly stressed killer', in the sense that a defendant could receive a manslaughter verdict if the particular form of stress in question was pathologised as diminished responsibility. This trend is also reflected in prominent domestic violence cases of the early 1990s featuring the controversial 'Battered Woman's Syndrome'. Such forms of interpretation have been described as a 'benign conspiracy' which stretched the notion of 'abnormality of mind', to enable a verdict to meet the perceived justice of the case. The restriction of the law to internationally medically recognised and documented conditions brings the possibility of a defendant (for example a 'mercy-killer') being convicted of murder and given a mandatory life sentence, despite his or her responsibility for the killing being far removed from 'the gangland executioner and the serial killer who likes to torture his victims first'.

So although the introduction of 'recognised medical condition' may promote the principle of clarity, conversely, it draws into question the fairness of the situation for the offender pleading diminished responsibility. Should both the court and the expert utilise a strict interpretation of the phrase, the likelihood of a 'mercy killer' being brandished a 'murderer' and sentenced to life imprisonment increases. Thus, the new law of diminished responsibility has a potentially damaging impact on a particular group of offenders who could have availed of the partial defence under the original definition.

Time will tell how the system responds to this particular circumstance in practice. It may well be the case that the courts will likewise stretch their interpretation of the term 'recognised medical condition', or the experts their diagnoses, in order to enable the 'benign conspiracy' to continue, albeit in a slightly different guise. Should this be the case, whether or not the clarity of the law relating to diminished responsibility has been improved [...] would be brought into question.

Gibson argues that the benign conspiracy *will* continue under the new version of the diminished responsibility defence.[24] A combination of expert generosity and jury benevolence will, he suggests, allow mercy killers to link a stressful or emotional state with a recognised medical condition, such as reactive depression. However, the continuation of the benevolent conspiracy presents a fundamental challenge to the integrity of the reformed defence:

> Any manipulation of these requirements therefore risks diluting, if not *subverting*, the medical emphasis of the revamped defence. This is ironic given that greater medical precision was a distinct goal of diminished responsibility reform. A further irony materialises when it is recalled that such accuracy was intended to aid medical experts in presenting their evidence. The continuation of the benevolent conspiracy requires them to expand the borders of the defence *more* artificially than under the former plea. If one aim of the 2009 Act was to bring the legal and medical professions closer together, then this is a perverse prospect. Such an aim will be frustrated.

A study by Mackay and Mitchell examined a total of 90 cases decided under the new version of the diminished responsibility defence. They contrasted their findings with those of an older study, which examined a total of 157 cases decided under the old version of the defence. The following extract outlines their principal findings and offers some indication of the practical impact that the changes to the defence have had.

---

[24]Gibson, M. (2017) 'Pragmatism Preserved? The Challenges of Accommodating Mercy Killers in the Reformed Diminished Responsibility Plea' 81 *Journal of Criminal Law* 177.

## EXTRACT

Read the following extract, which contrasts data from cases decided under the new version of the defence (the 'CPS cases') with data from cases decided under the old version (the 'Law Commission cases'). According to the study, have the changes to the defence led to an increase or a decrease in the proportion of cases with a contested plea? And, have the changes resulted in an increase or decrease in the proportion of cases resulting in a murder conviction?

### Mackay, R. and Mitchell, B. (2017) 'The New Diminished Responsibility Plea in Operation: Some Initial Findings' *Criminal Law Review* 18

The "official" view has been that the old s.2 was in need of clarification and modernisation and that the reformulation contained in the revised section was designed to achieve that and nothing more. However, this study could be regarded as casting some doubt on this "official" view of the new s.2, the operation of which may be giving rise to unintended consequences. In particular, what is of note is that 43.3% of the CPS cases under the new plea were contested compared to 22.9% under the old plea. In addition, in 65.6% (n=59) the finding was one of diminished responsibility, of which 13.5% (n=8) were contested. In the Law Commission study in 80.3% of the cases (n=126) the finding was one of diminished responsibility, of which 6.3% (n=8) were contested. In short, the new plea seems to have resulted in more contested pleas with convictions for murder being returned in 34.4% of these cases compared to a murder conviction rate of 14% under the old plea. While an increase in the number of convictions for murder was one of the clear reasons for abolishing provocation and introducing a new "loss of control" plea this was not true for diminished responsibility in that no such increase in murder convictions was ever suggested as a reason for reformulating s.2.

### 3. The defendant's abnormality of mental functioning substantially impaired his ability to do one of the things listed in subsection (1A)

The old law required that the defendant's 'mental responsibility' must have been 'substantially impaired'. But it provided no further guidance on what this meant. This was criticised by the Law Commission:[25]

> 5.110 [T]he definition says nothing about what is involved in a "substantial impairment [of] mental responsibility". The implication is that the effects of an abnormality of mind must significantly reduce the offender's culpability. The Act neither makes this clear, nor says in what way the effects of an abnormality of mind can reduce culpability for an intentional killing, such that a manslaughter verdict is the right result.

The new law seeks to remedy this ambiguity by stating that the defendant's abnormality of mental functioning must have substantially impaired his ability to do one of three things. These three things are listed in subsection (1A) of section 2. We will work through them in turn.

---

[25]Law Commission (2006) *Murder, Manslaughter and Infanticide* (Report No 304) HC 30.

### i. The defendant's ability to understand the nature of his conduct

The first possibility is that the defendant's abnormality of mental functioning substantially impaired his ability to understand the nature of his conduct. This is similar to one of the limbs of the *M'Naghten* rules, which, as we saw earlier in the chapter, applies when the defendant did not know the nature and quality of his actions. But there is an important difference. The *M'Naghten* rules apply where the defendant lacked *any* understanding of the nature and quality of his actions. By contrast, for diminished responsibility the defendant must show that his ability to understand the nature of his conduct was *substantially* impaired. So a defendant who had only a partial understanding of the nature of his conduct will not be able to plead insanity, but may be able to plead diminished responsibility.

The Law Commission gave the following example of when this type of diminished responsibility might apply:[26]

> [A] boy aged 10 who has been left to play very violent video games for hours on end for much of his life, loses his temper and kills another child when the child attempts to take a game from him. When interviewed, he shows no real understanding that, when a person is killed they cannot simply be later revived, as happens in the games he has been continually playing.

### ii. The defendant's ability to form a rational judgement

The second possibility is that the defendant's abnormality of mental functioning substantially impaired his ability to form a rational judgement. One of the examples given by the Law Commission to illustrate when this would apply was:[27]

> [A] woman suffering from post traumatic stress disorder, consequent upon violent abuse suffered at her husband's hands, comes to believe that only burning her husband to death will rid the world of his sins.

The Court of Appeal considered the meaning of the term 'ability to form a rational judgment' in *R v Conroy* [2017] EWCA Crim 81. Jason Conroy had autism spectrum disorder, learning difficulties, and attention deficit hyperactivity disorder. He lived in a special residential home. He developed an obsessive interest in one of the other residents, Melissa Mathieson. One evening he waited until Melissa was asleep and went to her room. His plan was to strangle her, take her to his room and then have sex with her. When he tried to take Melissa to his room he dropped her. A member of staff heard the bang, went to investigate, and found Melissa's unconscious body. She died four days later. Conroy was charged with murder and sought to rely on diminished responsibility. Four medical experts gave evidence at his trial. They all agreed that Conroy suffered from an abnormality of mental functioning which arose from a recognised medical condition (autism). The key issue, on which the experts disagreed, was whether this abnormality substantially impaired his ability to form a rational judgement. In his direction to the jury the trial judge drew a distinction between a defendant's thought processes and the outcome of those processes. He told the jury that they should concentrate on the thought processes, not the outcome, and consider whether the thought processes were irrational. The jury subsequently rejected the diminished responsibility defence and convicted Conroy of murder. He appealed, arguing that the trial judge misdirected the jury.

---

[26] Law Commission (2006) *Murder, Manslaughter and Infanticide* (Report No 304) HC 30, para 5.121.
[27] Law Commission (2006) *Murder, Manslaughter and Infanticide* (Report No 304) HC 30, para 5.121.

**EXTRACT**

Read the following extract from the judgment of Davis LJ. Should the jury in a case like this consider the defendant's thought processes, the outcome of those processes, or both? What reasons does Davis LJ give for this decision?

## *R v Conroy* [2017] EWCA Crim 81

### Davis LJ

30 In truth, as it seems to us, one cannot always neatly separate the "decision-making process" [...] from the actual ultimate decision: although of course it can be accepted that a jury may need, as part of its overall consideration, to consider how it was that in the particular defendant's mind the decision was arrived at. There may be cases where an entirely "irrational" decision may be taken: for example, to kill one's neighbour because of a fixed belief that he is an alien from Mars intent on blowing up innocent people in the village. But that decision and the motivation for it may then be accompanied, in terms of giving effect to the decision, by ostensibly logical and rational decisions with a view to carrying out the intended killing: for example by buying a knife, by waiting for the neighbour to be at home alone and so on.

[...]

35 [W]e revert to the judge's summing-up in this particular case. By his instruction to the jury he had in effect told them that the "outcome" need not be part of their deliberations. It has to be said that there is imprecision here in the judge's use of the word "outcome". On one view the outcome is simply the death of M. Another way perhaps of putting it is that the outcome is the act of killing M: which is not to be equated simply with her death. But the judge in fact added a yet further element, to the effect that the outcome was the killing of M "so that he could have sex with her": which is hardly just an outcome but also an additional statement of what the appellant's motivation and intention was. But be that as it may, the judge having so stated, he then went on to say that "on any view" this was an irrational "outcome": and the jury were therefore to focus on the appellant's thought processes that had led to that outcome.

36 It is that aspect which Mr Smith challenges on behalf of the appellant. He says that the judge had wrongly separated out the decision-making process from the outcome whereas the jury should have been invited to look at the position as a whole [...]

37 [...] As it seems to us, while of course any jury will need in the light of the available psychiatric evidence to assess a defendant's thinking processes in the context of assessing his ability to form a rational judgment, it is likely to be over-refined to divorce that consideration relating to a defendant's thinking processes from the actual outcome. Indeed, in some cases it may actually be extremely difficult to separate out the thought processes on the one hand from the "outcome" on the other hand. In some cases it may well be that the two may be entirely enmeshed. In our view, there is a potential danger in a direction such as this straying beyond what is actually stated in section 2 itself. The elements of section 2 should so far as possible not be glossed in a summing-up to the jury.

So any attempt to distinguish between thought processes and outcome is mistaken. The jury should consider the position as a whole when deciding whether the defendant's ability to form a rational judgement was substantially impaired. Note also that Davis LJ stressed that when directing juries trial judges should, so far as possible, stick to the statutory wording and avoid undue elaboration. As far as Conroy was concerned, however, the Court of Appeal concluded that the trial judge's misdirection did not impact the safety of the murder conviction, and so dismissed Conroy's appeal.

An example of a case in which the defendant's ability to form a rational judgement was found to have been substantially impaired is *R v Blackman* [2017] EWCA Crim 190. The defendant, Alexander Blackman, was an Acting Colour Sergeant in the Royal Marines. He was in command of a group of Marines in Helmand Province, Afghanistan. In September 2011, insurgents attacked a neighbouring command post. A helicopter was called in. It located one of the insurgents in a field and opened fire. Thinking the insurgent had been killed, a foot patrol led by Blackman embarked on a battle damage assessment. They found the insurgent badly wounded, but still alive. Blackman disarmed him, waited for the helicopter to move away, and then shot the insurgent at point blank range, saying, 'There you are, shuffle off this mortal coil, you cunt'. He then said to the other Marines, 'Obviously this doesn't go anywhere, fellas. I've just broke the Geneva Convention'. In 2013 Blackman was convicted of murder. In the light of fresh psychiatric evidence, the case was subsequently referred to the Court Martial Appeal Court. This evidence showed that Blackman had been suffering from an adjustment disorder. This had been caused by a number of factors, including the death of his father, the loss of other members of his unit, and his perception that he was receiving insufficient support from senior officers. The Court Martial Appeal Court held that the adjustment disorder had substantially impaired Blackman's ability to form a rational judgement. Although some of his actions were calculated, such as waiting for the helicopter to move away before shooting the insurgent, the Court stated:

> that type of planning is quite distinct from the effect of an adjustment disorder which can affect the ability to form a rational judgement about (1) the need to adhere to standards and the moral compass set by HM Armed Forces and (2) putting together the consequences to himself and others of the individual actions he is about to take. In our view, the adjustment disorder had put the appellant in the state of mind to kill, but the fact that he acted with apparent careful thought as to how to set about the killing had to be seen within the overarching framework of the disorder which had substantially impaired his ability to form a rational judgement ([111]).

### iii. The defendant's ability to exercise self-control

Here we see another difference between insanity and diminished responsibility. A defendant who is unable to exercise self-control falls outside the *M'Naghten* rules and so cannot plead insanity. But an inability to exercise self-control may form the basis of a defence of diminished responsibility. This is illustrated by *R v Byrne* [1960] 2 QB 396. The defendant, Patrick Byrne, strangled a young woman and mutilated her dead body. The unanimous medical evidence was that Byrne was a sexual psychopath who suffered from violent perverted sexual desires which he found difficult or impossible to control. It was agreed that Byrne fell outside the scope of the *M'Naghten* rules, since he knew the nature and quality of his actions and he knew that they were wrong. But at his trial the judge ruled that he could not plead diminished responsibility either. Byrne was therefore convicted of murder. He appealed. The Court of Appeal held that the trial judge's ruling was wrong. Lord Parker CJ explained that diminished responsibility is broader than insanity, and is available to defendants whose ability to exercise self-control is substantially impaired. Byrne's murder conviction was therefore quashed and replaced with a manslaughter conviction (though he was still sentenced to life imprisonment).

The new law confirms the decision in *R v Byrne*. It expressly states that diminished responsibility is available to a defendant whose abnormality of mental functioning substantially impaired his ability to exercise self-control. The Law Commission offered the following example of when this would apply:[28]

> [A] man says that sometimes the devil takes control of him and implants in him a desire to kill, a desire that must be acted on before the devil will go away.

A further example is *R v Blackman*, which we looked at a moment ago. The Court Martial Appeal Court held that Blackman's adjustment disorder had also substantially impaired his ability to exercise self-control. The Court pointed out that, on previous deployments, Blackman had managed to control his anger and hatred for the insurgents, and his decision to kill on this occasion 'was probably impulsive' ([112]). Commenting on this decision, Gibson suggests that it '[dilutes] the ability to exercise self-control limb to vanishing point [by] ruling that self-control may be sufficiently impaired even where no loss of self-control is externally discernible'.[29]

### iv. The meaning of 'substantially impaired'

So to establish diminished responsibility a defendant must show that his ability to do one of the three things listed in subsection (1A) was substantially impaired. We have looked at each of these three abilities. But what does the term 'substantially impaired' mean? This was discussed by the Supreme Court in *R v Golds* [2016] UKSC 61. In this case the Court considered two possible meanings of the word 'substantial'.

## EXTRACT

Read the following extract from the judgment of Lord Hughes. What does he say are the two possible meanings of 'substantial'? Which meaning applies to the diminished responsibility defence? What reasons does he give for saying that this is the correct meaning?

According to Lord Hughes, why was it necessary for the Supreme Court to explain the meaning of the word 'substantially'? Should trial judges always give this explanation to juries?

### *R v Golds* [2016] UKSC 61

#### Lord Hughes

27 The admirably concise submissions of Mr Etherington QC for the appellant correctly point out that as a matter simply of dictionary definition, "substantial" is capable of meaning either (1) "present rather than illusory or fanciful, thus having some substance" or (2) "important or weighty", as in "a substantial meal" or "a substantial salary". The first meaning could fairly be paraphrased as "having any effect more than the merely trivial", whereas the second meaning cannot. It is also clear that either sense may be used in law making. In the context of disability discrimination, the Equality Act 2010 defines disability in section 6 as an impairment which has a substantial and long-term effect on day to day activities, and by the interpretation section, section 212, provides that "'Substantial' means more than minor or trivial." It thus uses the word

---

[28]Law Commission (2006) *Murder, Manslaughter and Infanticide* (Report No 304) HC 30, para 5.121.
[29]Gibson, M. (2017) 'Diminished Responsibility in *Golds* and Beyond: Insights and Implications' *Criminal Law Review* 543.

in the first sense. Conversely, the expression "significant and substantial" when used to identify which breaches by the police of the Codes of Practice under the Police and Criminal Evidence Act 1984 will lead to the exclusion of evidence (see for example *R v Absolam* (1988) 88 Cr App R 332 and *R v Keenan* [1990] 2 QB 54) is undoubtedly used in the second sense. It is to be accepted that the word may take its meaning from its context. It is not surprising that in the context of triggering a duty to make reasonable adjustments to assist the disabled, the first sense should be used by the Equality Act; the extent of adjustments required varies with the level of disability and a wide spectrum of both is to be expected. Mr Etherington additionally submits that this usage shows that the first sense does not entirely strip the word "substantially" of meaning.

...

36 [The use of the expression in the second of the senses identified above] accords with principle. Diminished responsibility effects a radical alteration in the offence of which a defendant is convicted. The context is a homicide. By definition, before any question of diminished responsibility can arise, the homicide must have been done with murderous intent, to kill or to do grievous bodily harm, and without either provocation or self-defence. Whilst it is true that at one end of the scale of responsibility the sentence in a case of diminished responsibility may be severe, or indeed an indefinite life sentence owing to the risk which the defendant presents to the public, the difference between a conviction for murder and a conviction for manslaughter is of considerable importance both for the public and for those connected with the deceased. It is just that where a substantial impairment is demonstrated, the defendant is convicted of the lesser offence and not of murder. But it is appropriate, as it always has been, for the reduction to the lesser offence to be occasioned where there is a weighty reason for it and not merely a reason which just passes the trivial.

## Directing juries: good practice

37 As Mr Perry QC for the Crown rightly submitted, there are many examples of ordinary English words incorporating questions of degree, which are left to juries to apply without attempts at further definition. No-one attempts to define "reasonable" in the many contexts in which it appears. Nor should there be any further sophistication applied to the standard of proof required, that the jury be "sure", at least beyond the comparable expression "leaving no reasonable doubt". The same principle of leaving an ordinary word alone was applied by the House of Lords in *Brutus v Cozens* [1973] AC 854 to the expression "insulting", and would apply equally, no doubt, to its sister expressions "abusive" and "threatening". In all these cases the understandable itch of the lawyer to re-define needs to be resisted. Any attempt to find synonyms for such ordinary English expressions, although they involve questions of degree, simply complicates the jury's exercise, and leads to further semantic debate about the boundaries of meaning of the synonym.

38 Where, however, as here, there are two identifiable and different senses in which the expression in question may be used, the potential for inconsistent usage may need to be reduced. The existence of the two senses of the word "substantially" identified above means that the law should, in relation to diminished responsibility, be clear which sense is being employed. If it is not, there is, first, a risk of trials being distracted into semantic arguments between the two. Secondly, there is a risk that different juries may apply different senses. Thirdly, medical evidence (nearly always forensic psychiatric evidence) has always been a practical necessity where the issue is diminished responsibility. If anything, the 2009 changes to the law have emphasised this necessity by tying the partial defence more clearly to a recognised medical condition, although in practice this was always required. Although it is for the jury, and not for the doctors, to determine whether the partial defence is made out, and this important difference of function is well recognised by responsible forensic psychiatrists, it is inevitable that they may express an opinion as to whether the impairment was or was not substantial, and if they do not do so in their reports, as commonly many do, they may be asked about it in oral evidence. It is therefore important that if they use the expression, they do so in the sense in

which it is used by the courts. If there is doubt about the sense in which they have used it, their reports may be misunderstood and decisions made upon them falsified, and much time at trials is likely to be taken up unnecessarily by cross examination on the semantic question

[...]

40 It does not follow that it is either necessary or wise to attempt a re-definition of "substantially" for the jury. First, in many cases the debate here addressed will simply not arise. There will be many cases where the suggested condition is such that, *if* the defendant was affected by it at the time, the impairment could only be substantial, and the issue is whether he was or was not so affected. Second, if the occasion for elucidation does arise, the judge's first task is to convey to the jury, by whatever form of words suits the case before it, that the statute uses an ordinary English word and that they must avoid substituting a different one for it. Third, however, various phrases have been used in the cases to convey the sense in which "substantially" is understood in this context. The words used by the Court of Appeal in the second certified question in the present case ("significant and appreciable") are one way of putting it, providing that the word "appreciable" is treated not as being synonymous with merely recognisable but rather with the connotation of being considerable. Other phrases used have been "a serious degree of impairment" (*Seers*), "not total impairment but substantial" (*Ramchurn*) or "something far wrong" (*Galbraith*). These are acceptable ways of elucidating the sense of the statutory requirement but it is neither necessary nor appropriate for this court to mandate a particular form of words in substitution for the language used by Parliament. The jury must understand that "substantially" involves a matter of degree, and that it is for it to use the collective good sense of its members to say whether the condition in the case it is trying reaches that level or not.

So, for the purposes of diminished responsibility, 'substantial' means important or weighty, and whether the impairment of the defendant's ability to do one of the things listed in subsection (1A) was substantial or not is a question for the jury (though, as noted above in *R v Brennan*, if there is uncontradicted and unchallenged expert evidence juries may not depart from this unless there is a rational basis for doing so). The Supreme Court in *R v Golds* also stated that in some cases the trial judge should explain the meaning of 'substantially' to the jury – such as where an expert witness or counsel may have caused confusion by mentioning the expression 'more than merely trivial' – but added that it is not always 'either necessary or wise' to define the word for the jury. In the following extract, Karl Laird criticises this position.

### EXTRACT

Read the following extract from Laird's commentary. According to Laird, how did the Supreme Court's judgment undermine its stated aim of ensuring the term 'substantially' is applied consistently?

## Laird, K. (2017) 'Case Comment, Homicide: *R v Golds (Mark Richard)'* *Criminal Law Review* 316

The Supreme Court expressed concern about the possibility that different juries may attribute different meanings to "substantially". The court took the view that it was imperative to reduce the potential for inconsistent usage of this term. The court's judgment does little to bring consistency, however. The court concluded that, ordinarily, judges should *not* define the meaning of "substantially" for the jury. The possibility of inconsistent interpretations of the term therefore remains, which not only undermines the court's aim, but also has the potential to be deeply unfair. If, to adopt the expression used by the Supreme Court, the trial judge feels that a risk has arisen that the jury has misunderstood the import of the expression "substantial", he will have to direct the jury that a more than merely trivial impairment is insufficient to make out the defence. If, however, no such risk has arisen, the jury may assume that a more than merely trivial impairment suffices. All things being equal, it will be easier for the defendant in the latter scenario to plead the defence than the defendant in the former. To achieve consistency in application and parity between defendants, the Supreme Court should have held that a direction must be given in *every* case. The court's failure to do so is especially surprising, given that it held that the inclusion of the term "substantially" fulfils an important function by ensuring that defendants are not found guilty of manslaughter rather than murder in the absence of sufficiently weighty reasons.

As we saw above, the old law simply said that the defendant's 'mental responsibility' must have been 'substantially impaired'. This was criticised for being imprecise and vague. The new law was designed to provide greater clarity. But some have expressed concerns about the specificity of the new law.

## EXTRACT

Read the following extract from Mackay's article 'The Coroners and Justice Act 2009 – Partial Defences to Murder: (2) The New Diminished Responsibility Plea'. What concerns does he express about the changes introduced by the new law?

### Mackay, R. D. (2010) 'The Coroners and Justice Act 2009 – Partial Defences to Murder: (2) The New Diminished Responsibility Plea' *Criminal Law Review* 290

However, the new plea's approach of spelling out what abilities need to be impaired inevitably means that "abnormality of mental functioning" is now narrower than "abnormality of mind" in that the only activities of the mind which are included are the three specified things in subs.(1A) of the 1957 Act as amended. In addition, there is a legitimate concern that these three specified things will, taken together, prove to be more limited in scope than those which fell within the original plea. This was certainly the view of Baroness Murphy who, during debate on the Bill in the House of Lords, put forward an amendment to allow for,

"distortion of thinking or perception as a basis for a successful plea of diminished responsibility where the defendant was able to exercise self-control".

This would have more readily accommodated those whose mental disorder substantially impairs his or her perception of reality. It might also have included those with personality disorders, a condition which is now unlikely to fall within the new plea unless the defendant's ability to exercise self-control can be proved to have been substantially impaired. In any event, this amendment was roundly rejected by the Attorney General who said:

"In the unlikely event of cases arising where a defendant's perception of reality is substantially impaired but his ability to understand the nature of his conduct, form a rational judgment and exercise self-control are not, we do not consider that he should benefit from the partial defence as these issues go right to the heart of the case for reduced responsibility in homicide cases where there is an abnormality of mental function."

However, what this remark fails to acknowledge is that under the original s.2 of the 1957 Act there was nothing in principle to prevent a substantial impairment of perception of reality from falling within its scope owing to the flexibility/obscurity of the plea's drafting.

## 4. The defendant's abnormality of mental functioning provides an explanation for the defendant's participation in the killing

The fourth and final requirement is found in section 2(1)(c). It is that the abnormality of mental functioning provides an explanation for the defendant's participation in the killing. Subsection (1B) provides further guidance, stating that the abnormality provides an explanation if 'it causes or is a significant contributory factor in causing' the defendant to participate in the killing. In other words, there must be a causal link between the defendant's mental abnormality and his participation in the killing.

This is a new requirement. There was no equivalent provision under the old law. The rationale for this addition was to ensure that the defence would not be used where the killing had nothing to do with the defendant's mental abnormality. The Law Commission explained:[30]

5.124 The final choice of particular words is a matter for those drafting the legislation. However, we have framed the issue in these terms: the abnormality of mind [...] must be shown to be 'an explanation' for D's conduct. This ensures that there is an appropriate connection (that is, one that grounds a case for mitigation of the offence) between the abnormality of mental functioning [...] and the killing. It leaves open the possibility, however, that other causes or explanations (like provocation) may be admitted to have been at work, without prejudicing the case for mitigation.

This new requirement has, however, been criticised. Mackay has pointed out that there is now a disparity between the defences of diminished responsibility and insanity:[31]

The *M'Naghten Rules* do not contain any such similar causal requirement. All the Rules require is "a defect of reason, from disease of the mind". What is necessary is that a "disease of the mind" cause "a defect of reason". There is no additional need to prove that the "disease of the mind" *caused or was a significant contributory factor in causing, D to carry out his conduct.* As a result one is compelled to ask whether it will not now be easier for a defendant whose mental state at the time of the offence satisfies all the elements of both pleas (with the exception of this causal requirement) to prove insanity within the *M'Naghten Rules* rather than the new diminished responsibility plea.

It has also been suggested that the new causal requirement is too strict.[32] Imagine a defendant – who has a long history of schizophrenia – kills someone. Under the old law

---

[30]Law Commission (2006) *Murder, Manslaughter and Infanticide* (Report No 304) HC 30.

[31]Mackay, R.D. (2010) 'The Coroners and Justice Act 2009 – Partial Defences to Murder: (2) The New Diminished Responsibility Plea' *Criminal Law Review* 290.

[32]Simester, A.P., Spencer, J.R., Stark, F., Sullivan, G.R. & Virgo, G.J. (2016) *Simester and Sullivan's Criminal Law: Theory and Doctrine* (6th edn) Oxford: Hart Publishing, 751–754.

the defendant could plead diminished responsibility if his schizophrenia substantially impaired his mental responsibility. But under the new law the defendant may only plead diminished responsibility if he can also show that there was a causal link between his schizophrenia and the killing. So the fact that the defendant had a history of schizophrenia which substantially impaired his mental responsibility is no longer *in itself* regarded as a sufficient reason to reduce his responsibility from murder to manslaughter. Simester and Sullivan accordingly state:[33]

> The new section 2 is undoubtedly a more clearly worded, more schematic provision than the earlier version. There is now a much clearer divide between the loss of control partial defence (as a partial condonation for persons in stressful circumstances) and diminished responsibility which looks to D's abnormal functioning. Yet if that new tidiness comes at the price of murder convictions and mandatory life sentences for schizophrenics and others in like case, who may never receive adequate treatment for their symptoms in a prison setting, it is hardly an exercise in liberal and humane law reform.

## ACTIVITY

- Looking back over our study of diminished responsibility, what were the objectives of the changes introduced by the Coroners and Justice Act 2009? In your opinion, do the changes achieve these objectives?
- What are the drawbacks of the changes introduced by the Coroners and Justice Act 2009? In your opinion, do the benefits of these changes outweigh the costs?

### 5. Diminished responsibility and voluntary intoxication

Now that we have studied the four requirements for diminished responsibility, we need to look at two particular types of difficult case. The first of these is where the defendant suffers from an abnormality of mental functioning but was also voluntarily intoxicated at the time of the killing.

The leading case here is *R v Dietschmann* [2003] UKHL 10. In 1998 the defendant, Anthony Dietschmann, began a relationship with his aunt Sarah. They lived together until he was remanded in custody in November 1998. Whilst Dietschmann was in prison Sarah died. After his release, he began to drink heavily. One evening he was at a party with three other men, including the victim, Nicholas Davies. The men were dancing when Dietschmann's watch (which had been a gift from Sarah) fell off his wrist. He accused Davies of breaking the watch. A fight ensued. Dietschmann punched Davies and, when Davies fell over, Dietschmann stamped on his head several times and kicked him repeatedly. Davies died. At the time of the killing Dietschmann was not only drunk. Psychiatrists said that he was also suffering from a mental abnormality: an adjustment disorder which was a depressed grief reaction to Sarah's death. At trial the judge told the jury that Dietschmann could only plead diminished responsibility if they were satisfied that he would still have killed Davies even if he had not been drunk. He was convicted of murder and his appeal reached the House of Lords. The House of Lords held that the trial judge had misdirected the jury, and set out the correct test to apply in cases like this one.

---

[33]Simester, A.P., Spencer, J.R., Stark, F., Sullivan, G.R. & Virgo, G.J. (2016) *Simester and Sullivan's Criminal Law: Theory and Doctrine* (6th edn) Oxford: Hart Publishing, 753–754.

## EXTRACT

Read the following extract from the judgment of Lord Hutton (with which the rest of the House of Lords agreed). What test does he set out for juries to apply in cases where the defendant was both voluntarily intoxicated and had a mental abnormality?

### R v Dietschmann [2003] UKHL 10

### Lord Hutton

41 [...] [W]ithout attempting to lay down a precise form of words as the judge's directions are bound to depend to some extent on the facts of the case before him, I consider that the jury should be directed along the following lines:

"Assuming that the defence have established that the defendant was suffering from mental abnormality as described in section 2, the important question is: did that abnormality substantially impair his mental responsibility for his acts in doing the killing? You know that before he carried out the killing the defendant had had a lot to drink. Drink cannot be taken into account as something which contributed to his mental abnormality and to any impairment of mental responsibility arising from that abnormality. But you may take the view that both the defendant's mental abnormality and drink played a part in impairing his mental responsibility for the killing and that he might not have killed if he had not taken drink. If you take that view, then the question for you to decide is this: has the defendant satisfied you that, despite the drink, his mental abnormality substantially impaired his mental responsibility for his fatal acts, or has he failed to satisfy you of that? If he has satisfied you of that, you will find him not guilty of murder but you may find him guilty of manslaughter. If he has not satisfied you of that, the defence of diminished responsibility is not available to him."

Although *R v Dietschmann* was decided under the old law, the same approach still applies today. So when considering a possible defence of diminished responsibility in a case like this the first step is to decide whether the defendant was suffering from an abnormality of mental functioning which arose from a recognised medical condition (the first two requirements we looked at earlier). If so, then when you get to the third requirement you should apply *R v Dietschmann*. So the test for the third requirement is not: has the defendant proved that he would still have killed the victim even if he had not been intoxicated? The correct test is: disregarding the effect of the defendant's voluntary intoxication, did the mental abnormality alone substantially impair the defendant's ability to do one of the things listed in subsection (1A)? If so, the final step is to apply the fourth requirement – was there a causal link between the mental abnormality and the killing? – in order to decide whether the defence is established.

## 6. Diminished responsibility and alcoholism

There is a second type of difficult case. Earlier we studied *R v Dowds* and saw that voluntary acute intoxication cannot form the basis of a diminished responsibility plea. Here we are concerned with a different scenario: not whether a defendant may plead diminished responsibility on the basis of voluntary acute intoxication (a temporary state), but whether a defendant may plead diminished responsibility on the basis of alcoholism (an ongoing condition).

The Court of Appeal considered this in *R v Wood (Clive)* [2008] EWCA Crim 1305. The defendant, Clive Wood, killed the victim, Francis Ryan, with a meat cleaver and hammer after Ryan had made sexual advances towards him. On the day of the offence Wood had been drinking from the moment he woke up, and had consumed two to three litres of cider, several cans of lager, brandy and vodka. He was extremely drunk. Medical evidence also showed that he suffered from alcohol dependency syndrome. At trial Wood was convicted of murder. On appeal, the Court of Appeal explained the test that juries should apply in cases like this one.

## EXTRACT

Read the following extract from the judgment of Sir Igor Judge P. What approach does he set out for deciding whether the mental responsibility of an intoxicated alcoholic was substantially impaired?

### R v Wood (Clive) [2008] EWCA Crim 1305

### Sir Igor Judge P

41 [...] In deciding that question the jury should focus exclusively on the effect of alcohol consumed by the defendant as a direct result of his illness or disease and ignore the effect of any alcohol consumed voluntarily. Assuming that the jury has decided that the syndrome constitutes an abnormality of mind induced by disease or illness, its possible impact and significance in the individual case must be addressed. The resolution of this issue embraces questions such as whether the defendant's craving for alcohol was or was not irresistible, and whether his consumption of alcohol in the period leading up to the killing was voluntary (and if so, to what extent) or was not voluntary, and leads to the ultimate decision, which is whether the defendant's mental responsibility for his actions when killing the deceased was substantially impaired as a result of the alcohol consumed under the baneful influence of the syndrome.

This approach takes the logic of the judgment in *R v Dietschmann* and applies it in this specific context. So you begin by asking whether the first two requirements for diminished responsibility are satisfied: was the defendant suffering from a recognised medical condition (alcoholism) and did this condition cause an abnormality of mental functioning?[34] If so you should then apply the reasoning from *R v Wood (Clive)* when considering the third requirement: did the defendant's mental abnormality substantially impair his ability to do one of the three things listed in subsection (1A)? As Ashworth has commented, this is a 'fearsomely difficult question' in this context.[35] The Court of Appeal in *R v Wood (Clive)* stated that the jury should focus exclusively on the effect of the alcohol that was consumed as a direct result of the defendant's condition and disregard the effect of any alcohol that was consumed voluntarily. So the jury must first of all look back over the defendant's alcohol consumption and try to determine which drinks were consumed voluntarily and which were consumed as a result of alcoholism. Having done this, the jury must then focus exclusively on the alcohol that was consumed as a result of alcoholism and ask whether that alone substantially impaired the defendant's ability to do one of the three things listed in subsection (1A). If so, the jury must then apply the final requirement: was there a causal link between the defendant's alcoholism and the killing?

---

[34]The Court of Appeal in *R v Wood (Clive)* ruled that in order to establish an abnormality of mental functioning it is not necessary to prove observable brain damage.

[35]Ashworth, A. (2008) 'Commentary on *R v Wood*' *Criminal Law Review* 977.

In the subsequent case *R v Stewart* [2009] EWCA Crim 593 the Court of Appeal elaborated on the test set out in *R v Wood (Clive)*. In the following extract Lord Judge CJ suggests guidance that could be given to juries who are applying the substantially impaired test to defendants with alcoholism.

## EXTRACT

Make a list of the factors Lord Judge CJ suggests juries should consider when distinguishing alcohol that was consumed voluntarily from alcohol that was consumed as a result of the defendant's condition. To what extent do you think this reduces the difficulty of the jury's task?

### *R v Stewart* [2009] EWCA Crim 593

#### Lord Judge CJ

33 Finally, and assuming that the particular defendant's alcohol dependency syndrome did indeed constitute an abnormality of [mental functioning] due to disease or illness, which was present at the time of the killing, directions about whether the defendant's mental responsibility for what he did was substantially impaired should be addressed in conventional terms. The jury should be assisted with the concept of substantial impairment, and may properly be invited to reflect on the difference between a failure by the defendant to resist his impulses to behave as he actually did, and an inability consequent on it to resist them.

34 In answering their questions, the jury should be directed to consider all the evidence, including the opinions of the medical experts. The issues likely to arise in this kind of case and on which they should be invited to form their own judgment will include (a) the extent and seriousness of the defendant's dependency, if any, on alcohol, (b) the extent to which his ability to control his drinking or to choose whether to drink or not, was reduced, (c) whether he was capable of abstinence from alcohol, and if so, (d) for how long, and (e) whether he was choosing for some particular reason, such as a birthday celebration, to decide to get drunk, or to drink even more than usual. Without seeking to be prescriptive about considerations relevant to an individual case, the appellant's pattern of drinking in the days leading to the day of the killing, and on the day of the killing itself, and notwithstanding his consumption of alcohol, his ability, if any, to make apparently sensible and rational decisions about ordinary day-to-day matters at the relevant time, may all bear on the jury's decision whether diminished responsibility is established in the context of this individual defendant's alcohol dependency syndrome.

35 We acknowledge that this decision will rarely be easy. Indeed it is fair to say that diminished responsibility has always raised complex and difficult issues for the jury, not least because the defence usually involves conflicting medical evidence addressing legal, not medical concepts, for a jury of lay persons to decide. The jury is often called upon to confront problems relating to the operation of the mind with which they will be unfamiliar. Nevertheless the resolution of these problems continues to be the responsibility of the jury, and when addressing their responsibility they are inevitably required to make the necessary judgments not just on the basis of expert medical opinion but also by using their collective common sense and insight into the practical realities which underpin the individual case.

So whether or not the defendant's mental abilities were substantially impaired is ultimately a question for the jury to answer. As well as using the medical evidence, they should use 'their collective common sense and insight into the practical realities which underpin the individual case'.

In *R v Stewart* the defendant, Patrick Stewart, had an alcohol dependency that was at the extreme end of the spectrum. At the time of the killing his blood-alcohol level was four times the legal limit for driving. The medical experts agreed that he was a chronic alcoholic. The defence's expert witness stated that Stewart had lost the ability to voluntarily control his drinking. By contrast the prosecution's expert witness stated that Stewart could choose whether or not to drink, pointing to periods in the past where Stewart had been alcohol-free. When determining what alcohol (if any) Stewart consumed voluntarily the jury were therefore faced with conflicting expert opinion. The possibility of conflicting medical evidence compounds the difficulty that juries face in cases involving alcoholics. Commenting on the judgment in *R v Stewart*, Ashworth has stated:[36]

> Lord Judge recognises that the jury's decision will not be easy in cases of this kind, particularly where (as in this case) the two expert witnesses disagree on the issue of substantial impairment. In effect, this judgment still requires the same kind of decision as did *Wood,* and is afflicted with the same problem of determining whether D's apparent choices of when and what to drink were real choices, or actions stemming chiefly from his alcohol dependency. It is telling that Lord Judge refers to "apparently sensible and rational decisions about ordinary day to day matters", the word "apparently" begging the key question. Some of the things said and done by D in this case after he gave himself up to the police might appear to be "sensible and rational", but a sample taken at the time showed that the level of alcohol in his blood was about four times the drink/driving limit. With people who are accustomed to consuming large amounts of alcohol, appearances may not always be a good guide.

However difficult the jury's task in cases like this, the approach set out in *R v Stewart* was endorsed by the Court of Appeal in the conjoined appeals *R v Joyce*; *R v Kay* [2017] EWCA Crim 647. The second of these cases involved both a psychiatric illness (as in *R v Dietschmann*) and alcohol/drug dependency (as in *R v Wood (Clive)* and *R v Stewart*). The defendant, Kay, was a paranoid schizophrenic. He had a long history of alcohol and drug abuse, even though drug use triggered and exacerbated his schizophrenia. In June 2015 he went on a three day 'bender', drinking large amounts of alcohol and taking multiple unlawful drugs including cocaine, heroin and amphetamines. In the grip of a psychotic episode, he stabbed the victim to death. At trial, Kay sought to rely on the defence of diminished responsibility. He argued that it was his schizophrenia that was primarily responsible for his psychotic state at the time of the killing. He also claimed that he had an alcohol and drug dependency syndrome and so his intoxication was involuntary. His defence was unsuccessful and he was convicted of murder. On appeal against his conviction, defence counsel claimed that *R v Stewart* left the jury 'with a stark binary choice: schizophrenia and dependency syndrome equals guilty of manslaughter, schizophrenia and voluntary intoxication equals guilty of murder' ([14]). Rejecting this argument, the Court of Appeal explained that, in Kay's case, there were three possibilities. First, that his schizophrenia was so severe that it alone substantially impaired his ability to do one of the things listed in subsection (1A). The difficulty with this in Kay's case was that there was no medical evidence that suggested that, absent alcohol or drug abuse, his schizophrenia impaired these abilities substantially. The second possibility was that a combination of schizophrenia and alcohol and drug dependency substantially impaired Kay's ability to do one of the things listed in subsection (1A). The difficulty with this was that the jury at Kay's trial had rejected this possibility. That left the final possibility, which was that his psychotic episode arose not from a recognised medical condition, but from

---

[36]Ashworth, A. (2009) 'Commentary on *R v Stewart*' *Criminal Law Review* 808.

voluntary intoxication. It followed that the defence of diminished responsibility was unavailable. Hallett VP summarised the Court's conclusion as follows:

> 20. [W]e see no reason to depart from the approach in *Stewart*. Coupled with the provisions of section 2(1) of the Homicide Act (as amended), it provides a clear and sensible approach for directing the jury. The approach is neither binary nor simplistic but is flexible enough to encompass a wide variety of factual circumstances in a manner that is fair to all. It takes full account of the kind of mental health issues under consideration and our increased understanding of them. In our view, it rightly does not necessarily provide even a partial defence to everyone diagnosed with schizophrenia, who, well aware of the possible consequences, chooses to abuse drink and drugs to excess and then kills.

## ● ● ● Conclusion

Figure 10.1 presents an overview of the relationship between the three defences we have studied in this chapter.

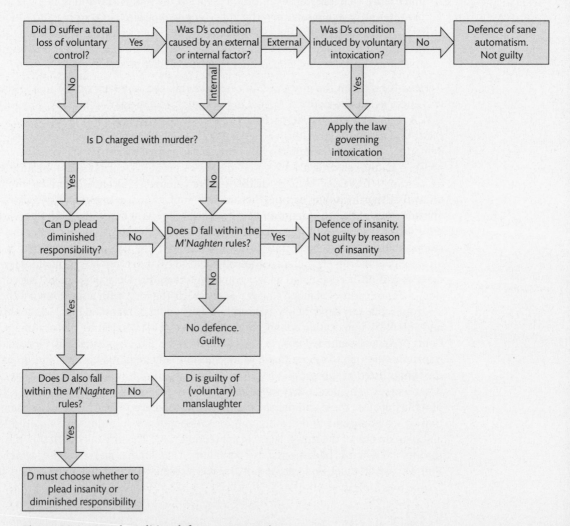

**Figure 10.1.** Mental condition defences: an overview

As you can see from this diagram, in a murder case it is possible that a defendant may satisfy the requirements for both insanity and diminished responsibility. The defendant must then choose which of the two to plead. Experience has shown that most defendants would prefer to be convicted of manslaughter on the grounds of diminished responsibility rather than be found not guilty by reason of insanity. Note, however, that if the defendant chooses to plead diminished responsibility it is open to the prosecution to argue that the defendant should instead be found not guilty by reason of insanity (and vice versa).[37]

Similarly, as we have seen in a number of cases in this chapter such as *R v Sullivan* and *R v Hennessy*, a defendant may sometimes have to choose between a defence of insanity and entering a guilty plea. Many defendants would prefer to plead guilty, especially if the crime they have been charged with is a minor one, in order to avoid possible hospitalisation.

Lastly, remember that even if the defendant cannot rely on any of the three defences we have studied in this chapter, it may still be possible for the defendant to argue that he lacked *mens rea*. We saw an example of this in *R v Clarke*. So remember to consider this possibility when answering an exam problem question!

## Self-test questions

1. Billy, a diabetic, is distraught. His wife has just been sentenced to two years' imprisonment for burglary. He is so distracted that, when he injects his normal dose of insulin, he inadvertently injects significantly more than normal. Although he eats some food shortly afterwards, he suffers hypoglycaemia. When his neighbour, Max, says to him 'What's it like being married to a jailbird?' Billy punches Max in the face giving him a black eye. Medical evidence later shows that Billy had no awareness of what he was doing during the hypoglycaemic episode.

   Discuss Billy's criminal liability. How (if at all) would your answer change if Billy had been so distracted that he had instead forgotten to take his normal dose of insulin?

2. Charlie is a big sports fan and is on his way to watch a match between his favourite team, the Wizards, and their biggest rivals, the Dragons. Discuss Charlie's criminal liability in the following scenarios:
   a. Charlie is a schizophrenic. As a result of a schizophrenic delusion, when Jim (a Dragons fan) walks towards him he mistakenly believes that Jim is a dragon about to attack him. Charlie attacks Jim, striking and kicking him repeatedly. Jim dies.
   b. Charlie is a schizophrenic. As a result of a schizophrenic delusion, Charlie believes he has been ordered to kill all Dragons supporters. When he sees Jim (who is wearing a Dragons scarf) he attacks him and kills him.
   c. Charlie has a mental condition which makes it very difficult for him to control feelings of anger and aggression. When he hears Jim (a Dragons fan) singing derogatory songs about the Wizards he erupts with anger, attacks Jim and kills him.

   How (if at all) would your answers to each of these scenarios be different if Jim had suffered serious injuries but not died?

3. Mildred is celebrating her 40th birthday in her local pub. One of her guests is Dale, an alcoholic who drinks at least a bottle of wine every day. After several glasses of wine Dale's urge to drink begins to subside, but Mildred orders another two

---

[37]Criminal Procedure (Insanity) Act 1964, s.6.

bottles and encourages him to keep drinking by saying, 'C'mon mate, it's my birthday!' A little later (by which time Dale has drunk three more glasses and is beginning to slur his speech) Mildred's brother, Patrick, says to Dale, 'It's time for you to head home you old drunk'. Angered by this, Dale replies, 'What did you call me?' 'An old drunk', Patrick retorts. At this Dale picks up one of the empty wine bottles and hits Patrick on the head with it as hard as he can, causing a deep gash. A fight breaks out, in the course of which Mildred (who was already very drunk) falls over and bangs her head. When she gets up she punches Dale in the face, giving him a black eye.

Patrick is taken to hospital where, as a result of the carelessness of a junior doctor, he is given a drug to which he is allergic. He suffers a severe reaction and dies.

Dale later states that, although he was aware of what he was doing when he struck Patrick, his consumption of alcohol had affected his powers of self-control. Meanwhile Mildred states that she was completely unaware of what she was doing for some time after falling and banging her head. Medical evidence subsequently shows that Mildred was both drunk and concussed when she struck Dale.

Discuss the criminal liability of Dale and Mildred.

4. 'The law governing diminished responsibility has been vastly improved by the changes introduced by the Coroners and Justice Act 2009. Before these changes the law in this area was ambiguous and insufficiently grounded in a medical diagnosis. This has now been rectified. As a result the law is now easier for juries to apply and arbitrary, inconsistent verdicts are unlikely.'

Discuss the extent to which you agree with this statement.

## Mental condition defences checklist

Having worked through this chapter, you should now have:

✓ An understanding of the meaning of automatism

✓ An understanding of the distinction between sane and insane automatism

✓ An understanding of the requirements for the defence of sane automatism

✓ An understanding of the requirements for the defence of insanity

✓ An understanding of the requirements for the defence of diminished responsibility

✓ A knowledge of the changes made to the diminished responsibility defence by the Coroners and Justice Act 2009

✓ An ability to critically discuss the changes made to the diminished responsibility defence by the Coroners and Justice Act 2009.

## Further reading

Gibson, M. (2017) 'Pragmatism Preserved? The Challenges of Accommodating Mercy Killers in the Reformed Diminished Responsibility Plea' 81 *Journal of Criminal Law* 177.

Kennefick, L. (2011) 'Introducing a New Diminished Responsibility Defence for England and Wales' 74 *Modern Law Review* 750.

Law Commission (2006) *Murder, Manslaughter and Infanticide* (Report No 304) HC 30.

Mackay, R.D. (2000) 'Diminished Responsibility and Mentally Disordered Killers' in A. Ashworth and B. Mitchell (eds) *Rethinking English Homicide Law*. Oxford: OUP.

Mackay, R.D. (2010) 'The Coroners and Justice Act 2009 – Partial Defences to Murder: (2) The New Diminished Responsibility Plea' *Criminal Law Review* 290.

Mackay, R. and Mitchell, B. (2017) 'The New Diminished Responsibility Plea in Operation: Some Initial Findings' *Criminal Law Review* 18.

Wake, N. (2012) 'Recognising Acute Intoxication as Diminished Responsibility? A Comparative Analysis' 76 *Journal of Criminal Law* 71.

# 11

# Substantive defences

## Chapter objectives

By the end of this chapter you should have:

- An understanding of the requirements for establishing the substantive defences of necessity, duress by threats, duress of circumstances, prevention of crime and private defence
- An ability to apply the relevant law to a hypothetical set of facts to determine whether any of these substantive defences can be established
- An ability to critically discuss whether duress should be available as a defence to murder.

# Introduction

Imagine you are discussing a defendant's criminal liability. You began by identifying the relevant criminal offence. You then worked through the *actus reus* and *mens rea* requirements of the offence and have concluded that they are all established. At this point it might seem that the defendant is liable for the crime. But this is not the end of the matter. There is a further stage, which is to consider whether the defendant can rely on a substantive defence. As we saw in Chapter 2, the anatomy of a crime is as shown in Figure 11.1.

$$\textbf{Actus reus} \; + \; \textbf{Mens rea} \; - \; \textbf{Substantive defence} \; = \; \textbf{Criminal offence}$$

**Figure 11.1.** The anatomy of a crime

When a defendant successfully relies on a substantive defence, we are effectively saying: 'Yes, you perpetrated the *actus reus* of the crime with the necessary *mens rea*, but we are nonetheless prepared to find you not guilty.' In other words, a substantive defence justifies or excuses commission of the crime.

In this chapter we examine five substantive defences: necessity; duress by threats; duress of circumstances; prevention of crime and private defence. We begin with necessity.

# Necessity

Suppose someone commits a crime in order to prevent something even worse from happening. In other words, the commission of the crime was the lesser of two evils. Should he be found guilty of the crime he committed? Or should he be able to argue that committing the crime was *necessary*?

In this section we begin by examining whether or not the criminal law recognises a defence of necessity. We then look at the difficult issue of whether necessity should be available as a defence to murder, before finally asking what test is used to determine whether the defence is available.

## 1. Is there a general defence of necessity?

A house is on fire. A man is trapped at an upstairs window. A fire engine has been called. The fire engine is just 200 metres away from the house when it reaches a set of traffic lights. The lights are red. The driver checks both directions, sees that the road is clear and so drives through the red light in order to save the man. If the driver of the fire engine was later charged with jumping the red light, should he be able to plead a defence of necessity?

This example was discussed by Lord Denning in *Buckoke v GLC* [1971] Ch 655. You may be surprised to learn that, although Lord Denning said the driver should be 'congratulated', he stated that the driver would not have a defence of necessity in law.

Lord Denning made these comments more than 40 years ago, and things have changed since then.[1] This example is nonetheless a powerful illustration of the courts'

---

[1] In the years since *Buckoke v GLC* specific provisions have been enacted for situations like these. In emergencies drivers of fire engines, police cars and ambulances may regard red traffic lights as warnings to give way and may exceed speed limits: Traffic Signs Regulations 2002 (SI 2002/3113), reg. 36; Road Traffic Regulation Act 1984, s.87.

reluctance, for much of the twentieth century, to recognise the existence of a general defence of necessity.

Why were the courts so wary of a defence of necessity? To help us answer this question we can look at another of Lord Denning's judgments, this time in *Southwark LBC v Williams* [1971] Ch 734.

## EXTRACT

Read the following paragraph from Lord Denning's judgment and then explain, in your own words, his reasons for not recognising the existence of a defence of necessity.

### Southwark LBC v Williams [1971] Ch 734

#### Lord Denning

The reason is because, if hunger were once allowed to be an excuse for stealing, it would open a way through which all kinds of disorder and lawlessness would pass. So here. If homelessness were once admitted as a defence to trespass, no one's house could be safe. Necessity would open a door which no man could shut. It would not only be those in extreme need who would enter. There would be others who would imagine that they were in need, or would invent a need, so as to gain entry. Each man would say his need was greater than the next man's. The plea would be an excuse for all sorts of wrongdoing. So the courts must, for the sake of law and order, take a firm stand. They must refuse to admit the plea of necessity to the hungry and the homeless: and trust that their distress will be relieved by the charitable and the good.

Although Lord Denning insisted that the courts should 'refuse to admit the plea of necessity', there were others who seemed prepared to allow necessity as a defence in some, limited, circumstances. For example, in the same case (*Southwark LBC v Williams*) Edmund Davies LJ stated:

> [... O]ne thing emerges with clarity from the decisions, and that is that the law regards with the deepest suspicion any remedies of self-help, and permits those remedies to be resorted to only in very special circumstances. The reason for such circumspection is clear: necessity can very easily become simply a mask for anarchy. As far as my reading goes, it appears that all the cases where a plea of necessity has succeeded are cases which deal with an urgent situation of imminent peril.

## ACTIVITY

In this paragraph Edmund Davies LJ envisages an exception to the general rule that necessity should not be a defence. What title would you give to this exception?

There were other cases in which the courts seemed prepared to recognise a defence of necessity. In *Johnson v Phillips* [1976] 1 WLR 65 a driver stopped his car behind a parked ambulance in a narrow one-way street. There had been an incident in a nearby pub, and other ambulances were expected to help remove people that had been injured. Since the driver's car was getting in the way a policeman asked the driver to reverse back along the street to clear the way for the other ambulances. The driver refused. He said that driving the wrong way down a one-way street is a criminal offence, and he was worried he might be prosecuted. He was subsequently convicted of wilfully obstructing the policeman in the execution of his duty. At his appeal against conviction the principal issue was whether the policeman was acting in the execution of his duty, which in turn depended on whether the policeman could lawfully tell the driver to disobey traffic regulations.

The driver's appeal was unsuccessful. On behalf of the Court Wien J stated:

> The law protects the liberty of the subject, but it must recognise that in certain circumstances which have to be carefully considered by the courts a constable may oblige persons to disobey a traffic regulation and not only in those cases that are explicitly dealt with by Parliament. In the judgment of this court a constable would be entitled, and indeed under a duty, to give such instruction if it were reasonably necessary for the protection of life or property.

So here we again see a willingness to recognise a defence of necessity.

These three cases give us a brief insight into the uncertainty that prevailed for much of the twentieth century as to whether a general defence of necessity existed. A key development came in 1989, when the House of Lords issued its judgment in *Re F (Mental Patient: Sterilisation)* [1990] 2 AC 1. This case involved a 36-year-old mentally handicapped woman who had the mental age of a small child. She was a patient in a mental hospital and had formed a sexual relationship with a male patient. The hospital staff did not want to restrict her (already limited) freedom by preventing sexual activity, but were anxious about the potentially disastrous effects pregnancy might have on her. As there were difficulties with all other methods of contraception the hospital concluded that she should be sterilised. As F was incapable of granting her consent to a sterilisation operation, F's mother applied to the courts for a declaration that F could be sterilised without her consent.

The House of Lords held that the doctors performing the sterilisation operation would not be acting unlawfully.

## EXTRACT

The following extract is from the judgment of Lord Brandon. He said that there are two situations in which adult patients may be given medical treatment, even though they have not consented, provided that the treatment is in their best interests. What are these situations?

Lord Brandon then goes on to consider the underlying principle which justifies this position. What is this principle?

### Re F (Mental Patient: Sterilisation) [1990] 2 AC 1

### Lord Brandon

At common law a doctor cannot lawfully operate on adult patients of sound mind, or give them any other treatment involving the application of physical force however small ("other treatment"), without their consent. If a doctor were to operate on such patients, or give them other treatment, without their consent, he would commit the actionable tort of trespass to the person. There are, however, cases where adult patients cannot give or refuse their consent to an operation or other treatment. One case is where, as a result of an accident or otherwise, an adult patient is unconscious and an operation or other treatment cannot be safely delayed until he or she recovers consciousness. Another case is where a patient, though adult, cannot by reason of mental disability understand the nature or purpose of an operation or other treatment. The common law would be seriously defective if it failed to provide a solution to the problem created by such inability to consent. In my opinion, however, the common law does not so fail. In my opinion, the solution to the problem which the common law provides is that a doctor can lawfully operate on, or give other treatment to, adult patients who are incapable, for one reason or another, of consenting to his doing so, provided that the operation or other treatment concerned is in the best interests of such patients. The operation or other treatment will be in their best interests if, but only if, it is carried out in order either to save their lives, or to ensure improvement or prevent deterioration in their physical or mental health.

Different views have been put forward with regard to the principle which makes it lawful for a doctor to operate on or give other treatment to adult patients without their consent in the two cases to which I have referred above. The Court of Appeal in the present case regarded the matter as depending on the public interest. I would not disagree with that as a broad proposition, but I think that it is helpful to consider the principle in accordance with which the public interest leads to this result. In my opinion, the principle is that, when persons lack the capacity, for whatever reason, to take decisions about the performance of operations on them, or the giving of other medical treatment to them, it is necessary that some other person or persons, with the appropriate qualifications, should take such decisions for them. Otherwise they would be deprived of medical care which they need and to which they are entitled.

Lord Brandon's judgment focuses on medical treatment. His comments may therefore be understood as relating specifically to *medical necessity*. This may be contrasted with the judgment of Lord Goff, who advanced a broader conception of necessity that was not restricted to the context of medical treatment.

## EXTRACT

Lord Goff explains that necessity might apply in three types of situation. What are these? Which one was relevant to the female patient in *Re F*?

Is Lord Goff's third type of situation limited to emergencies? If not, what are the requirements which Lord Goff says must be satisfied for a case to fall in the third of his categories?

### Re F (Mental Patient: Sterilisation) [1990] 2 AC 1

### Lord Goff

That there exists in the common law a principle of necessity which may justify action which would otherwise be unlawful is not in doubt. But historically the principle has been seen to be restricted to two groups of cases, which have been called cases of public necessity and cases of private necessity. The former occurred when a man interfered with another man's property in the public interest – for example (in the days before we could dial 999 for the fire brigade) the destruction of another man's house to prevent the spread of a catastrophic fire, as indeed occurred in the Great Fire of London in 1666. The latter cases occurred when a man interfered with another's property to save his own person or property from imminent danger – for example, when he entered upon his neighbour's land without his consent, in order to prevent the spread of fire onto his own land.

There is, however, a third group of cases, which is also properly described as founded upon the principle of necessity and which is more pertinent to the resolution of the problem in the present case. These cases are concerned with action taken as a matter of necessity to assist another person without his consent. To give a simple example, a man who seizes another and forcibly drags him from the path of an oncoming vehicle, thereby saving him from injury or even death, commits no wrong. But there are many emanations of this principle, to be found scattered through the books. These are concerned not only with the preservation of the life or health of the assisted person, but also with the preservation of his property (sometimes an animal, sometimes an ordinary chattel) and even to certain conduct on his behalf in the administration of his affairs.

[...]

[W]hen a person is rendered incapable of communication either permanently or over a considerable period of time (through illness or accident or mental disorder), it would be an unusual use of language to describe the case as one of "permanent emergency" – if indeed such a state of affairs can properly be said to exist. In truth, the relevance of an emergency is that it may give rise to a necessity to act in the interests of the assisted person, without first obtaining his consent. Emergency is however not the criterion or even a pre-requisite; it is simply a frequent origin of the necessity which impels intervention. The principle is one of necessity, not of emergency.

[...]

[T]he basic requirements, applicable in these cases of necessity, [are] that, to fall within the principle, not only (1) must there be a necessity to act when it is not practicable to communicate with the assisted person, but also (2) the action taken must be such as a reasonable person would in all the circumstances take, acting in the best interests of the assisted person.

Having recognised a defence of necessity in *Re F*, nine years later the House of Lords confirmed the existence of the defence in *R v Bournewood Community and Mental Health NHS Trust* [1999] 1 AC 458. In this case a mentally incompetent patient, L, was informally admitted, detained and treated without invoking the procedure set out in the Mental Health Act 1983. The House of Lords unanimously agreed that this was justified by necessity. Lord Goff stated that 'all the steps in fact taken [...] were in fact taken in the best interests of L and, in so far as they might otherwise have constituted an invasion of his civil rights, were justified on the basis of the common law doctrine of necessity'. This made it clear that a defence of necessity does exist.

## 2. Is necessity available as a defence to murder?

Our starting point here is the famous case *R v Dudley and Stephens* (1884–85) LR 14 QBD 273.[2] The two defendants, the 17-year-old victim and a fourth man were cast away in an open boat 1,600 miles from land after their yacht, the *Mignonette*, sank. The only food

---

[2]For more information on the case, see Simpson, A.W.B. (1984) *Cannibalism and the Common Law.* Chicago: University of Chicago Press.

they had was two tins of turnips. On their sixteenth day adrift (having had no food for eight days and no water for six days) the two defendants killed the victim. They fed upon his body and blood for the following four days until (on their twentieth day adrift) they were picked up by a passing vessel. The boy was weak and unable to resist, but did not agree to being killed.

The jury found that the following were fact:

- If the men had not fed upon the boy they probably would not have survived the four days.
- The boy was likely to die first.
- At the time of the killing there was no reasonable prospect of relief.
- It appeared to the defendants that they would die of starvation unless one of the castaways was killed.
- There was no appreciable chance of saving life except by killing.

The sole issue in the case was whether the defendants could rely on a defence of necessity. The Court held that they could not.

## EXTRACT

Read the following extract from the judgment of Lord Coleridge CJ. List the reasons he gives for not allowing Dudley and Stephens to plead necessity.

### R v Dudley and Stephens (1884–85) LR 14 QBD 273

### Lord Coleridge CJ

Now it is admitted that the deliberate killing of this unoffending and unresisting boy was clearly murder, unless the killing can be justified by some well-recognised excuse admitted by the law. It is further admitted that there was in this case no such excuse, unless the killing was justified by what has been called "necessity." But the temptation to the act which existed here was not what the law has ever called necessity. Nor is this to be regretted. Though law and morality are not the same, and many things may be immoral which are not necessarily illegal, yet the absolute divorce of law from morality would be of fatal consequence; and such divorce would follow if the temptation to murder in this case were to be held by law an absolute defence of it. It is not so.

[...]

It is not needful to point out the awful danger of admitting the principle which has been contended for. Who is to be the judge of this sort of necessity? By what measure is the comparative value of lives to be measured? Is it to be strength, or intellect, or what? It is plain that the principle leaves to him who is to profit by it to determine the necessity which will justify him in deliberately taking another's life to save his own. In this case the weakest, the youngest, the most unresisting, was chosen. Was it more necessary to kill him than one of the grown men? The answer must be "No"

(Being guilty of murder, the defendants were initially sentenced to death. However, their sentences were later commuted to six months' imprisonment.)

There has been some debate as to the *ratio decidendi* of *Dudley and Stephens*. Some have argued that the correct interpretation of the case is that necessity is *never* available as a defence to murder. As we'll see later in the chapter, this was how the House of Lords appeared to interpret *Dudley and Stephens* in their decision in *R v Howe* [1987] AC 417. The issue in *R v Howe* was whether duress should be available as a defence to murder. Their Lordships held that it should not be. One of the reasons they gave was that, since the court in *Dudley and Stephens* had held that necessity is never a defence to murder, duress should not be a defence to murder either. For example, Lord Mackay in *R v Howe* stated:

> [F]or this House now to allow the defence of duress generally in response to a charge of murder would be to effect an important and substantial change in the law. In my opinion too, it would involve a departure from the decision in the famous case of *Reg. v. Dudley and Stephens.*

But Lord Mackay's statement rests upon a particular interpretation of *Dudley and Stephens*. There are others who have argued that *Dudley and Stephens* should be interpreted more narrowly. They argue that, whilst necessity will not normally be available as a defence to murder, there are some, limited, circumstances in which it may still apply.

One possible example can be found in Joe Simpson's book *Touching the Void* (which has also been made into a film). This book tells the story of Simpson's attempt to climb the 6344-metre Siula Grande in the Peruvian Andes with his friend Simon Yates. On the descent Simpson slipped down an ice cliff, landed awkwardly, and broke his right leg. With bad weather closing in they needed to descend quickly to the glacier below. They tied themselves together, and Yates then began to lower Simpson down the mountain a bit at a time. As the storm conditions worsened and the daylight faded, Yates inadvertently lowered Simpson off a cliff. The pair were stuck. Simpson could not climb back up the rope, and Yates could not pull him up. They remained in this position for some time, until it became obvious that they were both going to be pulled to their deaths. Yates had no choice but to cut the rope.

Miraculously, Simpson survived. (He fell 50 metres into a deep crevasse. After regaining consciousness he managed to climb out, and over the next three days hopped and crawled the eight kilometres back to base camp.) But suppose Simpson had not been so fortunate. Suppose after Yates had cut the rope Simpson had fallen to his death. Would Yates have been guilty of murder?

## ACTIVITY

- Suppose Yates has been charged with murder, and you are his defence lawyer. Yates was a factual and legal cause of Simpson's death (see the discussion of causation in Chapter 3), but you wish to argue that he lacked the *mens rea* of murder. Produce a brief skeleton argument which explains why Yates should be found not to have intended to kill, or cause serious harm to, Simpson.

- Your alternative submission is that Yates has a defence of necessity. For this argument to succeed, you need to be able to distinguish *Dudley and Stephens*. Produce a brief skeleton argument which explains why Yates' situation is distinguishable from *Dudley and Stephens*.

In *Re A (Children) (Conjoined Twins: Surgical Separation)* [2001] Fam 147 Brooke LJ discussed a similar example. This was also a true story. On the night of 6 March 1987, shortly after leaving the Belgian port of Zeebrugge, the car and passenger ferry the *Herald of Free Enterprise* capsized. In total 193 people died.

## EXTRACT

Read the following extract from Brooke LJ's judgment, which describes the incident which occurred during the Zeebrugge disaster. Look at the reasons you gave for distinguishing Simon Yates' case from *Dudley and Stephens*, and then compare these to Brooke LJ's reasons (taken from a lecture given by Sir John Smith) for distinguishing the army corporal's actions from *Dudley and Stephens*. Did you manage to come up with the same arguments?

### Re A (Children) (Conjoined Twins: Surgical Separation) [2001] Fam 147

#### Brooke LJ

At the coroner's inquest conducted in October 1987 into the Zeebrugge disaster, an army corporal gave evidence that he and dozens of other people were near the foot of a rope ladder. They were all in the water and in danger of drowning. Their route to safety, however, was blocked for at least ten minutes by a young man who was petrified by cold or fear (or both) and was unable to move up or down. Eventually the corporal gave instructions that the man should be pushed off the ladder, and he was never seen again. The corporal and many others were then able to climb up the ladder to safety.

In his third lecture, "Necessity and Duress" [part of the 1989 Hamlyn Lecture series, published under the title "Justification and Excuse in the Criminal Law"], Professor Smith evinced the belief, at pp 77–78, that if such a case ever did come to court it would not be too difficult for a judge to distinguish *R v Dudley and Stephens* 14 QBD 273. He gave two reasons for this belief. The first was that there was no question of choosing who had to die, the problem which Lord Coleridge CJ had found unanswerable in *R v Dudley and Stephens*, at p 287, because the unfortunate young man on the ladder had chosen himself by his immobility there. The second was that, unlike the ship's boy on the *Mignonette*, the young man, although in no way at fault, was preventing others from going where they had a right, and a most urgent need, to go, and was thereby unwittingly imperiling their lives.

I would add that the same considerations would apply if a pilotless aircraft, out of control and running out of fuel, was heading for a densely populated town. Those inside the aircraft were in any event "destined to die". There would be no question of human choice in selecting the candidates for death, and if their inevitable deaths were accelerated by the plane being brought down on waste ground the lives of countless other innocent people in the town they were approaching would be saved.

So, according to Brooke LJ, the *ratio decidendi* of *Dudley and Stephens* is *not* that necessity is never a defence to murder. In *Dudley and Stephens* any one of the four onboard the lifeboat could have been sacrificed in order to give the others a better chance of survival. Dudley and Stephens exercised some degree of selection. They decided that the victim should die in order to improve their own chances. To allow necessity as a defence in situations like this would open the door to all sorts of difficult questions. As Lord Coleridge CJ asked, 'Who is to be the judge of this sort of necessity? By what measure is the comparative value of lives to be measured?'

By contrast, neither of our two examples involved an element of selection. Yates did not choose between Simpson and himself. Simpson was self-selecting by virtue of the fact that he was hanging off the cliff. Similarly, the young man on the rope ladder was self-selecting by virtue of the fact that he was blocking the only escape route. In situations like these, where the defendant does not exercise any element of selection, there is a strong argument for saying that necessity should be available as a defence to murder.

It was on this basis that Brooke LJ held that the doctors separating the conjoined twins Jodie and Mary would not be committing murder.[3]

### EXTRACT

*Re A (Children) (Conjoined Twins: Surgical Separation)* [2001] Fam 147

#### Brooke LJ

I have considered very carefully the policy reasons for the decision in *R v Dudley and Stephens* 14 QBD 273 supported as it was by the House of Lords in *R v Howe* [1987] AC 417. These are, in short, that there were two insuperable objections to the proposition that necessity might be available as a defence for the *Mignonette* sailors. The first objection was evident in the court's questions: who is to be the judge of this sort of necessity? By what measure is the comparative value of lives to be measured? The second objection was that to permit such a defence would mark an absolute divorce of law from morality. In my judgment, neither of these objections are dispositive of the present case. Mary is, sadly, self-designated for a very early death. Nobody can extend her life beyond a very short span. Because her heart, brain and lungs are for all practical purposes useless, nobody would have even tried to extend her life artificially if she had not, fortuitously, been deriving oxygenated blood from her sister's bloodstream.

It is true that there are those who believe most sincerely – and the Archbishop of Westminster is among them – that it would be an immoral act to save Jodie, if by saving Jodie one must end Mary's life before its brief allotted span is complete [...] But there are also those who believe with equal sincerity that it would be immoral not to assist Jodie if there is a good prospect that she might live a happy and fulfilled life if this operation is performed. The court is not equipped to choose between these competing philosophies. All that a court can say is that it is not at all obvious that this is the sort of clear-cut case, marking an absolute divorce from law and morality, which was of such concern to Lord Coleridge CJ and his fellow judges.

In the case of the conjoined twins, there was no element of selection. The doctors were not selecting whether to save Jodie or Mary. Sadly, Mary was 'self-designated' for death. The choice was whether both twins should die, or whether Jodie should be given a chance of survival.

The principle from this case was summarised succinctly by Sir John Smith ([2001] Crim LR 400, 405):

> Where A is, as the defendant knows, doomed to die in the near future but even the short continuation of his life will inevitably kill B as well, it is lawful to kill A, however free of fault he may be.

Whilst it is possible to distinguish the *Conjoined Twins* case from *Dudley and Stephens*, Brooke LJ's judgment has been criticised. Whilst Mary may have been 'self-designated' for death, if the twins had not been separated Mary still had up to a few months of life left. The upshot of Brooke LJ's reasoning, therefore, was that denying Mary of these months of life was a lesser evil than denying Jodie a chance of survival. It has been suggested that such an approach opens the door to utilitarian assessments of the relative value of lives.[4]

---

[3]We examined the facts of this case in Chapter 4.
[4]Michalowski, S. (2002) 'Sanctity of Life – Are Some Lives More Sacred Than Others?' 22 *Legal Studies* 377.

**ACTIVITY**

Jodie is desperately ill. Unless she receives a heart transplant within a week she will die. Meanwhile, another patient in the same hospital, Mary, is terminally ill with only three weeks left to live. However, Mary's heart is healthy. Suppose that a doctor killed Mary, so that Jodie could receive Mary's heart and be saved. Applying Brooke LJ's approach, would the doctor be able to plead necessity as a defence to murder? How (if at all) is this case distinguishable from the *Conjoined Twins* case?

Critics of Brooke LJ's judgment argue that the approach of Ward LJ, which we study later in the chapter, is a better way to justify separating the conjoining twins.

Finally, before moving on, it is worth noting the decision of the Supreme Court in *R (on the application of Nicklinson) v Ministry of Justice* [2014] UKSC 38. Tony Nicklinson suffered from locked-in syndrome. He was left paralysed after suffering a stroke in June 2005. He wanted to die but was unable to end his own life without assistance. He sought a declaration that necessity would be available as a defence to anyone who assisted him to commit suicide or committed euthanasia. In its judgment the Court of Appeal held that the defence of necessity would not apply, stating that there is an important difference between killing a person in order to save the life of another (as in *Re A (Children) (Conjoined Twins: Surgical Separation)*) and killing a person because that person wishes their life to end. Only Parliament could extend the defence of necessity to cases of assisted suicide and euthanasia.[5] Although the issue was not pursued before the Supreme Court, Lord Neuberger indicated his agreement with the Court of Appeal's decision ([130]).

## 3. The test for the defence of necessity

Whilst the *Re F* and *Bournewood Trust* cases clarified that a defence of necessity does exist, neither case told us very much about the conditions which must be present for the defence to apply. So, what test should be used to determine whether a defendant may plead necessity?

In the *Conjoined Twins* case Brooke LJ employed the following three-part test, which had originally been set out by the jurist Sir James Stephen in the late nineteenth century:

> According to Sir James Stephen there are three necessary requirements for the application of the doctrine of necessity: (i) the act is needed to avoid inevitable and irreparable evil; (ii) no more should be done than is reasonably necessary for the purpose to be achieved; (iii) the evil inflicted must not be disproportionate to the evil avoided.

However, this test is problematic, for it is too broad in scope.

**ACTIVITY**

Trevor grabs hold of Derek and says, 'Go and kill Victor. Otherwise I'll kill you'. Petrified, Derek kills Victor. Does Derek satisfy the three parts of the test approved by Brooke LJ?

At the very beginning of our examination of necessity, we saw that the defence is designed for situations in which the commission of the crime is the lesser of two evils. In

---

[5]*R (on the application of Nicklinson) v Ministry of Justice* [2013] EWCA Civ 961.

this example it is difficult to argue that Victor's death is a lesser evil than Derek's death, because this would seem to involve comparing the value of two people's lives. In other words, it should not be possible for Derek to argue that it was necessary to kill Victor in order to save himself, just as it was not possible for Dudley and Stephens to argue that it was necessary to kill their victim in order to save themselves. Yet both Derek and Dudley and Stephens seem to satisfy Brooke LJ's three-part test. This demonstrates that the test is over-inclusive.

So where does this leave us? Given the historic uncertainty over the defence of necessity, and the lack of any agreed-upon test, the only way forward seems to be to allow the defence to develop on a case-by-case basis.

## Duress

Armed with a baseball bat Trevor walks up to Derek and says, 'I'm going to beat you up unless you go and beat up Victor'. As we've seen, if Derek beats up Victor he will not be able to plead necessity because it is not possible to say that Victor suffering serious harm is a lesser evil than Derek suffering serious harm. But all is not lost for Derek. He may instead be able to plead duress.

The defence of duress applies where a defendant commits a crime in order to avoid an immediate threat of death or serious harm. The following extract, taken from the judgment of Lord Widgery CJ in *R v Hudson and Taylor* [1971] 2 QB 202, explains the rationale for the defence:

### EXTRACT

Using this extract, explain the reasons for allowing Derek (in our example above) a defence of duress.

### *R v Hudson and Taylor* [1971] 2 QB 202

#### Lord Widgery CJ

[D]uress provides a defence [...] if the will of the accused has been overborne by threats of death or serious personal injury so that the commission of the alleged offence was no longer the voluntary act of the accused [...] It is essential to the defence of duress that the threat shall be effective at the moment when the crime is committed. The threat must be a 'present' threat in the sense that it is effective to neutralise the will of the accused at that time

However, the defence of duress also raises important policy considerations. As Lord Bingham explains in the following extract from *R v Hasan* [2005] UKHL 22, these policy considerations require that the courts take a strict approach towards the test for the defence:

[T]he defence of duress is peculiarly difficult for the prosecution to investigate and disprove beyond reasonable doubt [...] The prosecution's difficulty is of course the greater when, as is all too often the case, little detail of the alleged compulsion is vouchsafed by the defence until the trial is under way [...] I must acknowledge that [these features of duress] incline me, where policy choices are to be made, towards tightening rather than relaxing the conditions to be met before duress may be successfully relied on.

As we work our way through the defence we will see examples of this tension between, on the one hand, the principle that a defendant should not be held responsible for behaviour that was not freely chosen and, on the other hand, the concern that the defence should be carefully circumscribed.

We begin by distinguishing two types of duress – duress by threats and duress of circumstances. We will then work through the two-limbed test that is used for the defence, before examining the position where a defendant voluntarily exposed himself to the threat, why the courts have held that duress is not available as a defence to murder and, finally, the relationship between duress of circumstances and necessity.

## 1. The distinction between duress by threats and duress of circumstances

So for duress to apply there must be an immediate threat of death or serious harm. When there is an express threat – such as when Trevor says 'I'm going to beat you up unless you go and beat up Victor' – the relevant type of duress is duress by threats. When there has been no expressly made threat, and the threat emanates instead from the situation the defendant finds himself in, the relevant type of duress is duress of circumstances. An example would be Lord Denning's hypothetical fireman, mentioned earlier. He jumped the red light because there was an immediate threat of death to the man trapped in the burning building.

Sometimes it can be difficult to distinguish between duress by threats and duress of circumstances.[6] In practice, however, the distinction between these defences does not matter since the same rules govern both. This was made clear by Woolf LJ in *R v Conway* [1989] QB 290 (the case which first recognised the existence of duress of circumstances).[7] So whether the threat of death or serious harm emanates from an expressly made threat or the situation the defendant finds himself in, the same test applies.

## 2. The test for duress

The test for duress was set out by the Court of Appeal in *R v Graham* [1982] 1 WLR 294 and was subsequently confirmed by the House of Lords in *R v Howe* [1987] AC 417. The test is as follows:

(1) Was the defendant, or may he have been, impelled to act as he did because, as a result of what he reasonably believed [T] had said or done, he had good cause to fear that if he did not so act [T] would kill him or [...] cause him serious physical injury?
(2) If so, have the prosecution made the jury sure that a sober person of reasonable firmness, sharing the characteristics of the defendant, would not have responded to whatever he reasonably believed [T] said or did by taking part in the killing?

---

[6]To illustrate how fine the distinction can be, compare the following two scenarios: (1) D, who is banned from driving, is told by a menacing gang, 'Drive this car or we'll kill you' (duress by threats); and, (2) D sees the gang running towards him with shouts of 'kill him', and the only way he can escape is by driving the car (duress of circumstances) (Ormerod, D. and Laird, K. (2014) *Smith and Hogan's Text, Cases, and Materials on Criminal Law* (11th edn) Oxford: OUP, p358).
[7]He stated: 'What is important is that, whatever it is called, [duress of circumstances] is subject to the same limitations as the "do this or else" species of duress.'

(For cases involving duress of circumstances the test is simply amended to refer to the 'situation' instead of what 'T had said or done': see *R v Martin* [1989] 1 All ER 652.)

For convenience, we'll label the first part of this test the subjective limb and the second part the objective limb.

### i. The subjective limb

So the subjective limb asks whether D may have been impelled to act as he did because, as a result of what he reasonably believed T had said or done, he had good cause to fear that if he did not so act T would kill him or cause him serious physical injury.

*The subjective limb ... but with an objective streak*

I've labelled this part of the test the 'subjective' limb because it focuses on whether the defendant reasonably *believed* he faced an immediate threat of death or serious physical injury. What someone believed is obviously subjective. But don't be fooled by the label. Although it's the subjective limb, this part of the test does still require some objective assessment. First, the defendant's belief must have been 'reasonable'. And second, as a result of what he reasonably believed, the defendant must have had 'good cause' to fear death or serious harm.

In the early 2000s some Court of Appeal decisions questioned the requirement that the defendant's belief must have been reasonable.[8] But in *R v Hasan* Lord Bingham rejected these suggestions. In keeping with his insistence that the defence of duress should be carefully circumscribed, he stated:

> It is of course essential that the defendant should genuinely, i.e. actually, believe in the efficacy of the threat by which he claims to have been compelled. But there is no warrant for relaxing the requirement that the belief must be reasonable as well as genuine.

### ACTIVITY

Only one of the following three defendants could satisfy the subjective limb of the test for duress. Which one?

- As a result of a misunderstanding, D1 believes T has threatened to kill him unless he smashes V's car windows. In fact, T did not threaten D1, and D1's mistake was unreasonable.

- D2 has made a mistake. He believes T is going to kill him unless he smashes up V's laptop. An ordinary, reasonable person in D2's situation would have made the same mistake.

- T tells D3 that he will kill him unless he smashes up V's greenhouse. An ordinary, reasonable person in D3's situation would have had good cause to fear T's threat, but D3 dismisses it as nonsense.

*A threat of death or serious physical injury*

This is another example of the courts' strict approach to the defence of duress. The threat must have been of death or serious physical injury. Nothing else will suffice. So, whilst the Court of Appeal has stated, *obiter*, that a threat of rape amounts to a threat of serious physical injury,[9] it has rejected the argument that duress should be available where the

---

[8] *R v David Paul Martin* [2000] 2 Cr App R 42; *R v Safi* [2003] EWCA Crim 1809.
[9] *R v A* [2012] EWCA Crim 434.

defendant feared serious psychological harm,[10] and it has stated that a threat of false imprisonment will not suffice.[11]

In *R v Quayle* [2005] EWCA Crim 1415 the three defendants had been charged with offences under the Misuse of Drugs Act 1971. They had each been growing cannabis. It was for their own personal use, in order to alleviate serious levels of pain. One of the issues the Court of Appeal had to consider was whether the subjective limb of the test for duress should be broadened to encompass not just serious physical injury, but also serious levels of pain.

### EXTRACT

In the following extract, what reasons does Mance LJ give for refusing to broaden the subjective limb?

### *R v Quayle* [2005] EWCA Crim 1415

#### Mance LJ

There is, on any view, a large element of subjectivity in the assessment of pain not directly associated with some current physical injury. The legal defences of duress by threats and [duress] by circumstances should in our view be confined to cases where there is an imminent danger of physical injury. In reaching these conclusions, we recognise that hard cases can be postulated, but these, as Lord Bingham said, can and should commonly be capable of being dealt with in other ways. The nature of the sentences passed in the cases before us is consistent with this.

### ACTIVITY

Think back to Lord Denning's hypothetical fireman. If the burning building had been empty, but the fireman had jumped the red light in order to stop the fire from spreading to neighbouring buildings, would the fireman be able to plead duress of circumstances? In your opinion, should he be able to?

#### *A threat of death or serious physical injury to anyone*

In many cases – like our original example ('I'm going to beat you up unless you go and beat up Victor') – the threat will be made against the defendant. But the defence may still apply where the threat is made against someone else. This is entirely appropriate. A threat to kill or seriously injure the defendant's spouse or children may be just as (if not even more) compelling.

What if the threat is made against someone the defendant has never met before? May the defence still apply? In *R v Hasan* Lord Bingham addressed this question, and stated:

> the threat must be directed, if not to the defendant or a member of his immediate family, to a person for whose safety the defendant would reasonably regard himself as responsible.

---

[10] *R v Baker* [1997] Crim LR 497.
[11] *R v Joseph* [2017] EWCA Crim 36.

It is important to point out that the defendant's sense of responsibility for the other person may stem from the threat itself. This was confirmed by Lord Woolf CJ in *R v Shayler* [2001] EWCA Crim 1977:

> the evil must be directed towards the defendant or a person or persons for whom he has responsibility or, we would add, persons for whom the situation makes him responsible [… For example] the situation where the threat is made to set off a bomb unless the defendant performs the unlawful act. The defendant may have not have had any previous connection with those who would be injured by the bomb but the threat itself creates the defendant's responsibility for those who will be at risk if he does not give way to the threat.

## ACTIVITY

An armed robber walks into a bank, points a gun at a customer, and says to the cashier, 'Hand over the money or I'll shoot this customer'. The cashier hands over the money. Suppose the cashier was charged with assisting the robbery. Could she plead duress, even though the customer the robber threatened to kill was a man she had never met before?

### The threat must have been unavoidable and immediate (or almost immediate)

We began our study of duress by noting the tension between, on the one hand, the principle that a defendant should be excused from criminal liability if he was compelled to act by a threat of death or serious physical injury, and, on the other hand, the concern that the defence should be carefully circumscribed. Nowhere is this tension more apparent than the case law on the unavoidability and immediacy of the threat.

Our starting point is the Court of Appeal's decision in *R v Hudson and Taylor* [1971] 2 QB 202. A man called Wright was on trial for wounding. Hudson, aged 17, and Taylor, aged 19, were the principal witnesses for the prosecution. In the build-up to Wright's trial Hudson was approached by a group of men which included a man called Farrell, who had a reputation for violence. Farrell warned Hudson that if she 'told on Wright in court' they would 'cut her up'. Hudson passed this warning on to Taylor. Afraid of what might happen to them if they testified against Wright, they both decided to lie. This decision was confirmed when they arrived at court to give evidence and saw Farrell sitting in the public gallery. When giving evidence both Hudson and Taylor denied knowing Wright and, as a result, he was acquitted. In due course Hudson and Taylor were charged with perjury. At their trial the judge told the jury that Hudson and Taylor could not plead duress because the threat made by Farrell was not a 'present immediate threat capable of being then and there carried out'. They appealed, arguing that this was a misdirection.

## EXTRACT

Read the following extract from the judgment of Lord Widgery CJ. According to Lord Widgery CJ, was the trial judge's ruling that Farrell's threat was insufficiently immediate correct? How did Lord Widgery CJ suggest we should test whether a threat is sufficiently imminent for the defence of duress?

It was also suggested that Hudson and Taylor should not be permitted to plead duress because the threat they faced was avoidable. Outline this argument. Why did Lord Widgery CJ reject it?

## *R v Hudson and Taylor* [1971] 2 QB 202

### Lord Widgery CJ

This appeal raises two main questions; first, as to the nature of the necessary threat and, in particular, whether it must be "present and immediate"; secondly, as to the extent to which a right to plead duress may be lost if the accused has failed to take steps to remove the threat as, for example, by seeking police protection.

It is essential to the defence of duress that the threat shall be effective at the moment when the crime is committed. The threat must be a "present" threat in the sense that it is effective to neutralise the will of the accused at that time. Hence an accused who joins a rebellion under the compulsion of threats cannot plead duress if he remains with the rebels after the threats have lost their effect and his own will has had a chance to re-assert itself: *Rex v. M'Growther* (1746) Fost. 13; *Attorney-General v. Whelan* [1934] I.R. 518. Similarly a threat of future violence may be so remote as to be insufficient to overpower the will at that moment when the offence was committed, or the accused may have elected to commit the offence in order to rid himself of a threat hanging over him and not because he was driven to act by immediate and unavoidable pressure. In none of these cases is the defence of duress available because a person cannot justify the commission of a crime merely to secure his own peace of mind.

When, however, there is no opportunity for delaying tactics, and the person threatened must make up his mind whether he is to commit the criminal act or not, the existence at that moment of threats sufficient to destroy his will ought to provide him with a defence even though the threatened injury may not follow instantly, but after an interval [...]

In the present case the threats of Farrell were likely to be no less compelling, because their execution could not be effected in the court room, if they could be carried out in the streets of Salford the same night. In so far, therefore, as the recorder ruled as a matter of law that the threats were not sufficiently present and immediate to support the defence of duress we think that he was in error. He should have left the jury to decide whether the threats had overborne the will of the appellants at the time when they gave the false evidence.

Mr. Franks, however contends that the recorder's ruling can be supported on another ground, namely, that the appellants should have taken steps to neutralise the threats by seeking police protection either when they came to court to give evidence, or beforehand. He submits on grounds of public policy that an accused should not be able to plead duress if he had the opportunity to ask for protection from the police before committing the offence and failed to do so. The argument does not distinguish cases in which the police would be able to provide effective protection, from those when they would not, and it would, in effect, restrict the defence of duress to cases where the person threatened had been kept in custody by the maker of the threats, or where the time interval between the making of the threats and the commission of the offence had made recourse to the police impossible. We recognise the need to keep the defence of duress within reasonable bounds but cannot accept so severe a restriction upon it. The duty, of the person threatened, to take steps to remove the threat does not seem to have arisen in an English case but, in a full review of the defence of duress in the Supreme Court of Victoria (*Reg. v. Harley and Murray* [1967] V.R. 526), a condition of raising the defence was said to be that the accused "had no means, with safety to himself, of preventing the execution of the threat."

In the opinion of this court it is always open to the Crown to prove that the accused failed to avail himself of some opportunity which was reasonably open to him to render the threat ineffective, and that upon this being established the threat in question can no longer be relied upon by the defence. In deciding whether such an opportunity was reasonably open to the accused the jury should have regard to his age and circumstances, and to any risks to him which may be involved in the course of action relied upon.

In our judgment the defence of duress should have been left to the jury in the present case, as should any issue raised by the Crown and arising out of the appellants' failure to seek police protection. The appeals will, therefore, be allowed and the convictions quashed

The immediacy of the threat was also the principal issue in *R v Abdul-Hussain* [1999] Crim LR 570. The defendants in this case were Shiite Muslims from southern Iraq. They had fled Iraq to live in Sudan. Fearing that the Sudanese authorities would deport them back to Iraq, where they faced being tortured and killed, they hijacked a plane bound for Jordan and forced it to fly to England. At their subsequent trial for hijacking they pleaded duress.

In this case the threat was less immediate than in *R v Hudson and Taylor*. The trial judge pointed out that the threat depended on a number of 'contingent and consequential steps'. First, the defendants would have had to have been detected in Sudan. Second, the Sudanese authorities would have had to decide to arrest them. Third, having arrested them, the Sudanese authorities would have had to decide to deport them. And fourth, they would have had to have actually been deported. The trial judge said that the defence of duress requires the presence of a threat 'so close and immediate as will give rise to what is virtually a spontaneous reaction to the physical risk arising'. He accordingly withdrew the defence of duress from the jury. The defendants appealed against this ruling. The Court of Appeal held that the trial judge had been wrong to withdraw the defence of duress from the jury's consideration. The Court said that for duress to be available the threat must have been 'imminent', but need not have been 'immediate'. In this case the threat was an imminent one because it was hanging over the defendants when they hijacked the aircraft. The Court gave the following illustration in support of its reasoning:

> If Anne Frank had stolen a car to escape from Amsterdam and been charged with theft, the tenets of English law would not, in our judgment, have denied her a defence of duress of circumstances, on the ground that she should have waited for the Gestapo's knock on the door.

The reasoning in *R v Hudson and Taylor* and *R v Abdul Hussain* was criticised by Lord Bingham in *R v Hasan*. Stressing the policy concern that there should be strict limits on the defence of duress, Lord Bingham opined that in both cases there had been an unacceptable relaxation of the requirements that the threat must have been both immediate and unavoidable.

## EXTRACT

According to Lord Bingham, was the threat the defendants faced in *R v Hudson and Taylor* unavoidable? Why/why not?

Notice that Lord Bingham's restatement of the immediacy requirement does qualify it slightly – he says the threat must have been immediate or 'almost' immediate. Is this of much practical significance?

## *R v Hasan* [2005] UKHL 22

### Lord Bingham

26. The recent English authorities have tended to lay stress on the requirement that a defendant should not have been able, without reasonably fearing execution of the threat, to avoid compliance. Thus Lord Morris of Borth-y-Gest in *Director of Public Prosecutions for Northern Ireland v Lynch* [1975] AC 653, 670, emphasised that duress

> "must never be allowed to be the easy answer of those who can devise no other explanation of their conduct nor of those who readily could have avoided the dominance of threats nor of those who allow themselves to be at the disposal and under the sway of some gangster-tyrant."

Lord Simon of Glaisdale, at p 687, gave as his first example of a situation in which a defence of duress should be available: "A person, honestly and reasonably believing that a loaded pistol is at his back which will in all probability be used if he disobeys ... " In the view of Lord Edmund-Davies, at p 708, there had been "for some years an unquestionable tendency towards progressive latitude in relation to the plea of duress".

27. In making that observation Lord Edmund-Davies did not directly criticise the reasoning of the Court of Appeal in its then recent judgment in *R v Hudson* [1971] 2 QB 202, but that was described by Professor Glanville Williams, *Textbook of Criminal Law*, 2nd ed (1983), p 636, as "an indulgent decision", and it has in my opinion had the unfortunate effect of weakening the requirement that execution of a threat must be reasonably believed to be imminent and immediate if it is to support a plea of duress [...]

I can understand that the Court of Appeal in *R v Hudson* had sympathy with the predicament of the young appellants but I cannot, consistently with principle, accept that a witness testifying in the Crown Court at Manchester has no opportunity to avoid complying with a threat incapable of execution then or there. When considering necessity in *R v Cole* [1994] Crim LR 582, 583, Simon Brown LJ, giving the judgment of the court, held that the peril relied on to support the plea of necessity lacked imminence and the degree of directness and immediacy required of the link between the suggested peril and the offence charged, but in *R v Abdul-Hussain* [1999] Crim LR 570 the Court of Appeal declined to follow these observations to the extent that they were inconsistent with *R v Hudson*, by which the court regarded itself as bound.

28 [...] It should [...] be made clear to juries that if the retribution threatened against the defendant or his family or a person for whom he reasonably feels responsible is not such as he reasonably expects to follow immediately or almost immediately on his failure to comply with the threat, there may be little if any room for doubt that he could have taken evasive action, whether by going to the police or in some other way, to avoid committing the crime with which he is charged.

Since three of the other four Law Lords in *R v Hasan* expressly agreed with Lord Bingham's judgment, it seems clear that the approach taken in *R v Hudson and Taylor* and *R v Abdul-Hussain* should no longer be followed. The threat must have been both unavoidable and immediate (or almost immediate).

### Indirectly conveyed threats

Suppose a defendant only learns of a threat secondhand. For example, Derek says to Denise, 'Trevor said he will beat us up unless we go and beat up Victor'. If Denise helps Derek attack Victor, should the defence of duress be unavailable to Denise because the threat from Trevor was communicated to her indirectly?

This issue was considered by the Court of Appeal in *R v Brandford* [2016] EWCA Crim 1794. The case concerned a drugs line run between London and Portsmouth. The co-defendants, Olivia Brandford and her partner Dean Alford, were in Alford's car when they were stopped by police in Portsmouth. Brandford was found to have concealed cocaine and heroin with a street value of between £1,500 and £2,300 in her vagina. They were charged with conspiring to supply controlled drugs. Brandford sought to rely on the defence of duress. She said that, the day before they were arrested, in London, Alford had told her that he needed to go to Portsmouth to sell drugs. He explained that he had inherited a debt from a friend of his who had been murdered. Alford asked Brandford to help him, saying that his life would be at risk if he lost any of the drugs. At trial, the trial judge ruled that the defence of duress was unavailable because Brandford had no firsthand knowledge of the threat made against Alford. Brandford appealed against her conviction, arguing that the trial judge's ruling was wrong.

## EXTRACT

Read the following extract from the judgment of Gross LJ. Was the trial judge correct to rule that the defence of duress is unavailable in cases where the threat is communicated to the defendant indirectly? Why/why not?

The Court of Appeal nonetheless concluded that 'the circumstances fell well short of the exacting requirements of the defence of duress' ([45]). Why?

### R v Brandford [2016] EWCA Crim 1794

### Gross LJ

39 [...] It is striking that amongst the limits on duress canvassed in the authorities to which we have referred, the indirect relaying of a threat is nowhere mentioned. For our part, we can envisage a situation where a threat is indeed very real, regardless of the fact that it is indirectly relayed. Take a threat made to a hypothetical D and her family by a messenger from an organised crime group, conveying a threat from a "crime boss" or the equivalent passing on of a threat from an emissary of a terrorist group. In our judgment, the question is not whether the threat was directly or indirectly relayed which is of significance, so much as its immediacy, imminence, the possibility of taking evasive action, the question of whether D reasonably believed the threat, his/her response to that threat and questions as to the response of a sober person of reasonable firmness sharing D's characteristics. It is very likely that the more directly a threat is conveyed, the more it will be capable of founding a defence of duress: e.g., the telling example of the loaded pistol in the back, given by Lord Simon of Glaisdale in *Director of Public Prosecutions for Northern Ireland v Lynch* [1975] AC 653, at p. 687. Conversely, the more indirectly the threat is relayed the more, all other things being equal, a defendant will struggle to satisfy the requirements of the defence, or (put in burden of proof terms) the more readily the prosecution will disprove it. However, the mere fact that the threat was conveyed indirectly does not seem to us to constitute a fatal bar to the defence. All must depend on the circumstances, of which the manner in which the threat is conveyed is but one, however important it may be ...

46 [...] Even on Brandford's account, there was vagueness in the threat – she was never given the names of those making them. The threats were only ever conveyed indirectly, via Alford. He himself did not threaten her and no one whom she believed was threatening him ever directly threatened her. There was plainly no *immediate* threat on the drive or in London that evening. In

London, she was able to go out – on her own – to purchase the latex gloves and other items. Over that night, she watched Alford prepare the drugs. She suggested going to the police but neither she nor Alford acted on this suggestion. She contemplated her father paying off those threatening Alford – thus necessarily accepting that there was an opportunity to contact him. The next day, the 27th August, she and Alford were not under any immediate threat on the drive from London to Portsmouth. They were further able to stop, to enable Alford to dispose of the drugs he was carrying. Still, Brandford persisted in carrying the drugs. Taking Brandford's evidence at its highest but having regard to the tenor of Lord Bingham's speech in Hasan (supra) at [28], together with his disapproval of Hudson and Taylor (Hasan, at [27]), these threats simply lacked the immediacy to preclude Brandford taking evasive action, most obviously by going to the police. The inescapable inference is that she persisted out of love, infatuation or under pressure from Alford – but without the foundation of immediate threat essential for the defence of duress. Again, as observed in Hasan (at [26]), duress must never be allowed to be an "easy answer".

So, whilst the reasoning of the trial judge had been mistaken, it was correct that the jury had not been asked to consider the defence of duress. A jury would have been bound to find the defence disproved, because the immediacy requirement set out by the House of Lords in *R v Hasan* was clearly not satisfied. Moreover, as we will see shortly, there was also a second reason why the defence would have been bound to fail.

### Mixed motives

Sometimes people have more than one reason for committing a crime. Suppose Trevor points a gun at Derek and says, 'If you help me commit this robbery I'll give you £100,000. If you don't I'll kill you'. Derek is terrified of being killed but also really wants to buy a new sports car, so he helps Trevor commit the robbery. Should Derek be able to plead duress even though he was in part motivated by the desire to buy a new car?

This issue of mixed motives was considered by the Court of Appeal in *R v Valderrama-Vega* [1985] Crim LR 220. The defendant had been charged with importing cocaine. He gave three reasons for committing the offence: (1) a mafia-type organisation had threatened him and his family with death or serious injury; (2) he was heavily in debt and under severe financial pressure and (3) he had been threatened with disclosure of his homosexual inclinations. Of these three reasons, only the first could form the basis of a defence of duress. The Court held that the threat of physical violence need not have been the defendant's sole motivation for committing the offence. The correct approach is to apply a 'but for' test. But for the threat of physical violence would the defendant have committed the offence? If not, then he is entitled to plead duress.

### ACTIVITY

If you were the judge in Derek's case above, how would you direct the jury on the mixed motives issue?

### Desisting once the threat has ceased

Someone who is compelled into committing a crime by an immediate threat of death or serious physical injury must stop committing the crime as soon as the threat has ceased. Once the threat has ceased the defence of duress will no longer be available. This is illustrated by *DPP v Mullally* [2006] EWHC 3448 (Admin).

Late one night Anne Mullally had reason to believe that her sister's partner was going to attack her sister. So she got in her car and drove to her sister's house. When Mullally arrived her sister's partner assaulted her and threatened to throw her down an external stairway. Mullally went back into the street outside and phoned the police. Her sister's partner had followed her, so she walked 100 metres up the road to her parked car. She got in, drove back past her sister's house and, having seen that the police had arrived, headed home. On her way home she was stopped by police and asked to take a breath test. She was found to be over the legal limit and so was charged with drink-driving. She argued that she had been acting under duress. The Court said that when Mullally left her sister's house, got into her car and drove off there was an immediate threat of serious physical injury. However, 'from the moment she was aware that the police had attended at the premises, it ceased being necessary for her to continue to drive whilst over the limit in order to avoid a serious assault'. The Court accordingly directed that Mullally should be convicted of drink-driving.

### ii. The objective limb

The second part of the test for duress is the objective limb. In this part of the test the jury must decide whether they are sure that a sober person of reasonable firmness, sharing the characteristics of the defendant, would not have responded to whatever he reasonably believed T said or did by taking part in the killing.

In *R v Graham* Lord Lane CJ explained the rationale underlying this part of the test. He said, 'As a matter of public policy, it seems to us essential to limit the defence of duress by means of an objective criterion formulated in terms of reasonableness'. The law should, he said, 'require [the defendant] to have the steadfastness reasonably to be expected of the ordinary citizen in his situation'.

#### '... sharing the characteristics of the defendant ...'

I have labelled this part of the test for duress the 'objective' limb because the jury have to assess the defendant's actions against the standard of the reasonable person. But, again, don't be fooled by the label. Although it is the objective limb, the jury may still take into account some of the characteristics of the defendant. But which ones? The leading case on this question is *R v Bowen* [1997] 1 WLR 372.

Cecil Bowen had been charged with a deception offence. He claimed that he had been acting under duress. He said that two men had accosted him in a pub and threatened to petrol bomb him and his family if he did not commit the offence. A psychologist gave evidence that Bowen had an IQ of 68 (which would have placed him in the lowest two per cent of the population) and that he was abnormally suggestible and vulnerable. The issue for the Court of Appeal was whether these characteristics could be taken into account when applying the objective limb of the test for duress. Stuart-Smith LJ reviewed the case law and then summarised the relevant principles as follows:

### EXTRACT

#### *R v Bowen* [1997] 1 WLR 372

#### Stuart-Smith LJ

What principles are to be derived from these authorities? We think they are as follows.

(1) The mere fact that the defendant is more pliable, vulnerable, timid or susceptible to threats than a normal person is not a characteristic with which it is legitimate to invest the reasonable/ordinary person for the purpose of considering the objective test.

(2) The defendant may be in a category of persons whom the jury may think less able to resist pressure than people not within that category. Obvious examples are age, where a young person may well not be so robust as a mature one; possibly sex, though many women would doubtless consider they had as much moral courage to resist pressure as men; pregnancy, where there is added fear for the unborn child; serious physical disability, which may inhibit self protection; recognised mental illness or psychiatric condition, such as post-traumatic stress disorder leading to learnt helplessness.

(3) Characteristics which may be relevant in considering provocation, because they relate to the nature of the provocation itself, will not necessarily be relevant in cases of duress. Thus homosexuality may be relevant to provocation if the provocative words or conduct are related to this characteristic; it cannot be relevant in duress, since there is no reason to think that homosexuals are less robust in resisting threats of the kind that are relevant in duress cases.

(4) Characteristics due to self-induced abuse, such as alcohol, drugs or glue-sniffing, cannot be relevant.

(5) Psychiatric evidence may be admissible to show that the defendant is suffering from some mental illness, mental impairment or recognised psychiatric condition provided persons generally suffering from such condition may be more susceptible to pressure and threats and thus to assist the jury in deciding whether a reasonable person suffering from such a condition might have been impelled to act as the defendant did. It is not admissible simply to show that in the doctor's opinion a defendant, who is not suffering from such illness or condition, is especially timid, suggestible or vulnerable to pressure and threats. Nor is medical opinion admissible to bolster or support the credibility of the accused.

(6) Where counsel wishes to submit that the defendant has some characteristic which falls within (2) above, this must be made plain to the judge. The question may arise in relation to the admissibility of medical evidence of the nature set out in (5). If so, the judge will have to rule at that stage. There may, however, be no medical evidence, or, as in this case, medical evidence may have been introduced for some other purpose, e.g. to challenge the admissibility or weight of a confession. In such a case counsel must raise the question before speeches in the absence of the jury, so that the judge can rule whether the alleged characteristic is capable of being relevant. If he rules that it is, then he must leave it to the jury.

(7) In the absence of some direction from the judge as to what characteristics are capable of being regarded as relevant, we think that the direction approved in *Reg. v. Graham (Paul)* [1982] 1 W.L.R. 294 without more will not be as helpful as it might be, since the jury may be tempted, especially if there is evidence, as there was in this case, relating to suggestibility and vulnerability, to think that these are relevant. In most cases it is probably only the age and sex of the accused that is capable of being relevant. If so, the judge should, as he did in this case, confine the characteristics in question to these.

The Court then applied these principles to Cecil Bowen. Applying the first principle, it held that the evidence that Bowen was abnormally suggestible and vulnerable could not be taken into account. Applying the fifth principle, it held that Bowen's low IQ could not be taken into account either: 'We do not see how low IQ, short of mental impairment or mental defectiveness, can be said to be a characteristic that makes those who have it less courageous and less able to withstand threats and pressure.'

**ACTIVITY**

Looking at the principles set out in *R v Bowen*, decide whether the characteristics of the following three defendants would be taken into account in the objective limb:

- Psychiatric evidence shows that the defendant is unusually pliant and susceptible to pressure.[12]
- A 28-year-old male forces the defendant, an elderly lady, to shoplift.
- As a result of years of drug abuse, the defendant is a particularly paranoid and timid individual.

*Voluntary intoxication may not be considered*

In *R v Graham* Lord Lane CJ stated clearly that:

> The fact that a defendant's will to resist has been eroded by the voluntary consumption of drink or drugs or both is not relevant to this test.

### 3. Voluntary exposure to the threats

Derek is keen to join a local gang of anti-capitalism protestors, even though he has heard stories of some gang members being forced to commit minor acts of criminal damage against major financial institutions. A couple of weeks after joining the gang's leader, Trevor, says to Derek, 'Go and graffiti the bank in the High Street or I'm going to kill you'. Terrified, Derek sprays graffiti all over the bank. When he is subsequently arrested and charged with criminal damage Derek pleads duress.

In a situation like this should someone like Derek be allowed to plead duress? Or should the defence be unavailable because Derek voluntarily chose to associate with the people that subsequently threatened him, knowing that they might force him to commit criminal damage? In *R v Hasan* the House of Lords held that 'the defendant may not rely on duress to which he has voluntarily laid himself open'. So in our example, the defence of duress would not be available to Derek.

Now imagine a slightly different example. Suppose Trevor had instead said to Derek: 'I'm planning an armed robbery of the bank in the High Street tonight and I want you to help me. If you don't I'll kill you.' Terrified, Derek takes part in the armed robbery. Does the principle from *R v Hasan* still apply? When Derek joined he was aware that there was a chance he might be forced to commit minor acts of criminal damage. But he did not foresee that he might be forced to take part in an offence as serious as armed robbery.

The House of Lords also considered this issue in *R v Hasan*. Hasan worked as a driver and minder for a woman called Claire Taeger, who ran an escort agency and was involved in prostitution. A man called Frank Sullivan, who had a reputation for violence and being a drug dealer, became Taeger's boyfriend. Shortly after this Hasan stopped working for Taeger but he remained in contact with Sullivan. A couple of months later Sullivan forced Hasan to commit a burglary, saying that if he didn't he and his family would be harmed. Hasan was subsequently charged with aggravated burglary and pleaded duress.

In its judgment the House of Lords considered whether a defendant like Derek in our example should be able to plead duress if: (1) he voluntarily exposed himself to the risk of some pressure to commit crimes; but (2) was not aware that the pressure would be to commit an offence of the type he was forced to commit. Pointing to the policy reasons for carefully circumscribing the defence, and the fact that a defendant who pleads duress is

---

[12]Based on *R v Horne* [1994] Crim LR 584.

'seeking to be wholly exonerated from the consequences of a crime deliberately committed', Lord Bingham held that the defence should be unavailable. Since a defendant like Derek has 'voluntarily surrendered his will to the domination of another', he said that 'Nothing should turn on foresight of the manner in which, in the event, the dominant party chooses to exploit the defendant's subservience'. Lord Bingham then stated the following general principle:

> The policy of the law must be to discourage association with known criminals, and it should be slow to excuse the criminal conduct of those who do so. If a person voluntarily becomes or remains associated with others engaged in criminal activity in a situation where he knows or ought reasonably to know that he may be the subject of compulsion by them or their associates, he cannot rely on the defence of duress to excuse any act which he is thereafter compelled to do by them.

Two conditions must be satisfied for this principle to apply. The first is that the defendant 'voluntarily becomes or remains associated with others engaged in criminal activity'. The second is that the defendant 'knows or ought reasonably to know that he may be the subject of compulsion by them or their associates'.

The House of Lords held that this principle applied to Hasan. The defence of duress was therefore unavailable and Hasan's conviction for aggravated burglary was upheld. The principle was also applied in *R v Brandford*. As we saw above, in this case the Court of Appeal stated that there were two reasons why Brandford's defence of duress would inevitably have failed. The first was that the threat lacked immediacy. The second reason was that Brandford had voluntarily associated with Dean Alford, even though she was aware of Alford's previous conviction for dealing in Class A drugs, knew that Alford's friend had been murdered six months earlier, and knew that Alford himself had been attacked twice in the previous eight months. Gross LJ stated that 'Brandford must have appreciated that with serious violence as the norm or a regular feature, the risk of coercion was self-evident. Nevertheless, Brandford remained the partner of Alford …' ([46]).

---

## ACTIVITY

Derek chooses to spend most evenings in his local pub. Other regulars at the pub include a local gangster, Trevor, who has a reputation for violence. If Derek sees Trevor he says 'Hello', but generally does his best to keep his distance. One day, at closing time, Trevor points a gun at Derek and forces him to take part in an armed robbery. Has Derek voluntarily associated with Trevor?

Which of the following three sentences correctly states the second of the two conditions for the principle from *R v Hasan* to apply?

- The defendant knew – or ought to have known – that he might be compelled to commit a crime of the type he foresaw.
- The defendant knew – or ought to have known – that he might be compelled to commit a crime (of any type).
- The defendant knew – or ought to have known – that he might be compelled to do something he didn't want to do (criminal or non-criminal).

Suppose it never occurred to the defendant that the people he chose to associate with might subject him to compulsion, but if he had thought about it properly this possibility would have been obvious to him. Does the principle still apply?

## 4. To which crimes is duress available as a defence?

Duress is a general defence, so in principle it is available as a defence to any crime. However, there are some exceptions. In *R v Howe* the House of Lords held that duress is not available as a defence to murder or being an accessory to murder. And in *R v Gotts* [1992] 2 AC 412 the House of Lords held, by a majority of three to two, that duress is also not available as a defence to attempted murder.

There are some strong arguments in favour of allowing duress as a defence to murder. In fact, in *R v Hasan* Lord Bingham said that the 'logic of this argument is irresistible'. In the following extract, taken from the Law Commission's consultation paper *A New Homicide Act for England and Wales?*, the Law Commission argue that the refusal to allow duress as at least a partial defence to murder risks causing injustice.

(NB: Para 7.7 in the extract must now be read in the light of the Supreme Court's judgment in *R v Jogee*, which we study in Chapter 13)

### EXTRACT

### Law Commission (2005) A *New Homicide Act for England and Wales? A Consultation Paper* (Consultation Paper No 177)

7.5 [...] The following hypothetical examples, however, demonstrate the potential for injustice which can result from the present position.

EXAMPLE 1: D sees her violent husband speeding towards her, waving a gun, as she is waiting in her car at the lights. She speeds off even though she realises she will crash into a pedestrian who is crossing in front of her. She realises that she will cause him serious injury. The pedestrian dies as a result of his injuries.

EXAMPLE 2: D1, a psychopathic father, compels his eleven year old son, D2, through threat of death to participate in the murder of one of D1's rivals. D2 does no more than hold his father's gun whilst his father forces open the door to the rival's house prior to the killing.

7.6 In Example 1 D is liable for murder and accordingly she faces the mandatory life sentence. The absence of a defence of duress of circumstances means that the law cannot take into account the fact that she was acting under threat of death or serious harm and that at the time of acting she had no realistic alternative but to speed ahead.

7.7 In Example 2 D1 may be convicted of manslaughter on the basis of diminished responsibility but D2 must be convicted of murder if he was aware of what his father might do with the gun.

7.8 A blanket rule that duress can never apply as a defence to murder can cause injustice for particular groups of defendants. There is a very strong case that juveniles and young persons, who are much less mature than adults, and hence less able to withstand a threat of death, should be able to rely on the defence.

7.9 Under the present rule, by which the defendant incurs liability for murder notwithstanding that he did not intend to kill but only intended really serious harm, he has no defence of duress. This is potentially unjust where the defendant has acted under threat of death to himself.

### ACTIVITY

- Do you agree with the Law Commission that in their two examples it would be unjust for D and D2 to be convicted of murder and receive the mandatory life sentence?

If there are strong reasons for allowing duress as a (full or partial) defence to murder, why did the House of Lords in *R v Howe* hold that it is unavailable?

## EXTRACT

Milgate has identified the following seven reasons for the House of Lords' decision (Milgate, H.P. (1988) 'Duress and the Criminal Law: Another About Turn by the House of Lords' 47 *Cambridge Law Journal* 61). Read the following extracts from the judgments of Lords Hailsham, Bridge, Griffiths and Mackay in *R v Howe* and then write a short description of each argument:

- The heroic argument
- The comparison with necessity
- The legislative argument
- The prosecution argument
- The executive action argument
- The charter for terrorists
- The uncertainty argument.

## *R v Howe* [1987] AC 417

### Lord Hailsham

In general, I must say that I do not at all accept in relation to the defence of murder it is either good morals, good policy or good law to suggest, as did the majority in *Lynch* and the minority in *Abbott* that the ordinary man of reasonable fortitude is not to be supposed to be capable of heroism if he is asked to take an innocent life rather than sacrifice his own. Doubtless in actual practice many will succumb to temptation, as they did in *Dudley and Stephens*. But many will not, and I do not believe that as a "concession to human frailty" the former should be exempt from liability to criminal sanctions if they do. I have known in my own lifetime of too many acts of heroism by ordinary human beings of no more than ordinary fortitude to regard a law as either "just or humane" which withdraws the protection of the criminal law from the innocent victim and casts the cloak of its protection upon the coward and the poltroon in the name of a "concession to human frailty."

[...]

I am not so shocked as some of the judicial opinions have been at the need, if this be the conclusion, to invoke the availability of administrative as distinct from purely judicial remedies for the hardships which might otherwise occur in the most agonising cases. Even in *Dudley and Stephens* in 1884 when the death penalty was mandatory and frequently inflicted, the prerogative was used to reduce a sentence of death by hanging to one of six months in prison. In murder cases the available mechanisms are today both more flexible and more sophisticated [...] The Parole Board will always consider a case of this kind with a High Court judge brought into consultation. In the background is always the prerogative and, it may not unreasonably be suggested, that is exactly what the prerogative is for. If the law seems to bear harshly in its operation in the case of a mandatory sentence on any particular offender there has never been a period of time when there were more effective means of mitigating its effect than at the present day. It may well be thought that the loss of a clear right to a defence justifying or excusing the deliberate taking of an innocent life in order to emphasise to all the sanctity of a human life is not an excessive price to pay in the light of these mechanisms.

[...]

Unlike the doctrine of provocation, which is based on emotional loss of control, the defence of duress, as I have already shown, is put forward as a "concession to human frailty" whereby a conscious decision, it may be coolly undertaken, to sacrifice an innocent human life is made as an evil lesser than a wrong which might otherwise be suffered by the accused or his loved ones at the hands of a wrong doer.

## Lord Bridge of Harwich

[... My conviction that duress should be unavailable as a defence to murder] is now immensely strengthened by the knowledge that Parliament, even against the background of the plainly unsatisfactory present state of the law, has in ten years taken no action on the Report of the Law Commission, No. 83. If duress is now to be made available generally as a defence to murder, it seems to me incontrovertible that the proper means to effect such a reform is by legislation such as that proposed by the Law Commission. Not only is it for Parliament to decide whether the proposed reform of the law is socially appropriate, but it is also by legislation alone, as opposed to judicial development, that the scope of the defence of duress can be defined with the degree of precision which, if it is to be available in murder at all, must surely be of critical importance.

## Lord Griffiths

But what, I think, is significant is the fact that although the [Law Commission's] report clearly recognised that English law did not extend the defence of duress to the actual killer and recommended that the law should be changed, Parliament never acted upon this advice. The report was laid before Parliament by Lord Elwyn-Jones L.C. in July 1977 but no steps have been taken to introduce a Bill upon the lines they recommended. This must at least be some indication that the community at large are not pressing for a change in the law to remedy a perceived injustice.

Against this background are there any present circumstances that should impel your Lordships to alter the law that has stood for so long and to extend the defence of duress to the actual killer? My Lords, I can think of none. It appears to me that all present indications point in the opposite direction. We face a rising tide of violence and terrorism against which the law must stand firm recognising that its highest duty is to protect the freedom and lives of those that live under it. The sanctity of human life lies at the root of this ideal and I would do nothing to undermine it, be it ever so slight.

[...]

I am not troubled by some of the extreme examples cited in favour of allowing the defence to those who are not the killer such as a woman motorist being hijacked and forced to act as getaway driver, or a pedestrian being forced to give misleading information to the police to protect robbery and murder in a shop. The short, practical answer is that it is inconceivable that such persons would be prosecuted; they would be called as the principal witnesses for the prosecution.

[...]

But the sentence for murder although mandatory and expressed as imprisonment for life, is in fact an indefinite sentence, which is kept constantly under review by the parole board and the Home Secretary with the assistance of the Lord Chief Justice and the trial judge. I have confidence that through this machinery the respective culpability of those involved in a murder case can be fairly weighed and reflected in the time they are required to serve in custody.

### Lord Mackay of Clashfern

To change the law in the manner suggested by counsel for the appellants in the present case would, in my opinion, introduce uncertainty over a field of considerable importance.

So far I have referred to the defence of duress as if it were a precisely defined concept but it is apparent from the decisions that it is not so [...] To say that a defence in respect of which so many questions remain unsettled should be introduced in respect of the whole field of murder is not to promote certainty in the law.

[...]

Since the decision in *Lynch* the Law Commission have published in their Report No. 83, to which I have referred, the result of an extensive survey of the law relating to duress and have made recommendations upon it which have been laid before Parliament. In my opinion, the problems which have been evident in relation to the law of murder and the availability of particular defences is not susceptible of what Lord Reid described as a solution by a policy of make do and mend. While I appreciate fully the gradual development that has taken place in the law relating to the defence of duress I question whether the law has reached a sufficiently precise definition of that defence to make it right for us sitting in our judicial capacity to introduce it as a defence for an actual killer for the first time in the law of England. Parliament, in its legislative capacity, although recommended to do so by the report of the Law Commission, has not taken any steps to make the defence of duress available generally to a charge of murder even where it has the power to define with precision the circumstances in which such a defence would be available.

In his article Milgate argues that none of the seven reasons advanced by the House of Lords in *R v Howe* is convincing.

## EXTRACT

Read the following extract from Milgate's article and summarise why he rejects each of the House of Lords' reasons.

### Milgate, H.P. (1988) 'Duress and the Criminal Law: Another About Turn by the House of Lords' 47 *Cambridge Law Journal* 61

#### (1) The heroic argument

This argument can be expressed quite simply. The "ordinary man," if asked to take innocent life to save his own, will not necessarily yield to temptation and comply with the demand. The law should encourage this high standard of human behaviour by exposing to criminal sanctions those who fail to live up to it [...]

Emotion aside, there are a number of problems with this argument. In the first place, it is out of step with general principle. Apart from a few exceptional cases, there is no duty in the criminal law to be a hero. Unless a special relationship exists, we can watch a child drown without fear of prosecution for murder; unless asked by the police to assist, we have no duty to wade in and tackle an armed robber. Moreover, even where the charge against the defendant arises from his own positive act of conduct, he will almost invariably be judged by the standard of the reasonable man and not the hero. So, for example, where a defendant has killed in self-defence he will avoid conviction if he used only such force as was reasonable under the circumstances.

Secondly, as the self-defence example shows, the criminal law does recognise that the reasonable man may justifiably take the life of an aggressor [...] Heroism is of course to be encouraged, but by religious or moral law, not by the criminal law.

[...] Furthermore, the House ignored the fact that the path of heroism may not always be clear. The case in which D's life is threatened unless he shoots V, an innocent third party, is, in an analytical sense, an easy one. But what if D's child is threatened? What if all three of his children are threatened? In this terrorist age these examples are not far-fetched. Are we really to deny D the defence of duress if he pulls the trigger and kills V? If so, are we genuinely giving supreme importance to the value of human life? Regrettably, not one of their Lordships discussed these difficult questions.

## (2) The comparison with necessity

In 1884, in *Dudley and Stephens*, the House of Lords decided that necessity could not be a defence to murder, whatever the degree of participation. Since then it has been argued strongly that necessity and duress are analogous and that duress cannot be available on a murder charge whilst *Dudley and Stephens* remains part of the common law.

[... W]hilst parallels undoubtedly do exist between duress and necessity, these parallels are arguably no stronger than those that exist between duress and provocation. As Lord Lane pointed out in *Graham:* "Provocation and duress are analogous. In provocation the words or actions of one person break the self-control of another. In duress the words or actions of one person break the will of another." Why then was the analogy with necessity so persuasive in *Howe?* The high standard of conduct imposed by *Dudley and Stephens* is, as we have seen, exceptional, and it therefore seems strange that the House should be so heavily influenced by the case. Regrettably, Lord Mackay was vague on this point. He felt that even if there was merit in the analogy with provocation their Lordships "would not be justified in the present state of the law in introducing for the first time into our law the concept of duress acting to reduce the charge to one of manslaughter ..." Lord Hailsham offered rather more explanation. Although in his view both defences involved a "concession to human frailty," they were not analogous. The essence of provocation was that the killer had acted without self control. Duress, on the other hand, involved "a conscious decision" to do the relevant act. This distinction was vital and justified a divergent approach to the two defences. With respect to Lord Hailsham, this distinction seems too fine. Theoretically the man who kills under duress may make "a conscious decision" to kill, but in practice his will may be subject to enormous pressure. It is not obvious why his "human frailty" in succumbing to that pressure should be ignored, whilst the "human frailty" of the man who is provoked to kill may reduce murder to manslaughter.

## (3) The legislative argument

Ten years ago the Law Commission recommended that duress should be available in *all* cases of murder. However, since then, Parliament has taken no action to implement that recommendation. Lords Bridge and Griffiths therefore argue that there is neither the legislative will nor the public pressure to extend the defence to the actual killer. This argument can easily be turned on its head. *Lynch* [which allowed duress as a defence to someone charged as an accessory to murder before it was overruled in *R v Howe*] was decided over twelve years ago and in all that time Parliament has done nothing to interfere with that decision. If Parliament was really so anxious that duress should not be available to a participant in murder, would it not have acted? In any event, is it part of the judicial function to second-guess Parliament in this way? In truth, the legislative argument gets us nowhere.

## (4) The prosecution argument

The rule that duress can never be a defence to murder is clearly capable of operating harshly, particularly where the defendant who has acted under threat has played a very minor part in the killing. The House in *Howe* gave two reasons why in practice the law would not operate unjustly. I shall label these "the prosecution argument" and "the executive action argument" respectively [...]

Unfortunately, experience shows [the prosecution argument] to be over-optimistic. For example, the prosecution the subject of the appeal in *Anderton* v. *Ryan* was exactly the kind of prosecution which the Law Commission had predicted would never be brought. It is a complete evasion of the responsibilities of the House of Lords to avoid dealing with difficult cases on the basis that they will never get to court. They do. In fact, until a case is heard and the evidence tested, it may not be possible for the prosecutor to accept the truth of the defendant's exculpatory story; indeed, until then, he may not even be aware of it!

## (5) The executive action argument

The executive action argument arises because a life sentence must, by law, be imposed if a defendant is found guilty of murder. Unlike manslaughter, there is no discretion: human frailty is ignored not only in reaching a verdict but also at the sentencing stage. However, Lord Griffiths again argues that the harshness of this position is more theoretical than real:

> ... the sentence for murder although mandatory and expressed as imprisonment for life, is in fact an indefinite sentence, which is kept constantly under review by the parole board and the Home Secretary with the assistance of the Lord Chief Justice and the trial judge. I have confidence that through this machinery the respective culpability of those involved in a murder case can be fairly weighed and reflected in the time they are required to serve in custody.

Others have not shared this confidence, for example Lord Wilberforce in *Lynch:*

> A law, which requires innocent victims of terrorist threats to be tried for murder and convicted as murderers, is an unjust law even if the executive, resisting political pressures, may decide, after it all, and within the permissible limits of the prerogative to release them. Moreover, if the defence is excluded in law, much of the evidence which would prove the duress would be inadmissible at the trial, not brought out in court, and not tested by cross-examination. The validity of the defence is far better judged by a jury, after proper direction and a fair trial, than by executive officials; and if it is said that to allow the defence will be to encourage fictitious claims of pressure I have enough confidence in our legal system to believe that the process of law is a better safeguard against this than inquiry by a government department.

Such argument is compelling, but was not even considered in *Howe*. One has to be concerned that a decision of this magnitude is based on such a superficial discussion of an important issue.

## (6) The charter for terrorists

This argument is not a new one. It was raised by Lord Simon in his dissenting judgment in *Lynch* when he sounded a warning about the dangers of allowing a general defence of duress:

> Would it not enable a gang leader of notorious violence to confer on his organisation by terrorism immunity from the criminal law? ... your Lordships should hesitate long lest you may be inscribing a charter for terrorists, gang-leaders and kidnappers.

It is notable that this argument has not prevented duress being available as a defence to crimes other than murder. Nonetheless, it resurfaces in the speeches of Lords Hailsham and Griffiths in *Howe*, to support the view that duress should not be available to the murderer. Whilst no-one would deny the problems posed by terrorism in the nineteen-eighties, the "charter for terrorism" argument is now considerably weaker than it was in Lord Simon's day.

First, implicit in Lord Simon's argument is the assumption that, once raised, the defence of duress will almost invariably succeed. However, as Lord Hailsham admits in *Howe*, "juries have been commendably robust" in rejecting duress where appropriate, as the verdicts in the trials of Howe, Bannister and Burke clearly demonstrate. Moreover, the House of Lords in *Howe* itself has made the "automatic acquittal" even less likely by confirming that there is an objective element in the duress defence. The House held that where the defence of duress applies the accused is to be judged by the standard of the reasonable man, or more accurately by the "sober person of reasonable firmness sharing the defendant's characteristics." If duress were allowed as a defence to murder this objective element would provide a safeguard against the unmeritorious defendant.

Secondly, the charter for terrorism argument has lost much of its force as a result of recent Court of Appeal decisions which, in fairness, were reported after the House handed down its decision in *Howe*. It is now clear that where the defendant voluntarily joins a terrorist group or criminal gang, and is forced by pressure of violence to commit an offence for that group or gang, he cannot raise the defence of duress if, when he joined the gang, he knew that it took part in violent crime or that violence might be used against him to compel him to take part in the gang's activities. To that extent duress is not a charter for terrorists whatever the crime charged.

## (7) The uncertainty argument

Finally, it is argued that duress should not be available on a charge of murder because it is too uncertain [...]

This is the weakest argument of all, given that it undermines the very basis on which common law operates. Common-law principles are not born fully developed from a single judicial statement; instead they evolve on a case by case basis as new factual situations arise. Recent case law on self-defence, and indeed on duress itself, shows this phenomenon operating in the context of the criminal law. The answer to uncertainty is to cure it-either by further case law or, if necessary, by legislation. Lord Mackay's comments can also be criticised on a narrower ground. Most of the uncertainties associated with duress apply whatever the crime charged [...] If duress is available on a rape charge, despite these uncertainties, it is difficult to see why it should be denied just because the charge is murder. In short, the uncertainty argument best exposes the decision in *Howe* for what it is – a major piece of judicial legislation, based on an apparently cursory examination of principle and policy.

---

The following three developments have all occurred in the years since Milgate wrote his article. All three strengthen his critique of the reasoning in *R v Howe*:

- **The comparison with necessity:** As we saw earlier in the chapter, it now appears to be accepted that necessity may sometimes be a defence to murder. So the *ratio decidendi* of *R v Dudley and Stephens* is narrower than the House of Lords in *R v Howe* envisaged.

- **The executive action argument:** The minimum period that must be spent in custody by those convicted of murder is now governed by the Criminal Justice Act 2003. This was designed to reduce the discretion of sentencing judges. For the least heinous category of murders, the presumption is that a minimum of 15 years should be served before consideration for parole. This framework reduces the extent to which concessions can be made when sentencing those who kill under duress.

- **The charter for terrorists:** The strict principle expounded by the House of Lords in *R v Hasan* addresses the concern that members of terrorist groups or criminal gangs might effectively be able to confer immunity on one another.

## 5. The relationship between duress of circumstances and necessity

Earlier on we examined the relationship between duress by threats and duress of circumstances. Before we conclude our study of duress, it is also important to consider the relationship between duress of circumstances and necessity.

As we've worked through the defence of duress you may have noticed some similarities between the defences of duress of circumstances and necessity. Indeed, to some extent the two defences do overlap. In fact, the reluctance to recognise a defence of necessity for individuals like Lord Denning's fireman is probably one of the reasons why the courts created duress of circumstances in the first place. There are, however, the following important differences between the two defences:

- As we saw above, it appears that necessity may be a defence to murder in some, limited circumstances. By contrast, duress of circumstances is never available as a defence to murder.

- Unlike duress of circumstances, necessity is not limited to threats of death or serious physical injury. It might also apply, for example, in cases involving property damage.

- Duress of circumstances is only available if the threat was an immediate one. Necessity is not limited in this way.

- A defendant who mistakenly believed he faced an immediate threat of death or serious physical injury may still plead duress of circumstances, as long as his belief was a reasonable one. Necessity is not available in cases involving a mistaken belief.

- Necessity is only available if commission of the crime was the lesser of two evils. Duress of circumstances is not limited in this way.

### ACTIVITY

Figure 11.2 depicts the overlap between necessity and duress and circumstances. Match each of the five scenarios (a) to (e) (listed below) to an appropriate arrow on the diagram.

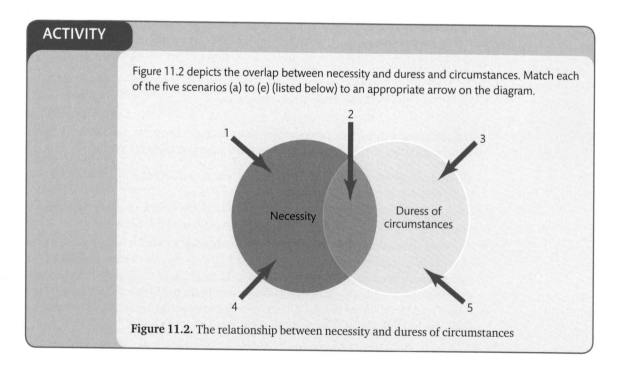

**Figure 11.2.** The relationship between necessity and duress of circumstances

a.  Lord Denning's hypothetical fireman (from *Buckoke v GLC* [1971] Ch 655)
b.  Dorothy, who is elderly and very frail, sees a group of young men walking towards her car shouting loudly. Believing they are going to attack her she drives off, well above the speed limit. In fact, the group were not going to attack her, but her mistake is found to have been a reasonable one.
c.  *Re A (Children) (Conjoined Twins: Surgical Separation)* [2001] Fam 147
d.  *Re F (Mental Patient: Sterilisation)* [1990] 2 AC 1
e.  The only way for Dave to avoid serious physical injury is if he causes Victor serious physical injury instead. Dave seriously injures Victor and escapes unharmed.

## Prevention of crime and private defence

These defences are often referred to as self-defence, but in fact this is slightly misleading. The defences apply not only when the defendant was defending himself against an act of violence, but also when the defendant was protecting another person from violence, when the defendant was protecting his own or someone else's property and when the defendant was preventing the commission of a crime. So, for example, the defences may apply where a taxi driver uses force to stop a passenger from running away without paying.[13]

Prevention of crime and private defence are both complete defences. Successfully pleading either defence will result in the defendant being found not guilty. They are also general defences. They are available as a defence to any charge involving the use of force against people or property, including murder.[14]

We begin by looking at the differences between prevention of crime and private defence and the relationship between them. We then move on to examine the test that is used for both of them.

### 1. The relationship between prevention of crime and private defence

Prevention of crime is a statutory defence.[15] It is found in section 3 of the Criminal Law Act 1967:

### EXTRACT

#### Section 3 of the Criminal Law Act 1967

#### 3. Use of force in making arrest, etc.

(1)  A person may use such force as is reasonable in the circumstances in the prevention of crime, or in effecting or assisting in the lawful arrest of offenders or suspected offenders or of persons unlawfully at large.

(2)  Subsection (1) above shall replace the rules of the common law on the question when force used for a purpose mentioned in the subsection is justified by that purpose.

---

[13]*R v Morris* [2013] EWCA Crim 436.
[14]For example, in *R v Riddell* [2017] EWCA Crim 413 the Court of Appeal held that the defence is available in cases involving driving offences (such as dangerous driving), so long as on the facts of the case the defendant used force in response to an actual or perceived threat.
[15]In *R v Jones (Margaret) & others* [2006] UKHL 16 the House of Lords held that the word 'crime' in section 3 is limited to crimes under English law. It does not cover crimes under international law.

Private defence, on the other hand, is a common law defence. There is a long- established common law right to use force in private defence.

You're probably already thinking, don't these defences often overlap? Suppose Trevor is armed with a gun and is about to kill your best friend. Heroically, you grab hold of Trevor, wrestle the gun from him, and your friend escapes unharmed. This looks like both prevention of crime (you prevented Trevor from committing murder) and private defence (you came to the defence of your friend).

Where the two defences overlap like this, which one applies? The answer is found in section 3(2) of the Criminal Law Act 1967 (above). The statutory prevention of crime defence supersedes the common law right of private defence, so when the two defences overlap you should apply the prevention of crime defence.

This does not render private defence redundant, for there may be some situations in which the prevention of crime defence would not be available because the threatened attack is not unlawful. Suppose that Trevor in our example was insane (and so would not be guilty of any crime by reason of insanity). You would then have to rely on the common law right of private defence. The same would apply if Trevor was below the age of criminal responsibility (i.e. if he was nine years old or younger). So whilst you should apply the prevention of crime defence if possible, there may sometimes be occasions where it is necessary to invoke the common law right of private defence.

Earlier in the chapter we saw how Brooke LJ applied the defence of necessity in *Re A (Children) (Conjoined Twins: Surgical Separation)*. Ward LJ employed different reasoning. He held that the doctors separating the twins would not be guilty of murdering Mary because they could invoke the common law right of private defence:

## EXTRACT

### *Re A (Children) (Conjoined Twins: Surgical Separation)* [2001] Fam 147

#### Ward LJ

The reality here – harsh as it is to state it, and unnatural as it is that it should be happening – is that Mary is killing Jodie. That is the effect of the incontrovertible medical evidence and it is common ground in the case. Mary uses Jodie's heart and lungs to receive and use Jodie's oxygenated blood. This will cause Jodie's heart to fail and cause Jodie's death as surely as a slow drip of poison. How can it be just that Jodie should be required to tolerate that state of affairs? One does not need to label Mary with the American terminology which would paint her to be "an unjust aggressor", which I feel is wholly inappropriate language for the sad and helpless position in which Mary finds herself. I have no difficulty in agreeing that this unique happening cannot be said to be unlawful. But it does not have to be unlawful. The six-year-old boy indiscriminately shooting all and sundry in the school playground is not acting unlawfully for he is too young for his acts to be so classified [... I]n law killing that six-year-old boy in self-defence of others would be fully justified and the killing would not be unlawful. I can see no difference in essence between that resort to legitimate self-defence and the doctors coming to Jodie's defence and removing the threat of fatal harm to her presented by Mary's draining her lifeblood. The availability of such a plea of quasi-self-defence, modified to meet the quite exceptional circumstances nature has inflicted on the twins, makes intervention by the doctors lawful.

## 2. The test for the defences

So there is a slight difference in the scope of the two defences. But there is no difference in the test that is used to decide whether the defences are available.[16] As for duress, the test for prevention of crime and private defence has two limbs: the subjective limb and the objective limb.

### i. The subjective limb

The subjective limb asks whether the defendant genuinely believed the use of force was required in order to prevent crime (or in private defence). Since this limb of the test focuses on the defendant's belief I have labelled it the subjective limb.

*Mistaken beliefs*

In *R v Williams (Gladstone)* [1987] 3 All ER 411 a man called Mason saw a youth snatch a woman's handbag. He chased the youth and got hold of him, intending to take him to a police station. But the youth managed to break free and ran off. Mason chased and managed to get hold of him once again. This time he knocked the youth to the ground and held him in an arm-lock. The defendant, Williams, only saw the latter stages of the incident and so to him it looked like Mason was attacking the youth. When Williams asked Mason what he was doing, Mason replied that he was a police officer and he was arresting the youth. This was untrue. When Mason was unable to produce identification Williams punched Mason in the face. Williams was charged with assault occasioning actual bodily harm.

This was obviously a case involving a mistaken belief. Williams believed that Mason was attacking the youth, but in fact Mason was trying to stop the youth from escaping. At Williams' trial the judge told the jury that Williams' mistake could only be taken into account if it was a genuine *and* reasonable belief. Williams was convicted and appealed, arguing that this was a misdirection. So the issue for the Court of Appeal was whether a mistaken belief must have been both genuine and reasonable in order to be taken into account.

### EXTRACT

According to the following extract from the Court of Appeal's judgment, may the jury take into account: (a) only genuinely held beliefs which were reasonable; or (b) all genuinely held beliefs, whether they were reasonable or not?

If the answer is (b), how (if at all) is the reasonableness of the mistaken belief relevant?

### *R v Williams (Gladstone)* [1987] 3 All ER 411

#### Lord Lane CJ

What then is the situation if the defendant is labouring under a mistake of fact as to the circumstances? What if he believes, but believes mistakenly, that the victim is consenting, or that it is necessary to defend himself, or that a crime is being committed which he intends to

---

[16]As David Ormerod observes: 'If D goes to the defence of E whom V is trying to murder, he is exercising the right of private defence but he is also seeking to prevent the commission of a crime. It would be absurd to ask D whether he was acting in defence of E or to prevent murder being committed and preposterous that the law should differ according to this answer' (Ormerod, D. & Laird, K. (2015) *Smith and Hogan's Criminal Law* (14th edn) Oxford: OUP, p443).

prevent? He must then be judged against the mistaken facts as he believes them to be. If judged against those facts or circumstances the prosecution fail to establish his guilt, then he is entitled to be acquitted.

The next question is, does it make any difference if the mistake of the defendant was one which, viewed objectively by a reasonable onlooker, was an unreasonable mistake? In other words should the jury be directed as follows: "Even if the defendant may have genuinely believed that what he was doing to the victim was either with the victim's consent or in reasonable self-defence or to prevent the commission of crime, as the case may be, nevertheless if you, the jury, come to the conclusion that the mistaken belief was unreasonable, that is to say that the defendant as a reasonable man should have realised his mistake, then you should convict him."

[...]

The reasonableness or unreasonableness of the defendant's belief is material to the question of whether the belief was held by the defendant at all. If the belief was in fact held, its unreasonableness, so far as guilt or innocence is concerned, is neither here nor there. It is irrelevant. Were it otherwise, the defendant would be convicted because he was negligent in failing to recognise that the victim was not consenting or that a crime was not being committed and so on. In other words the jury should be directed first of all that the prosecution have the burden or duty of proving the unlawfulness of the defendant's actions; secondly, if the defendant may have been labouring under a mistake as to the facts, he must be judged according to his mistaken view of the facts; thirdly, that is so whether the mistake was, on an objective view, a reasonable mistake or not

The decision of the Court of Appeal in *R v Williams (Gladstone)* has been placed on a statutory footing by section 76 of the Criminal Justice and Immigration Act 2008. The relevant subsections are (3)–(5).

## EXTRACT

These subsections identify one situation where the principle from *R v Williams (Gladstone)* does not apply. What is this situation?

## Section 76 of the Criminal Justice and Immigration Act 2008

### 76 Reasonable force for purposes of self-defence etc.

(1)  This section applies where in proceedings for an offence–

  (a)  an issue arises as to whether a person charged with the offence ("D") is entitled to rely on a defence within subsection (2), and

  (b)  the question arises whether the degree of force used by D against a person ("V") was reasonable in the circumstances.

(2)  The defences are–

  (a)  the common law defence of self-defence;

  (aa) the common law defence of defence of property; and

  (b)  the defences provided by section 3(1) of the Criminal Law Act 1967 (c. 58) or section 3(1) of the Criminal Law Act (Northern Ireland) 1967 (c. 18 (N.I.)) (use of force in prevention of crime or making arrest).

(3)  The question whether the degree of force used by D was reasonable in the circumstances is to be decided by reference to the circumstances as D believed them to be, and subsections (4) to (8) also apply in connection with deciding that question.

(4)  If D claims to have held a particular belief as regards the existence of any circumstances–

    (a)  the reasonableness or otherwise of that belief is relevant to the question whether D genuinely held it; but

    (b)  if it is determined that D did genuinely hold it, D is entitled to rely on it for the purposes of subsection (3), whether or not–

        (i)  it was mistaken, or

        (ii)  (if it was mistaken) the mistake was a reasonable one to have made.

(5)  But subsection (4)(b) does not enable D to rely on any mistaken belief attributable to intoxication that was voluntarily induced.

An example of the type of situation in which subsection (5) might apply is *R v O'Grady* [1987] QB 995. O'Grady had spent the day drinking with his friends McCloskey and Brennan. They fell asleep at O'Grady's flat. When Brennan woke up the next morning O'Grady was covered in blood and McCloskey was dead. McCloskey had severe bruising, a fractured rib and more than 20 wounds on his face. He had bled to death from these wounds. O'Grady had a number of cuts to his head, hands and legs. O'Grady stated: 'I was awakened by a bang on the head and I jumped up and put my hand to my head and the blood was running down. I am not sure if it was one bang I got or more. I saw Eddie [McCloskey] standing up ... he had a piece of glass in one hand ... I made for him to stop him hitting me again. I picked up a piece of glass and I hit him. We were both standing up facing each other ... We struggled ... He was getting the better of me, trying to knock me over. I hit him to stop him hitting me again ... I did not want to kill him. I wanted him alive, not dead. I had no enmity to him. If I had not hit him I would be dead myself.' At trial O'Grady was convicted of manslaughter.

One of the questions of fact the jury had to consider was whether O'Grady's belief that McCloskey was attacking him was mistaken. At his appeal against conviction the Court of Appeal held that if O'Grady had formed a mistaken belief, and this mistake was due to voluntary intoxication, the mistaken belief must be disregarded:

> We have come to the conclusion that where the jury are satisfied that the defendant was mistaken in his belief that any force or the force which he in fact used was necessary to defend himself and are further satisfied that the mistake was caused by voluntarily induced intoxication, the defence must fail [... A] defendant is not entitled to rely, so far as self-defence is concerned, upon a mistake of fact which has been induced by voluntary intoxication

Although mistaken beliefs which are the result of voluntary intoxication must be disregarded, mistaken beliefs which are the result of mental illness are taken into account when applying the subjective limb. So, for example, suppose a defendant being held in a police station suffers a psychotic delusion. As a result he believes that the police officers are evil spirits intent on harming him, and so punches them in order to escape. At this stage of the test, his mistaken beliefs must be taken into account.[17]

---

[17] *R v Oye* [2013] EWCA Crim 1725.

### ii. The objective limb

With the exception of 'householder cases' (where, as we'll see below, special rules apply[18]), the objective limb of the test asks whether the amount of force the defendant used was reasonable in the circumstances as he believed them to be. It is important to be clear that the test is not whether the defendant thought the amount of force used was reasonable. It is whether the amount of force used was objectively reasonable.

Subsections (6), (7) and (8) of section 76 of the Criminal Justice and Immigration Act 2008 provide some guidance on the application of the objective limb.

---

## EXTRACT

### Section 76 of the Criminal Justice and Immigration Act 2008

(6)   In a case other than a householder case, the degree of force used by D is not to be regarded as having been reasonable in the circumstances as D believed them to be if it was disproportionate in those circumstances.

[...]

(7)   In deciding the question mentioned in subsection (3) the following considerations are to be taken into account (so far as relevant in the circumstances of the case)–

(a)  that a person acting for a legitimate purpose may not be able to weigh to a nicety the exact measure of any necessary action; and

(b)  that evidence of a person's having only done what the person honestly and instinctively thought was necessary for a legitimate purpose constitutes strong evidence that only reasonable action was taken by that person for that purpose.

(8)   Subsections (6A) and (7) are not to be read as preventing other matters from being taken into account where they are relevant to deciding the question mentioned in subsection (3).

---

Subsection (6) makes it clear that (in non-householder cases) it will always be deemed unreasonable to use a disproportionate amount of force. However, it is important to remember that in many cases involving prevention of crime or private defence the defendant will have to act in the heat of the moment. He will have to act instinctively, and will not have time to stop and ponder the amount of force that it would be reasonable to use. Subsection (7) makes some concession for this. It requires a jury to take into account the fact that the defendant may not have had the chance to 'weigh to a nicety the exact measure of any necessary action'. And it states that the fact that the defendant only did what they 'honestly and instinctively thought was necessary' to prevent crime or for private defence is 'strong evidence' that the amount of force used was reasonable.

### Householder cases

Subsection (5A) explains that the application of the objective limb differs in householder cases:

(5A) In a householder case, the degree of force used by D is not to be regarded as having been reasonable in the circumstances as D believed them to be if it was grossly disproportionate in those circumstances.

---

[18]These were inserted by section 43 of the Crime and Courts Act 2013.

So whilst subsection (6) tells us that in non-householder cases it will always have been unreasonable to have used a disproportionate amount of force, subsection (5A) raises this threshold for householder cases. It tells us that in such cases it will always have been unreasonable to have used a *grossly disproportionate* amount of force. The Ministry of Justice explained the rationale of subsection (5A) as follows:[19]

> The provision is designed to give householders greater latitude in terrifying or extreme situations where they may not be thinking clearly about the precise level of force that is necessary to deal with the threat faced.

The interpretation of subsection (5A) was considered in *R (on the application of Collins) v Secretary of State for Justice* [2016] EWHC 33 (Admin).

## EXTRACT

Read the following extract from the judgment of Sir Brian Leveson P. According to this, if a defendant in a householder case used a disproportionate (but not grossly disproportionate) amount of force, does it automatically follow that the force used was reasonable?

In a householder case, how should the trial judge direct the jury on the objective limb?

## R (on the application of Collins) v Secretary of State for Justice [2016] EWHC 33 (Admin)

### Sir Brian Leveson P

18 [...] It is clear from the section that s. 76(3) adopts and preserves the second limb of self-defence at common law. As it has been for many years, the central question (and the standard) remains whether the degree of force that a defendant used was "reasonable in the circumstances as the defendant believed them to be". The standard remains that which is reasonable: the other provisions (and, in particular, s. 76(5A) and (6) of the 2008 Act) provide the context in which the question of what is reasonable must be approached. The test in the statute is not whether the force used was proportionate, disproportionate or grossly disproportionate.

19 The operation of s. 76(5A) automatically excludes a degree of force which is grossly disproportionate from being reasonable in householder cases. If the degree of force was not grossly disproportionate, s. 76(5A) does not prevent that degree of force from being considered reasonable within the meaning of the second self-defence limb. On the other hand, it does not direct that any degree of force less than grossly disproportionate is reasonable. Whether it was or was not reasonable will depend on the particular facts and circumstances of the case.

20 Thus, s. 76(5A), read together with s. 76(3) and the common law on self-defence, requires two separate questions to be put to the jury in a householder case. Presuming that the defendant genuinely believed that it was necessary to use force to defend himself, these are:

(i)  Was the degree of force the defendant used grossly disproportionate in the circumstances as he believed them to be? If the answer is "yes", he cannot avail himself of self-defence. If "no", then;

(ii) Was the degree of force the defendant used nevertheless reasonable in the circumstances he believed them to be? If it was reasonable, he has a defence. If it was unreasonable, he does not

---

[19]Ministry of Justice (2013) *Use of force in Self Defence at Place of Residence* (Circular no 2013/02 26 April 2013).

The Court went on to state that, understood in this way, subsection (5A) does not violate Article 2 of the European Convention on Human Rights (the right to life).

Having considered the law that applies in householder cases, the next question is, what constitutes a 'householder case'? This is explained in subsections (8A)–(8F):

---

**EXTRACT**

## Section 76 of the Criminal Justice and Immigration Act 2008

(8A) For the purposes of this section *"a householder case"* is a case where–

    (a)  the defence concerned is the common law defence of self defence,

    (b)  the force concerned is force used by D while in or partly in a building, or part of a building, that is a dwelling or is forces accommodation (or is both),

    (c)  D is not a trespasser at the time the force is used, and

    (d)  at that time D believed V to be in, or entering, the building or part as a trespasser.

(8B) Where—

    (a)  a part of a building is a dwelling where D dwells,

    (b)  another part of the building is a place of work for D or another person who dwells in the first part, and

    (c)  that other part is internally accessible from the first part, that other part, and any internal means of access between the two parts, are each treated for the purposes of subsection (8A) as a part of a building that is a dwelling.

(8C) Where–

    (a)  a part of a building is forces accommodation that is living or sleeping accommodation for D,

    (b)  another part of the building is a place of work for D or another person for whom the first part is living or sleeping accommodation, and

    (c)  that other part is internally accessible from the first part, that other part, and any internal means of access between the two parts, are each treated for the purposes of subsection (8A) as a part of a building that is forces accommodation.

(8D) Subsections (4) and (5) apply for the purposes of subsection (8A)(d) as they apply for the purposes of subsection (3).

(8E) The fact that a person derives title from a trespasser, or has the permission of a trespasser, does not prevent the person from being a trespasser for the purposes of subsection (8A).

(8F) In subsections (8A) to (8C)–

*"building"* includes a vehicle or vessel, and

*"forces accommodation"* means service living accommodation for the purposes of Part 3 of the Armed Forces Act 2006 by virtue of section 96(1)(a) or (b) of that Act.

---

The key points to note are as follows:

- The defendant must have been defending himself or another person (subsection (8A)(a)). So if the defendant was protecting property or preventing crime, but not defending himself or another, the case is a non-householder one.

- Householder cases include those where the defendant lives and works in the same building (subsection (8B)) and those where the defendant was a member of the armed forces and was in forces accommodation (subsection (8C)).

- The defendant must have been in, or partly in, the relevant building when the force was used (subsection (8A)(b)). So if the defendant was defending himself against an attack on the street, the case is a non-householder one.

### Use of excessive force

If the defendant passes both the subjective and objective limbs the defence succeeds and the defendant is not guilty. But if the amount of force used by the defendant was not reasonable, then the defence fails. It is all or nothing.

This is particularly important in homicide cases. An example is *R v Clegg* [1995] 1 AC 482. Clegg was a soldier in Northern Ireland. Whilst on patrol a stolen car approached his patrol at speed. He fired three shots at the windscreen, and a fourth after the car had passed. The last shot, which was fired when the car was 15 metres down the road, killed a rear-seat passenger. Clegg argued that he had fired in defence of himself and a fellow soldier.

The case reached the House of Lords. It was argued that if the defendant genuinely believed the use of force was necessary, but the amount of force used was excessive (i.e. the defendant passed the subjective limb of the test, but failed the objective limb), he should be convicted of manslaughter, not murder. In other words, it was suggested that there should be a partial defence to murder of excessive force. The House of Lords rejected this suggestion.

## EXTRACT

Read the following extract from Lord Lloyd's judgment. Why did he refuse to recognise a partial defence of excessive force?

### *R v Clegg* [1995] 1 AC 482

#### Lord Lloyd

In other words, there is no half-way house. There is no rule that a defendant who has used a greater degree of force than was necessary in the circumstances should be found guilty of manslaughter rather than murder [... I]t is all or nothing. The defence either succeeds or it fails. If it succeeds, the defendant is acquitted. If it fails, he is guilty of murder.

[...]

I am not averse to judges developing law, or indeed making new law, when they can see their way clearly, even where questions of social policy are involved. A good recent example would be the affirmation by this House of the decision of the Court of Appeal (Criminal Division) that a man can be guilty of raping his wife (*Reg. v. R.* [1992] 1 A.C. 599). But in the present case I am in no doubt that your Lordships should abstain from law-making. The reduction of what would otherwise be murder to manslaughter in a particular class of case seems to me essentially a matter for decision by the legislature, and not by this House in its judicial capacity. For the point in issue is, in truth, part of the wider issue whether the mandatory life sentence for murder should still be maintained. That wider issue can only be decided by Parliament. I would say the same for the point at issue in this case. Accordingly I would answer the certified question of law as follows. On the facts stated, and assuming no other defence is available, the soldier or police officer will be guilty of murder, and not manslaughter. It follows that the appeal must be dismissed.

## ACTIVITY

If a similar case occurred today, would the defendant be able to plead the partial defence of loss of control?

### Characteristics of the defendant

In 1999 a case involving Norfolk farmer Tony Martin hit the headlines and sparked a national debate. Martin's farmhouse, Bleak House, was extremely remote and had been burgled many times in the past. On 20 August 1999 two men, 16-year-old Freddie Barras and 30-year-old Brendan Fearon, broke into Bleak House. Armed with an unlicensed pump action shotgun, Martin shot at the intruders at least three times. Fearon was shot in the legs, and Barras was shot in the legs and in the back. Barras died from his injuries. Martin was charged with murder. At trial Martin argued that he acted in self-defence, but the jury rejected this and convicted him of murder.

At Martin's subsequent appeal fresh psychiatric evidence was produced. According to this evidence, Martin had a long-standing paranoid personality disorder. As a result of this disorder, Martin's perception of the threat the two intruders posed to his physical safety would have been much greater than the perception of the average person. One of the principal issues for the Court of Appeal in *R v Martin (Tony)* [2003] QB 1 was whether psychiatric conditions like this can be taken into account when applying the objective limb of the test for prevention of crime and private defence.

## EXTRACT

According to the following extract from the judgment of Lord Woolf CJ, which of the defendant's characteristics can be taken into account when applying the objective limb and which cannot?

### *R v Martin (Tony)* [2003] QB 1

#### Lord Woolf CJ

67. We would accept that the jury are entitled to take into account in relation to self-defence the physical characteristics of the defendant. However, we would not agree that it is appropriate, except in exceptional circumstances which would make the evidence especially probative, in deciding whether excessive force has been used to take into account whether the defendant is suffering from some psychiatric condition

So Martin's condition could be taken into account when applying the subjective limb, but not the objective limb. In other words, a defendant's psychiatric condition may be considered when deciding whether the defendant genuinely believed that the use of force was necessary to respond to a threat, but may not be considered when assessing whether the amount of force used in response to the threat was reasonable. This fine distinction has been criticised by commentators.[20]

It is worth noting three further points about the judgment in *R v Martin (Tony)*:

- First, you will have noticed in the extract from Lord Woolf CJ's judgment above that he stated that psychiatric conditions may be considered in 'exceptional circumstances'. The Court of Appeal commented on this in *R v Oye* [2013] EWCA Crim 1725. In this case the defendant, Seun Oye, was being held in a police station custody suite when he suffered a psychotic delusion. As a result of the delusion he believed that the police officers in the station were evil spirits intent on harming him, and so he punched them in order to escape. Referring to Lord Woolf's judgment, defence counsel argued that there were exceptional circumstances which meant that Oye's delusion should be taken into account when applying the objective limb. The Court of Appeal rejected this. Davis LJ stated:

> 53. [...] Quite what Lord Woolf had in mind in his reference to "exceptional circumstances" is unexplained. But at all events if Martin was not considered an exceptional case then we do not see how or why the present case should be.

It seems clear from this that Lord Woolf's reference to "exceptional circumstances" will rarely be applied in practice.

- Second, Martin's case predated the new rules regarding householder cases. So if a similar case occurred today, the jury would have to apply the rules set out in subsection (5A) of section 76 of the Criminal Justice and Immigration Act 2008.

## ACTIVITY

Imagine a jury was applying the new rules regarding householder cases to the facts of Tony Martin's case. In your opinion, would Martin still be convicted? Or would Martin's claim of self-defence now succeed?

- Third, although the Court of Appeal rejected Martin's plea of self-defence it did hold that the paranoid personality disorder was an abnormality of the mind for the purposes of diminished responsibility. The Court therefore quashed Martin's murder conviction and substituted a manslaughter conviction on the grounds of diminished responsibility. Martin was sentenced to five years' imprisonment for manslaughter, and was released from custody in July 2003. In 2009, on the tenth anniversary of the offence, an unrepentant Martin said in an interview, 'I don't have any regrets at all, I don't see why I should'.[21]

### Pre-emptive strikes

A defendant may be able to plead prevention of crime or private defence where he has acted pre-emptively. As Lord Griffiths stated in the Privy Council case *Beckford v*

---

[20]The authors of *Simester and Sullivan's Criminal Law*, for example, describe it as 'spurious' (Simester, A.P., Spencer, J.R., Stark, F., Sullivan, G.R. & Virgo, G.J. (2016) *Simester and Sullivan's Criminal Law: Theory and Doctrine* (6th edn) Oxford: Hart Publishing, p701).

[21]"'I don't regret killing that teenage burglar'", says vigilante farmer Tony Martin *Daily Mail* 21 August 2009.

*The Queen* [1988] AC 130, 'A man about to be attacked does not have to wait for his assailant to strike the first blow or fire the first shot; circumstances may justify a pre-emptive strike'.

In *Attorney-General's Reference (No 2 of 1983)* [1984] QB 456 the defendant owned a shop in an area where there had been two nights of rioting. The defendant's shop had been damaged and goods had been looted. Fearing further attacks, the defendant made ten petrol bombs. He explained, 'I had no intention to injure anyone but to use purely as a last resort to keep them away from my shop'. At trial the defendant was acquitted of an offence under the Explosive Substances Act 1883. The Attorney-General referred to the Court of Appeal the question whether someone in a situation like the defendant's could plead self-defence. Whilst parts of the Court's reasoning are problematic,[22] the Court made it clear that a defendant may act pre-emptively where there is a threat of an imminent attack. Lord Lane CJ stated:

> It may be a reasonable excuse that the carrier is in anticipation of imminent attack and is carrying the weapon for his own personal defence [...] In our judgment a defendant is not left in the paradoxical position of being able to justify acts carried out in self-defence but not acts immediately preparatory to it.

### A duty to retreat?

In *R v Bird* [1985] 1 WLR 816 the defendant, Debbie Bird, was celebrating her 17th birthday at a house party. Bird's ex-boyfriend, Darren Marder, showed up at the party with his new girlfriend. A little later an argument broke out between Bird and Marder. She claimed that Marder grabbed hold of her and held her against a wall. To defend herself, she struck him with her hand. In the heat of the moment, she said it did not occur to her that the hand she struck him with was holding a glass. The glass smashed in Marder's face, and as a result he lost an eye. Bird was charged with malicious wounding under section 20 of the Offences Against the Person Act 1861.

At Bird's trial the judge told the jury that 'it is necessary that a person claiming to exercise a right of self-defence should demonstrate by her action that she does not want to fight'. In other words, there is a duty to retreat before using force in order to prevent crime or for private defence. Failure to try and retreat will result in these defences being unavailable. The issue for the Court of Appeal at Bird's appeal against conviction was whether this was a misdirection.

## EXTRACT

According to the following extract from the judgment of Lord Lane CJ, is there a duty to retreat before using force in order to prevent crime or for private defence?

If not, then how (if at all) is a defendant's attempt or failure to retreat relevant to the objective limb of the test?

---

[22]In particular, Lord Lane CJ's statement that, 'He may still arm himself for his own protection, if the exigency arises, although in so doing he may commit other offences'. As Ormerod and Laird argue, it appears to be inconsistent to say 'He may do it – but he will commit an offence if he does' (Ormerod, D. & Laird, K. (2015) *Smith and Hogan's Criminal Law* (14th edn) Oxford: OUP, p450).

## *R v Bird* [1985] 1 WLR 816

### Lord Lane CJ

The matter is dealt with accurately and helpfully in *Smith and Hogan Criminal Law*, 5th ed. (1983), p. 327:

> "There were formerly technical rules about the duty to retreat before using force, or at least fatal force. This is now simply a factor to be taken into account in deciding whether it was necessary to use force, and whether the force was reasonable. If the only reasonable course is to retreat, then it would appear that to stand and fight must be to use unreasonable force. There is, however, no rule of law that a person attacked is bound to run away if he can; but it has been said that– '... what is necessary is that he should demonstrate by his actions that he does not want to fight. He must demonstrate that he is prepared to temporise and disengage and perhaps to make some physical withdrawal' [*Reg. v. Julien* [1969] 1 W.L.R. 839, 842]. It is submitted that it goes too far to say that action of this kind is *necessary*. It is scarcely consistent with the rule that it is permissible to use force, not merely to counter an actual attack, but to ward off an attack honestly and reasonably believed to be imminent. A demonstration by [the defendant] at the time that he did not want to fight is, no doubt, the best evidence that he was acting reasonably and in good faith in self-defence; but it is no more than that. A person may in some circumstances so act without temporising, disengaging or withdrawing; and he should have a good defence."

We respectfully agree with that passage. If the defendant is proved to have been attacking or retaliating or revenging himself, then he was not truly acting in self-defence. Evidence that the defendant tried to retreat or tried to call off the fight may be a cast-iron method of casting doubt on the suggestion that he was the attacker or retaliator or the person trying to revenge himself. But it is not by any means the only method of doing that

As a result of the misdirection, the conviction was quashed.

The decision in *R v Bird* has now been placed on a statutory footing, in subsection (6A) of section 76 of the Criminal Justice and Immigration Act 2008:[23]

> (6A) In deciding the question mentioned in subsection (3), a possibility that D could have retreated is to be considered (so far as relevant) as a factor to be taken into account, rather than as giving rise to a duty to retreat.

### *The defendant was the initial aggressor*

The issue in *R v Bird* was whether there is a duty to retreat. *R v Rashford* [2005] EWCA Crim 3377 concerned a slightly different scenario. Imagine that Derek has just discovered that his wife has been having an affair with Victor. Furious, he sets off to Victor's house to confront him. When he arrives he grabs Victor by the scruff of the neck and yells angrily at him. Victor retaliates violently. He knocks Derek to the floor and kicks him several times. To escape, Derek trips Victor over and punches him in the face. Suppose that Derek is charged with an offence for punching Victor in the face. Should he be able to plead self-defence? Or should the defence be unavailable to him because he sought Victor out in the first place? In other words, should the defence be available to a defendant who was the initial aggressor?

---

[23]For detailed discussion of the duty to retreat, see Mark Dsouza, 'Retreat, Submission, and the Private Use of Force' (2015) 35 *Oxford Journal of Legal Studies* 727.

## EXTRACT

The following extract is taken from the judgment of Dyson LJ in *R v Rashford*. If the defendant was the initial aggressor, is the defence automatically unavailable? If not, then in what circumstances may the initial aggressor plead self-defence?

### *R v Rashford* [2005] EWCA Crim 3377

### Dyson LJ

19 [... T]he mere fact that a defendant goes somewhere in order to exact revenge from the victim does not of itself rule out the possibility that in any violence that ensues self-defence is necessarily not available as a defence. It must depend on the circumstances [...] There may be a temptation whenever it is open to a jury to conclude that the defendant went to an incident out of revenge or was the aggressor to direct the jury that if they reach that conclusion then self-defence cannot avail the defendant. But if the judge wishes to give a direction along these lines the facts will usually require something rather more sophisticated where the possibility exists that the initial aggression may have resulted in a response by the victim which is so out of proportion to that aggression as to give rise to an honest belief in the aggressor that it was necessary for him to defend himself and the amount of force that he used was reasonable

So the fact that the defendant was the initial aggressor does not necessarily bar him from relying on the defence.

The Court of Appeal revisited this issue in *R v Keane* [2010] EWCA Crim 2514, and provided further guidance. The defendant, Daniel Keane, had been on a night out at the pub. The victim was giving Keane and two women a lift home. On the way they stopped at a petrol station. Whilst the victim was inside paying for the petrol Keane got into an argument with one of the women, during which he pushed her over. When the victim got back he asked Keane what was going on. There was a conversation, which ended with the victim saying 'Just don't do it again'. As the victim turned to walk away Keane said, 'What are you going to do about it?' The victim stopped and turned back, and as he did so he began to take his hand out of his pocket. Thinking that the victim was going to hit him, Keane punched him in the face. The victim fell back and suffered a serious blow to the back of his head. At trial Keane was convicted of maliciously inflicting grievous bodily harm (section 20 Offences Against the Person Act 1861).

At Keane's appeal against conviction the Court of Appeal had to consider whether Keane could claim he was acting in self-defence. The Court reiterated the approach set out in *R v Rashford*.

## EXTRACT

In the following extract, what test does the Court set out for deciding whether the initial aggressor may claim self-defence?

### R v Keane [2010] EWCA Crim 2514

#### Lord Justice Hughes

17 [... S]elf-defence may arise in the case of an original aggressor but only where the violence offered by the victim was so out of proportion to what the original aggressor did that in effect the roles were reversed.

[...]

18 [... I]t is not enough to bring self-defence into issue that a defendant who started the fight is at some point during the fight for the time being getting the worst of it, merely because the victim is defending himself reasonably. In that event there has been no disproportionate act by the victim [...] The victim has not been turned into the aggressor. The tables have not been turned in that particular sense. The roles have not been reversed

Dismissing Keane's appeal, the Court emphasised a further principle, which was particularly relevant to Keane saying 'What are you going to do about it?'

### EXTRACT

Read the following extract. What was the further principle the Court set out? Why was it relevant to Keane saying 'What are you going to do about it?'

### R v Keane [2010] EWCA Crim 2514

#### Lord Justice Hughes

19 [...] We need to say as clearly as we may that it is not the law that if a defendant sets out to provoke another to punch him and succeeds, the defendant is then entitled to punch the other person. What that would do would be to legalise the common coin of the bully who confronts his victim with taunts which are deliberately designed to provide an excuse to hit him.

#### The use of force on an innocent third party

Can a defendant inflict force on an innocent third party in order to prevent someone else from committing a crime? This was considered by the Court of Appeal in *R v Hichens* [2011] EWCA Crim 1626.

When Hichens lost his hostel placement Kathleen Brown allowed him to stay in her flat. Brown had previously had an on-off relationship with a man called John Oliver. One day Oliver turned up at the flat acting abusively, threatening to beat Hichens up. The next morning he returned, again acting abusively. The police warned Oliver to stay away, and advised Brown not to let Oliver in if he showed up again. Later that evening Oliver turned up at the flat. Brown wanted to let him in, but Hichens stopped her from doing so. He grabbed Brown's arm, threw her on to the sofa, and then put his hand around her throat causing her to lose consciousness. He also threatened to break her jaw.

Hichens argued that he could rely on the prevention of crime defence. He argued that he assaulted Brown in order to prevent Oliver from entering the flat and beating him up. At Hichens' trial the judge withdrew the prevention of crime defence from the jury's consideration, and Hichens was convicted of battery. He appealed, arguing that the judge had been wrong to withdraw the defence from the jury.

## EXTRACT

Read the following extract from the judgment of Gross LJ. Is it correct to say that a defendant who used force on an innocent third party in order to prevent someone else from committing a crime may never plead the prevention of crime defence?

The Court of Appeal concluded that the trial judge was wrong to withdraw the prevention of crime defence from the jury's consideration, but nonetheless upheld Hichens' conviction. How did the Court justify this?

### R v Hichens [2011] EWCA Crim 1626

### Gross LJ

30. It is next convenient to focus on two separate strands. The first is whether self-defence at common law and the use of force in the prevention of crime under s.3 of the Criminal Law Act 1967 are capable of extending to the use of force, against an innocent third party, to prevent a crime being committed by someone else. If and in so far as the judge thought that these defences were not capable of extending to the use of force against an innocent third party, we respectfully disagree, and indeed Mr Wicks did not seek to contend otherwise. Although we suspect that the facts capable realistically of giving rise to such a defence will only rarely be encountered, examples can be adduced and two will suffice:

1.  a police constable bundles a passerby out of the way to get at a man he believes about to shoot with a firearm or detonate an explosive device;

2.  Y seeks to give Z car keys with Z about to drive. X, believing Z to be unfit to drive through drink, knocks the keys out of Y's hands and retains them.

As ever the fact that the defence is capable of being advanced is of course a very different question from whether it would succeed

[...]

33 [... W]e are wholly unable to contemplate a reasonable jury, properly directed, with a suitable and forceful emphasis on the question of remoteness, acquitting the appellant. Even on the most favourable view of the evidence for the appellant, we underline: (i) Miss Brown was doing what she was perfectly entitled to do, whether wisely or not; (ii) there was no risk to the appellant from Miss Brown, the victim of the slapping; (iii) there was, at the most, a possibility of a crime being committed by Oliver should he be admitted to the flat; (iv) at the time of the slapping no crime was being committed and Oliver was not in the flat; (v) the appellant had known that Oliver might be coming to the flat for some time before the incident; (vi) the appellant had obvious options including calling the police or leaving the flat and, in our judgment, ample time to exercise them. It follows that the appeal against conviction must be dismissed. We have no doubt that the conviction was safe.

## Conclusion

In this chapter we have studied a total of five defences: necessity; duress by threats; duress of circumstances; prevention of crime and private defence. As we have seen during the chapter, sometimes the different defences may overlap. For example:

- It may sometimes be difficult to distinguish between duress by threats and duress of circumstances, because it may be plausible to describe the facts of some cases in either way.
- There is a considerable overlap between prevention of crime and private defence.
- The defences of necessity and duress of circumstances may sometimes overlap. For example, Lord Denning's hypothetical fireman could potentially plead either necessity or duress of circumstances.
- The defences of necessity and private defence may sometimes overlap. For example, we saw that in the *Conjoined Twins* case Brooke LJ applied the defence of necessity, whilst Ward LJ applied the common law right of private defence.

One question that students often ask when answering exam problem questions is, in a case where the defences overlap, which one(s) should I discuss? So to conclude the chapter, here is some guidance:

- As we have seen, the test for the defence of duress is the same whether the case involves duress by threats or duress of circumstances. So if the facts could be presented in either way, you should simply explain this point and then apply the test for duress.
- We also saw earlier that if prevention of crime and private defence overlap, you should apply prevention of crime. This is a statutory defence and supersedes the common law right of private defence (Criminal Law Act 1967, section 3(2)).
- There remains uncertainty over the defence of necessity, particularly regarding the test that should be used for the defence. As we saw above, it seems that the courts will leave the defence to develop on a case-by-case basis. So if the problem question you are answering has similar facts to one of the existing cases on necessity, it would be sensible to begin with this defence and argue that it should apply by analogy. But if the facts are not closely analogous, and there are other defences that could be used, it would be sensible to begin with these other defences instead. This is not to say that you shouldn't mention necessity at all. Rather, you should mention it as an alternative, more speculative, possibility.

## Self-test questions

1. Ken, William and Theresa are at a nightclub. Shortly after midnight a fire breaks out, and Ken, William and Theresa find themselves trapped in the chill-out room. The only escape route is through a small window. Ken begins to climb through the window, but becomes stuck. As the smoke and heat become more and more intense, William realises that he and Theresa will die if they do not get out quickly – but the only way for them to escape is to cut off Ken's arm and push him through the window. Despite Ken's loud protestations, William cuts off Ken's arm. As a result, all three of them manage to escape.

   Discuss William's criminal liability. How (if at all) would your answer be different in each of the following three situations?
   i. The fire brigade had arrived at the nightclub and begun to tackle the blaze. When William said that he would have to cut off Ken's arm, Theresa had replied,

'We don't need to cut off his arm. The fire brigade are here. They will rescue us'. William ignored Theresa's remarks, saying, 'We can't wait any longer', and cut off Ken's arm, enabling the three of them to escape through the window. Evidence subsequently shows that at the time William cut off Ken's arm, the fire brigade had the fire under control and would have been able to rescue William and Theresa from the chill-out room.

ii. Ken suffered a substantial loss of blood and as a result died shortly afterwards.

iii. Ken had insisted that he should climb through the window first, and pushed William and Theresa out of the way. After Ken got stuck the room quickly filled with smoke. William and Theresa died from smoke inhalation, but Ken was successfully rescued. (NB: In this scenario you should discuss the criminal liability of Ken, not William.)

2. Teenager Tom lives with his parents. One day he is on his way home from college when Vito, a member of a local gang, walks up to him, points a knife at him, and says, 'Do as I say and you won't get hurt. I want you to break into Carlo's flat, find his wallet, and bring it to me'. Tom is too stunned to say anything. Vito continues, 'I'll wait here. Off you go. And don't think you can run away because I know where you live'. Terrified, Tom runs all the way to Carlo's flat – which is a quarter of a mile away – breaks in, finds Carlo's wallet, runs back to Vito and hands over the wallet.

Discuss Tom's criminal liability. How (if at all) would your answer be different in each of the following four situations?

i. Vito had gone to Carlo's flat with Tom, and stood by the front door keeping watch while Tom searched for Carlo's wallet.

ii. When Vito pointed the knife at Tom he had said, 'Do it or I'll slash the tyres on your dad's car'.

iii. Carlo happened to be one of Tom's neighbours, and Tom intensely disliked him. Tom felt no remorse about breaking into Carlo's flat, and in fact helped himself to a few of Carlo's DVDs while he was there.

iv. Even though Vito's reputation for violence was well-known, a week earlier Tom had seen Vito at the local pub and had a drink with him.

3. Doug has just discovered that his wife Tessa has been having an affair with Vinnie. Furious, he storms round to Vinnie's house to confront him. When Vinnie opens his front door Doug begins to shout insults at him. Vinnie responds by pushing Doug over, and then jumps on top of him and begins to punch him. To get him to stop, Doug manages to pick up a stone from Vinnie's front garden and strikes Vinnie on the head with it, as hard as he can. Vinnie suffers a fractured skull, and has to spend several weeks in hospital.

Discuss Doug's criminal liability. How (if at all) would your answer be different in each of the following three situations?

i. Doug had a personality disorder. As a result of this personality disorder, when Vinnie was on top of Doug punching him Doug was certain that Vinnie was going to kill him.

ii. Instead of picking up a stone, Doug had managed to get to his feet and started to run away. Seeing that Vinnie was chasing him, Doug pushed a passing pedestrian called Alice out of his way. Alice fell over and landed awkwardly, breaking her wrist.

iii. Doug had taken a knife with him. He didn't intend to use it, he just wanted to get his own back on Vinnie by scaring him. As Doug shouted insults at Vinnie, Vinnie had picked up a toy gun and pointed it at Doug. Although most people would have realised it was a toy, in the heat of the moment Doug thought Vinnie was going to shoot him, so he pulled out the knife and fatally stabbed Vinnie.

4.  'It is impossible to justify the House of Lords' decision, in *R v Howe* [1987] AC 417, that duress should not be available as a defence to murder.'

How far (if at all) do you agree with this statement?

# Substantive defences checklist

Having worked through this chapter, you should now have:

✓ An understanding of the Courts' historical reluctance to recognise a defence of necessity, and an awareness of the types of situation in which such a defence has been recognised

✓ An ability to critically discuss *R v Dudley and Stephens* and whether necessity is ever available as a defence to murder

✓ An understanding of the two-limbed test for duress

✓ An understanding of the principle stated in *R v Hasan* for cases in which the defendant has voluntarily exposed himself to duress

✓ An ability to critically discuss the House of Lords' reasons in *R v Howe* for holding that duress is not available as a defence to murder

✓ An understanding of the differences between necessity and duress of circumstances and when to apply which defence

✓ An understanding of the relationship between prevention of crime and private defence and when to apply which defence

✓ An understanding of the two-limbed test for prevention of crime and private defence.

# Further reading

Arenson, K.J. (2014) 'The Paradox of Disallowing Duress as a Defence to Murder' 78 *Journal of Criminal Law* 65.

Clarkson, C.M.V. (2004) 'Necessary Action: A New Defence' *Criminal Law Review* 81.

Gardner, S. (2005) 'Direct Action and the Defence of Necessity' *Criminal Law Review* 371.

Leverick, F. (2006) *Killing in Self-Defence.* Oxford: OUP.

Michalowski, S. (2002) 'Sanctity of Life – Are Some Lives More Sacred Than Others?' 22 *Legal Studies* 377.

Milgate, H.P. (1988) 'Duress and the Criminal Law: Another About Turn by the House of Lords 47 *Cambridge Law Journal* 61.

Rogers, J. (2001) 'Necessity, Private Defence and the Killing of Mary' *Criminal Law Review* 515.

Thomas, M.P. (2016) 'Defenceless Castles: The Use of Grossly Disproportionate Force by Householders in Light of *R (Collins) v Secretary of State for Justice* [2016] EWHC 33 (Admin)' 80 *Journal of Criminal Law* 407.

# 12

# Inchoate offences

## Chapter objectives

By the end of this chapter you should have:

- An understanding of the requirements for establishing criminal liability for: (a) encouraging or assisting crime; (b) conspiracy and (c) criminal attempts
- An ability to apply the relevant law to a hypothetical set of facts and discuss whether criminal liability may be established for any of the offences listed above
- An ability to critically discuss the 'more than merely preparatory' test for the *actus reus* of attempts and the courts' application of this test.

# ⬤ ⬤ ⬤  Introduction

In Chapter 2, I explained that the criminal law would be seriously defective if it only contained offences like murder, rape, assault and theft. It needs a broader scope, in two respects. First, since the criminal law aims to prevent crimes as well as to punish those who commit them, it should also apply to preparatory actions. Second, the criminal law should encompass those who assist and encourage others to commit crimes, as well as those who actually commit them. This chapter and the next one look at each of these in turn. The next chapter focuses on accessories. This chapter focuses on inchoate offences. The word 'inchoate' means: at an early stage, just begun, undeveloped. In other words, inchoate offences are ones which apply where the defendant has embarked on a plan to commit a crime, but has not yet actually committed it.

The inchoate offences that we study in this chapter are set out on the timeline in Figure 12.1. The first two offences we study are encouraging or assisting crime and conspiracy. These target the early stages of plans to commit crime, such as words of persuasion, offers of help and verbal agreements. The third offence we study is criminal attempts. This applies where the defendant has gone beyond mere preparation, but has not yet committed the planned offence.

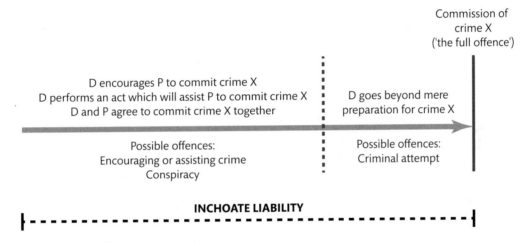

**Figure 12.1.** Inchoate offences: a timeline

Inchoate crimes have a preventative rationale. They enable the authorities to arrest, prosecute and punish would-be offenders without having to wait for them to carry out the crime they had planned. One difficult issue that this raises is how early we should intervene. On the one hand there are some strong arguments in favour of having broad inchoate offences in order to enable early intervention, but on the other hand there are also good reasons for ensuring inchoate liability is tightly confined. Later in the chapter we will examine these competing principles and policy concerns when we evaluate the *actus reus* of criminal attempts.

Before turning to the offences themselves, it is helpful to clarify the meaning of one term that will appear throughout the chapter: 'full offence'. When we use this term we are referring to the crime that the defendant had planned to commit (or encourage or assist someone else to commit). So if two defendants agree to rob a post office together they are guilty of conspiracy to rob. The relevant inchoate offence is conspiracy and the relevant full offence is robbery. Or if a defendant tries unsuccessfully to have non-consensual sexual intercourse with someone else, he is guilty of attempted rape. The relevant inchoate offence is attempt and the relevant full offence is rape. Hopefully this will save any confusion later in the chapter!

# Encouraging and assisting crime

Part 2 of the Serious Crime Act 2007 abolished the old common law offence of incitement and replaced it with three new offences which involve encouraging and assisting crime. These new offences were designed to be slightly broader than the offence of incitement. Like incitement, they apply to those who encourage others to commit a crime. But they also cover the defendant who assists someone else to commit a crime without actually encouraging them to do so (e.g. the defendant who provides vital equipment in exchange for payment).

The three offences are set out in sections 44, 45 and 46 of the Act.

---

## EXTRACT

### Sections 44, 45 and 46 of the Serious Crime Act 2007

#### 44 Intentionally encouraging or assisting an offence

(1)  A person commits an offence if –

    (a)  he does an act capable of encouraging or assisting the commission of an offence; and

    (b)  he intends to encourage or assist its commission.

(2)  But he is not to be taken to have intended to encourage or assist the commission of an offence merely because such encouragement or assistance was a foreseeable consequence of his act.

#### 45 Encouraging or assisting an offence believing it will be committed

A person commits an offence if –

    (a)  he does an act capable of encouraging or assisting the commission of an offence; and

    (b)  he believes –

        (i)   that the offence will be committed; and

        (ii)  that his act will encourage or assist its commission.

#### 46 Encouraging or assisting offences believing one or more will be committed

(1)  A person commits an offence if –

    (a)  he does an act capable of encouraging or assisting the commission of one or more of a number of offences; and

    (b)  he believes –

        (i)   that one or more of those offences will be committed (but has no belief as to which); and

        (ii)  that his act will encourage or assist the commission of one or more of them.

(2)  It is immaterial for the purposes of subsection (1)(b)(ii) whether the person has any belief as to which offence will be encouraged or assisted.

(3) If a person is charged with an offence under subsection (1) –

    (a) the indictment must specify the offences alleged to be the "number of offences" mentioned in paragraph (a) of that subsection; but

    (b) nothing in paragraph (a) requires all the offences potentially comprised in that number to be specified.

(4) In relation to an offence under this section, reference in this Part to the offences specified in the indictment is to the offences specified by virtue of subsection (3)(a).

These offences have been described by David Ormerod and Rudi Fortson as 'some of the most convoluted offences in decades'.[1] So if you find some of the next few pages hard, don't worry. Be reassured by the fact that even leading commentators have found these offences difficult!

There are five requirements which must be satisfied to establish liability for one of these offences. The first key point is that the *actus reus* of all three offences is identical. To establish the *actus reus*, the following requirement must be satisfied:

1. The defendant did an act that was capable of encouraging or assisting the commission of an offence.

The *mens rea* consists of three requirements. The first *mens rea* requirement is what distinguishes the three offences from each other, and is what makes section 44 the most serious of the three:

2. The defendant had *mens rea* in relation to the behaviour part of the full offence.

The next two *mens rea* requirements are the same for all three offences:

3. The defendant had *mens rea* in relation to the consequence and circumstance parts of the full offence.

4. The defendant had *mens rea* in relation to the *mens rea* part of the full offence.

The final requirement is found in section 50 of the Act (set out below). This section creates a reasonableness defence:

5. No offence is committed if it was reasonable for the defendant to act as he did.

When answering an exam problem question, it is advisable to work through the requirements in this order. Begin with the *actus reus*, then identify which of the three offences applies in the particular case by applying the first *mens rea* requirement, then work through the other two *mens rea* requirements and finally, if both *actus reus* and *mens rea* are established, consider the reasonableness defence. We will accordingly work through the five requirements in this order.

## 1. The defendant did an act that was capable of encouraging or assisting the commission of an offence

To examine this *actus reus* requirement we need to look at the meaning of five key words: act; capable; encouraging; assisting and offence.

---

[1]Ormerod, D. and Fortson, R. (2009) 'Serious Crime Act 2007: The Part 2 Offences' *Criminal Law Review* 389.

### i. An act …

Sections 44 to 46 each use the word 'act'. But in this context the word has a broader meaning than its ordinary dictionary meaning, in three respects. First, section 65(2)(b) states:

---

**EXTRACT**

## Section 65(2)(b) of the Serious Crime Act

(2)   A reference in this Part to a person's doing an act that is capable of encouraging or assisting the commission of an offence includes a reference to his doing so by –

[…]

(b)   failing to take reasonable steps to discharge a duty.

---

So a defendant may commit these three offences by omission, if he had a legal duty to act and failed to take reasonable steps to discharge this duty. An example is a security guard who deliberately fails to turn on a burglar alarm at his employer's premises in order to help burglars steal from the premises.

Second, section 67 states:

---

**EXTRACT**

## Section 67 of the Serious Crime Act 2007

### 67 Course of conduct

A reference in this Part to an act includes a reference to a course of conduct, and a reference to doing an act is to be read accordingly.

---

So although the word 'act' suggests that the prosecution must point to some specific single action, in fact the prosecution may point to a series of actions which amount to a course of conduct.

And third, section 66 states:

---

**EXTRACT**

## Section 66 of the Serious Crime Act 2007

### 66 Indirectly encouraging or assisting

If a person (D1) arranges for a person (D2) to do an act that is capable of encouraging or assisting the commission of an offence, and D2 does the act, D1 is also to be treated for the purposes of this Part as having done it.

---

This section was drafted with criminal gangs in mind. Suppose that a gang leader, Vito, tells one of the gang members, Michael, to persuade Sonny to commit a murder. Michael does so. Section 66 states that, since Vito arranged for Michael to persuade Sonny, Vito may be treated as if he had performed the acts of encouragement himself. So Vito would be guilty of intentionally encouraging Sonny to commit murder.

### ii. … that was capable …

There are three important points to note here.

First, since these three offences are inchoate crimes it is not necessary to show that the encouragement or assistance actually led to the full offence being committed. This is confirmed by section 49(1):

---

**EXTRACT**

## Section 49 of the Serious Crime Act 2007

### 49 Supplemental provisions

(1)  A person may commit an offence under this Part whether or not any offence capable of being encouraged or assisted by his act is committed.

---

So if Vito encourages Michael to murder Philip, there is no need to show that Michael actually committed the murder.

Second, it is also not necessary to show that the defendant's act did in fact provide encouragement or assistance. All that needs to be shown is that the act was *capable* of providing encouragement or assistance. Suppose that Vito posts a letter to Michael which encourages him to murder Philip. The letter gets lost in the post and never arrives. Although Michael did not receive the encouragement, Vito may still be convicted of intentionally encouraging murder since posting the letter was an act that was capable of providing encouragement.

Third, when framing the charge there is no need to specify the particulars of the full offence that the defendant encouraged or assisted. So the defendant would be charged with 'encouraging or assisting murder', not with 'encouraging or assisting the murder of Philip'. This was explained by the Law Commission as follows:

---

**EXTRACT**

## Law Commission (2006) *Inchoate Liability for Assisting and Encouraging Crime* (Law Commission Report No 300) Cm 6878

### D's liability is for encouraging or assisting an abstract and not a particular principal offence

5.13 D may not know the details of the prospective principal offence. Thus, D may provide P with a baseball bat believing that P will use it to rob V1. Instead, P uses it to rob V2. Alternatively, D may provide the baseball bat believing that P will use it to commit robbery but have no belief as to the identity of the victim. It matters not that D lacks knowledge or belief as to the details of the prospective principal offence. D is guilty of encouraging or assisting P to commit robbery rather than encouraging or assisting P to rob V.

---

This would be relevant in cases where the planned offence turns out to be impossible. Suppose that, unbeknown to Vito, Philip is already dead. Vito would simply be charged with intentionally encouraging murder, *not* with intentionally encouraging the murder of Philip. The fact that Philip is already dead would therefore be irrelevant.

---

### ACTIVITY

In the following three examples, does Vito do an act that is capable of encouraging or assisting murder?

- Vito says to Michael, 'If you kill Philip I'll pay you £1,000'. Michael rejects the offer.
- Vito writes a letter which encourages Michael to murder Philip. But on his way to the post box Vito changes his mind and, instead of posting the letter, he rips it up.
- Michael has decided to kill Philip. He asks Vito for Philip's address. Vito gives him an address in New York, which he thinks is where Philip lives. But, unbeknown to Vito, Philip has recently moved house and gone to live in Sicily.

---

iii. ... of encouraging ...

In this context the word 'encouraging' has a broader meaning than its ordinary sense of instigating or persuading. Section 65(1) states:

---

### EXTRACT

### Section 65 of the Serious Crime Act 2007

#### 65 Being capable of encouraging or assisting

(1)  A reference in this Part to a person's doing an act that is capable of encouraging the commission of an offence includes a reference to his doing so by threatening another person or otherwise putting pressure on another person to commit the offence.

---

The case law on the old common law offence of incitement is also helpful in understanding the meaning of encouragement. The following two cases illustrate that: (1) the encouragement may be by words or by conduct, and may be express or implied; and (2) the encouragement need not be addressed to a particular person, and could be addressed to the world at large.

---

### EXAMPLE

- *Invicta Plastics v Clare* [1976] RTR 251: The defendant company produced a device called Radatec, which let out a high-pitched whine when within 800 yards of wireless telegraphy transmissions including those used for police radar speed traps. At the time of the case a licence was needed to use such devices. The company advertised Radatec in a motoring magazine. The advert had a picture of a car with the Radatec device fitted to its windscreen and a speed limit sign in the background. The advert read, 'You ought to know more about Radatec. Ask at your accessory shop or write for name of nearest stockist'. The Divisional Court held that, looking at the advert as a whole, it impliedly encouraged unlicensed readers to use Radatec.

- *R v Marlow* [1997] Crim LR 897: Michael Marlow produced a book which gave advice on how to grow and produce cannabis. The book was advertised and about 500 copies were sold. Some of those who bought the book were subsequently found to have attempted to produce cannabis using the methods described in the book. The Court of Appeal held that the book 'amounted to an active and widespread encouragement of others to engage in the production and use of cannabis'.

The courts have also considered a further issue. Suppose that Michael goes to Vito and says, 'I've decided to kill Philip'. Vito congratulates him and encourages him to go through with it. Can Vito be convicted of encouraging murder even though Michael had already made his mind up to commit the crime? This was considered by the Court of Appeal in *R v Goldman* [2001] EWCA Crim 1684.[2] In this case a company called ESV placed an advert on the Internet advertising pornographic materials for sale, including paedophilic ones. The defendant, Terence Goldman, wrote to ESV and asked for photographs of girls aged 7 to 13. At trial he was convicted of inciting ESV to distribute indecent photographs of children under 16. He appealed against his conviction, arguing that he could not be guilty of inciting ESV to distribute the materials because ESV had already offered them for sale.

### EXTRACT

Read the following extract from the judgment of Clarke LJ. Had Goldman encouraged ESV to distribute indecent photographs? Explain Clarke LJ's reasoning.

### *R v Goldman* [2001] EWCA Crim 1684

#### Clarke LJ

23. In the instant case, the appellant offered to buy indecent photographs for £75. As we have indicated, the provision of the photographs would have been a criminal offence. In our judgment that offer was a suggestion or proposal or persuasion or inducement to commit that offence. It is true that ESV had advertised its wares and that it was thought to be willing to provide the photographs. However in our judgment that is nothing to the point. ESV would not have sent the photographs except in response to an offer, and probably only in response to an offer which included a cheque. In ordinary language it required an element of persuasion or encouragement in the form of an offer before it would distribute the video tapes. It follows, in our judgment, that the letter of 9th June was an inducement to commit the offence. It was a suggestion or proposal or inducement to commit the offence and at the very least an attempt to incite it.

---

[2]See also *O'Shea v Coventry Magistrates' Court* [2004] Crim LR 948: in this case D had accessed websites featuring child pornography. The Divisional Court upheld his conviction for inciting the company maintaining the website to distribute indecent photographs of children. By accessing the website D had encouraged the company to maintain it.

So in our example Vito would be guilty of intentionally encouraging murder, notwithstanding the fact that Michael had already resolved to kill Philip before speaking to Vito.

Finally, note that it does not matter if no one else is aware of the defendant's acts of encouragement or assistance. So in our earlier example in which Vito posts a letter of encouragement to Michael which never arrives there is the *actus reus* of this offence even though no one else knew that Vito had posted the letter.[3]

### iv. ... or assisting ...

The Serious Crime Act 2007 does not contain any definition of the word 'assist'. The ordinary meaning of the word should therefore be applied. The case law on 'aiding' can also be used (we study this in the next chapter). Note also that it does not matter if the defendant's acts of assistance were very minor. The Act does not contain any requirement that the defendant provided substantial assistance.[4]

The Act does deal with one particular type of situation.

---

### EXTRACT

### Section 65 of the Serious Crime Act

(2)  A reference in this Part to a person's doing an act that is capable of encouraging or assisting the commission of an offence includes a reference to his doing so by –

   (a)  taking steps to reduce the possibility of criminal proceedings being brought in respect of that offence;

[...]

(3)  But a person is not to be regarded as doing an act that is capable of encouraging or assisting the commission of an offence merely because he fails to respond to a constable's request for assistance in preventing a breach of the peace.

---

Two examples of when section 65(2)(a) might apply are: providing advice to someone on how to avoid detection and providing a gun for the perpetrators to use against any eye-witnesses.[5] But note that section 65(2)(a) will only apply if the act of assistance occurs before the offence is complete. Suppose that Michael kills Philip, and then tells Vito what he has done. Vito helps Michael flee the country. Vito cannot be guilty of assisting murder because he only assisted Michael after Philip was already dead. In such circumstances other offences would be used, such as perverting the course of justice.

### v. ... the commission of an offence

A defendant may be guilty of encouraging or assisting any of the offences we have studied in Chapters 5, 6, 7 and 8 of this text. When answering an exam problem question, it is important to specify which offence the defendant encouraged or assisted. So don't just write 'D is guilty of intentionally encouraging crime'. You must write 'D is guilty of intentionally encouraging theft' or 'D is guilty of intentionally assisting rape'.

---

[3]Cf: *State v Tally* 15 So 722 [1894], discussed in Chapter 13.

[4]In its report Law Commission (2006) *Inchoate Liability for Assisting and Encouraging Crime* (Law Commission Report No 300) Cm 6878, the Law Commission stated: 'D should be liable if his or her act is capable of assisting (or encouraging) another person to any extent. The marginal nature of any assistance or encouragement can be reflected in the sentence' (para 5.51).

[5]Law Commission (2006) *Inchoate Liability for Assisting and Encouraging Crime* (Law Commission Report No 300) Cm 6878, para A.91.

A defendant may also be guilty of encouraging or assisting someone to be an accessory to a crime. Suppose Vito encourages Michael to help Sonny kill Philip. Vito could be charged with intentionally encouraging Michael to be an accessory to murder.[6]

A defendant may also be charged with encouraging or assisting an inchoate offence. This is known as double inchoate liability. Note, however, that section 49 states that double inchoate liability is only possible if the defendant is charged with the section 44 offence. This means that the potential forms of double inchoate liability are:

- Intentionally encouraging or assisting a person to encourage or assist someone else to commit a crime[7]

- Intentionally encouraging or assisting a person to conspire to commit a crime

- Intentionally encouraging or assisting a person to attempt to commit a crime.

Finally, a person cannot be charged with encouraging or assisting an offence if the offence in questions exists for their protection. This is set out in section 51 of the Act:

## EXTRACT

### Section 51 of the Serious Crime Act 2007

#### 51 Protective offences: victims not liable

(1) In the case of protective offences, a person does not commit an offence under this Part by reference to such an offence if –

   (a) he falls within the protected category; and

   (b) he is the person in respect of whom the protective offence was committed or would have been if it had been committed.

(2) "Protective offence" means an offence that exists (wholly or in part) for the protection of a particular category of persons ("the protected category").

Suppose that a 14-year-old girl encourages her 26-year-old boyfriend (who knows her age) to have sexual intercourse with her. Her boyfriend is charged with the offence of sexual activity with a child.[8] The girl cannot be charged with intentionally encouraging her boyfriend to commit sexual activity with a child, because she was the victim of the sexual offence and the offence exists for her protection.

## 2. The defendant had *mens rea* in relation to the behaviour part of the full offence

The *actus reus* requirement is the same for each of the section 44, 45 and 46 offences. It is this first *mens rea* requirement that invites you to identify which one of the three offences applies to the facts of a particular case.

---

[6]This example is similar to the earlier one involving section 66. The key difference is that section 66 states that it only applies 'If a person (D1) arranges for a person (D2) to do an act that is capable of encouraging or assisting the commission of an offence, *and D2 does the act* [...].' So, in our example, if Michael ignored Vito section 66 would not apply. The prosecution would then have to charge Vito with intentionally encouraging Michael to be an accessory to murder.

[7]Note that the charge would need to specify whether the defendant was intentionally encouraging/assisting the person to commit the section 44, 45 or 46 offence.

[8]Sexual Offences Act 2003, s.9.

In Chapter 2, we saw that the *actus reus* of criminal offences can be divided into three separate parts: behaviour; consequences and circumstances. This distinction is important here. You need to begin by looking at the *actus reus* of the full offence and identify the behaviour part. The defendant must then be shown to have had *mens rea* in relation to this. The specific requirements are set out in the first four subsections of the 'tortuous'[9] section 47:

---

## EXTRACT

### Section 47 of the Serious Crime Act 2007

#### 47 Proving an offence under this Part

(1) Sections 44, 45 and 46 are to be read in accordance with this section.

(2) If it is alleged under section 44(1)(b) that a person (D) intended to encourage or assist the commission of an offence, it is sufficient to prove that he intended to encourage or assist the doing of an act which would amount to the commission of that offence.

(3) If it is alleged under section 45(b) that a person (D) believed that an offence would be committed and that his act would encourage or assist its commission, it is sufficient to prove that he believed –

  (a) that an act would be done which would amount to the commission of that offence; and

  (b) that his act would encourage or assist the doing of that act.

(4) If it is alleged under section 46(1)(b) that a person (D) believed that one or more of a number of offences would be committed and that his act would encourage or assist the commission of one or more of them, it is sufficient to prove that he believed –

  (a) that one or more of a number of acts would be done which would amount to the commission of one or more of those offences; and

  (b) that his act would encourage or assist the doing of one or more of those acts.

[...]

(7) In the case of an offence under section 44 –

[...]

  (b) D is not to be taken to have intended that an act would be done in particular circumstances or with particular consequences merely because its being done in those circumstances or with those consequences was a foreseeable consequence of his act of encouragement or assistance.

---

So suppose Vito has encouraged Michael to commit rape. The behavioural element of the *actus reus* of rape is that the defendant penetrated the vagina/anus/mouth of the victim with his penis. To identify whether the section 44, 45 or 46 offence is the most appropriate, you should work through subsections (2) to (4) of section 47.

Begin with the section 44 offence since this is the most serious of the three. Section 47(2) states that for the section 44 offence the prosecution must prove that the defendant intended to encourage or assist the behaviour part of the full offence. Importantly,

---

[9]Ormerod, D. and Fortson, R. (2009) 'Serious Crime Act 2007: The Part 2 Offences' *Criminal Law Review* 389, 407.

sections 44(2) and 47(7)(b) explain that in this context the meaning of intention is limited to direct intention.[10] In other words, it must have been the defendant's purpose to encourage or assist the behaviour part of the full offence. So in our example, for the section 44 offence to apply the prosecution must show that Vito's purpose was to encourage or assist Michael's act of penile penetration.

If the section 44 offence does not apply you should consider the section 45 and 46 offences instead. Both offences use the *mens rea* concept of belief. The difference between them is that section 45 applies where the defendant believes a specific full offence will be committed, whereas section 46 applies where the defendant believes that one of several full offences will be committed but is unsure which one.[11] So if Vito gives Michael a baseball bat believing Michael will use it to beat Philip up, rob Philip or smash the windows on Philip's Ferrari, but is not sure which, the relevant offence is section 46. However, if Vito simply believes Michael will use the baseball bat to beat Philip up the relevant offence is section 45.

Once you have determined whether section 45 or section 46 applies, the defendant must be shown to have had the following two beliefs:

1. For the section 45 offence the defendant must have believed that the behaviour part of the full offence would be committed (s.47(3)). For the section 46 offence the defendant must have believed that the behaviour part of one of the anticipated full offences would be committed (s.47(4)). As we saw in Chapter 4, to believe something is to have mentally accepted it as true.[12] So a belief is more than merely a suspicion. If the defendant only suspected that the behaviour part of the full offence would be committed he is not guilty of either offence. In our initial example this means that, if Vito thought Michael might commit the act of penile penetration, but concluded that he probably would not, Vito would not satisfy this *mens rea* requirement.

2. The defendant must have believed that his actions would encourage or assist commission of the behaviour part of the full offence. Note that it is not enough to show that the defendant believed his actions might provide encouragement or assistance. He must have believed that they *would* do so.

Figure 12.2 summarises how to approach this *mens rea* requirement.

## ACTIVITY

Use Figure 12.2 to answer the following question:

One day Michael comes to Vito's home. Extremely agitated, he says, 'This time I've had enough' and angrily demands to borrow Vito's handgun. Vito's knows that Michael has long held a grudge against Philip, and is worried about what Michael might use the gun for. In spite of this he lends Michael the weapon. How would you advise a prosecutor deciding whether to charge Vito for the section 44, 45 or 46 offence?

---

[10]We examined the different types of intention in Chapter 4.
[11]This interpretation of section 46 was adopted by the Court of Appeal in *R v Sadique* [2013] EWCA Crim 1150, effectively overruling the different interpretation adopted in *R v Sadique and another* [2011] EWCA Crim 2872.
[12]*R v Forsyth* [1997] 2 Cr App R 299.

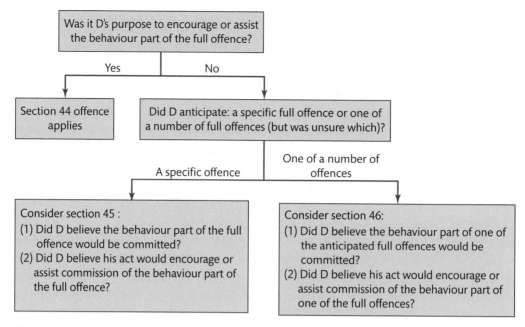

**Figure 12.2.** An overview of the section 47 *mens rea* requirement

### 3. The defendant had *mens rea* in relation to the consequence and circumstance parts of the full offence

Here we move on to subsection 5(b) of section 47:

---

**EXTRACT**

## Section 47(5)(b) of the Serious Crime Act 2007

### 47 Proving an offence under this Part

[...]

(5) In proving for the purposes of this section whether an act is one which, if done, would amount to the commission of an offence –

[...]

    (b) if the offence is one requiring proof of particular circumstances or consequences (or both), it must be proved that –

        (i) D believed that, were the act to be done, it would be done in those circumstances or with those consequences; or

        (ii) D was reckless as to whether or not it would be done in those circumstances or with those consequences.

[...]

(7) In the case of an offence under section 44 –

    (a) subsection (5)(b)(i) is to be read as if the reference to "D believed" were a reference to "D intended or believed"; but

(b) D is not to be taken to have intended that an act would be done in particular circumstances or with particular consequences merely because its being done in those circumstances or with those consequences was a foreseeable consequence of his act of encouragement or assistance.

To illustrate this *mens rea* requirement we can return to our example in which Vito has encouraged Michael to commit rape. The *actus reus* of rape includes a circumstance element: the penile penetration must have been non-consensual. According to section 47(5)(b), the prosecution must therefore show either:

- That Vito believed that, when Michael penetrated the victim's vagina/anus/mouth with his penis, he would do so without the consent of the victim (s.47(5)(b)(i)); In the case of the section 44 offence, it will also suffice for the prosecution to show that Vito directly intended that the penetration would be non-consensual (s47(7)); or
- That Vito was reckless as to whether or not Michael would penetrate the victim's vagina/anus/mouth with his penis without the consent of the victim (s.47(5)(b)(ii)).

The same applies where the *actus reus* of the full offence has a consequence element. Suppose Vito encourages Michael to kill Philip. The *actus reus* of murder includes a consequence element: death of the victim. So according to section 47(5)(b), the prosecution must show either:

- That Vito believed that, when Michael committed the act, it would cause Philip's death (s.47(5)(b)(i)); Again, in the case of the section 44 offence direct intention will also suffice (s47(7)); or
- That Vito was reckless as to whether or not Michael's act would cause Philip's death (s.47(5)(b)(ii)).

So when applying this *mens rea* requirement to an exam problem question, you first need to identify the circumstance and consequence elements of the *actus reus* of the full offence. Remember that not all crimes have a circumstance and/or consequence element. Once you have identified the relevant circumstances and consequences you should then apply section 47(5)(b) to these.

## 4. The defendant had *mens rea* in relation to the *mens rea* part of the full offence

The final *mens rea* requirement is that the defendant had *mens rea* in relation to the *mens rea* part of the full offence. This is governed by subsection (5)(a) of section 47.

### EXTRACT

#### Section 47(5)(a) of the Serious Crime Act

(5) In proving for the purposes of this section whether an act is one which, if done, would amount to the commission of an offence –

   (a) if the offence is one requiring proof of fault, it must be proved that –

      (i) D believed that, were the act to be done, it would be done with that fault;

      (ii) D was reckless as to whether or not it would be done with that fault; or

      (iii) D's state of mind was such that, were he to do it, it would be done with that fault; and

[...]

(6) For the purposes of subsection (5)(a)(iii), D is to be assumed to be able to do the act in question.

To illustrate this *mens rea* requirement we can once again use our example in which Vito encourages Michael to commit rape. Rape has two *mens rea* requirements: (1) that the defendant intentionally penetrated the victim's vagina/anus/mouth with his penis; and, (2) that the defendant lacked a reasonable belief in consent. According to section 47(5)(a), the prosecution must therefore show either:

- That Vito believed that Michael would intentionally penetrate the victim's vagina/anus/mouth with his penis, and that Michael would do so without a reasonable belief that the victim was consenting (s.47(5)(a)(i));

- That Vito was reckless as to whether Michael would intentionally penetrate the victim's vagina/anus/mouth with his penis, and as to whether Michael would do so without a reasonable belief that the victim was consenting (s.47(5)(a)(ii)); or

- That if Vito had committed the act of sexual intercourse himself, he would have intentionally penetrated the victim's vagina/anus/mouth with his penis and would have lacked a reasonable belief that the victim was consenting (s.47(5)(a)(iii)).

Section 47(6) deals with a very specific type of scenario. Suppose that Carmela encourages Michael to commit rape. As we saw in Chapter 7, women cannot commit the offence of rape as principals. At first it would therefore seem that section 47(5)(a)(iii) cannot apply. However, section 47(6) states that, in this context, the defendant 'is to be assumed to be able to do the act in question'. It follows that if Carmela intended penile penetration of the victim's vagina/anus/mouth and lacked a reasonable belief that the victim would consent she would satisfy this *mens rea* requirement by virtue of section 47(5)(a)(iii).

## 5. No offence is committed if it was reasonable for the defendant to act as he did

Finally, the defendant cannot be convicted of the section 44, 45 or 46 offences if it was reasonable for him to act as he did. The reasonableness defence is set out in section 50:

---

**EXTRACT**

### Section 50 of the Serious Crime Act 2007

#### 50 Defence of acting reasonably

(1)  A person is not guilty of an offence under this Part if he proves –

    (a)  that he knew certain circumstances existed; and

    (b)  that it was reasonable for him to act as he did in those circumstances.

(2)  A person is not guilty of an offence under this Part if he proves –

    (a)  that he believed certain circumstances to exist;

    (b)  that his belief was reasonable; and

    (c)  that it was reasonable for him to act as he did in the circumstances as he believed them to be.

(3)  Factors to be considered in determining whether it was reasonable for a person to act as he did include –

    (a)  the seriousness of the anticipated offence (or, in the case of an offence under section 46, the offences specified in the indictment);

    (b)  any purpose for which he claims to have been acting;

    (c)  any authority by which he claims to have been acting.

Note the following two points:

- The test is whether the defendant's actions were objectively reasonable. It is *not* whether the defendant thought his conduct was reasonable.

- The burden of proof for this defence rests on the defendant. He must prove on the balance of probabilities that: (1) he knew the relevant circumstances existed; and (2) it was reasonable for him to act as he did in those circumstances (s.50(1)). Or, if he had made a mistake, he must prove that: (1) the mistaken belief was genuine; (2) the mistake was an objectively reasonable one and (3) it was reasonable for him to act as he did in the circumstances as he believed them to be (s.50(2)).

Commentators have criticised the reasonableness defence for being vague and ill-defined.[13]

## ACTIVITY

Do you think the reasonableness defence would be available in the following two situations? Should it be?

- The defendant works in a hardware store. A customer asks to buy some rope, tape and a knife. The defendant believes that the customer will use the items to kidnap someone, but his boss tells him to stop being stupid and so he completes the sale.

- The defendant is driving in the right-hand lane on the motorway. In his rear view mirror he notices a speeding car approaching fast. The defendant moves into the middle lane in order to let the speeding car continue unobstructed.

# Conspiracy

There are three different types of conspiracy offence: statutory conspiracy; conspiracy to defraud and conspiracy to corrupt public morals or outrage public decency. In this chapter we study just the first of these: statutory conspiracy. The simple reason for this is that the vast majority of conspiracies are statutory conspiracies.

---

[13]Ormerod, D. and Fortson, R. (2009) 'Serious Crime Act 2007: The Part 2 Offences' *Criminal Law Review* 389.

Statutory conspiracy is governed by section 1 of the Criminal Law Act 1977:

> ## EXTRACT
>
> ### Section 1 of the Criminal Law Act 1977
>
> #### 1 The offence of conspiracy
>
> (1) Subject to the following provisions of this Part of this Act, if a person agrees with any other person or persons that a course of conduct shall be pursued which, if the agreement is carried out in accordance with their intentions, either—
>
>     (a) will necessarily amount to or involve the commission of any offence or offences by one or more of the parties to the agreement, or
>
>     (b) would do so but for the existence of facts which render the commission of the offence or any of the offences impossible,
>
> he is guilty of conspiracy to commit the offence or offences in question.

This tells us that the offence has three requirements:

1. An agreement …
2. … that a course of conduct shall be pursued which will necessarily amount to or involve the commission of an offence by one or more parties to the agreement
3. An intention that the crime will be carried out as planned.

In some circumstances (which are explained below) there will also be a fourth requirement:

4. Intention or knowledge of essential facts or circumstances.

Numbers 1 and 2 are *actus reus* requirements. Numbers 3 and 4 are *mens rea* requirements. We will work through them in turn.

## 1. An agreement ...

Agreement is the essence of a conspiracy. To establish an agreement it is not enough to show that one defendant encouraged the other to commit a crime himself. It must be shown that the defendants had decided to commit the unlawful plan as a joint collaborative project. In *R v Mehta* [2012] EWCA Crim 2824, for example, Toulson LJ stated, 'A conspiracy requires that the parties to it have a common unlawful purpose or design' ([36]).

For there to have been an agreement the defendants must have gone beyond the stage of negotiation. But once an agreement has been reached the crime of conspiracy is complete. In *R v Saik* [2006] UKHL 18 Lord Nicholls said: 'The offence therefore lies in making an agreement […] The offence is complete at that stage' ([3]). This means that there is no need to prove that the planned full offence was carried out. In fact, there is no need to prove that the defendants even began to put their plan into operation. So if Vito and Michael agree to commit a murder, but later change their minds, they are nonetheless guilty of conspiracy to murder.

The agreement may be a continuing one. Suppose Vito and Michael agree to commit a robbery in two weeks' time. A few days before the planned robbery they recruit Sonny. Sonny becomes a party to the agreement, and all three are guilty of conspiracy to rob.

There can also be an agreement even if some of the details of the planned offence still need to be worked out. So if Vito and Michael agree to rob a petrol station in two weeks' time, they are guilty of conspiracy to rob even if they haven't yet agreed which petrol station to rob or whether to commit the offence during the day or at night.

Note also that it is not necessary for all parties to the conspiracy to have communicated with one another. As long as all the defendants share the same common unlawful purpose it is not necessary for them all to have met, or have communicated with, each other.

---

**EXAMPLE**

- **Wheel conspiracies**: In a wheel conspiracy one central figure, D1, communicates with all of the other parties to the agreement. D2, D3, D4, D5 and D6 never actually communicate with one another.
- **Chain conspiracies**: In a chain conspiracy D1 communicates with D2, D2 communicates with D3, D3 communicates with D4 and so on.

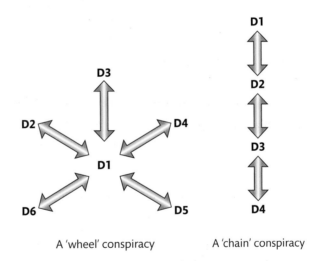

A 'wheel' conspiracy          A 'chain' conspiracy

**Figure 12.3.** Wheel and chain conspiracies

It is possible for there to be one general conspiracy, with related sub-conspiracies. An example is *R v Ali (Ahmed) & others* [2011] EWCA Crim 1260. This case involved a terrorist plot to blow up transatlantic flights using explosives in plastic drinks bottles. All seven men were convicted of conspiracy to murder. However, although four of the men (the four would-be suicide bombers) knew that the plan was to use explosive devices to kill people, it was uncertain whether they knew that the intended target was transatlantic flights. For this reason, only the other three men – Ali (the ringleader), Tanvir Hussain (Ali's right-hand man) and Sarwar (the explosives expert) – were convicted of the more serious charge of conspiracy to murder by detonating explosive devices on transatlantic aircraft. The Court of Appeal held that these were distinct conspiracies. There was one general agreement between the seven men to commit murder, and a separate sub-agreement between three of them as to the method and scale of the murder to be carried out.

So there can be wheel conspiracies, chain conspiracies and sub-conspiracies. Whatever type of conspiracy is involved, however, it is essential to show that the parties shared a common unlawful purpose. Without a shared common unlawful purpose there can be no conspiracy. This is illustrated by *R v Griffiths & others* [1966] 1 QB 589. Griffiths and his co-defendants were all farmers who used the same accountant, a man named Booth. Booth showed each of the farmers various ways of dishonestly obtaining subsidies from the Ministry of Agriculture. Each farmer then made fraudulent claims to the Ministry. At trial, the farmers were convicted of all being parties to one large conspiracy to defraud the Ministry of Agriculture. They appealed, arguing that they had not all been parties to one conspiracy.

## EXTRACT

Read the following extract from the judgment of Paull J. Were the farmers all parties to one conspiracy? Why/why not?

### *R v Griffiths & others* [1966] 1 QB 589

#### Paull J

The matter can be illustrated quite simply. I employ an accountant to make out my tax return. He and his clerk are both present when I am about to sign the return. I notice an item in my expenses of £100 and say: 'I don't remember incurring this expense.' The clerk says: 'Well, actually I put it in. You didn't incur it, but I didn't think you would object to a few pounds being saved.' The accountant indicates his agreement to this attitude. After some hesitation I agree to let it stand. On those bare facts I cannot be charged with 50 others in a conspiracy to defraud the Exchequer of £100,000 on the basis that this accountant and his clerk have persuaded 500 other clients to make false returns, some being false in one way, some in another, or even all in the same way. I have not knowingly attached myself to a general agreement to defraud.

*R v Griffiths & others* was applied in *R v Mehtab* [2015] EWCA Crim 1665. A group of people, including the ringleaders Ibrahim Mahter and Abdulgrani Makrani and a woman named Kubrah Saiyed, organised sham marriages to assist unlawful immigration into the UK. In 2011, the defendant, Syed Mehtab, married Saiyed. There was some evidence that the marriage was a sham. For example, they married within two months of meeting and the marriage certificate stated that they lived at different addresses. Crucially, Mehtab was charged with being a party to the wider conspiracy. His submission of no case to answer was rejected by the trial judge, and he was convicted. On appeal, the Court of Appeal held that the submission should have been accepted, and quashed the conviction. Whilst there was some evidence that Mehtab's marriage to Saiyed was a conspiracy to evade immigration laws, this was not the conspiracy with which he had been charged. He had been charged with being a party to the wider conspiracy led by Mahter and Makrani, but there was no evidence that Mehtab's marriage to Saiyed had been organised by Mahter and Makrani or even that Mehtab was aware of the wider conspiracy.

These decisions can be contrasted with *R v Bhatti & others* [2015] EWCA Crim 1305. The three defendants set up an organisation called Middlesex College, which offered various courses to overseas students. But in fact, the college provided no real education. Instead, it provided documents to non-EU foreign nationals that purported to show that they were studying at Middlesex College, in order to allow them to enter, or remain in, the UK as students. In other words, it offered bogus immigration status. A large number of people had used the service offered by the College. The defendants were convicted of conspiring to facilitate a breach of immigration law. They appealed, arguing that, as in *R v Griffiths & others*, the evidence did not reveal one single conspiracy, but rather a very large number of similar, but separate, conspiracies with individual students. The Court of Appeal rejected this argument, distinguishing *R v Griffiths & others*. Simon J explained that students who entered into an agreement with Middlesex College knew that others were doing the same thing in pursuance of the same criminal purpose. So, unlike Syed Mehtab and the farmers in *R v Griffiths & others*, the students had a shared purpose and knew that there was a wider scheme that went beyond the particular offence in which they were involved.

Lastly, there are some situations in which people might agree to commit a crime and yet not be guilty of conspiracy. These are set out in section 2(2) of the Criminal Law Act 1977:

---

### EXTRACT

## Section 2(2) of the Criminal Law Act 1977

### 2 Exemptions from liability for conspiracy.

[...]

(2)  A person shall not by virtue of section 1 above be guilty of conspiracy to commit any offence or offences if the only other person or persons with whom he agrees are (both initially and at all times during the currency of the agreement) persons of any one or more of the following descriptions, that is to say–

(a)  his spouse or civil partner;

(b)  a person under the age of criminal responsibility; and

(c)  an intended victim of that offence or of each of those offences.

---

### ACTIVITY

- Vito and Michael want Philip to be sent to prison, so they agree that Vito should break Michael's arm and then frame Philip. Are Vito and Michael guilty of conspiring to cause GBH with intent?

- Vito, Vito's wife Carmela and Vito's nine-year-old son Michael agree to beat up Philip. Are they guilty of conspiracy? Would your answer be any different if Michael is 11 years old?

The scope of section 2(2)(a) was considered in *R v Suski* [2016] EWCA Crim 24.[14] The defendant and his co-accused were unmarried, but they lived together and had children together. The defendant argued that section 2(2)(a) should be read down, to include couples in a relationship akin to a marriage. The Court of Appeal rejected this argument and applied the express terms of the statute. McCombe LJ commented, 'There are very good grounds why a court trying a charge of conspiracy should not have to inquire closely into the nature of personal relationships of alleged conspirators, infinitely variable as they are likely to be from case to case. Nor, in our judgment, should the criminal law turn upon such vagaries' ([23]).

### 2. ... that a course of conduct shall be pursued which will necessarily amount to or involve the commission of an offence by one or more parties to the agreement

The first *actus reus* requirement focused on whether or not there was an agreement. The second *actus reus* requirement focuses on the content of the agreement. For this require-ment to be satisfied, it must be shown that the defendants agreed on a course of conduct that necessarily involved at least one of them committing a crime.

A defendant may be charged with conspiracy to commit any of the offences we have studied in Chapters 5, 6, 7 and 8. A defendant may also be charged with conspiracy to commit an inchoate offence. This means the following charges are all theoretically possible:

- Conspiracy to commit one of the three encouraging or assisting offences we studied earlier in the chapter
- Conspiracy to conspire to commit an offence
- Conspiracy to attempt to commit an offence.

In practice, however, it is hard to imagine circumstances in which it would be appro-priate to charge a defendant with 'conspiring to conspire' or 'conspiring to attempt!' Very unusual facts would be needed!

Note also that there is no offence of conspiring to be an accessory to an offence.[15]

It is important to note that section 1(1)(a) states that the conspirators must be the ones who are going to commit the planned offence. Suppose that Vito and Michael agree that they will ask Sonny to murder Philip. On these facts, Vito and Michael are not guilty of conspiracy to murder. Their plan is for Sonny to commit the murder, and Sonny is not a party to the agreement. Instead, Vito and Michael would be guilty of conspiring to intentionally encourage Sonny to commit murder.

Section 1(1)(a) also uses the word 'necessarily'. It states that parties to an agreement are only guilty of conspiracy if their plan necessarily involves the commission of an offence. So what if the defendants' agreement was conditional, so that they will only commit the full offence if certain circumstances exist at the time? Can they argue that their agreement did not necessarily involve the commission of a crime? This was the issue in *R v Jackson* [1985] Crim LR 442. A man named Whitlock was on trial for bur-glary. Whitlock agreed with three of his friends – Jackson, Golding and Jackson – that if he was convicted they should shoot him in the leg. The idea was that the sentencing court

---

[14]See also *R v Bala* [2016] EWCA Crim 560, in which the Court of Appeal held that section 2(2)(a) does extend to a spouse under a polygamous marriage that is recognised as valid under English law.

[15]*R v Kenning* [2008] EWCA Crim 1534.

would show Whitlock some leniency if it believed he had been the victim of a shooting. Whitlock was subsequently convicted. His friends shot him. Whitlock was left permanently disabled and his friends were convicted at trial of conspiring to pervert the course of justice. On appeal against their convictions they argued that their plan had not necessarily involved the commission of a crime. Whitlock might have been acquitted of burglary, in which case they would not have shot him and attempted to pervert the course of justice. The Court of Appeal rejected their appeal. Purchas LJ stated:

> Planning was taking place for a contingency and if that contingency occurred the conspiracy would necessarily involve the commission of an offence. 'Necessarily' is not to be held to mean that there must inevitably be the carrying out of an offence. It means, if the agreement is carried out in accordance with the plan, there must be the commission of the offence referred to in the conspiracy count.

There are two final points to note about the content of the agreement. First, section 2(1) states:

---

**EXTRACT**

## Section 2(1) of the Criminal Law Act 1977

### 2 Exemptions from liability for conspiracy

(1)   A person shall not by virtue of section 1 above be guilty of conspiracy to commit any offence if he is an intended victim of that offence.

---

This is similar to section 51 of the Serious Crime Act 2007, which we looked at for encouraging or assisting crime. Suppose that a 14-year-old girl and her 26-year-old boyfriend (who knows her age) agree to have sexual intercourse. According to section 2(1) of the Criminal Law Act 1977, the girl is not guilty of conspiracy to commit sexual activity with a child.[16] She was the intended victim of the conspiracy, and section 2(1) states that someone cannot be guilty of conspiring to commit an offence if they themselves were the intended victim.

Second, defendants may be guilty of conspiracy even if the planned full offence is, unbeknown to them, factually impossible. This is stated in section 1(1)(b). So if Vito and Michael agree to murder Philip, but unbeknown to them Philip had in fact been killed in a road accident earlier in the day, they are nonetheless guilty of conspiracy to murder. The fact that their planned crime was factually impossible is no defence.

## 3. An intention that the crime will be carried out as planned

This *mens rea* requirement derives from the wording of section 1(1) of the Criminal Law Act 1977, which assumes that the conspirators must have intended that their agreement would be carried out. In spite of this, this *mens rea* requirement was thrown into doubt by the judgment of the House of Lords in *R v Anderson* [1986] AC 27.

The defendant, William Anderson, had been remanded in custody. So too had Ahmed Andaloussi. They spent one night in the same cell. Anderson told Andaloussi that he expected to be released on bail the next day. Andaloussi said that he was

---

[16]Sexual Offences Act 2003, s.9.

awaiting trial for serious drugs offences and that he wanted to try and escape from prison. The two men reached an agreement. Anderson would be paid £20,000. In return he would supply equipment, including diamond cutting wire, to Andaloussi's brother and friend who would smuggle the equipment into the prison and pass it on to Andaloussi.

The next day Anderson was released on bail as expected. He subsequently received a down payment of £2,000 before being injured in a road accident. The plan never got any further, but in evidence Anderson stated that he intended to supply the diamond wire once he received a further £10,000. He was then going to go and live in Spain and play no further part in Andaloussi's attempts to escape.

At trial Anderson was convicted. He appealed, claiming that he lacked the *mens rea* of conspiracy. He said that his sole interest was receiving the money for supplying the diamond wire. He did not want the plan to be put into action and in fact he was sure that the plan could not possibly succeed. The case reached the House of Lords.

## EXTRACT

According to the following extract from the judgment of Lord Bridge, can a defendant be guilty of conspiracy if he lacked any intention that the agreement be carried out?

What does Lord Bridge say is the only *mens rea* requirement for the offence of conspiracy?

### R v Anderson [1986] AC 27

### Lord Bridge

I am clearly driven by consideration of the diversity of roles which parties may agree to play in criminal conspiracies to reject any construction of the statutory language which would require the prosecution to prove an intention on the part of each conspirator that the criminal offence or offences which will necessarily be committed by one or more of the conspirators if the agreed course of conduct is fully carried out should in fact be committed. A simple example will illustrate the absurdity to which this construction would lead. The proprietor of a car hire firm agrees for a substantial payment to make available a hire car to a gang for use in a robbery and to make false entries in his books relating to the hiring to which he can point if the number of the car is traced back to him in connection with the robbery. Being fully aware of the circumstances of the robbery in which the car is proposed to be used he is plainly a party to the conspiracy to rob. Making his car available for use in the robbery is as much a part of the relevant agreed course of conduct as the robbery itself. Yet, once he has been paid, it will be a matter of complete indifference to him whether the robbery is in fact committed or not. In these days of highly organised crime the most serious statutory conspiracies will frequently involve an elaborate and complex agreed course of conduct in which many will consent to play necessary but subordinate roles, not involving them in any direct participation in the commission of the offence or offences at the centre of the conspiracy. Parliament cannot have intended that such parties should escape conviction of conspiracy on the basis that it cannot be proved against them that they intended that the relevant offence or offences should be committed.

There remains the important question whether a person who has agreed that a course of conduct will be pursued which, if pursued as agreed, will necessarily amount to or involve the commission of an offence is guilty of statutory conspiracy irrespective of his intention, and, if not, what is the *mens rea* of the offence. I have no hesitation in answering the first part of the question in the negative. There may be many situations in which perfectly respectable citizens, more particularly those concerned with law enforcement, may enter into agreements that a course of conduct shall be pursued which will involve commission of a crime without the least intention of playing any part in furtherance of the ostensibly agreed criminal objective, but rather with the purpose of exposing and frustrating the criminal purpose of the other parties to the agreement. To say this is in no way to encourage schemes by which police act, directly or through the agency of informers, as agents provocateurs for the purpose of entrapment. That is conduct of which the courts have always strongly disapproved. But it may sometimes happen, as most of us with experience in criminal trials well know, that a criminal enterprise is well advanced in the course of preparation when it comes to the notice either of the police or of some honest citizen in such circumstances that the only prospect of exposing and frustrating the criminals is that some innocent person should play the part of an intending collaborator in the course of criminal conduct proposed to be pursued. The *mens rea* implicit in the offence of statutory conspiracy must clearly be such as to recognise the innocence of such a person, notwithstanding that he will, in literal terms, be obliged to agree that a course of conduct be pursued involving the commission of an offence.

I have said already, but I repeat to emphasise its importance, that an essential ingredient in the crime of conspiring to commit a specific offence or offences under section 1(1) of the Act of 1977 is that the accused should agree that a course of conduct be pursued which he knows must involve the commission by one or more of the parties to the agreement of that offence or those offences. But, beyond the mere fact of agreement, the necessary *mens rea* of the crime is, in my opinion, established if, and only if, it is shown that the accused, when he entered into the agreement, intended to play some part in the agreed course of conduct in furtherance of the criminal purpose which the agreed course of conduct was intended to achieve. Nothing less will suffice; nothing more is required.

Applying this test to the facts which, for the purposes of the appeal, we must assume, the appellant, in agreeing that a course of conduct be pursued that would, if successful, necessarily involve the offence of effecting Andaloussi's escape from lawful custody, clearly intended, by providing diamond wire to be smuggled into the prison, to play a part in the agreed course of conduct in furtherance of that criminal objective. Neither the fact that he intended to play no further part in attempting to effect the escape, nor that he believed the escape to be impossible, would, if the jury had supposed they might be true, have afforded him any defence.

Lord Bridge's answers to each of these two questions were both novel and controversial. We shall examine each in turn.

### i. Can a defendant be guilty of conspiracy if he lacked any intention that the agreement be carried out?

Lord Bridge stated that it was not necessary to prove that Anderson intended that the agreement would be carried out. But if this is taken to its logical conclusion, the result is that there can be a conspiracy even if none of the conspirators intends to carry out the agreement! The point has been made forcefully by David Ormerod:

> If no intention needs to be proved on the part of conspirator A, then none needs to be proved on the part of another, B. But if A and B are the only parties, and neither has

the intention that it should be carried out, how can there be a crime of conspiracy? A conspiracy which no one intends to carry out is an absurdity, if not an impossibility.[17]

As the extract from Lord Bridge's judgment showed (in particular the hire car example), he was concerned that defendants like Anderson might escape liability for the crime of conspiracy if the prosecution is required to show that each conspirator had an intention that the agreement would be carried out. However, there was a more satisfactory way of addressing this policy concern. Anderson's conviction could have been upheld on the basis that he was an accessory to the conspiracy to help Andaloussi escape. Anderson unquestionably had the *mens rea* of accessorial liability, and as we shall see in the next chapter an accessory can be tried, indicted and punished as a principal offender.

In the years since the House of Lords' judgment the Court of Appeal has not followed *R v Anderson* on this issue. An example is *R v McPhillips* [1990] 6 BNIL.[18] In this case the police stopped a car at about 11 pm. A man named Drumm was driving and the defendant, McPhillips, was in the passenger seat. Behind the driver's seat was a bomb. McPhillips admitted that they had agreed to place the bomb on the roof of a nearby hotel where there was a disco taking place, but he claimed that he had intended to give a telephone warning to the police so that the hotel could be evacuated before the bomb exploded. This was accepted as being true by the trial judge. The Court of Appeal of Northern Ireland therefore held that McPhillips could not be convicted of conspiracy to murder since he lacked any intention that the crime of murder be carried out. Lord Lowry CJ explained:

> [T]he accused must agree with another that murder will be committed and must intend that this will happen. The guilty act is the agreement that the crime contemplated will be committed; the guilty mind is the intention that that crime will be committed [... T]he agreed course of conduct was the planting of a 'no warning' bomb at the Seagoe Hotel and persons who had agreed to that course of conduct intending it to be carried out would be guilty of conspiracy to murder because, if the agreement had been carried out in accordance with their intentions it would (unless all the patrons of the disco had gone home or had a miraculous escape) necessarily involve the commission of murder. But, on the facts found here, this result would not have been in accordance with the intention of [McPhillips]. Therefore he was not guilty of conspiracy to murder.

(McPhillips was, however, convicted of conspiracy to cause an explosion and other explosives offences.)

**ACTIVITY**

If a case like *R v McPhillips* happened today, could the defendant be convicted of one of the offences under the Serious Crime Act 2007 that we studied earlier in the chapter?

Another example of the Court of Appeal not following *R v Anderson* on this issue is *R v Goddard & another* [2012] EWCA Crim 1756. The defendants, Daniel Goddard and Robin Fallick, were charged with conspiring to rape a child under 13. They exchanged text messages after meeting on a gay chat line (they had never met each other in person). The

---

[17]Ormerod, D. and Laird, K. (2015) *Smith and Hogan's Criminal Law* (14th edn) Oxford: OUP, p503.
[18]Another example is *R v Edwards* [1991] Crim LR 45.

prosecution case focused on the following series of text messages which Fallick sent to Goddard (the messages which Goddard sent to Fallick were not available):

09:35 I need some help rapin a 6yo

09:37 Next friday night

09:39 Its rob in slough

09:41 tis ok. So your in?

10:46 He's about 4ft dark hair and eyes, slim, toned stomach tight round ass and perfect legs. Really soft smooth skin and ruby red lips.

11:02 He'll be with me, he's 6

11:09 Next friday. Yes we can do stuff but we need to make sure he doesn't drop us in it. i'm best friends with his mum, drug him is a poss?

At trial the two men were convicted. They appealed, arguing that the text message conversation was nothing more than a fantasy from which they both gained sexual pleasure and that they never had any intention of carrying out the plan. Quashing their convictions, the Court of Appeal concluded that there was insufficient evidence for any reasonable jury to be able to conclude beyond reasonable doubt that the two men had intended to carry out the agreement. Aikens LJ explained:

40 We have concluded that no reasonable jury, taking the prosecution evidence at its highest, could surely infer that the defendants intended to carry out the agreement. The evidence is all equivocal; it is as consistent with fantasy as with an intent to carry out the plan. It is particularly striking that these men never met at any stage, either before or after the text exchange nor did they even suggest meeting to discuss the plan further. Nor is there any evidence that they took any steps to advance the plan beyond suggesting "Friday night". No place or time or other practical details are identified. Nothing at all happened after the exchange of text messages. We appreciate that their silence in interviews and failure to mention that this was all a fantasy can be taken into account. But that is of very little weight given the other facts or rather lack of them.

So in spite of Lord Bridge's judgment in *R v Anderson*, it is now safe to say that a defendant can only be guilty of conspiracy if he had an intention that the agreement be carried out.[19]

### ii. Must the defendant have intended to play some part in the agreed course of conduct?

According to Lord Bridge in *R v Anderson*, what must be shown to establish the *mens rea* of conspiracy is an intention to play some part in the agreed course of conduct. This was a radical suggestion which was strongly criticised by commentators. Suppose that Vito tells Michael and Sonny to go and murder Philip. Applying Lord Bridge's approach it would seem that Michael and Sonny are guilty of conspiracy to murder (since they intend to play an active part in the plan), but Vito is not (since he was not going to play any active part). This would be very difficult to justify. Not only is it at odds with the focus of the offence of conspiracy on the fact of an agreement. It would also 'place the godfathers of criminal conspiracies even further beyond the reach of the criminal justice system'.[20] The Court of Appeal revisited this issue in *R v Siracusa & others* (1989) 90 Cr App R 340. This case involved a conspiracy to smuggle massive amounts of heroin (with a street value of more than £15m) from Kashmir to Canada via England, hidden in secret

---

[19] This conclusion is reinforced still further by Lord Nicholls' statement in *R v Saik* [2006] UKHL 18 that 'The conspirators must intend to do the act prohibited by the substantive offence' ([4]).

[20] Fitzpatrick, D. (1993) 'Variations on Conspiracy' 143 *New Law Journal* 1180.

compartments in furniture. At trial the four defendants were all convicted of conspiracy to import heroin. They appealed against their convictions. In its judgment the Court of Appeal discussed Lord Bridge's judgment in *R v Anderson*.

## EXTRACT

According to the following extract from the judgment of O'Connor LJ, what is required to establish 'an intention to play some part in the agreed course of conduct'?

Applying O'Connor LJ's approach to our example of Vito telling Michael and Sonny to go and murder Philip, does Vito have 'an intention to play some part in the agreed course of conduct'?

### R v Siracusa & others (1989) 90 Cr App R 340

#### O'Connor LJ

We think it obvious that Lord Bridge cannot have been intending that the organiser of a crime who recruited others to carry it out would not himself be guilty of conspiracy unless it could be proved that he intended to play some active part himself thereafter. Lord Bridge had pointed out [...] that

> "in these days of highly organised crime the most serious statutory conspiracies will frequently involve an elaborate and complex agreed course of conduct in which many will consent to play necessary but subordinate roles, not involving them in any direct participation in the commission of the offence or offences at the centre of the conspiracy."

[...] Participation in a conspiracy is infinitely variable: it can be active or passive. If the majority shareholder and director of a company consents to the company being used for drug smuggling carried out in the company's name by a fellow director and minority shareholder, he is guilty of conspiracy. Consent, that is the agreement or adherence to the agreement, can be inferred if it is proved that he knew what was going on and the intention to participate in the furtherance of the criminal purpose is also established by his failure to stop the unlawful activity. Lord Bridge's *dictum* does not require anything more.

O'Connor LJ's reasoning pays only lip service to Lord Bridge's judgment in *R v Anderson*. Failing to stop an unlawful activity is hardly the same as playing an active part! But Lord Bridge's approach is so problematic that it is likely that *R v Siracusa* will be followed on this issue.

So we have effectively come full circle! We have looked at two key questions: (i) Can a defendant be guilty of conspiracy if he lacked any intention that the agreement be carried out? and (ii) Must the defendant have intended to play some part in the agreed course of conduct? We have seen that the House of Lords in *R v Anderson* answered 'Yes' to both questions, but subsequent case law has undermined the precedential status of this case such that today the answer to both questions seems to be 'No'!

There is one final point to note. A person can only be convicted of conspiracy if at least one of the other parties to the agreement also had the *mens rea* of conspiracy.[21] Suppose that Vito and Michael agree that Michael should have sexual intercourse with Sandra. Vito knows that Sandra is only 15 years old, but Michael reasonably believes that she is 16. Michael lacks the *mens rea* of conspiracy to commit sexual activity with a child. This means that Vito cannot be guilty of conspiracy to commit this offence since he had not formed an agreement with another person who had the necessary *mens rea*.

---

[21]Criminal Law Act 1977, s.1(2).

### 4. Intention or knowledge of essential facts or circumstances

Section 1(2) specifies an additional *mens rea* requirement. However, this only applies if the following two conditions are satisfied:

1. The full offence which the defendants planned to commit has a circumstance element as part of its *actus reus*

2. The definition of the full offence specifies a *mens rea* requirement for this circumstance element which is less than knowledge or intention.

An example of when section 1(2) applies is conspiracy to commit rape. The definition of rape has a circumstance element as part of its *actus reus* (the victim was not consenting) and the definition of rape specifies a *mens rea* requirement for this circumstance element which is less than knowledge or intention (lack of a reasonable belief in consent).

> **EXTRACT**
>
> ## Section 1(2) of the Criminal Law Act 1977
>
> (2)   Where liability for any offence may be incurred without knowledge on the part of the person committing it of any particular fact or circumstance necessary for the commission of the offence, a person shall nevertheless not be guilty of conspiracy to commit that offence by virtue of subsection (1) above unless he and at least one other party to the agreement intend or know that that fact or circumstance shall or will exist at the time when the conduct constituting the offence is to take place.

In other words, a defendant can only be convicted of conspiracy if he had intention or knowledge in relation to each circumstance element of the *actus reus* of the full offence he planned to commit.[22] So on a charge of conspiracy to rape, the defendant can only be convicted if he intended that the victim would not consent or knew that the victim would not consent. Lack of a reasonable belief that the victim would consent might suffice for the offence of rape, but not for the offence of conspiracy to rape.[23]

 ## Attempts

The law of criminal attempts is governed by section 1(1) of the Criminal Attempts Act 1981:

> **EXTRACT**
>
> ## Section 1(1) of the Criminal Attempts Act 1981
>
> ### 1 Attempting to commit an offence.
>
> (1)   If, with intent to commit an offence to which this section applies, a person does an act which is more than merely preparatory to the commission of the offence, he is guilty of attempting to commit the offence.

---

[22] This interpretation of section 1(2) was confirmed by the House of Lords in *R v Saik* [2006] UKHL 18. In this case the defendant was charged with conspiracy to launder money. He admitted that he suspected the money represented the proceeds of crime. However, the House of Lords held that suspicion as to this circumstance element of the full offence was insufficient. It had to be shown that he knew the money was the proceeds of crime.

[23] In its 2009 report *Conspiracy and Attempts* (Report No 318) HC 41, the Law Commission proposed simplifying and relaxing the requirements contained in section 1(2). See further part 2 of its report.

This tells us that the offence has two requirements:

1.  The defendant did an act that was more than mere preparation for the commission of the full offence

2.  The defendant intended to commit the full offence.

Number 1 is an *actus reus* requirement. Number 2 is a *mens rea* requirement. We will work through them in turn.

## 1. The defendant did an act that was more than mere preparation for the commission of the full offence

Our examination of this *actus reus* requirement is broken down into three parts. First we examine the 'more than merely preparatory' test, before briefly looking at which offences it is a crime to attempt and impossible attempts.

### i. The 'more than merely preparatory' test

Section 1(1) of the Criminal Attempts Act 1981 states that a defendant only satisfies the *actus reus* of an attempt if he has gone beyond mere preparation. As the timeline in Figure 12.4 illustrates, this means that there is an all-important distinction to be drawn between 'mere preparation' and 'more than mere preparation'.

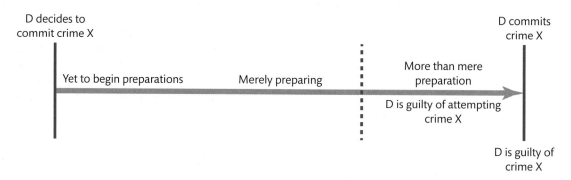

**Figure 12.4.** Criminal attempts: a timeline

Whether a defendant has gone beyond mere preparation in a particular case is a question of fact for the jury to decide. However, the trial judge may only leave this issue to the jury if there is sufficient evidence for a reasonable jury to be able to convict. If there is no evidence that the defendant has gone beyond mere preparation he must be found not guilty.

We are going to look at five cases in which the Court of Appeal has had to decide whether there was any evidence that the defendant had gone beyond mere preparation.[24] Examining these cases will help you: (1) understand the distinction between mere preparation (= no liability for a criminal attempt) and more than mere preparation (= liable for a criminal attempt); and (2) evaluate whether the criminal law has drawn this dividing line appropriately. First, though, consider the following scenario.

---

[24]Other cases include: *R v Bowles and Bowles* [2004] EWCA Crim 1608; *Mason v DPP* [2009] EWHC 2198 (Admin); and *R v K* [2009] EWCA Crim 1931.

## ACTIVITY

Vito has decided to kill Philip. At which of the following six stages do you believe the criminal law should impose liability for attempted murder? Why?

a.  The day before the planned killing, Vito goes out and buys a gun on the black market.

b.  Before leaving his house to go and kill Philip, Vito puts some bullets in his pocket and tucks his gun in his belt.

c.  Vito follows Philip home from the pub.

d.  While Philip (who is in a drunken stupor) fumbles around trying to find his front door key, Vito loads his gun.

e.  Philip finally finds his front door key, and puts it in the lock. Vito crooks his finger round the trigger of the gun and takes aim.

f.  Vito fires the gun, but misses.

Remember your answer to this question: you will shortly be able to use this to decide whether the law is as you believe it should be.

The first case for us to examine to see how the courts have applied the distinction between mere preparation and more than mere preparation is *R v Gullefer* [1990] 1 WLR 1063. Ian Gullefer was at a Greyhound race meeting in Romford. It was the last race of the night. The dog that Gullefer had bet on was losing, so he climbed over the fence onto the track and waved his arms at the dogs. He thought that if he could distract them the stewards would declare the race void and the bookmakers would have to refund his stake. In the event, the dogs were not distracted and the race was not declared void. At trial Gullefer was convicted of attempted theft. He appealed to the Court of Appeal, arguing that his actions had not gone beyond mere preparation.

## EXTRACT

In the following extract from Lord Lane CJ's judgment he explains that before the 1981 Act there were two different sets of cases which applied different tests for the *actus reus* of an attempt. What tests did these lines of authority use? How is the 'more than merely preparatory test' different to these other two tests? How did Lord Lane CJ paraphrase the 'more than merely preparatory' test?

According to the Court of Appeal, had Gullefer gone beyond mere preparation?

### R v Gullefer [1990] 1 WLR 1063

### Lord Lane CJ

Was the appellant still in the stage of preparation to commit the substantive offence, or was there a basis of fact which would entitle the jury to say that he had embarked on the theft itself? Might it properly be said that when he jumped on to the track he was trying to steal £18 from the bookmaker?

Our view is that it could not properly be said that at that stage he was in the process of committing theft. What he was doing was jumping on to the track in an effort to distract the dogs, which in its turn, he hoped, would have the effect of forcing the stewards to declare "no race," which would in its turn give him the opportunity to go back to the bookmaker and demand the £18 he had staked. In our view there was insufficient evidence for it to be said that he had, when he jumped on to the track, gone beyond mere preparation

[...]

Since the passing of the Act of 1981, a division of this court in *Reg. v. Ilyas* (1983) 78 Cr.App.R. 17, has helpfully collated the authorities [which preceded the Act]. As appears from the judgment in that case, there seem to have been two lines of authority. The first was exemplified by the decision in *Reg. v. Eagleton* (1854) 5 Dears C.C. 515. That was a case where the defendant was alleged to have attempted to obtain money from the guardians of a parish by falsely pretending to the relieving officer that he had delivered loaves of bread of the proper weight to the outdoor poor, when in fact the loaves were deficient in weight.

Park B., delivering the judgment of the court of nine judges, said, at p. 538:

> "Acts remotely leading towards the commission of the offence are not to be considered as attempts to commit it, but acts immediately connected with it are; and if, in this case, after the credit with the relieving officer for the fraudulent overcharge, any *further step* on the part of the defendant had been necessary to obtain payment, as the making out a further account or producing the vouchers to the Board, we should have thought that the obtaining credit in account with the relieving officer would not have been sufficiently proximate to the obtaining the money. But, on the statement in this case, no other act on the part of the defendant would have been required. It was the last act, *depending on himself*, towards the payment of the money, and therefore it ought to be considered as an attempt."

Lord Diplock in *Director of Public Prosecutions v. Stonehouse* [1978] A.C. 55, 68, having cited part of that passage from *Reg. v. Eagleton*, added: "In other words the offender must have crossed the Rubicon and burnt his boats."

The other line of authority is based on a passage in *Stephen's Digest of the Criminal Law*, 5th ed. (1894), art. 50: "An attempt to commit a crime is an act done with intent to commit that crime, and forming part of a series of acts which would constitute its actual commission if it were not interrupted." As Lord Edmund-Davies points out in *Director of Public Prosecution v. Stonehouse*, at p. 85, that definition has been repeatedly cited with judicial approval: see Byrne J. in *Hope v. Brown* [1954] 1 W.L.R. 250, 253 and Lord Parker C.J. in *Davey v. Lee* [1968] 1 Q.B. 366. However, as Lord Parker C.J. in the latter case points out, at p. 370G, *Stephen's* definition falls short of defining the exact point of time at which the series of acts can be said to begin.

It seems to us that the words of the Act of 1981 seek to steer a midway course. They do not provide, as they might have done, that the *Reg. v. Eagleton* test is to be followed, or that, as Lord Diplock suggested, the defendant must have reached a point from which it was impossible for him to retreat before the actus reus of an attempt is proved. On the other hand the words give perhaps as clear a guidance as is possible in the circumstances on the point of time at which *Stephen's* "series of acts" begin. It begins when the merely preparatory acts come to an end and the defendant embarks upon the crime proper. When that is will depend of course upon the facts in any particular case.

The judgment of Lord Lane CJ in *R v Gullefer* was followed by the Court of Appeal in *R v Jones (Kenneth)* [1990] 1 WLR 1057. Kenneth Jones had been having an affair with a woman named Lynn Gresley. She began a relationship with another man, Michael Foreman, and two months later broke off her relationship with Jones. As a result, Jones decided to kill Foreman. On the day of the offence Foreman took his daughter to school as normal. After she had got out of the car Jones jumped into the rear seat. He introduced himself and said he wanted to sort things out. Foreman drove off, and subsequently pulled over on a grass verge. Jones then handed Foreman a letter he had received from Lynn. While Foreman was reading it Jones pulled a sawn-off shotgun out of the bag he was carrying. It was loaded. He pointed it at Foreman and said, 'You're not going to like this'. Foreman quickly grabbed the end of the gun and pointed it sideways. A struggle ensued, and Foreman managed to escape.

At trial Jones was convicted of attempted murder. He appealed to the Court of Appeal. He argued that a defendant has only gone beyond mere preparation if he has performed the 'last act' within his power towards commission of the full offence. Since he still had to perform at least three more acts before he could have committed murder (remove the safety catch, put his finger on the trigger and pull the trigger) he claimed that he had not performed the last act and so had not gone beyond mere preparation.

## EXTRACT

Read the following extract from the judgment of Taylor LJ. Did the Court of Appeal accept Jones' arguments? Why/why not?

### *R v Jones (Kenneth)* [1990] 1 WLR 1057

#### Taylor CJ

The words "an act which is more than merely preparatory to the commission of the offence" would be inapt if they were intended to mean "the last act which lay in his power towards the commission of the offence."

Looking at the plain natural meaning of section 1(1) in the way indicated by the Lord Chief Justice [in *R v Gullefer*], the question for the judge in the present case was whether there was evidence from which a reasonable jury, properly directed, could conclude that the appellant had done acts which were more than merely preparatory. Clearly his actions in obtaining the gun, in shortening it, in loading it, in putting on his disguise, and in going to the school could only be regarded as preparatory acts. But, in our judgment, once he had got into the car, taken out the loaded gun and pointed it at the victim with the intention of killing him, there was sufficient evidence for the consideration of the jury on the charge of attempted murder. It was a matter for them to decide whether they were sure those acts were more than merely preparatory. In our judgment, therefore, the judge was right to allow the case to go to the jury, and the appeal against conviction must be dismissed.

Next are three cases which have generated controversy. The first is *R v Geddes* [1996] Crim LR 894. The defendant, Gary Geddes, was found in the boys' toilets in a school in Brighton. He had no right to be there, and had with him a large knife, some rope and a roll of masking tape. The prosecution alleged that Geddes had intended to kidnap a pupil. At trial, he was convicted of attempted false imprisonment. He appealed, arguing that his conviction should be quashed on the basis that he had not gone beyond mere preparation. His case reached the Court of Appeal.

## EXTRACT

Read the following extract from the judgment of Lord Bingham CJ. How did he paraphrase the 'more than merely preparatory' test?

According to the Court of Appeal, had Geddes gone beyond mere preparation? Why/why not? What is your reaction to the outcome of this case?

### R v Geddes [1996] Crim LR 894

### Lord Bingham CJ

This appeal is concerned not with the correctness of the jury's decision of fact, but the correctness of the judge's ruling of law. Was the evidence summarised in the admissions sufficient in law to support a finding that the appellant did an act which was more than merely preparatory to the commission of the offence charged? The cases show that the line of demarcation between acts which are merely preparatory and acts which may amount to an attempt is not always clear or easy to recognise. There is no rule of thumb test. There must always be an exercise of judgment based on the particular facts of the case. It is, we think, an accurate paraphrase of the statutory test and not an illegitimate gloss upon it to ask whether the available evidence, if accepted, could show that a defendant has done an act which shows that he has actually tried to commit the offence in question, or whether he has only got ready or put himself in a position or equipped himself to do so.

In the present case, as already indicated, there is not much room for doubt about the appellant's intention. Furthermore, the evidence is clearly capable of showing that he made preparations, that he equipped himself, that he got ready, that he put himself in a position to commit the offence charged [...] But was the evidence sufficient in law to support a finding that the appellant had actually tried or attempted to commit the offence of imprisoning someone? Had he moved from the realm of intention, preparation and planning into the area of execution or implementation? [...] Here it is true that the appellant had entered the school; but he had never had any contact or communication with any pupil; he had never confronted any pupil at the school in any way. That may well be no credit to him, and may indeed reflect great credit on the vigilance of the school staff. The whole story is one which fills the court with the gravest unease. Nonetheless, we cannot escape giving an answer to the fundamental legal question [...] So, for this purpose, must the contents of the rucksack, which give a clear indication as to what the appellant may have had in mind, but do not throw light on whether he had begun to carry out the commission of the offence. On the facts of this case we feel bound to conclude that the evidence was not sufficient in law to support a finding that the appellant did an act which was more than merely preparatory to wrongfully imprisoning a person unknown. In those circumstances we conclude that the appeal must be allowed and the conviction quashed.

The next case is *R v Campbell* (1990) 93 Cr App R 350. The police had received a tip-off that a post office in London was going to be robbed. After keeping watch of the post office for several days they saw the defendant, Tony Campbell, arrive on a motorbike. He was dressed in a motorcycle suit, crash helmet and gloves, and hung around in front of the post office for a while. Then he walked off. Half an hour later he reappeared. He walked towards the post office and, when he was a yard from the front door, the police stopped and searched him. He was found to be in possession of an imitation firearm, sunglasses and a threatening note. Campbell admitted that he had originally intended to rob the post office but claimed that by the time he was arrested he had changed his mind. He said he had decided that the dangers of committing the robbery were too great and simply not worth it.

At trial Campbell was convicted of attempted robbery. He appealed, arguing that he had not gone beyond mere preparation. The case reached the Court of Appeal.

## EXTRACT

According to the following extract from the judgment of Watkins LJ, had Campbell gone beyond mere preparation? Why/why not? What is your reaction to the outcome of this case?

### *R v Campbell* (1990) 93 Cr App R 350

#### Watkins LJ

Looking at the circumstances here it was beyond dispute that the appellant, at the material time, was carrying an imitation firearm which he made no attempt to remove from his clothing. He was not, as he had done previously that day, wearing, as a form of disguise, sunglasses. It was not suggested that he had, in the course of making his way down the road past the post-box, turned and, so to speak, moved towards the door of the post office so as to indicate that he intended to enter that place.

In order to effect the robbery it is equally beyond dispute it would have been quite impossible unless obviously he had entered the post office, gone to the counter and made some kind of hostile act – directed, of course, at whoever was behind the counter and in a position to hand him money. A number of acts remained undone and the series of acts which he had already performed – namely, making his way from his home or other place where he commenced to ride his motor cycle on a journey to a place near a post office, dismounting from the cycle and walking towards the post office door – were clearly acts which were, in the judgment of this court, indicative of mere preparation, even if he was still of a mind to rob the post office, of the commission that is of the offence of robbery. If a person, in circumstances such as this, has not even gained the place where he could be in a position to carry out the offence, it is extremely unlikely that it could ever be said that he had performed an act which could be properly said to be an attempt.

The outcome in *R v Campbell* may be contrasted with *R v Tosti & White* [1997] Crim LR 746. The defendants were seen walking to the door of a barn and examining the padlock. They realised they were being watched and ran off. Some oxygen-cutting equipment was found hidden nearby. The defendants were convicted of attempted burglary. They appealed, arguing that they had not gone beyond mere preparation. Their convictions were upheld by the Court of Appeal. Beldam LJ explained:

> [The defendants] had committed acts which were preparatory, but not merely so – so that it could be said the acts of preparation amounted to acts done in the commission of the offence.

On the face of it the conduct of Tosti and White seems very similar to Campbell's. Like Campbell, they were loitering outside a building that they planned to steal from. Yet Campbell's conviction for attempted robbery was quashed whilst Tosti's and White's were upheld. The key to reconciling the two cases is the different offences the men were charged with. Campbell was charged with attempted robbery. As we saw in Chapter 8, the essence of robbery is theft with violence. He had not embarked on this offence because he was never in a position where he could carry it out. By contrast, Tosti and White were charged with attempted burglary. The essence of burglary is entry as a trespasser with intent to steal. By examining the padlock on the barn door Tosti and White had embarked on gaining entry and so had begun to carry out the burglary. So it is possible to reconcile the two cases. However, the distinction between them is a fine one. In fact, Simester and Sullivan suggest that it 'may be considered so faint as to be invisible'.[25]

## ACTIVITY

Look back over the five cases we have studied on the 'more than merely preparatory' test and list the key principles expounded by the Court of Appeal.

Think back to our earlier example involving Vito and Philip. Applying the principles set out by the Court of Appeal, at which of the following six stages does Vito go beyond mere preparation and commit a criminal attempt?

a.  The day before the planned killing, Vito goes out and buys a gun on the black market.

b.  Before leaving his house to go and kill Philip, Vito puts some bullets in his pocket and tucks his gun in his belt.

c.  Vito follows Philip home from the pub.

d.  While Philip (who is in a drunken stupor) fumbles around trying to find his front door key, Vito loads his gun.

e.  Philip finally finds his front door key, and puts it in the lock. Vito crooks his finger round the trigger of the gun and takes aim.

f.  Vito fires the gun, but misses.

How does your answer compare to your earlier answer (at which stage should Vito be liable for attempted murder)?

A number of commentators have criticised the outcome in *R v Geddes* and *R v Campbell*. The following extract is taken from Christopher Clarkson's article 'Attempt: The Conduct Requirement'. Although he regards the outcomes of these cases as 'highly unsatisfactory', Clarkson argues that the 'more than merely preparatory' should be retained, not replaced. What is needed, he says, is a reformulation of the test backed up with a set of illustrative examples.

---

[25]Simester, A.P., Spencer, J.R., Stark, F., Sullivan, G.R. and Virgo, G. J. (2016) *Simester and Sullivan's Criminal Law: Theory and Doctrine* (6th edn) Oxford: Hart Publishing, p343.

## EXTRACT

What problems does Clarkson identify with the existing law of attempts?

Clarkson explains that the law of attempts must balance two sets of competing principles and policy concerns. What are the principles and policy concerns which support a narrow law of attempts? What are the principles and policy concerns which support a broader law of attempts?

In your own words, explain Clarkson's proposal. What reasons does he give for this proposal?

## Clarkson, C. (2009) 'Attempt: The Conduct Requirement' 29 *Oxford Journal of Legal Studies* 25

The leading decision on what constitutes acts which are 'more than merely preparatory' is *Gullefer* where it was ruled that the defendant had to have 'embarked on the crime proper'. An examination of many of the subsequent decisions suggests that the courts (in most cases) have tended to the view that there can only be an attempt where there has been a 'confrontation' with the victim (in cases of attempted rape, injury/death, kidnapping, false imprisonment, etc.) or with the property (in cases of attempted burglary, criminal damage, etc.). One can hardly have embarked on the crime proper without at least confronting the victim or property. For example, the defendant in *Jones*, intending to kill, had jumped into his victim's car armed with a loaded gun; he had confronted the victim when he got in the car and was liable for attempted murder. Similarly, in the attempted rape cases of *Attorney-General's Reference (No 1 of 1992)*, *Dagnall* and *Patnaik* the defendants were liable; in each of these cases there had been a confrontation with the person the defendant was planning to rape. The same approach has been adopted in a series of attempted burglary cases where the 'crime proper' involves an entry. In *Boyle and Boyle*, the defendants were liable for attempted burglary when they had broken down a door in their effort to gain entry to a building. Similarly, the defendant in *Tosti*, in examining the padlock with a view to gaining entry, had 'confronted' the building and embarked on the process of entry. Again, in *Toothill* the defendant who knocked at the proposed victim's door was liable for attempted burglary.

On the other hand, in cases where there has been no confrontation the defendants have tended to escape liability. In *Geddes*, the defendant trespassed on to school premises and was waiting in a boy's lavatory equipped with a knife, rope and masking tape with a view to capturing and restraining a boy when one entered the lavatory. It was held that he could not be liable for attempted false imprisonment as he had not 'actually tried' to commit the offence. The defendant could not have embarked on the crime of false imprisonment without at least confronting a boy. In *Campbell*, the defendant, wearing a partial disguise and carrying an imitation gun and threatening note, was arrested one yard from the door of a post office which he planned to rob. It was held that he had not progressed sufficiently far to be liable for attempted robbery. Robbery involves theft with force or threatened force. Without confronting the cashier he could not be said to have embarked on the crime proper. The defendant in *Gullefer*, who had disrupted a dog race in an effort to have the race declared void so that his stake would be refunded, had not confronted the bookmaker from whom it was alleged he had attempted to steal and so was not liable.

This approach, while it might explain most of the decisions, is nevertheless highly unsatisfactory in that too many offenders (such as those in *Geddes* and *Campbell*) who are on the point of committing the crime have escaped liability. The strictness of this approach is underlined when one recalls that in these cases the Court of Appeal has ruled that the actions of the defendants *could not* be 'sufficient in law' to amount to an attempt. Even if it had been ruled that these actions could amount to an attempt, there would still be a second hurdle to be overcome in that the jury would then have to consider 'as a question of fact' whether the acts were sufficient for an attempt.

[...]

There are several commonly stated rationales of the law of attempt. These are sometimes categorized as being either objectivist or subjectivist theories. Under an objectivist perspective, the defendant by intending to commit the crime and by committing acts closely connected with the crime has crossed a moral threshold ('crossed the Rubicon') and is displaying a degree of moral culpability similar to that involved in the commission of the full offence. Further, the actions involved in an attempt display 'vivid danger' and a 'clear threat of harm'. There is a manifest threat to the security interests of others. The victim in *Jones* was threatened or unnerved by the defendant's actions. This infringement of his security rights is a 'second-order harm'. These rationales suggest the defendant must come close to committing the crime. It was not until the defendant in *Jones* entered the car brandishing a loaded gun that his actions constituted this 'vivid danger' and that he had crossed a threshold making him sufficiently morally culpable for such a serious offence.

On the other hand, under a 'subjectivist' rationale the main emphasis is on the mental element of the defendant. If someone intends to commit a crime, they are dangerous and need restraining; they also need rehabilitation and punishment is necessary to deter them and others from embarking on criminal plans. Under this approach, all that is required is some conduct corroborative of this intention. Accordingly, liability can be imposed at a much earlier stage. Even before entering the car, the defendant in *Jones* had, by shortening the gun and setting off in disguise to kill his victim, indicated his dangerousness. At this stage punishment is also appropriate to deter others from such actions. And, of course, the law should be structured so as to facilitate police intervention to prevent crimes. When a person planning robbery and armed with a gun or an imitation firearm, as was the defendant in *Campbell*, is only one yard from the door of the building wherein the robbery is planned, the police should not be forced to wait until he has entered the building and produced his gun to the victim.

In striking the balance between these rationales the competing interests of individual freedom and the countervailing interests of society have to be placed in the scales. As the Law Commission state: 'In a free and democratic society where the right to privacy, freedom of conduct and civil liberties generally are respected, the balance may come down firmly against imposing criminal liability.'

The weight to be given to these competing interests depends on the seriousness of the offence of attempt. If attempts are to continue to be treated as being as serious (in terms of potential punishment) as the complete offence, the balance should only be struck at a point when the defendant's moral culpability can be regarded as broadly equal to that of the person who commits the full crime. On the other hand, if the offence were to be regarded as less serious, liability could be imposed for conduct at an earlier stage. The emphasis would then be not so much on the broadly comparable culpability of the attempter but rather on the dangerousness of such an actor and the need to facilitate police intervention. In short, the less serious the offence of attempt, the earlier could the line be drawn.

There are strong reasons why the crime of attempt should continue to be regarded as being of (almost) comparable gravity to the complete offence. The labels attempted murder and attempted rape have a strong resonance with the public as being very serious offences. In many cases it could be sheer luck that the crime was not completed. The defendant has broadly the same *mens rea* (or greater) than that required for the full offence. There is, of course, an argument that attempts should generally be punished less severely than completed offences, as is done in many other jurisdictions. Put simply, it is worse to kill someone than try to kill someone and worse to rape someone than try to rape someone. However, most of those supporting this view still recognize the seriousness of the crime of attempt and that in some cases the penalty imposed should be the same as for the complete offence. For example, Duff has proposed that while the penalty imposed for an attempt should generally be lighter than that which would have been imposed had the offence been completed, nevertheless a person convicted of an attempt should potentially be liable to the same penalty as for the completed offence and 'in exceptional cases' should be punished at that level.

A further argument for insisting that conduct comes close to the actual commission of the crime is that it affords intending criminals an opportunity to abandon the criminal enterprise. In doing this, we are according the person respect as a responsible agent 'who is in principle susceptible to rational persuasion'.

Finally, drawing the line at an earlier point would result in an unwarranted extension of the criminal law. Any 'respectable theory of criminalisation' needs to accept the 'last resort principle'. This principle applies not only to the creation of new offences but to the expansion of existing offences. In order to respect freedom, civil liberties and privacy, any expansion of the criminal law should involve a thorough investigation into whether it is necessary. Such an investigation is easier when criminalizing specific acts of preparation, in that one is operating within a specific context with a clearly defined harm being targeted. Simply to allow the line at which conduct should be criminalized to drift backwards risks infringing this basic principle.

Accordingly, it is suggested that the primary rationale of a reformulated offence of attempt should be, as at present, that of punishing a person whose moral culpability can be regarded as broadly comparable to that of the completer. This is similar to Duff's proposal that the conduct required for an attempt should be 'constitutive of the agent's criminality'. Culpability being broadly comparable or constitutive of criminality is not the same as requiring it to be equal to that of the completer. Such equality would only exist when the defendant has done *all* she needs to do to commit the crime. To be broadly comparable or constitutive of criminality, the defendant must have crossed *a* (relevant) threshold and have commenced, *or be about to commence*, on the execution of the crime. What is needed is a test that captures this crossing of a threshold and conduct displaying a 'vivid danger' that the full offence will be committed. The defendant in *Jones*, by entering the car and pointing a loaded gun at the victim had crossed this psychological threshold and displayed sufficient moral culpability and vivid danger to be liable for attempted murder.

Such a reformulated test needs to free itself from the present effective requirement that there must be a confrontation with, or 'attack' on, the victim or object of the crime. From the moment the defendant in *Geddes* trespassed on to school property, armed with his tools for capturing a boy, he had crossed the threshold towards the crime of false imprisonment; his actions displayed a vivid danger and he should be liable for an offence of attempted false imprisonment.

More controversial is whether a test reformulated along such lines should catch the [defendant in *Campbell*]. The key here involves fleshing out what is meant by 'crossing a threshold' and displaying 'vivid danger'. Crossing what threshold and a vivid danger of what? The answer lies in the charge the defendant is facing which will have been framed with reference to the defendant's established or alleged *mens rea*. The defendant's actions can only be understood and interpreted in the light of this *mens rea*. Given his *mens rea* (he was intending to commit robbery), did the defendant in *Campbell* cross a moral threshold towards *robbery* and did his actions display a vivid danger of *robbery* being committed? Views on this might differ but there is a strong argument that the test is satisfied once he, with his disguise, note and imitation firearm, approached the building in which the robbery was planned to take place.

[...]

Of course, a major problem will be how to capture this new degree of proximity. Legislation cannot be framed in terms of vague concepts, such as crossing thresholds or displaying a vivid danger. This is where the use of examples becomes important. What is needed is a general reformulation of the *actus reus* of attempt backed up by a series of examples. It has been suggested that such a test should require the defendant to have 'embarked on the commission of the offence' or be 'in the process of executing his or her plan to commit an intended offence'. However, such tests are capable of being construed too narrowly as requiring a need for confrontation with the victim or object. On a literal view, the defendant in *Geddes* had not embarked on the commission of the offence. Equally, they could be construed too broadly. At what point does one 'embark on the commission of the crime'. Did the defendant in *Jones* not commence on the execution of the crime when he left home in disguise with a loaded gun – or even when he simply bought the gun? This should not be enough for attempted murder. At this stage no relevant threshold had been crossed and no vivid danger displayed.

A possible reformulation could run along the lines of imposing liability for attempt when a person: 'does an act which is more than merely preparatory to, and is closely connected to, the commission of the offence in terms of time, location and acts under the control of the accused remaining to be accomplished'. Such a test is necessarily broad and open to the accusation of vagueness and being capable of generating uncertainty. However, this test has the advantage of stressing that mere preparatory acts will not suffice. The actions of the defendant in *Jones* in buying and shortening his gun and in setting forth armed with his gun are all merely preparatory acts. Further, unlike the present law, it emphasizes that the defendant must have come close to committing the offence but not so close as to have embarked on the crime. In terms of time and location and remaining acts to be done, the actions of the defendant in *Campbell* were closely connected to the full offence. With the aid of examples it would ensure that defendants in the controversial cases discussed above (such as *Geddes*) would be brought within its ambit. It is beyond the scope of this article to suggest a full list of examples. The important point is that, once one has established the rationale of the reformulated offence and its level of seriousness, the flavour of the examples becomes apparent.

Others have also warned of the dangers of an overly broad definition of the *actus reus* of attempts. Simester and Sullivan warn that it would 'carry an undue risk of oppressive policing and unsafe convictions based on dubious confessions'.[26] They point out that Campbell was convicted for possession of an imitation firearm (for which he received a sentence of three years' imprisonment), and that following *R v Geddes* Parliament introduced the offence of trespass with intent to commit a sexual offence.[27] 'It is better', they argue, 'to proceed in this piecemeal way than to resort to a broad and vague law of attempt susceptible to uncertainties of interpretation and oppressive modes of enforcement'.[28]

This area of the criminal law was reviewed by the Law Commission in its 2009 report *Conspiracy and Attempts* (Report No 318) HC 41. The following extract sets out the Commission's conclusions.

---

[26]Simester, A.P., Spencer, J.R., Stark, F., Sullivan, G.R. and Virgo, G.J. (2016) *Simester and Sullivan's Criminal Law: Theory and Doctrine* (6th edn) Oxford: Hart Publishing, p360.
[27]Sexual Offences Act 2003, s.63.
[28]Simester, A.P., Spencer, J.R., Stark, F., Sullivan, G.R. and Virgo, G.J. (2016) *Simester and Sullivan's Criminal Law: Theory and Doctrine* (6th edn) Oxford: Hart Publishing, p360.

EXTRACT

What did the Law Commission recommend? What reasons did it give for these recommendations? Do you agree with them?

## Law Commission (2009) *Conspiracy and Attempts* (Report No 318) HC 41

8.78 In the light of the mixed response we have received from consultation, and the absence of any consensus amongst our consultees, we have reached the conclusion that it would be inappropriate for us to recommend that the present offence of attempt should be redefined and supported by a list of examples for guidance.

8.79 Section 1(1) of the 1981 Act should therefore be retained without amendment. As explained above, we are mindful of the fact that there have been many cases [such as *R v Tosti*] in which the Court of Appeal has accepted that the present offence of attempt should be interpreted broadly, contrary to the narrow approach exemplified by *Geddes*. Bearing in mind the absence of any broad support from our consultees, and given that Parliament may intervene to rectify any future problems by creating new context-specific offences of preparation, we have concluded that the problem with the present law is insufficiently serious to warrant reform in the way we originally proposed.

8.80 It is worth adding, in closing, that the flexibility inherent in the present definition of the offence of attempt means that the courts currently have the power to draw the line separating mere preparation (incurring no liability) from attempt differently depending on the nature of the harm intended.

8.81 Where the line separating attempt from non-criminal preparation is drawn under the current law may depend on how serious, damaging and anti-social the intended offence is. In other words, it may be that the line will be drawn further back from the commission of the intended offence in proportion to the seriousness and/or anti-social nature of that offence. We accept that, if this is the approach which the courts adopt, consciously or otherwise, there is no compelling need for guiding examples. The inherent flexibility of the present inchoate offence, whatever label it bears, means that, by and large, the right decision will be reached for the type of offence intended.

8.82 On this view, cases such as *Geddes* should be seen as aberrations or deviations from the proper approach, and dealt with, as we suggest, by the creation of new context-specific offences where necessary.

### ii. Which offences can be attempted?

Section 1(4) of the Criminal Attempts Act 1981 states:

(4) This section applies to any offence which, if it were completed, would be triable in England and Wales as an indictable offence, other than —

    (a) conspiracy (at common law or under section 1 of the Criminal Law Act 1977 or any other enactment);

    (b) aiding, abetting, counselling, procuring or suborning the commission of an offence;

This means that:

- A defendant can be convicted of attempting any of the crimes we have studied in Chapters 5, 6, 7 and 8 of this text, except for assault and battery (since these are summary offences).

- There is no offence of attempting to conspire. Nor is there an offence of attempting to be an accessory. But a defendant can be convicted of attempting to commit one of the three encouraging or assisting offences we studied earlier in the chapter.

It is also important to note that section 1(1) says 'If, with intent to commit an offence to which this section applies, *a person does an act* [...]'. This means that a defendant cannot be held liable for an attempt in respect of an omission.

Note also that a defendant can be convicted of an attempt even if the attempt was in fact successful and the defendant committed the full offence.[29] So if for some reason Vito is on trial for the attempted murder of Philip even though Philip has died (perhaps because Philip died from his injuries whilst the trial was in progress), it is no defence for Vito to say that he murdered Philip. The policy reasons for this are obvious!

### iii. Impossibility

There are two basic types of impossibility: legal impossibility and factual impossibility.

Legal impossibility is where the defendant believes he is attempting a crime, but he is not. Suppose that Vito commits adultery, believing that adultery is a crime. He is not guilty of a criminal attempt. There is no offence of attempted adultery because adultery is not a crime!

Factual impossibility is different. There are two types of factual impossibility:

- **Inadequate means:** this is where the crime could potentially have been committed, but the means used by the defendant were simply incapable of success. Examples would be if Vito decides to kill someone, but mistakenly administers a harmless substance to the victim instead of deadly poison, or if Vito fires his gun at the victim without realising that the victim is just too far away and out of the range of his gun.

- **Physical impossibility:** this is where the situation was such that commission of the crime was simply not possible. Examples would be if Vito decides to steal the contents of a safe, but when he opens the safe discovers that it is empty, or if Vito stabs someone that he thinks is asleep but is in fact already dead.

Cases involving factual impossibility are governed by sections 1(2) and 1(3) of the Criminal Attempts Act 1981.

---

**EXTRACT**

## Section 1 of the Criminal Attempts Act 1981

(2) A person may be guilty of attempting to commit an offence to which this section applies even though the facts are such that the commission of the offence is impossible.

(3) In any case where —

    (a) apart from this subsection a person's intention would not be regarded as having amounted to an intent to commit an offence; but

    (b) if the facts of the case had been as he believed them to be, his intention would be so regarded,

    then, for the purposes of subsection (1) above, he shall be regarded as having had an intent to commit that offence.

---

[29] Criminal Attempts Act 1981, s.6(4).

These sections mean that factual impossibility is no defence to a charge of attempt. So in our four examples above, Vito would be guilty of three counts of attempted murder and one count of attempted theft.

The leading case on factual impossibility is *R v Shivpuri* [1987] AC 1. The defendant, Pyare Shivpuri, was arrested and found to be in possession of a powdered substance. When he was interviewed he said that the substance was either heroin or cannabis. However, when it was analysed the substance was found to be snuff. Shivpuri was charged with attempting to deal with illegal drugs. Drawing on sections 1(2) and 1(3) of the Criminal Attempts Act 1981, the House of Lords said that Shivpuri had to be judged on the basis of the facts as he believed them to be. His conviction was therefore upheld.

## 2. The defendant intended to commit the full offence

In many cases of attempted crime all that distinguishes the defendant's criminal actions from wholly innocent ones is his guilty intention. Suppose that Dave kicks a football and it hits his neighbour's greenhouse. The ball bounces off the glass panes without breaking them. Did Dave attempt to cause criminal damage? Or did he have a lucky escape from an unfortunate accident? It all depends on whether or not Dave intended to smash the glass. As Lord Goddard CJ stated in *R v Whybrow* (1951) 35 Cr App R 141, in an attempt 'the intent becomes the principal ingredient of the crime'.

The central importance of intention is reflected in the Criminal Attempts Act 1981. Section 1(1) states that in order to be guilty of an attempt the defendant must have intended to commit the full offence. So, according to the statute, nothing less than an intention to commit the full offence will suffice. This means that sometimes the *mens rea* of the full offence is different to the *mens rea* of an attempt.

### EXAMPLE

- In Chapter 5, we saw that the *mens rea* of murder is an intention to kill or cause GBH. By contrast, the *mens rea* of attempted murder is an intention to kill. For attempted murder an intention to cause GBH will not suffice.

- In Chapter 8, we saw that the *mens rea* of criminal damage is an intention to damage the property or recklessness whether the property is damaged. By contrast, the *mens rea* of attempted criminal damage is an intention to damage the property. Recklessness will not suffice.

Intention here means either direct intention or oblique intention.[30] We studied these two types of intention in Chapter 4.

### ACTIVITY

In Chapter 6, we studied the crime of malicious infliction of GBH (Offences Against the Person Act 1861, s.20). What is the *mens rea* of attempted infliction of GBH? How is this different to the full offence?

---

[30] *R v Mohan* [1976] QB 1. See also *R v Pearman* (1984) 80 Cr App R 259 and *R v Walker and Hayles* (1989) 90 Cr App R 226.

So the general rule is that only intention suffices for the *mens rea* of an attempt. However, for some of the crimes we have studied in this text things are not quite this straightforward! For some crimes the courts have been willing to accept something less than intention in relation to circumstance and consequence elements of the full offence.

The first example is the Court of Appeal's decision in *R v Khan* [1990] 1 WLR 813 on attempted rape. The victim in this case met one of the defendants at a disco. Afterwards she accompanied him to a nearby house. At the house three men had non-consensual sexual intercourse with her. They were subsequently convicted of rape. The four defendants also tried to have sexual intercourse with her but failed. They were convicted at trial of attempted rape. They appealed to the Court of Appeal. The case focused on the *mens rea* of attempted rape.

## EXTRACT

Read the following extract from the judgment of Russell LJ. How (if at all) is the *mens rea* for attempted rape different to the *mens rea* for rape? What reasons did Russell LJ give for this conclusion?

### *R v Khan* [1990] 1 WLR 813

#### Russell LJ

The only difference between the two offences is that in rape sexual intercourse takes place whereas in attempted rape it does not, although there has to be some act which is more than preparatory to sexual intercourse. Considered in that way, the intent of the defendant is precisely the same in rape and in attempted rape and the *mens rea* is identical

[...]

If this is the true analysis, as we believe it is, the attempt does not require any different intention on the part of the accused from that for the full offence of rape. We believe this to be a desirable result which in the instant case did not require the jury to be burdened with different directions as to the accused's state of mind, dependent upon whether the individual achieved or failed to achieve sexual intercourse.

This judgment was delivered several years before the introduction of the Sexual Offences Act 2003. The combined effect of *R v Khan* and the 2003 Act is that a defendant has the *mens rea* of attempted rape if he intended to penetrate the victim's vagina, anus or mouth with his penis and lacked a reasonable belief in consent. In other words, it is identical to the *mens rea* of rape (which we studied in Chapter 7).

The second example is the Court of Appeal's judgment in *A-G's Reference (No 3 of 1992)* [1994] 1 WLR 409. This case focused on attempted aggravated criminal damage. Four people were sitting in a parked car talking to two others who were standing on the pavement, when the four defendants drove past and threw a petrol bomb at them. The petrol bomb missed the parked car and hit a neighbouring wall. No one was injured and no property was damaged. The defendants were charged with attempted aggravated criminal damage.

In Chapter 8, we saw that the crime of aggravated criminal damage has two *mens rea* requirements. One relates to property damage (intention to damage property or recklessness whether property is damaged). The other relates to endangering life (intention to endanger life or recklessness whether life is endangered). At the defendants' trial the trial judge stated that for attempted aggravated criminal damage only intention will suffice in respect of both of these. Since the prosecution had produced no evidence that the defendants had an intention to endanger life she directed that the charges be dismissed.

The Attorney-General subsequently referred the issue to the Court of Appeal for clarification.

## EXTRACT

Read the following extract from the judgment of Schiemann J. What *mens rea* does he say must be shown in relation to: (a) property damage; and (b) endangering life?

Was the trial judge right to dismiss the charges against the defendants?

### A-G's Reference (No 3 of 1992) [1994] 1 WLR 409

#### Schiemann J

[...] In the present case, what was missing to prevent a conviction for the completed offence was damage to the property [...] Such damage is essential for the completed offence. If a defendant does not intend to cause such damage he cannot intend to commit the completed offence. At worst he is reckless as to whether the offence is committed. The law of attempt is concerned with those who are intending to commit crimes. If that intent cannot be shown, then there can be no conviction.

However, the crime here consisted of doing certain acts in a certain state of mind in circumstances where the first named property and the second named property were the same, in short where the danger to life arose from the damage to the property which the defendant intended to damage. The substantive crime is committed if the defendant damaged property in a state of mind where he was reckless as to whether the life of another would thereby be endangered. We see no reason why there should not be a conviction for attempt if the prosecution can show that he, in that state of mind, intended to damage the property by throwing a bomb at it. One analysis of this situation is to say that although the defendant was in an appropriate state of mind to render him guilty of the completed offence the prosecution had not proved the physical element of the completed offence, and therefore he is not guilty of the completed offence. If, on a charge of attempting to commit the offence, the prosecution can show not only the state of mind required for the completed offence but also that the defendant intended to supply the missing physical element of the completed offence, that suffices for a conviction. That cannot be done merely by the prosecution showing him to be reckless. The defendant must intend to damage property, but there is no need for a graver mental state than is required for the full offence.

The trial judge in the present case, however, went further than this, and held that not merely must the defendant intend to supply all that was missing from the completed offence – namely, damage to the first named property – but also that recklessness as to the consequences of such damage for the lives of others was not enough to secure a conviction for attempt, although it was sufficient for the completed offence. She held that before a defendant could be convicted of attempting to commit the offence it had to be shown that he intended that the lives of others should be endangered by the damage which he intended.

She gave no policy reasons for so holding, and there is no case which bound her so to hold. The most nearly relevant case is *Reg. v. Khan (Mohammed Iqbal)* [1990] 1 W.L.R. 813. [...]

What was missing in *Reg. v. Khan (Mohammed Iqbal)* was the act of sexual intercourse, without which the offence was not complete. What was missing in the present case was damage to the first named property, without which the offence was not complete. The mental state of the defendant in each case contained everything which was required to render him guilty of the full offence. In order to succeed in a prosecution for attempt, it must be shown that the defendant intended to achieve that which was missing from the full offence. Unless that is shown, the prosecution have not proved that the defendant intended to commit the offence. Thus in *Reg. v. Khan (Mohammed Iqbal)* [1990] 1 W.L.R. 813 the prosecution had to show an intention to have sexual intercourse, and the remaining state of mind required for the offence of rape. In the present case, the prosecution had to show an intention to damage the first named property, and the remaining state of mind required for the offence of aggravated arson.

Schiemann J's reasoning has been labelled the 'missing element' test. It draws a distinction between those elements of the full offence which were missing and those which were present. The defendant must have intended to supply the missing elements of the full offence. But for those elements which were present the *mens rea* of an attempt is the same as for the full offence. So, applying this to the case:

- **Endangering life:** Intention or recklessness suffices for the full offence. Since this part of the offence was present, intention or recklessness was also sufficient for an attempt.
- **Property damage:** This part of the offence was missing, so an intention to damage property was required.

In *R v Pace & Rogers* [2014] EWCA Crim 186 the Court of Appeal cast some doubt on the reasoning employed in *R v Khan* and *A-G's Reference (No 3 of 1992)*. Davis LJ stated:

> 62 Turning, then, to [section 1(1) of the Criminal Attempts Act 1981] we consider that, as a matter of ordinary language and in accordance with principle, an "intent to commit an offence" connotes an intent to commit all the elements of the offence. We can see no sufficient basis, whether linguistic or purposive, for construing it otherwise.

Importantly, Davis LJ emphasised that *R v Pace & Rogers* concerned an impossible attempt.[31] The defendants worked at a scrap metal yard. Undercover police officers offered to sell them scrap metal, telling them that it was stolen. The defendants accepted the metal and paid for it. They were charged with attempted conversion of criminal property. At trial the judge ruled that it was sufficient that the defendants had a suspicion that the metal was stolen, since suspicion is sufficient for the full offence. Of course, the scrap metal was not stolen since it was owned by the police. Moreover, the fact that the police owned the metal meant that commission of the full offence was impossible. The Court of Appeal allowed the defendants' appeals against conviction, ruling that suspicion that the metal was stolen was insufficient for a criminal attempt. Only an intention or knowledge that the metal was stolen would suffice.

So we now have competing approaches to the *mens rea* of criminal attempts. On the one hand we have *R v Pace & Rogers*, which insists that only intention or knowledge will suffice for all elements of the offence, whilst on the other hand we have *R v Khan* and *A-G's Reference (No 3 of 1992)*, both of which are prepared to accept something less than intention in relation to circumstance and consequence elements of the full offence. One way of reconciling the cases is to say that *R v Khan* and *A-G's Reference (No 3 of 1992)* apply to possible attempts, whereas *R v Pace & Rogers* applies to impossible attempts.[32]

---

[31]At [54].

[32]A distinction which has been criticised as incoherent: Child, J.J. and Hunt, A. (2014) 'Pace and Rogers and the *mens rea* of criminal attempt: *Khan* on the scrapheap?' 78 *Journal of Criminal Law* 220.

## ⬭⬭⬭ Conclusion

In this chapter we have studied three types of inchoate offence: encouraging or assisting crime; conspiracy and attempts. To conclude, here are three pieces of advice for answering exam problem questions:

- When you state which offence the defendant would be charged with, be sure to include details of the full offence. It is not enough to write 'D would be charged with conspiracy' or 'D would be charged with a criminal attempt'. You need to state which offence the defendant encouraged, assisted, attempted or conspired to commit. So write, 'D would be charged with conspiracy to rob' or 'D would be charged with attempted rape'.

- Sometimes it might be possible to charge a defendant with more than one of the offences we have studied in this chapter. Some students find this confusing, and when answering problem questions are unsure which offence they should focus on. As a rule of thumb, it is preferable to charge the defendant with a criminal attempt since this conveys greater proximity to commission of the full offence. If the defendant did not go beyond mere preparation: you should charge conspiracy if the defendants agreed to commit the unlawful plan as a joint collaborative project, and encouraging or assisting crime if they did not.

- There is another potential source of confusion. There is a large overlap between: (a) the encouraging or assisting crimes and conspiracy; and (b) the law governing accessories (which we study in the next chapter). As a result students are sometimes unsure which of these offences to discuss. As a rule of thumb, if the principal never went beyond mere preparation you should charge the defendant with an inchoate offence. But if the principal committed the full offence, you should charge the defendant with being an accessory. This gives due recognition to the fact that the full offence did occur.

## ⬭⬭⬭ Self-test questions

1. Vito has just found out that Philip is having an affair with his wife. Furious, he says to Michael, 'I want revenge'. Discuss the criminal liability of Vito and Michael in the following situations:

   a. Vito says to Michael, 'I'm going to beat Philip up'. Wanting to protect Philip, Michael replies, 'Don't do that'. He then hands Vito a brick and says, 'Smash the windows on his Ferrari instead'. Vito takes the brick and sets off to Philip's house. By the time he arrives there he has calmed down and decides not to retaliate.

   b. Vito says to Michael, 'Will you drive me to Philip's house? I want to break his nose'. At first Michael replies, 'Leave me out of it. It's nothing to do with me'. But when Vito says, 'I'll give you £1,000 to drive me to Philip's', Michael changes his mind. He drives Vito to Philip's house and drops him off outside. Unbeknown to Vito and Michael, however, Philip is away on a business trip and does not return home that evening.

   c. Michael and Vito agree to kill Philip. Unbeknown to them, Philip was killed in a road accident earlier that day. Would your answer be any different if Michael and Vito agreed to pay Trevor to kill Philip (but when they ask, Trevor refuses)?

   d. Vito, armed with a gun, says to Michael, 'Will you drive me to Philip's house? I'm going to kill him'. Michael agrees to take Vito to Philip's house. On the way there they are stopped by the police, who confiscate Vito's gun and arrest him. Michael tells the police that, after dropping Vito off, he planned to telephone Philip to warn him not to go home and then telephone the police.

e.  Vito and Michael agree to go and beat Philip up. They set off to his house. When they arrive, Vito looks through the living room window and sees Philip sitting watching TV. As he tries to open the window, which he discovers is locked, he is apprehended by a passing policeman.

f.  Vito and Michael agree to try and frighten Philip in order to 'warn him off'. So they make a petrol bomb, drive to Philip's house and lie in wait. When Philip arrives home from work in his car Vito throws the petrol bomb into the road close to Philip's car. No one is harmed and no property is damaged.

2.  'The case law on the "more than merely preparatory" test contained in section 1(1) of the Criminal Attempts Act 1981 is confused and inconsistent. Moreover, the statutory test is too limited in its scope. This results in defendants who should be convicted of a criminal attempt escaping liability.'

Discuss the extent to which you agree with this statement.

## Inchoate offences checklist

Having worked through this chapter, you should now have:

✓  An understanding of the requirements for the three encouraging or assisting crime offences

✓  An understanding of the requirements for the crime of statutory conspiracy

✓  An understanding of the requirements for a criminal attempt

✓  An ability to critically discuss the 'more than merely preparatory' test for the *actus reus* of criminal attempts and the courts' application of this test.

## Further reading

Child, J.J. and Hunt, A. (2014) '*Pace and Rogers* and the *mens rea* of criminal attempt: *Khan* on the scrapheap?' 78 *Journal of Criminal Law* 220.

Clarkson, C. (2009) 'Attempt: The Conduct Requirement' 29 *Oxford Journal of Legal Studies* 25.

Donnelly, B. (2010) 'Possibility, Impossibility and Extraordinariness in Attempts' 23 *Canadian Journal of Law and Jurisprudence* 47.

Duff, R.A. (1996) *Criminal Attempts*. OUP: Oxford.

Glazebrook, P. (1969) 'Should We Have a Law of Attempted Crime?' 85 *Law Quarterly Review* 28.

Law Commission (2006) *Inchoate Liability for Assisting and Encouraging Crime* (Law Commission Report No 300) Cm 6878.

Law Commission (2009) *Conspiracy and Attempts* (Law Commission Report No 318) HC 41.

Ormerod, D. and Fortson, R. (2009) 'Serious Crime Act 2007: The Part 2 Offences' *Criminal Law Review* 389.

Rogers, J. (2008) 'The Codification of Attempts and the Case for "Preparation"' *Criminal Law Review* 937.

# 13

# Accessories

## Chapter objectives

By the end of this chapter you should have:

- An understanding of the requirements for establishing that an individual is criminally liable as an accessory
- An ability to apply the relevant law to a hypothetical set of facts and discuss whether an individual may be criminally liable as an accessory
- An ability to critically discuss the decision of the Supreme Court in *R v Jogee*.

# Introduction

Consider the following four scenarios:

- A group of soldiers stand and watch as some of their fellow soldiers rape a young woman. They do not say or do anything: not to encourage or assist the rapists, nor to try and stop them. Are they accessories to the rape?

- A thief is trying to break into a van when he is interrupted by a passer-by. The thief gets into his getaway vehicle, which is being driven by his brother. The passer-by tries to stop them escaping. The thief sits in the passenger seat as the getaway driver murders the passer-by by running him over. Is the thief an accessory to the murder?

- A man guides a group of terrorists to a pub. He knows that the terrorists plan to attack the pub, but is unsure what form the attack will take. Is the man an accessory to the subsequent bomb attack?

- A man is on a night out with his friends. At the end of the evening, he and his friends start a fight with another group. The man punches and kicks members of the other group. One member of the other group is knocked to the floor. While the member of the other group is on the floor, one of the man's friends stamps on his head, killing him. Is the man an accessory to the murder?

These scenarios are all taken from cases that we will study in this chapter. They illustrate the challenging and diverse fact scenarios to which the law on accessories applies. By the end of the chapter you will be able to explain the outcomes in each of these cases and discuss whether or not the relevant law is satisfactory.

The chapter begins by explaining how and why we distinguish accessories from principals. It then sets out the *actus reus* and *mens rea* requirements for being an accessory. The next part of the chapter then focuses on an area of law that has generated a lot of attention in recent years: joint enterprise. The penultimate part of the chapter looks at the derivative principle – the notion that a defendant cannot be guilty as an accessory if the principal did not in fact commit the full offence – and outlines a couple of exceptions to this principle. Finally, the chapter examines what a defendant must do in order to withdraw from a criminal enterprise that he has previously encouraged or assisted.

Before turning to the law, there are two quick terminological points to clarify. First, accessorial liability is often referred to as secondary liability. Some of the extracts in this chapter accordingly refer to accessories as secondary parties. Second, for reasons we will see in a moment, when a defendant is an accessory to an offence most case law and literature on this topic will simply refer to him as being guilty of the offence and not say that he is guilty of being an accessory to the offence. For example, instead of saying that the defendant is guilty of 'being an accessory to murder' most would simply say that the defendant is guilty of 'murder'. In order to try and prevent confusion, in this chapter I do not adopt this approach. Instead, I will always refer in full to 'being an accessory to …', but as you read the quoted extracts and other literature on this topic you should bear this point in mind.

# The distinction between principals and accessories

The principal is the person who perpetrated the *actus reus* of the offence, whereas an accessory is someone who provided the principal with assistance or encouragement. So, to give a simple example, if Freddie breaks into Jack's house and steals all his valuables Freddie is guilty of burglary as a principal. If Ronnie stands outside Jack's house and keeps watch for Freddie, then Ronnie is an accessory to the burglary.

In most cases distinguishing the accessories from the principal will be straightforward. However, there are some situations in which the distinction is more difficult. Before considering these it is useful to begin by looking at section 8 of the Accessories and Abettors Act 1861, which states:

> Whosoever shall aid, abet, counsel, or procure the commission of any indictable offence, whether the same be an offence at common law or by virtue of any Act passed or to be passed, shall be liable to be tried, indicted, and punished as a principal offender.

(Section 44 of the Magistrates' Court Act 1980 contains an equivalent provision for summary offences.)

So the law treats accessories and principals identically for the purposes of procedure and punishment. An accessory to murder, for example, will receive the mandatory life sentence just as the principal will. If an accessory is to be tried, indicted and punished as a principal offender, you may well ask: is it really necessary to distinguish accessories from principals? There are at least two reasons why the distinction is important:

- The *actus reus* and *mens rea* requirements that the prosecution must prove differ according to whether the defendant is charged as a principal or an accessory. To give a simple example, a defendant can be guilty of drink-driving as a principal without any proof of *mens rea*. It is a strict liability offence. But for a defendant to be guilty of being an accessory to drink-driving, the prosecution must prove that he had the *mens rea* of being an accessory.

- For some offences there are classes of person who cannot be held liable as a principal. For example, women cannot commit rape as principals. But a woman can be convicted of being an accessory to rape. Similarly, although it is not a criminal offence for a person to commit suicide, someone who assists or encourages another person to do so can be convicted of being an accessory to suicide.[1]

Having explained why we distinguish accessories from principals, we can now look at four situations in which the distinction is not so straightforward:

- **Innocent agents**: Innocent agency is where the defendant uses someone, who is unaware of the significance of his actions, to perpetrate the *actus reus* of the offence. Suppose Freddie invites Jack for dinner. Freddie knows that Jack has a serious peanut allergy, but nonetheless asks his wife to cook a dish containing peanuts. Jack eats the meal, suffers a severe allergic reaction and dies. Freddie's wife was an innocent agent. In a case like this one, the actions of the innocent agent are treated as being the actions of the defendant. So Freddie would be liable for Jack's death as a principal.

- **Joint principals**: Suppose that Ronnie and Freddie attack Jack and Jack dies. If one of the men inflicts a specific wound that can be identified as the cause of death, then he will be the principal and the other an accessory. So if Freddie pulls out a knife and

---

[1] Suicide Act 1961.

inflicts a fatal stab wound, then Freddie is the principal and Ronnie is the accessory. But if there is no specific wound that can be identified as the cause of death, and Jack dies from the cumulative effect of all his injuries, then Ronnie and Freddie will be liable as joint principals. So if they each attacked Jack with the *mens rea* of murder, they will each be guilty of murder as a principal.

- **The prosecution can prove that the defendant was either a principal or an accessory, but cannot prove which**: This was the position in *R v Giannetto* [1997] 1 Cr App R 1. The Court of Appeal held that the defendant could be convicted, notwithstanding the fact that there was uncertainty over whether he was a principal or an accessory. This was because the prosecution had proved that he was either one or the other. So suppose that the prosecution prove that Ronnie either killed Jack himself or paid Freddie to do it for him, but cannot prove which. Ronnie would be convicted of murder.

- **The prosecution can prove that one of two people committed the offence, but cannot prove which one**: In this situation neither person can be convicted of the offence. Suppose Ronnie, Freddie and Jack are housemates. One day Jack is found dead. The prosecution can prove that the killer was either Ronnie or Freddie, but cannot prove which. On these facts, Ronnie cannot be convicted since the prosecution cannot show, beyond reasonable doubt, that he was the killer. Nor can Freddie be convicted since the prosecution cannot show, beyond reasonable doubt, that he was the killer either. (Things would be different if the prosecution could prove that both Ronnie and Freddie were at least accessories. Then the principle from *R v Giannetto* would apply to both men.)

## The *actus reus* and *mens rea* of being an accessory

A combination of case law and section 8 of the Accessories and Abettors Act 1861 tells us that the offence of being an accessory has the following three requirements:

1. The defendant must have aided, abetted, counselled or procured the commission of the offence

2. The defendant must have intended to aid, abet, counsel or procure the commission of the offence

3. The defendant must know or intend the essential elements of the principal's offence.

Number 1 is an *actus reus* requirement. Numbers 2 and 3 are *mens rea* requirements. We will work through them in turn.

### 1. The defendant must have aided, abetted, counselled or procured the commission of the offence

To establish the *actus reus* of accessorial liability, it is necessary to show that the defendant participated in the offence committed by the principal. Section 8 of the Accessories and Abettors Act 1861 specifies four forms of participation: aiding; abetting; counselling and procuring. We will look at the meaning of each of these in turn. First, though, it is worth noting the following observations, which were offered by Lord Widgery CJ in *Attorney-General's Reference (No 1 of 1975)* [1975] QB 773.

*Attorney-General's Reference (No 1 of 1975)* [1975] QB 773

### Lord Widgery CJ

We approach section 8 of the Act of 1861 on the basis that the words should be given their ordinary meaning, if possible. We approach the section on the basis also that if four words are employed here, "aid, abet, counsel or procure," the probability is that there is a difference between each of those four words and the other three, because, if there were no such difference, then Parliament would be wasting time in using four words where two or three would do. Thus, in deciding whether that which is assumed to be done under our reference was a criminal offence we approach the section on the footing that each word must be given its ordinary meaning.

Lord Widgery CJ states that the words 'aid', 'abet', 'counsel' and 'procure' should be given their 'ordinary meaning'. What do you understand to be the ordinary meaning of: (a) aiding; (b) abetting; (c) counselling and (d) procuring?

According to Lord Widgery CJ, it may be assumed that the words 'aid', 'abet', 'counsel' and 'procure' each have their own distinctive meaning. At the same time, however, it is clear that there is a significant degree of overlap. It is important to point out, therefore, that a jury may convict a defendant as long as they agree that the defendant satisfies at least one of the four modes of participation. It is not necessary for the jury to agree on which mode of participation is the most apt to the case in hand. For example, suppose a defendant is charged with 'abetting and counselling murder'. Six jurors conclude that the defendant abetted the murder. The other six conclude that the defendant counselled the murder. The defendant may be convicted of being an accessory to the murder, since the jury unanimously agree that he participated in the offence. It does not matter that there was a difference of opinion as to the most relevant form of participation.

With these introductory points in mind we can turn to examine the four forms of participation.

### i. Aid

Aiding means to help or to assist. A simple example would be where Ronnie lends Freddie a baseball bat to use to smash Jack's car windows. Ronnie would be guilty of aiding the criminal damage offence committed by Freddie.

In *Attorney-General v Able* [1984] QB 795 the five defendants were members of the executive committee of the Voluntary Euthanasia Society. The Society published a booklet titled 'A Guide to Self-Deliverance'. The booklet was aimed at people considering suicide. It began with a section titled 'Why you should think again'. This advised readers to think carefully and for a long period of time about whether to commit suicide and encouraged them to consider whether their problems could be overcome in other ways, such as medical treatment or way-of-life changes. It then set out five methods of 'self-deliverance'. In less than 18 months the Society sold over 8,000 copies. The Attorney-General applied to the courts for a declaration that supplying the book constituted the offence of aiding, abetting, counselling or procuring the suicide of another. In the High Court Woolf J held that supplying the booklet would amount to this offence in certain circumstances.

Four important points emerge from Woolf J's judgment. First, to establish that a defendant aided an offence it is not necessary to show that the assistance was a factual cause of the principal's offence. In other words, it is not necessary to show that, but for the assistance, the principal would not have committed the crime. Woolf J stated:

> [I]t does not make any difference that the person would have tried to commit suicide anyway. Nor does it make any difference, as the respondents contend, that the information contained in the booklet is already in the public domain.

So if Freddie says to Ronnie, 'I'm going to smash Jack's car windows' and Ronnie responds by lending Freddie his baseball bat, Ronnie is an accessory to the subsequent criminal damage offence even though Freddie would still have committed the crime without Ronnie's help.

This leads on to the second point from *Attorney-General v Able*. Whilst it is not necessary to prove factual causation, it is necessary to prove that the defendant provided some assistance. Woolf J stated:

> There will also be cases where, although the recipient commits or attempts to commit suicide, the booklet has nothing to do with the suicide or the attempted suicide; for example, a long period of time may have elapsed between the sending of the booklet and the attempt. In such a case, again, I would agree [...] that there would not be a sufficient connection between the attempted suicide and the supply of the booklet to make the supplier responsible.

Similarly, if Ronnie lends Freddie his baseball bat but Freddie leaves the bat at home and instead uses a brick to smash Jack's car windows, then Ronnie's actions have not provided any actual assistance. In this case, a prosecutor should instead consider charging Ronnie with abetting or counselling the criminal damage offence, since lending Freddie the bat could be deemed to be an act of encouragement.

The third point to note from *Attorney-General v Able* is that a defendant can be guilty of being an accessory without being present at the scene of the crime. Woolf J confirmed that those who published the booklet could be guilty of being accessories to suicide even though they would not be present when the principal ended his life. By the same token, Ronnie could be guilty of being an accessory to criminal damage even if he was not present when Freddie smashed Jack's car windows.

Finally, it is clear from *Attorney-General v Able* that the act of assistance need not have occurred at the time of the principal's offence. The booklet could have provided assistance even if the principal read it some weeks before choosing to end his life. This was confirmed by the Court of Appeal in *R v Stringer* [2011] EWCA Crim 1396, with Toulson LJ explaining:

> 46 [...] It is one thing to say that D cannot be liable as an aider or abettor unless P acted with D's assistance or encouragement when he committed the offence. It is quite another to suggest that the act or words providing the assistance or encouragement must be performed or said at the moment of the commission of the offence. Such a limitation would exclude, for example, a person who supplied a murder weapon in advance of the crime knowing the purpose for which P wanted it. The law would be defective if an aider and abettor could escape liability by seeing that there was a gap in time between his conduct and the conduct of P.

Before moving on, it is worth noting one further point: that a defendant may aid an offence even if the principal is unaware of the assistance he has provided. This may be illustrated using the facts of the US case *State v Tally* 102 Ala 25, 15 So 722 (1894). Judge Tally knew that his brothers-in-law had set out to kill the victim. He also knew that someone had sent a telegram to warn the victim. So Judge Tally ordered the telegraph operator not to deliver the telegram. The telegraph operator complied, and the brothers-in-law committed the offence. The judge was convicted of aiding the murder, even though the brothers-in-law were unaware of the judge's assistance when they killed the victim.

### ii. Abet

The word 'abet' means to incite, instigate or encourage. Whilst each of the four modes of participation listed in the 1861 Act overlaps, there is a particularly large degree of overlap between the words 'abet' and 'counsel'. One way of distinguishing between them is to use the word 'abet' to refer to encouragement given at the time of the principal's offence, and to use the word 'counsel' to refer to encouragement given at an earlier stage. But this is not a hard-and-fast rule and there is nothing to prevent the word 'abet' from being used to refer to encouragement given before the principal commits his offence.

One important issue which has arisen here is whether a defendant abets a crime simply by being present at the scene whilst the offence is being committed. The leading case is *R v Clarkson* [1971] 1 WLR 1402. The defendants, David Clarkson and Joseph Carroll, were members of the army. One evening there was a party at their barracks. The victim, an 18-year-old girl named Elke von Groen, went to the party. Sometime after midnight the two defendants heard screaming and moaning coming from one of the rooms in the barracks. They entered the room and found Elke being repeatedly raped by a group of their fellow soldiers. They remained in the room for some time. Whilst they were in the room, there was no evidence that Clarkson and Carroll did anything to participate in the rape or to encourage it. But neither did they do anything to try and stop it.

At trial they were convicted of being accessories to rape. They appealed against their convictions. The case reached the Court Martial Appeal Court. The key issue in the case was whether the defendants had encouraged the rape merely by their presence in the room. The Court Martial Appeal Court allowed the defendants' appeal. Megaw LJ explained that being present at the scene of a crime is not, in itself, sufficient for the *actus reus* of being an accessory. As we saw when we studied omissions in Chapter 3, there is no general duty to prevent crime. It is not a crime to simply stand by and watch someone else commit an offence. Megaw LJ said that to establish the *actus reus* of being an accessory, the prosecution must prove that there was in fact assistance or encouragement. In the present case, the prosecution had failed to produce any evidence that Clarkson and Carroll had encouraged the rapists:

> [T]here was no evidence on which the prosecution sought to rely that either of the defendants Clarkson or Carroll had done any physical act or uttered any word which involved direct physical participation or verbal encouragement. There was no evidence that they had touched the girl, helped to hold her down, done anything to her, done anything to prevent others from assisting her or to prevent her from escaping, or from trying to ward off her attackers, or that they had said anything which gave encouragement to the others to commit crime or to participate in committing crime.

Admittedly the defendants' presence might have provided encouragement. But this had to be proved with evidence. In the absence of such evidence, the convictions had to be quashed.

This principle was also applied in *R v Willett* [2010] EWCA Crim 1620. The defendant, Tommy Willett, and his brother, Albert, went to a car park intending to steal items from the cars parked there. Tommy Willett was attempting to break into a Mercedes van when the owner, Balbir Matharu, saw him and began to shout. Willett got back into Albert's car and they attempted to drive off, but Matharu stood in the way of the exit to block their escape. A witness said that Albert's car edged forward. Matharu was banging on the bonnet, but then appeared to trip. Albert drove forward and Matharu went under the car. Albert continued to drive. Matharu was dragged along the road and killed. Albert was convicted of murder. Tommy Willett was charged with being an accessory to the murder. At trial the judge told the jury that, in order to convict, they had to be sure that Tommy had provided either 'actual or tacit encouragement'. Willett was subsequently convicted. He appealed to the Court of Appeal, arguing that the trial judge had been wrong to tell the jury that tacit encouragement was sufficient. The Court of Appeal agreed. Moses LJ reiterated that mere presence is insufficient. There must be encouragement in fact:

## EXTRACT

### *R v Willett* [2010] EWCA Crim 1620

#### Moses LJ

18 It is difficult to see that merely continuing to sit in the passenger seat of the Mondeo amounted to any encouragement to the driver to run over Mr Matharu. Events happened fast. There was an opportunity, at the last minute, we suppose, for the appellant to get out of the vehicle and remonstrate with Mr Matharu. But his failure to do so cannot, we think, be said to be an encouragement to the driver to run him over. The speed and turn of events makes such a suggestion unrealistic.

[...]

24 The difficulty in the judge's ruling lies in his apparent acceptance that "tacit" encouragement would be enough. We do not agree. Indeed, we are not sure what he meant by "tacit encouragement" in the context of this case. The danger with that expression is that it suggests that this appellant's continued presence was sufficient. For the reasons we have given, it was not.

Neither Clarkson and Carroll, nor Tommy Willett, had made prior arrangements to be present at the scene of the offence. Clarkson and Carroll only entered the room where the rapes were occurring when they heard sounds coming from inside, and when Willett got into his brother's car he did not know that their escape route would be blocked or that Albert would kill the victim. This raises the question: does the principle from these cases apply when the defendant actually made prior arrangements to be present at the scene of the crime? Or is the fact that the defendant purposely arranged to be present sufficient to establish the *actus reus* of being an accessory?

This was the issue in *R v Coney* (1882) 8 QBD 534. The defendant went to watch an illegal prize-fight. The fighters were each convicted of assault. Coney was charged with being an accessory to the assaults. At trial the judge stated that Coney's voluntary attendance to watch the prize-fight was conclusive evidence of encouragement. The jury therefore convicted Coney. Coney appealed against his conviction. By a majority of 8–3, the Divisional Court held that the trial judge had misdirected the jury. The majority explained that, whilst voluntary, non-accidental presence at the scene of a crime is evidence of encouragement, it is not conclusive evidence. In other words, the same approach applies here as in *R v Clarkson* and *R v Willett*: the prosecution must prove that there was assistance or encouragement in fact. The fact that a defendant arranged to go and watch an offence being committed is evidence that he provided encouragement – indeed, it may be powerful evidence as if there had been no spectators the prize-fight would presumably not have gone ahead – but voluntary attendance is not in itself conclusive. The jury must also look at any other relevant evidence and decide whether the defendant did in fact provide encouragement. Since the trial judge had misdirected the jury, Coney's conviction was quashed.

An example of a case in which a defendant was convicted of being an accessory after watching an illegal performance is *Wilcox v Jeffery* [1951] 1 All ER 464. This case involved the famous US saxophonist Coleman Hawkins. Hawkins came to London to play a concert. The concert was in fact illegal: Hawkins was only given permission to enter the UK on condition that he undertook no employment, paid or unpaid. The defendant, William Wilcox, was the owner and editor of a jazz magazine, *Jazz Illustrated*. Wilcox attended the concert and was subsequently convicted of being an accessory to the illegal performance. The Divisional Court dismissed his appeal against conviction, stating that there was ample evidence that Wilcox's presence at the concert had encouraged the performance. Not only had he voluntarily arranged to attend. He paid for a ticket. He did not boo or protest during the performance. He had also been at the airport to welcome Hawkins, and he later wrote a glowing review of the concert in his magazine.

*Wilcox v Jeffery* illustrates one further point: as with aiding, abetting does not require proof of factual causation. So whilst it is necessary to establish actual encouragement, it is not necessary to show that but for the abetting the principal would not have committed the crime. This is clear from *Wilcox v Jeffery*: even if Wilcox had not attended the concert, the illegal performance would still have gone ahead.

### iii. Counsel

The meaning of counsel was considered by the Court of Appeal in *R v Calhaem* [1985] QB 808. Parker LJ stated:

> We must therefore approach the question raised on the basis that we should give to the word "counsel" its ordinary meaning, which is, as the judge said, "advise," "solicit," or something of that sort.

So if Ronnie says to Freddie, 'I really think you need to teach Jack a lesson. You should beat him up' – and Freddie later acts on this and punches Jack in the face, giving him a black eye – Ronnie would be guilty of counselling the offence of assault occasioning ABH committed by Freddie. Similarly, if Freddie tells Ronnie that he plans to break Jack's leg, and Ronnie advises him, 'The best time to attack him would be when he leaves the pub tomorrow night', Ronnie would be guilty of counselling Freddie's subsequent offence.

In *R v Calhaem* Parker LJ went on to offer some further guidance on the meaning of counselling:

## EXTRACT

### *R v Calhaem* [1985] QB 808

#### Parker LJ

There is no implication in the word itself that there should be any causal connection between the counselling and the offence. It is true that [...] the actual offence must have been committed, and committed by the person counselled. To this extent there must clearly be, first, contact between the parties, and, secondly, a connection between the counselling and the murder. Equally, the act done must, we think, be done within the scope of the authority or advice, and not, for example, accidentally when the mind of the final murderer did not go with his actions. For example, if the principal offender happened to be involved in a football riot in the course of which he laid about him with a weapon of some sort and killed someone who, unknown to him, was the person whom he had been counselled to kill, he would not, in our view, have been acting within the scope of his authority; he would have been acting entirely outside it, albeit what he had done was what he had been counselled to do.

Three important points emerge from this extract. First, Parker LJ explained that there must be 'contact between the parties'. A defendant cannot be held to have counselled the principal if his words of encouragement were never received. The position here is different to the position with acts of assistance. As we saw above, a principal can receive assistance without being aware of it (as *State v Tally* illustrated). But a person cannot receive encouragement if he is unaware of the encouragement! So if Ronnie sends Freddie a text message urging him to kill Jack, but unbeknown to Ronnie Freddie has recently changed his number and so never receives the message, there can be no counselling since Freddie never received the words of encouragement.

Second, whilst the words of encouragement must have been received, it is not necessary to show that they were a factual cause of the principal's offence. In other words, as with both aiding and abetting, there is no requirement to show that, but for the counselling, the principal would not have committed the offence. So if Ronnie encourages Freddie to kill Jack, Ronnie can be guilty of counselling murder even if Freddie had already made up his mind to carry out the killing. This is confirmed by the following example from the Court of Appeal's judgment in *R v Giannetto* [1997] 1 Cr App R 1:

> Supposing somebody came up to [the defendant] and said, 'I am going to kill your wife', if he played any part, either in encouragement, as little as patting him on the back, nodding, saying, 'Oh goody', that would be sufficient to involve him in the murder, to make him guilty, because he is encouraging the murder.

The third point from *R v Calhaem* is that there must be some 'connection' between the principal's offence and the counselling. The principal's offence must be 'within the scope of the authority or advice'. Parker LJ explained this point in the extract above using the example of the principal killing someone during a riot who just happened, by sheer coincidence, to be the person the defendant had counselled him to kill. On these facts there would not be any sufficient connection between the counselling and the principal's offence. In *R v Calhaem* itself, the defendant, Kathleen Calhaem, hired a man named Julian Zajac to murder Shirley Rendell (Rendell was having an affair with a man that Calhaem was infatuated with). Zajac testified that, on the day of the murder, he went to Rendell's house with no intention of killing her. He said that he intended to act out a charade, so that both Rendell and Calhaem would think that he had attempted to kill Rendell. However, when he forced his way into Rendell's house she began to scream. Zajac said that her screams caused him to go 'berserk'. He hit her several times with a hammer and stabbed her. The Court of Appeal upheld Calhaem's conviction for counselling murder, on the basis that Zajac had acted within the scope of Calhaem's authority and advice.

## ACTIVITY

In the light of the guidance from *R v Calhaem*, do you think that counselling can be established in the following two scenarios:

- Freddie has a long-standing feud with Jack. Ronnie is aware of this, and sends Freddie an email urging him to kill Jack. For some reason, the email goes straight to Freddie's spam folder. Even though he never sees the email, Freddie kills Jack.
- Ronnie pays Freddie £10,000 to kill Jack. Freddie takes the money, even though he does not plan to kill Jack. Instead he intends to beat Jack up and then disappear with Ronnie's money. However, Freddie later discovers that Jack has been having an affair with his girlfriend. Incensed, he confronts Jack and kills him.

### iv. Procure

The meaning of 'procure' was considered by the Court of Appeal in *Attorney-General's Reference (No 1 of 1975)* [1975] QB 773. In this case the defendant secretly spiked his friend's drinks with alcohol, even though he knew that his friend would shortly be driving home. His friend was subsequently convicted of drink-driving. The defendant was charged with procuring the drink-driving offence. At trial the trial judge ruled that there was no case to answer (on the basis that there was no shared intention between the two men). Believing this to have been mistaken, the Attorney-General referred the case to the Court of Appeal as raising a point of law of general importance.

## EXTRACT

Read the following extract from the judgment of Lord Widgery CJ. How does he define 'procure'?

According to Lord Widgery CJ, to establish procurement is it necessary to show: (a) that there was a shared intention between the principal and the accessory; and (b) that there was a causal link between the accessory's actions and the principal's offence?

### *Attorney-General's Reference (No 1 of 1975)* [1975] QB 773

#### Lord Widgery CJ

To procure means to produce by endeavour. You procure a thing by setting out to see that it happens and taking the appropriate steps to produce that happening. We think that there are plenty of instances in which a person may be said to procure the commission of a crime by another even though there is no sort of conspiracy between the two, even though there is no attempt at agreement or discussion as to the form which the offence should take. In our judgment the offence described in this reference is such a case.

If one looks back at the facts of the reference: the accused surreptitiously laced his friend's drink. This is an important element and, although we are not going to decide today anything other than the problem posed to us, it may well be that, in similar cases where the lacing of the drink or the introduction of the extra alcohol is known to the driver, quite different considerations may apply. We say that because, where the driver has no knowledge of what is happening, in most instances he would have no means of preventing the offence from being committed. If the driver is unaware of what has happened, he will not be taking precautions. He will get into his car seat, switch on the ignition and drive home and, consequently, the conception of another procuring the commission of the offence by the driver is very much stronger where the driver is innocent of all knowledge of what is happening, as in the present case where the lacing of the drink was surreptitious.

The second thing which is important in the facts set out in our reference is that, following and in consequence of the introduction of the extra alcohol, the friend drove with an excess quantity of alcohol in his blood. Causation here is important. You cannot procure an offence unless there is a causal link between what you do and the commission of the offence, and here we are told that in consequence of the addition of this alcohol the driver, when he drove home, drove with an excess quantity of alcohol in his body.

Giving the words their ordinary meaning in English, and asking oneself whether in those circumstances the offence has been procured, we are in no doubt that the answer is that it has. It has been procured because, unknown to the driver and without his collaboration, he has been put in a position in which in fact he has committed an offence which he never would have committed otherwise.

It is clear from the facts of this case that it is not necessary to prove there was a shared intention in order to establish procurement. The principal had no idea that his drinks had been spiked. However, to prove procurement it is necessary to establish factual causation. It must be shown that, but for the defendant's actions, the principal would not have committed the offence. This was readily apparent in *Attorney-General's Reference (No 1 of 1975)*; if the defendant had not spiked his friend's drinks, his friend would not have committed the drink-driving offence. In this respect, then, procurement is quite different to aiding, abetting and counselling – since none of these other forms of participation require proof of factual causation.

It is important to distinguish procurement from two other, similar scenarios:

- Procurement must be distinguished from innocent agency. As we saw above, in a case of innocent agency the actions of the innocent agent are treated as being the actions of the defendant. The defendant is therefore guilty of the offence in question as a principal, not as an accessory. In a case involving procurement, by contrast, there is no innocent agent and so the defendant is guilty as an accessory, not a principal. In *Attorney-General's Reference (No 1 of 1975)*, for example, the defendant's friend was not an innocent agent. He was guilty of drink-driving as a principal. The defendant was an accessory to this offence.

- Procurement does not apply if there was a break in the chain of causation between the accessory's actions and the principal's offence. Therefore, procurement does not apply if the principal made a voluntary choice to commit the offence.[2] So suppose Ronnie offers to buy Freddie a drink. Freddie asks for something non-alcoholic. In spite of this, Ronnie buys him an alcoholic drink. Freddie decides to drink it, even though he knows it is alcoholic and he knows he has to drive home later. Freddie is subsequently convicted of drink-driving. Ronnie could not be convicted of procuring the drink-driving offence, since Freddie's voluntary choice to drive home breaks the chain

---

[2] As we saw in Chapter 3, a voluntary choice is one which was free, deliberate and informed (*R v Pagett*).

of causation between Ronnie buying the drink and Freddie drink-driving. However, this does not mean Ronnie escapes liability as an accessory! The prosecution could instead argue that Ronnie aided the drink-driving offence, since he provided assistance by buying Freddie the drink.

### v. Participation by omission?

Whether or not it is possible to be an accessory to an offence simply by doing nothing is an important question, particularly in cases like *R v Clarkson* and *R v Willett* which involve presence but no positive acts of assistance or encouragement. There are two types of situation in which an omission may satisfy the *actus reus* of being an accessory.

The first is illustrated by *Rubie v Faulkner* [1940] 1 KB 571. The defendant, George Rubie, was teaching a man called Percy James to drive. As they approached a bend, James attempted to overtake a horse and cart even though he could not see what was coming round the bend. He pulled out to the other side of the road, a lorry came around the bend and James stalled the car, resulting in a collision. Even though Rubie could see the manoeuvre James was going to perform, he did not intervene. James was convicted of driving without due care and attention. Rubie was convicted of being an accessory to this offence. Rubie appealed against his conviction, arguing that he had not done or said anything to encourage the dangerous manoeuvre. His appeal against conviction was dismissed. The Divisional Court explained that, since Rubie was supervising a learner driver, he had a legal duty to intervene. By failing to do so he had breached this duty, and so he was an accessory to James' offence.

So it is clear from *Rubie v Faulkner* that a person may be an accessory to an offence by omission, if he breaches a legal duty to intervene. A further example would be where a child's father stands and watches as the mother deliberately injures the child. As we saw in Chapter 3, the father has a legal duty to intervene. His failure to do so is a breach of this duty and so he satisfies the *actus reus* of being an accessory.

It seems that a defendant may also be guilty as an accessory, even though he had no legal duty to intervene, if he had a legal power or right to do so. In *Du Cros v Lambourne* [1907] 1 KB 40 the defendant, Du Cros, owned a Mercedes car. He allowed his friend, Victoria Goodwin, to drive the car whilst he sat in the passenger seat. Goodwin was convicted of a speeding offence. Du Cros was convicted of being an accessory to the speeding offence. He appealed, arguing that he had done nothing but sit passively in the passenger seat. His appeal was dismissed by the Divisional Court. The Court held that:

> [Du Cros was] in control of the car, and that he could, and ought to, have prevented her from driving at this excessive and dangerous speed, but that he allowed her to do so and did not interfere in any way.

So if a defendant has the power or right to control the principal's actions, and fails to do so, he satisfies the *actus reus* of being an accessory.

### ACTIVITY

Ronnie owns a flat. He has a lodger, Freddie. He knows that people visit Freddie at the flat in order to buy and sell drugs, but turns a blind eye since Freddie always pays the rent on time. Freddie is convicted of drugs offences. Is Ronnie an accessory to these offences?

### vi. The timing of the participation

There is one final point to note about the *actus reus* of being an accessory, which concerns the timing of the defendant's participation. A person cannot be liable as an accessory to an offence if the assistance or encouragement he provides comes after the offence is already complete. Suppose that Ronnie, Freddie and Jack are housemates. Ronnie arrives home one day, only to discover that Freddie has just murdered Jack. Ronnie agrees to help Freddie dispose of the body. On these facts, Ronnie is not liable as an accessory to Jack's murder because the assistance he provides comes after the murder was already complete. This is not to say that Ronnie has committed no crime at all – there are specific offences aimed at those who help to conceal crimes that have been committed[3] – the key point is that the assistance came too late for Ronnie to be an accessory to the murder that had already occurred.

## 2. The defendant must have intended to aid, abet, counsel or procure the commission of the offence

There are two *mens rea* requirements for being an accessory, which must both be satisfied at the time of the defendant's assistance/encouragement. The easiest way to understand the difference between them is to remember that one of them relates to the defendant's thoughts about his own actions, whilst the other relates to the defendant's thoughts about the actions of the principal. We will begin by looking at the first of these: the defendant must have intended, by his actions, to aid, abet, counsel or procure the commission of the crime.

There are two points to note about this *mens rea* requirement. First, it asks whether the defendant intended to assist or encourage the principal to commit the offence. It does not ask whether it was the defendant's intention that the principal would go ahead and commit the offence. This may seem like a fine distinction, so imagine the following example.[4] The defendant, a shopkeeper, sells a customer a gun knowing that the customer might use it to commit a murder. The shopkeeper does not care whether the customer commits the murder or not. All the shopkeeper cares about is the profit he will make from the sale. On these facts, the shopkeeper does intentionally provide assistance. This may not be his direct intention (i.e. his purpose). But it is his oblique intention, since he realises that assistance is the inevitable consequence of completing the sale (see the *R v Woollin* direction, which we studied in Chapter 4). So, if the customer goes ahead and commits the murder, whether or not the shopkeeper is guilty of being an accessory to the murder will depend on whether he satisfies the final *mens rea* requirement, which we will look at shortly.

The second point to note about this *mens rea* requirement is that only intention will suffice. Recklessness is insufficient. This is particularly important in cases involving questions of oblique intention, like the shopkeeper example we just discussed, since the jury will have to decide whether the defendant foresaw assistance/encouragement as virtually certain (oblique intention) or whether the defendant only foresaw assistance/encouragement as a risk (even a grave risk) (recklessness). As we saw in Chapter 4, the dividing line between a risk and a virtual certainty is a difficult one.

---

[3]See, for example, sections 4 and 5 of the Criminal Law Act 1967.
[4]Similar examples were discussed in *National Coal Board v Gamble* [1959] 1 QB 11 and *R v Jogee* [2016] UKSC 8.

Ronnie invites a number of friends to his house for dinner. Even though Ronnie knows that Freddie will be driving home later that evening, he gives Freddie a large glass of wine and refills it several times during the meal. Freddie later drives home. He is stopped by police and subsequently convicted of drink-driving. Ronnie is charged with being an accessory to the drink-driving offence. In your opinion, does he satisfy this *mens rea* requirement?

## 3. The defendant must know or intend the essential elements of the principal's offence

Whilst the previous *mens rea* requirement focused on the defendant's thoughts about his own actions, this *mens rea* requirement focuses on the defendant's thoughts about the actions of the principal. In *Johnson v Youden* [1950] 1 KB 544, Lord Goddard CJ explained that 'Before a person can be convicted of aiding and abetting the commission of an offence he must at least know the essential matters which constitute that offence'. Whilst some previous decisions of the Court of Appeal suggested that something less than knowledge may be sufficient,[5] the Supreme Court in *R v Jogee* [2016] UKSC 8 reiterated that the defendant must have had 'knowledge of any existing facts necessary for [the principal's actions] to be criminal' ([9]).

There are three issues to address in respect of this *mens rea* requirement. The first concerns the word 'knowledge'. In cases where the defendant provides assistance or encouragement at the time of the principal's offence, the word 'knowledge' will be unproblematic, such as where Ronnie sees Freddie attacking Jack and shouts encouragement. On these facts, when Ronnie provides encouragement he knows the essential elements of Freddie's offence. But in many cases the defendant will offer assistance or encouragement in advance of the principal's offence, such as where Ronnie provides Freddie with detailed information on a building Freddie is planning to burgle. In these cases, using the word 'knowledge' is awkward since a person cannot have knowledge of something that is yet to occur. So in these cases it is better to use the language of intention.[6] You begin by asking whether the defendant's purpose (direct intention) was for the principal to go ahead and commit the offence. If it was, this *mens rea* requirement is satisfied. If it was not, then you should ask whether the defendant knew that it was virtually certain that the principal would commit the offence (oblique intention). If he did, then this *mens rea* requirement is satisfied. If he did not, then this *mens rea* requirement would seem not to be satisfied (there is some ambiguity here because, as we will see later in the chapter, in *R v Jogee* the Supreme Court did not clearly state whether or not the *R v Woollin* threshold of virtual certainty applies in this context).

The second point to note is that it is not enough to show that the defendant knew that some prohibited conduct or consequence would occur. It must be established that the defendant knew that the principal was committing the relevant offence, or intended that he would do so. This is an important distinction. It means that the defendant must have known or intended *both* that the principal would perpetrate the conduct specified in the *actus reus* of the relevant offence *and* that the principal would act in this way possessing the relevant *mens rea*. The point can be illustrated using the following two examples.

---

[5]E.g. *R v Bryce* [2004] EWCA Crim 1231, in which the Court said that it was sufficient to show that the defendant realised there was a real or substantial risk that the principal would commit the offence.
[6]Ormerod, D. and Laird, K. (2016) '*Jogee*: Not the End of a Legal Saga but the Start of One?' *Criminal Law Review* 539.

**EXAMPLE**

- Freddie murders Jack. Ronnie is charged with being an accessory to the murder. It would not be enough to show that Ronnie intended that Freddie would perform the actions that caused Jack's death. Ronnie must also have intended that Freddie would commit these actions with the *mens rea* of murder. So the prosecution would have to show that Ronnie intended: (1) that Freddie would attack Jack; and, (2) that Freddie would carry out the attack with an intention to kill Jack or cause him serious harm.
- Ronnie is charged with being an accessory to Freddie raping Jack. It would not be enough to show that Ronnie intended that Freddie would have sexual intercourse with Jack. The prosecution would have to show that Ronnie intended: (1) that Freddie would have non-consensual sexual intercourse with Jack; and (2) that Freddie would penetrate Jack intentionally and lack a reasonable belief that Jack was consenting.

**ACTIVITY**

Ronnie and Freddie are playing football in the street, using their neighbour's wall as a goal. Freddie kicks the ball at the wall as hard as he can. The ball goes much higher than he intended and smashes an upstairs window. Freddie is charged with criminal damage of the window. Ronnie is charged with being an accessory to criminal damage. Make a list of everything the prosecution must prove in order for Ronnie to be convicted.

The third issue we need to address is: how much knowledge must the defendant have of the details of the principal's offence? At one extreme, must the defendant know all the specific details, that is, when, where and how the offence will be committed? Or, at the other extreme, is it enough that the defendant merely knew that something unlawful would occur? The courts' answer is somewhere between these two positions.

The leading case is *R v Bainbridge* [1960] 1 QB 129. The defendant, Alan Bainbridge, purchased oxygen-cutting equipment. Six weeks later the equipment was used to break into a Midland bank in Stoke Newington. Bainbridge was charged with being an accessory to the break-in. In evidence, Bainbridge said that he had bought the equipment for a man named Shakeshaft. He admitted that he suspected Shakeshaft wanted it for something illegal, but he said he thought Shakeshaft would use the equipment to dispose of stolen goods, not to break into a bank. At trial Bainbridge was convicted. He appealed, and the case reached the Court of Appeal.

**EXTRACT**

Read the following extract from the judgment of Lord Parker CJ. According to Lord Parker CJ, for this *mens rea* requirement to be satisfied what must the defendant have known?

### R v Bainbridge [1960] 1 QB 129

#### Lord Parker CJ

The court fully appreciates that it is not enough that it should be shown that a man knows that some illegal venture is intended. To take this case, it would not be enough if he knew – he says he only suspected – that the equipment was going to be used to dispose of stolen property. That would not be enough. Equally, this court is quite satisfied that it is unnecessary that knowledge of the particular crime which was in fact committed should be shown to his knowledge to have been intended, and by "particular crime" I am using the words in the same way in which [counsel for the defence] used them, namely, on a particular date and particular premises.

[...]

[The trial judge] in this case, in the passage to which I have referred, makes it clear that there must be not merely suspicion but knowledge that a crime of the type in question was intended, and that the equipment was bought with that in view. In his reference to the felony of the type intended it was, as he stated, the felony of breaking and entering premises and the stealing of property from those premises. The court can see nothing wrong in that direction.

So, on the facts of *R v Bainbridge*, the prosecution would not have to show that the defendant knew that the principal planned to break into the Stoke Newington branch of the Midland bank. But equally it is not enough to show that the defendant merely knew that something illegal was planned. The prosecution have to show that the defendant knew or intended that the principal would commit a crime of that type, that is, breaking and entering and theft. The jury at Bainbridge's trial had concluded that Bainbridge knew this type of crime would be committed, and so his appeal against conviction was dismissed.

A similar case is *DPP for Northern Ireland v Maxwell* [1978] 1 WLR 1350. Here, the House of Lords dealt with a slightly different scenario: where the defendant knows that the principal will commit one of several different offences, but is unsure which. The defendant, James Maxwell, was a member of a terrorist organisation in Northern Ireland. Members of the organisation told him to guide a group of men, who were strangers to the area, to a particular pub. Having reached the pub, Maxwell left. He knew that a terrorist attack was planned, but was unsure what form the attack would take. In fact, the men attempted (unsuccessfully) to bomb the pub. Maxwell was convicted of being an accessory to the attack. His appeal against conviction reached the House of Lords. In his judgment Lord Scarman explained the relevant principle as follows:

> [A defendant] may have in contemplation only one offence, or several: and the several which he contemplates he may see as alternatives. An accessory who leaves it to his principal to choose is liable, provided always the choice is made from the range of offences from which the accessory contemplates the choice will be made.

Since the attack on the pub was within the range of offences Maxwell had contemplated, his conviction was upheld.

## Joint enterprise

Suppose that Ronnie and Freddie work together to burgle Jack's house. Ronnie acts as lookout whilst Freddie enters Jack's house and steals all his valuables. Freddie will be guilty of burglary. As for Ronnie, establishing the *actus reus* and *mens rea* of being an accessory to the burglary will be straightforward: (1) he abetted (encouraged) Freddie by embarking on the crime with him; (2) he did so with an intention to abet Freddie; and, (3) he provided encouragement with the intention that Freddie would commit the burglary. Cases like this one – in which two or more people act together with the shared purpose of committing a particular crime (or crimes) – are often referred to as a joint enterprise (even though 'joint enterprise' is not in fact a legal term[7]).

Cases involving a joint enterprise become far more difficult when one party steps outside the common purpose and commits some other offence. For example, suppose that, whilst Ronnie and Freddie were burgling Jack's house, Jack arrived home and disturbed them. Freddie had told Ronnie that he was going to take a gun with him for situations like this. Ronnie had urged him not to, but when Freddie insisted Ronnie said, 'Ok, as long as you only use it for show and don't shoot anyone'. But, upon seeing Jack, Freddie took out the gun and fatally shot him. On these facts, Freddie is straightforwardly guilty of murder. But is Ronnie guilty as an accessory to the murder? In a line of cases that began with the Privy Council's decision in *Chan Wing-Siu v The Queen* [1985] AC 168, and included the House of Lords' decision in *R v Powell & Daniels*; *R v English* [1999] 1 AC 1, the courts held that where two people have a shared purpose to commit crime A, and during the commission of this crime one of them commits crime B, the other person will be liable as an accessory to crime B if the following four conditions are satisfied:

1. The parties must have been embarked on a joint enterprise
2. The offence must have been an incident of the joint enterprise
3. The defendant must have foreseen that the principal might commit the offence
4. The offence must have been of a type that the defendant foresaw.[8]

Applying this to our example, Ronnie and Freddie were embarked on a joint enterprise and the murder was an incident of this. The prosecution would point to Ronnie's statement '… don't shoot anyone' to argue that Ronnie foresaw that Freddie *might* commit murder if they were disturbed during the burglary, and the killing was of the type that Ronnie foresaw (a shooting). So, under the law set out in *Chan Wing-Siu* and *R v Powell & Daniels*; *R v English*, Ronnie could be found guilty of being an accessory to the murder committed by Freddie. This became known as 'parasitic accessory liability'.[9]

Parasitic accessory liability was very controversial, particularly in homicide cases. For a principal like Freddie to be guilty of murder he must have intended to kill or cause GBH. But in cases of parasitic accessory liability, a defendant could be guilty of being an accessory to murder as long as he *foresaw* that the principal *might* commit murder (requirement 3 on the list above). In other words, a defendant like Ronnie could be guilty of being an accessory to murder – and therefore receive the mandatory life sentence – notwithstanding the fact that he had no intention that the victim should be killed or suffer GBH, nor any intention to assist or encourage the principal to commit murder.

In *R v Jogee* [2016] UKSC 8, *Ruddock v The Queen* [2016] UKPC 7, the Supreme Court was asked to reconsider the law set out in *Chan Wing-Siu* and *R v Powell & Daniels*;

---

[7]In *R v Jogee* [2016] UKSC 8, *Ruddock v The Queen* [2016] UKPC 7, the Supreme Court confirmed that 'the expression "joint enterprise" is not a legal term of art' ([77]). This leaves uncertain the precedential status of the decision of the (seven member) Supreme Court in *R v Gnango* [2011] UKSC 59 (which was covered in detail in the first edition of this book (pp 508–513)).

[8]For a detailed description of these four conditions, see pages 508–520 of the first edition of this book.

[9]A term first used by Sir John Smith QC ('Criminal Liability of Accessories: Law and Law Reform' 113 *Law Quarterly Review* 453, 455).

*R v English*. The certified point of general public importance was whether this law 'over-criminalises secondary parties'. In a judgment described as being of 'seminal' importance,[10] the Supreme Court rejected the approach taken in *Chan Wing-Siu*. In this section we are going to examine and evaluate the Supreme Court's judgment.

## 1. The law before *R v Jogee*

Before looking at the decision in *R v Jogee* itself, it is first worth examining in greater detail why parasitic accessory liability was so controversial.

### EXTRACT

In the following extract Wilson and Ormerod discuss Simester's attempt to justify parasitic accessory liability. What justification did Simester offer? Why do Wilson and Ormerod disagree with Simester? Who do you agree with, and why?

### Wilson, W. and Ormerod, D. (2015) 'Simply Harsh to Fairly Simple: Joint Enterprise Reform' *Criminal Law Review* 3

Particularly in the case of murder, there is a significant injustice arising from the present state of the law founded on the joint enterprise approach. A conviction for being party to a joint enterprise may mean that D suffers all the consequences of a murder conviction, including the offence label and the mandatory sentence (ratcheted up in real terms by the Sch.21 tariffs to the Criminal Justice Act 2003), without necessarily having demonstrated any of the culpability or wrongdoing of the principal offender. Given that the wrong in murder is to kill with malice aforethought, to convict a secondary party of that crime simply upon proof of his contemplation or foresight that this may be what his principal has in mind takes considerable justification.

Simester offers one justification: it is not, in principle, wrong to punish D for the actions of P. By joining with P in a common criminal enterprise which has death as a foreseen outcome D changes his normative position in relation to that outcome. Rough justice it may be, he implies, but justice nevertheless, no less than GBH murder is [GBH murder is where someone is convicted of murder on the basis of the GBH rule]. We cannot absolve ourselves from responsibility for the consequences of our actions by blaming an unruly fate. That is not how our moral universe is organised. The problem with this argument in the context of PAL [parasitic accessory liability], however, is, as has been explained, that it fails to pay full regard to a central and defining feature underpinning criminal doctrine: that we must take responsibility for our own choices and their outcomes, not the choices of others and their outcomes. Standard accessorial liability accommodates this problem to a degree by basing the liability of secondary parties on their lending (unconditional) support to the criminal projects of the principal. This is why contemplation alone sufficed in *DPP of Northern Ireland v Maxwell*. In *Maxwell* D did not know precisely the crime to be committed, but by assisting P in the knowledge that P might intentionally commit one of a number of crimes, D was deemed, quite fairly, to have lent his support to any of those crimes, if committed. The unknown crime constitutes their common purpose. But in PAL, having lent support to one *crime*, D is also deemed to lend support to another merely because, although it forms no part of their common purpose, he has foreseen,

---

[10]*R v Anwar* [2016] EWCA Crim 551, [20].

out of the corner of his eye, the possibility that P might commit this further crime. Unconditional support is lent only to crime A and only constructive support, in effect, to crime B, a crime indeed which D may even have counselled his principal *not* to commit or which was at the periphery of his thinking when lending his support to crime A. What moral principle demands that I take responsibility not simply for the consequences of my own choices and those choices of my co-adventurer which I happen to share but also those which I do not share but happen to contemplate that he may, with a following wind, make at some stage in the future? In the specific context of murder, of course, the problem is exacerbated. D is liable despite not having chosen to kill; and not even having chosen to cause serious injury. D's choice, and *pace* Simester admittedly he makes one, is simply not to back out of a criminal enterprise when he realises that P may have more on his mind than what has been agreed. A conviction for murder, rather than manslaughter, is, given the power of the label and the mandatory sentence, not rough justice. It is injustice.

The extract from Wilson and Ormerod focuses on whether the rules governing parasitic accessory liability meant that, in homicide cases, defendants could be convicted of being an accessory to murder even though they were not sufficiently culpable to deserve the label 'murderer' and the mandatory life sentence. The following extract, taken from a report published by the House of Commons Justice Committee, discusses this issue in a broader context.

## EXTRACT

Read the following extract from the Justice Committee's report and make a list of the concerns expressed by the witnesses to their enquiry. How did the Government respond to these concerns?

### House of Commons Justice Committee (2014) *Joint Enterprise: Follow-Up*, Fourth Report of Session 2014–15, HC 310

#### Joint enterprise as a social policy tool and a deterrent

26 Several of our witnesses used the metaphor of a "dragnet" to describe the operation of joint enterprise, claiming that it was hoovering up young people from ethnic minority communities who have peripheral, minor or even in some cases non-existent involvement in serious criminal acts, along with the principal perpetrators of those acts, and imposing draconian penalties on them. Melanie McFadyean argued that the doctrine was:

a blunt powerful instrument operated crucially and centrally for social policy reasons as stated repeatedly in appeal court judgments and elsewhere, its remit to be tough on crime and to be seen to be so.

In oral evidence she cited a number of judgments and other sources in support of her contention. Other witnesses made similar arguments. Dr Dyson claimed that "The reason for the core of joint enterprise was almost certainly not normative or moral, but simply evidential and driven by policy. In particular, how do you deal with crimes with multiple defendants". Simon Natas of Irvine Thanvi Natas Solicitors argued that "The use of punitive law and order policies to combat youth crime is a blunt instrument which runs the risk of making matters worse, not only because young people are much less likely to cooperate with the authorities if they perceive the legal system to be unjust, but also because custodial sentences have been shown to increase, not reduce, reoffending".

27 A claim made in support of the use of joint enterprise is that it has the desirable effect of deterring young people from becoming involved in criminal activities associated with gangs. In 2009 the Metropolitan Police produced a video which has been shown in many schools in London to warn young people of the possible consequences for them of joint enterprise if they engage in gang activities; there has also been considerable publicity about some joint enterprise cases in recent years. Nevertheless, some of our witnesses expressed scepticism about the existence of a deterrent effect. Dr Crewe, for example, argued that:

> For deterrence to work, at least two conditions need to be met. One is that people are aware of the sanction or the penalty. As others have said, our experience in undertaking the research is that very few of our interviewees said that they had any idea of what joint enterprise was, or they had heard of it but understood it only vaguely, which is not surprising as it is difficult to understand ...

> The second condition that needs to be met is that, even among those who are aware of the sanction, it would have to have some impact on their behaviour ... We know from the research literature on deterrence that thinking that you will be caught has more of a deterrent effect than the length of sentence or the severity of the sanction.

28 We put to the Minister claims that the application of joint enterprise was being driven by social policy considerations, including the aim of deterring young people from involvement in criminal gang activities because of the severity of the penalties they might face. He said:

> We would all want people to think very carefully before they were involved in any crime, and the consequence of being involved in crime is the whole principle, I hope, of what we are looking at today. If it has an effect on gang culture, so be it. At the end of the day, my view – a non-legalistic view – is around justice. Justice for the victim is the most important thing.

29 We consider that there is a danger in justifying the joint enterprise doctrine on the basis that it sends a signal or delivers a wider social message. The application of the doctrine should be such as to ensure that people are found guilty of offences in accordance with the law as it currently stands, which includes the threshold of foresight for secondary participants. It is self-evident that if people are aware of the risk of conviction under joint enterprise, they should also recognize that involvement in gang activities which could lead to criminal offences may result in them being charged and convicted.

...

## Joint enterprise and murder

36 One of the main influences on opinions about the fairness of the joint enterprise doctrine is the fact that, when a jury finds a secondary participant guilty of murder, a life sentence has to be imposed. Although the sentencer has some discretion in determining the tariff (the minimum term which must be served before a person is eligible for parole), a life sentence is potentially what its name indicates and release on completion of tariff is far from certain. The requirement to impose a life sentence in murder cases makes it all the more important that prosecutors exercise discriminatory judgment in deciding which charges to bring against each individual in cases where groups of people are involved and a death occurs. Because life sentences must be imposed on all those convicted of joint enterprise murder in such cases, it compounds the sense of injustice on the part of those who believe that a convicted person did not intend that murder or serious harm should take place. They and their families contrast their secondary participation

not only with person who dealt the fatal blow but also with murderers in other cases, and do not see it as appropriate that they have the same sentence. The mandatory life sentence also magnifies concerns over the *mens rea* threshold of foresight, through the contrast between the lowness of that threshold with the severity of the sentence on conviction. This contrast has been accentuated by the rise in the average minimum term of imprisonment imposed for a mandatory life sentence, from 12 years in 2003 to 21 years in 2013.

37 We asked the Minister whether the lack of flexibility and discretion in sentencing murder cases meant that it would be sensible to consider whether the doctrine of joint enterprise should be employed in those cases. He replied:

> That has been looked at, not only after previous reports from the Committee, but also by previous Secretaries of State. It is a really difficult decision. When people go to prison for a very long time, it has a huge effect on them and their families, but we have to balance that against their involvement under the legislation (*sic*). I understand where you are coming from, but it is a balance that has to be made to protect the public and to protect the victims.

## 2. The judgment in *R v Jogee*

Having looked at the criticisms of the old law, we can now turn to the judgment in *R v Jogee* [2016] UKSC 8, *Ruddock v The Queen* [2016] UKPC 7. The facts of these two cases, which the Supreme Court heard together, were as follows:

- Ameen Jogee spent the evening of 9 June 2011 with his co-defendant, Mohammed Hirsi. Shortly before midnight Jogee and Hirsi went to the home of a woman named Naomi Reid. There was an argument. Reid told them to leave and warned that her partner, Paul Fyfe, would be home soon. Jogee and Hirsi left, but added that they would be back later. A little later Hirsi returned to Reid's house alone. Reid phoned Jogee and told him to come and take Hirsi away. Jogee arrived, and the two men left. But soon after they returned to Reid's home once again. By now, Fyfe had also arrived at Reid's house. Whilst Fyfe was upstairs Hirsi went to the kitchen and picked up a knife. Jogee was armed with a bottle. When Fyfe came downstairs there was an angry exchange, during which Hirsi fatally stabbed Fyfe with the knife. At trial, Hirsi was convicted of murder and Jogee was convicted of being an accessory to the murder.
- Shirley Ruddock was convicted of being an accessory to the murder of Pete Robinson. Ruddock and his co-defendant, a man named Hudson, had stolen Robinson's car. Robinson was later found with his hands and feet tied and his throat cut. Hudson pleaded guilty to the murder. The prosecution's case was that Ruddock had assisted the murder by tying Robinson's hands and feet.

The Supreme Court's judgment, handed down by Lord Hughes and Lord Toulson JJSC, began by recounting a line of cases, from *R v Collison* (1831) 4 Car & P 565 to *R v Reid (Barry)* (1975) 62 Cr App R 109. These cases had established an important point, they explained, that parties to a joint enterprise could only be guilty of being an accessory to murder if they intentionally encouraged or assisted the principal to commit murder. In *Chan Wing-Siu*, however, the Privy Council departed from these authorities. According to *Chan Wing-Siu*, if P and D agree to commit crime A, and in the course of it P commits crime B, D may be convicted of being an accessory to crime B even if he did not intend for crime B to be committed, as long as he foresaw it as a possibility. Lords Hughes and Toulson said that this fails to distinguish between foresight and intention:

[T]he rule in *Chan Wing-Siu* makes guilty those who foresee crime B but never intended it or wanted it to happen. There can be no doubt that if D2 continues to participate in crime A with foresight that D1 may commit crime B, that is evidence, and sometimes powerful evidence, of an intent to assist D1 in crime B. But it is evidence of such intent (or, if one likes, of "authorisation"), not conclusive of it ([66])

Having concluded that in *Chan Wing-Siu* the 'law took a wrong turn' ([87]), the next question for the Supreme Court in *R v Jogee* was whether to reverse 'a statement of principle which has been made and followed by the Privy Council and the House of Lords on a number of occasions' ([79]). The Court offered five reasons for so doing:

## EXTRACT

### *R v Jogee* [2016] UKSC 8, *Ruddock v The Queen* [2016] UKPC 7

#### Lord Hughes and Lord Toulson JJSC

80 Firstly, we have had the benefit of a much fuller analysis than on previous occasions when the topic has been considered. In *Chan Wing-Siu* only two English cases were referred to in the judgment – *Anderson and Morris* and *Davies*. More were referred to in the judgments in *Powell and English*, but they did not include (among others) *Collison*, *Skeet*, *Spraggett* or notably *Reid*.

81 Secondly, it cannot be said that the law is now well established and working satisfactorily. It remains highly controversial and a continuing source of difficulty for trial judges. It has also led to large numbers of appeals.

82 Thirdly, secondary liability is an important part of the common law, and if a wrong turn has been taken, it should be corrected.

83 Fourthly, in the common law foresight of what might happen is ordinarily no more than evidence from which a jury can infer the presence of a requisite intention. It may be strong evidence, but its adoption as a test for the mental element for murder in the case of a secondary party is a serious and anomalous departure from the basic rule, which results in over-extension of the law of murder and reduction of the law of manslaughter. Murder already has a relatively low *mens rea* threshold, because it includes an intention to cause serious injury, without intent to kill or to cause risk to life. The *Chan Wing-Siu* principle extends liability for murder to a secondary party on the basis of a still lesser degree of culpability, namely foresight only of the possibility that the principal may commit murder but without there being any need for intention to assist him to do so. It savours, as Professor Smith suggested, of constructive crime.

84 Fifthly, the rule brings the striking anomaly of requiring a lower mental threshold for guilt in the case of the accessory than in the case of the principal.

85 As to the argument that even if the court is satisfied that the law took a wrong turn, any correction should now be left to Parliament, the doctrine of secondary liability is a common law doctrine (put into statutory form in section 8 of the 1861 Act) and, if it has been unduly widened by the courts, it is proper for the courts to correct the error.

The Supreme Court then set out the correct approach. It emphasised that 'joint enterprise' is not a legal term and there are no special rules that apply to so-called joint enterprise cases. In all cases, the 'ordinary principles of secondary liability' should be applied ([76]). In other words, even in a case which might be described as a joint enterprise you should apply the same *actus reus* and *mens rea* requirements as for any other case involving accessories. These are the three requirements that we worked through earlier in the chapter.

As well as clarifying the correct approach, the Supreme Court offered some guidance on the application of the *actus reus* and *mens rea* requirements of being an accessory in joint enterprise cases. Five points are worth noting. First, if the prosecution is able to prove the existence of a common purpose, this is likely to be sufficient to constitute proof of the *actus reus* and *mens rea* requirements of being an accessory:

> 78 As we have explained, secondary liability does not require the existence of an agreement between D1 and D2. Where, however, it exists, such agreement is by its nature a form of encouragement and in most cases will also involve acts of assistance. The long established principle that where parties agree to carry out a criminal venture, each is liable for acts to which they have expressly or impliedly given their assent is an example of the intention to assist which is inherent in the making of the agreement. Similarly, where people come together without agreement, often spontaneously, to commit an offence together, the giving of intentional support by words or deeds, including by supportive presence, is sufficient to attract secondary liability on ordinary principles. We repeat that secondary liability includes cases of agreement between principal and secondary party, but it is not limited to them.

As this extract illustrates, however, it is possible to establish the *actus reus* and *mens rea* requirements of being an accessory without proving that the parties shared a common purpose. Accordingly, in some cases – such as those involving a spontaneous outbreak of violence – it may be better to avoid the language of joint enterprise and common purpose:

> 95 In cases where there is a more or less spontaneous outbreak of multi-handed violence, the evidence may be too nebulous for the jury to find that there was some form of agreement, express or tacit. But, as we have said, liability as an aider or abettor does not necessarily depend on there being some form of agreement between the defendants; it depends on proof of intentional assistance or encouragement, conditional or otherwise. If D2 joins with a group which he realises is out to cause serious injury, the jury may well infer that he intended to encourage or assist the deliberate infliction of serious bodily injury and/or intended that that should happen if necessary. In that case, if D1 acts with intent to cause serious bodily injury and death results, D1 and D2 will each be guilty of murder.

Second, earlier in the chapter we considered the example of the shopkeeper who sells a customer a gun knowing that the customer might use it to commit a murder, not caring whether the customer commits the murder or not. The customer subsequently commits the murder. We saw that the shopkeeper satisfied the first *mens rea* requirement of being an accessory: he (obliquely) intended to assist the customer to commit the murder. His liability therefore hinges on the second *mens rea* requirement. It was not the shopkeeper's direct intention that the murder would be committed. His purpose was to make a profit on the sale, and he would not have considered it a failure if the victim had not been killed. Nor was it his oblique intention to assist the murder. He knew the customer might commit the offence, but he did not foresee it as virtually certain. The Supreme Court in *R v Jogee* seemed to confirm this analysis:

> [10] … [T]here can be cases where D2 gives intentional assistance or encouragement to D1 to commit an offence and to act with the mental element required of him, but without D2 having a positive intent that the particular offence will be committed. That may be so, for example, where at the time that encouragement is given it remains uncertain what D1 might do; an arms supplier might be such a case.

Third, the Court noted that the defendant's intention may be conditional – indeed, in cases involving joint enterprises, it often will be:

> 92 In cases of secondary liability arising out of a prior joint criminal venture, it will also often be necessary to draw the jury's attention to the fact that the intention to assist, and indeed the intention that the crime should be committed, may be conditional. The bank robbers who attack the bank when one or more of them is armed no doubt hope that it will not be necessary to use the guns, but it may be a perfectly proper inference that all were intending that if they met resistance the weapons should be used with the intent to do grievous bodily harm at least. The group of young men which faces down a rival group may hope that the rivals will slink quietly away, but it may well be a perfectly proper inference that all were intending that if resistance were to be met, grievous bodily harm at least should be done.

Fourth, we saw above that under the old law the final requirement of parasitic accessory liability was that the offence that the principal committed was of a type that the defendant foresaw. This often required juries to consider whether the attack that occurred was of a different type to the attack that the defendant foresaw, in particular, whether an attack with one weapon (such as a gun) was of a different type to an attack with a different weapon (such as a knife). In *R v Jogee* the Supreme Court stated that the emphasis should shift away from the weapon used and towards whether the defendant intended to assist or encourage the crime committed:

> 98 … The tendency which has developed in the application of the rule in *Chan Wing-Siu* to focus on what D2 knew of what weapon D1 was carrying can and should give way to an examination of whether D2 intended to assist in the crime charged. If that crime is murder, then the question is whether he intended to assist the intentional infliction of grievous bodily harm at least, which question will often, as set out above, be answered by asking simply whether he himself intended grievous bodily harm at least. Very often he may intend to assist in violence using whatever weapon may come to hand. In other cases he may think that D1 has an iron bar whereas he turns out to have a knife, but the difference may not at all affect his intention to assist, if necessary, in the causing of grievous bodily harm at least. Knowledge or ignorance that weapons generally, or a particular weapon, is carried by D1 will be evidence going to what the intention of D2 was, and may be irresistible evidence one way or the other, but it is evidence and no more.

Lastly, the Supreme Court discussed the position in a homicide case in which P and D violently attack the victim, P is guilty of murder, but D lacked the *mens rea* of being an accessory to murder. The Court stated that 'If a person is a party to a violent attack on another, without an intent to assist in the causing of death or really serious harm, but the violence escalates and results in death, he will be not guilty of murder but guilty of manslaughter' ([96]). This would normally be because D intended to assist or encourage the infliction of some harm falling short of GBH, but is not limited to such cases. It is sufficient that D knew or intended that P would commit an act that was unlawful and which the reasonable person would have realised involved a risk of some harm (see the dangerousness test for unlawful act manslaughter, detailed in Chapter 5). In fact, in such a case, the Court stated that D would only escape liability for being an accessory to manslaughter if the death was 'caused by some overwhelming supervening act by the perpetrator which nobody in the defendant's shoes could have contemplated might happen and is of such a character as to relegate his acts to history' ([97]). This would not apply if the cause of death was simply the 'escalation of a fight' ([33]).

So, in cases involving fights between rival gangs, if D did not form the *mens rea* necessary to be convicted of being an accessory to murder, he will almost inevitably be convicted of being an accessory to manslaughter instead. The Supreme Court said that this undermined one of the key policy reasons for the decision in *Chan Wing-Siu*. In that case, the Privy Council stated 'Where a man lends himself to a criminal enterprise knowing that potentially murderous weapons are to be carried, and in the event they in fact are used by his partner with an intent sufficient for murder, he should not escape the consequences'. The Court in *R v Jogee* stated that this wrongly implied that, were it not for the decision in *Chan Wing-Siu*, D 'would escape all criminal liability' ([74]). Moreover, the Court added, 'There was no consideration in *Chan Wing-Siu*, or in *Powell and English*, of the fundamental policy question whether and why it was necessary and appropriate to reclassify such conduct as murder rather than manslaughter. Such a discussion would have involved, among other things, questions about fair labelling and fair discrimination in sentencing' ([74]). The Court continued:

> 75 In *Powell and English* Lord Hutton referred to the need to give effective protection to the public against criminals operating in gangs (at p 25), but the same comments apply. There does not appear to have been any objective evidence that the law prior to *Chan Wing-Siu* failed to provide the public with adequate protection. A further policy reason suggested by Lord Hutton for setting a lower *mens rea* requirement for the secondary party than for the principal was that the secondary party has time to think before taking part in a criminal enterprise like a bank robbery, whereas the principal may have to decide on the spur of the moment whether to use his weapon. But the principal has had an earlier choice whether to go armed or not. As for the secondary party, he may have leisure to think before going out to rob a bank, but the same is not true in many other cases (for example, of young people who become suddenly embroiled in a fight in a bar and may make a quick decision whether or not to help their friends).

So, if you are answering a problem question that involves a joint, fatal, violent attack, when discussing the liability of the secondary parties you should begin by considering whether they are guilty of being an accessory to murder. Here you apply the normal *actus reus* and *mens rea* requirements of being an accessory, as follows:

1. Did D aid, abet, counsel or procure the commission of murder by P? (I.e. did D's actions in fact provide encouragement or assistance to P?)

2. Did D intend to aid, abet, counsel or procure the commission of murder by P? (I.e. did D intend to aid, abet, counsel or procure either the intentional killing of V by P, or the intentional causing of GBH to V by P?)

3. Did D know or intend the essential elements of P's offence? (I.e. was it D's direct intention that P should intentionally kill or cause GBH to V? If not, did D know that it was virtually certain that P would intentionally kill or cause GBH to V?)

If the defendant lacks the necessary *mens rea* of being an accessory to murder, then you should instead consider whether he is guilty of being an accessory to manslaughter. The relevant type of manslaughter will be unlawful act manslaughter, and so the *actus reus* and *mens rea* requirements will be as follows:

1. Did D aid, abet, counsel or procure the commission of manslaughter by P? (I.e. did D's actions in fact provide encouragement or assistance to P?)

2. Did D intend to aid, abet, counsel or procure the commission of manslaughter by P? (I.e. did D intend to aid, abet, counsel or procure the intentional commission by P of an act, where that act was unlawful, dangerous and was the cause of V's death?)

3. Did D know or intend the essential elements of P's offence? (I.e. was it D's direct intention that P should intentionally commit the unlawful, dangerous act that caused V's death? If not, did D know that it was virtually certain that P would intentionally commit the unlawful, dangerous act that caused V's death?)

Having set out the correct approach, the Supreme Court then considered the position of the two defendants, Jogee and Ruddock. At the trials of both men, the trial judge had given a jury direction based on the *Chan Wing-Siu* principle. As such, their murder convictions could not stand. Jogee was subsequently retried. At his retrial, the jury acquitted him of being an accessory to murder but convicted him of being an accessory to manslaughter.[11] In Ruddock's case, the Jamaican Court of Appeal concluded that there should not be a retrial, and instead substituted a conviction of being an accessory to manslaughter.[12]

## 3. Evaluation of *R v Jogee*

In its judgment in *R v Jogee*, the Supreme Court addressed the concern that the effect of its decision would be 'to render invalid all convictions which were arrived at over many years by faithfully applying the law as laid down in *Chan Wing-Siu* and in *Powell and English*' ([100]). Rejecting this concern, the Court explained:

> 100 … The error identified, of equating foresight with intent to assist rather than treating the first as evidence of the second, is important as a matter of legal principle, but it does not follow that it will have been important on the facts to the outcome of the trial or to the safety of the conviction. Moreover, where a conviction has been arrived at by faithfully applying the law as it stood at the time, it can be set aside only by seeking exceptional leave to appeal to the Court of Appeal out of time. That court has power to grant such leave, and may do so if substantial injustice be demonstrated, but it will not do so simply because the law applied has now been declared to have been mistaken

So, whilst for appeals against conviction brought within time (i.e. within 28 days) the key criterion is whether the conviction is unsafe, for appeals brought out of time an extra hurdle applies. Leave to appeal will only be granted if 'substantial injustice' can be demonstrated. As the Supreme Court indicated, this is a high threshold.

The 'invidious task of determining how this concept [substantial injustice] ought to be applied in the context of an individual who has been convicted of a serious criminal offence, often murder, based upon what the Supreme Court has since characterised as being a legal wrong turn'[13] fell to the Court of Appeal in *R v Johnson* [2016] EWCA Crim 1613. In this case, the Court of Appeal considered the cases of 13 men. Between them, these 13 men had been involved in a total of six separate incidents of violence. Five of the six victims died; the other was stabbed. Twelve of the men were convicted of being accessories to murder, the other was convicted of wounding with intent to cause GBH.[14] All 13 were convicted prior to the Supreme Court's judgment in *R v Jogee* and sought leave to appeal against their convictions.

---

[11]'Ameen Jogee Jailed for Manslaughter in Joint Enterprise Test Case' *The Guardian*, 12 September 2016.
[12]*Shirley Ruddock v R* [2017] JMCA Crim 6.
[13]Laird, K. (2017) 'Commentary on *R v Johnson' Criminal Law Review* 216, 218.
[14]Offences Against the Person Act 1861, s. 18. He was convicted on the basis that the prosecution had established that he was either a principal or an accessory.

## EXTRACT

Read the following extract from the Court of Appeal's judgment. What are the policy reasons for the 'substantial injustice' requirement? What factors will the courts take into account when determining whether this requirement is met?

### R v Johnson [2016] EWCA Crim 1613

### Lord Thomas CJ, Sir Brian Leveson P and Lady Hallett LJ, V-P

18 In our view, as was accepted, the fact that there has been a change in the law brought about by correcting the wrong turning in *Chan Wing-Siu* and *R v Powell, R v English* is plainly, in itself, insufficient. As the Supreme Court stated at paragraph 100, a long line of authority clearly establishes that if a person was properly convicted on the law as it then stood, the court will not grant leave without it being demonstrated that a substantial injustice would otherwise be done. The need to establish substantial injustice results from the wider public interest in legal certainty and the finality of decisions made in accordance with the then clearly established law. The requirement takes into account the requirement in a common law system for a court to be able to alter or correct the law upon which a large number of cases have been determined without the consequence that each of those cases can be re-opened. It also takes into account the interests of the victim (or the victim's family), particularly in cases where death has resulted and closure is particularly important.

...

21 In determining whether that high threshold has been met, the court will primarily and ordinarily have regard to the strength of the case advanced that the change in the law would, in fact, have made a difference. If crime A is a crime of violence which the jury concluded must have involved the use of a weapon so that the inference of participation with an intention to cause really serious harm is strong, that is likely to be very difficult. At the other end of the spectrum, if crime A is a different crime, not involving intended violence or use of force, it may well be easier to demonstrate substantial injustice. The court will also have regard to other matters including whether the applicant was guilty of other, though less serious, criminal conduct. It is not, however, in our view, material to consider the length of time that has elapsed. If there was a substantial injustice, it is irrelevant whether that injustice occurred a short time or a long time ago. It is and remains an injustice.

The guidance in *R v Johnson* makes it clear that the substantial injustice requirement will only be met in the 'rarest of cases'.[15] Indeed, the Court of Appeal refused all 13 men leave to appeal against their convictions.[16]

---

[15]Laird, K. (2017) 'Commentary on *R v Johnson*' *Criminal Law Review* 216, 220. Similarly, in *R v Anwar* [2016] EWCA Crim 551 the Court of Appeal emphasised that 'the same facts which would previously have been used to support the inference of *mens rea* before the decision in *Jogee* will equally be used now. What has changed is the articulation of the *mens rea* ...' ([22]), and so it is 'difficult to foresee circumstances in which there might have been a case to answer under the law before *Jogee* but, because of the way in which the law is now articulated, there no longer is' ([20]).

[16]Similarly, in *R v McLeod & others* [2017] EWCA Crim 800 the Court of Appeal held that the substantial injustice threshold had not been met, because the inference of the necessary intention was 'irresistible' and so a *R v Jogee* compliant direction 'would not have made a difference' ([48]).

The extract from *R v Johnson* above states that, when applying the substantial injustice requirement, the primary factor to consider is whether the outcome at the defendant's trial would have been any different had the jury been asked to apply the law as stated in *R v Jogee* instead of *Chan Wing-Siu*. Here, the notion of conditional intention may play a significant role. One of the incidents considered in *R v Johnson* involved a man named Michael Hall. The violence in Hall's case occurred outside a pub late at night, and was between two groups. One group included Michael Hall, a woman named Laura Mitchell (who we will discuss later in the chapter), and the eventual killer, Carl Holmes. The other group included the victim, Andrew Ayres, and two brothers, Craig and Dean Powell. The incident began with an argument over a taxi. Hall, Mitchell and Holmes were all involved in the violence, punching and kicking members of the other group. There was then a lull in the violence. Some of Hall and Mitchell's group (but not Hall and Mitchell themselves) walked down the road to a friend's house, where they collected a knuckleduster, a CS spray canister and a medieval mace. When they returned, the members of the other group realised that they were about to be attacked again and tried to run away. Craig Powell escaped, but Hall caught Dean Powell, pulled him to the ground and punched and kicked him. Andrew Ayres was also caught and knocked over. Carl Holmes then stamped on Ayres' head with such force that he died from his injuries. At trial Hall and Mitchell were both convicted of being accessories to Ayres' murder.

In *R v Johnson* Hall argued that he would not have been convicted of being an accessory to Ayres' murder had the prosecution been required to prove that he intended to encourage or assist the infliction of serious injury on the victim (as required by *R v Jogee*), and so therefore his conviction was unsafe. The Court of Appeal rejected this, stating:

> The jury must by their verdict have concluded that [Hall] foresaw that Holmes would attack the third member of the group, the deceased, with intent to cause really serious bodily injury. In the circumstances it would have been open to them to infer that he had the necessary conditional intent now required ([189]).

Therefore, the Court said, there was not 'a sufficiently strong case that the defendant would not have been convicted of murder if the law had been explained to the jury as set out in *Jogee*', and so substantial injustice had not been established ([191]). In the following extract, Stark discusses the Court's reasoning, particularly its use of the notion of conditional intention.

## EXTRACT

In this extract Stark suggests that the approach to conditional intention in *R v Johnson* means that few instances of substantial injustice will be found, and that *R v Jogee* may have changed little. Why?

### Stark, F. (2017) 'The Taming of *Jogee*?' 76 *Cambridge Law Journal* 4

Those appeals heard in *Johnson* that engaged the two-crime analysis characteristic of PAL [parasitic accessory liability], and where the jury was directed in terms of foresight of crime B, were scuppered by the Court's willingness to use *D1*'s foresight to find a conditional intention on his part to assist or encourage *D2* intentionally to cause (at least) GBH, if such violence proved necessary. *Jogee* is clear that such conditional intention will suffice for accessorial liability for murder. If such a conditional intention is found on the facts, then it will not be possible to argue that manslaughter was a more appropriate verdict.

A good example of the Court's broad approach to conditional intention is the appeal in *Hall*. That the defendant "foresaw that [D2] would attack [V] ... with intent to cause really serious bodily injury" was found to be consistent with a finding of conditional intention to assist or encourage the intentional causing of GBH (at [189]). Here (despite the Court's vague reference to "the circumstances" of the case), conditional intention looks suspiciously like foresight of crime B combined with a decision to continue with the original plan to commit crime A, namely PAL. If conditional intention to assist or encourage offending can easily be found in such cases, the impact of *Jogee* on past convictions will be limited: few will be unsafe, and few instances of "substantial injustice" will be found, because the jury will (having applied *Chan Wing-Siu*, etc.) have been sure that the defendant foresaw crime B's possible commission in the course of crime A's commission. *Johnson* may also suggest that, in the future, convictions for murder could legitimately be returned routinely – on the post-*Jogee* basis of conditional intention – in cases where the defendant foresaw the possibility of GBH being caused intentionally, and continued with an underlying criminal plan nonetheless. This will be particularly the case where the defendant knew that the principal was armed (e.g. at [21]). In short, *Jogee* may have changed little.

As well as looking suspiciously like the *Chan Wing-Siu* test of foresight,[17] there is a further, conceptual, problem with the courts' approach to conditional intention in *R v Jogee* and *R v Johnson*. As Simester has explained,[18] if D has a conditional intention, that intention must relate to a future action by D himself (such as where D opens the back door of a lorry intending to steal the contents, should they turn out to be valuable). D cannot have a conditional intention that relates to the future action of someone else. If D lends P a baseball bat for P to use to attack his business partner, V, should V continue to help himself to money from their business, then it is P whose intention is conditional. Importantly, once D has passed the baseball bat to P, the *actus reus* of accessorial liability has occurred. D has aided P. The question is whether D intended to assist P to attack V. D either had such an intention or he didn't. He cannot have had a conditional intention to assist, because he had already provided assistance!

So, suppose that Jack owes Freddie some money. Freddie wants to be paid, so asks Ronnie to come with him to 'rough Jack up a bit'. Although Ronnie knows that Freddie is carrying a knife, he agrees to go with him because Freddie says he will only use the knife if 'Jack pulls a knife on me first'. But, when they confront Jack, Freddie immediately pulls out the knife and fatally stabs him. If Ronnie was charged with being an accessory to the murder, the first step would be to establish the *actus reus*. If Ronnie was found to have provided assistance or encouragement by agreeing to go with Freddie, the *actus reus* would be established. The next question would be whether, when he provided this assistance/encouragement, Ronnie had an intention to assist or encourage Freddie to kill or cause GBH to Jack. Properly analysed, this is not an instance of conditional intention, for the reason explained above. The correct approach is to begin by asking whether, when he

---

[17]A similar example is *R v Agera* [2017] EWCA Crim 740, in which the Court of Appeal concluded: 'Once the jury concluded that Lansana knew that Agera might use the knife to stab (i.e. he had that conditional intent), its size could only lead the jury to conclude that he intended that, if used, at least serious bodily injury would be caused' ([36]).

[18]Simester, A. (2017) 'Accessory Liability and Common Unlawful Purposes' 133 *Law Quarterly Review* 73.

agreed to go with Freddie, it was Ronnie's direct intention to assist or encourage Freddie to intentionally kill or cause GBH to Jack. If not, the next question is whether it was Ronnie's oblique intention.

This brings us to another criticism of the reasoning in *R v Jogee*. The Supreme Court stated clearly that foresight must be distinguished from intention. Foresight is evidence from which (oblique) intention may be inferred.[19] Yet it did not explicitly state the degree of foresight that is required for (oblique) intention to be inferred. In particular, it did not say whether the *R v Woollin* direction should be used in this context. This omission is discussed by Ormerod and Laird in the following extract.

## EXTRACT

In the following extract, what is the omission to which Ormerod and Laird refer? What issues do they say arise as a result of this omission?

### Ormerod, D. and Laird, K. (2016) '*Jogee*: Not the End of a Legal Saga but the Start of One?' *Criminal Law Review* 539

What the Supreme Court failed to mention is the fact that the common law, in the context of murder at least, imposes a high threshold on the types of foresight from which a jury will be entitled to infer intent. After over 25 years or so of incremental narrowing (i.e. from *Hyam – Woollin*), the House of Lords finally agreed in *Woollin* that: (1) the defendant can be guilty of murder as a principal offender where he intended to kill or cause really serious harm; (2) intention is not limited to purpose or desire; (3) a jury is not entitled to "find" that the defendant intended to kill or cause really serious harm unless they conclude that death or really serious harm was a virtually certain consequence, barring some unforeseen intervention, and the defendant appreciated that this was the case; (4) there is a threshold on foresight – anything less than foresight of virtual certainty will not be sufficient to entitle the jury to find intention; and (5) foresight is merely evidence and does not equal intention, given that the Court of Appeal subsequently confirmed in *Matthews and Alleyne* that the law has not yet reached a definition of intent in murder in terms of appreciation of a virtual certainty. Therefore the jury retains its "moral elbow room".

In *Jogee*, the Supreme Court concluded that: (1) the defendant can be guilty of murder as a secondary offender where he intended to assist or encourage the principal to kill or cause really serious harm with intent; (2) intention is not limited to purpose or desire; and (3) a jury may "infer" that the defendant possessed the requisite intent if they conclude that he foresaw the principal's intentional conduct. Crucially, however, there is no explicit statement as to what threshold of foresight the defendant must possess before the jury will be entitled to infer the requisite intent – will the defendant's foresight of even the slightest possibility of the principal intentionally acting in the proscribed way be sufficient for a jury to be entitled to infer that he possessed the requisite intention? Alternatively, does there have to be a high level of foresight before the jury will be entitled to infer from this foresight that he possessed the requisite intention? It is the failure to specify what intention means in this context that could lead to difficulty.

...

---

[19]Note that the Supreme Court in *R v Jogee* repeatedly used the word 'infer', notwithstanding the fact that the House of Lords preferred the word 'find' instead of 'infer' in the *R v Woollin* direction (see Chapter 4).

It is unclear whether it is safe to conclude from this omission that the Supreme Court did not intend for some version of the *Woollin* direction to apply. The House of Lords in *Woollin* did expressly state that its decision applied only to murder and did not state whether it extended to accessorial liability. Indeed, Lord Steyn prefaced his judgment in *Woollin* by remarking that intention does not necessarily have the same meaning in every context of the criminal law. To the extent that the restatement of the law in *Jogee* applies in non-murder cases, a different formulation may therefore be applicable anyway. There will, we suggest, be considerable reluctance to apply the virtual certainty test, because if applied rigorously that test will mean that it will be difficult to secure convictions for murder for any participant.

It is submitted that there are three issues arising as a result of this uncertainty around foresight and intention. First, it is unclear how judges are to direct juries on the law. Different judges may direct juries in different ways, which makes resolution of this issue a priority. Secondly, as a matter of principle, there is lack of clarity on whether there ought to be parity as to the level of foresight required of the principal and the accessory. Resolution of this issue is made more complicated by the fact that two different questions are being asked. In relation to the principal, the issue relates to a consequence, whereas for the accessory, the issue is partly about someone else's state of mind. Thirdly, without speedy resolution by the Court of Appeal there is the danger that the debate the House of Lords sought to put an end to in *Woollin* will be replayed which would be undesirable as the law would be thrown into a state of confusion.

Returning to the example involving Freddie and Ronnie, imagine that they were standing trial as co-defendants: Freddie charged with the murder of Jack; and, Ronnie charged as an accessory to this murder. Now imagine that the trial judge deems it necessary to explain the meaning of 'oblique intention' to the jury. If you were a juror, you would probably find it confusing to be told that: (1) if Ronnie foresaw that Freddie might kill or cause GBH to Jack, you may 'infer' from this that he (obliquely) intended to assist or encourage Freddie to kill or cause GBH; but, (2) you may only 'find' that Freddie (obliquely) intended to kill or cause GBH to Jack if he foresaw death or GBH as a virtual certainty (as per *R v Woollin*). As Ormerod and Laird state, it is not clear why there should be this disparity between principals and accessories, and there is a danger that some – but not all – trial judges will direct juries in accordance with *R v Woollin* in respect of both principals and accessories, resulting in uncertainty and dissimilar treatment of similar cases. At the same time, however, Ormerod and Laird acknowledge that there will be 'considerable reluctance' to apply the *R v Woollin* direction to defendants like Ronnie because it will make it difficult for prosecutors to secure convictions of secondary parties in such cases. Ronnie, for example, would argue that he did not foresee death or GBH as virtually certain because he believed Freddie would only use the knife if Jack pulled out a knife first.

There is a further question about the Supreme Court's decision in *R v Jogee* that should be considered: whether the Court was, in fact, merely correcting a 'wrong turn' taken in the earlier decision in *Chan Wing-Siu*. In a detailed examination of the case law, Stark offers an 'alternative history' according to which parasitic accessory liability was not an invention of the Privy Council in *Chan Wing-Siu*. In fact, he argues, parasitic accessory liability had existed in some form since at least the sixteenth century. As the following extract explains, the significance of *Chan Wing-Siu* was that it confirmed that, where P and D agree to commit crime A together, and during the commission of crime A P commits crime B, D must have *subjectively* foreseen the possibility of P committing crime B (as opposed to the previous approach of asking whether crime B was a probable outcome of pursuing crime A).

## EXTRACT

According to Stark, how does the reaction at the time to the decision in *Chan Wing-Siu* support his claim that the Privy Council in that case did not misstate the law?

If the decision in *R v Jogee* was not correcting a 'wrong turn', how does Stark say the decision should be understood? Why is this significant, in his opinion? Do you agree?

### Stark, F. (2016) 'The Demise of "Parasitic Accessorial Liability": Substantive Judicial Law Reform, Not Common Law Housekeeping' 75 *Cambridge Law Journal* 550

In light of the discussion above, the thesis that the Privy Council's decision in *Chan Wing-Siu* bucked a clear trend in endorsing intention as the fault element in *all* instances of secondary liability, and introduced a "new principle" that changed "the common law in a way which made it more severe ... widening the scope of secondary liability by the introduction of new doctrine", is highly suspect. Although it was claimed in *Jogee* that *Chan Wing-Siu* was "based on an incomplete, and in some respects erroneous, reading of the previous case law", the Supreme Court/Privy Council cannot escape a similar charge. The court cited selectively, giving the most sympathetic view of history that it could. On the alternative history argued for in this article, which it is submitted explains more of the decided cases, *Chan Wing-Siu* (despite the Privy Council citing few cases) simply confirmed what was already becoming clearer in the case law: there was a "wider principle" (i.e. PAL) beyond standard aiding and abetting, "whereby a secondary party is criminally liable for acts by the primary offender of a type which the former foresees but does not necessarily intend". Indeed, the appellants in *Chan Wing-Siu* do not seem to have argued otherwise, basing their case on the requirement of *foresight of a probability* of collateral offending, rather than suggesting intention was the relevant standard (although they maintained the intellectual muddle of claiming there to be "tacit agreement" regarding Crime B where in fact there was none).

...

Indeed, had the decision in *Chan Wing-Siu* been as revolutionary and flawed as the Supreme Court/Privy Council suggested, one might have expected this to be noticed. Yet, in 1984, J.C. Smith described the Privy Council's decision as "a valuable restatement and clarification of ... the law". This was not simply a case of the significance of the decision being missed in its immediate aftermath. In 1997, Smith stated that "It would be quite wrong to suppose that parasitic accessorial liability ... is a recent development in the law, an innovation by the Privy Council in *Chan Wing-Siu*". Similarly, Spencer, writing in 1985, thought that the Privy Council's decision was consistent with the contemporary English approach, not a new development. The 1985 edition of *Archbold* mentions *Chan Wing-Siu* only once, without adverse comment. Although the case was not initially applied universally, the Court of Appeal endorsed it fairly promptly.

...

The claim that *Chan Wing-Siu* was a "wrong turn", and departing from it was in large part a matter of precedent (and therefore constitutionally straightforward), is thus unconvincing. The more compelling reading of *Jogee* is that the Supreme Court/Privy Council engaged in substantive law reform. This could have been made explicit, and the decision sold as a continuation of the historical narrowing of PAL. Just as the law had moved from a focus on: (1) furthering the common purpose, to (2) probable collateral offending, to (3) contemplated/

foreseen collateral offending, it was now moving to focus on (4) intentional encouragement/assistance of the collateral crime, thus rendering PAL conceptually identical to ordinary aiding and abetting (and redundant). Many would have viewed such a judicial change as desirable, regarding PAL – a judicial development – as the genesis of much injustice. Being explicit about the change would, however, have meant engaging more directly with the proper process of revisiting previous decisions, and raised more clearly constitutional concerns about judicial activism. Although the Supreme Court/Privy Council is no doubt right that *corrections* of clear common law "errors" are largely unproblematic constitutionally, there are clearer concerns raised by more substantive reform of even the common law (as the prosecution maintained in *Jogee*). The reasons the change in *Jogee* is problematic, once the alleged precedential "error" has been dismissed as a smokescreen, are as follows: (1) the law as stated (defensibly, as shown above) in *Chan Wing-Siu* had been relatively settled for over 30 years; (2) requiring intentional encouragement or assistance for all secondary liability was not a reform the Law Commission had proposed when it had considered accessorial liability; and (3) Parliament had not apparently contemplated reforming the law, despite recent encouragement to do so. Once that shield of precedent and history has been shattered, the question is whether the *other* reasons provided by the Supreme Court/Privy Council in *Jogee* justified such dramatic law reform being undertaken by the courts, not the legislature. It is unfortunate that this question was so easily avoided in *Jogee*, but this paper opens up the possibility for it to be addressed more straightforwardly in the future. *Jogee* should be seen for what it is: significant judicial law reform, not common law housekeeping.

Stark's argument raises the question whether the abolition of parasitic accessory liability in *R v Jogee* was, in fact, desirable. Interestingly, in *Miller v The Queen* [2016] HCA 30 the High Court of Australia chose not to follow *R v Jogee* and instead affirmed the existence of parasitic accessory liability.[20] In the following extract, Simester explains why, in his opinion, the High Court of Australia was right not to follow *R v Jogee*.

## EXTRACT

Read the following extract. What is Simester's opinion on each of the following issues:

- Whether embarking on a joint criminal enterprise is a distinctive wrong;
- The lower *mens rea* that parasitic accessory liability requires of the defendant, compared to the principal;
- Whether parasitic accessory liability is draconian; and,
- The difficulties in requiring proof of abiding/abetting/counselling/procuring in all cases involving accessories?

Do you agree with Simester's critique? Should English law recognise a distinctive form of liability for secondary parties involved in a joint enterprise?

---

[20]Krebs, B. (2017) 'Accessory Liability: Persisting in Error' 76 *Cambridge Law Journal* 7.

## Simester, A.P. (2017) 'Accessory Liability and Common Unlawful Purposes' 133 *Law Quarterly Review* 73

In order to understand the latest divide between our jurisdictions, we need to specify more precisely what the Supreme Court did in *Jogee*. Most prominently, the court abolished what in Australia is called the doctrine of *extended joint criminal enterprise*, sometimes known in England as "parasitic accessorial liability". According to that doctrine, where S, the secondary party, and P, the perpetrator, form a common unlawful purpose to commit a crime (crime A), and set out together to pursue it, then in addition to any liability S may have regarding crime A, S becomes liable as a party to any further crime (crime B) committed by P in the pursuance of crime A, provided S realises that a crime of that further type is a possible upshot of their carrying out the common purpose. Extended joint criminal enterprise liability therefore supplies a distinct channel of complicity liability, separate from aiding and abetting because it does not require the prosecution to prove specifically that S has assisted or encouraged crime B. Indeed, as the House of Lords recognised in *Powell*, it operates to sustain liability even where S has actively discouraged P from committing crime B, but proceeded nonetheless with the plan to commit crime A.

That boat has now sailed from English shores. No longer can S become guilty of foreseen ancillary crimes by pursuing a shared criminal purpose with P. S must be a party *directly* to any crime of which S is convicted. *Extended* joint criminal enterprise liability is thus interred, at least for now.

So much is well known. What may be less obvious is that the doctrine of *joint criminal enterprise* itself – of "plain vanilla" joint enterprises, as Lord Hoffman once called them – is also abolished. Suppose that S and P decide to attack V. They find and confront V, who is punched by P. Prior to *Jogee*, S could be convicted of battery just in virtue of the fact that S had a common purpose with P that the battery be committed. No more. From the perspective of complicity liability, a common unlawful purpose is no longer doctrinally significant (although it may still have evidential significance). What must now be shown, under English law, is that S *aided, abetted, counselled, or procured* P's crime. Of course, the practical effects of this second difference are small. Doubtless, S can still be convicted of battery, since it will usually be straightforward to prove that one who joins in a common purpose thereby encourages the perpetrator. (More on this below.) But this is now a matter to be proved in its own right. In terms of formal doctrine, it is the encouragement, not the shared purpose, that must now be shown

...

There are no simple solutions in the field of complicity law. The problems are complex and nuanced. Rational arguments can be made both for and against the merits of extended joint criminal enterprise liability. Those arguments are not knock-down ones, and it is not helpful to suggest otherwise. The High Court [of Australia], while embracing the grip of precedent, addressed those arguments somewhat indirectly. Endorsing the earlier discussion in *R. v Powell; English*, the court pointed to evidential difficulties associated with group wrongdoing, as well as to its inherent dangerousness and tendency to escalate. *Miller v The Queen* also acknowledges the distinctive normative character of the wrong involved in embarking on a joint criminal enterprise.

On the other hand, the Supreme Court [in *Jogee*] made virtually no effort to argue against joint enterprise liability at the level of principle. It merely pointed to the so-called "anomaly" of requiring a "lower" *mens rea* standard for S than for P. But the *mens rea* standard isn't lower. It is different. As the well-known case of *Callow v Tillstone* illustrates, sometimes S's *mens rea* can be far more stringent than is demanded of P. Given that *actus reus* requirements differ between accessories and principals, it is hardly surprising that the *mens rea* elements also differ. S needs to *intend* his or her own act of involvement, *and* have *mens rea* regarding P's acts *as well as* regarding P's *mens rea*. More generally, it is a mistake to think that S's culpability must equal P's. What matters is whether S is *sufficiently* culpable to be held guilty of P's crime.

Still, there is the broader worry that extended joint criminal enterprise law may be Draconian in practice. Curiously, the law in jurisdictions such as Australia, Canada, and New Zealand has not generated parallel controversy to that in England. The High Court in *Miller v The Queen* was not presented with evidence that it has become a state weapon of systematic injustice. Albeit without citing any such evidence, the Supreme Court saw things differently. The decision in *Jogee* is clearly informed by a sense that the application of extended joint criminal enterprise liability rules has in recent years produced significant injustice.

Given the lack of analysis of this problem, it is plausible that the difficulty may arise not from common purpose liability doctrine per se but from how it has been applied: from over-zealous findings of shared criminal purposes – with foresight – against those on the periphery of wrongdoing. Common purpose liability should be a form of guilt by *enterprise*, not by association; a point emphasised forcefully by the High Court in *Miller v The Queen*. If extended joint criminal enterprise doctrines have indeed been abused, or indeed are prone to abuse, that certainly supplies *a* reason to see them off. But one should always hesitate before casting out the baby with the bathwater. Extended joint criminal enterprise doctrines could instead have been tweaked to avoid overreach, for instance by tightening the definition of joint enterprises and, perhaps, by requiring that S foresaw P's further crime as *probable*; or by limiting convictions to cases where S was certain that the collateral offence would be committed by P in the event of particular, foreseen circumstances. Such revisions would, of course, depart from existing case law, but not to the radical extent that *Jogee* does.

Alas, once joint enterprise liability was castigated as an egregious error in law, it had to go. The Supreme Court backed itself into a corner. That is unfortunate because it meant that the court never took seriously the question whether common unlawful purpose *should* have legal significance. In principle, having two distinct channels of complicity liability affords the law greater flexibility and moral sensitivity when determining whether S is a participant in P's crime. Direct aiding/abetting doctrines are simply too blunt by themselves to capture, without substantial over- or under-inclusion, all forms of association with P's crime that warrant a finding of guilt alongside P.

Despite the attention lavished upon them, the key features of common unlawful purpose liability are not its *mens rea* elements. They are (i) a distinctive *actus reus*, i.e. joining in a common purpose, which cannot simply be reduced to assistance or encouragement; (ii) the unlawfulness of that *actus reus* in its own right; and (iii) S's presence in the pursuance of their common purpose. By collapsing common purpose liability into mere aiding/abetting, the law obviates – and so loses sight of – these crucial features, which are not shared by acts of aiding/abetting. Lending P a jemmy is not anti-social at all *until* we know that P's plans for its use are wrong. Setting out with P on a criminal enterprise is entirely a different matter.

The High Court of Australia was right to point to the discussion of merits in *R. v Powell; English*. As Lord Steyn observed in that case, joint criminal enterprises are dynamic and often escalate. Unlike aiding/abetting scenarios, S signs up to that dynamic character on an ongoing basis. As such, common unlawful purpose doctrine responds to contingencies of scope, which is what really matters here, rather than contingencies of S's intention. It allows the common law to accommodate fast-moving developments, provided they occur in the pursuance and within the foreseen scope of the criminal enterprise (in which S has a non-contingent intention to engage), and in the presence of S. Moreover, as Lord Steyn also noted, the doctrine allows the courts to overcome at least some of the traditional evidential difficulties associated with group wrongdoing.

The Court in *Jogee* overestimates the capacity of aiding/abetting law to accommodate such difficulties. Joint criminal enterprises are a distinct moral phenomenon. Indeed, only by recognising that can we adequately protect the law of aiding and abetting. Absent legislative reform, the inadequacy of traditional aiding/abetting doctrine to deal with the complexity of multi-party wrongdoing will inevitably generate pressure, either to restore joint criminal enterprise liability or – disastrously – to water down the *mens rea* requirements of aiding and abetting itself. Let us hope that London opts for the former, and ultimately realigns itself with Canberra.

## ACTIVITY

Look back over the extracts you have read in this section on joint enterprise, and make a list of the arguments for and against the decision in *R v Jogee*. In your opinion, which set of arguments is the strongest?

## To which offences may a defendant be an accessory?

A defendant can be convicted of being an accessory to any of the offences we studied in Chapters 5, 6, 7 and 8 of this text. He may also be convicted of being an accessory to the offences we studied in Chapter 12. So, for example, a defendant could be convicted of being an accessory to a conspiracy,[21] or of being an accessory to a criminal attempt.[22]

There is, however, one restriction on when a defendant may be guilty as an accessory. If a statutory offence was designed to protect a specific class of persons, a member of that class cannot be liable as an accessory to the offence. For example, in *R v Tyrrell* [1894] 1 QB 710 the principal, Thomas Ford, had sexual intercourse with the defendant, Jane Tyrrell. Tyrrell was under the age of 16. She was convicted of being an accessory to Ford's offence of having sexual intercourse with a girl aged between 13 and 16. The conviction was quashed. Tyrrell could not be convicted as an accessory to this offence since she was a member of the class of persons that the offence existed to protect.

## The derivative principle

Freddie asks his friend Ronnie for some information on a property he intends to burgle. Ronnie gives Freddie all the information he needs. The day before the burglary, Freddie has a change of heart and decides not to go through with it. On these facts, Ronnie may be guilty of an inchoate offence such as intentionally encouraging and assisting

---

[21]*R v Anderson* (1984) 80 Cr App R 64. This was the Court of Appeal judgment in the House of Lords case *R v Anderson* [1986] AC 27. We saw in the previous chapter that it would arguably have been more appropriate to have charged William Anderson with being an accessory to the conspiracy to help Andaloussi escape from prison.
[22]*R v Hapgood and Wyatt* (1870) LR 1 CCR 221.

burglary.[23] But Ronnie cannot be convicted of being an accessory to burglary, because the burglary never took place. You cannot be an accessory to an offence that did not occur!

This is a simple illustration of the derivative principle. According to the derivative principle, an accessory's liability derives from the liability of the principal. So if the principal is not guilty of any offence, the accessory cannot be either.

Whilst the law on accessories is based on the derivative principle, there are two exceptions in which a defendant may be liable as an accessory even though the principal is not guilty:

- The first exception is where the reason the principal is not guilty of the relevant offence is because a substantive defence applies. This is illustrated by *R v Bourne* (1952) 36 Cr App R 125. The defendant twice forced his wife to have sexual intercourse with a dog. His wife was not guilty of any offence against the dog because she had a defence of duress. But the Court of Appeal upheld the defendant's conviction for being an accessory to a sexual offence against the dog.

- The second exception is where the reason the principal is not guilty of the relevant offence is because he lacked the necessary *mens rea*. This is illustrated by *R v Cogan & Leak* [1976] QB 217. The defendant, Michael Leak, terrorised his wife into submitting to sexual intercourse with John Cogan. Leak then told Cogan that his wife would consent to sex with him. Cogan had sex with Mrs Leak believing that she was consenting. Cogan's conviction for rape was quashed on appeal on the basis that he lacked the *mens rea* of rape.[24] But Leak's conviction for being an accessory to rape was upheld.

Note that, although the principal had not committed any crime in either of these cases, the *actus reus* of the relevant offence did still occur. So in cases like *R v Bourne* and *R v Cogan & Leak* the liability of the accessory is best understood as deriving from the fact that the defendant procured the *actus reus* of the offence in question.[25]

## Withdrawal

Suppose that a defendant provides assistance or encouragement, but then has a change of heart. If the principal has not yet committed the relevant offence, it is possible for the defendant to withdraw and avoid accessorial liability. In this section we will look at some case law which identifies the factors to take into account when deciding whether a defendant's purported withdrawal was in fact effective. As we look at the cases, remember that whether or not a purported withdrawal is effective is a question of fact, to be determined by the jury having regard to the features of the particular case before it.[26]

The first case to consider is *R v Becerra & Cooper* (1975) 62 Cr App R 212. Antonio Becerra, John Cooper and a third man broke into the home of an elderly lady, Mrs Francis, in the early hours of the morning. Becerra was carrying a knife. Cooper entered the

---

[23]Serious Crime Act 2007, section 44 (see Chapter 12).

[24]At the time the *mens rea* of rape was lack of a genuine belief in consent. As we saw in Chapter 7, today the *mens rea* is lack of a reasonable belief in consent. Since the jury in the case found that Cogan had no reasonable grounds for his belief that Mrs Leak was consenting, if the case had occurred today Cogan would have been guilty of rape.

[25]See the judgment of the Court of Appeal in *R v Millward* [1994] Crim LR 527.

[26]*R v O'Flaherty & others* [2004] EWCA Crim 526.

building first, climbing in through Mrs Francis' bedroom window. Mrs Francis turned her bedside light on. Cooper went over to her, punched her, jumped on top of her and covered her head with a pillow. Becerra and the other man then entered and Becerra cut the telephone wires. Cooper then said to Becerra, 'Give me the knife in case somebody jumps me'. Becerra handed the knife over. At this point Mr Lewis, who lived in a first floor flat in the house and had heard noises from below, came downstairs. Becerra and the third man heard him, climbed out of the window and ran away. Before leaving, Becerra called to Cooper, 'Come on, let's go'. Cooper tried to exit via the back door, but found it was locked. He was confronted by Mr Lewis. There was a struggle. Cooper stabbed Mr Lewis four times. One of the wounds was fatal. Becerra and Cooper both pleaded guilty to burglary. At trial, Cooper was convicted of murder and Becerra was convicted of being an accessory to the murder. Becerra appealed against his conviction, arguing that he had withdrawn before Cooper murdered Mr Lewis. The appeal reached the Court of Appeal.

## EXTRACT

Read the following extract from the judgment of Roskill LJ. Is it sufficient for an effective withdrawal for a defendant to change his mind and leave the scene of the crime?

Roskill LJ cites with approval a passage from a Canadian case, *Whitehouse*. This passage identifies one 'essential element' for an effective withdrawal. What is this?

Roskill LJ then refers to an English case, *Croft*. The passage from this case identifies another requirement for an effective withdrawal. What is this?

Applying these requirements to the facts of *R v Becerra & Cooper*, does Roskill LJ conclude that Becerra's purported withdrawal was effective? Why/why not?

### *R v Becerra & Cooper* (1975) 62 Cr App R 212

#### Roskill LJ

[Counsel for the defence] referred us to several Canadian cases, to only one of which is it necessary to refer in detail, a decision of the Court of Appeal of British Columbia in *Whitehouse* (alias *Savage*) (1941) 1 W.W.R. 112. I need not read the headnote. The Court of Appeal held that the trial judge concerned in that case, which was one of murder, had been guilty of misdirection in his direction to the jury on this question of "withdrawal." The matter is, if I may most respectfully say so, so well put in the leading judgment of Sloan J. A., that I read the whole of the passage at pp. 115 and 116: "Can it be said on the facts of this case that a mere change of mental intention and a quitting of the scene of the crime just immediately prior to the striking of the fatal blow will absolve those who participate in the commission of the crime by overt acts up to that moment from all the consequences of its accomplishment by the one who strikes in ignorance of his companions' change of heart? I think not. After a crime has been committed and before a prior abandonment of the common enterprise may be found by a jury there must be, in my view, in the absence of exceptional circumstances, something more than a mere mental change of intention and physical change of place by those associates who wish to dissociate themselves from the consequences attendant upon their willing assistance up to the moment of the actual commission of that crime. I would not attempt to define too closely what must be done in criminal matters involving participation in a common unlawful purpose to break the chain of causation and responsibility. That must depend upon the circumstances of each case but it seems to me that one essential element ought to be established in a case of this kind: Where practicable and reasonable there must be timely communication of the intention to abandon the common purpose from those who wish to dissociate themselves from the contemplated crime to those who desire to continue in it. What is 'timely communication' must be determined by the facts of each case but where practicable and reasonable it ought to be such communication, verbal or otherwise, that will serve unequivocal notice upon the other party to the common unlawful cause that if he proceeds upon it he does so without the further aid and assistance of those who withdraw. The unlawful purpose of him who continues alone is then his own and not one in common with those who are no longer parties to it nor liable to its full and final consequences." The learned judge then went on to cite a passage from 1 Hale's Pleas of the Crown 618 and the passage from Saunders and Archer (supra) to which I have already referred.

In the view of each member of this Court, that passage, if we may respectfully say so, could not be improved upon and we venture to adopt it in its entirety as a correct statement of the law which is to be applied in this case.

The last case, an English one, is Croft (1944) 29 Cr.App.R. 169; [1944] 1 K.B. 295, a well known case of a suicide pact where, under the old law, the survivor of a suicide pact was charged with and convicted of murder. It was sought to argue that he had withdrawn from the pact in time to avoid liability (as the law then was) for conviction for murder.

The Court of Criminal Appeal, comprising Lawrence J. (as he then was), Lewis and Wrottesley JJ. dismissed the appeal and upheld the direction given by Humphreys J. to the jury at the trial. Towards the end of the judgment Lawrence J. said, at p. 173 (pp. 297 and 298): "... counsel for the appellant complains – although I do not understand that the point had ever been taken in the court below – that the summing-up does not contain any reference to the possibility of the agreement to commit suicide having been determined or countermanded. It is true that the learned judge does not deal expressly with that matter except in a passage where he says: 'Even if you accept his statement in the witness-box that the vital and second shot was fired when he had gone through that window, he would still be guilty of murder if she was then committing suicide as the result of an agreement which they had mutually arrived at that that should be the fate of both of them, and it is no answer for him that he altered his mind after she was dead and did not commit suicide himself.' ... the authorities, such as they are, show in our opinion, that where a person has acted as an accessory before the fact, in order that he should not be held guilty as an accessory before the fact, he must give express and actual countermand or revocation of the advising, counselling, procuring, or abetting which he had given before."

It seems to us that those authorities make plain what the law is which has to be applied in the present case.

We therefore turn back to consider the direction which the learned judge gave in the present case to the jury and what was the suggested evidence that Becerra had withdrawn from the common agreement. The suggested evidence is the use by Becerra of the words "Come on let's go," coupled, as I said a few moments ago, with his act in going out through the window. The evidence, as the judge pointed out, was that Cooper never heard that nor did the third man. But let it be supposed that that was said and the jury took the view that it was said.

On the facts of this case, in the circumstances then prevailing, the knife having already been used and being contemplated for further use when it was handed over by Becerra to Cooper for the purpose of avoiding (if necessary) by violent means the hazards of identification, if Becerra wanted to withdraw at that stage, he would have to "countermand," to use the word that is used in some of the cases or "repent" to use another word so used, in some manner vastly different and vastly more effective than merely to say "Come on, let's go" and go out through the window.

So for Becerra's withdrawal to have been effective, he would have needed to unequivocally communicate notice of his withdrawal to Cooper and to have done something 'vastly more effective' to countermand his actions than simply saying 'Come on, let's go' and running off.

So generally, in order to withdraw effectively, a defendant must: (1) unequivocally communicate notice of his withdrawal; and (2) take steps to countermand (i.e. negate) his assistance/encouragement. Notice, though, that there is no requirement for the defendant to show that he took reasonable steps to prevent the principal from committing the offence.[27] This was significant in *R v Grundy* [1977] Crim LR 543, in which the courts said there was evidence of an effective withdrawal. The defendant in this case had provided information to two men about premises they planned to burgle. But two weeks before the planned burglary the defendant had a change of heart. During these two weeks he tried to persuade the men not to go ahead with the burglary. At trial the judge ruled there was insufficient evidence of an effective withdrawal for the issue to be left to the jury. The Court of Appeal said that this was wrong and quashed Grundy's conviction. There was evidence of an effective withdrawal, and so the jury should have been left to decide whether Grundy's purported withdrawal was effective or not.

It is also important to note that the requirements for an effective withdrawal may not be as strict in cases involving spontaneous, as opposed to preplanned, violence. In *R v O'Flaherty & others* [2004] EWCA Crim 526 the three defendants – Errol O'Flaherty, Phillip Ryan and Mitchell Toussaint – had been to a nightclub. After the club shut, violence broke out between two groups of young men: one which included the three defendants and another which included the victim, Marcus Hall. Importantly, the violence occurred in two locations. First, the three defendants and others exchanged blows with Marcus Hall in a road called Flowers Way outside the nightclub. O'Flaherty was armed with a cricket bat, Ryan was armed with a beer bottle and Toussaint was armed with a claw hammer. Hall then ran around the corner into Park Street West, chased by a number of the group including O'Flaherty but not Ryan or Toussaint. In Park Street West Hall was struck and stabbed. O'Flaherty stood within a few feet of the attack, holding the cricket bat. At trial, the three defendants were all convicted of being accessories to the murder. They appealed against their convictions. On appeal, one of the issues the Court of Appeal had to consider was whether the defendants had withdrawn from the course of violence before the fatal blow was struck.

### EXTRACT

Read the following extract from the judgment of Mantell LJ. What distinction does he draw between cases of spontaneous violence and cases of preplanned violence?

What reasons does Mantell LJ give for allowing the appeals of Ryan and Toussaint?

What reasons does Mantell LJ give for dismissing the appeal of O'Flaherty?

### *R v O'Flaherty & others* [2004] EWCA Crim 526

#### Mantell LJ

61 [... T]he decision in *R v Mitchell and King* (1998) 163 JP 75, so far as we can see, an authority not brought to the attention of the judge, shows that in a case of spontaneous violence in

---

[27] *R v O'Flaherty & others* [2004] EWCA Crim 526.

principle it is possible to withdraw by ceasing to fight, throwing down one's weapons and walking away. In that case one of Mitchell's defences was that he had withdrawn before the fatal injuries had been inflicted. It was stated by the Court (p. 81) that in those circumstances the jury had to be directed (a) that they must be satisfied that the fatal injuries were sustained whilst the joint enterprise was continuing and that the defendant was still acting within that joint enterprise, and (b) that they must be satisfied that the acts which caused the death were within the scope of the joint enterprise.

62 In *R v Mitchell and King* this Court also considered Soan J.A.'s statement in *R v Whitefeld* that "where practicable and reasonable there must be timely communication of the intention to abandon the common purpose". It held that while communication of withdrawal is a necessary condition for disassociation from pre-planned violence it is not necessary when the violence is spontaneous.

[...]

65 It is not arguable that the learned judge should have withdrawn the case of O'Flaherty from the jury. The fact that he followed the group to Park Street West still armed with the cricket bat provided an evidential foundation for the jury to conclude, if properly directed, that he was "still in it". There are significant differences so far as Ryan and Toussaint are concerned. In a case of spontaneous violence such as this where there has been no prior agreement the jury will usually have to make inferences as to the scope of the joint enterprise from the knowledge and actions of the individual participants. Ryan and Toussaint were solely in the fray in Flowers Way, and in Ryan's case only for some 7 seconds. There was no evidence from which it could be inferred that pursuit was part of any joint enterprise by them. Since there was no evidence that any injury causative of death was inflicted in Flowers Way, there was no evidence concerning them on the charge of murder to go to the jury. Accordingly their cases should have been withdrawn

66 We turn to the effect of the directions. We are clear that even had it been proper to leave Ryan and Toussaint's cases to the jury the effect of the failure to direct the jury that the fatal injuries had to have been sustained when the joint enterprise was continuing and that the particular defendant was still acting within that joint enterprise would have rendered their convictions unsafe. The position of O'Flaherty differs. He followed the group to Park Street West holding the cricket bat. He was present carrying the cricket bat as the group attacked Hall. Although it is right to say that the jury would have to be satisfied that he was present and at the very least providing encouragement or prepared to lend support it would seem to this court that no other conclusion would have been available to a reasonable jury than was arrived at by this jury.

A final case to consider here is *R v Mitchell* [2008] EWCA Crim 2552. We saw the facts of this case earlier in the chapter in our discussion of *R v Johnson*. The case involved an outbreak of violence late at night between two groups, one of which included Michael Hall (who we examined previously), Laura Mitchell, and the eventual killer, Carl Holmes. Mitchell was centrally involved in the initial outbreak of violence, kicking and punching several members of the other group. There was then a lull in the violence, during which time Mitchell stayed in the pub car park. She had lost both her shoes and was trying to find them. When the rest of Mitchell's group returned they attacked the members of the other group again, and the victim, Andrew Ayres, was killed. At trial Mitchell was convicted of being an accessory to the murder. She appealed against her conviction on two grounds, both of which were rejected by the Court of Appeal:

- First, she argued that there were in fact two separate joint enterprises: the original attack, which she participated in and which had come to an end; and a second attack which she had not participated in. The Court rejected this, saying that the jury at her trial had been entitled to find that there had been one ongoing joint enterprise which had had a temporary lull whilst the group members collected weapons.

- Second, she argued that she had withdrawn from the joint enterprise. She only remained in the pub car park to find her shoes, and had not taken part in the further incidents of violence. The Court rejected this also, saying that the jury had been entitled to find that she had not withdrawn from the joint enterprise. She had played a leading role in starting the violence, and had remained present at the scene of the violence.

Finally, when answering an exam problem question remember the following two points:

- A defendant can only withdraw before the principal commits the relevant offence. It is not possible to withdraw once the principal has committed the crime.
- Even if the defendant did withdraw effectively, he may still be liable for some other offence, such as the inchoate offences of conspiracy or encouraging and assisting crime.

## Conclusion

The topics we have covered in this chapter include some of the most difficult material in the whole text. So to conclude the chapter, here are three pieces of advice for answering exam problem questions:

- Before considering the liability of any possible accessories, you should always begin by discussing the liability of the principal. As we have seen, the liability of an accessory derives from the liability of the principal. So, unless one of the exceptions to the derivative principle applies, if the principal is not guilty of any offence there can be no accessorial liability!

- Always remember to specify the offence that the defendant was an accessory to. In exams it is quite common for students to write something like 'The defendant would be guilty of being an accessory'. This doesn't provide enough information. You need to write 'The defendant would be guilty of being an accessory to murder' or 'The defendant would be guilty of being an accessory to theft'.

- There is a considerable overlap between the law on accessories and the inchoate offences. This leaves some students unsure which offences they should discuss. As a rule of thumb, you should discuss accessorial liability before considering inchoate offences. This is because finding a defendant guilty as an accessory recognises that the full offence actually occurred.

## Self-test questions

1. Ronnie and Freddie are members of a criminal gang. Jack is the leader of a rival gang. Discuss the criminal liability of Ronnie and Freddie in the following situations:

   a. Freddie suggests to Jack that they meet up at his local pub for a drink to resolve their differences. When Jack arrives, Ronnie and Freddie are in the middle of a game of pool. Jack walks over to them and Freddie immediately attacks him, striking him repeatedly with his pool cue. Ronnie stands and watches, not doing or saying anything. Jack suffers serious injuries, including a broken arm. Ronnie later tells police that he had no idea that Freddie had invited Jack to the pub.

   How (if at all) would your answer be different in each of the following two scenarios: (i) Ronnie had known that Freddie had invited Jack so that he could attack him and Ronnie had gone to the pub in order to watch; and (ii) Ronnie owned the pub in which the attack occurred?

   b. Freddie asks Ronnie to find out where Jack lives. Ronnie does so and gives Freddie the address. Ronnie expects some sort of violence, but is unsure what form this will take. That evening Freddie breaks into Jack's house planning to kill him. Unbeknown to Freddie, Jack had been killed in a road accident earlier that day.

   c. Ronnie and Freddie agree to go and beat Jack up with wooden posts. They drive to Jack's house in Ronnie's car. When they arrive, Ronnie says to Freddie, 'I'm not sure this is such a good idea. I'm going home'. Freddie replies, 'I'm going through with it'. Ronnie leaves. Freddie attacks Jack. Jack suffers serious injuries.

   d. Ronnie and Freddie agree to go and beat up Jack with wooden posts. Ronnie says to Freddie, 'For goodness' sake don't kill him'. They attack Jack. Freddie relentlessly hits Jack on the head as hard as he can with a wooden post. Jack dies.

   How (if at all) would your answer be different in each of the following two scenarios: (i) medical evidence shows that Jack died from the cumulative effect of all of the injuries the men inflicted; and, (ii) unbeknown to Ronnie, Freddie had taken a knife with him. After striking Jack with the wooden posts, Freddie pulls out the knife and fatally stabs him?

2. 'The decision of the Supreme Court in *R v Jogee* [2016] UKSC 8, *Ruddock v The Queen* [2016] UKPC 7 should be applauded. Parasitic accessory liability produced harsh results that it was impossible to justify. The law that now applies to so-called joint enterprises is both fairer and more coherent.'

   Discuss the extent to which you agree with this statement.

## Accessories checklist

Having worked through this chapter, you should now have:

✓ An understanding of how to distinguish accessories from principals

✓ An understanding of the requirements that must be satisfied for a defendant to be convicted of being an accessory to an offence

✓ A knowledge of the Supreme Court judgment in *R v Jogee* and an ability to critically discuss it

✓ An understanding of the derivative principle and the exceptions to it

✓ An understanding of the requirements for a defendant to withdraw effectively from a criminal enterprise.

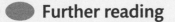 **Further reading**

House of Commons Justice Committee (2012) *Joint Enterprise* (11th Report of Session 2010–12) HC 1597.

House of Commons Justice Committee (2014) *Joint Enterprise: Follow-Up* (4th Report of Session 2014–15) HC 310.

Law Commission (2007) *Participating in Crime* (Law Commission Report No 305) Cm 7084.

Ormerod, D. and Laird, K. (2016) '*Jogee*: Not the End of a Legal Saga but the Start of One?' *Criminal Law Review* 539.

Simester, A.P. (2017) 'Accessory Liability and Common Unlawful Purposes' 133 *Law Quarterly Review* 73.

Stark, F. (2016) 'The Demise of "Parasitic Accessorial Liability": Substantive Judicial Law Reform, Not Common Law Housekeeping' 75 *Cambridge Law Journal* 550.

Sullivan, G.R. (2008) 'Participating in Crime: Law Com No 305 – Joint Criminal Ventures' *Criminal Law Review* 19.

Wilson, W. (2008) 'A Rational Scheme of Liability for Participating in Crime' *Criminal Law Review* 3.

Wilson, W. and Ormerod, D. (2015) 'Simply Harsh to Fairly Simple: Joint Enterprise Reform' *Criminal Law Review* 3.

# Index

Note: Page numbers followed by n represent foot notes.